A HISTORY
OF PHILOSOPHY
IN AMERICA

Volume II

Elizabeth Flower
and Murray G. Murphey

Capricorn Books, New York
G. P. Putnam's Sons, New York

Vol. I SBN: 399-11650-8
Vol. II SBN: 399-11743-1

Library of Congress Cataloging in Publication Data

Flower, Elizabeth.
  A history of philosophy in America.

  Bibliography: p.
  Includes index.
  1. Philosophy, American—History. I. Murphey,
Murray G., joint author. II. Title.
B851.F56   1976   191   75-40254

PRINTED IN THE UNITED STATES OF AMERICA

Acknowledgments

We are grateful for permission to quote from the following:

The Manuscript Journals of Amos Bronson Alcott, by permission of The Houghton Library, Harvard University.

"The Technometry of William Ames," by Lee W. Gibbs, unpublished dissertation, Harvard University, 1967, by permission of the author.

Freedom of the Will, by Jonathan Edwards, edited by Paul Ramsay, by permission of Yale University Press.

Images and Shadows of Divine Things, by Jonathan Edwards, edited by Perry Miller, by permission of Yale University Press.

The Philosophy of Jonathan Edwards, edited by Harvey Townsend, University of Oregon Monographs, 1955, by permission of University of Oregon Books.

"The Mind" of Jonathan Edwards, by Leon Howard, copyright © 1963 by The Regents of the University of California, by permission of University of California Press.

The Papers of Benjamin Franklin, edited by L. Labaree, by permission of Yale University Press.

The Thought and Character of William James, by Ralph Barton Perry, by permission of Alexander R. James.

Samuel Johnson, President of King's College, His Career and Writings, edited by Herbert and Carol Schneider, volumes I, II, and III, Columbia University Press, 1929, by permission of Columbia University Press.

The Manuscripts of Charles Sanders Peirce, by permission of the Department of Philosophy, Harvard University.

The Collected Papers of Charles Sanders Peirce, volumes 1-6, edited by Charles Hartshorne and Paul Weiss, The Belknap Press of Harvard University Press, 1931-1935; volumes 7-8, edited by Arthur Burks, The Belknap Press of Harvard University Press, 1958, by permission of Harvard University Press.

Royce's Logical Essays, by Josiah Royce, edited by Daniel Robinson, by permission of The Christopher Publishing House.

Fugitive Essays, by Josiah Royce, Introduction by J. Loewenberg, 1920, by permission of Harvard University Press.

The World and the Individual, Second Series, by Josiah Royce, by permission of Dover Publications, Inc.

For both inspiration and the forging of the tools with which the writers have worked there is a preeminent obligation on the part of both of us to Herbert Schneider and Perry Miller.

Contents
Volume I

CONTENTS

Volume II

Chapter Eight

The Absolute Immigrates to America: The St. Louis Hegelians

Chapter Eight

The Absolute Immigrates
to America

Hegel's Absolute Idealism came to the United States under the official sponsorship of the St. Louis Hegelians, who also supervised its naturalization here. Perhaps these Westerners are of marginal interest today;[1] undergraduates are seldom assigned their original articles, while not a single catchphrase of theirs (such as the pragmatists' "will to believe" or the "fixation of belief") perpetuates them even in cocktail conversation. For all of this, they and their connections have left a profound mark on American education from kindergarten to graduate school and they had an important, perhaps decisive, political role in building the nation during and after the Civil War. More importantly in the present context, they gave philosophy such a fresh sense of power and historicity that it was moved out of the genteel world of clerics and colleges into the realms of public affairs. For them, philosophy was a calling (in the sense of Fichte's *Bestimmung des Menschen*) rather than a mere profession. Amateurs in the most cordial sense of that term, they studied, talked, and worked with incredible intensity. Above all, they translated philosophic classics so indefatigably that the undergraduate who does not know their articles stands a fair chance of using editions of German philosophers prepared by them or their near associates. And if he has work to do in Plato or Aristotle, medieval logic or theory of education, that same undergraduate (or scholar) runs the risk of missing fruitful insights if he overlooks their investigations.

After a discussion of alternative approaches to these Hegelians (1), we proceed in a leisurely fashion to discuss the gathering of the group in St. Louis under its central figures Harris and Brokmeyer shortly before the Civil War (2). A review of its main European philosophic debts (3) is followed by an account of how the group, reassembled after the war and strengthened by such newcomers as Snider, Davidson, and Howison, becomes active in social and educational reform (4); and founds a journal with a cultural mission (5). Finally, we turn to the relation of St. Louis and Concord (6).

1. The St. Louis Hegelians in Different Perspectives

Now there are various ways of approaching the St. Louis Hegelians, for they intersect diverse intellectual currents: as a robust extension of Trancendentalism to the Western frontier; as an important part of the larger story of German culture in America; or, in their own terms, as a "Moment" in the dialectic by which the Western Spirit was to join the nation to the mainstream of continental thought. While this last is the course we shall follow, it is worth indicating where the other options might have taken us.

It is fairly easy to see why both Alcott and Harris regarded the St. Louis Hegelians as an extension of or "complement to" Eastern Transcendentalism. Harris and Brokmeyer took their initial inspirations from New England's idealism, and the various groups that formed about them kept alive those contacts which were further bonded by visits from Emerson and Alcott. In the end, Harris and many of his associates (excepting Brokmeyer, on principle) returned to Concord— there to write an epilogue to Transcendentalism, and to help bridge it to Harvard's academic idealism.

Emerson and Alcott seldom held themselves strictly responsible to the German originals. Less inclined to strip the texts for their precise lessons, they used them where they matched or supplemented their own insights; the Concord philosophers read even Kant himself with a hearty Platonism that was starched with Common Sense Realism. In the process, they dulled finer distinctions so attractive to German metaphysics. Further, the proper Transcendentalists were cautious about being identified with post-Kantian philosophy and theology lest the charge of infidelity launched against the latter aggravate their own precariously balanced position vis-à-vis orthodoxy. They were more sanguine about associating themselves with the cautious French restatements of German thought, particularly Cousin's *Course of the History of Modern Philosophy;* and of course they were happy enough to acknowledge the influence of Coleridge and Carlyle. Yet all of these, in one way or another, were seeking to overcome in some higher synthesis the difficulties left by Kant: Cousin, in his eclecticism, Coleridge in his own logic,

Fichte and Schelling by their versions of objective idealism, and Emerson and Alcott in the ways explored in the previous chapters. Of the Germans, the Transcendentalists found Schleiermacher most to their taste, on personal and philosophic grounds—especially insofar as he emphasized *Vernunft* as a way of direct access or intuition, in contrast to *Verstand,* mere scientific understanding. Schleiermacher, in fact, stood to one side of the main course of German idealism which hindsight finds climaxed in Hegel. He was, however, closer to the deepest concern of the Trancendentalists, for he saw religion not as an institutional matter but as a matter of direct experience, particularly the experience of dependence. Even so, many Transcendentalists worried that even Schleiermacher was too dangerously pantheistic.

Still there were others in New England, in and out of Transcendentalism, who took a more scholarly attitude toward German texts. Even before George Bancroft complained that he could find no German-English dictionary or grammar to prepare him for the German trip that was to begin the Harvard-Göttingen axis, Moses Stuart at Andover was attempting to show that a staunch Calvinism could be maintained even when using the tools of German higher criticism. Yet both Stuart and his student James Marsh were often put on the defensive. On the whole, German philosophy of this time *was* bound in the same volume with radical theology, philology, and the science of history, and orthodox Americans could reasonably suspect it of pantheism. And if there were any doubt where Hegelianism and the higher criticism might lead, it was dissipated in America by Bancroft's report that Hegel's classes were "blasphemous." (Perhaps this attitude of Bancroft's was not entirely uninfluenced by Schleiermacher, who was the American's host in Germany, at a time when the break between Schleiermacher and Hegel's philosophy of religion was still a stylish scandal.) At any rate, suspicions about Hegel's pantheism were converted into certainties when an acknowledged disciple of Hegel, David Strauss, published his *Das Leben Jesu* (1835). Whereas Schleiermacher's stress on the dependence-experience as the essence of Christianity merely minimized the importance of the institutional structure of religion, Strauss saw Jesus, the Christ-myth, as a poetic symbol of the divine in man. Rapidly, after that, left-wing German philosophy went on to challenge not only the historicity of the Gospels and of Jesus, but also the objective reference of religious conceptions, including "God." Their project became one of explaining the rise of religious institutions naturalistically, i.e., psychologically and anthropologically.

Among those who traveled in the Trancendentalist orbit, the most influential in St. Louis (Emerson and Alcott aside) were their outstanding scholars—Hedge, Parker, and Cabot, the beginning, middle, and end, as it were, of Trancendentalism. Frederick Hedge was but a teenage charge of Bancroft's on the German trip, and thus received youthful training in German literature and thought. As a Unitarian minister in Providence and a professor of modern languages at Harvard, Hedge became a major source for really reliable information about German thought. One of his articles in *The Christian Examiner* (1833), although ostensibly on Coleridge, gives a neat précis of the development of philosophy from Kant (who "sets the method" as an examination of experience) through Fichte and Schelling (who further elaborate the system and rework the difficulties). Theodore Parker, like Hedge a minister with broad interests in German literature, was also a reliable source for translations, especially of Schelling, and for articles on German idealism in general. The most controversial of these was an examination of *Das Leben Jesu*.[2] At the time of writing, Parker was unwilling to go all the way with Strauss's mythologizing of Jesus, but he used it to good effect to distinguish Christianity as religious experience from dogma, ritual, and mummery. But both Parker and Hedge stopped short of sympathy for Hegel, and we shall see later that the threat of Hegel's pantheism also exercised Harris. Nonetheless Hedge, in his *Prose Writers of Germany,* added sections of Hegel's *Philosophy of History* and his ironic essay, "Who Thinks Abstractly?" to the predictable selections from Kant's *Critiques* and his essay on *Perpetual Peace.* Fichte was also represented in part by the *Destination of Man* in an especially powerful translation. While of course there were no chapters on Strauss, Feuerbach, or the Socialists, the inclusion of Hegel had as fateful consequences as any of the romantic historians could have wished. The "anonymous friend" who prepared the selection distances himself from Hegelianism in the introduction, but writes that "Hegel's disciples allege that this philosophy is shaped to what Christianity offers by faith" and that they claim that it is the culmination of all other systems, recapitulating the whole progress of the human mind, the course of history, the phenomena of nature, and all problems of speculation.

> There is one *Absolute Substance* pervading all things. That Substance is *Spirit.* This Spirit is endowed with the power of development; it produces from itself the opposing powers and forces of the universe. All that we have to do is to stand by and see the process going on. . . . [It] goes on from stage to stage until the Absolute Spirit has passed through all the stadia of its evolution, and is exhibited in its highest form in the Hegelian system. . . . The system comprises three departments: . . . Logic is the science of the Absolute Idea, in its abstract character; in the Philosophy of Nature we have the same Absolute in another, an external form; in the Philosophy of Spirit we have its highest stage. Here it manifests itself as the Subjective Spirit, the Objective Spirit, and the Absolute Spirit. The Absolute Spirit, in fine, has three stages of development, which are religion, art, and philosophy.[3]

Reports vary, but it is likely that the "anonymous friend" was plural and included H. B. Smith as well as James Elliot Cabot who was admittedly the translator of almost all of the considerable section on Kant. Cabot, later to become an overseer of Harvard, a sometime lecturer in ethics there, and a kind of literary executor for Emerson, encouraged and supported the St. Louis crowd and, even more than they, approached Kant and the Post-Kantians without idiosyncrasy. Perhaps by the time Cabot started to write, Hegel was becoming more respectable in Boston (or perhaps a Cabot didn't need to worry about such matters). But he put Hegel on a more substantial footing with a brilliant and enthusiastic review in Parker's *Massachusetts Quarterly Review* of Stallo's *General Principles of the Philosophy of Nature,* a pioneer book in the Hegelian style. Later he gave favorable publicity to the house organ of the St. Louis Hegelians, their *Journal of Speculative Philosophy,* in the brahmin *North American Review.* This is a notable, if rather dry, confrontation of John Stuart Mill's inductive logic with the kind of methodological problems raised easily by Hegel's critique of empirical psychology. Cabot also published in the *Journal* his part of the controversy with William James on the categories of time and space. By nature Cabot was a genteel adversary, committed to philosophic inquiry without the aura of ego involvement and vehemence; he remained unperturbed by the rising tide of empirical psychology, for, if one views philosophy *sub specie Hegelianitatis,* the pendulum must swing back to idealism again.

The Westerners came to think that New England's affair (Cabot excepted) with German philosophy was anemic and emasculated. The most striking difference between St. Louis and eastern Massachusetts was of course the former's confidence in Hegel, which carried along with it a related preference for Aristotle over Plato. Those who like Harris remained close in mood and problem to the East struggled with Hegel's pantheism and ultimately succeeded in bringing it into line with their own brand of Christianity—helped by such German post-Hegelians as Daub and Rosenkranz. It goes without saying that these and other Hegelian moderates, such as the Italian Augusto Vera, were to be given copious space in the pages of the journal which the St. Louis intellectuals shortly founded.

Although pantheism was a continuing concern of Harris's throughout the years, his own interests changed under the pressures of the evolutionary sciences. An early paper is preoccupied with pantheism in the context of the relation between God and man. Because God is free and independent He is essentially a creator.

> His self-knowledge is therefore the creation of the world, and of man as an image, or reflection of Himself. The World, or created Universe is not God, but His Image, his Reflection, his Creation.[4]

Harris thinks that he is properly interpreting Hegel by holding that God is transcendent over nature and not identical with anything in nature, save what is the consequence of his activity. History, especially human history, reflects the person, the will, intellect, and heart of God; yet man preserves his identity because he also is self-conscious and free. Of course Harris's problem is to show how these two claims are compatible. Others among the St. Louisans didn't see the problem, for they thought that God needs us as badly as we need Him.

In an article written some ten years later, as a part of a symposium on the relation between science and religion,[5] Harris attempts to show that neither pantheism nor atheism (which clearly can't account for the patent experience of dependence), but theism is entailed by modern science. Theism now, however, seems to involve merely a necessary appeal to some kind of unity. Even in the case of the physical sciences mere observation could never be forged into a scientific theory; what counts is the organizational feature by which hypothesis determines the relevant and systematic connections of observations. Harris gets his best ammunition not from the physical sciences, but from the historical and social ones. It is obvious that a set of observations of the successive stages by which a seedling becomes a tree would never capture its unity through time. Not even the teleology of survival, as in Darwin, could be understood without the prerequisite unifying principles. When we turn from biology to sociology and the principles which determine the historical development of human institutions, of art, religion, or even philosophy itself, the kind of natural laws to be found in physics simply don't come to grips with the matter; some appreciation of self-determined activity is necessary, some account of the cumulative intelligence which is expressed in the history of human culture. Harris has yet another arrow in his quiver, for he shows that science itself is institutional; it depends on the social transfer of knowledge, the division of labor, and the share of each in the profits of the experience of all. Few scientists appreciate how socially determined are their aims, assumptions, and behavior. Harris's conclusion is that science implies theism insofar as the latter means the relational character and interdependence of all features of the universe.

There were others, generally native Westerners, who were spared the agony over Hegel's alleged pantheism either, as in the case of Brokmeyer, because they ignored the problem or because they had reversed the problem—to put it informally, by making the personality of God immanent in history and thereby "spiritualizing" nature. But Harris's dilemma remains more poignantly, because how then can the individual be saved from being "swallowed up" by God; how can the individual's autonomy be salvaged from the spiritual determinism of the Absolute and leave both God and man as Persons?

The St. Louis Hegelians stand out in a different way when viewed as a part of the story of German influence on America. Of course Bancroft's claim that he couldn't prepare himself adequately for his trip to Germany is a canard. Perhaps (putting it unkindly) the complaint stems from an old man's memory magnifying the obstacles to his own achievements. After all, Moses Stuart and James Marsh found no such obstacles to learning German and there appear to have been German holdings in Harvard's own library from colonial times that survived the various fires. In any case, there were obvious resources in New York and Pennsylvania. For example, in Pennsylvania, quite apart from individual German-Americans who contributed to our intellectual life, there had been pre-Revolutionary communities which preserved German traditions of literacy, printing, and education. Particularly their ministers and physicians were well trained, often in German universities. Further, there were German studies at the University of Pennsylvania (and Columbia) and occasionally illustrious professors such as Kunze who were probably inspirations for the rather surprising number of references to Kant, Wolff, and Leibniz even before 1800.

It seems plausible to infer the continuity of knowledgeable groups from the eighteenth to the nineteenth century. In addition to anti-intellectual communities of Mennonites and Amish, among others, there were cultivated Germans such as Frederick A. Rauch.[6] He lectured at Mercersburg Seminary and Marshall College, and if we may presume his *Psychology* (1840) was comprehensible to those who kept it in publication, then his was a very sophisticated audience. Rauch had studied in Germany with Daub, Hegel's literary executor, and he attempted to weld Hegelian insights with empirical psychology. It is difficult to believe that Rauch himself, or the Mercersburg School of Theology of which he was the forerunner, found any deep inconsistency between Hegelianism and Christianity (Yale's Murdock to the contrary[7]).

Theology is not our main concern, however, for the German influence in America had, in the long run, considerable secular effect as well. Peter Kaufmann is an example.[8] He speaks with a new social voice decades ahead of the conservative economic spirit of German visitors like List and Lieber. Almost immediately upon his arrival in Philadelphia he established the first Labor-for-Labor store. Presumably he knew Robert Owen (who was in Philadelphia at the time), but his own philosophy is closer to that of the early Continental Christian Socialists. His exotic and Tolstoy-like Utopianism emphasized the involvement of the individual in the social setting. Society as presently organized is not only economically inefficient, but is also subversive of the development of natural social harmony. The social gospel is no counsel of perfection; it must be taken quite literally and acted upon immediately. In fact it requires the present realization of justice and the setting up of Socialism. Kaufmann carried this message westward in steps, coming to settle finally in Canton, Ohio, where he worked as a publicist. Although he turned rather late to the formal study of German idealism, his Socialism shares the Hegelian view of history as a process in which good emerges from evil through alterations and reform of the social institutions which transmit and mold values. This, of course, contrasts the prevalant New England view that social reform depends upon the individual's change of heart.

Kaufmann, as well as others who traveled west from the Eastern seaboard, joined a larger and more direct stream of German immigration that was pouring into the Middle West in the thirties and forties. These were predominantly farmers and artisans, but at midcentury they were augmented by "forty-eighters," victims of the failure of liberal revolutionary hopes in Europe. These latter, relatively few in number, brought a professional but nonclerical class to such cities as Canton, Chicago, Detroit, and that "Athens of the West," Milwaukee (where the indispensable adjunct of philosophizing was first brewed in 1840). The forty-eighters were not merely intellectuals; they were men of action. They belonged to the generation which had cherished the social ideals of the French Revolution, freedom and self-determination, translated now into economic terms. And they preserved the romantic aspirations of Fichte and early Hegel of a nation as a cultural unity no less than as a political one. Many had been schooled in a sturdier socialism than Kaufmann's Christian Socialism and some had been associated with the Communist League. These last included Willich, Weitling, and Weydemeyer, to mention only some "Ws." All in Germany had seen the collapse in the fall of 1848 of the republican aspirations which had been so hopeful in the spring. Americans read the history of the revolutionary drama and the distress of the political refugees as it was vividly drawn by Marx in Greeley's *New York Tribune.* Insofar as Hegel figured in their philosophies it was the young and revolutionary Hegel now tempered by the left-wing theorists and utilized by Feuerbach and Marx. Hegel's reputation as a conservative "Law and Order" man was only later entrenched by the German conservative backlash; in such later right-wing theorists as the historian Treitschke, Hegel is portrayed as a nationalist in a modern competitive sense, and it is this interpretation of Hegel that survives in the twentieth century, at least till the rediscovery of the early Hegel.

Cincinnati and St. Louis received the brunt of this German cultural migration. By the time Willich settled in Cincinnati, befriended by Stallo, it was already an industrial and urbane city, complete with libraries, foreign booksellers, music festivals, and a consolidated German community. There were sizable samplings of German and French Catholics, Jews, Calvinists, and Unitarians, many of whom had set up their own resources for higher education. The prevailing sentiment was liberal and when President Lyman Beecher forbade the students at Lane Theological Seminary to discuss slavery, their abolitionist sympathies led them to remove virtually en masse to Oberlin. But where Stallo's use of Hegelian themes was geared to science and the evolution of the natural order, Willich was a left-wing Hegelian who had come to edit the liberal German language newspaper, the *Cincinnati Republikaner.*

Willich is a good illustration of the way Hegel's philosophy, compounded with others, entered into the Western *Weltanshauung.* Willich was a foster son of Schleiermacher and must have been part of the household when Bancroft was hosteled there. He entered the Prussian army as an officer but quickly became disgusted with the caste system that separated the privilege of the officers from the degradation of the soldier. He then came to see this conflict as a reflection of the larger exploitation of the people, and when he carried the new spirit of democratization into the army, he quickly found himself in anticipatable trouble. Soon he was fighting with the revolutionaries and as soon sharing their exile.

In London, while identified with the Communist League, he became estranged from Marx who called him a "true socialist." This remark was of course no compliment because it suggested, and correctly, that Willich still had faith that a social revolution might be brought off, completely disregarding Marx's insistence on the indispensable preparation of society itself before an ultimate victory could be possible. Willich had faith not only in an immediate revolution but in the workers themselves. Society is alienated against itself, the worker has lost his humanity in his servitude. Yet the worker can be educated to see the need to determine the conditions of his employment, and to liberate himself from the whims and interests of the factory owner who controls capital and credit. He could be educated as well to the power he has to initiate social reform. It is this education and the establishing of workingmen's associations across national boundaries that are the avenues to social justice—not the capturing of governments and the nationalizing of the means of production.

The estrangement with Marx was overcome, but not before the American public was entertained by exchanges in which, for example, Marx calls Willich the "magnanimous" man in Hegel's ironic sense. Willich firmly publicizes the continuity between Hegel and Marx, a continuity which Engels developed so carefully:

> Marx was and is the only one who could undertake the work of extracting from Hegel's logic the kernel which comprised Hegel's genuine discoveries in this area and construct the dialectical method, divested of its idealistic trappings, in the simple form in which it becomes the only correct form of the development of thought. The working out of this method which forms the foundation of Marx's critique of political economy we consider a result scarcely less important than his basic materialistic perspective.[9]

He is particularly impressed with Engels' exposition of the Hegelianism that so influenced Marx's political economy—the fact that truth lies in the historical evolution of knowledge, not in a set of dogmas, the fact that each stage is necessary for its time and conditions and yet unjustifiable with respect to the newer and higher conditions evolving out of its internal structure.[10]

Now it would be predictable that the St. Louis group which had held to the middle of the road as regards Christian theory would enlist Hegel's social philosophy in the service of the moderate political center, and as predictable that they would avoid association with the German-American left and the labor movement generally. Indeed their condescending willingness to include "laborers only if they are 'properly philosophic' " sounds somewhat snide. And although they made Willich (and Stallo) associates of the *Journal of Speculative Philosophy,* Weydemeyer, who was for a time editor of the *St. Louis Neue Zeit,* is absolutely ignored. Even so their commitment to an organic view of society and the state distinguishes them from New England's academic laissez-faire atomism. Yet they were not happy with the Concord Transcendentalism that led to Brook Farm. Active intervention, not withdrawal, social unity of interdependent interests that makes morally right actions possible, not moral salvation via an inner light. Hegel in the light of such aims has become a democrat—a kind of La Follette progressive.

The important lesson to be learned from these ways of approach is that Hegelianism, in one or another of its varieties, did not need to wait for the St.

Louisans to find its way into America. What they did provide for Hegel was a voice and an organization. There is one further caution needed lest the label "St. Louis Hegelians" mislead: just as the Hegelian influence was geographically broader than St. Louis, so interest in St. Louis was intellectually broader than Hegel. They followed the full sweep of German Objective Idealism from Kant through Fichte and Schelling to Hegel and even beyond him to philosophers like Trendelenburg and Ulrici, who in the close skirmishes of German philosophy appeared as critics of Hegel but who were seen in America as sharers of the general viewpoint. The great figures of German philosophy also joined the Westerners to the great figures of German intellectual history—to Goethe, Schiller, and the Schlegels, with an enthusiasm and a virility that distinguishes them from the Transcendentalists, and to Greek culture—to Plato, Aristotle, and to the tragedians and historians. Indeed they were even reintroduced to a nineteenth-century Shakespeare in the Tieck-Schlegel translations, and in *Wilhelm Meister.*

Yet St. Louis and Hegel did have the stellar roles, for the story begins in the most unpretentious meeting of Harris and Brokmeyer one winter evening in 1858 in the St. Louis Mercantile Library. William Tory Harris (1835-1909) was afterward to rise through the school system to become United States Commissioner of Education, and Hans Conrad Brokmeyer (1828-1906) was to become lieutenant governor of Missouri; but on that first encounter they were modest, not to say impoverished, figures. Harris was but recently arrived from the East, having left Yale by mutual consent with its president, Noah Porter, to seek his fortune in the West. If his assets were financially insignificant, at least they included an odd assortment of talents from a reasonable competence in the classics, experience in managing a gymnasium, a knowledge of shorthand, a love of Goethe's *Wilhelm Meister,* and a tremendous will to get to the bottom of Kant's philosophy. Among his more tangible resources were Cousin's essays on the history of philosophy to guide him to the last. It was not Noah Porter who led him to philosophy but Emerson and Alcott; the latter, a personal friend, had stiffened his interest away from an incipient theosophy toward somewhat more serviceable and orthodox problems. The time was to come when Harris would educate them both in Hegelianism.

That part of Emerson's education was still in the future when Harris finished an informal lecture, though presumably a philosophically respectable one, in St. Louis's Mercantile Library. Brokmeyer, dressed in foundry clothes, challenged his defense of Cousin. This was the first of many discussions that were to last till early morning. Even at that first meeting Brokmeyer held out Hegel and especially the *Larger Logic* as the "key to virtually every philosophic puzzle from the understanding of Kant to the reconstruction of social institutions." Rough looking though he may have been, Brokmeyer was as skilled a dialectician and as charismatic a figure as was to appear among American philosophers. Brokmeyer had come from Germany in 1844, too young to have studied philosophy in the Old World, but not too young to make a fortune on his westward travel. He tried out

Georgetown College (Kentucky) but when encouraged by its authorities to leave, he talked his way into Brown University. That experience did not prove a total success either, for after engaging President Wayland in pyrotechnic debate, he left that university as well, cockily determined "Ich bin meine eigene Universität." The Brown venture, however, was a success in another way, for there he met Frederick Hedge, who was a minister at the time in Providence. Hedge's *Prose Writers of Germany* initiated him into German philosophy, and although conversations with the conservative Hedge may have strengthened his knowledge, they were most unlikely to have converted him to his lifelong devotion to Hegel. Brokmeyer returned to the West, taking seriously the Transcendentalists' injunction to be and know yourself, to live the Fichtean vocation of man; but the measure of his involvement was a Walden of two years on the harsh frontier beyond St. Louis in the company of Hegel, Kant, Goethe, Descartes, and a gun for hunting. It was here that Brokmeyer began the translation of Hegel's *Logic* that he revised for nearly half a century; although it was never published, it was copied by hand in its entirety many times and circulated widely and parts of it were taken down in phonography by Harris. In a way, Harris and Brokmeyer are the contrast (which Harris himself saw) of the ways that Wilhelm Meister and Faust approach the vocation of man. Harris, the Wilhelm Meister, prepares for a life in this world with a limited outlook. He is torn between poetry and business during his *Lehrjahre* or apprenticeship and he is blocked in his progress toward becoming a whole man by abortive and external associations. His *Wanderjahre,* or journeyman years, see him still struggling with the problem of education and self-education, seeking a more ample self-view in good and harmonious living, but not attempting to alter the social order drastically. The end is still open, for the *Meisterjahre* is not told, but the title, of course, gives a reason for optimism. Brokmeyer is rather the Faustian figure preparing for a more cosmic life; at the outset the earth spirit, the world, is too much for him and he grapples with an ideal, struggling for the knowledge that will allow him to bring the world and the ideal in touch with one another. He feels no indignation at the sufferings of individuals, e.g., for the old couple whose lands must be flooded, but sees rather the subordination of the individual to the social ideal. The contrast is carried over in their views against slavery, for where Harris is morally incensed, Brokmeyer works unsentimentally toward that reconstruction of society which will eventually make the institution unnecessary.

Brokmeyer's first retreat to the wilderness was not the last, but between these withdrawals he found time to practice law, enter politics, become a mayor (it is said). His leadership in the German community helped hold Missouri for the Union and crystallize its progressive sentiment. His influence was later important in electing Carl Schurz to the Senate and in getting Stallo's diplomatic appointment; his greatest service to Missouri was less as lieutenant governor (and acting governor, 1876-77) than his hand in drafting the State Constitution of 1875 which guaranteed education to *all* from the sixth to the twentieth year. Throughout he was sensitive and knowledgeable about political movements; practical policies and Hegel's logic were all of a piece, since philosophy was to be tested in social and political reality.

2. The Group Forms in St. Louis

St. Louis also had its role in these philosophic developments. It was a frontier town, a gateway to those who would seek their futures in the farther West and the point of return for those who, like Harris's own father, had tried there and failed. Yet it was much more than that, it was a cosmopolitan city which cherished aspirations of one day becoming the capital of a United States of America that stretched from one ocean to the other. French culture had left its trace in taste, religion, and above all in the Catholic schools and university. A small but educated group of Italians and a sizable German population mingled with homesteaders from the East whose various denominations set about founding their colleges, the most famous of which was the Unitarians' Washington University (1839). Between 1846 and 1856, St. Louis was culturally enriched by the forty-eighters—journalists, physicians, soldiers, jurists, and artists who set high standards of social practice. Also, as in Cincinnati, they brought a nonpuritanical and romantic interest in art, literature, and music. There appears to have been more cooperation between segments of the German and native-born community than in Cincinnati, for neither the Germans nor the native Americans who provided the setting for the St. Louis Hegelians were concerned merely with transplanting German culture, nor for that matter with creating an American philosophy as such. Their interest in German philosophy was their interest in resources, to make available to American thinkers the full range of world culture and experience.

Perhaps this solidarity was fostered in part by the special and long-standing tensions that beleaguered and disrupted the city: St. Louis was surrounded on almost all sides by slaveholders and Confederate sympathizers. The city itself, however, was strongly antislavery. Though loyal to the Union during the war, its people were as deeply committed to preserving the larger Union as Hegel had been to making of Germany a nation. They saw their role as synthesizers, and after the war they were equally concerned lest the Union destroy the states, even the Southern states.

St. Louis, with its enterprise, and refugees, its conflicts and cultural and political aspirations, was then an important part of the setting of the meeting of Brokmeyer and Harris. That meeting was only a beginning, for around them there arose a Kant Club, the first of a variety of associations and discussion groups the history of which is so indefinite and so unreliably remembered that its exact development can not be reconstructed. In any case, it is their collective impact which is of importance. Membership of the first Kant Club is approximate; it seems to have included Woerner, afterward a judge, and Kroeger, who in addition to a staggering number of philosophic translations, served as a reporter for the *New York Tribune.* Although meetings of the Kant Club were given over to a discussion of philosophic texts (Hegel as well as Kant), attention was given also to the multidimensional problems which then beset St. Louis, especially the difficulties set by the developing political and social community, and those created by the forward shadow of civil war. From the first, they appreciated the critical role of their city: theirs was to be the destiny of leaders who held the Union fast, of compromisers and synthesizers engaged in building up a nation. Of course the war, when it came, dampened their activities; it was felt closely and early. The members of the Kant Club, including Brokmeyer, served the Union cause by organizing brigades and helping the war effort: certainly the preservation of the Federal Arsenal in St. Louis and the northern victory at Camp Jackson (though a small engagement)[11] were factors in Missouri's commitment to the Union cause. Harris, who had lost the sight of one eye as a boy, remained in the school system and wrote extensive articles for the newspapers. His was a steady, sober (if a somewhat pedantic) voice, urging union and freedom for all men. He sought especially to explain the conflict, to understand how from its tragedy, a higher victory might emerge. Had men only been better educated, he thought, the agony of war might have been avoided. Industry might have transformed a more willing South gradually if both North and South had understood the nature and laws of institutional growth—in short, if the Hegelian view had been taken more to heart.[12] Harris was persuaded that even tragic history was not blind but a providential working out of a rational plan, and if we only could comprehend it we might take a hand and direct it in a more orderly way. This already represented a departure from Hegel, for we have therefore more to do than to witness the process going on, as the quoted introduction to Hegel in the *Prose Writers* put it. As Harris's interests widened, he resolved the conflicts between loyalty to the West and the pull of New England by assuming national responsibilities first as president of the National Teachers Association and then as Commissioner of Education (1889-1906). Like Wilhelm Meister, he was seeking his vocation through education. Harris's years of greatest philosophic leadership, however, were spent in St. Louis. After the war had receded from the West, Harris and Brokmeyer organized the St. Louis Philosophical Society, and a Kant Club, heir presumptive to the old one. The West in general, and St. Louis in particular, was again favored by an influx of professional people, both immigrants and Easterners. A kind of mystique had grown up concerning the destiny of the city, which had multiplied in population by twenty times between 1840 and 1870. This corporate pride, which fitted well with certain aspects of Hegelian philosophy, made fertile soil for the civic and social activities of these men. The connections of the St. Louis group became more extensive; they exchanged personal visits, and corresponded with such individuals as Stallo and Willich and with philosophic clubs in Jackson and Quincy, Illinois.[13] Somewhat later they intellectually "colonized" Milwaukee, Terre Haute, and even the rival city of Chicago. Many of the newcomers were educators who brought with them enthusiasms which broadened the intellectual interests of the group, transforming an initial strong political bias into the broader concern for social institutions and culture. Among the most important newcomers (for our purposes) were Denton J. Snider, who with Thomas Davidson came to teach in the public schools, and George Howison, who taught at Washington University.

3. A Sketch of the European Background

We shall follow the activities of these three, but first we need to look to Fichte and Schelling and, so the *Prose Writers* tells us, the climax in Hegel. This Idealistic tradition forms the basic fabric, but it was embroidered, stretched, and rewoven so thoroughly that the resultant idealism became as much American as derivative, and it dominated the American academic philosophy by the century's end. Not to understand it is to impoverish our understanding of Royce, Dewey, and Mead, as well as the significance of such problems as the knower and the known, the flow of consciousness, the importance of action in knowledge, the relation between psychology and philosophy, and the revolt against dualism, to be found even in Peirce, James, and modern realists. England, too, had its wave of German philosophic migration, which it naturalized after its fashion, in British neo-Hegelianism (which included—for a short period—even Bertrand Russell). And in both America and England, for a brief moment, philosophy seemed on the point of deserting its empirical interests. But powerful scientific developments (especially stimulated by Darwinian biology) restored the balance, and the subsequent philosophical return to empiricism was richer as a consequence. Snider was to trace the dialectic of this development from Hegelianism and the Absolute to a corrective antithesis in Darwin. He foresaw a synthesis in psychology, the study of man. The assimilation of Objective Idealism by the St. Louis group is thus the story of an intellectual migration. And as with migration studies generally, the story moves from the homeland and the ways the immigrant brings with him to the manner in which these ways are modified in the new land, and sometimes return to have an effect on the source. We shall look at the German tradition from the Western perspective, attempting to reconstruct it from their problems, articles, and translations rather than as present scholarship sees it. The review is necessarily skimpy and selective, but this procedure has advantages for both the reader and the authors since we can then relegate to a note a discussion of Hegel's *Logic,* the arcane concern of the in-group, in favor of the *Phenomenology of Spirit* which had broader and more exuberant appeal.

Kant provides the stimulus, not only by his positive philosophy, but by the host of difficulties he bequeathed to the next generation. Above all, the chasm which Kant left between the noumenal and phenomenal worlds establishes an absolute dichotomy between that which is knowable by science and the understanding, and that which is permanently unavailable—the knowledge of the world as it *really* is,

of God, immortality, and the freedom and purpose of the moral order. The
Romantic tradition often picks up clues which were provided by Kant himself,
although it is clear he would not have licensed much that was developed from such
clues. No chasm exists, the Romantics argue, between being and thought—for the
two are merely reality under different forms. Reality is knowable because whatever *is*, is spiritual. Such a doctrine will require slight adjustments in what is
"knowable." For if reality is not cognizable by the understanding, still some
higher faculty of insight (will, faith, feeling) has access through morals, history,
art, religion, and of course philosophy, to the ultimate reality. Man's capacity for
such larger insights shows that there is more to his person than mere understanding
and science. Understanding makes generalizations and applies categories. Only
this larger insight gives the relation of facts to a totality, reveals their interconnec-
tions and dynamics. In all of this, they believed that they were developing Kant's
notion of "reason" (as beyond the understanding), and as we have seen this is
Emerson's project as well.

Hedge's *Prose Writers* included a section on Fichte's *Bestimmung des
Menschen,* which was nicely translated as *The Destination of Man* rather than the
currently more usual *Vocation of Man.* In this most popular of Fichte's works, his
doctrine is least esoterically stated. Its message is that man's vocation is not merely
to know but to do in the light of that knowledge. Not speculation but action is the
end of being. Moral duty unfolds to us, as individuals and as a race, a destination
worthy of all our powers and love; through the exercise of moral duty our own
identity and continuity of being are secured, and both God and an external world
are restored to us. The Eastern readers of Hedge were especially concerned with
the theological implications and the most mystical appeal to faith at the end of this
work. We have noted the different uses to which Brokmeyer and Harris put the
notion of vocation.

The interest of the Western Hegelians was directed also to the epistemological
questions which Fichte[14] developed starting with the tension between Kant's
Critique of Pure Reason and the *Critique of Practiçal Reason.* Now Kant had
shown that the unity of knowledge was gained by the activity of a self, imposing
categorical forms upon the content or sensous manifold; but the synthetic unity as a
condition and the categories and the content were all different things, and
moreover, there was no demonstrated necessity for their connection. Fichte sought
to show that all of these were derivable from the nature of consciousness itself—it
provides the necessary conditions thus for the deduction of the categories and
generates the content. The self is already a function or activity, not a faculty or an
entity. To understand the necessary steps in the development of consciousness
toward self-consciousness, the evolution of rational self-consciousness, is the end
of Reason. This evolution takes place through oppositions and their resolutions.
The primary fact or assumption is that of the activity of the self. Its first awareness
is of itself. Such self-consciousness is the minimal step, merely asserting the
reality of the self. Then the self posits a not-self or object which is opposed to it.

Yet through this opposition the character of self develops. Finally such opposition is resolved in the larger knowledge that after all both self and not-self are constructions of the activity of the self.

Just what Fichte is getting at is clearer when we realize that the world or the nonego which the self is creating is primarily the world of moral and legal entities. This alien world of our conflicts is constructed so that through our striving and conflicts with other egos and objects, the realization of our own freedom and progressive self-consciousness can take place. We see the moral world and duty initially as something opposed or alien to ourselves—our wants clash with those of others and our duty is opposed to our inclinations. But the next stage in the drama of self-realization comes when we see that the moral demands are imposed by ourselves, that we are autonomous moral beings. Then the acknowledgment of the autonomy and the dignity of others leads us to identification with the moral community, in which our doing is informed by knowledge and where all men are free through such knowledge and identification of interest. Such a theory represents a challenge to the brittle individualism of laissez faire, and it moves into Fichte's nationalism and tentative Socialism.

Schelling[15] similarly starts with objections to the Kantian dichotomy between noumena and phenomena, but he, like most of the Americans, felt that Fichte's answer was too subjectivistic—the idea that we construct a world merely as a theater for our moral drama was not at all persuasive nor properly appreciative of science, of art, nor, for that matter, of the intransigence of nature. Schelling's thought passed through many stages, and though initially a friend of Hegel's, he became critical of him after Hegel's death. Loyalty to Schelling appears to account in some part for New England antipathy to Hegel since the threat of pantheism is equally forceful in both.

The stage of his philosophy that was important to both East and West is called the *Identity* philosophy. Schelling holds that the ideal and the real, soul and matter, are aspects of a single and greater reality somewhat after the manner of Spinoza. But unlike Spinoza he holds that there is a dynamic and creative principle or world soul which is immanent in the world and operates in all nature according to the single law of dialectical evolution. Consciousness, not that of any particular person, seeks to realize itself in and through matter. All things represent some stage in the development of consciousness, but mankind is the highest product, and man alone is self-conscious. We know the world of nature because we are like it; categories of thought and being are one and the same.

Important to the St. Louis Hegelians, even beyond the place he makes for science, is Schelling's aesthetic theory. By dissolving the distinction between the ideal and the real, Schelling takes the final step so that the world of nature and of art are both evidences of the ideal. Thus the question of the subjectivity of aesthetic judgment is relieved. Aesthetic experience—both that of the artist and of the spectator—is legitimized as a unique kind of insight or knowledge. Art and its understanding is not just pastime, it is a critical feature of education.

Hegel, in his turn, built on the philosophies of Fichte and Schelling.[16] He welcomes their breakthrough with respect to Kant. In his hands idealism becomes fashioned into a full and systematic account on the order of a Plato and an Aristotle, but the romanticism of Fichte and Schelling is rejected in favor of a classic or Greek ideal of reason. From Fichte he takes the notion of method or dialectic, but regards the subjectivism as merely descriptive of the subjective phase of a world objective process. By maintaining the identity of thought and being he shares much with Schelling, but disavows his mysticism to make a larger place for science. But Hegel did not inherit just metaphysical and epistemological problems left over by Kant and mulled over by the post-Kantians. Hegel was united, and the Americans with him, to larger problems and traditions which he wove organically into his metaphysics and epistemology. Through Fichte he was united to philosophic problems of history, culture, and politics, to the tradition of Herder and the social geographers. Through the problems of Fichte, Hegel is reminded not only of morality as an institution, and the family and education as institutional forces, but above all of the function of philosophy in social reform. Through Schelling Hegel is literally and personally joined to one of the most exciting moments of German literary and cultural history. The contrast between classicism and romanticism was in full swing, but it was made amiable because, although Goethe calls himself a classicist, the philosophers—Schelling, the Schlegels, and Hegel—defined romantic as everything from and including Shakespeare, with of course Goethe as the key figure.

It was the great virtue of Hegel that he accepted the problems of literary criticism and of art and religion, of the development of social and political institutions, into his philosophy not as isolated problems but as organic and integrative to the whole sweep of his cosmic system.

The key to Hegel's philosophy is its dialectic method. This may be summarized briefly by saying that it is at once genetic and world-historical. Every social and cultural item, from family to religion and myth, from style and form of art to economic institutions, emerges at a particular time and in a particular context, as a historical convergence of factors. It is thus a process of becoming, which always embodies the past and points to the future. No abstract formula can express its essence, for every abstraction and universal is one-sided and static. Institutions, in the broadest possible connotation, covering all patternings of the self and all cultural forms, can be understood only by reference to the direction of the general historical flow.

That total flow or process is the mark of *Geist* (Spirit, God, Idea, or Absolute). The rationale of history, covering the evolution of absolutely everything, is found not only in the fact of its direction, but also in this: that the laws of dialectic which characterize the process winnow out whatever is inadequate at each stage, leaving only what is genuinely valuable to be incorporated as a part of some later stage. This is part of what Hegel meant by the slogan, "The real is rational and the rational, real." On some interpretations this is read as the justification of any existing thing or state of affairs, relative to its time, because it will survive or continue to obtain only so long as it meets the demands made upon it, and become inoperative when it fails to do so. Man is free insofar as he understands the laws of this march of reason through History—laws which are simultaneously those of being and of thought (reason). The dialectic moves from a triadic base: each thesis has its antithesis, and these two are always resolved in some higher synthesis. Each of these units (e.g., each thesis, antithesis, or synthesis) may in turn be broken down triadically; at some lower level, it will turn out also to be composed of thesis, antithesis, and synthesis. Thus in his philosophy of art, Hegel distinguishes as the thesis Oriental art (whose characteristic is symbolism); the antithesis is classic or Greco-Roman art, and the synthesis is "modern" or romantic art.[17]

The Phenomenology of Spirit (1807), an early work, gives the gist of Hegel's system as a whole. It was this that appealed to the less esoterically minded among the St. Louis Hegelians, to the teachers, judges, and doctors. It is a book so rich in allusions, in breadth of reference and cultural scope, that any Westerner who troubled to master it would be more than a match for Alcott's *Orphic Sayings*. The *Phenomenology* appealed to the Westerners, not only because of its aesthetic character, but also because it struck in them the chord of their historical appreciation of events, an insight that seems virtually absent in the East. The Midwest was closer to Europe, and knew and felt the catastrophes of that overseas drama—both in the actual experience of its citizens and in their imaginative reconstructions of European history. They could not escape the role of conflict, tragedy, and success; they were witnesses of governments replaced, of the rise and destruction of institutions, and they heard through Hegel's echo of Fichte the appeal for the development of community and nation. In the *Phenomenology,* "institution" is a very broad term: chivalry rises and falls sardonically in the person of Quixote; romanticism is cut to pieces and satirized in pitiless romantic dialectic: "it is a book written in romantic style which destroys romanticism."[18]

Hegel's *Phenomenology* is the natural history of consciousness, *Geist,* or the Absolute; reality is seen as a developmental process in which Reason achieves its full self-consciousness. The book is, as it were, the autobiography of the World-Spirit, and this is the meaning of the references in the St. Louis writers to "voyages of discovery of the Spirit." Hegel was carrying the manuscript on his person when, at Jena in 1806, he witnessed Napoleon's preparations for battle. He later remarked that he saw that day the World-Spirit on horseback, and Snider added that he might justly have claimed to "be carrying the Absolute in his pocket!"

The distinctive merit of Hegel's metaphysics, as viewed by Harris and the rest, was not its idealism; after all, idealism was familiar to them from the work of the post-Kantians and the Transcendentalists. It is the dynamic character of Hegel's philosophy which fascinated them. To appreciate this dynamism, one may compare Hegel with Aristotle (a comparison which constantly appears in the work of the St. Louis writers[19]) for Hegel, as the St. Louis group was quick to notice, was enthusiastically responsive to Greek culture.

Both Aristotle and Hegel offered teleological explanations of process—the arguments of the former involve the notion of a separate and inherent plan for each species including man, but there is no master plan; interactions between different species are accidental and contingent. Hegel, on the other hand, argues that there is a unified purpose or plan, implicating not only all species, but also the totality of all events and processes. The Greek and the German agree that self-conscious thought is the highest reality: but while for Aristotle, God was pure thought thinking itself, eternal, unchanging, and external to the world, for Hegel, the Idea or Absolute was immanent in the process and continually undergoing a sort of development. Neither held that activity was merely "material movement." Activity in Aristotle ultimately meant the actualization of form, while movement was an incomplete actualization; the highest actualization is pure thought. In Hegel, self-activity (not a mere matter of movement) is described in terms of growth: self-consciousness is active in that it grows. Because all history is just this development of one self-consciousness, the practical and the active are not severed from the theoretical.

From this special sense of activity, Hegel derives his special sense of freedom. Developing self-consciousness and increasing freedom go hand in hand. Hegel is not identifying freedom with the notion of a willing spirit (thought of as opposing a completely determined matter); nor is he treating of Kant's "sense of freedom," which is located only in the noumenal world while the phenomenal world remains completely determined; nor, finally, is his conception of freedom to be identified with the activist notion, according to which the growth of self-consciousness becomes the increasing power to control, determine, or arrange the future through knowledge. Hegelian freedom emerges through the individual operating as a social being in a world-historical unfolding activated by conflict.

Self-realization and the realization of freedom occur through the processes of history, for Reason works its way through institutions, which are the rational objectifications of will. In the Oriental world only one man is free—the potentate; in the Greek and Roman world, some are free with slaves to serve them; in the modern world, all are progressively attaining to freedom. This modern freedom consists, minimally, in the increased scope of activity which is made possible by improved social organization and the cumulative results of technology. But there is more to Hegel's notion of freedom than the increased scope of activity. The individual has a role in the cosmic process; he has a will which embraces his needs, inclinations, desires, etc., and his reason is expressed in purposes designed to satisfy these. On the face of it such an individual, working for his own goals, would seem to be in opposition to a rational plan of history. But Reason is cunning, and the conflict of men's passions and limited purposes is the device by which Spirit achieves Its realization.

Men are citizens, persons, victims, or heroes. Citizens are the bearers of the morality of their age and generally act in accordance with its teachings. Persons, of whom Socrates is the prime example, appreciate the weight of customary morality but seek to understand its rationale and to make it more reasonable. The hero is the decisive vehicle of the World-Spirit at its critical turning points, while the victims are those who have no role at all—the dropouts who are simply used by history. But the irony, as suggested above, is that heroes even such as Napoleon are themselves but the victims of the cunning of Reason. Their appearance on the world scene is an accident of their time and context; driven by personal aims and ambitions they seldom appreciate their true role and when their job is done they disappear from the scene or, as in the case of the Little Corporal, are discarded.

4. The Group Reassembles after the War

This background provided a kind of *lingua franca* for those centered in St. Louis, although they were quick to modify it to their own ends. Thus (as suggested above) none was to take to heart this Hegelian irony—that men are passive witnesses to the processes of history. Snider, Davidson, and even Howison were interveners and they saw public education as the most powerful instrument for giving rational direction to social processes. Denton Snider (1841-1925) was one of the more joyous and flamboyant figures in our intellectual history. A native Midwesterner of German background, he saw, as a student, the costly but courageous stand of the abolitionist Oberlin faculty against the Fugitive Slave laws and he early learned that principles could be clothed in effective action. His particular concerns were political theory and literature, but these for him were not disparate interests since the sweep of history and the emergence of social institutions with their conflicts, climaxes, and resolutions was simply the most vast and heroic of dramas.

Certainly less schooled in scholastic discussion, his influence was widely exerted on generations of high-school students. At a time when the teaching of literature was a cold affair and translation a matter of parsing and grammar, Snider succeeded in making it a passionate and quickening experience. He brought the wholeness of Schelling's view of art and nature and the broad modes of Hegelian literary critique to the appreciation of Shakespeare, Dante, Goethe, and the Greek tragedians and historians. Long after graduation, clubs of former students continued to meet in serious confrontations with a work or an author. He proselytized the Hegelian literary gospel from Washington to Milwaukee and even to the camp of the Transcendentalists, to the Concord school.

Of equal importance was his concern about personality or personhood which he also found in the post-Kantian tradition. Thus while teaching psychology in Chicago he gave impetus to the kindergarten movement and such European educational philosophies as those of Pestalozzi and Froebel. This movement involved a tremendous humanistic shift in the view of the development of the child's capacities toward making a whole person and socializing him. Educational institutions and educators are critical in determining the future quality of a community. The training of youth and the humane relation between student and teacher require education at a college level for prospective teachers. This opened a major opportunity for women to acquire higher education when other avenues were closed.

Snider was the historian of the St. Louis group (though his *The St. Louis Movement* was written after a lapse of many years and deals with history in a rather cavalier fashion). We glean from his writings an intimate picture of the exchanges between East and West, of the confrontation of Alcott and Emerson with Brokmeyer.[20]

[Mr. Alcott] gave quite a full exposition of his doctrine of the lapse of the soul, from the Primal One dropping in its descent the various orders of creating down to matter. It was the Alcottian redaction of the Neo-Platonic theory of the universe. . . . [Brokmeyer] was courteous and appreciative, but he showed the Alcottian lapse to be hardly more than a relapse to Oriental emanation, which had been long since transcended, while he put stress upon the opposite movement of philosophy, namely, Occidental evolution, with its principle of freedom.

[Emerson] opened the talk in a vein of urbane irony: "Is it not strange that we keep finding deeper and deeper meanings in Shakespeare, and that we have come to know more about his plays than he ever knew himself?" The implied criticism was familiar to me, and I had already engaged in many sharp skirmishes along the same line. "Oh yes," I replied, "Shakespeare, like Nature whom he so completely represents, is continually unfolding into fresh meanings, being reflected new in every age, so that he is sure to have a line of successive interpreters reaching down time, to doomsday, of whom I only pretend to be one. Shakespeare, too, is in the process of evolution."[21]

Unfortunately, academicians are in the habit of patronizing nonprofessional philosophers, and (judged by these standards) it must be admitted that Snider is "popular." Yet he was thoroughly familiar with the texts, and one who has glanced at his *Modern European Philosophy* will see him as the forerunner of all those modern professors who point out that (a) philosophic convictions have their roots in the more general culture around them, and (b) that the full sweep of ideas has a dynamic of its own, a cumulative and self-correcting facet. Snider would have been the first to agree that philosophy must be "relevant" to the problems of society.

Thomas Davidson (1840-1900) was the maverick, at least so far as respect for Hegel was concerned. He shared Snider's enthusiasm for things Greek to such an extent that it was whispered that he preferred Aristotle to Hegel and Greek culture to Christianity. Davidson, although from the poorest of Scottish families, had taken a degree at St. Andrews with the highest honors. His wanderings had taken him to St. Louis and he was teaching classics in the high school when the

Philosophical Society was formed. During his stay there he became the focus for many who wished to study Greek texts, especially Aristotle, and for the less philosophically oriented whose concern was with Greek art and architecture. Basically a peripatetic, Davidson withdrew from academic teaching without withdrawing from the academic world. William James was altogether right in feeling that "Davidson would not run well in academic harness." Indeed, just as James and Cabot were engaged in the delicate task of arranging for Davidson to teach Greek at Harvard, Davidson published a savage critique of its classics department in the *Atlantic Monthly*. Needless to say, this cost Davidson a future at Harvard but left him undismayed, since he had never intended to settle down as a professor, planning rather to spend the rest of his life shuttling between Europe and America. As a matter of fact, even this allocation of time in America was not always worked out. His return was often vainly awaited in the Concord School.

Davidson's knowledge of Greek art was neither casual nor secondhand. He lived for months at a time in Greece, and his writings about architecture are insightful and philosophical (especially his essay on the Parthenon frieze). He was one with the rest of the Hegelians at least in his belief that aesthetics is a fully philosophic enterprise, and that the fine arts are as susceptible of analysis as literature.

Davidson's permanent and central love was Aristotle, and his many translations are of literary and philosophic importance. In 1887 he was in Italy, at Domo d'Ossola, examining medieval commentaries on Aristotle. There he became interested in the philosophy of Antonio Rosmini-Serbati (1797-1855) and the contemporary Italian discussion it aroused. Davidson's interest in Rosmini and the translations which he did of his work are further evidences of the cosmopolitan interests of members of the St. Louis group.[22] On the other hand, it was not a distraction from the main problems with which they were concerned, for Italian philosophy was developing in the same general pattern as German philosophy and its American reflection. Italy had had its empiricism and its criticism, and it was to have its Hegelianism, especially as represented by Augusto Vera who was in personal contact with the St. Louis group. Rosmini's philosophy is a kind of intermediate step, representing something of the direction of Schelling and Fichte; yet it must have been attractive to Davidson because it also held strong overtones of the Scottish philosophy which he had known at St. Andrews. Rosmini worked with the problem of the objectivity of knowledge. Like Kant, he found in knowledge an element which is universal, necessary, and contributed by the mind itself; however, instead of being merely subjective, this element, so Rosmini argued, is objective. Ideas are ideas *of* something and every idea carries with it existential reference. This resembles the Scottish commonsense realist's position about the knowability of an external world. Thus the idea and its object are as inseparable as seeing is from the light. Such judgments of objective reality are specific and infallible. Error arises only in judgment since the mind by reflection and inference constructs its knowledge and of course is fallible. There is truth when there is knowledge of what exists really. Thus as in Aristotle the categories of reality and thought are conjoined, but as in Hegel this conjunction, being dynamic, is only realized through history.

More than the Rosminians, however, Davidson was concerned with the relation not only between thinking and being, but of these with action. Benefiting from Rosmini's identification of thought and being, Davidson took something of the attitude of a scientist prepared to acquiesce at once in the limits of our knowledge in science; this is not skepticism but the beginning of inquiry. What distinguished Davidson's ethics from the Rosminian and from Socialism was the emphasis he put on the need to develop the individual and to prepare him to *understand* the world rather than to change it. In this education of the individual, philosophy has a central role. It is not a cold intellectualism that he intends by "understanding," but that kind of knowledge or intellect which becomes a spring of action by its power to see that there is a world of values, that one thing is better and to be preferred to another. In his theory of the individual he makes a metaphysical category out of feeling, using it in the broad sense that James used. An individual then is simply feeling or sensibility, modified by influences that are not self-originated. Such modifications when grouped are the individual's world, and each individual then is a sentient unity of a sensible world. Feeling made active is desire, and for Davidson the interaction of one individual with another is simply a fact, indeed, the fundamental moral fact. In rather the way of Fichte or Schelling, this moral world is a construction or an ordering of our experience.

Though these worlds are constructed, not all worlds are equally satisfying. The aim of education through philosophy is to help enlarge the domain of our experience and our modes of organizing it into the most harmonious and ideal world. The important fact of history and its drama is the role of the self-dependent individual; he is master of his own destiny and is determined neither by things nor by the providence of an all-inclusive God. Hegel's neglect of such individualism and pluralism was constantly offered by Davidson to Harris as evidence of Hegel's shortcomings. And idealism of this individualistic sort was shortly to become a hallmark of American thinking.

The Rosminians also attracted Davidson for another reason which was to become important to the course of philosophic instruction in America. Rosmini had established an order dedicated to the education of youth and to charity, emphasizing moral and intellectual aids as well as material wants. His commitment to education as integral to the tasks of philosophy is shared by all the St. Louis Hegelians. Davidson was forever establishing centers that aimed at securing the betterment of man's world through his acquisition of culture, thereby allowing him to enlarge his vista and to refashion himself. In England, e.g., he founded the Fellowship of the New Life, which had as its ideal a community of fully developed moral beings, culturally sensitive and engaged in the continual discovery of values in themselves and in their communal life. Although the title and objectives may appear quaint—like a social version of Benjamin Franklin's plan for self-improvement—we must not forget that the early 1880s witnessed the growth of a social conscience in America and England which was a prelude to social reform. And in fact this quaintly named organization soon became the Fabian Society of the Webbs and Bernard Shaw. Davidson by that time had abandoned this child of his own creating, for he thought that they had subverted the moral perfection of the individual to an excessive concern for improving his material environment.

In America he learned from workmen of the Lower East Side that some accommodation of his objectives was required. When he told a labor audience that the culture of the world lay ready for any man who, after his day's work, would go home to his table and books, the audience immediately protested that they neither had a room for themselves nor a table nor money for books, that, in short, the world of culture was unavailable to them. Davidson immediately, if somewhat rashly, offered to conduct classes, and out of this the Breadwinners College was born. The response was enthusiastic, hundreds of people, especially Jewish immigrants, joined the classes which read Plato and Dante, Aristotle, and even the inscrutable Hegel himself. Students grew into professionals and teachers, and the list of those associated with the college reads like a *Who's Who* of the next generation's intelligentsia and reformers. Davidson lectured not only at Snider's schools, but when he made it, at Alcott's Concord School. Finding that the Concord atmosphere was becoming too rarefied, he established his own philosophic center in the Adirondacks. The lasting importance of this effect lay in the professional exchanges which it promoted between such men as Dewey, Royce, and James, and some of the associates of the Breadwinner's College, for example, Morris R. Cohen.[23]

In many respects George H. Howison (1834-1916) places the same emphasis on the individual as does Davidson. The doctrine that finally emerges, after two years of study in Germany with Lotze, Michelet, and Paulsen, is more explicit and more academically formulated. Whereas Davidson was knowledgeable on a broad front, Howison was a genuine scholar of modern philosophy; Kant and Fichte especially fascinated him. Doubtless in the long run Howison was the more influential, not because he established a school, but because he trained at the University of California a large number of next-generation professors.

An undergraduate of Marietta College, Howison then attended the Lane Theological Seminary where Hegel was discussed but he did not sympathize with him. Thus when Howison arrived in St. Louis he was more inclined to "debate" than to accept the philosopher of the day. In St. Louis his sympathies were strongly Kantian and Leibnizian; perhaps these interests were tied to his expertise in mathematics and in the more formal aspects of logic. While teaching mathematics at Washington University, he wrote quite an impressive book on analytic geometry, which Chauvenet regarded as an original contribution to the field. This interest in mathematics persisted throughout his career, even when he devoted himself to philosophy proper. He wrote articles defining the domain of mathematics, and he also taught what appear to be the first courses on the philosophy of science and the logic of grammar at MIT.

Howison was the first of the group to leave St. Louis. In 1878, hoping to teach philosophy in the Boston area, he left the security of friends and position to accept a high-school teaching post there. He had known Emerson and Alcott for some time, and quickly became a member of the Trancendentalist "Family." William James, who took all the St. Louis writers to be Hegelians, always regarded him with affection mixed with formality. Howison wrote back to St. Louis that he had heard Cabot's lectures on Kant in the same audience with Emerson and Henry James, Sr. From its beginning he took an active part in the Concord School, including participation in a famous symposium on science and pantheism with Peirce, Fiske, and Abbot.

He achieved his ambition temporarily by teaching at MIT. Unfortunately, the depression of the late 1870s forced MIT to cut down its humanistic offerings and Howison was once again without a position in philosophy. By 1880, when Harris had come east and joined the Concord summer school, Howison contributed lectures as a member of the original faculty. In the way of a stopgap after leaving MIT, Howison was invited by C. C. Everett, dean of the Harvard Divinity School, to lecture on German philosophy. Still in the pursuit of philosophic wisdom, Howison went next to Germany to study. The two years he spent there helped him crystallize his own philosophic outlook. Though modestly regarding himself as a student, he became a real part of intellectual life there. He was deeply moved by Michelet's lectures, held in the same auditorium where Fichte and Hegel had once lectured. He formed friendships in Germany with psychologists as well as philosophers, and corresponded with them the rest of his life. Michelet, who was one of the staunch Hegelians and who supervised the publication of Hegel's works in Germany, expected Howison to hold aloft the banner of Hegel in America. Howison worked with Vaihinger as an American representative of the *Kant Studien,* and found time to chat with Hegel's widow about more intimate details of the philospher's life. Although more than an acquaintance of Zeller, Paulsen, and Ebbinghaus, he was most intimately acquainted with Eucken. In England too he became friends with Neo-Hegelians such as the Cairds, and Stirling, but he also was in friendly conversation with F. C. S. Schiller, the embattled standard bearer of pragmatism in England.

Howison was thus in touch with most of the important themes of idealism and also those that were shortly to challenge it. He was knowledgeable in empirical psychology and shared the pluralism of James and Schiller, but his own view, which he called Personal Idealism, retained the strong flavor of rational theism and the concerns he shared with Harris in St. Louis. This Personal Idealism was developed largely in the decades that followed his return to America.[24] For after a year at Michigan—Howison was the predecessor there of Dewey—he went to California. Here he created a philosophical establishment at Berkeley, the

Philosophical Union. In the spirit of the St. Louis clubs, he reached beyond the university. He sought to mobilize the philosophical resources of the entire bay area, his own students and those who had graduated, scientists, and intellectuals generally. They would choose a topic and work extensively at it, meeting monthly during the year; the climax would be the visit of a distinguished philosopher and the publication that signalized the year's work. Foreign visitors such as John Watson from Toronto, Rashdall, Ward, and McTaggart from Britain, and Americans such as Palmer, James, and Dewey, all had their turn. But the most publicized discussion was that of 1897, which ended in a symposium by LeConte, Mezes, Howison, and Royce on the conception of God. Even *The New York Times* and the *Tribune* covered this debate. Howison's criticism of Royce is that the individual self is "swallowed up" in the Absolute, with the consequence that the individual—the person, in Howison's view—loses his reality. In saving the individual Howison was in effect making personality the test of reality. Hence God, too, would have to be a Person. What is thereby regarded as Howison's extremism in the idealist camp is thus forced on him by his fundamental endeavor. The way Howison sets the question of the limits of scientific knowledge vis-à-vis religion and philosophy is somewhat unfashionable, but most of the men of his generation, James and Peirce not excepted, were anxious about how deeply science cuts into philosophy. Howison is out to preserve human freedom (in the face of scientific determinism) and the moral value of action (in the valueless world of science). Of course evolution is a powerful and respectable scientific theory, but it is extended beyond its proper limits when it attempts to explain all phenomena and when it is thought to exhaust philosophic method. Those who exaggerate in this way often resort to the principle of conservation of energy as well as that of evolution; they tend to reduce the account of the world to a single principle so operating that the higher functions of mind are presumed derivable from physiological functions. Thus all genuine transcendence becomes impossible, and what is more, since the system operates as a single whole there is not even a place for a responsible moral individual. For example, the evolutionary theory aims only to provide a holistic plan for the evolution of species and to allow nothing to the individual's ingenuity. Hence the impact of science tends to be either outrightly materialistic or—and this he regards as philosophically more mature—completely pantheistic, the only place for God or spirit being immanence, as with the Hegelians.

Science, says Howison, is not entitled to such all-encompassing philosophic conclusions. Its method can leave it at most agnostic on the profounder questions of religion, morality, and the nature of knowledge itself. Spencer and the evolutionists tried to explain in evolutionary terms how the Kantian categories of knowledge evolved. Such attempts are inherently bound to fail, for knowledge itself as a construction of mind exhibits the element of transcendence; in order to construct a theory of evolution the scientist must presuppose such categories as time, space, and causation.

For the primacy of mind over Nature, the legislative relation of mind to the world, has been found to be the real presupposition of science itself, and the tacit recognition of this truth to be the clue to the first sudden advance of modern science, and to its unparalleled subsequent progress.[25]

Quoting Kant, he points out that science interrogates nature not as a pupil but as a judge, forcing it through experiment to answer questions of science's own construction. As Howison elsewhere expresses his basic theme, mind (including science) is not the offspring of nature, but rather the offspring of mind's true nature.

Science, restricting itself to what is empirically given, renders freedom and immortality impossible by its very initial assumptions. The incontrovertible fact which science cannot reach is the authenticity of the individual's moral struggle and the genuineness of his responsibility in the relation between act and thought.

The heart on which the vision of a possible moral perfection has once arisen, and in whose recesses the still and solemn voice of Duty has once resounded with its majestic sweetness, can never be reconciled to the decree, though this issue never so authentically from Nature, that bids it count responsible freedom an illusion and surrender existence on that mere threshold of moral development which the bound of our present life affords.[26]

Howison, in effect, begins where Fichte had begun—with the practical reason of Kantian philosophy. He too deals with the conflict between the noumenal and phenomenal worlds, between the natural law governing the latter and the transcendent freedom of the former. Howison, like Fichte, not only regards the world as a moral construction of the individual, a stage for moral drama, but also holds that man's very vocation is that of moral self-perfecting and doing.

For Howison, morality is social. Men interact as minds; i.e., they have common purposes. Since it is necessary, if "moral struggle" is to have any meaning, that there be obligations among autonomous individuals—God, who according to Howison is also moral, must be an individual among individuals, with obligations and regrets. Howison went so far in this direction as to argue that the personal God did not create persons, but rather that persons are the ultimate realities, the eternally existent metaphysical substances. The relation between man and God is not an efficient causal relation, but a final one: individuals are attracted to God as their perfect final cause. Our individual lives are purposive only as we strive toward that guiding perfection. Our common human striving guarantees that there will be no ultimate basic human conflict, in spite of the singularity of the individual and the diversity of human ideals. God is absolved by Howison from responsibility for evil; systems of "pantheism" and Hegelian idealism, according to him, have proven themselves weak by the fact that they ascribe this awful responsibility to the Deity. Natural evil is a product of the nondivine minds themselves, when these ultimate metaphysical constituents of the universe fail to will in accordance with their rational visions.

Howison's was only one among a variety of idealisms that dominated the American philosophic scene in the first generation of academicians after the Scottish Realists. Undoubtedly the closest to Howison among the younger idealists was Bowne, whose lineal descendants are of influence today. And the most famous and comprehensive was Josiah Royce. These idealisms developed independently of British Neo-Hegelianism, though in friendly enough competition with it. The distinctive mark of American idealisms was a voluntaristic individualism, a philosophic reflection of the general cultural climate which even Royce could not help but preserve and which becomes more explicit after Howison's work. At Cornell, meanwhile, Schurman and Creighton (educated in Britain) were spreading the British version of Neo-Hegelianism among American students.

5. The Journal and the Cultural Mission

The foregoing illustrates that neither a particular interpretation of Hegel, a doctrine, nor even a problem united the St. Louis groups. Indeed, it is hard to say that they were all German idealists; still, if Davidson, dissenting, preferred Aristotle, his was a very Hegelianized one, while Harris's Hegel was a very Aristotelianized one—quite in keeping with his sometime claim that Aristotle holds the key to Hegel. Of course they were all "Hegelians" to James's disrespectful pen, but in fact their only common cause was philosophizing in the broad cultural Hegelian sense. Even the New Englanders who cherished philosophy's connections with religion moved toward an institutional interpretation of it. And to a man the St. Louisans looked to philosophy for an understanding of the political tensions of their day and for guidance in social action. Thus it was that they stressed, especially after the Civil War, philosophy as "education," meaning thereby education as a personal vocation, as the mode of cultural transmission and social reconstruction.

This overriding interest in education was expressed in an organizational pursuit of knowledge. We have already seen how long-term and short-term groups formed to study Kant, Aristotle, and Hegel, literature, pedagogy, and fine art; how they established connections with other like-minded groups or colonized other centers. Indefatigable in lecturing, they spread the gospel wherever they went, although it was not always the same gospel save as it preached the need to "spiritualize" America, i.e., to join her to the mainstream of continental kultur.

What gave the group its coherence and influence was the dedication to publishing as the way of educating the English-reading public in the German sources either directly through translations or indirectly through articles and book-length studies on the history of philosophy. Thus Americans came to participate in the historical mood that was so important an aspect of German idealism insofar as it sought to make the history of philosophy significant not merely as scholarship but as philosophy. The translations and commentaries from which we constructed the German background were but the smallest part of their outpourings. Their crowning achievement was the *Journal of Speculative Philosophy* (called familiarly "JoSP") whose intensely packed volumes were the voice of the St. Louis Philosophical Society for more than two decades.

Early in their association Brokmeyer and Harris had established the custom of keeping their translations and essays in a tin box. In 1866, Harris sent an article on Spencer's "Unknowable," a topic which was par for the philosophic course of those days, to the prestigious *North American Review*. Charles Eliot Norton, with Chauncey Wright concurring, rejected it with rather strong comments about style which seemed all too gratuitous to the Westerners. Then and there they resolved to publish their own journal, which became the first periodical in English to be devoted exclusively to philosophy. It first appeared in 1867, with the article on Spencer duly included in the first volume. Analytically solid, its literary quality more than justified the acid criticisms of Messrs. Norton and Wright; in fact the reversal of priorities aptly marks the difference between the *JoSP* and its Eastern competitors.

The *Journal* continued for more than twenty years before it faded out. It was truly an extraordinary undertaking, and except for professional journals there is nothing to match it today. It helped make the center of an international exchange of ideas. In addition to the Westerners, such New Englanders as Cabot, Hedge, Alcott, and Emerson were contributors. British Hegelians, e.g., Stirling and Caird, joined the venture as associates and as contributors together with other Englishmen like James Ward who were less seriously committed to Idealism. Drs. Rosenkranz (of Königsberg) and Hoffman (of Würzburg) debated Hegel's interpretation of God and freedom.

The readers could follow in its pages controversies which raged over Trendelenburg's critique of Hegel which implicated French and Italian scholars as well. Articles and translations were not limited of course to the German greats; above all there were the translations of classic Greek philosophy with a steady preference for Aristotle. Some of these books and translations are valuable even today, sometimes because they are the only translations, sometimes because they are the best to date. Of course preference was given to speculative philosophy but there was room for correspondence from Darwin, articles on the philosophy of mathematics and even empirical psychology. Thus Peirce wrote some of his significant articles for the *Journal* and others, e.g., Jastrow, wrote on the developments in symbolic logic. Dewey's first article appeared in vol. XVIII, "On Kant and Philosophic Method," and it is likely that this contained the kernel of his Ph.D. thesis, written under G. S. Morris at Johns Hopkins. The English Hegelians were also well represented, as were a host of others who, in retrospect, make strange bedfellows: Nicholas Murray Butler and even William James (who, for all his opposition to the Hegelians, published a fair number of the chapters from his *Psychology* there).

Yet with all the emphasis on Hegel and the enthusiasm among the group for Brokmeyer's translation of the *Logic,* it was never gotten into adequate shape for the *Journal.* Snider regarded this as a tragedy that was in no wise remedied by Harris's final publication of a slim volume, *A Critical Exposition of Hegel's Logic,* in the Griggs Series edited by G. S. Morris.

These New World Hegelians were busy in practical affairs beyond publishing, translating, and teaching. Were the impact of the larger group to be assessed properly, it would carry us well into the annals of American public affairs. The Pulitzers sought political reform through their journalism; Carl Schurz (and Stallo) entered the diplomatic corps via public office. Less well known, Hosmer's *History of the Jews,* with its sympathetic admiration for that people, had its lesson of tolerance for a critical moment of nineteenth-century anti-Semitism; while Kroeger's work as correspondent for *The New York Times* (at roughly the time that Marx was writing for the *Tribune*) was supplemented through ill-fated but competent service as a city official. Judge Woerner's legal career was as influential as his writings in the West. Within the inner circle we have already seen something of the consequences of Davidson's socialism as the forerunner of Fabianism, and we have already noted that Brokmeyer's political involvements took him to the lieutenant governorship of Missouri. Harris, as U.S. Commissioner of Education and as mainstay of the National Education Association, was extraordinarily influential at the time when university education was coming of age, and teachers as a group were beginning to take social initiative. Still they made their greatest effects through education, although they would hardly have been willing to draw a line between educational and noneducational ventures, regarding as they did all institutions as educative. Underlying the work and action of the narrower and wider groups are commitments to a Hegelian social philosophy—diluted and interpreted, selected, pummeled, and sometimes mauled.

An issue-by-issue comparison of their social philosophy with that of Hegel's would show the manner of their reliance on it less clearly than their uses of Hegel relative to their own social problems. This is so because they were quite loose with their interpretations; in practical matters their Hegelianism often lost its identity as such, becoming fused with other social attitudes. This happens, for example, when the context was a needed legislative restraint on railroads or a governmental stimulus to the education of blacks, or kindergarten children. Yet they were equally anxious about Federal encroachment into the private areas of society, or into the matters best left to the states. Of course, as befits men who had succeeded within the system, they feared the threats of the labor movement, syndicalism, and Communism. But they were not insensitive to the dangers of monopolists carefully operating under a protective blanket of laissez-faire. In a somewhat larger context, they wanted to steer a middle road between a Calvinist Social Darwinism and the materialistic interpretation of history. At the same time they wanted to preserve a sense of providential destiny and of accumulating values expressed in history. Always they opposed the hedonism and individualism of laissez-faire, although free enterprise generally found its way into their organic view of the state.

Now these may seem to be odd issues to which to apply the wisdom of Hegel, but it needs remembering that Hegel could mean almost all things to all men. This is not particularly because Hegel was inconsistent, but is rather a consequence of the richness of the social philosophy. As a philosophy of process, each feature of institutional growth, each concrete moment of history, must find its niche. After all, America was not alone in putting Hegel into the categories of its own needs. As everyone knows, Hegel's social philosophy (no less than his epistemology and religious philosophy) was polarized on the European scene. Politically, the conservative right glorified the state and a Marxist left sought through human action to hurry the inevitable dialectic of history. It is often said that Marx saved only the dialectic, dispensing with the idealism, but the heritage of Hegel in Marx is much stronger than that. Strictly speaking, Hegel's philosophy could (and did) open onto state interference and control, as well as to the faith that history will ultimately make the state unnecessary. In England, this split was less extreme, with liberals such as T. H. Green using Hegel's "social mind" to temper extreme individualism, while the conservative wing of the Neo-Hegelians (especially Bradley and Bosanquet) gloried the social totality. Bosanquet's *Philosophical Theory of the State* became the source book of conservative ideology.

Thus it is scarcely surprising that America also should have its several Hegelianisms. The vocabulary is often recognizable in the rhetoric of manifest destiny or even of white supremacy; while in less objectionable settings, e.g., that of Bancroft's histories, there is a sense of purpose and direction which is clearly Hegelian. More obviously, Hegel had his indirect influence on left-wing social and labor movements. Even Whitman and Dewey, Willich and Weydemeyer, unlike in so many other respects, agreed that only a dynamic philosophy such as Hegel's could adequately treat of democracy. Easterners either read his philosophy in a religious context, or when they took his social philosophy straight, it seemed to have no more effect on their opinions than Marx. Even for the Transcendentalists, the history of Europe was no cataclysmic conflict of institution against institution, no drastic change of forms of government, nor change in the seat of authority, which allowed the emergence of more vital institutions. In the American West, however, the situation was dramatically different. Fichte's *Addresses to the German People* and Hegel's romantic philosophy spoke intimately to their condition. They felt that the Easterners could not even read "mit Verstand" the *Phenomenology* with its cosmic wit and all-embracing allusions to European historical experience. After all there were similarities in the situation which the St. Louisans faced and those which the Germans had fronted. Fichte and Hegel had dreamed of forging a genuine national personality out of political and cultural fragments, a national identity that would assume a role in world history.

The New World Hegelians shared that dream even during that fierce tempering of the American spirit by the Civil War. On the very first page of the *JoSP*, Harris wrote:

> . . . it will be acknowledged that the national consciousness has moved forward onto a new platform during the last few years. The idea underlying our form of government had hitherto developed only one of its essential phases—that of brittle individualism—in which national unity seemed an external mechanism, soon to be entirely dispensed with, and the enterprise of the private man or of the corporation substituted for it. Now we have arrived at the consciousness of the other essential phase, and each individual recognizes his substantial side to be the State as such. The freedom of the citizen does not consist in the mere Arbitrary, but in the realization of the rational conviction which finds expression in established law.

Such a quotation is readily matched with Hegel's assessment of America's future in the introduction to *The Philosophy of History*. This also found a place in an early volume.[27] Hegel remarks on the enormous resources which allowed the prosperous increase of population, agriculture, and industry, of civil order and the firm freedom in North America. A healthy community arose initially out of the necessities that bind man to man—the desire for repose, the establishment of civil rights, security, and freedom. The external character of the state as an aggregation of individuals or atomic constituents functioning to safeguard property was tempered by the Protestant sense of mutual confidence and trust in all members and in all activities. Thus this unique example of a permanent Republican constitution also had an aspect of subjective unity. Doubtless there remained too much legalism divorced from probity as well as an excess of subjective or religious feeling. Further, the conditions for a real state were still lacking ". . . real Government arise(s) only after a distinction of classes has arisen, when wealth and poverty have become extreme, and when such a condition of things presents itself that a large portion of the people can no longer satisfy its necessities in the way it has been accustomed to do so." The object and existence of the American state are still undetermined; nonetheless America is ". . . the land of the future, where, in the ages that lie before us, the burden of the World's History shall reveal itself . . . It is a land of desire for all those who are weary of the historical lumber-room of old Europe. . . . It is for America to abandon the ground on which hitherto the History of the World has developed itself."

Hegel's view allowed these Westerners to confront the entrenched views of progress and history and to challenge the going views of laissez-faire and natural right. In the first place, progress is not linear but dialectically growing through conflict. The great social forces which are the internal determinants of history are not readily amenable to man's will and designing; nor are their complex interplay with the environment easily open to man's understanding. Indeed the understanding of the laws of development itself becomes a part of the phenomena to be understood (e.g., where economic theory itself is a partial determinant of economic forces and partly a product of those same forces). Knowledge of these laws of human history, the very history of philosophy itself, adds a new dimension in the development of institutions. The individual comes to see himself not as an isolated atom, but as an interrelated part of a social context, his social role defines his character, his self-awareness, and the possibilities of his growth. History, moreover, is irreversible; what eventuates is unique; the emergence of industrial societies with a vivid sense of nationalism is the finest available evidence of this state of affairs. Both the modern state and the understanding of it (in terms of political theory) are consequences of natural growth and evolution. It never was contractual; to explain the state in terms of a social contract is merely to project individual relationships onto the larger framework of the state. The national state was a product of its special germinal factors, arising at a particular time in history because there was a "reason" that it should so arise. Any given state is a living consequence of a particular historical past, and of the customs, laws, and *Volksgeist* of a people. Only genetically can the "reason" be understood.

The problems that worried the St. Louis Hegelians are set in this context. They share the general Hegelian commitment to an organic view of society and the "spiritual" character of history, as taxed now by peculiar American problems and colored by American political and social tradition. What is the relationship between the individual and the community (and, indeed, what is the nature of the individual person, given that the psychology of Locke and Bentham is inadequate)? What is the nature of individual freedom, and what is its relation to authority? What is needed by way of a methodology to handle the complexity, values, and direction of social phenomena? Surely the physical model of a Newton, the biological model of a Spencer, and the psychological laws of British associationism (themselves pale reflections of physical laws) are grossly inadequate. The laws which they were seeking were still to be "natural," but they looked to a dynamic view of nature, wherein God's immanence is manifest not only in natural processes (narrowly), but also in the directional history of institutions and their progressive realization as well.

Now such questions may be answered from the political and social right or left; but the solutions urged by St. Louis run the full gamut of the center. Their slogan might have been "Reform, yes; revolutionary change, no!" It was appropriate for them to turn not to the *Phenomenology,* written in Hegel's youth, but rather to *The Philosophy of Right* (1821) and *The Philosophy of History* (published posthumously) which were works of the mature Hegel when he too was a part of the Prussian Establishment, in fact, the official philosopher of an autocratic state. The dominant themes of all three books are shared, for they present the same view of freedom and culture. What has changed is the mood and the detail; in the latter two the view of freedom has hardened and stress falls on the role of moral and political institutions as they foster the development of freedom within a stable social order. Freedom, still the freedom to know, not to do, emerges in the clash of self and society, as private inclination, private role, and private decision war with externally imposed objectives, socially defined positions, and externally imposed order. His moral theory is corrective of a Kantian (and New England) ethics which regards the individual as autonomous and without a social context, while his political theory is corrective of an individualism in which the government's responsibilities and decisions have no more rationale than the summing of the interests of its constituents. Collectively the moral, social, and political institutions through which freedom evolves are seen by Hegel as Objective Mind with its dialectic of Abstract Right (the thesis), Morality (the antithesis), and Social Morality (the synthesis).

For the first time in world history, freedom is potentially open to all. While the Greeks were the first to know freedom, they thought it was only for the few and they accepted slavery. It is only when this notion of freedom is coupled with the Christian notion of religious equality that the slavery of anyone at all becomes heinous. Finally, only in the emergence of the modern state, does religious equality become social freedom.

In the first stage of Abstract or Legal Right, the individual is circumscribed by the external environment, which includes his relations to others. The only moral rule is the noninfringement of the other person. Then the individual objectifies his person in things, or mixes labor with objects. Freedom in this fashion becomes the liberty to possess and exchange property through contract. Morality at this point is essentially a matter of promise-keeping and the honoring of contracts as well as respect for the life of the agent. The widening of moral right is also a widening of the domain of wrong; contract-keeping implicates the notion of contract-breaking and of sanction. The notion of punishment as a corrective is itself fraught with contradictions; because, although the criminal may not wish to be punished, strictly speaking and insofar as he is a contract-making and responsible citizen, he has a right to be punished; and insofar as he has a moral conscience he will approve of such punishment.

Thus far, the community is concerned only with outward appearances and with the keeping of a customer morality. Freedom is assured by external compulsion, until the last Moment when the criminal acquiesces in his just punishment. But conscience, internalized compulsion, and approval beyond self-interest usher in a new dimension which is in many ways the antithesis of Abstract Right. In this next stage, Morality, the agent first regards himself as responsible merely for his purpose (*Vorsatz*), for his immediate objective. With greater maturity he comes to regard himself as responsible for his full intention, i.e., for all the foreseeable consequences which were not directly purposed. He begins to see that objective social relations generate broader duties than the mere "luxury" of private conscience. This, then, is the point at which Morality ends in a conflict between a universal and abstract moral obligation, external to the agent, and the agent's own internal private good. This is the larger question of moral good and evil.

The final stage, that of Social Morality (*Sittlichkeit*) is a resolution of the antagonisms between Abstract Right and individual or Abstract Morality. In this stage obligation and duty are not external but represent the individual truly as identified with a social group; his good and his freedom are to be found in the social context. And here there is a union between freedom and necessity since the individual's freedom is gained by the identification of his will with a universal will. His acts are free and autonomous because he is self-determining, while his actions are necessary because there is neither caprice nor arbitrariness in the plan by which social or psychological laws unfold.

In this final stage, morality is institutionalized in the family, in the civil community, and in the state. The family has a unity in which the interests of the members are organically related and reinforced by affection. As the individual matures, his interests and loyalties are directed outward into the associations of business, clubs, religious organizations, etc.; the loyalties that represent external interests may come in conflict with the emotionally supported family loyalties. The state builds both on the kind of feeling which cements the family and the shared rational objectives which make for other associations. It is the final stage of social organization and it reaches its climax in the emergence of the modern national state. Where civil society is merely tuned to satisfying needs and interests, the state is the end-all, holding every right over individuals since it is rationality manifest in the historical life of a people. Freedom is only attainable under its authority. As the source of all morality, it itself is not to be judged by the canons of a private morality. While *The Philosophy of Right,* with its emphasis on the emergence of stable institutions, orderly growth, and constitutional law has a somewhat different tone than *The Philosophy of History* which traces out the succession through conflict of historical states, still they share a common pessimism (at least as the Americans see it). Wisdom and philosophy are quite literally reflective; they can only appreciate the cosmic justification of evil and the cumulative character of good in the historical process after the action is over. "The Owl of Minerva takes to flight only when the dusk has fallen." Only after the fact can we recognize that all that happens is not merely not without God, but actually God's realization.

Hegel's social philosophy is interwoven in the discussions of the St. Louis Hegelians and their wider fellowship.[28] The parallels between their concrete situation and that which Hegel faced, however, did not obscure the need for adaptations. As they recognized, the finer-grained dissimilarities were enormous —from class and interest structure, the climate of competing ideologies, the potential power of organized labor, the mix of cultures, the ready fields for entrepreneurs, to the limitless frontiers for expansion. Factors such as these, combined with the very specific crises of national identity, were nowhere felt more disturbingly than in Missouri. Further, of course, they had no mind to compromise their own democratic tradition but only to supplement it. Thus their uses of the Hegelian themes were often not so much adaptations as refashionings and sometimes total retoolings of the message. Witness the shift of heroes; it is not a

Napoleon expressing unwittingly the rationale of history but a Lincoln self-consciously entering and altering its course.

As might be expected, they followed no line. Howison shows as a New England conservative, unreconstructed by the West, even the Far West. How extraordinary his views on "The Duty of the University to the State"[29] would sound today if repeated from the same University of California base. Quite calmly he gives a recipe for the enthrallment of education to politics and to the interest of government. The shallow moderns (he mentions Spencer) have come to consider liberty as the unconditional right of individuals to do as they see fit. Liberty lies in the obedience to law. Since all of what is peculiarly human depends on "that organized and supreme directive intelligence and conscience" which is the State, we owe to it (as to God) absolute allegiance. A university community not only owes that allegiance, but has the special duty of mastering its grounds and of preaching them to all classes of citizens. Davidson, as we have seen, turned away from the Fabians when he thought they overstressed material betterment, while Harris shrank from any form of Socialism, except of course governmental responsibility for education. Snider and Brokmeyer were more involved with the social reformers; the first out-Hegels Hegel in his vivid dialectic of the Civil War[30] and the latter in political action.

Whatever their individual differences, uniformly they rejected Hegel's view of self-activity and his pessimism, which latter they saw as a genetic restatement of Calvinistic determinism and of the darker faces of Social Darwinism. After all, they themselves had a hand in creating businesses, communities, schools, courts (where even stenography could be essential), states, and even a federal union. They assigned a clear and effective role to the individual as regards his moral and political efficacy. Their notion of self-activity implies that man is not a passive agent, but can enter the stream of history as an originator. He is not a tool of the cunning of history, but a self-consciously causal and responsible element in his own destiny. History can go wrong; the point of knowing the laws of social change is that the future may be modified by intelligent choice. Some phase of decision, individual and cosmic, lies outside the determinism of the dialectic. This view of purposive activity and responsibility separates them not only from Hegel, but also the Marxists (at least on their interpretation) and the Utopians who would jump the intervening steps of historical preparation, as in the New Harmony, Oneida, and Waldenesque experiments. Their major target, however, was popular laissez-faire, which after midcentury was taking support from biological evolution. The objections are predictable: the atomism of associational psychology stereotypes individual, economic, and political behavior and simply ignores personal growth, the creative search for goals, and authentic social ties; government and law do not function merely as traffic directors removing obstacles to individual action nor as brokers negotiating the conflicts of interest. While individuals do make social institutions, reciprocally institutions are forming the character of individuals.

Meanings are social; what we are, and even our individual potentialities, have no meaning outside of the social context which provides the theater for the self to grow and to realize those potentialities. Thus social institutions, but not particularly the state, must seek to overcome the alienation of individuals left unintegrated in the fabric of society—the slave, the laborer, the disenfranchised woman. More positively, society must create the conditions that further the growth of human personality. Where the empiricists' stereotype leaves most areas of personal growth to individual initiative and unwittingly closes down the nature of human needs and satisfactions to those which are generated by the cultural *status quo,* the Hegelians see such growth and the opportunities for self-realization as essential ingredients in the quality of a society. As societies self-critically develop they may replace outworn notions by even richer ones, including even the vision of what human potentialities are. Their view of the valuational character of history and the merging of the moral, economic, cultural, and social potentialities forges a quite different tool of social criticism and active reform than Liberalism. Although they insisted that such reform should be orderly, they saw too that social institutions, including the supporting political philosophy, not uncommonly entrenched the interests of their purveyors.

Innovations about the effects of intelligent decision on an individual's career and the efficacy of social critique make for progressively larger deviations from Hegel as the Americans work through the dialectic of institutions. They are closest to Hegel in their view of the family, and where they differ is in the direction of the intimate and the romantic. Brokmeyer, e.g., in his "Letters on Faust" contrasts the Old World obstacles to love brought about by hardened social inequalities with the openness of the West. "A true American, born in the free West . . . if he is poor and Sally is the daughter of a United States Senator, and her mother in consequence deadly opposed to the match, quietly works his way into the legislature of the State, defeats the old man for the Senate, and asks the old lady how she would like to be his mother-in-law now. For he is a free American citizen, containing, by virtue of his birth, all the social possibilities between the gallows and the presidential chair."[31] Throughout, their comments on the family suggest rich personal experiences, especially since they were writing before Freud made us self-conscious about revealing ourselves. Like Hegel they are repelled by Kant's view of marriage as the mutual lease of the sexual organs. The relation which signalizes marriage is not contractual nor, in its first intent, economic; on the contrary it begins in a warm personal relation making for intellectual, physical, emotional, and spiritual fulfillment. In fact this social union is the primitive case where individuals enlarge, not sacrifice, their personalities and freedom. Marriage is thus an ethical relation. While they scarcely envisaged the role of woman in a modern "liberation" sense, nonetheless they regarded her as an authentic person contributing necessary and unique capacities to the relation. The moral essence of marriage could even be sustained in a free love situation so long as it involved consenting, one-to-one monogamy; their criticism turned more vigorously against the Mormons and the "exotic" communes. As a primary institution the family functions as the decisive educational milieu for children. (This is another reason for providing for the education and self-realization of women.) Elementary and secondary schooling was to continue what began in the home, fostering not merely the learning of skills but the development of personality as well. The critical importance of education beyond that was witnessed at all their efforts at adult education—from the Breadwinners' Colleges to their own clubs. Yet they also saw that formal education of whatever kind and level could cut itself off from the other educative processes of a society only at the risk of irrelevance and failure.

The family also provides the basis for property as well as education. They were never to challenge the institution as such, but to introduce a justification radically different from that advanced by the Socialists working in the shadow of the Mercantile Library or the Eastern seaboard economists. Private property does not depend upon divine or natural right; it does not even arise primarily in response to needs; therefore the social good will not be a social welfare function. Property is a social institution; mere possession is not enough, the person must see himself objectified in it; further, the recognition of ownership depends on acknowledgment by others and thus is embedded in a system of social relations. Thus, as above, the quality of property depends upon the character of the society of which it is a feature. Yet if property is the objectification of the individual will, Hegel and the American Hegelians face a dilemma, since each will seems to require so unfettered a scope for its own activities that unreconcilable conflicts with other wills will result. The system of private enterprise if left to itself thus contains the seeds of its own dissolution because it possesses no mechanism for generating a common interest, including what would be necessary to preserve the system itself. Governments do impose external regulations, but what is needed is something to provide an internalized acquiescence and the grounds for loyalty to the total good. Where Hegel found the required institution in the state, the Americans looked to resources other than political sovereignty, viz., a broadly based moral and democratic society itself and what Snider at least regarded as the mediating middleman. Here they are speaking jointly out of philosophic commitments and experiences in the West.

St. Louis itself, and Missouri, were expanding economically. The railroads had begun to ensure the relations of St. Louis to the East, just as the river had earlier oriented it to the South. St. Louis was changing from a relay point for agricultural products to a center for the processing of raw materials. They began to appreciate their manufacturing and mining potential and to look to the industrial East as a market. For the most part a poor man like Sally's suitor could have aspirations to economic independence, and so the St. Louis Hegelians spoke more of functions and interests than of classes. The producers on the one hand and the providers of capital on the other are mediated by the middleman who organizes production, gathering capital and labor and relating them. In a complex society all three roles are indispensable. Capital need not be exploitive; its surpluses can be plowed back for the strengthening of the whole economy. Labor's potentiality for exploitation through organization and strike is dampened as capital is used constructively. The role of the middleman as organizer has the dangers of concentrated irresponsible power; still, if this group fulfills its mediatorial role in creating production and markets, in allocating and distributing resources, it can fulfill a central moral role in the creating of a nation. Since they can most easily understand the needs of the whole, they are in the best position to be the guardians of social well-being. Just as men had tamed the natural laws of the physical world and turned them into opportunities of human construction and enjoyment, so the economic laws are equally natural and through understanding can be also tamed to human good, wanting only knowledge, initiative, and education. The rich need not inevitably grow richer and the poor poorer in a moral society.

Revisionist views such as these about the strength of a moral society, the resources of the competitive system to correct itself, and the place assured individual initiative call for further departures from Hegel's account of morality and the state. The concept of freedom they were attempting to maintain allies them to a Kantian or Common (i.e., shared) Moral Sense theory and politically to the notions of individual liberty that were the heritage of British political institutions. The core is the moral individual, acting on the dictates of his private conscience or will. Still the matter is not simple: sincere individuals with the best wills in the world may internalize or will moral principles (e.g., the golden rule) without arriving necessarily at the same view of what ought to be done. Each one stands in a network of intersecting and obligation-demanding roles. The lone conscience has a difficult time respecting and ordering these diverse and legitimate loyalties—he may at once be a Republican, teacher, abolitionist, Missourian, Unitarian, Southerner, and an American. The temptation is arrogantly to absolutize one loyalty at the cost of the others when what is needed is a synthesis involving a kind of maximizing, or give-and-take, in a long-sighted program. The needed integration is supplemented and mediated by society and the state, which of course is not equivalent to a particular government or office.

The Americans thus stressed constructive compromise and development through cooperation rather than conflict. The synthesis they sought lay between individual and social morality, between political pluralism and a genuine national interest. They saw a clear analogy between the individual and the state and between the several states and the Federal union. The reciprocal relation of the individual and the state they see as strikingly represented when the union, made by the states, in turn becomes state-making (the original states even abrogating their westward claims to a Federal government and relinquishing specific powers in the Constitution). Because the United States are not monolithic, the union could serve as the moral mediator, reaching the citizen, guiding the interplay among the states, but most importantly wedding state and Federal government for the fulfillment of both.

The men centered in St. Louis were then painfully alert to the divisiveness that prefaced the open hostilities of the Civil War and to the shattering antagonisms of its aftermath. The dialectic was not without usefulness here. Snider interprets the Southern cause as *Abstract Right,* for of course the owners had quite literally a property right in their slaves. Yet of course the freedom of individuals is transgressed. Insofar as the Northerners acknowledged the equal need of men for freedom and self-realization, they represent *Abstract Morality,* yet they failed to look beyond their incensed consciences to see the state as more than a collection of private ethical individuals. Government is neither a contract nor a system of checks and balances; it is not even the summed interests of groups; it is the national consciousness institutionalized in a political constitution. The synthesis, *Sittlichkeit,* or *The Ethical State,* is embodied in the American Constitution. It was precisely because Lincoln rested his case on the constitutional issue that he was their hero. Given their philosophic insights, their vocations as educators, and even their historical location in time and place (Missouri was still associated with compromise, albeit an inadequate one), they saw their office as synthesizers between an industrial North and an agricultural South, a conservative East, and a progressive West, between those who would sacrifice the integrity of the several states to an overpowering national authority and those who would crush central authority into atomized state power.

For all that they saw the Civil War as a large social movement turning on constitutional issues, their sentiments were strongly antislavery. After all, Harris was from Connecticut, Brokmeyer a leader in mobilizing the antislavery feelings among the German population, and Snider had early taken his stand when he saw his professors imprisoned for harboring fugitive slaves. They read Hegel's analysis of slavery in the *Phenomenology*—the master is more enslaved than the slave—with enthusiasm. They felt that the collapse of slavery as a system of labor was inevitable; had they been able to educate both the South and the North to an understanding of this inevitability, social forces could have been harnessed on a rational rather than a warlike foundation. Hopefully after the war the educators would not fail their part in reconstructing the nation.

By this point they have put some distance between themselves and Hegel. Snider was not even above playing lightly with the dialectic and turning it around sardonically on Hegel's own writings, noting that they move toward autocratic political philosophy as the "philosopharch" rises in Berlin to philosophic dictatorship. Distinguishing between the absolute philosopher and the philosophy of the absolute, Snider points to the latter as the thesis of an emerging triad, with the Darwinian view of nature as the corrective antithesis and with a psychologically oriented study of man as the synthesis of the future.

Their independence is shown in a more serious matter: In absolute contrast to Hegel's world dominant state, they went on to project the model of the United States onto a World Federation. And because they envisaged a noncompetitive nationalism and a common world, they differ absolutely from Hegel's view that wars are inevitable and even serviceable in stimulating patriotism. In the world exchange of goods and invention, of art and social experience and of philosophy, they saw the basis of international peace.

Now the St. Louis Hegelians saw the political problem of the relation between the individual and the group as only one side of a larger logical, metaphysical, and religious problem. This larger issue was to be an anxious focus for their successors who—as time faded the specter of pantheism as well as the constraints of conventional Christianity—often found the religious component somewhere in the relationship of individual to community, interpreting the latter as Nature, the body of fellowmen or as God personalized. This later philosophic generation, e.g., Royce and James, worked with a more sophisticated logic, psychology, and biology. At the same time methods of political and social analysis were to come of age in such institutionally oriented writers as Veblen, Beard, and, of course, Dewey. There is a real generation gap between the St. Louis amateurs (in the congenial sense noted above) and the professionals, but the work of the former and eventually their diaspora were critical in the greening of American thought. If their journal published translations, it also published the early articles of Peirce and William James, of Royce and Dewey. And if, Howison excepted, they did not supervise directly the move to professionalization, members of their extended family did bridge the generation gap.

One of the intermediaries, George Sylvester Morris (1840-1889), played a curiously pivotal part. He was a transitional figure as much because of an unfinished career as from the date of birth. While not belonging to the group from St. Louis he was intimately related to them, for he shared their enthusiasm for German philosophy, wrote for the *Journal*, and cited *JoSP* extensively for the bibliography in his edition of Ueberweg's *History of Philosophy*. With them he brought a goodly portion of Germanizing to the Concord meetings and they advised him on the Griggs series of philosophic books of which he was the editor.

Still Morris writes in a new vein. Education at Dartmouth and especially at Union Theological Seminary under H. B. Smith (one of the anonymous translators of Hegel cited at the beginning) had already prepared him for the hassles of the German scene when he went there to finish his studies. Of some importance in the sequel his sympathies were enlisted by such post-Hegelians as Ulrici, Trendelenburg, and of course Ueberweg. Thus he was not merely looking back to the admitted climax of German thought from Kant through Hegel, but also to the disputes which they inspired. Of immediate interest here is the unpublished preface which he wrote to his *Hegel's Philosophy of the State and of History* (1887),[32] an interpretation of Hegel rather than a summary. The real adversary to an adequate social science is the tradition which was begun by Hobbes but which was represented in the nineteenth century by Bentham and the utilitarians, Buckle and Bagehot. These rival themes are familiar enough: The projection of the Newtonian model onto psychology and social relations, and therefore the appropriateness of the physicomathematical model. Individuals are like the hypothetical abstractions of physics, associating under the play of mechanical forces. All that bespeaks of human personality and of free and spontaneous community is simply closed out of consideration. Man is set against nature; it is to be struggled with and overcome. The human and the organic are left discontinuous, or, when Spencer came to buttress utilitarianism, man is become a mere appendix to evolution. History is thus merely social mechanics; it is valueless and pointless. Even the much flaunted place of freedom leads to a paradox. "Thought . . . is viewed exclusively as the dependent function and instrument of physical processes. 'Ideas and justice' are held to be determined by the physical evolution of society; they are not comprehended as at once the final and efficient causes of social development. . . . Man and nature are of the same spiritual household. The dependence of the former on the latter . . . is like the 'dependence' of an organism on one of its own members. Instead of prejudicing the freedom of man, it is one of the conditions of the latter. The freedom of man fulfills, rather than contradicts, the prophecies of nature.'"33

Aristotle and Hegel are the protagonists. Morris, of course, does not deny that men are physical beings, and insofar as they are, the methods are appropriate, but this is to ignore the truly relevant aspects of man as human. Nature is not alien, man is in the most intimate, one might almost say social, intercourse or communion with it. Man is interacting and fashioning it even as he is in part fashioned by it. Initially thought may be determined by objects but in the end objects are determined by thought as men utilize the laws of nature and cooperate with them to invent and plan and reshape the world. Morris is operating on the idealist assumption that nature can become successfully the object of thought because thought is already in nature.

Biological organisms rise to a new level in the way natural energies are utilized. Mechanical explanations are not up to accounting for growth, development, maturation, and the functional interplay of parts so essential to the workings of any organism. It is this functional interaction of organisms, rather than the mechanical model, which must be the paradigm for the world of nature generally. Man is therefore not a mechanical product of nature, he is not an accident but a fulfillment. Man is uniquely capable of bending natural energies toward self-determined and self-directed objectives.

But whereas the language of nature is voiceless, communion with other human beings is enriched by significant language. The fact that language is social and that it guides practice toward common objectives means that it is central to creating a common consciousness. Men only know themselves as specifically human when there is intercourse between them and when they see the image of themselves in the mirror of others.

The greatest oversight of the utilitarian tradition is its failure to see the degree to which personality is social. Furthermore it is precisely because men are a part of the world, yet social, that they can conceive of an ideal and project it back onto nature. Ideals thus become effective agents in history. The ideal of a perfected humanity involves man in a moral struggle discarding and warding off what is not congruent with his notions of justice and good. But this struggle is necessarily institutionalized, and this gives the true point of history; it is teleological. Social institutions are the embodiments of men's ideals; the *res interna* of human nature becomes the *res publica.* Political and moral institutions are all of a piece with other institutions to form the culture; and the culture of any given moment will bear the mark of this underlying moral struggle.

Thus there is a continuity between man's relation to nature and his interactive relation with society. Continuous with these relations also is man's relation to God. This too is a social relation. Providence is no small-trade special force intervening in a particular man's interest; it is a providential direction of history itself in which God and men work cooperatively in the realization of moral objectives.

6. St. Louis and Concord

The idealist community which we have surveyed in this chapter formed a remarkable group. Chiefly amateurs, passionately devoted to philosophy, and exhibiting an astonishing range of beliefs, these people were scattered geographically across the nation rather than concentrated in the urban centers of the East. St. Louis, Cincinnati, and Ann Arbor were only the most prominent of Western cities in which idealists met to discuss and debate Hegel, Greek philosophy, and social reform. In Jacksonville, Illinois—the self-styled Athens of the West—Dr. Hiram K. Jones founded a Plato Club in 1865. Jones was a man of remarkable vigor and organizational ability: he founded the Jacksonville Historical Society, the American Akademe, and was cofounder of a Microscopic Society, in addition to being professor of physiology and philosophy at Illinois College.[34] Similarly, at Quincy, Illinois, Mrs. Sarah Denman organized in 1866 a group called the Friends in Council, which devoted itself to philosophic studies and particularly to Plato. Four years later, Samuel Emery organized a Plato Club in Quincy. A New Englander by birth who had studied briefly at Harvard and Amherst, Emery was a man of considerable philosophic acumen. His interest in the subject was first aroused by hearing Emerson lecture, and he rapidly progressed from Emerson's works to Plato's. Emery of course knew Harris and read the *Journal of Speculative Philosophy,* in which he published occasional articles. Through Harris he became interested in Hegel and in 1875 he succeeded in having a copy of Brokmeyer's translation of the *Logic* made for himself. From that point on he seems to have moved rapidly into the Hegelian camp. Both Denman and Emery were close friends of Emerson and Alcott, who frequently visited Quincy on their tours, of Jones and the Jacksonville group, and of the St. Louis idealists.[35] And what was true of Quincy and Jacksonville was doubtless true of other Midwest towns as well.

What the idealist community lacked most notably was any central institutional base from which their doctrines and concerns could be propagated. True, Howison was ensconced in California and Morris, until an early death cut short his career, held the chair at Michigan, but these were almost the only exceptions to the rule. It was not for nothing that Emerson and Alcott had dreamed in the 1840s of establishing a school of philosophy of their own in some New England town where their group could bring its full force to bear upon education. "Do you not see," Emerson had written to Margaret Fuller, "that if such a thing were well and happily done for twenty or thirty students only at first, it would anticipate by years the education of New England?"[36] But it was not until the 1870s that an attempt was made to transform this dream into a reality. In the summer of 1878, Hiram Jones and Sarah Denman visited Bronson Alcott in Concord, and there in discussion with Emerson and Franklin Sanborn the decision was reached to establish a summer school of philosophy in Concord. The school was to draw upon the resources of the whole idealist community, Western as well as Eastern, and to furnish an institutional platform for idealisms of every variety. If it represented, as it surely did, the realization of the hopes which Emerson and Alcott had nourished for forty years, it also embodied the passion for education which so characterized the St. Louis group.

The Concord School opened with a six-week session in the summer of 1879. Alcott served as dean of the school, Samuel Emery, who with his brother-in-law Edward McClure had just moved to Concord and entered Harvard Law School, served as moderator, and Sanborn as secretary-treasurer. The chief lecturers that summer were Hiram Jones, W. T. Harris, Alcott, Mrs. Cheney, and David Wasson. Emerson gave seven lectures, while Sanborn, Benjamin Peirce, Cyrus Bartol, Thomas Davidson, and others also lectured. The school thus drew together in its staff and faculty the leading figures from the various idealist groups and presented a forum for the exposition of the leading idealistic positions: Platonism, represented by Jones, New England Transcendentalism, represented by Emerson and Alcott, and Hegelianism, represented by Harris. It was then in a very real sense the culmination of the idealistic movement in America during the first seven decades of the nineteenth century.

The Concord School continued until 1888, and was an astonishingly successful enterprise. Among those who lectured there, in addition to the names above, were Noah Porter of Yale, James McCosh of Princeton, John Bascom, then president of the University of Wisconsin, Howison, G. S. Morris, William James, Snider, John Fiske, and Edward Montgomery. The four years from 1879 through 1882 were the most successful period of the school. Harris moved to Concord in 1880 so as to be continuously on the scene, and quickly emerged as the strongest lecturer on the faculty. His expositions of Hegel were popular and he steadily outdrew his Platonic rivals. But Jones made an effective presentation of Plato, and Emerson still drew large crowds. Snider joined the staff in 1880 and Howison in 1882, and both Porter and McCosh lectured there in 1882—a sure indication of the importance that the school had attained. But 1882 was clearly the crest. Emerson died in April of that year, and in October Alcott suffered a stroke which ended his effective leadership. With the New England leadership thus weakened, Jones proposed that the location of the school be moved to the West for the next year. The New Englanders and the St. Louis group insisted on keeping the Concord site, and so Jones and his group did not return in 1883, founding instead the American Akademe in Jacksonville, which during the next nine years provided a forum for Platonism. The Concord School continued with a four-week session in 1883 and a staff featuring Harris, Howison, Snider, Sanborn, and William James. But thereafter the emphasis on philosophic subjects declined somewhat and increasing attention was given to literature. The program of 1884 was devoted almost exclusively to Emerson, that of 1885 to Goethe. In 1886 the session lasted only two weeks and was divided between Dante and Plato. In 1887, Harris, Sanborn, and Davidson devoted the two-week session to Aristotle and dramatic poetry. That was the last session of the school. On March 4, 1888, Alcott died and the school died with him.[37]

All things considered, the school was remarkably successful. Sanborn estimated that it drew at least two thousand people during the nine years of its operation, and there is no reason to doubt that estimate. It assembled a distinguished faculty and provided an effective forum for the discussion of philosophic issues and the exposition of the varying, although predominantly idealistic, philosophic positions. But the influence of the school went far beyond the formal sessions at Concord. For in drawing the leadership of the idealistic community to New England, it brought these men into the philosophic discussion clubs which then flourished in Boston and Cambridge where they were in direct contact with men who were to dominate professional philosophy in America during the next twenty years.

We still do not know how many of these philosophic discussion clubs there were, but certainly the most famous of them was the Metaphysical Society which Charles Peirce organized in Cambridge, Massachusetts, in 1871. This club numbered among its members William James, Oliver Wendell Holmes, Chauncey Wright, Nicholas St. John Green, Joseph Warner, John Fiske, and Francis Ellingwood Abbot, and it was at a meeting of this club in November of 1872 that Peirce first proposed the doctrine which later came to be known as pragmatism. Of the members of this celebrated group, Peirce and Abbot were the only idealists, and from what we know of its meetings it was certainly not devoted to the discussion of idealistic philosophy. But the club expired in late 1874 or early 1875: Chauncey Wright died in 1875, Peirce went to Europe, and the group ceased to meet.[38] It was quickly revived however in 1875 chiefly by Thomas Davidson, who had come to Cambridge that year where he was serving as tutor to the children of James Eliot Cabot—a philosopher of idealistic persuasions, a friend of Emerson who was to become his literary executor and memorialist, and an overseer of Harvard College. Cabot drew Davidson's attention to Green's edition of Hume's *Treatise* which had appeared the year before, and Davidson saw in Green's introduction the focus for a debate between British Empiricism and rational idealism. Accordingly, Davidson set out to organize a philosophical society, drawing upon what was left of the old Metaphysical Club and upon some new resources. James, Holmes, Green, Warner, and Abbot were enlisted, together with Cabot, Bowen, C. C. Everett of the divinity school, and F. H. Hedge, and two relative newcomers—Francisco Fenollosa, then a graduate student, and G. H. Howison, who had been teaching at MIT since 1871. Davidson and Howison were of course veterans of the St. Louis clubs, and although Davidson's ardor for Hegel had cooled, Howison was still deeply imbued with German idealism. Bowen had been moving from Hamiltonianism to German idealism for some time, and Cabot represented a strong link to Transcendentalism, while the members of Peirce's old Metaphysical Club, Abbot excepted, were firm in the empiricist faith. G. Stanley Hall, G. H. Palmer, and David Wasson later joined the club, while others were periodically absent, but the discussions seem to have continued briefly until at least April of 1879. All of the activity thus preceded the opening of the Concord School, and served to stimulate both philosophic discussion in general and a growing interest in idealism in particular which made a receptive climate for the Concord venture.

During its career, the Concord School brought to Concord a variety of idealist leaders from over the country. Interest in idealism was already strong at Harvard and in the Cambridge club. Palmer had begun studying Hegel with Caird the year before, and was, as James remarked, "fully enrolled in the white-winged band of seraphim *illuminati.*"[39] In 1880-81 Palmer offered a seminar on Hegel at Harvard. Emery and McClure both attended, as did James. The seminar concentrated on Hegel's *Logic*—a subject for which Emery, armed with Brokmeyer's translation, was admirably prepared. James, assuming the role of the defender of empiricism against the rising tide of Hegelian idealism, battled Palmer in the seminar, and was stimulated by it to write his article "On some Hegelisms"—an open attack on the Hegelian position.

By 1880 Harris was in residence in Concord, where he assumed the chief role as champion of the Hegelian position. This role was quickly extended to Boston and Cambridge, when in late 1881 Harris organized a Hegel Club. Emery and McClure were members, as were Abbot, James, Cabot, Hall, Palmer, Howison, Everett, and Charles Ames—a young businessman who had known Harris in St. Louis. Although the membership of this club was as variable as the others, it continued to meet regularly until 1885, and intermittently until 1887. As long as the club existed, Harris seems to have been its dominant figure and the teaching of Hegel's logic its principal function.[40]

The Concord School was not responsible for introducing either idealism or Hegel at Harvard; developments which were clearly destined to lead to that result were well under way before the Concord School opened. Nor is it correct to regard

Harvard idealism as having been imported from the West: the first seminar in Hegel taught at Harvard was taught by Palmer and there is no evidence that Palmer was influenced by the Westerners. Nevertheless, such St. Louis alumni as Davidson and Howison played an important role in the Cambridge club of the late seventies, and the Concord School by bringing to a focus the idealistic forces throughout the country certainly increased the influence of idealism at Harvard.

Notes—Chapter Eight

1. How erratic are the winds of philosophic interest can be seen from the fact that since this was written there has been an emerging interest exhibited in books, articles, and even in conferences. For example, see: William H. Goetzmann, ed., *The American Hegelians: An Intellectual Episode in the History of Western America* (New York: Alfred A. Knopf, 1973); John O. Riedl, "The Hegelians of St. Louis, Missouri and Their Influence in the United States," *Proceedings of the Marquette Hegel Symposium*, 1970. (Professor Riedl's interest in the St. Louis Hegelians is a long-standing one, and he is planning to publish Brokmeyer's translation of Hegel's *Larger Logic,* which we shall see in the chapter provided the leitmotiv of the movement. It had a curious career of use and nontranslation.)

This rising interest seems to express a number of themes: the emergence of a self-consciousness of the Midwest as constituting a vital part of the intellectual tradition in America (cf. Lloyd D. Easton, *Hegel's First American Followers: The Ohio Hegelians* [Athens, Ohio: Ohio University Press, 1966]); the revival of Hegelian studies; and the increased interest in Socialism and Marx (cf. Albert Fried, ed., *Socialism in America: From the Shakers to the Third International* [Garden City, L.I.: Doubleday & Co., 1970]; David Herreshoff, *American Disciples of Marx* [Detroit: Wayne State University Press, 1967]). An astonishing omission of reference to Socialists characterizes the traditional bibliographies, as well as the *Dictionary of American Biography;* although the latter includes the most minor of ministers, it includes of the Socialists only Stallo, who after all was converted to the Establishment. Considerably more work is needed to fill in the history of Socialism in America.

All students of the St. Louis Hegelians, however, begin with the monumental work of Henry A. Pochmann, *German Culture in America, Philosophical and Literary Influences, 1600-1900* (Madison, Wis.: University of Wisconsin Press, 1961). This is in the best tradition of German scholarship, and furnishes a comprehensive bibliography. We have also found useful Harvey G. Townsend's *Philosophical Ideas in the United States* (New York: American Book Co., 1934), chap. 8; and the source materials arranged and edited by Charles M. Perry, *The St. Louis Movement in Philosophy* (Norman, Okla.: University of Oklahoma Press, 1930). We are also indebted to Philip Mullen and the late David Green for their assistance in the research.

2. *The Christian Examiner*, 1839, XXVIII, pp. 272-313.

3. Frederick Hedge, *Prose Writers of Germany* (Philadelphia: Carey and Hart, 1848), p. 446.

4. *Journal of Speculative Philosophy* 9:332 (1875).

5. Symposium on "Is Pantheism the legitimate outcome of Modern Science?" *JoSP*, vol. 19 (1885). Participants included John Fiske, F. E. Abbot, and Howison.

6. Cf. Howard J. B. Ziegler, *Frederick Augustus Rauch, American Hegelian* (Lancaster, Pa.: Franklin and Marshall College Studios, #8, The Sentinel Printing House, 1953).

7. James Murdock, *Sketches of Modern Philosophy, Especially Among the Germans* (Edinburgh: Thomas Clark, 1843). There is a separate chapter on Dr. Rauch, after American Transcendentalism. Murdock seems to think that Hegel and Christianity cannot be brought together.

8. Easton, *Ohio Hegelians*, esp. pp. 95-122.

9. *Ibid.*, p. 182. This material is being reproduced by Willich from the *Cincinnati Republikaner*.

10. The reference to Engels is to his discussion of the transition from Hegel to Feuerbach. Cf. Frederick Engels, *Ludwig Feuerbach and the Outcome of Classical German Philosophy* (New York: International Publishers, 1935), pp. 21-22.

11. Sherman and Grant, as Harris told Emerson, were in St. Louis to witness this victory. Harris believed they were so heartened by the solidarity of pro-Union sentiment and support for the liberal cause that they threw in their lots for the North.
   When Harris later visited New England, he was astonished to find Alcott and his group unmindful of the West's role in the war; apparently they believed that New England had won it single-handedly.

12. *Missouri Republican*, October 8, 1861.

13. The Easterners looked rather condescendingly on the Western cultural efforts. Thus Louisa May Alcott reports with some glee an exchange, shortly after her father had become dean of the Concord School:

Father, the dean. He has his dream realized at last, and is in glory, with plenty of talk to swim in. People laugh, but will enjoy something new in this dull old town; and the fresh Westerners will show them that all the culture in the world is not in Concord. I had a private laugh when Mrs.————asked one of the new-comers, with her superior air, if she had ever looked into Plato. And the modest lady from Jacksonville answered, with a twinkle at me, "We have been reading Plato in *Greek* for the past six years." Mrs.———— subsided after that. (Louisa May Alcott, *Her Life, Letters and Journals,* ed. Ednah D. Cheney [Boston: Little, Brown, 1928], p. 267.)

14. This picture of Fichte rests on materials in *JoSP,* e.g. (all translation or commentary by A. E. Kroeger):
"Fichte's Introduction to the Science of Knowledge," I: 23-36 (1867).
"A Criticism of Philosophic Systems," I: 79-86, 137-59 (1867).
"Fichte's 'Sun-clear Statement,' " II: 3-15, 65-82, 129-40 (1868).
"New Exposition of the Science of Knowledge by Fichte," III: 1-31, 97-133, 193-241, 289-317 (1869).

15. This picture of Schelling rests on materials in *JoSP,* e.g.:
Thomas Davidson, trans., "Schelling's Introduction to the Philosophy of Nature," I: 193 (1867).
Ella S. Morgan, trans., "Schelling, F. W. J. von, On the Science of Fine Arts," XV: 152 (1881).
Thomas Davidson, trans., "Schelling's Introduction to Idealism," I: 159 (1867).

16. This picture of Hegel rests on materials in *JoSP,* e.g.:
W. T. Harris, "Analysis of Hegel's Phenomenology," II: 99 (1868).
Brokmeyer and Harris, trans., "Hegel's Phenomenology of Spirit," II: 94 (1868).
"Hegel's First Principle," III: 344 (1869). This is taken from a work published in 1840, which is substantially the outline of Hegel's course given in 1808. (See Harris's note, p. 166.)
W. T. Harris, trans., "Hegel on the Philosophy of Aristotle," V: 61 (1871).
G. S. Hall, trans., "Rosenkranz on Hegel's Psychology," VII: 17 (1873).
J. A. Martling, trans., "Bénard's Essay on Hegel's Aesthetics," I: 36, 91, 169, 221 (1867); II: 39, 157; III: 31, 147, 281, 317 (1869).
G. S. Hall, trans., "Rosenkranz on Hegel's Aesthetics," VII: 44 (1873).
Thomas Davidson, trans., "Trendelenburg on Hegel's System," V: 349 (1871), (continued in vol. VI).

17. It is interesting to note that the translation in Hedge's *Prose Writers of Germany* inverts the final dialectic triad, giving religion, art, philosophy, rather than Hegel's art, religion, philosophy (see quotation p.466, above).

18. Denton J. Snider, *Modern European Philosophy* (St. Louis: Sigma Publishing Co., 1904), p. 691.

19. There is considerable convergence on the comparison of Aristotle and Hegel. For example, Harris translated Hegel on the philosophy of Aristotle in vol. V (1871) of *JoSP*, while in the same volume Davidson translated Trendelenburg's examination of Hegel's system. Trendelenburg was not only an expositor of Hegel, but also a distinguished Aristotelian scholar, who dealt seriously with Aristotle's biology and categories alike. Trendelenburg's influence on Dewey is recognized, and has somewhat altered the view as to which Hegel characterized Dewey's early Hegelianism. Trendelenburg was widely influential, and his lectures at the time were widely discussed in Berlin. Herbert Schneider has surmised that Marx may well have known the lectures, and a resonance of that influence is to be found in the *Manifesto*.

20. Denton Jaques Snider, *The St. Louis Movement in Philosophy, Literature, Education, Psychology, with Chapters of Autobiography* (St. Louis: Sigma Publishing Co., 1920).

21. Denton J. Snider, *A Writer of Books in His Genesis* (St.Louis: Sigma Publishing Co., 1910), pp. 341 and 429.

22. Thomas Davidson, *The Philosophical System of Antonio Rosmini-Serbati, translated with a sketch of the Author's Life, Bibliography, Introduction and Notes* (London: Kegan Paul, Trench and Co., 1882). Davidson says in the preface (p. vi) that the book is also intended as an introductory handbook to the study of modern Italian thought. The scope of Davidson's interests can be seen from his contributions to *JoSP*, which include such varied themes as: "Winkelmann's Remarks on the Torso of Hercules" (translation), II: 187 (1868); "Sentences of Porphyry the Philosopher" (translation), III: 46 (1869); "Conditions of Immortality according to Aristotle," VIII: 143 (1877).

23. Cf. Morris Raphael Cohen, *A Dreamer's Journey* (Glencoe, Ill.: Free Press, 1949).

24. See his *The Limits of Evolution and Other Essays Illustrating the Metaphysical Theory of Personal Idealism*, 2d ed. (New York: Macmillan, 1904).

25. J. W. Buckham and G. M. Stratton, *George Holmes Howison, Philosopher and Teacher* (Berkeley: University of California, 1934), contains most of *The Limits of Evolution,* etc. The quotation is from 219f.

26. *Ibid.,* p. 205.

27. *JoSP,* vol. VI (1872), "Hegel's Philosophy of History," trans. G. S. Hall from an article by Rosenkranz. The reference to America is in Hegel's *The Philosophy of History,* introduction.

28. Cf. Frances A. Harmon, *The Social Philosophy of the St. Louis Hegelians* (New York: Columbia University Press, 1943).

29. Josiah Royce, Joseph LeConte, G. H. Howison, and Sidney Edward Mezes, *The Conception of God* (New York: Macmillan Co., 1902).

30. Denton J. Snider, *The American Ten Years War (1855-1865)* (St. Louis: Sigma Publishing Company, 1906).

31. *JoSP* XXI: 57.

32. Of special interest is the unused introduction to the book. It is appendix B in Marc Edmund Jones, *George Sylvester Morris* (Philadelphia: David McKay, 1948).

33. *Ibid.*, p. 391.

34. Paul Anderson, "Hiram K. Jones and Philosophy in Jacksonville," *Journal of the Illinois State Historical Society* 33: 478-520 (1940).

35. Paul Anderson, "Quincy, an Outpost of Philosophy," *Journal of the Illinois State Historical Society* 34: 50-83 (1941).

36. F. B. Sanborn and W. T. Harris, *A. Bronson Alcott, His Life and Philosophy* (Boston: Roberts Bros., 1893), II: 508.

37. Henry A. Pochmann, *New England Transcendentalism and St. Louis Hegelianism* (Philadelphia: Carl Schurz Memorial Foundation, 1948); F. B. Sanborn, *Recollections of Seventy Years* (Boston: Richard Badger, 1909), chap. 21; Sanborn and Harris, II: 506ff.

38. Max Fisch, "Was There a Metaphysical Club in Cambridge?" *Studies in the Philosophy of Charles Saunders Peirce,* ed. Moore and Robin (Amherst: University of Massachusetts Press, 1964), pp. 3-32.

39. Max Fisch, "Philosophical Clubs in Cambridge and Boston," *Coranto* 2:24 (Spring 1965).

40. Max Fisch, "Philosophical Clubs in Cambridge and Boston/ I" *Coranto* II, no. 1 (Fall 1964): 12-23; II, no. 2 (Spring 1965): 12-25; III, no. 1 (Fall 1965): 16-29; George Herbert Palmer, *The Autobiography of a Philosopher* (Boston: Houghton Mifflin, 1930); Ralph Barton Perry, *The Thought and Character of William James* (Boston: Little, Brown, 1935), vol. 1, chaps. 44-48.

Chapter Nine

The Evolutionary Controversy

Chapter Nine

The Evolutionary Controversy

1. Introduction

To the New England Puritans no axiom was more self-evident than the principle that knowledge is one. The theory of technologia was based upon the assumption that the diverse "arts" that constitute our ectypal knowledge form a consistent whole which reflects, however inadequately, the perfectly self-consistent archetypal plan in the mind of God. The Newtonian revolution did not disturb this axiom, for although Newton, Boyle, Franklin, and others substituted a new physical science for the old, and Locke and the Scottish Realists a new psychology and epistemology, these developments were viewed as advancing our knowledge of certain aspects of the underlying plan—not as challenging the existence of the plan. Newton took his theological studies as seriously as his scientific studies, and saw no inconsistency in pursuing both.[1] It is accordingly incorrect to interpret the effects of the Newtonian revolution upon the established world view in terms of a controversy between science and religion. Whatever difficulties arose in reconciling new scientific findings with traditional beliefs, virtually no one seriously doubted that such a reconciliation was possible and that true science and theology were perfectly consistent. The Protestant churches not only supported science— they enjoined the scientific study of nature as a duty, and many of the early American scientists were ministers. Similarly, the scientists themselves were overwhelmingly orthodox and viewed their discoveries as revealing the divine wisdom embodied in nature. Until the evolutionary controversy erupted, there was no warfare between science and theology in America.

Nevertheless, the attempt to integrate the new scientific doctrines into the

517

established world view did encounter certain difficulties. A number of these have already been treated in preceding chapters, but it will be useful to summarize some of the major points of stress. First, Newtonian science required a reconceptualization of the relation between natural events and human behavior. The Puritans had interpreted a large class of natural events as divine judgments upon human behavior: hence, although these events were predestined, as was the human behavior, they could not be predicted or explained without reference to human conduct. But the triumphs of physics in the eighteenth and nineteenth centuries and the general adoption of the Newtonian model as descriptive of physical reality virtually eliminated this class of "special providences" by showing that their occurrence was explicable without reference to human behavior. Accordingly, a redefinition of the relation of nature to God and to us was required. Second, if special providences were banished from physical nature, were they also banished from the realm of human affairs? Franklin had helped to prove that physical nature obeyed the Newtonian model, yet he also insisted that human affairs were governed by a "particular providence" and that without a belief in such a particular providence morality would collapse. And third, some method was required which could reconcile the Biblical accounts of such events as the sun's stopping for Joshua with the findings of the new sciences. These issues arose directly from the acceptance of the Newtonian model, but equally important problems were raised by the new psychology and epistemology. First, in Puritan psychology, certain faculties, e.g., reason, will, and conscience, are specific to the immortal soul, while others, e.g., common sense, imagination, and memory, are faculties of the sensitive soul and so are common to man and beast. It is therefore perfectly clear in Puritan thought which psychological phenomena represent the action of the immortal soul and which do not. But Locke's rejection of the faculty psychology has the consequence that the human understanding becomes a unitary agent: hence the dual nature of man is not clearly reflected in the operations of his mind. Locke asserted that thinking is the action of a spiritual agent,[2] yet since many actions of this spirit are analogous to those of the animal mind, and since it is only the power of framing abstract ideas which "puts a perfect distinction betwixt man and brutes,"[3] the result is that the categorical division between the spiritual and the animal upon which the Puritans insisted becomes much less clear in Lockean psychology. Thus one line of development leads from Locke through Hume and Hartley toward a purely mechanistic concept of man, while another leads through the Scottish writers toward the "intellectual and moral science" of Porter and McCosh who view psychology as the study of the soul. The question of which psychological phenomena are of a spiritual character and which are not was obviously a crucial question for men who believed themselves possessed of a nature which was part animal and part spirit, but it was a question to which Lockean psychology returned no very clear answer. Second, even if it be granted that certain functions of the mind are spiritual in character, Locke gave no clear explanation of how these functions can be known. As we have seen repeatedly,

Locke's "ideas of reflection" proved a mare's nest of troubles for those who came after him. The nature of the "ideas" through which the mind knows itself remained one of the most perplexing epistemological problems facing American philosophers. Furthermore, since Locke regards the idea of spirit as a complex idea built out of simple ideas of reflection,[4] the difficulties involved in the concept of ideas of reflection also infect ideas of spirits. The Puritans had insisted that spirits could only be conceived as intelligible species wholly abstracted from sense, but there is no process of abstraction in Locke's theory which can obtain a purely intelligible concept from sensory ideas. Hence unless simple ideas of reflection are ideas of spiritual attributes to begin with there can be no concept of spirits. The problem of spiritual knowledge therefore centers upon the nature of self-consciousness and the ideas of reflection, and it is this issue which is the central problem in integrating Lockean empiricism and Protestant theology.

By 1850 acceptable answers had been found for most of these issues. There were it is true dissidents like Emerson who rejected the prevailing synthesis as superficial, but such critics were few. The problem of the religious interpretation of nature was solved for the eighteenth and early nineteenth centuries by the natural theology. There was of course nothing new about the natural theology— that nature was a revelation of God was a traditional Christian doctrine, and was a fundamental article of the Puritan creed. What was new in the eighteenth- and nineteenth-century natural theology was the ever-increasing emphasis upon the orderliness and regularity of nature, rather than upon miraculous events or special providences. When Cotton Mather had celebrated the birth of the Newtonian world in *The Christian Philosopher,* he was able to combine his examples of celestial order with enough instances of terrestrial disorder to show the existence both of immutable decrees and of providential interventions. But the rapid and spectacular successes of science in establishing order and regularity throughout nature made it clear that the age of miracles was past. Accordingly, the traditional distinction between "natural religion" and "revealed religion" took on in this period a new and deeper significance. "Natural theology" dealt with observable nature as described by science, and sought to derive from the scientific findings evidence concerning the nature and intentions of God. And since what science found most striking in nature was order and regularity, the natural theology tried to make order and regularity the distinguishing marks of the divine. To accomplish this, the theologians made use of certain principles which were largely taken for granted rather than argued—particularly, that order implies an orderer, that the effect must resemble the cause, that the laws of nature describe the mode of operation of the divine power, and that final causes are empirically identifiable. From these axioms, it is possible to argue that regularities in nature are means to identifiable ends and so must have been designed for those purposes by an intelligent creator, whose mode of action is described in the statement of the regularity. From the character of the end produced, and of the means used, one may then establish the attributes of the orderer, as, e.g., his goodness, justice, mercy, power, wisdom, skill, etc. So interpreted, order and regularity become themselves marks of divinity, and the findings of science become bulwarks of orthodoxy.[5] But nature revealed only certain general characteristics of God and the law—the distinctive doctrines of Christianity could not be learned from nature alone but required the further revelation granted to men through the Scripture. "Revealed theology" therefore dealt with the Scriptural revelations, and with the evidence for those revelations. And these evidences were exactly the opposite of order and regularity. As Paley put it, "Now in what way can a revelation be made but by miracles? In none which we are able to conceive."[6] It was therefore precisely the violation of natural order which was the proof of supernatural revelation. That this committed theology to two contradictory descriptions of the behavior of nature was not a critical problem in the eighteenth century because the descriptions applied to different eras and because each rested upon a body of evidence which was largely independent of the other. Thus the proofs of the orderliness of nature came from sciences such as astronomy, mechanics, physiology, and chemistry—sciences whose applicability to the ancient past was based chiefly upon the presumed generality of their laws rather than upon historical evidence—while the proofs of miracles rested upon documentary historical evidence. And while a few men such as Hume[7] and Paine[8] pressed this inconsistency to a denial of miracles, most men, having agreed to the principle of the natural theology that a law of nature merely describes the mode of action of the divine power, saw no impossibility in the Lord's occasionally acting out of the ordinary course.

The miracles are a special class of the providential events recorded in the Bible: the deluge presumably was accomplished through secondary causes rather than by the direct exertion of divine power. The historical evidences thus supported not only miracles, but also a multitude of special providences as well. Even though Newtonian science had shown that such special providences do not now occur in nature, the Biblical proofs that they had occurred were important, for they supported the belief that providential intervention had occurred in the affairs of men. Since men were not themselves a part of nature, and since there was clear evidence of God's having exercised direct control over their fate sometimes, the present invariability of the natural order posed no contradiction to the continued existence of a particular providence in human affairs. So long as the historical evidences remained secure, so long as the higher criticism could be rejected, and so long as science itself did not become historical and begin to inquire into the events of the past, so long this perilous balance could be maintained. And meanwhile, the further progress of science merely strengthened the arguments of the natural theology that all nature illustrated a divine plan.

Yet it was a curious fact that the area which should have illustrated the creator's workmanship most clearly, and which did show it admirably with respect to particulars, failed to evidence a coherent overall plan. This was biology. The exquisite design of particular organs and organisms was among the favorite proofs of intelligent order used by the natural theology. Every treatise on the subject included descriptions of such organs as the eye and the hand, showing the marvelous workmanship and perfect adaptation of means to ends which these organs were held to involve.[9] Yet the overall plan of the plant and animal kingdoms somehow failed to emerge. It is true that the eighteenth century had inherited the classical doctrine of the great chain of being, and that this theory did purport to define the master plan of the natural world. Specifically, the doctrine of the great chain held that created beings form a linear series ordered with respect to perfection which extends from the inanimate up to God, with man occupying an intermediate position between the beasts and the angels. In the classical form, the series was regarded as continuous and complete, so that every possible grade of perfection has been created, and as static in time, so that neither extinction nor evolution was possible. But by the eighteenth century, the belief that creation had been by distinct and fixed species—a belief which harmonized far more easily with the Biblical account of creation—led to the conceptualization of the chain as a series of natural classes, and it was admitted that various species might have been created at different times.[10] Nevertheless, the concept of the chain of being is at best a characterization of the type of order which nature presents rather than a specific scheme of classification, and it was a type of order into which the systematic biologists of the eighteenth century found it very difficult to fit their data. For among the results of the great "age of discovery" which had so vastly extended the geographical horizons of the fifteenth, sixteenth, and seventeenth centuries were new plant and animal species hitherto completely unknown in Europe, and as descriptions and specimens of these new forms poured in, systematic biologists were swamped by a mass of data for which they had no adequate classifications. As a result, the search for systems of classification became the major enterprise of eighteenth-century systematic biology. A number of such classifications were produced, those of Linnaeus being the most famous and the most widely used, yet all of these systems were recognized to be arbitrary and "artificial." The goal of Linnaeus and of the other systematists was a "natural" system of classification—one based on species as "real classes" and showing the "natural affinities" of these species, but despite their lifelong labors no such system was forthcoming.[11] To eighteenth- and nineteenth-century men it was obvious that such an order must really exist—God could not have worked without a plan—and the Bible showed (and the assumed infertility of hybrids confirmed) that the species was the basic unit.[12] Yet the order did not emerge, and speculative minds wondered why.

There were other facts that helped them wonder. Newton's work had wrought a revolution in the concept of the universe, but it had had little immediate effect on the views relating to time and creation. Most men in the eighteenth century believed that the world was created in 4004 B.C. and that it would end "soon"— i.e., within a time period comparable in years to its past. And virtually all men of that time accepted the Christian thesis that time was "essentially the divine

medium in which a great play—the drama of the human Fall and Redemption—
was being played out upon the stage of the world. This drama was unique and not
repetitious."[13] Yet as the eighteenth century wore on, new results and new
theories began to accumulate which called these beliefs into question. Among the
first of these was the nebular hypothesis, first proposed by Kant in 1755,[14] and
subsequently by Laplace in 1796.[15] The form which Laplace gave to the theory
became widely known and accepted, and formed the basis for most cosmological
speculations in the nineteenth century. But the thesis that the solar system had
evolved through the condensation of a rotating nebula of course projected a
creative process contrary to the Biblical one, and implied an age for the earth
which the traditional Christian theory precluded. Accordingly, the theory was
denounced as heretical and contrary to Scripture.

The nebular hypothesis was at best a highly speculative theory based on slender
evidence, but a more serious threat to the traditional view was raised by geology.
Since geology dealt directly with the structure and history of the earth, it was to be
expected that its findings would be consistent with the Biblical account of creation,
and that traces of such providential events as the deluge would be found. And for
most of the eighteenth century this seemed to be the case. The discovery of marine
fossils even on mountain tops gave clear evidence that at some time the sea had
covered the land, and this fact was at once interpreted as evidence of Noah's flood.
Similarly, the so-called Neptunist geology of Abraham Werner and his followers
attempted to account for the existence and character of geological strata by a
process of precipitation from a primeval sea. The stages of this "creation" were
assumed to match the Biblical "days," and Noah's flood became one among
many deluges which the earth had known.[16] But with the publication of James
Hutton's *Theory of the Earth* in 1788,[17] a new science of geology emerged. Hutton
was not concerned with the origin of the earth but with its structure and operation.
He thought of the earth as a great machine which, like the Newtonian universe, had
achieved a stable equilibrium. Two forces operated to define this equilibrium. One
was erosion, by which particles of earth were carried from more to less elevated
portions of the earth's surface by the action of water. Over a sufficiently long
period of time, erosion would thus wear away the more elevated land areas and
deposit their debris at the bottom of the sea. Here the second force—subterranean
heat—operated in two ways. First, Hutton attributed the solidification of the debris
into strata to the action of heat. Second, he regarded the subterranean heat as
providing the power by which the sea's bed was elevated to form new landmasses.
These reciprocal processes Hutton conceived as acting continually throughout
unlimited time, old continents being destroyed and new ones built over and over
again, world without end. "We find no vestige of a beginning—no prospect of an
end."[18] The theory has of course serious inadequacies: Hutton's account of the
formation of strata is not satisfactory, and his account of the elevation of continents
by the action of subterranean heat was open to catastrophist interpretations.[19] But
his theory did explain a wide variety of phenomena, ranging from volcanic action

to the presence of marine fossils in mountains, and was scientifically far superior to any of its predecessors. Moreover, Hutton's work was thoroughly religious, for in the action of this superb machine he saw clear evidence of the designing hand of the creator.[20] He even went so far as to argue that the final cause of the world machine was the maintenance of organic life, that erosion was a necessary effect of the processes required for that purpose, and hence that the self-restoring character of the world machine illustrated the creator's provision for the welfare of the creation.[21] Nevertheless, Hutton's "uniformitarian" theory was furiously attacked, not only on Neptunist grounds, but on religious grounds as well.[22] It was not just because Hutton contradicted the Biblical account of creation, for Hutton's theory had nothing to say about origins, nor was it simply that his theory required a far greater expanse of time for its operation than Christian doctrine could allow. The real issue was that Hutton's theory was directly historical—that it extended the reign of natural order and regularity, and so of natural causes, into the indefinite past, and so for the first time brought the weight of science against the occurrence of miracles and providential events. In Hutton's theory, although continents rose and fell, there was no universal deluge.

Yet there were facts that Hutton's uniformitarian theory had difficulty in explaining. There were, e.g., dislocations and distortions of strata which appeared to evidence sudden and violent upheavals of a catastrophic character. Hutton had argued that the power producing these elevations of strata was subterranean heat, but despite his uniformitarian principle he left the door open to catastrophist interpretations. But more crucial was the relation between fossils and strata. In the 1790s William Smith discovered the correlation of fossils with strata, thus making it possible for the first time to reconstruct in detail the sequence of organic forms which had inhabited a specific region.[23] In the early years of the nineteenth century, Georges Cuvier applied comparative anatomy to the study of the fossil remains excavated from the Paris basin, thereby virtually creating the field of vertebrate paleontology.[24] Combining stratigraphy and paleontology, Cuvier discovered what appeared to be radical discontinuities between the flora and fauna of different geological periods, with no evidence of intervening forms. On the basis of these findings, he propounded the doctrine of catastrophism. Cuvier held that the earth had experienced a series of catastrophies, each resulting in massive extinctions of existing species, and each followed by the creation of new species. The species themselves were for Cuvier fixed and immutable classes, created by God at a particular point in time and terminated at another point in time through catastrophe. The last of these catastrophes was of course the Biblical deluge.[25] The theory was based upon solid empirical evidence, and Cuvier was universally acknowledged to be one of the great scientists of his time. But the appeal of the theory was more than scientific. Not only did the theory confirm essential features of the Biblical account—it asserted the existence of past events which, Cuvier held, could not have been produced by any natural causes currently operating in nature.[26] Thus catastrophist geology seemed for a time to bring science to the aid of revealed religion and to prove the contention of the theologians—that miraculous events had indeed occurred once upon a time.[27]

In 1830 Charles Lyell began the publication of the *Principles of Geology.*[28] Thoroughly and meticulously, Lyell established the uniformitarian case, showing that the geological phenomena which Cuvier had claimed could only be explained by the catastrophes could also be explained by the action of presently operating processes over sufficiently long periods of time. The massive array of evidence which Lyell produced virtually ended the geological argument for the deluge, and left the catastrophist position dependent, not upon geology, but upon paleontology. For although Lyell was a uniformitarian in geology, he adhered to the doctrine of fixed species, so that the discontinuities in the successions of organic forms remained untouched by his arguments. After Lyell, it was impossible to claim that there was geological evidence for divine intervention: the only remaining events which appeared to require miraculous support were the origins of the species.[29]

Lyell's views, like Hutton's, aroused strong opposition, and won acceptance only slowly. Their progress in America was particularly slow, owing to the prevailing Wernerian and catastrophist views of the leading American geologists, Maclure, Eaton, Cleaveland, and Silliman.[30] Moreover, the influence of catastrophist theories in the United States was greatly strengthened by the arrival here in 1846 of Louis Agassiz—one of Cuvier's most outstanding disciples. A brilliant scientist, a great teacher, and an adroit manipulator, Agassiz quickly became the leading naturalist in the United States and maintained this position until the Civil War. As professor of zoology and geology at Harvard, and director of the Harvard museum, Agassiz exerted a great influence on both professional and public opinion in America, and all of his influence was used to support the immutability of species and the catastrophist geology. His famous "Essay on Classification" which appeared in 1857 was an attempt to revise Cuvier's system in the light of more recent findings, but without any modification of the essential principles of that system.[31]

The failure of eighteenth-century systematists to establish a satisfactory classification by immutable species led men to wonder why such a classification could not be found. One explanation was that nature had no order, but no rationalist took that possibility seriously; a more plausible thesis was that species were not immutable. Speculations of this sort began long before Charles Darwin—indeed, Darwin's grandfather, Erasmus Darwin, argued for a form of evolution.[32] But the most persuasive of those early theories—certainly the one most often invoked as an alternative to Charles Darwin's theory—was that of Jean Baptiste Lamarck. In 1802 Lamarck advanced a theory of evolution based upon environmental adaptation and the inheritance of acquired characteristics. In order to survive, Lamarck argued, the organism must be able to obtain satisfactions for its biological needs from its environment. In striving to obtain these satisfactions, the organism makes differential use of its members and abilities: those which are most used are strengthened by exercise and those which are rarely used tend to atrophy. Lamarck supposes these increments in strength and weakness to be inheritable, so that over a sufficiently large number of generations some organs may waste away while others are developed into such radically altered forms that their possessors appear to belong to new species. But although it is the goal-directed striving of the organism which produces these changes, the guiding principle of Lamarck in evolution is the environment, for it is the environment which determines the conditions to which the organism must adapt, and so which members and abilities will be used. The theory permits extinction if changes in the environment are too swift to allow adaptation, but when combined with a uniformitarian geology it should lead to gradual adaptive changes corresponding to the gradual alterations in the environment. The theory is thus both teleological, since the organism is goal directed in seeking satisfaction, and deterministic, since the environment determines the behavior and changes of the organism.[33] The Lamarckian theory was not popular before Darwin published, but because its blend of teleology and determinism was compatible with traditional views of nature and because its emphasis upon adaptation rather than selection was consistent with the view that experience is a providential discipline, it was often adopted after Darwin as a compromise position.

Then in 1859 Darwin published the *Origin of Species*.[34] Like Newton, Darwin had fully developed his theory long before he published, and had devoted years to perfecting it and to assembling data to support it.[35] When he did publish, therefore, the *Origin of Species* contained not only a presentation of his theory, but also a vast array of supporting evidence which gave the work an authority which no mere hypothesis would have had. Those who opposed Darwinian evolution found themselves confronted not just by a persuasive theory but by thoroughly marshaled empirical data which they could neither deny nor explain away.

The Darwinian theory differed from its predecessors in combining effectively two principles: fortuitous variation and natural selection. The principle of fortuitous variation holds that offspring always exhibit slight variations from the form of the parents, that these variations, whatever their unknown determinants may be, appear to us wholly "fortuitous" or random, and that they are inheritable. It is true that Darwin equivocated over the question of whether or not the environment can affect the degree of variation, and did sometimes hold that drastic changes in the environment can stimulate the tendency to variation in the organism, but the variations themselves remain apparently random deviations from the parental norm. The process of fortuitous variation should therefore lead to an endless proliferation of forms diverging in every way from the original parental stock: it thus accounts admirably for the diversity of organic forms, but not for the direction of the known successions of these forms. To account for the direction, Darwin introduced various forms of selection, of which the chief was what he called "natural selection." Following Malthus, Darwin held that organisms reproduce at a rate which far exceeds that by which their supply of food and other necessities of life can be increased. Accordingly, there must result a competition among the organisms for the limited supply of necessities available. In this competition, or struggle for existence, cumulative variations come to play a critical role, for some of the variations will be more advantageous to their owners than others. Those organisms which are thus advantaged will survive to reproduce and so transmit their good fortune to their successors; those which are disadvantaged will not so survive, and their unfortunate variations will then die with them. Thus nature, or the environment, "selects" those organisms which by good luck are well adapted and eliminates those which are not. Natural selection is not the only selective agency Darwin recognized—sexual selection was also important—but he considered it by far the most important and fundamental, and the twin principles of fortuitous variation and natural selection were the basic principles of the theory.[36]

When the *Origin of Species* appeared in 1859, it encountered at first strong opposition within scientific circles. Despite the massive evidence which Darwin and his defenders marshaled for the theory, there were serious difficulties which they could meet only imperfectly. First, the principle of fortuitous variation was a purely descriptive generalization concerning similarities and differences among organisms: it did not provide any explanation of the process of inheritance involved. Darwin did indeed attempt to formulate a theory of heredity—the pangenesis theory—but this theory remained much more speculative than the principle it was to support, and was in critical respects inadequate for its purpose. Lacking such a theory of heredity, Darwin found it difficult to defend his denial of the inheritance of acquired characteristics or to prove the fortuitous character of variation, and his opponents were not slow to exploit this lacuna in the theory.[37] Second, despite the many evidences of variation which he had, Darwin could not come close to reconstructing the entire evolutionary sequence of the major species, and he was therefore required to postulate a degree of incompleteness in the geological record, which had been unsuspected before and which looked to his opponents all too much like special pleading.[38] This incompleteness was particularly clear with respect to man, and was one reason why Darwin delayed the publication of the *Descent of Man* until 1871.[39] As Eiseley has remarked,

It is a matter of considerable historical interest that Darwin postulated his theory and extended it to man without having available as evidence a single subhuman fossil by which, on the basis of his theoretical views, he could have satisfactorily demonstrated the likelihood of man's relationship to the world of subhuman primates.[40]

Third, Darwin had assumed, on the basis of the work of Lyell and Hutton and of Laplace's demonstration of the stability of the solar system, that the period during which evolution could have operated was virtually unlimited. Accordingly, Darwin drew freely upon this boundless past in framing his theory, and the processes he postulated required immense time periods for their operation. But no sooner was the *Origin of Species* in print than Lord Kelvin attacked the problem of the age of the solar system from the standpoint of thermodynamics. Experiments by Herschel and Pouillet in 1837[41] had revealed for the first time how immense the sun's annual expenditure of heat really was, and had raised the question of how this heat was produced and maintained. The nebular hypothesis appeared to offer a solution to this problem, for the condensation and contraction of the nebula afforded an apparent means of converting energy into heat which might be sufficient to account for the sun's expenditures. In 1854 Helmholtz showed that a contraction by the sun of 1/10,000 part of its radius would be sufficient to supply the heat it radiated for over two thousand years.[42] In the early 1860s, Kelvin used similar arguments to determine the age of the earth and reached a figure which was completely inconsistent with both uniformitarian geology and Darwinian evolution.[43] Because of Kelvin's prestige, and the apparent certainty and precision of the physical theory upon which he based his conclusions, this objection was one of the most difficult and embarrassing the Darwinians had to meet.

Despite these objections to the Darwinian theory, the evidence for it was sufficiently overwhelming so that by the end of the 1860s the scientific acceptance of the theory was all but complete. In America the most powerful and fervent opponent of the theory was Louis Agassiz—himself a great naturalist and the leading biologist in the United States before the Civil War. Agassiz opposed the Darwinian theory with all the resources at his command, yet by the time he died in 1873 all of his own students had already gone over to the Darwinian camp.[44]

But if evolution had triumphed in science, it encountered continuing and angry opposition from religious and philosophic writers. For the orthodox churches, evolution posed a fundamental threat on at least three major issues. First, it struck directly at the foundations of revealed religion. Having wedded an empiricist epistemology, American Protestantism was compelled to prove the supernatural authority of revelation by empirical evidences. And that meant, as Emerson and Alcott had pointed out thirty years before, that if the historical evidences were overthrown, revelation—and so the supernatural authority of Christianity—went with it. What the higher criticism had done to the New Testament miracles, uniformitarian geology and Darwinian evolution had done far more thoroughly to the providential events of the Old Testament. If, as Paley said, revelation must be by miracles, the churches were in serious trouble. Second, the Darwinian theory carried appalling consequences for the natural theology. It was not that Darwin had failed to find order in nature; it was rather the character of the order he found. In place of the perfect order and economy of the Newtonian world, Darwin postulated an incredibly wasteful process of random proliferation and ruthless extinction. In place of the benevolent harmony in which all nature conspires to the happiness of the creation, Darwin presented "nature red in tooth and claw." If indeed order bespeaks an orderer, if like produces like, if natural law is but the mode of divine action, if all effects are intended, what conclusions follow respecting a deity who would design a world on the model of a slaughterhouse where most perished horribly, where the "saving remnant" was saved by chance adaptation alone, and where the meek would never live to inherit anything? For those who had made the natural theology the foundation of their reconciliation of religion and science, the Darwinian theory suddenly opened the abyss beneath their feet.

But beyond this there lay an even more fundamental issue—the nature of man himself. Traditional Christianity had always maintained that man possessed a dual nature: he might be part animal but he was also part angel. That man's animal body had affinities to the higher primates no literate Christian would deny; that man's immortal soul had such affinities no true Christian could ever admit. Darwin had nothing whatever to say about the immortal soul, but he had a great deal to say about the descent of man and about the evolution of those rational powers which had always been recognized as signifying the presence of the immortal soul.[45] If these higher powers of man had evolved by purely natural processes from analogous characteristics of higher primates, then there was no empirical evidence to support the postulate of the existence of a spiritual factor in man. But should that once be admitted, then orthodox Christianity would be at an end.

The question of whether man is a purely natural or partly spiritual creation was the fundamental issue of the controversy. Upon it rested ultimately all the other issues—moral, religious, and social. Without an indwelling spiritual principle, the religious held, man could possess neither immortality nor freedom. Furthermore, if man were wholly natural, and if, as geology and evolutionary biology claimed, the reign of natural law extended into the indefinite past, then there was no basis for believing in a providential government even in human affairs. Hence the moral order, if there was a moral order, could have no effective relation to human fate. The critical question then was the nature of man, and this issue quickly came to center upon that feature of man in which he most transcended the brute—his mind. Were the distinctive attributes of the human mind—reason, conscience, and consciousness of self—different in kind from those of the animal mind: this was the crucial question between science and religion in the post-Darwinian era. The literal truth of the Bible could be surrendered and religion survive; the argument from design could be surrendered and religion survive; but that man was somehow different in kind from the animal world—that the powers of the mind were not purely natural—that could not be surrendered and religion survive.

2. Herbert Spencer

Darwin's *Origin of Species* was a technical treatise which was read chiefly by specialists. Most Americans learned about evolution, not from Darwin himself, but from popularizers and interpreters, and among these the most influential was Herbert Spencer. Born in Derby, England, in 1820, Spencer became an engineer and subsequently an editor of the *Economist*. He was an advocate of evolution before the *Origin of Species* appeared, and so was well prepared to become its popular champion afterward. In 1860 Spencer announced his intention to construct what he called the "Synthetic Philosophy"—an all-embracing evolutionary system which was to unite all science and philosophy. This system was elaborated in a series of volumes, beginning with the *First Principles*[46] in 1864 and proceeding through the *Principles of Biology,*[47] the *Principles of Sociology,*[48] the *Principles of Ethics,*[49] etc. It was from Spencer rather than Darwin that the American people learned about evolution.[50]

Spencer claimed that his "Synthetic Philosophy" could not only "unify" all the sciences, but also reconcile science and religion as well. This modest ambition he hoped to fulfill by showing, first, that science and religion both assume the existence of an unknowable reality, which Spencer identifies with the divine, and, second, by "deriving" all the sciences from certain "first principles" which he attempts to lay down. The argument for the unknowable is based upon Hamilton's Law of the Conditioned. Spencer first distinguishes between real and symbolical conceptions. By a real conception, Spencer means that which can be both conceived and imagined. By a symbolical conception he means a concept not also imaginable. Hence "great magnitudes, great durations, great numbers, are none of them actually conceived, but are all of them conceived more or less symbolically."[51] The formation of symbolical conceptions Spencer holds to be a necessary and highly useful process, but in some cases this process can lead us to concepts which are not only unimaginable but also incomprehensible. Such he holds to be the concepts of infinity, continuity, and the absolute.[52] Spencer then invokes Hamilton's Law of the Conditioned to show that such incomprehensible concepts must have some real referents. Recalling that, by the conditioned, Hamilton means what can be positively thought, his statement of the law is

> The conditioned is the mean between two extremes—two inconditionates, exclusive of each other, neither of which *can be conceived as possible,* but of which, on the principles of contradiction and excluded middle, one *must be admitted as necessary.*[53]

Thus space must be infinite or finite, but we cannot conceive space as infinite, nor can we conceive it as finite. Yet by the law of excluded middle it must be one or the other. From such cases, Hamilton concludes

> We are thus taught the salutary lesson, that the capacity of thought is not to be constituted into the measure of existence; and are warned from recognizing the domain of our knowledge as necessarily co-extensive with the horizon of our faith. And by a wonderful revelation, we are thus, in the very consciousness of our inability to conceive aught above the relative and finite, inspired with a belief in the existence of something unconditioned beyond the sphere of all comprehensible reality.[54]

Although Hamilton holds that the unconditioned can be conceived only negatively, Spencer claims that we can have a positive though "indefinite" consciousness of it. That is, Spencer conceived the unconditioned as a substance from which all "conditioned"—i.e., limited—predicates are abstracted. We cannot have any definite concept of such a substance, for there is no definite predicate through which to think it, but we have nevertheless an indefinite concept of it.[55] Hence we do in some sense know the unconditioned, though we cannot say anything about it except what it is not.

Spencer applies this argument to show that the Unknowable is a necessary presupposition of both science and religion. The proof consists in showing that the entities postulated by science and religion must have incomprehensible properties. That this is true of God is easily shown since God must be both absolute and infinite.[56] The same type of argument is applicable to time, space, matter, and force; time, like space, must be either finite or infinite, yet neither possibility is conceivable,[57] and matter must be either infinitely divisible or finitely divisible, and again neither possibility is conceivable.[58] That force is incomprehensible Spencer asserts on the ground that on the one hand it is impossible that centers of force should act upon each other at a distance without some intermediary, while on the other hand every intermediary itself consists of centers of force which also act at a distance.[59] That this "contradiction" is generated only by assuming that all matter is composed of atomic centers of force—i.e., by asserting that a continuous distribution of force in space is impossible—simply testifies to the degree to which Spencer assumed the validity of the Newtonian model of reality. On the basis of these arguments, Spencer holds that we are forced to the conclusion that in both religion and science the fundamental concepts refer to an unknowable reality of which we know only the phenomenal effects. And since that reality is unknowable, science and religion cannot contradict each other, for neither can make positive assertions about anything but appearances.[60]

Having established the existence and indefinite character of the unknowable, Spencer turns to the knowable. He is a thoroughgoing empiricist and holds that all our positive knowledge is derived from our sensory experience. The ideas of space and time he regards as abstracted from the relations of coexistence and succession which we find among our sensations.[61] The concept of matter, or mass, he derives from the experience of resistance.

> Our conception of Matter, reduced to its simplest shape, is that of co-existent positions that offer resistance; as contrasted with our conception of Space, in which the co-existent positions offer no resistance . . . Whence it becomes manifest that our experience of *force,* is that out of which the idea of Matter is built. Matter as opposing our muscular energies, being immediately present to consciousness in terms of force; and its occupancy of Space being known by an abstract of experiences originally given in terms of force; it follows that forces, standing in certain correlations, form the whole content of our idea of Matter.[62]

If matter is nothing but force, it is clear that motion is resolvable into successive locations of forces at a series of space-points.[63] It is force, then, which is the ultimate concept characterizing changeable reality as we know it, but since force itself is unintelligible, Spencer claims that we must regard it as a direct manifestation of the divine. "Force, as we know it, can be regarded only as a certain conditioned effect of the Unconditioned Cause—as the relative reality indicating to us an Absolute Reality by which it is immediately produced."[64] Spencer thus obtains, by arguments which are obviously heavily indebted to Hamilton, a set of basic concepts—time, space, and force localized at time-space points—which he regards as sufficient to characterize knowable reality. These concepts are essentially those of mechanics, with mass translated into force, and as this suggests Spencer's model of the knowable is entirely mechanistic. Yet Spencer's position is more properly described as a form of Berkeleyan Idealism, for matter is defined in terms of force, and force is regarded as the direct action of God upon us.

Since Spencer regards the primitive concepts of science as referring to the Unknowable, it is not surprising that he should regard the axioms in the same light. His justification for this claim is based on his theory of explanation, which again is borrowed directly from Hamilton. To explain a fact means, according to Spencer, to subsume it under a more general principle. But if this be so, then either we have a regress, or explanation must at some point involve a most general principle which is itself not subsumed under any more general principle. From this fact Spencer draws the conclusion:

> Manifestly, as the *most* general cognition at which we arrive cannot be reduced to a more general one, it cannot be understood. Of necessity, therefore, explanation must eventually bring us down to the inexplicable. The deepest truth which we can get at, must be unaccountable.[65]

This "deepest truth" or ultimate principle upon which all science rests Spencer asserts to be the principle of the "persistence of force." This principle is held to include the laws of the conservation of energy and of matter, for according to Spencer matter is simply a special form of force. But since force itself is incomprehensible, the principle is really a statement about the Unknowable.

> Hence the force of which we assert persistence is that Absolute Force of which we are indefinitely conscious as the necessary correlate of the force we know. By the Persistence of Force, we really mean the persistence of some Cause which transcends our knowledge and conception. In asserting it we assert an Unconditioned Reality, without beginning or end . . . The sole truth which transcends experience by underlying it, is thus the Persistence of Force.[66]

To achieve his synthesis of all knowledge, Spencer first attempted to generalize established results in the special sciences into broad general laws, and then to "derive" these laws from his principle of the persistence of force. The procedure may be briefly illustrated. From the nebular hypothesis in astronomy, the Darwinian theory of evolution, Von Baer's formula in embryology,[67] and various alleged facts of chemistry,[68] social history,[69] and other fields, Spencer arrived at a general "law of evolution" which he states in the following form:

> Evolution is an integration of matter and concomitant dissipation of motion; during which the matter passes from an indefinite, incoherent homogeneity to a definite, coherent heterogeneity; and during which the retained motion undergoes a parallel transformation.[70]

Spencer then "derives" this law from the principle of the persistence of force.[71] The "derivation" of course is not a logical one: the premises actually employed include the whole of mechanics, as well as such remarkable principles as that space cannot be unlimited because "unlimited space is inconceivable,"[72] and the connection between the premises and the conclusion remains at best obscure. Nevertheless, Spencer claims to have effected such a "derivation" and so to have "unified" our knowledge by showing that the results of our empirical investigations necessarily follow from "the law that transcends proof."[73]

Since Spencer conceives knowable reality in terms of mechanics, his "law of evolution" is an attempt to reduce all evolution to a mechanical process analogous to that described by the nebular hypothesis. To apply this law to organic nature, he must therefore define biological organisms as mechanical devices. By a living organism, Spencer means an unstable material organization which sustains itself by a continual adjustment of internal to external relations.[74] The adjustive process by which the organism is maintained may be purely automatic and inflexible, as in instinctive behavior of the sort which characterizes the lower forms of life, or it may involve the ability to modify behavior as a result of experience, as in learning, but in either case the process is conceived as one of mechanically determined adjustment. Spencer's psychology is thus a crude form of behaviorism. He regards the learning process as a direct copying of external sequences through association, so that the mind really consists in the power of memory and is completely determined by the environment.[75] The absolute determinism of mechanics thus applies without remission to the operation of the mind, and the organism is regarded as utterly incapable of any sort of creative response to its surroundings.

Spencer also extended his "law" of evolution to social development—indeed, it was the applicability of evolutionary ideas to social questions which first interested him in biology. In his first major work, *Social Statics*,[76] published in 1850—nine years before the *Origin of Species*—Spencer stated his social views in their starkest form. These views were subsequently modified and developed in the three volumes of the *Principles of Sociology* which began appearing in 1876, but the essential doctrines remained unchanged. Spencer's social philosophy may be most succinctly described as an evolutionary interpretation of the doctrine of natural rights. He conceives social evolution as the development of organized society out of a primitive state which is virtually a state of nature, and the course of this development is the same for all people. There is therefore one linear scheme of social evolution, with respect to which the progress of any present society can be evaluated. Spencer's description of the primitive state of mankind is completely governed by his belief that primitives are less developed physically, psychologically, and socially than civilized men. He describes them as childlike, as governed by impulse and lacking emotional controls, as excessively concrete in thinking and lacking abstract concepts—in short, as "less evolved" than modern man.[77] Primitive social life consists according to Spencer of small nomadic tribes leading a predatory existence[78]—very nearly as the war of all against all. Spencer regards natural rights as based upon "the truth that if life is justifiable, there must be a justification for the performance of acts essential to its preservation; and, therefore, a justification for those liberties and claims which make such acts possible."[79] In the predatory life of primitives these liberties and claims are unrestricted, so that warlike characteristics constitute part of the necessary equipment of the primitive.[80] To this predatory state Spencer holds that primitive man is well adapted, but expanding population and the amalgamation of groups, either through conquest or by other means, compel the development of increasingly complex social conditions for which this primitive adaptation is inadequate.[81] Social evolution—i.e., the evolution of more "advanced" sociocultural systems—thus implies a corresponding evolution of human nature itself—an evolution made possible for Spencer by the inheritance of acquired characteristics, by natural selection, and by his psychological theories according to which the adaptation of the organism to the environment is an automatic result of experience. But as the mind's adjustment follows changes in the environment, it is clear that while the social conditions themselves are changing, the adaptation of man to these conditions will be imperfect, and it is to this failure of adaptation that Spencer attributes all the evils of the world. "All evil results from the non-adaptation of constitution to conditions," Spencer wrote in *Social Statics*,[82] thereby identifying adaptation with the good, and since adaptation is the law of nature it is clear that in the long run the good will triumph. "Progress, therefore, is not an accident, but a necessity."[83] If in the meantime maladaptations are severe, Spencer's answer is that the only remedy is the automatic working of the evolutionary process of adjustment. Attempts to interfere with the evolutionary process cannot be successful, for the mind cannot rule the process by which it is itself ruled, and will merely result in perpetuating the unfit. Spencer had the courage of his convictions and did not flinch from their implications.

It seems hard that widows and orphans should be left to struggle for life or death. Nevertheless, when regarded not separately but in connexion with the interests of the univeral humanity, these harsh fatalities are seen to be full of the highest beneficence—the same beneficence that brings to early graves the children of diseased parents, and singles out the low-spirited, the intemperate, and the debilitated as the victims of an epidemic.[84]

The lesson which this "salutory pain" is designed to teach us is that the exercise of each individual's natural rights must be restricted so that the natural rights of others are not infringed. As Spencer put it in *Social Statics,* the "law of right social relationships, [is] that—*Every man has freedom to do all that he wills, provided he infringes not the equal freedom of any other man."*[85] When this "law" has been learned, as it must inevitably be, society will assume an ideal form which Spencer calls the "industrial society."[86] With the elimination of man's predatory characteristics—i.e., his desires to infringe the rights of others—war will also have ceased, and so except for minor police functions the state will wither away.[87] What will remain will be a society of free moral individuals engaged in peaceful, voluntary cooperation to produce needed goods and services. Each man will be secure in his own rights, and will be checked from invading the rights of others by internalized moral controls.[88] Thus Spencer concludes:

The ultimate man will be one whose private requirements coincide with public ones. He will be that manner of man who, in spontaneously fulfilling his own nature, incidentally performs the functions of a social unit; and yet is only enabled so to fulfill his own nature by all others doing the like.[89]

The synthetic philosophy was a program rather than a system. Spencer never seriously attempted to derive biology, psychology, and sociology from mechanics in any rigorous sense. The "synthesis" rather consisted in framing highly general formulae, such as the above-quoted "law" of evolution, which were sufficiently broad to subsume a number of more specific hypotheses. Nevertheless, the popularity of Spencer's work in America was phenomenal. By the time he died in 1903, 368,755 volumes of his writings had been sold in this country[90]—a fantastic sale for the time and the nature of the works. Moreover, Spencer's influence was not limited to his own writings. He quickly acquired American champions who undertook to publicize his work and to spread his doctrine throughout the land. E. L. Youmans, whose journals, *Appleton's Journal* and the *Popular Science Monthly,* were chiefly devoted to publishing the gospel according to Spencer, was only the most active of a list which ranged from Andrew Carnegie to Jack London.[91] Nor is it difficult to see why Spencer should have been so popular. The publication of the *Origin of Species* had badly shaken the established world view, particularly with respect to the relation between science and moral and religious doctrines. There was accordingly an acute demand for a reintegration of the world view which would bring evolution into harmony with more traditional beliefs. This synthesis Spencer undertook to perform, and his immense popularity testified less to the correctness of his conclusions than to the felt need which his works met. If the doctrine of the Unknowable did not satisfy orthodox theologians, it did permit a compromise between science and religion which many people found highly useful. Moreover, by making mechanics the basis of his synthesis, Spencer resolved the disturbing new theories into special cases of a familiar and accepted theory, and by then using Hamilton to establish what amounted to an idealistic interpretation he brought purpose and design back into nature. Evolution thus became a form of God's providence, and nature was once again the expositor of the divine mind. Finally, Spencer's social theories were admirably suited to post-Civil War America. The transformation of the American economy which resulted from the introduction of the industrial technology had become sufficiently extensive by the 1860s so that some of its major implications were apparent. Natural law theory and laissez-faire economics, which had provided so admirable a conceptualization of the small farm and craft-shop culture of an earlier era, were already proving inadequate to deal with the emerging industrial society, yet these intellectual systems had acquired so fundamental a place in the American world view that they were virtually the only theories available in terms of which the new situation could be interpreted. Spencer's social philosophy is precisely such an interpretation of the new conditions in established terms. The ideal society he envisaged was an embodiment of the natural rights and laissez-faire doctrines, and his description of the "ultimate man" could have been written by Thomas Jefferson. By showing that industrialism, with all its horrors, was a necessary means to such a goal, he provided a rationale which persuaded many that they understood what was happening and that the old verities still applied to the new situation. The popularity of Herbert Spencer in America is in fact a testimonial to the degree of entrenchment which the older world view had attained, and an indication of how difficult a road lay before those who were to seek new answers to the modern world.

3. Chauncey Wright

Of the defenders of evolution in America, Chauncey Wright was one of the ablest. Wright was born in Northampton, Massachusetts, in 1830, the son of a grocer of modest means. With the aid and encouragement of family friends, Wright went to Harvard, from which he graduated in 1852. As a student, he distinguished himself in physical science and mathematics, and after graduation, he took a position as a computer for the *Nautical Almanac*. Although the pay was very modest, Wright kept this position until 1872, when an inheritance freed him from the necessity of working. He died in 1875, at the age of forty-five, having lived in Cambridge almost continuously since entering college.[92]

After graduating from college, Wright became captivated by the philosophical writings of Sir William Hamilton. As one of his friends remarked, "Chauncey's relation to Hamilton in those days was in a way like that of a devout Christian to his Bible."[93] Wright read everything Hamilton had written, and, as his correspondence with Francis Abbot shows,[94] he became a defender of Hamilton's views, including, of course, the famous Law of the Conditioned. For Wright as for many others, Hamilton's curious combination of Scottish Realism and Kantianism provided an empiricist philosophy compatible with strong commitments to science, while at the same time offering a seemingly sound basis for religious faith. Wright could thus pursue his work as a physical scientist, certain that no scientific findings could undermine his religious commitments.

When the *Origin of Species* appeared in 1859, Wright became converted to Darwin's position, although he also accepted such Lamarckian principles as the inheritance of acquired characteristics. From that time on, most of Wright's efforts were devoted to the defense of evolution. This defense took many forms, including new contributions to evolutionary theory, and defenses of the theory against theological and scientific objections. A review of the latter sort which Wright wrote in 1871 brought him into direct correspondence with Darwin, at whose request he undertook the investigation which led to the publication of his finest paper, the "Evolution of Self-Consciousness," in 1873.[95] By the time he died in 1875, Wright had made a considerable mark as a defender of evolution.

In 1865, J. S. Mill published his *Examination of Sir William Hamilton's Philosophy.*[96] For Wright, as for all followers of Hamilton, this event marked a major crisis. Mill's attack on Hamilton was among the most destructive ever executed by one philosopher upon another, and its success ended Hamilton's leadership in philosophic circles. The efforts of McCosh, Mansel, and others to defend Hamilton proved futile, and Mill and the school he represented thereafter emerged as the leaders of British empiricism. Wright was dismayed by his first reading of Mill's *Examination,*[97] and particularly by the evidence of inconsistency which Mill adduced, but he did not immediately abandon Hamilton's cause. In reviews of Mill's work in the *Nation*[98] and the *North American Review,*[99] he accused Mill of misinterpreting Hamilton's views on numerous points, and argued that some at least of the contradictions which Mill had charged against Hamilton were the products of Mill's own misunderstanding of Hamilton's doctrines. Thus it was not simply the negative effect of Mill's book which weaned Wright from Hamilton, although Wright admitted that Hamilton's stature was sadly diminished by the *Examination:*[100] rather, it was the marked superiority of Mill's psychological analysis over what Wright described as Hamilton's metaphysical approach to psychology. For Hamilton, the foundation of all philosophy was the philosophy of the mind, or psychology.[101] And the problem of psychology was, as Hamilton saw it, the analysis of cognitions to determine which elements are due to the knowing subject and which to the subject known.[102] Hamilton based his analysis upon the absolute authority of consciousness; whatever consciousness testifies to be the case must be the case.[103] In particular, those ultimate facts of consciousness which are universal, necessary, and "incomprehensible" (i.e., primitive) must be accepted as generic to the human mind,[104] and so a priori true. Wright was particularly struck by the contrast between this "metaphysical" approach to psychology and that of Mill, in which the presence of such "ultimate" facts of consciousness as the existence of matter were accounted for by known psychological principles such as the Law of Inseparable Association,[105] and he recognized in this contrast the scientific superiority of Mill's approach.[106] From that point on, Wright became increasingly a follower of Mill and Bain, interested in developing a truly scientific psychology—an effort which culminated in his famous paper on the "Evolution of Self-Consciousness" in which he undertook to present an evolutionary explanation of that very faculty of which Hamilton had said, "Consciousness is to the philosopher what the Bible is to the theologian."[107]

Although Wright gave several courses of lectures at Harvard, he never held a university appointment. He had apparently little ambition for place or fame, and his remarkable abilities were not employed in advancing his own career. Although he wrote articles and reviews for a number of journals, the slightness of his published writings was a source of great regret among his intimates. As James commented, "His best work has been done in conversation,"[108] for which he had apparently an extraordinary talent. He was involved in several philosophical discussion groups at various times, the most famous being the Metaphysical Club which included William James, Charles Peirce, Oliver Wendell Holmes, Nicholas St. John Green, Joseph Warner, John Fiske, and Frank Abbot, and before which in the early 1870s Peirce presented the idea of pragmatism.[109] In such informal gatherings Wright's abilities had full play, and his views exerted an important influence on James, Peirce, Abbot, and doubtless upon a number of others. As James remarked, "In the acts and writings of the many friends he influenced his spirit will, in one way or another, as the years roll on, be more operative than it ever was in direct production."[110]

The focal point of Wright's intellectual endeavors was the defense of evolution. We have noted above that one of the greatest problems the Darwinians faced was Kelvin's estimate of the age of the earth. In 1864 Wright published an article entitled "A Physical Theory of the Universe"[111] in which he attempted to meet this challenge. Recognizing that Kelvin's argument followed directly from the nebular hypothesis and that with the physics of that time it could not be refuted if that hypothesis was granted, Wright tried to formulate an explanation of the origin of the solar system and of the sun's heat on other grounds. Following the "meteoric" theory of Mayer,[112] Wright argued that the sun's heat could be produced by the fall of solid bodies into the sun—i.e., by the conversion of mechanical energy into heat. Wright further supposed that in this conversion the projectile body, and part of the sun's surface which received the impact, are vaporized, creating an expanding cloud of gas surrounding the sun. At the outer limits of this cloud, the temperature will have declined sufficiently to produce a condensation of the gas into solid form, at which point the reformed solid, under the action of gravity, falls once more into the sun. Thus Wright comments:

In these suppositions we have exactly reversed the nebular hypothesis. Instead of, in former ages, a huge gaseous globe contracted by cooling and by gravitation, and consolidated at its centre, we have supposed one now existing, and filling that portion of the interstellar spaces over which the sun's attraction predominates,—a highly rarefied continuous gaseous mass, constantly evaporated and expanded from its solid center, but constantly condensed and consolidated near its outer limits—constantly heated at its center by the fall of solid bodies from its outer limits, and constantly cooled and condensed at these limits by the conversion of heat into motion and the arrest of this motion by gravitation.[113]

Because of the analogy which this theory bears to terrestrial weather phenomena, Wright called it the theory of "cosmical weather."[114] The formation of the planets Wright seeks to account for in terms of aggregations of meteorites at certain points in the rotating gas cloud.[115] The theory is developed only in outline and in a nontechnical form, yet the purpose is clear, for what Wright is seeking to do is to offer a theory regarding the origins of the solar system and the sun's heat which will be consistent with known physical laws and at the same time will permit the existence of a past sufficiently extended to accommodate uniformitarian geology and biological evolution. The cosmic weather hypothesis is really a rejection of cosmology, in the sense of a history of the solar system from beginning to end, in favor of a directionless repetitive cosmic process which could be infinitely old.[116]

Wright also undertook the defense of evolution against the attacks of the theologians, both by attacking the natural theology and by an analysis of the relation of science and religion. In 1865, he published an article on "Natural Theology as a Positive Science"[117] in which he attacked the basic assumptions of those theologians, and he followed it with a number of later articles which taken together amount to a thorough destruction of the position.[118] Wright attacks in turn each of the principles upon which the natural theology rested. First, he maintains that it is impossible to identify final causes empirically.

For it is denied by the physical philosopher that causes and effects in natural phenomena can be interpreted into the terms of natural theology by any key which science itself affords. By what criterion, he would ask, can we distinguish among the numberless effects, that are also causes, and among the causes that may, for aught we can know, be also effects,—how can we distinguish which are the means and which are the ends? What effects are we warranted by observation in calling final, or final causes, or the ends for which the others exist?[119]

What in fact physical science disclosed are endless causal sequences: antecedent states lead to consequent "effects" which themselves are causes of further effects, and so on endlessly. With respect to the behavior of particular sentient beings, the concept of final cause has content, insofar as these beings are conceived to pursue specific goals in the achievement of which they are themselves the agents.[120] But with regard to nature as a whole, to designate any particular effect as an end whose causes are means to its production is to impose a distinction which has no empirical warrant at all—any other effect could just as legitimately have been chosen as the end sought. Accordingly, Wright held that the proof of order in nature is not a proof of design, for it cannot be shown that the order is designed to any particular end. Second, Wright subjected the principle that the effect must resemble the cause to a withering analysis. By a causal sequence, Wright argues, what is meant is that a certain aggregate of conditions is followed by an event. This aggregate of conditions is not usually denoted by a single name "the connotation of which would define its nature."[121] Accordingly, in order to refer to these conditions collectively as the "cause," they are often defined by some one condition or property deemed essential, which may be the property of producing this effect. In the latter case, and then only, does the nature of the effect appear as essential to the cause, and so it is "by refunding to the effect what we have thus borrowed from it that we arrive at the metaphysician's mathematical conception of causation, the transference of the nature of one thing, that is, the cause, to another thing, its effect."[122] "Yet," Wright remarks,

> for practical and scientific purposes this aggregate is best defined by the enumeration of the conditions that compose it, to which observation adds the fact, or nature, that it will whenever it exists be followed by a given or defined effect. In this case the conditions which constitute the cause do not constitute the effect. They are simply followed by the effect, whose nature is wholly unlike that of its cause, or is like and is implied in its cause only so far as the capacity of producing it may be thought of identically as a part of the nature of its cause.[123]

The alleged similarity of cause and effect is therefore an artifact of a particular mode of definition, and one which is not scientifically useful. Third, Wright presents a very clear analysis of the nature of scientific law. Wright does not hold that the laws of nature are simply invariable sequences, for there are invariable sequences among phenomena which clearly do not represent causal connections—e.g., day and night. The relation of causality is rather a species of invariable succession: "It means an *unconditional,* invariable succession; *independence* of other orders of succession, or of all orders not involved in it."[124] That is, a true scientific law asserts not only that an invariable sequence among phenomena does occur, but also that it always would occur. Wright is thus committed to the reality of possibility supporting counterfactuals, so his position is not as nominalistic as has sometimes been supposed. But Wright vigorously opposed the claim that scientific laws merely describe the operation of "powers" to whose agency ultimate causality is to be attributed.

> Metaphysics demands, in the interest of mystery, *why* an elementary antecedent is followed by its elementary consequent. But this question does not arise from that inquisitiveness which inspires scientific research. It is asked to show that it cannot be answered, and hence that all science rests on mystery. It is asked from the feelings that in the barbarian or the child forbid or check inquiry. But, being a question, it is open to answer; or it makes legitimate, at

least, the counter-question, When can a question be properly asked? or, What is the purpose of asking a question? Is it not to discover the causes, classes, laws, or rules that determine the existence, properties, or production of a thing or event? And when these are discovered, is there any further occasion for inquiry except in the interest of feelings which would have checked inquiry at the outset?[125]

Elementary connections among phenomena simply are: why they are can only be explained by deriving them from yet more elementary connections which then stand as ultimate facts. Beyond such elementary connections, there is nothing.

Wright's attack on the natural theology was intended to eliminate one class of religious objections to evolution. But Wright also attempted to develop a strategy which would free evolution, and science, from all religious objections. This strategy consists in drawing a sharp distinction between religion and theology, and in attributing all the contradictions between science and established religious doctrines to theology rather than to religion.

> That there is a fundamental distinction between the natures of scientific and religious ideas ought never to be doubted; but that contradiction can arise, except between religious and superstitious ideas, ought not for a moment to be admitted. Progress in science is really a progress in religious truth, not because any new reasons are discovered for the doctrines of religion, but because advancement in knowledge frees us from the errors both of ignorance and superstition . . . If the teachings of natural theology are liable to be refuted or corrected by progress in knowledge, it is legitimate to suppose, not that science is irreligious, but that these teachings are superstitious; and whatever evils result from the discoveries of science are attributable to the rashness of the theologian, and not to the supposed irreligious tendencies of science.[126]

By a theology Wright means a system of propositions concerning both God and nature, and purporting to "explain" at least some natural events in terms of divine decrees. That such a system can, and indeed must, sooner or later come into conflict with science is obvious, and reflects, so Wright holds, the arrogant presumption of the theologians. But religion has no necessary relation to theology.

> Religion (subjective) means a man's devotion—the complete assent and concentration of his will—to any object which he acknowledges to have a right to his entire service, and supreme control over his life. Religion (objective) means the object or objects whose claims to this supremacy are acknowledged. An irreligious man is, then, first, one who acknowledges no supreme ends or objects; or, secondly, one who, though he acknowledges, does not habitually submit his will to such a power.[127]

For Wright, religion consists in an ultimate concern or end, service to which is self-sanctioning: "if immediate happiness in doing his duty, or misery in not doing it, is the ultimate sanction, then his religion is real, or a part of his character."[128] But the choice of ultimate ends Wright considers to be a matter of sentiment or emotion which is not based upon empirical proof or disproof and which is therefore wholly independent of science. Thus between science as a system of knowledge and religion as an ultimate devotion there cannot be a contradiction—it is only when religion becomes entwined in the superstitions of theology that it can conflict with science and then the overthrow of these superstitions is really a service to religion.

This strategy was used effectively by the Darwinians to defend themselves against the attacks of orthodox religion, and is exemplified in the difference in wording of the titles of two highly influential books: in 1873 John William Draper published a *History of the Conflict between Religion and Science*[129] while in 1893 Andrew Dickson White published *A History of the Warfare of Science with Theology in Christendom.*[130] By shifting the attack from religion to theology, the Darwinians could defend science against theology while at the same time professing the compatibility of science with "true" religion. In effect, therefore, the strategy amounted to an offer of peace between science and the churches, on the condition that traditional theology be abandoned, and these terms the liberal Protestant churches generally accepted. From the Darwinian controversy until the emergence of neoorthodoxy in recent years, philosophical theology was virtually abandoned in America.[131] It was this desertion of the field that Royce attacked when he brought out *The Problem of Christianity* in 1913.[132]

But Wright had more than the theologians and the physicists to contend with— he had also to deal with the dogmatic metaphysical evolutionists, of whom Herbert Spencer was the most prominent. The advocacy of what they alleged to be the evolutionary cause by writers such as Spencer was a constant source of embarrassment to those who, like Wright, were engaged in the defense of Darwinian evolution as a scientific theory, and Wright's review of Spencer is one of the most slashing he ever wrote.[133] Wright attacked Spencer's attempt to discover ultimate truths by framing generalizations which "comprehend and consolidate the widest generalizations of Science"[134] as

. . . a method for the ascertainment of ultimate truths, which a positivist would regard as correct only on the supposition that the materials of truth have all been collected, and that the research of science is no longer for the enlargement of our experience or for the informing of the mind. Until these conditions be realized, the positivist regards such attempts as Mr. Spencer's as not only faulty, but positively pernicious and misleading.[135]

Spencer's method assumes that investigation is complete and that the function of scientific principles is merely to summarize facts already known. But this is not the function of scientific principles as Wright sees it: "nothing justifies the development of abstract principles in science but their utility in enlarging our concrete knowledge of nature.''[136] True scientific hypotheses are "finders, not merely summaries of truth.''[137] But Spencer's generalizations were not even adequate summaries, for instead of devising a precise set of axioms from which he then deduced the known results, he rather generalized the known results by rendering the statement of them so vague that roughly analogous findings appear to be instances of one general "law.''[138] Spencer's "law of evolution" was perhaps the most obvious case of this, but Wright was particularly incensed by Spencer's attempt to subsume all the conservation laws of physics under the "principle of the persistence of force"—a principle which Wright observed has more in common with "the old metaphysical 'Principle of Causality', or the impossibility of any change in the quantity of existence (whatever this may mean)''[139] than with the laws of physics. Moreover, Spencer's argument that the ultimate terms of science are unknowable and that its ultimate laws "transcend" empirical proof were indications to Wright that Spencer simply did not understand the methods of science. Wright regarded the verification principle as the basis of scientific proof, and he interpreted this principle in a way which fully allows for indirect proof and for theoretical constructs.

> But whatever be the origin of the theories of science . . . the *value* of these theories can only be tested, say the positivists, by an appeal to sensible experience, by deductions from them of consequences which we can confirm by the undoubted testimony of the senses. Thus, while ideal or transcendental elements are admitted into scientific researches, though in themselves insusceptible of simple verification, they must still show credentials from the senses, either by affording from themselves consequences capable of sensuous verification, or by yielding such consequences in conjunction with ideas which by themselves are verifiable.[140]

The fact that the primitive terms of a system are not explicitly defined within the system does not prevent their being implicitly defined,[141] and conservation laws, like all postulates, are susceptible of confirmation. Accordingly, Wright concluded that Spencer's Synthetic Philosophy was neither a scientific philosophy nor a philosophy of science, but a metaphysical system of "encyclopedic abstractions"[142] of no use to anyone.

In defending evolution as a scientific hypothesis, Wright found it necessary to combat both theology and metaphysics as equally dangerous enemies of science. Both represented to him superstitious interpretations of phenomena which were in fundamental contradiction to genuine scientific explanations and which therefore science must overthrow. Between science and philosophy, conceived as metaphysics or theology, Wright believed there could be no peace; but between science and philosophy, conceived as epistemology, he believed there could be no conflict. Thus Wright wrote to Abbot:

> Secondly, you surprise me by asking if Idealism is not "the very negation of objective science?" By objective science, I understand the science of the

objects of knowledge, as contradistinguished from the processes and faculties of knowing. Does Idealism deny that there are such objects? Is not its doctrine rather a definition of the nature of these objects than a denial of their existence? There is nothing in positive science, or the study of phenomena and their laws, which Idealism conflicts with. (See Berkeley.) Astronomy is just as real a science, as true an account of phenomena and their laws, if phenomena are only mental states, as on the other theory.[143]

If the various philosophical positions are conceived as accounts of the nature of phenomena, then so long as the accounts are self-consistent and comprehensive, they are equally compatible with science, for they involve no new statements of relations among phenomena, with which alone science is concerned, but only offer alternative ways of defining the phenomena themselves. Epistemologically therefore science is neutral, although it is opposed to all forms of metaphysics.

Although Wright's defense of Darwin's theory played a significant part in the evolutionary controversy, his most important works were his positive contributions to the theory of evolution. One of these was a technical paper in mathematical biology in which he attempted to account for the arrangement of leaves on the stem of a plant by evolutionary principles.[144] But his most important paper was the monograph on the "Evolution of Self-Consciousness"[145] which he published in 1873. The paper originated in a discussion between Wright and Darwin in September of 1872, of which Wright gave the following account:

> One point I may mention, however, of our final talk. I am some time to write an essay on matters covering the ground of certain common interests and studies, and in review of his "Descent of Man", and other related books, for which the learned title is adopted of *Psychozoölogy*,—as a substitute for "Animal Psychology", "Instinct", and the like titles,—in order to give the requisite subordination (from our point of view) of consciousness in men and animals, to their development and general relations to nature.[146]

In undertaking this work, Wright addressed himself to the central issue of the evolutionary controversy—the nature of the mind and particularly the nature of the mind's peculiar capacity for self-transcendence which had long been regarded as the undeniable evidence of an indwelling supernatural principle. The publication of the *Descent of Man* in 1871 made it imperative that this issue be met, and it is a tribute to Wright's abilities that Darwin should have asked him to do it.

The problem of self-consciousness as Wright conceived it is a problem of emergence: how can something "new" suddenly emerge in the course of evolution? Wright's answer is based upon two principles. The first is that the effect need not resemble the cause. The second is that true causal laws serve to define disposition properties. From the first principle, it follows that even a radical dissimilarity between two phenomena is no objection to one being the cause of the other; hence self-consciousness may well be the effect of antecedent conditions which are in no sense "like" their effect. From the second principle, it follows that if self-consciousness is the effect of certain antecedent conditions, then whenever those conditions are realized self-consciousness will result, and if it should be the case that those antecedent conditions are never simultaneously realized prior to a particular time, but are realized thereafter, then self-consciousness will "emerge," or first appear, at that particular time.[147] The problem of the evolution of self-consciousness thus becomes that of defining the antecedent conditions upon the occurrence of which self-consciousness ensues, and of showing how these conditions have come about.

When human beings are viewed in evolutionary perspective, it is clear that they represent one terminus of a series of organic forms whose behavior has ranged from the purely instinctive to the largely habitual. Wright was concerned to stress the continuity of this series, and the fact that he believed in the inheritance of acquired characteristics enabled him to interpose inherited "dispositions" between true instincts and individually acquired habits. Thus while he views instincts as purely automatic responses to stimuli he also believed that *"habit* properly so called, and *dispositions,* which are the inherited effects of habits, are not different in their practical character or modes of action from true instincts; but differ only in their origin and capacity of alternation through the higher forms of volition."[148] Wright does not present a detailed analysis of learning, but the brief comments he does give show that he subscribed to a form of reinforcement theory.

> . . . volitions are connections between the occasions, or external means and conditions of an action, and the production of the action itself through the *motive of the end,* and not through emotions or by any other ties instinctively uniting them. They are joined by the foreseen ulterior effect of the action, or else through a union produced by its influence. The desirableness of what is effected by an action connects its occasions, or present means and conditions, with the action itself, and causes its production through the end felt in imagination. The influence of the end, or ulterior motive in volition, may not be a consciously recognized part of the action, or a distinctly separated step in it, and will actually cease to be the real tie when a series of repeated volitions has established a habit, or a fixed association between them and their occasions, or external conditions. This connection in habits is, as we have said, closely similar to strictly instinctive connections, and is indistinguishable from them independently of questions of origin and means of alterations.[149]

Since habits result from repeated volitions, the connection of stimulus and response is initially mediated by the motive or goal desired, and it is the desirability of the goal for the attainment of which the response is instrumental which *creates* its relation to the stimulus. Habitual behavior therefore presupposes motivation or goal direction on the part of the organism.

To the extent that behavior is governed by habit, and so is instrumental to the

attainment of goals desired by the organism—i.e., is motivated—the organism
may be "spoken of as free, or unconstrained by an outward force, or necessity."[150] On the other hand, behavior which is instinctive only or which subserves
ends not desired by the organism itself may be said to be constrained or necessi-
tated.[151] This distinction between freedom and necessity is not the traditional one,
for Wright regards all behavior as causally determined[152]—the difference for him
relates only to whether or not the behavior is instrumental to the attainment of a
goal sought by the organism itself. The significance of the distinction therefore is
not philosophical but psychological, for it provides the basis for an elementary
form of self-consciousness. In its most rudimentary form, Wright regards the ego
or self as that which exercises this voluntary control over behavior and experience,
and so is sharply contrasted with that nonego which is not subject to such
control.[153] An awareness of this difference, and so a consciousness of self as a
cause distinguished from other causes, Wright regards as existing even in dogs, for
dogs can understand the reference of names to themselves[154] and can apprehend
"themselves as agents or patients with wills and feelings distinct from those of
other animals, and from the forces and interests of outward nature generally."[155]
Thus it would follow from Wright's analysis that the existence of the ego is a
function of the existence of voluntary behavior and hence of learned behavior, so
that the ego "emerges" with the capacity of the organism to formulate goals and
pursue them through habitual action. In this sense, an ego, and a consciousness of
the ego, must exist at a prehuman level.

Habitual behavior as Wright describes it implies the presence of signs. These
signs need not be linguistic: any image, feeling, or sound may serve as a sign if it
suggests the same thing to the mind that its object suggests.[156] Wright generally
uses the term "internal sign" to refer to such nonlinguistic mental imagery which
serves a representative function, and the term "external sign" to refer to spoken
linguistic signs or observable gestures.[157] Dumb animals may or may not possess
language, or "signs *purposely used* for communication,"[158] but they must possess
internal signs if they have habits. For in the first place, the habit is properly a
relation between a class of stimuli and a class of responses. The percept which
serves as the stimulus in a specific case must be "cognized"—i.e., recognized as
like or unlike prior percepts[159]—and this implies the determination of a representative image having mnemonic functions through which this classification is
made.[160] The animal of course is not aware of performing a classification or of
making an inference; upon presentation of the stimulus the animal makes the
suggested response without any awareness of an intermediary process. Hence
habitual action in animals is analogous to enthymematic reasoning.[161] The structure of the inference is

In every case of S, then R follows
This is a case of S
Therefore R follows.

But for the animal the major premise is implicit and the response is at once suggested by the particular stimulus. Nevertheless, the use of a representative image which serves as a conceptual interpretation of the percept is clearly implied in this behavior. And in the second place, Wright regards the formation of habit as a connection of stimulus and response through a motive. But the motive, or goal sought, though perhaps attained after the response is made, is not present in perception when the response is made. Hence the motive, and the instrumental relation of the behavior to the motive, must be represented in imagination, and this implies the use of some sort of mental sign.[162] Animals capable of habitual action therefore must possess "concepts" in some form—i.e., they must possess representative images having both mnemonic functions, in that they recall and classify as like past experiences, and directive or guiding functions, in that they lead on to a desired goal state.[163] Where these concepts exist as internal signs only without accompanying external signs, their functions, and very existence, are doubtless implicit and unrecognized, yet their existence appears to be a prerequisite to the presence of habitual behavior.

It is a question of considerable interest, and one which Wright is clearly loath to attempt to answer, whether the origin of language precedes or follows the emergence of self-consciousness. Concepts as we generally know them appear so closely related to linguistic or external signs that it is not easy to think of the concept apart from its linguistic formulation, and there is certainly no question that the introduction of external signs would greatly increase the animal's command over his representative images and his ability to attend to them as objects.[164] Wright remarks at one point that a gestural rather than verbal language might precede self-consciousness,[165] but he so phrases his argument that the question of which comes first is left open. But what is essential to self-consciousness is sufficient strength of memory and imagination so that the internal sign can be held before the mind and contrasted either with an external sign or a percept and its representative function recognized.

As soon, then, as the progress of animal intelligence through an extension of the range in its powers of memory, or in revived impressions, together with a corresponding increase in the vividness of these impressions, has reached a certain point (a progress in itself useful, and therefore likely to be secured in some part of nature, as one among its numerous grounds of selection, or lines of advantage), it becomes possible for such an intelligence to fix its attention on a vivid outward sign, without losing sight of, or dropping out of distinct attention, an image or revived impression; which latter would only serve, in case of its spontaneous revival in imagination, as a sign of the same thing, or the same event. Whether the vivid outward sign be a real object or event, of which the revived image is the counterpart, or whether it be a sign in a stricter meaning of the term,—that is, some action, figure, or utterance, associated either naturally or artificially with all similar objects or events, and, consequently, with the revived and representative image of them,—whatever the character of this outward sign may be, provided the representative image, or inward sign, still retains, in distinct consciousness, its power as such, then the outward sign may be consciously recognized as a substitute for the inward one, and a consciousness of simultaneous internal and external suggestion, or significance, might be realized; and the contrast of thoughts and things, at least in their power of suggesting that of which they may be coincident signs, could, for the first time, be perceptible. This would plant the germ of the distinctively human form of self-consciousness.[166]

Self-consciousness of the distinctively human sort means for Wright the recognition of thought as thought and the ability to reflect upon that thought. The conditions upon which such a recognition depends are strength of memory and imagination sufficient to permit attention to be focused upon internal signs, and their reprentative character recognized. Such a recognition would be facilitated by external signs, but it is perhaps possible without them. Thus the powers upon which human self-consciousness depends exist already in the animal mind, although not in a sufficiently developed form to produce this particular result. But their gradual strengthening to the point at which self-consciousness would emerge is clearly in line with established evolutionary principles.

One of Wright's most arresting insights is his recognition that human self-consciousness must be won.

That a dumb animal should not know itself to be a thinking being, is hardly more surprising than that it should not be aware of the circulation of its blood and other physiological functions; or that it should not know the anatomy of its frame or that of its nervous system. . . .[167]

The discovery that it possesses internal signs is only the germ of self-consciousness—that germ must be developed by reflection. The animal must explore this new domain of objects and so attempt to reduce them to some coherent order. In so doing it applies to the world of its thoughts the same powers of observation, analysis, and generalization which it employs in dealing with other experiences—reflection requires no new faculties of mind but only the employment of established faculties upon our thoughts as objects.[168] But precisely which of our experiences are our own thoughts and which are not is itself one of the things which reflection must discover. Thus Wright remarks:

These images, in their *individual* capacity, are not to be distinguished, even in human consciousness, from the object of perception. It is in their specific, or notative, function as signs, and as referring back to memories of like experiences, which they summarize, that they are separately and subjectively cognized.[169]

Experience per se is for Wright neither subjective nor objective—it simply is. The classification of experience as subjective or objective is made by us on the basis of its functions and behavior—its relations to other experiences and its subjection to or independence of our will. As a result of this process of classification we arrive at the *summa genera* which we call the I and the not-I. Wright summarizes this account of the gradual development of the concept of the I as follows:

> If, however, the theory above propounded be true, this greatest of human qualities, intelligent self-consciousness, understood in its actual and proper limits, would follow as a consequence of a greater brain, a greater, or more powerful and vivid, memory and imagination, bringing to light, as it were, and into distinct consciousness, phenomena of thought which reflective observation refers to the subject, already known in the dumb animal, or distinguished as an active cause from the forces of outward nature, and from the wills of other animals. The degrees of abstraction and the successively higher and higher steps of generalization, the process which, in scientific knowledge, brings not only the particulars of experience under general designations, but, with a conscious purpose, brings the less general under the more general, or gives common names not only to each and all resembling objects and relations, but also more general common names to what is denoted by these names, thus grouping them under higher categories,—this process brings together the several forms of self-consciousness. Willing, desiring, feeling, and lastly thinking, also, are seen in thought to belong together, or to the same subject; and by thinking they are brought under a common view and receive a common name, or several common names, to wit, "my mind," "me," "I," "my mental states."[170]

The I and the not-I are *summa genera* because no higher abstractions appear to be derivable: "nothing appears to be common to all my mental states, except their belonging together and acting on one another, along with their common independence of other existences in this mutual action."[171] The terms "I" and "not-I" are therefore merely names for two classes of experiences rather than descriptive predicates. Nor are they names for anything more than these classes of experiences. No metaphysical substrata are assumed in the classification itself, for by experiences belonging to the "same subject" Wright means only that they belong to the same class.

If self-consciousness arises by the process Wright describes, how is it that all men agree with respect to the content of the I and the not-I? It is a significant evidence for Wright's thesis that in fact all men do not agree and that "errors" respecting what experience is subjective and what objective do in fact occur.[172] Similarly, the seeming lack of self-consciousness in young children is also a point in Wright's favor.[173] Yet the overwhelming preponderance of agreement, at least within our culture, remains to be explained, and for this purpose Wright invokes the inheritance of acquired characteristics and evolution by natural selection. Since he holds that habits, including habits of classification, are inheritable in the form of dispositions to a like behavior in the offspring, it follows that a difference in classification in one generation will be repeated in subsequent generations, unless modified by further learning. It is not difficult to see that an erroneous classification of certain experiences as subjective which in fact were objective would result in severely corrective experiences, including possibly a rather rude termination of the classifier's career, so it may be presumed that over sufficient time adaptation and natural selection would produce a nearly uniform disposition respecting this classification in all survivors. Hence on these evolutionary grounds the general agreement can be accounted for.[174]

The fact that dispositions to classification are inheritable means that Wright is committed to a form of apriorism. Thus in a letter to Abbot, Wright wrote:

> This process [cognition] is not determined solely by the laws of association among the elements of the primitive impressions. There is always an *à priori,* or mnemonic element involved. Associations, either original to the mind or early established, control the formation of new ones. Of the manifold of a presentation, only parts are retained in the mind and remain adherent to one another; and this selection is determined *à priori,* by the orders of impressions already experienced or else by an order inherent in the very nature of the intellect.[175]

The *"à priori* or mnemonic"* element is a disposition to classify experiences as like or unlike, "for what is it in the intuition which is cognizable, unless it be its likeness or unlikeness to other intuitions?"[176] These dispositions may be the result of prior learning or they may be innate, yet since Wright regards even the innate dispositions as derived from the experience of earlier generations they are not independent of all experience, even though they do not originate in the experience of the particular individual who inherits them. Furthermore, dispositions, like habits, are modifiable by the experience of the individual—indeed, this is one of the features which distinguishes dispositions from instincts.[177] There is then an a priori element in knowledge in the sense that certain proclivities so to classify are present in the mind before experience, but these "categories" of the mind, including even the *summa genera,* are subject to revision in the light of experience. Thus Wright remarks that

> The abstract form of this knowledge, the laws of logic and grammar, and the categories of the understanding, which are forms of all scientific knowledge, are all referable to the action of a *purpose* to know, and to fix knowledge by precise generalization; just as the mechanical conditions of flight are referable to the purpose to fly and to secure the requisite means.[178]

The categories, or higher *genera* used in thinking, are tested functionally as means to the end of knowing, and the development over the history of the race of near uniformity with respect to such categories as science employs is to be explained both by natural selection and by adaptation through learning.

If Wright overestimated the role of biological inheritance in accounting for the a priori he did not underestimate the role of social inheritance. Language constitutes another source of a priori principles which he regarded as being at least as important as inherited dispositions. Since Wright subscribed to a theory of linear social evolution—a view all but universal in his day—and since he like Comte regarded science as a stage of intellectual culture subsequent to theology and metaphysics, much of what he has to say about the role of language as a purveyor of the a priori is couched in negative terms. Thus Wright remarks that

The languages employed by philosophers are themselves lessons in ontology, and have, in their grammatical structures, implied conceptions and beliefs common to the philosopher and to the barbarian inventors of language. . . .[179]

These "conceptions and beliefs," as Wright shows by a discussion of substance and accident and of the active and passive voices,[180] are often metaphysical and represent impediments to the progress of genuine scientific understanding. But the fact that Wright employed this function of language for polemic purposes should not obscure its positive contribution to our knowledge. Wright conceives knowledge as involving both a sensory given and a conceptual interpretation which together form a functioning whole instrumental to the survival of the organism. The conceptual system he regards as partly the creation of the individual organism and as partly derived from the historic experience of the race. That he thought of this derivation partly in terms of biological inheritance betrays his lingering Lamarckianism, but that he also recognized the extent to which language itself embodies this historic experience and structures our construction of the world shows a subtle appreciation of the role of culture. In pointing out that this conceptual schema is a priori for the individual while at the same time based upon historic experience, and that it is tested and modified in the light of its utility, Wright opened the way for James, Lewis, and their more modern followers.

"The Evolution of Self-Consciousness" was Wright's most brilliant paper. The question with which it dealt was the fundamental issue of the evolutionary controversy and Wright's treatment of it was not only subtle, but also showed a remarkable grasp of the problems involved. As a purely psychological paper, the work was notable for its naturalisic treatment of the mind, its reinforcement theory of learning, its analysis of concepts as both mnemonic and directional components of what Wright called the "train" of thought, and its halting steps toward a concept of the ego. These elements, together with the appreciation of the crucial role of psychology in the evolutionary controversy, were later to flower in James's *Principles of Psychology*.[181] But Wright was concerned with more than psychology—he was concerned with psychozoology. The question of the evolutionary continuity between the higher primates and man with respect to psychological characteristics was virtually unexplored in his time, and is only beginning to receive adequate treatment today.[182] Moreover, the psychological theories then available were extremely limited, and problems of the nature of heredity continually confused the picture. Nevertheless, Wright saw that the emergence of learned behavior as a means to desired satisfactions is related to voluntary control and so the ego functions, even though his concept of the ego was only vaguely defined. Similarly, his recognition that an animal need no more be conscious of itself as thinking than of itself as digesting led him to see that self-consciousness is only a partial awareness of some aspects of the mind's behavior and so to the brink of the question of the unconscious. And his discussion of the function of signs in thinking, and of the relation between language and self-consciousness raised questions of major interest in our own time. James's comment that "a treatise on psychology written by him [Wright] (could he have been spared and induced to undertake the drudgery) would probably have been the last and most accomplished utterance of what he liked to call the British school,"[183] may be accurate, but there are hints that Wright might have done considerably more. Finally, as a work in philosophy, Wright's paper must be accounted an important contribution to the empiricist tradition in America. The break with his Hamiltonian past was complete; not only was self-consciousness itself accounted for on evolutionary grounds, but the I and the not-I and other of Hamilton's ultimate facts of consciousness also were explained as evolutionary developments on the basis of known laws. This was the program of Mill and Bain, carried even further than they had carried it. Moreover, some of the ideas which Wright introduced in this paper were to have an important influence upon subsequent work: the concept of the neutral character of pure experience was to appear again in James's radical empiricism, and the concept of the functional a priori appears not only in James and Royce but particularly in Lewis.

We have seen above that although Wright believed science and theology to be implacable enemies, he regarded science and religion as independent of each other in such a sense that no conflict was possible. The same view obtains with respect to the relation between science and valuation. The choice of ultimate ends Wright held to be based solely on emotive factors and to be unarguable. "So far as a feeling is ultimate and an immediate source of human happiness or excellence, it is its own positive standard and sanction."[184] Wright did not believe that all ultimate ends were equal, but he regarded their ranking in terms of worth and dignity as depending entirely upon personal preference, and so as variable from individual to individual. Wright does not regard ultimate ends as being moral ends, for with respect to morality he is a thoroughgoing utilitarian, but he holds that utility can only be defined in terms of antecedently determined ultimate ends.

But it is not the beautiful alone or even pre-eminently, but the whole class of ends in themselves—all our pleasures and those of all sentient beings—that constitute the grounds of utility. It is a mistake . . . to suppose that the measure of a pleasure in this philosophy is simply its intensity as a feeling, and not also its rank or preferability in kind, or a certain dignity it has in the spiritual hierarchy independent of and antecedent to its proper moral rank. This moral rank is a derived dignity, and is determined by preferability or weight with the will on the whole and as compared with the *sum* of the pleasures or ends that are sacrificed for it, both in ourselves and others.[185]

Pleasure results from the achieving of the desired goal so that utility is indeterminate until the ultimate ends are specified. What the utilitarian maxim does do as Wright sees it is to impose a test of consistency upon ends.

Utility tests it [a motive] only negatively in its consistency with other interests and feelings, and with the maximum of all in all sentient beings measured both by intensity and rank,—not moral rank, for this is a resultant, an acquired or conferred dignity.[186]

So viewed, the utilitarian principle defines as moral that which maximizes the total pleasure of all, based upon the preference ordering of each, but it says nothing about those individual preference orderings except that they should be internally consistent, since otherwise the maximum may not exist. Thus Wright is both a utilitarian in ethics and an emotivist with respect to the grounds of values.[187]

Although Wright believed that preferences may be based in part upon inherited dispositions, he did not believe that evolution itself was a moral process, or that it tended in any automatic fashion to produce a moral order.

It is permissible to use the word Nature as the name of the harmony of things, but it is not permissible to confound the harmony in the whole, the laws of nature and the invisible orders both without and within us,—to confound the law of causation, whose formula is, "If thus, then so", with the harmony we seek as moral beings, which without our seeking would not, and does not, exist . . . The laws of this harmony are of a wholly different order, *different in meaning,* out of the other's sphere, neither contradictory to nor in conformity with those of the scientific cosmos; though involving them as the laws of the living structures involve those of matter generally, or as the laws of mechanical structures involve those of its materials and surrounding conditions.[188]

That there is ultimate order and harmony in nature Wright fully believed—the universality of the causal principle was an axiom of his philosophy—but that there is anything either moral or necessarily valuable about that order or its products Wright regarded as a purely gratuitous assumption. The moral order is for him the creation of intelligent beings and has no existence apart from them. Thus Wright accepted, as very few men of his day could, the division of knowledge into wholly separate and autonomous realms.

Wright's contributions to American philosophy are difficult to assess because of the fragmentary character of his work and because so much of what he did was so directly involved in the evolutionary controversy. Yet that controversy was of great importance for philosophy, for all of the questions of the relations among science, metaphysics, theology, religion, and ethics were involved in it. Until 1859, the fundamental unity of knowledge was assumed by virtually all serious writers in America. That the natural order revealed the divine will, and so presented a symbol of the moral law, was a thesis upon which all agreed, though they might disagree as to just how the divine will was revealed, or the moral lesson read out. What the controversy over evolution did was to shatter this unity of knowledge by revealing in nature an order which was not only different from what had been believed to be there, but which when explicated for its theological and ethical meanings according to the traditional canons of exegesis led to conclusions in flat contradiction to established doctrines. The disparate attempts of Spencer, Fiske, Abbot, Peirce, and many others to restore the unity of knowledge by creating grand cosmological syntheses in which evolution became a new form of divine providence are one mark of the felt urgency of the problem for men of that era. But Wright took precisely the opposite course. To free science from religious and moral entanglements, he denied, not only specific contradictions, but also the possibility of any contradiction. For Wright, valuation and religion are basically noncognitive subjects different in kind from the sciences: there cannot therefore be any conflict between them. This does not mean that Wright became an atheist, for the evidence suggests that he retained his religious commitments until his death, but it does mean that for Wright knowledge is not one: what is and what ought to be are forever severed, and there is no basis in nature for our spiritual and moral doctrines. For Peirce, James, and the others who came to philosophy in Darwin's wake, the gravest challenge of all was not Spencer with his crude mechanical determinism, nor Hegel with his Idealistic block universe; it was the cool, dispassionate analyst who said "behind the bare phenomenal facts . . . there is *nothing.*"[189]

Notes—Chapter Nine

1. John Maynard Keynes, "Newton, the Man" in *Essays and Sketches in Biography* (New York: Meridian, 1956), pp. 280-90.

2. Locke, *Essay*, I: 300f.

3. *Ibid.*, p. 208.

4. *Ibid.*, p. 406.

5. Cf. William Paley, "Natural Theology," in *The Works of William Paley, D.D.* (London: Henry Fisher, Son, and P. Jackson, 1828), vol. II. For later elaborations, see the *Bridgewater Treatises:* Thomas Chalmers, *On the Power, Wisdom, and Goodness of God as Manifested in the Adaptation of External Nature to the Moral and Intellectual Constitution of Man,* 2 vols. (London, 1833); John Kidd, *On the Adaptation of External Nature to the Physical Conditions of Man* (London, 1833); William Whewell, *Astronomy and General Physics, Considered with Reference to Natural Theology* (London, 1833); Sir Charles Bell, *The Hand, Its Mechanism and Vital Endowments, as Evincing Design* (London, 1833); Peter Mark Roget, *Animal and Vegetable Physiology, Considered with Reference to Natural Theology,* 2 vols. (London, 1834); William Buckland, *Geology and Minerology, Considered with Reference to Natural Theology,* 2 vols. (London, 1836); William Kirby, *On the Power, Wisdom, and Goodness of God as Manifested in the Creation of Animals, and in their History, Habits, and Instincts* (London, 1835); William Prout, *Chemistry, Meteorology, and the Function of Digestion* (London, 1834).

6. Paley, "Evidences of Christianity," *Works,* I: 1.

7. David Hume, "An Inquiry Concerning the Human Understanding," sec. 10, "Of Miracles," in *The Philosophical Writings of David Hume* (Boston: Little, Brown and Co., 1854), vol. IV.

8. Thomas Paine, "The Age of Reason," in *The Complete Writings of Thomas Paine*, ed. Foner (New York: Citadel, 1945), I: 463-604.

9. Paley, "Natural Theology," *Works*, II: 7ff; Bell, *The Hand, etc.*

10. The classic study of the concept of the chain of being is Arthur O. Lovejoy, *The Great Chain of Being* (Cambridge, Mass.: Harvard University Press, 1948). Cf. also Loren Eiseley, *Darwin's Century* (New York: Doubleday, 1958), chap. I; Charles Gillispie, *Genesis and Geology* (Cambridge, Mass.: Harvard University Press, 1951), pp. 17ff.

11. Knut Hagberg, *Carl Linnaeus* (London: Jonathan Cape, 1952), chap. 5; Erik Nordenskiöld, *The History of Biology* (New York: Tudor, 1949), pp. 203ff; Eiseley, *Darwin's Century*, pp. 16ff; A. Wolf, *Eighteenth Century*, pp. 426ff.

12. The discovery that not all hybrids were sterile was one of the first major blows to this thesis. When Linnaeus discovered that the peloria was capable of reproducing itself, he saw at once that "it is possible for new species to arise within the plant world" (Hagberg, *Linneaus*, p. 197). Lamarck considered this fact fatal to the doctrine of immutable species (Alpheus S. Packard, *Lamarck, The Founder of Evolution* [New York: Longman Green and Co., 1901], p. 284).

13. Eiseley, *Darwin's Century*, p. 60.

14. Sir William Dampier, *A History of Science* (Cambridge: University Press, 1949), p. 180; John Theodore Merz, *A History of European Thought in the Nineteenth Century* (Edinburgh: William Blackwood and Sons, 1928), II:282ff.

15. Dampier, *History*, p. 180; Merz, *History*, II: 284ff.

16. Gillispie, *Genesis and Geology*, pp. 41-46.

17. James Hutton, "Theory of the Earth," in *Transactions of the Royal Society of Edinburgh*, I: 209-304.

18. Hutton, *Theory*, p. 304.

19. Sir Charles Lyell, *Principles of Geology* (London: John Murray, 1875), I: 76.

20. Hutton, *Theory*, pp. 210ff.

21. *Ibid.*, pp. 294f.

22. Gillispie, *Genesis and Geology*, pp. 49ff.

23. *Ibid.*, pp. 91ff; Eiseley, *Darwin's Century*, pp. 75-81.

24. Eiseley, *Darwin's Century*, pp. 81-89.

25. Gillispie, *Genesis and Geology*, pp. 98ff.

26. Georges Cuvier, *Essay on the Theory of the Earth* (Edinburgh: William Blackwood, 1815), p. 24.

27. Gillispie, *Genesis and Geology*, p. 120.

28. Sir Charles Lyell, *Principles of Geology*, 3 vols. (London: John Murray, 1830-33).

29. Gillispie, *Genesis and Geology*, chap. 5.

30. George P. Merrill, *The First One Hundred Years of American Geology* (New Haven, Conn.: Yale University Press, 1924), pp. 57ff, 77ff, 82ff, 125ff, 146f, 231.

31. Edward Lurie, *Louis Agassiz* (Chicago: University of Chicago Press, 1960).

32. Eiseley, *Darwin's Century*, pp. 46ff.

33. Packard, *Lamarck*, chaps. 16-18.

34. Charles Darwin, *On the Origin of Species* (London: John Murray, 1859).

35. Eiseley, *Darwin's Century*, chaps. 6-7.

36. Darwin, *Origin*, chaps. 6-7; Eiseley, *Darwin's Century*, chaps. 6-7.

37. Eiseley, *Darwin's Century*, pp. 209ff; Nordenskiöld, *History*, chap. 12, pp. 472-73.

38. Darwin, *Origin*, chap. 10.

39. Charles Darwin, *Descent of Man* (New York: Appleton, 1871-72); Eiseley, *Darwin's Century*, chap. 10.

40. Eiseley, *Darwin's Century*, p. 256.

41. Merz, *History*, II: 357.

42. Dampier, *History*, p. 299; Merz, *History*, II: 357ff.

43. Dampier, *History*, p. 299; Merz, *History*, II: 363ff; Eiseley, *Darwin's Century*, pp. 238ff.

44. Lurie, *Agassiz*, chaps. 7-9.

45. Darwin, *Descent of Man,* chaps. 3-5.

46. Herbert Spencer, *First Principles* (New York: D. Appleton and Co., 1864).

47. Herbert Spencer, *Principles of Biology* (New York: D. Appleton and Co., 1864-67).

48. Herbert Spencer, *Principles of Sociology* (New York: D. Appleton and Co., 1876-85).

49. Herbert Spencer, *Principles of Ethics* (New York: Appleton and Co., 1879; 1891-93).

50. Richard Hofstadter, *Social Darwinism in American Thought* (Philadelphia: University of Pennsylvania Press, 1945), chap. 2.

51. Spencer, *First Principles,* p. 27.

52. *Ibid.,* pp. 30, 44ff.

53. Sir William Hamilton, "The Philosophy of the Unconditioned," in *Discussions on Philosophy and Literature, Education and University Reform* (New York: Harper and Bros., 1853), p. 22.

54. *Ibid.,* p. 22.

55. Spencer, *First Principles,* pp. 89-99.

56. *Ibid.,* pp. 38-48.

57. *Ibid.,* pp. 50ff.

58. *Ibid.,* pp. 52ff.

59. *Ibid.,* pp. 61ff.

60. *Ibid.,* pp. 100ff.

61. *Ibid.,* pp. 166ff.

62. *Ibid.,* pp. 169-70.

63. *Ibid.,* pp. 171-72.

64. *Ibid.,* pp. 173-74.

65. *Ibid.,* p. 75.

66. *Ibid.,* p. 200.

67. *Ibid.*, p. 347.

68. *Ibid.*, pp. 303ff.

69. *Ibid.*, pp. 326ff.

70. *Ibid.*, p. 407. Original in italics.

71. *Ibid.*, p. 562.

72. *Ibid.*, p. 440.

73. *Ibid.*, pp. 562-63.

74. *Ibid.*, p. 86.

75. *Ibid.*, pp. 86ff; Herbert Spencer, *Principles of Psychology* (New York: D. Appleton and Co., 1903), vol. I, pt. IV.

76. Herbert Spencer, *Social Statics* (London: Chapman, 1851).

77. Spencer, *Sociology*, I: 55; cf. chaps. 5-7.

78. Spencer, *Social Statics*, p. 31.

79. *Ibid.*, p. 398.

80. *Ibid.*, pp. 31ff; Spencer, *Sociology*, II: 473ff.

81. Spencer, *Social Statics*, pp. 31f; Spencer, *Sociology*, I: 464ff.

82. Spencer, *Social Statics*, p. 28.

83. *Ibid.*, p. 32. Spencer modified this extreme optimism in his later years. He recognized that progress was not inevitable for every society and that some backward societies would never reach the ideal state. Yet he believed that in the main, and despite regressions, progress toward the Industrial society would continue in the more "advanced" societies (*Sociology,* vol. III, chap. 24).

84. Spencer, *Social Statics*, p. 150.

85. *Ibid.*, p. 55.

86. Spencer, *Sociology*, vol. II, chap. 18.

87. *Ibid.*, pp. 606ff.

88. *Ibid.*, pp. 612ff.

89. *Ibid.*, III: 611.

90. Hofstadter, *Social Darwinism,* p. 21.

91. *Ibid.*, pp. 21, 30ff; Jack London, *Martin Eden* (New York: Macmillan, 1957), pp. 329f.

92. Edward H. Madden, *Chauncey Wright and the Foundations of Pragmatism* (Seattle: University of Washington, 1963).

93. James Bradley Thayer, ed., *Letters of Chauncey Wright* (Cambridge, Mass.: John Wilson and Son, 1878), p. 365.

94. *Ibid.*, pp. 55f.

95. Madden, *Wright,* p. 128.

96. John Stuart Mill, *An Examination of Sir William Hamilton's Philosophy and of the Principal Questions Discussed in his Writings* (London: Longmans, Green, Longmans, Roberts and Green, 1865).

97. Thayer, *Letters,* p. 84.

98. Chauncey Wright, "Mill on Hamilton," *Nation* 1:278ff (1865).

99. Chauncey Wright, "Mill on Hamilton," *North American Review* 103:250-60 (1866).

100. *Ibid.*, p. 260.

101. Francis Bowen, ed., *The Metaphysics of Sir William Hamilton* (Cambridge, Mass.: Sever and Francis, 1862), p. 38.

102. *Ibid.*, p. 106.

103. *Ibid.*, p. 175.

104. *Ibid.*, pp. 178-81.

105. Mill, *Examination,* chaps. 11-13.

106. Wright, "Mill on Hamilton," *North American Review,* pp. 258-59.

107. Bowen, *Hamilton,* p. 52. Original in italics.

108. Madden, *Wright,* p. 143.

109. Philip Wiener, *Evolution and the Founders of Pragmatism* (Cambridge, Mass.: Harvard University Press, 1949), chaps. 2-3; Max Fisch, "Was There a

Metaphysical Club in Cambridge?'' in *Studies in the Philosophy of Charles Sanders Peirce,* ed. Moore and Robin (Amherst: University of Massachusetts Press, 1964), pp. 3-32.

110. Madden, *Wright,* pp. 143-44; Wiener, *Evolution,* chap. 3. On Wright's biography, see Madden, *Wright,* chap. 1; Wiener, *Evolution,* chap. 3. Norton's biographical sketch in Chauncey Wright, *Philosophical Discussions,* ed. Charles Eliot Norton (New York: Henry Holt, 1877), pp. vii-xxiii.

111. Wright, *Discussions,* pp. 1-34. First published in the *North American Review,* July 1864.

112. *Ibid.,* pp. 80ff; Merz, *History,* II: 357-58.

113. Wright, *Discussions,* p. 25.

114. *Ibid.,* p. 10.

115. *Ibid.,* pp. 27ff.

116. *Ibid.,* p. 7.

117. *Ibid.,* pp. 35-42. First published in the *North American Review,* January 1865.

118. *Ibid.,* "A Fragment on Cause and Effect,'' pp. 406-13; "The Genesis of Species," pp. 126-67; "Evolution by Natural Selection," pp. 168-98, and others.

119. *Ibid.,* p. 36.

120. *Ibid.*

121. *Ibid.,* p. 410.

122. *Ibid.,* p. 409.

123. *Ibid.,* p. 410.

124. *Ibid.,* p. 245.

125. *Ibid.,* pp. 246-47.

126. *Ibid.,* p. 40.

127. Thayer, *Letters,* pp. 97-98.

128. *Ibid.,* p. 115.

129. John William Draper, *History of the Conflict between Religion and Science* (New York: D. Appleton and Co., 1875).

130. Andrew Dickson White, *A History of the Warfare of Science with Theology in Christendom* (New York: D. Appleton and Co., 1896).

131. See pp.746-55.

132. Josiah Royce, *The Problem of Christianity*, 2 vols. (New York: Macmillan, 1913).

133. Wright, "The Philosophy of Herbert Spencer," in *Discussions*, pp. 43-96. First published in the *North American Review*, April 1865.

134. Spencer, *First Principles*, p. 135.

135. Wright, *Discussions*, pp. 55-56.

136. *Ibid.*, p. 56.

137. *Ibid.*

138. *Ibid.*, p. 78.

139. *Ibid.*, p. 80.

140. *Ibid.*, pp. 46-47.

141. *Ibid.*, p. 77.

142. *Ibid.*, p. 96.

143. Thayer, *Letters*, p. 132.

144. Wright, "The Use and Origins of the Arrangement of Leaves in Plants," in *Discussions*, pp. 296-328, first published in *Memoirs of the American Academy of Arts and Sciences*, communicated October 10, 1871.

145. Wright, "Evolution of Self-Consciousness," in *Discussions*, pp. 199-266, first published in the *North American Review*, April 1873.

146. Thayer, *Letters*, p. 248.

147. Wright, *Discussions*, pp. 199ff.

148. *Ibid.*, p. 221.

149. *Ibid.*

150. *Ibid.* p. 222.

151. *Ibid.*

152. Thayer, *Letters,* pp. 73-75.

153. Wright, *Discussions,* p. 224.

154. *Ibid.,* pp. 224-25.

155. *Ibid.,* p. 225.

156. *Ibid.,* p. 210.

157. *Ibid.,* pp. 208-9.

158. *Ibid.,* p. 206.

159. Thayer, *Letters,* p. 128.

160. Wright, *Discussions,* pp. 208-19.

161. *Ibid.,* pp. 205-9.

162. *Ibid.,* p. 221.

163. *Ibid.,* pp. 216-17, 223.

164. *Ibid.,* p. 209.

165. *Ibid.,* p. 254.

166. *Ibid.,* p. 210.

167. *Ibid.,* p. 226.

168. *Ibid.,* p. 219.

169. *Ibid.,* pp. 228-29.

170. *Ibid.,* p. 227.

171. *Ibid.*

172. *Ibid.,* p. 231.

173. *Ibid.,* p. 225.

174. *Ibid.*, pp. 229, 231.

175. Thayer, *Letters*, p. 125.

176. *Ibid.*, p. 128.

177. Wright, *Discussions*, pp. 221, 239ff.

178. *Ibid.*, p. 226.

179. *Ibid.*, p. 235.

180. *Ibid.*, pp. 235-37.

181. William James, *The Principles of Psychology*, 2 vols. (New York: Henry Holt, 1890).

182. See A. I. Hallowell, "Self, Society, and Culture in Phylogenetic Perspective," in *The Evolution of Man*, ed. Tax (Chicago: University of Chicago Press, 1960), pp. 309-72.

183. Madden, *Wright*, pp. 144-45.

184. Thayer, *Letters*, p. 194.

185. *Ibid.*, p. 195.

186. *Ibid.*, p. 194.

187. Madden, *Wright*, chap. 3.

188. Thayer, *Letters*, p. 328.

189. Ralph Barton Perry, *The Thought and Character of William James* (Boston: Little, Brown and Co., 1935), I: 522.

Chapter Ten

Charles Sanders Peirce

Chapter Ten

Charles Sanders Peirce

1. Introduction

Charles Sanders Peirce was born September 10, 1839, in Cambridge, Massachusetts. His father was Benjamin Peirce, professor of mathematics and astronomy at Harvard, and the leading American mathematician of that time. Charles Peirce entered Harvard in 1855 and graduated with no particular distinction in 1859. The following year he entered the Lawrence Scientific School where he performed brilliantly and took an Sc. B. degree *summa cum laude* in 1863. In 1861 Peirce had begun a career of thirty years with the United States Coast and Geodetic Survey. During the 1860s and early 1870s he was assigned to the Harvard Observatory where he did outstanding work in astronomy. In 1878 Peirce published a book on his photometric astronomical researches in which he made substantive and methodological contributions which are of importance even today. Peirce's later work concerned the use of gravity pendulums to measure variations in the strength of gravity over the earth's surface—a problem of major importance in geodesy. He made a number of important contributions to this field, particularly with respect to the design and use of pendulums for this purpose and the sources of errors in the measurements obtained with them. By the time Peirce retired from the Coast Survey in 1891, he had earned a reputation as one of America's leading men of science.

But Peirce was also a philosopher. At least as early as 1857 he had begun working on philosophic questions, and in the late sixties he began to publish papers on philosophy and logic. During the 1860s Peirce gave several courses of lectures at Harvard on philosophic subjects. In the early 1870s, Peirce, Chauncey Wright,

567

William James, Oliver Wendell Holmes, Nicholas St. John Green, John Fiske, Francis Abbot, and others formed a philosophical discussion group in Cambridge which they called the Metaphysical Club. The club met for several years, usually at Peirce's or James's house, and it was before this group that Peirce first proposed the doctrine of pragmatism, sometime in 1872 or 1873. Thus, although Peirce was not professionally a philosopher at this time, he was in close touch with the best philosophic minds in America.

In 1876 The Johns Hopkins University was founded, and partly on James's recommendation Peirce was appointed lecturer in logic. The position was a part-time one, since Peirce continued to work for the United States Coast and Geodetic Survey, but it brought him into contact with a remarkable faculty and with one of the most brilliant groups of students ever assembled at an American university. Through his courses, and through a second "metaphysical society" which he founded there, Peirce was brought into contact with Christine Ladd-Franklin, Oscar Howard Mitchell, Thomas Craig, John Dewey, Thorstein Veblen, and many others. Peirce was an able teacher, and in 1883 he published a book of papers on logic written in his seminar which demonstrates both the high capacity of his students and the quality of his teaching.

Peirce was dismissed from Johns Hopkins in 1884 for reasons which have never been made clear. Thereafter he continued to work for the Coast Survey until 1891, when he retired to Milford, Pennsylvania, where he had purchased a home in 1887. For the last twenty-seven years of his life he lived in Milford, supporting himself on his writings, his dwindling inheritance, occasional lectures, and the charity of friends. Although he wrote thousands of pages on philosophy, little of his later work was published during his lifetime, and most of it remains only in the form of fragmentary manuscripts. By the time he died, in 1914, he was in penury. [1]

2. Peirce's Early Philosophy

Peirce came to philosophy a student of Kant, and it was from Kant that he acquired both his concept of the nature of philosophic systems and the basic components of his own early philosophy. In his "architectonic" theory of systematic knowledge, Kant held that it is possible so to characterize the entire domain of possible human knowledge that general theorems can be proven true of all that can ever be known. This can be done, according to Kant, because knowledge consists of propositions, and the logical forms of such propositions are both limited in number and precisely defined. We can thus know a priori that all propositions will involve certain logical forms—hence we can also know a priori that whatever can be an object of knowledge must be such that it can be known through propositions of these forms. Since Kant held that sense data—intuitions, as he called them—come to us in an unordered manifold which is synthesized into objects by the mind, and since only objects knowable in propositions can be objects of our knowledge, the synthesis of intuitions by which we construct objects must be subject to such forms that the resulting objects are knowable in propositions. Kant therefore "derived" from his table of logical forms, or "functions of judgment," a table of categories which he held to be the fundamental concepts in terms of which the synthesis of intuitions is made. It follows then that the categories are a priori true of all possible experience, for the objects of possible experience are constructed according to the categories.[2] This concept of the nature of systematic philosophy forms the starting point for Peirce's early work.

Peirce drew heavily upon Kant in constructing his own first system, but in his interpretation of Kant, he was greatly influenced by post-Kantian romanticism. The sources of this romanticism are not known: whether Peirce derived it from Schelling or Hegel, or from the New England Transcendentalists, with whom he certainly had contact, or developed it himself is not yet clear. What is clear is that by the late 1850s Peirce was trying to formulate a system which would combine elements of Kant's Transcendental Analytic with an extreme form of Platonism. Adopting from Kant the thesis that all our thoughts are representations, Peirce distinguished between the thought itself, or representation, and the thought-of, or object of the representation. He then employed this distinction to generate the following argument:

Proposition. All unthought is thought-of.
Proof. We can sometimes think of the unthinkable as thought; we have, for instance, a conception of the conception Infinity, though we cannot attain that conception.
To think of a thing is to think in such a way that our conception has a relation to that thing . . . any unthought which is not thought of as thought, is by the relation of complete negation, negatively thought of as unthought.
Cor. I. Only the phenomena can be thought of as thought, the things in themselves are thought of as unthought.
Cor. II. All *neumena* (things-in-themselves) are unconditioned because they cannot even be thought of as thought.
Cor. III. All thought is thereby thought of, for it would not be in our consciousness unless we were conscious of it. Hence, all things in heaven and earth are thought of, however small our experience may be.
Cor. IV. Whatever is unthought is apprehended, for as I showed before all falsehood is partial truth.*(*Whatever claims to be a representation (a portrait for example) is a representation. Truth is that which, claiming to be a representation, is a representation. Therefore Truth has no absolute antithesis. Falsehood also claims to be a representation. It is an imperfect *copy* of truth.)
Whatever is thought-of can be normally thought of. Normal thought is true. Therefore all the unconditioned is apprehended and may be so without error. To formulate it: Whatever is unintelligible is true.[3]

A thought is, for Peirce, a mental state which serves as a representation. Any thought may itself be thought of—i.e., may be made the object of another representation—and when thought of it is thought of as thought—i.e., as being a representation. Hence for Peirce, all phenomena are thought of as thought. But Peirce follows Kant in holding that some of our representations refer to the Transcendental object—i.e., to things-in-themselves, or noumena. Since we do not experience the transcendental object itself, we can only think of it as unthought—as not being a representation. We have therefore two classes of ontological objects: things thought-of as thought, or representations, and things thought-of as unthought, or things-in-themselves.

But Peirce holds that there is a third class of ontological objects—abstractions. These abstractions are not thoughts, for "the *necessity* for instance which I think today or tomorrow is not the same thing as that immutable, impersonal necessity which I am thinking *of.*"[4] Indeed, Peirce argues, an abstraction cannot be realized in consciousness at all. "An abstraction, however, is no longer a modification of consciousness at all, for it has no longer the accident of belonging to a special time, to a special person, and to a special subject of thought . . . Nobody can think pure abstraction on account of the necessity of doing it at a particular time, etc."[5] The abstraction must therefore be thought-of as unthought, yet it is certainly not a thing in the same sense as the transcendental object. Peirce describes it as an unthinkable idea, or as thought thought-of as unthought. Such abstractions can be referred to, though they cannot be realized in the mind.

Now the problem with this formulation is obvious: how can we have true knowledge of abstractions if we cannot think them? Peirce's answer is that there are two types of unthinkable conceptions: those which, like a four-sided triangle, are contradictory so that no such thing can be realized in consciousness; and those which, like infinity, are not contradictory but require powers of synthesis beyond our own.[6] In the latter case we may reason about the concept and even have true knowledge of it.

> . . . we call a judgement untrue when from its contradicting some other judgement, we conclude [that] in the framing of it, our faculties did not act in the normal way. Now to whatever is thought-of there is a normal way of thinking-of; and that normal way gives a true thought of the thing; and that is an apprehension of the thing. And so even when the normal way of thinking of a thing gives an unintelligible result, it is either because it can't be thought of or because we have an unconscious idea of it; In the first case, we have no thought of it by Corollary III it does not exist and therefore hence we have a true thought of it. In the latter case, the unconscious idea accords with the definition of a true representation.[7]

To know anything, we must have an idea of it: if that idea cannot be realized in consciousness, it must exist in us as an unconscious idea. And we can make true statements about things of which we have only unconscious ideas, even though the resulting statements are in a certain sense unintelligible. The criterion of truth here is consistency. If a proposition regarding infinity is consistent with our other knowledge, it is true. Indeed, any unintelligible statement is true since it can contradict nothing else.

But if consistency is the criterion of truth, what reason have we to think that our statements are true to things-in-themselves? Peirce elaborates his answer as follows:

> *Idealism*. The only possible definition of the person (self) is that which one thinks of when he closes his senses and excludes all thought but simple consciousness. That is, it is the thought-of, when the only thought-of is the thought. By Cor. III nothing external to the self exists.
>
> *Materialism*. Matter is substance whose existence is not subject to mental conditions. By Cor. II Nothing but matter exists and the soul is matter.
>
> *Realistic Pantheism*. From Idealism, it follows that nothing exists which is not of-thinkable as thought. From materialism, it follows that nothing but the unthought exists. That which being unthinkable is of-thinkable as thought is Perfection. In Chapter III of the Introduction, it was shown that Perfection is God. Hence, nothing exists but God.
>
> Here then we have three worlds Matter, Mind, God, mutually excluding and including each other . . .
>
> Synthesis
>
> Let us now restate the problem and see whether it answers itself. Given three worlds completely unrelated except in identity of substance. Everything which springs up freely in one of these, the Mind, does so from the very nature and substance thereof. Verity is unity of substance.* (*An invariable connection in the nature of things is unity of substance.) It is clear that these data answer the question, How Innate Notions can be True to External Fact. The connection between mind and matter is thus a pre-established Harmony.[8]

Peirce believed that universal propositions cannot be derived directly from experience.[9] Hence they are either inferred or innate. But Peirce also believed at this time that all inference is in Barbara,[10] so that universal propositions can only be inferred from other universal propositions. It follows that there must be some ultimate universal premises behind our knowledge which are neither inferred nor given in experience, and so must be innate. If our knowledge is consistent, then, all propositions we know must follow from or be consistent with these innate premises. But for our knowledge to be true of things-in-themselves, these innate premises must be true of things-in-themselves, and Peirce can only support that claim by appealing to a preestablished harmony.

Thus starting from the Kantian doctrine that all thoughts are representations, Peirce was led to distinguish three classes of entities: thoughts, things, and abstractions—or, mind, matter, and God. This tripartite ontology also has its origin in Kant, for it seems clear that Peirce derived it from Kant's transcendental sciences. According to Kant, ''The thinking subject is the object of *psychology,* the sum-total of all appearances (the world) is the object of *cosmology,* and the thing which contains the highest condition of the possibility of all that can be thought (the being of all beings) the object of *theology.*''[11] The objects of these sciences Peirce took to be his three classes of ontological objects. As early as 1857, Peirce began using the personal pronouns to designate these classes: matter is called It; mind, Thou; and God, I.[12] It was from this usage that Peirce later derived the names of his categories: First Person, Second Person, Third Person—or, First, Second, and Third.

Having divided all there is into three disjoint classes, Peirce now faced the problem of explaining how these classes are related. What constitutes our knowledge are thoughts, and thoughts presumably embody abstractions and refer to objects. But these relations of connection and denotation which connect the three classes require explanation. Peirce's problem is less a problem of truth, since he is prepared to invoke a preestablished harmony for that, than a problem of meaning and reference. And Peirce's answer to this problem is typically Platonic. The abstraction in the divine mind is embodied, or expressed, in material form so that it may be presented to us in experience.

> Abstraction, therefore, to become modification of consciousness needs to be combined with that which modification of consciousness as yet unrelated to any abstraction is, that is to the perfectly unthought manifold of sensation. Well, how shall abstraction be combined with manifold of sensation? By existing as a form for matter, by *expression.* The first condition of creation is then expression.[13]

Once the abstraction is expressed, we obtain our concept by abstracting from the symbolic objects presented. ''The abstraction must be expressed. Suppose that condition complied with, how does it pass into consciousness? By the operation of abstracting.''[14] There are thus two separate processes involved: one is the synthetic process of expression whereby the object is created; the other is the analytic process by which we derive the concept from experience.

The process of expression is a synthesis in intuition and not surprisingly Peirce tried to use Kant's categories to effect it. And the fact that he equated his three ontological classes with the objects of Kant's transcendental sciences led him to look closely at the relations which Kant asserted between the Transcendental Sciences and the categories. The fact that Kant divided his twelve categories into four sets of three, each set having a general heading, suggested to Peirce that the four headings—quantity, quality, relation, and modality—were the true categories of which the twelve are determinations.[15] Moreover, Kant himself remarked that certain relations obtain among the categories under each heading: ''. . . it may be observed that the third category in each class always arises from the combination of the second category with the first . . .''[16] And in the Dialectic, Kant trichotomizes the table of categories by the Transcendental Sciences, assigning one category from each class to each science. Thus the thinking subject is one, simple, substance, and related to possible objects, and so on for the other two.[17]

Developing these suggestions, Peirce concluded that quantity, quality, relation, and modality were the true categories; that each category when applied to the three ontological classes yielded three "stages" or subcategories;[18] and that the form of the category corresponding to mind resulted from the combination of the other two.[19] Accordingly, Peirce attempted to work out the process of synthesis in detail, but in so doing he became involved in logical difficulties. Peirce conceived of expression as essentially a type of predication: thus he writes,

> Even to be conscious of this thought it must be expressed. It must be realized in a substance. It implies a capacity of the substance to receive it. That is the subject must already have certain predicates as conditions to its receiving the given predicate.[20]

The problem here is that Peirce is trying to use the *nota notae* as a means of applying an abstract property to an object, and so is confusing membership and inclusion. Thus the abstract predicate is applied to the object by being implied by some other property of the object. But this process of application at once leads to an infinite regress, since every predicate must modify an already inhering predicate. And such a regress is very clearly present in some of Peirce's early papers on this subject, where to justify the application of each category he must invoke a prior category, and so is driven into a circle.[21]

By 1862 Peirce had come to the conclusion that the synthesis of three ontological classes could not be effected by the Kantian categories. By the architectonic principle, this fact implied either that Kant had wrongly deduced the categories from his logic, or that the logic itself was wrong. Peirce concluded that the error lay in the logic:[22]

> Kant first formed a table of the various logical divisions of judgment, and then deduced his categories directly from these . . . The correspondences between the functions of judgment and the categories are obvious and certain. So far the method is perfect. Its defect is that it affords no warrant for the correctness of the preliminary table, and does not display that direct reference to the unity of consistency which alone gives validity to the categories.[23]

Therefore, in 1862, Peirce embarked upon the intensive study of logic, and the authors to whom he turned were the scholastics. For the next two years Peirce read widely and well in scholastic philosophy and logic, and he found indeed a key to the solution of his problem.[24]

Kant's table of judgments was a logical classification of propositions. But from Scotus, Peirce learned that the significance of any particular propositional form depended upon the role which that form played in inference, and so came to regard the classification of syllogisms or arguments as primary.[25] Moreover, Peirce also learned that the traditional disjunctive and categorical propositions could be converted into hypotheticals,[26] so that the third triad of Kant's table of functions of judgment was proven to be less fundamental than Kant had thought. But the fact that these three types of propositions are interconvertible means that there is no significant difference between disjunctive, categorical, and hypothetical syllogisms, since this classification of syllogisms depends only on the form of the premises. Accordingly, the only fundamental classification of syllogisms appeared to be the division into the four figures. Yet here Peirce found himself confronting Kant's paper on "The Mistaken Subtlety of the Four Syllogistic Figures"[27] in which Kant claimed to have proven that all figures are reducible to the first, together with an immediate inference by conversion or contraposition. If Kant's argument were correct, all syllogistic inference would be reducible to the first figure and the categories would have to be based on that figure alone.

In 1866 Peirce published a "Memoranda Concerning the Aristotelian Syllogism"[28] in which he showed that Kant's argument of the "Mistaken Subtlety" was itself mistaken. For although it is true that the second and third figures can be reduced to the first and immediate inference, the syllogism in which the reduction is made must be in the figure which is being reduced. Thus Peirce could hold that there were three irreducible forms of inference: viz., the three figures. Moreover, by this time Peirce had also discovered that if induction were represented as a type of syllogistic reasoning, it took the form of inferring the major premises of a third figure syllogism from the minor and the conclusion:

$S_1 S_2 \ldots S_n$ are P
$S_1 S_2 \ldots S_n$ are M
Therefore P is M

This at once suggested to Peirce that there should be a type of inference which derives the minor premise from the major and conclusion, and this form he discovered would be in the second figure:

All M is P' P'' P'''
All S is P' P'' P'''
Therefore S is M

This type of inference he called hypothetical inference. Peirce accordingly concluded that the three figures were related to the three types of inferences—deduction, induction, and hypothesis.[29]

3. Peirce's Second System

But while Peirce was pursuing these studies of inference, he had also discovered an even more important fact: that the relations holding between subject and predicate, antecedent and consequent, and premises and conclusion are all variants of the sign relation. "The subject is a sign of the predicate, the antecedent of the consequent; and this is the only point that concerns logic."[30] Now if that is true, then propositions and syllogisms involve the same synthetic relation, and even if there are irreducible forms of inference, they are irreducible only in the sense of being distinct variations of one fundamental relation: signhood. To say that the abstraction is expressed in material form is to say that what we experience signifies the abstraction. To find the categories we must ask, how is representation possible?

As a result of these discoveries in logic, Peirce published in 1867-68 a series of four papers which contain a complete reformulation of his early position.[31] This reformulation may be taken to constitute his second philosophic system. In line with the architectonic principle, his first task was to define a list of categories, and this task he undertook in the first paper, entitled "On a New List of Categories." Having proven that propositions and syllogisms are both based upon the representative relation, it mattered little which example of this relation Peirce chose to analyze. He chose to work with the proposition. In doing so, however, he made a fundamental assumption: viz., that all propositions are of the subject-predicate type. This assumption was supported by the whole of traditional logic—particularly scholastic logic—and Peirce had no reason in 1868 not to accept it. As a result the subject-predicate theory of the proposition is one of the premises underlying his second system.

The traditional theory of the proposition which Peirce learned from the scholastics was the theory of supposition. This theory holds that in a proposition the predicate is affirmed of the object for which the subject stands. Thus Jean Buridan describes the doctrine as follows: "Supposition, as here understood, is the interpretation of a term in a proposition for some thing or things such that, if it or they be indicated by the pronoun 'this' or 'these' or an equivalent, that term is truly affirmed of the pronoun by way of the copula of that proposition."[32] The connection of predicate and thing is established by the predicate's being affirmed of the subject by the copula "is," and what is affirmed is that the subject and predicate refer to the same objects. Now this theory can easily lead to exactly the same regress that Peirce earlier encountered. For if the subject term is interpreted as a concept, then the application of the subject to the object requires that the subject term have supposition for a prior term referring to that object, etc. Moreover, Peirce's claim that categoricals and hypotheticals are all one, when combined with his confusion of membership and inclusion, leads to a similar result. For consider the categorical, $. \chi \epsilon A$. If this is convertible into a hypothetical, we have $\chi \epsilon A \equiv \gamma \epsilon \chi \rightarrow \gamma \epsilon A$ but then $\gamma \epsilon A$ becomes $Z \epsilon \gamma \rightarrow Z \epsilon A$, and so on. In short, the claim that all categoricals are equivalent to hypotheticals implies the identity of membership and inclusion and so leads to an endless regress in which every antecedent divides into a conditional. Thus Peirce's theory of predication is still involved in an infinite regress.

Not all infinite regresses are vicious, and by 1867 Peirce had found a way of combining this infinite regress with certain principles of the Kantian theory of knowledge which gave interesting results. Kant held that concepts arise only for the purpose of bringing the manifold of impressions to unity, and that it is the function of the syntheses in apprehension, reproduction, and recognition to effect this unification. Impressions alone do not refer—they simply are. Before they can refer, they must be apprehended and reproduced—i.e., they must be brought together before the mind by attention and recognized as something, as It. But, Peirce argues, such an operation upon the data is already a conceptual interpretation, however rudimentary, for the notion of "the present in general, of IT in general" is already a concept. Moreover, if we consider what is before the mind, it is clear that until we collect the impressions under this concept, we do not know the impressions themselves as objects at all. It is doubtless necessary to assume that they exist, but Peirce's point is that they are not known as such until apprehended, reproduced, and attended to, and so until they are already brought under concepts. From the standpoint of what is immediately known, therefore, we are compelled to say that there are no impressions as such, as given: we can at most begin with the concept of It.[33]

This doctrine is not as extreme as may at first appear. It is obvious that what Peirce is attacking is the traditional empiricist view that we begin with first impressions of sense which are directly given. What Peirce is arguing is that even if there are real things which produce effects in us, these first effects are neural stimulations of some kind—not images or concepts. By the time anything resembling an image or concept arises, we have already conceptually interpreted these neural stimulations, and it is impossible to single out what is given from what is interpreted. We may hypothesize that neural stimuli precede our concept, and that hypothesis may be supported by our knowledge of physiology, but this sensory given itself we never know as such. All phenomena therefore are inferences or interpretations, and so are to some degree conceptual. Combining this fact with the apparent regress involved in predication, Peirce drew the conclusion that all cognitions are the results of inference, and so are logically determined by prior cognitions of the same object. The fact that this involves an infinite regress Peirce accepted once he was convinced that the regress was not vicious.

Since we do not know first impressions of sense as such, we must begin with the manifold as apprehended and reproduced and so already conceptualized as what is present before us. Such a concept is as near to sense data as we can come. "That universal conception which is nearest to sense is that of *the present, in general.*"[34] Thus the manifold, at the point where it first comes before us, makes its appearance as the present in general, as "IT in general."[35] The reduction of the manifold is to be achieved by explaining "It," and this is done by predicating something of it. The problem then is to explain how the predicate and the subject are related.

The scholastic theory of supposition holds that the subject and predicate are connected by the subject standing for that for which the predicate stands.[36] Since Peirce defines a sign as that which stands for something to someone in some respect,[37] the theory of supposition implied to him that the subject and predicate are connected by a sign relation. And since Peirce held that the sign relation is irreducible, it is also clear that it cannot be analyzed into component parts; nevertheless, it is possible to describe and clarify this relation by attending successively to various aspects of it while ignoring others—a process Peirce calls "precision."[38] If the proposition "it is blue" is interpreted by the theory of supposition, it asserts that "it" stands for something for which "blue" stands. Clearly, one aspect of this relation is the notion of "standing for" or denoting another object or correlate. This aspect of denotation itself requires exploration: how does the term "blue" denote? Peirce's answer is, "a symbol *denotes* by virtue of *connoting* and not *vice versa.*"[39] That is, "blue" denotes whatever has the property of blueness. Accordingly, reference to such an abstract property, or "ground," as blueness is also an irreducible feature of this relation, without which denotation is impossible. But a predicate connoting "blue" can denote an object only if the object has the qualitative character in question, and that the object has the character can be known only if the object is compared to a correlate known to be blue and is recognized as similar. Hence, denotation requires also a reference of the object to a correlate. But how is such a comparison to be made? Peirce's answer is that the object is brought into relation to the predicate by the interpretative function of the predicate, or by the predicate serving as an interpreting representation, which asserts that the subject stands for something to which it already refers. Thus Peirce remarks, "every comparison requires, besides the related thing, the ground, and the correlate, also a *mediating representation which represents the relate to be a representation of the same correlate which this mediating representation itself represents.*"[40] This mediating representation or interpretant is the predicate, for Peirce asserts, "that to which a thing stands for something is that which brings the thing into comparison with that for which it stands."[41] Thus the interpretant (the predicate), by establishing through comparison that the relate (the manifold) and the correlate (the object) share the same property (blueness), asserts that the relate (the manifold) stands for the correlate (object) which lies in the extensional domain of the predicate, and thereby brings the manifold to unity. Hence, signhood involves essentially reference to an abstract property or ground, reference to a thing or correlate, and reference to an interpreting representation. These three conceptions Peirce called his new list of categories.[42]

Peirce's account of the reduction of the manifold to unity certainly implies that we have prior knowledge of blue things. Indeed, the proposition "it is blue" is properly the conclusion of the hypothetical syllogism

It is thus
Blue things are thus
It is blue[43]

In the "New List" Peirce tries to condense this inference into one proposition, with the result that the argument is difficult to follow. In other papers, however, it is clear that the unification of the manifold is made by substituting "blue" for the confused predicate "thus."[44] But this also makes it clear that "it is blue" is not a protocol sentence: it is what Peirce calls a constitutional, nominal hypothesis[45]—nominal, because it is the substitution of a new name "blue" for the thusness, a hypothesis, because it is the result of hypothetical inference; and constitutional, because the process of inference is purely automatic and unconscious.

But Peirce's analysis of signs leads to a further conclusion. If every sign must have an interpretant, and the interpretant is itself a sign, then the series of signs not only has no beginning—it also has no end. This conclusion, also, Peirce fully endorsed. The infinite series of signs may be interrupted by death or other factors, but of itself the sign process goes on forever. Thus thinking is an endless process of sign interpretation.[46]

Peirce's analysis of signhood defines three classes of referents which bear a marked similarity to the three ontological classes of his earlier system. The connection is made quite explicit in a paper of 1866:

> A symbol in general and as such has three relations. The first is its relation to the pure Idea or Logos and this (from the analogy of the grammatical terms for the pronouns I, IT, THOU) I call its relation to the first person, since it is its relation to its own essence. The second is its relation to the Consciousness as being thinkable, or to any language as being translatable which I call its relation to the second person, since it refers to its power of appealing to a mind. The third is its relation to its object, which I call its relation to the third person or IT.[47]

It seems likely that Peirce first derived the names First, Second, and Third from the pronouns, and only later connected them to the number of correlates. But the fact that the I always refers, not to the mind, but to the pure abstraction, and so to God, strongly suggests the doctrine of the greater self. That this suggestion is correct is made clear in the same paper:

> . . . it becomes important to distinguish two kinds of self-knowledge—two selves, if you please, one known immediately and the other mediately. The mediate knowledge of self is not the inner world . . . is not something presented to us but is a mere product of active thought. We find that every judgment is subject to a condition of consistency; its elements must be capable of being brought to a unity. This consistent unity since it belongs to all our judgments may be said to belong to us. Or rather since it belongs to the judgments of all mankind, we may be said to belong to it. But the world of self the world of feelings does not contain such a unity. [sic] Much rather does this unity contain the feelings.[48]

This passage makes quite clear the extent to which Peirce must be regarded as belonging to the tradition of post-Kantian romanticism. Like many other romantic idealists, he had interpreted Kant's statement that "there is one single experience in which all perceptions are represented as in thoroughgoing and orderly connection, just as there is only one space and one time in which all modes of appearance and all relation of being or not being occur,"[49] as meaning that all human experience is part of a single overall experience. Accordingly, Peirce has interpreted the Transcendental unity of apperception as the unity of consistency characterizing the universal experience or Universal Mind, and his use of the "I" to refer to God probably stems from this attribution of the "I think" to the divine mind. In the statement of the "New List" itself, this romanticism is suppressed: Peirce prefers to begin with the concept of signhood, to derive the categories from it, and to leave the nature and status of the referents themselves open for investigation. That this investigation was to be forthcoming is indicated by the fact that Peirce then defined three transcendental sciences of his own—speculative rhetoric, logic, and speculative grammar—each of which was to deal with the relation of signs to one of these referents.[50] But what Peirce is seeking to prove in the "New List" is that since signhood requires these three referents, if all knowledge is in signs, then these three referents are presupposed in all knowledge. What he must elaborate next is a theory of cognition which will show that all knowledge is in signs, and then a theory of truth and reality which will show how these presuppositions support our knowledge.

Peirce elaborated his theory of cognition in his papers in the *Journal of Speculative Philosophy*[51] in 1868. In the first two of these papers, he seeks to establish four propositions:

1. We have no power of Introspection, but all knowledge of the internal world is derived by hypothetical reasoning from our knowledge of external facts.
2. We have no power of Intuition, but every cognition is determined logically by previous cognitions.
3. We have no power of thinking without signs.
4. We have no conception of the absolutely incognizable.[52]

The meaning which Peirce gives to the term "intuition" here is not precisely Kant's and does not touch the question of whether or not cognition contains a sensory component. Peirce defines an intuition as a cognition not determined by a prior cognition but referring immediately to the transcendental object.[53] Thus the denial of intuition expressed in proposition two is an immediate consequence of the doctrines of the "New List." Against proposition two there are two arguments which Peirce must meet—one direct, and one indirect. The direct argument is that we can distinguish an intuition from an inferred cognition by inspection. Peirce shows that argument to be false by pointing to the numerous cases in which people are unable to distinguish what they have seen from what they have inferred.[54] If there are pure intuitions, then, they are not directly known to be such, so their existence must be inferred. But inferred from what? The only reason for inferring such intuitions, Peirce holds, is that since there exists a time before which we do not cognize an object, if we do cognize it later there must have been some time at which cognition of the object began and so a first cognition of the object not inferred from a prior one. But Peirce argues that if we assume that the series of cognitions is infinite and that there is no minimum finite interval between cognitions, then the necessity for postulating a first intuition is removed—we simply have an infinite series which does not contain its own limits. Hence there is no reason to postulate intuitions, and so they may be dispensed with.[55]

If we have no intuitions we cannot have intuitions of ourselves, and so there cannot be an intuitive introspection. In denying all introspection, however, Peirce means to say something more than this—he means also that our sensations, volitions, and thoughts first occur as responses to external stimuli, and that we only become aware of them afterward by abstraction and inference from our experience of outer things. Even self-consciousness, Peirce holds, arises as a hypothesis to explain the existence of error and ignorance. There are, therefore, for Peirce no ideas of reflection in Locke's sense: ideas of the mind and its operations are inferred from behavior.[56]

The denial of introspection is really a lemma by which Peirce seeks to establish the thesis that all thinking is in signs. Having overthrown intuition he has eliminated one objection to this principle, and by the denial of introspection he eliminates all arguments based on direct observation of the thinking process. We can only know thought and feeling by inference from the observation of behavior. But behavior cannot furnish us with thought not in signs.[57] Moreover, as the "New List" argues, all thought arising as a response to sense stimuli is in signs and Peirce holds that no other type of thought can be shown to exist.[58]

Finally, Peirce denies the existence of anything incognizable. He had, of course, held this doctrine since 1859. The argument for it here is based on the theory of the "New List":

. . . all our conceptions are obtained by abstractions and combinations of cognitions first occurring in judgments of experience. Accordingly, there can be no conception of the absolutely incognizable, since nothing of that sort occurs in experience.[59]

Nor does the fact that we can form the term "not-cognizable" alter this conclusion: "not" is either syncategorematic or else arises from experience; hence not-cognizable is either not a concept or is self-contradictory.[60]

If all thought is in signs and if we have no intuitions, then Peirce holds all cognitions are determined by prior cognitions.[61] But what is the nature of this "determination"? According to Peirce the determination is logical: every cognition is inferred from prior cognitions.[62] For since hypothetical inference infers minor premises, including even judgments of sensation, induction infers major premises, and deduction infers conclusions, there is no type of declarative statement which cannot be obtained by inference. And so far as our reasoning leads to true propositions, there is no reason to deny that we think by inferring. But Peirce has also to show that we think by inferring when our reasoning does not lead to true propositions. In order to do this, Peirce classifies the possible types of fallacious reasoning into four kinds: ''1. Those whose premisses are false; 2. Those which have some little force, though only a little; 3. Those which result from confusion of one proposition with another; 4. Those which result from the indistinct apprehension, wrong application, or falsity, of a rule of inference.''[63] These four kinds exhaust the possible cases, for any other case would involve a false conclusion being drawn from a true premise clearly understood by a valid rule, and this is impossible. But if the premises are false, the reasoning itself is either valid, or the error occurs in one of the other three ways. If the inference has some force, then the reasoning is valid probable inference. If the error is due to confusion, then the confusion must be due to a resemblance between two propositions—i.e., the identity of the two propositions is inferred from their having common characteristics. But such an inference is valid hypothetical reasoning. Finally, if the error results in the last way, it is due either to confusion over the rule, which makes it an error of the third type, or from the use of a false rule as a premise and so is an error of type one. ''In every fallacy, therefore, possible to the mind of man, the procedure of the mind conforms to the formula of valid inference.''[64]

But if every cognition is inferred, how is it possible that we should have singular terms? Peirce's answer is that there are two meanings to ''singular.'' In one sense, a term such as Socrates or the sun is singular, but this sense of singular is not opposed to general, and propositions involving such subjects were traditionally treated as universal. But ''singular'' can also mean absolutely determinate, such that every conceivable characteristic is either true or false of the object. In this sense, Peirce holds, we have no singular cognitions at all. Such a cognition would have to contain an infinity of absolutely determinate detail; yet we are never aware of such an infinity of detail, nor can we adduce any reason for believing it to exist. Thus Peirce concludes that all cognitions are partially indeterminate, though the degree of determinacy can be increased by attention or training.[65]

From these principles of cognition Peirce drew a further conclusion: a man is a series of signs. For as all thought is in signs and thinking is a sequence of signs, there are no mental phenomena aside from the sign series.

> We have seen that the content of consciousness, the entire phenomenal manifestation of mind, is a sign resulting from inference. Upon our principle, therefore, that the absolutely incognizable does not exist, so that the phenomenal manifestation of a substance is the substance, we must conclude that the mind is a sign developing according to the laws of inference.[66]

What differentiates a man from a sign? There is, to be sure, consciousness, and it may be admitted that consciousness is not itself a sign, but it is what Peirce calls a ''material quality'' of a thought-sign—i.e., just as the word ''man'' is composed of the Latin letters "m," "a," "n," which constitute its material cause, so the states of mind which are representations include consciousness as a component of their material cause.[67] Indeed, whatever the material characteristics of psychological states, so long as these states function as signs and there are no states which do not function as signs, Peirce's thesis can be supported. And the denials of introspection and of incognizables previously established now serve to eliminate any incognizable knower or self: what knows previous thought is a subsequent interpreting thought, and no other knower need be postulated.

Peirce believed that these arguments were sufficient to prove that all thinking is in signs, that all sign translation and so all thinking is inference, that the series of signs is doubly infinite and does not contain its own limits, that there is no intuition, no absolutely determinate cognition, and no incognizable, and that man himself is a sign. These propositions may be taken to constitute Peirce's cognitive theory of the late 1860s. If the theory stands, it will certainly support the contention of the "New List" that the categories, and the three classes of referents derived from them, are presuppositions of all knowledge. Indeed, what Peirce so far has created is really an extreme semiotic idealism which had clear affinities to Berkeley as well as to Kant. But Peirce also considered himself a realist, and in these papers of the late 1860s he attempts to set out a theory of reality which will guarantee the reality of both things and universals.

Since the position which Peirce has developed on the basis of his categorical and cognitive theories is quite clearly idealistic, it would seem at first that he cannot defend a realistic position. And it is certainly true that, since he denies the existence of intuitions, or of cognitions which relate directly to the transcendental object, he cannot hold that our knowledge is in any sense a copy of the cause of cognition. But to Peirce this did not constitute a denial of real objects: rather, it led him to define the real, not as the incognizable cause of cognition, but as the final result of cognition.[68] That is to say, the existence of real objects is a hypothesis introduced to account for the coherence of our experience. It turns out that we can unify the manifold of experience—i.e., make experience coherent—only by postulating that there exist objects which cause sensation in us. The existence of such objects is not given—it is inferred by hypothetical reasoning. It is, therefore, the end product or result of reasoning rather than the premise. Yet although our hypothesis is the final upshot of investigation, yet in the causal order which that hypothesis postulates, the object precedes and causes our experience.[69]

It is true, of course, that the same object does not invariably produce an identical effect upon us, for "our sensations are as various as our relations to the external things."[70] Nevertheless, by taking into account our relations to objects, we can define a series of conditionals relating the conditions of perceiving the object to its effects on us which will suffice to bring our experience to order. Thus we may reason that under given conditions the presence of a certain object produces particular sensations in us. If we then verify that we have those sensations and that these conditions prevail, it is a valid hypothetical inference that the object is

From this definition of the real object, Peirce concluded that universals, or generals, as he calls them, are real. For if the real object is that which we postulate to bring experience to coherence, then it must be as we hypothesize it to be, since it is only as we hypothesize it that it exists at all. But every judgment of ours involves general elements, for as Peirce has already established, there is no such thing as an absolutely determinate cognition. Hence, whatever real thing there may be must be to some degree general. So, if anything is real, generals are real.[72]

The fact that whatever is, is general, clearly implies that there is no such thing as a completely determinate individual. "The absolute individual," Peirce asserts, "can not only not be realized in sense or thought, but cannot exist, properly speaking."[73] From this, it follows that Peirce's realism is of an extreme rather than of a moderate form.

But it follows that since no cognition of ours is absolutely determinate, generals must have a real existence. Now this scholastic realism is usually set down as a belief in metaphysical fictions. But, in fact, a realist is simply one who knows no more recondite reality than that which is represented in a true representation. Since, therefore, the word "man" is true of something, that which "man" means is real. The nominalist must admit that man is truly applicable to something; but he believes that there is beneath this a thing in itself, an incognizable reality. His is the metaphysical figment. Modern nominalists are mostly superficial men, who do not know, as the more thorough Roscellinus and Occam did, that a reality which has no representation is one which has no relation and no quality. The great argument for nominalism is that there is no man unless there is some particular man. That, however, does not affect the realism of Scotus; for although there is no man of whom all further determination can be denied, yet there is a man, abstraction being made of all further determination. There is a real difference between man irrespective of what the other determinations may be, and man with this or that particular series of determinations, although undoubtedly this difference is only relative to the mind and not *in re.* Such is the position of Scotus. Occam's great objection is, there can be no real distinction which is not *in re,* in the thing-in-itself; but this begs the question for it is itself based only on the notion that reality is something independent of representative relation.[74]

Yet this is not the position of Scotus, even though Peirce evidently believed that it was. Scotus solves the problem of universals by holding that although the external correspondent of the universal is an individual thing, yet both universal and individual have a common nature. In itself the common nature is neither universal nor individual, but is rather prior to both. As it appears in the external object, the common nature is individuated not only by particularizing determinations, but also by a peculiar nonqualitative element called thisness, or *haecceity,* which is added to it. As it appears in the mind, the common nature is made universal by the action of the agent intellect. Both universals and individual things therefore have one common nature, but the common nature in the thing is not universal and the thing really is individual.[75] But as Peirce states the position, the object is not really individual: it contains a universal nature which can be obtained by merely abstracting from the particularizing determinations. It is true that after 1885 Peirce made certain changes in his position and introduced Scotus's concept of *haecceity* into his own system, but prior to that time there is neither *haecceity* nor individuality in Peirce's doctrine. Peirce's position of 1868 is thus an extreme realism, since the external correspondent of the universal is itself general.

To define the real as that the postulation of which is necessary to bring experience to coherence is to say that truth consists in coherence and that the real object is the object of a true proposition. But whose experience is brought to coherence, and when are we entitled to say coherence is achieved and truth established? Peirce's answer to this question is stated in the following passage:

> The real, then, is that which, sooner or later, information and reasoning would finally result in, and which is therefore independent of the vagaries of me and you. Thus, the very origin of the conception of reality shows that this conception essentially involves the notion of a COMMUNITY, without definite limits, and capable of a definite increase of knowledge. And so those two series of cognitions—the real and the unreal—consist of those which, at a time sufficiently future, the community will always continue to reaffirm; and of those which, under the same conditions, will ever after be denied. Now, a proposition whose falsity can never be discovered, and the error of which therefore is absolutely incognizable, contains, upon our principle, absolutely no error. Consequently, that which is thought in these cognitions is the real, as it really is. There is nothing, then, to prevent our knowing outward things as they really are, and it is most likely that we do thus know them in numberless cases, although we can never be absolutely certain of doing so in any special case.[76]

Now it is at once apparent that this passage contains two very different criteria of reality: what will ultimately be agreed upon, and what is independent of any group less than the community. The first criterion can be satisfied by any infinite series of investigations which leads to a unique result, and requires no reference to any community, while the second appears to involve the wholly gratuitous assumption of the reality of other minds. Yet since Peirce has deliberately combined these criteria, it must be assumed that he did so for a reason and we must try to discover what that reason was. One clue is furnished by the fact that the 1868 paper from which the above passage is quoted was based in part upon a lecture which Peirce gave in 1866:[77] The earlier paper contains the whole doctrine that man is a sign, and many phrases of the later paper are taken directly from the earlier. But in the earlier paper there is no reference to the community: instead, Peirce discusses the unity of consciousness in the divine mind.[78] This strongly suggests that in the 1868 paper the community stands for the Universal Mind. For since man himself is a sign, the community is a community of signs which are present to the Universal

Mind. But on Peirce's principle that the phenomenal manifestation of the substance is the substance itself,[79] it is clear that the phenomenal manifestation of the Universal Mind is the community of signs, and what is meant by saying that the Universal Mind knows itself is that the community has an interpreter which is a subsequent, or future, community of signs. And since all representations require an interpreting representation, this series is infinite so that the community of signs is unlimited in time.

We have already seen that Peirce regarded the transcendental unity of apperception as the consistent unity of the divine mind. In this reformulation of his position, the transcendental unity of apperception must appear as the consistent unity of the community—i.e., as the community consisting of a system of perfectly consistent signs. Hence, on any given matter the signs composing the community must agree. But for Kant, the transcendental unity of apperception is the foundation of all knowledge of objective reality, for it is the transcendental unity of apperception which gives us the concept of the transcendental object and so permits our representations to be referred to an objective reality.[80] Accordingly, in reformulating this doctrine, Peirce must hold that it is the agreement of the community which provides the concept of the objectively real. And this is precisely Peirce's position. The real is the object of the proposition which will be agreed upon by the community, and the existence of reality rests upon the alleged fact that this agreement will be reached. Thus the community now plays the part which had previously been assigned to the divine mind. It is, therefore, in one sense true that Peirce assumes the reality of other minds, but it would be more accurate to say that he assumes that there are symbols and that they can be brought to consistency. That there are separate individual minds at all is not a given fact but the result of an inference from the existence of ignorance and error, and if ignorance and error are eliminated—i.e., if the ultimate agreement is attained—separate individuality will also be eliminated.

The concept of an objectively real object is necessary to bring our experience to coherence, and that coherence warrants the hypothesis of the object. For the concept of the real object is that of something which causes sensation in us according to the laws of perception, and so by reasoning from those effects and those laws we can acquire knowledge of the object. But is the object anything more than our actual sensations of it? According to Peirce it is, for the object is conceived as a possibility of sensation—as having a power to cause sensations in us.[81] But as Peirce remarked in a review of Berkeley in 1871,

What is the POWER of external things, to affect the senses? To say that people sleep after taking opium because it has a soporific *power,* is that to say anything in the world but that people sleep after taking opium because they sleep after taking opium? To assert the existence of a power or a potency, is it to assert the existence of anything actual? Or to say that a thing has a potential existence, is it to say that it has an actual existence? In other words, is the present existence of a power anything in the world but a regularity in future events relating to a certain thing regarded as an element which is to be taken account of beforehand, in the conception of that thing? If not, to assert that there are external things which can be known only as exerting a power on our sense, is nothing different from asserting that there is a general *drift* in the history of human thought which will lead it to one general agreement, one catholic consent. And any truth more perfect than this destined conclusion, any reality more absolute than what is thought in it, is a fiction of metaphysics.[82]

What Peirce is asserting here is that the possible can only be known as actualized. To say that the real is a possibility of sensation is to say that sensations will occur in the future. The basis for this assertion is, of course, Peirce's attempt to combine realism and phenomenalism. Unless the possible sensations do become actual they cannot be cognized, and Peirce cannot admit that there is anything incognizable. Yet Peirce is equally anxious to avoid reducing the real to a mere set of phenomena, since to do so would leave him open to skeptical attack. What saves his position here from just such a reduction is the fact that the future is infinite.

In Peirce's system, the infinite future plays the part of the philosopher's stone; it transforms possibility into actuality without compromising either the inexhaustibility of the possible or the limitations of the actual. On the one hand, the real must be a permanent and inexhaustible possibility of sensation; on the other, it must be wholly cognized. These two statements can only be reconciled by postulating an infinite future in which those possibilities of sensation can be realized.[83]

If our cognitions of the object will continue to be received forever, then the agreement of the community concerning the object must also lie in the infinite future—indeed, the perfect consistency of our knowledge must constitute a limit toward which inquiry will converge. And this fact affords Peirce a very neat way of stating his doctrine, and also of adducing evidence for it. It is well known that if an infinite series is convergent, it is possible to prove this fact from the behavior of the terms of the series alone, and hence to prove that a limit exists even though the limiting value itself may not be known. So Peirce can define the truth as the limiting view to which an infinite series of cognitions will converge, and the real as the object of a true statement. If he can then prove that the series of cognitions is convergent, he will have succeeded in defining the real, and in proving that there are real things, on the basis of phenomenal experience alone, and so have made good his attempt to combine phenomenalism and realism.

But can Peirce prove that the infinite series of cognitions is convergent? Since all cognitions are signs, and all sign translation is inference, the problem is equivalent to that of proving that an infinite series of inferences must converge to a limit. And since that limit is by definition the truth, this is equivalent to the question of the validity of inference, and particularly of synthetic inference. Peirce presents his argument in terms of induction, although the same argument holds for hypothesis, and the argument is that a world in which induction would fail as often as lead to truth is impossible. For what could such a world be? It would have to be a world in which things have common characters, for otherwise the premises of an inductive syllogism would not apply. but in which no two characters are significantly associated. But this can only occur if every possible combination of characters occurs with equal frequency.

> But this would not be disorder, but the simplest order; it would not be unintelligible, but, on the contrary, everything conceivable would be found in it with equal frequency. The notion, therefore, of a universe in which probable arguments should fail as often as hold true, is absurd. We can suppose it in general terms, but we cannot specify how it should be other than self-contradictory.[84]

Accordingly, to define a universe in which induction would not lead to truth is to define a self-contradictory world. But now Peirce seeks to establish two further propositions: that his own idealistic theory of reality defines a world in which induction does hold good, and that no nonidealistic theory of reality defines such a world. The first proposition is argued as follows:

> . . . since all the members of any class are the same as all that are to be known; and since from any part of those which are to be known an induction is competent to the rest, in the long run any one member of a class will occur as the subject of a premise of a possible induction as often as any other, and, therefore, the validity of induction depends simply upon the fact that the parts make up and constitute the whole. This in its turn depends simply upon there being such a state of things than any general terms are possible. But it has been shown . . . that being at all is being in general. And thus this part of the validity of induction depends merely on there being any reality.[85]

The first assertion follows from the denial of incognizables, and is equivalent to saying that in the long run the population will be enumerated. The second assertion means that any members of the population may serve as subjects of the premises of an inductive syllogism respecting the population—a fact which follows from the form of the inductive syllogism. The conclusion that in the long run every member must occur as subject of a possible induction as often as any other is exceedingly obscure, but it seems to be a rather arcane way of saying that since the population consists only of the sum of the actually examined samples, the sample statistic cannot be a biased estimate of the population parameter: thus Peirce remarks that "the validity of induction depends simply upon the fact that the parts make up and constitute the whole." Hence Peirce concludes that the validity of induction depends upon there being real generals, and, one should add, nothing incognizable. But both of these principles are guaranteed by Peirce's theory of reality. On the other hand, they are not guaranteed by nonidealistic theories.

But now let us suppose the idealistic theory of reality, which I have in this paper taken for granted [,] to be false. In that case, inductions would not be true unless the world were so constituted that every object should be presented in experience as often as any other; and further, unless we were so constituted that we had no more tendency to make bad inductions than good ones. These facts might be explained by the benevolence of the Creator; but, as has already been argued, they could not explain, but are absolutely refuted by the fact that no state of things can be conceived in which probable arguments should not lead to the truth. This affords a most important argument in favor of that theory of reality, and thus of those denials of certain faculties from which it was deduced, as well as of the general style of philosophizing by which those denials were reached.[86]

Hence the proof of Peirce's theory of the real is that induction must be valid, that if Peirce's theory is true then induction is valid, and that on the nonidealistic theory induction need not be valid. As this implies, Peirce regarded the nonidealistic theory as self-contradictory, for he thought that any such theory involved belief in incognizable realities, and as we have already seen, he considered the concept of the incognizable to be self-contradictory.

By 1870 Peirce had elaborated a theory which accomplished most of the things he had set out to do in the late 1850s. Starting from the Kantian theory that all knowledge begins in the bringing of the manifold of sense to unity, he had in the "New List" shown that this unification was achieved through the sign relation, and he had then explicated the sign relation in such a way as to show that the sign necessarily involved triple reference to an object, an interpreting representation, and an abstraction. On this basis, Peirce elaborated a cognitive theory and a theory of reality which amount to an attempt to construct an extreme realism on the basis of a semiotic idealism. The human mind thus becomes identified with its phenomenal manifestation, the sign, and the Universal Mind with its phenomenal manifestation, the community; and the real object is defined as that which is postulated in the proposition which is the limit of an infinite series of investigations. The theory was certainly ingenious, and seemed to offer Peirce a way of constructing a philosophy of science on the basis of idealistic metaphysics. But then came De Morgan's paper.

4. The Logic of Relatives and the Theory of Inquiry

In the late 1860s Augustus De Morgan sent Peirce a copy of his paper on the logic of relations. Peirce at once set to work upon the new subject and within an astonishingly short time not only mastered it, but also made substantial advances in it.[87] Indeed, Peirce's greatest contributions to logic and philosophy were made in this area, and it is not too much to say that the modern logic of relations was largely his creation. But while the new logic opened up a new world for investigation, it also involved some very serious implications for Peirce's philosophy. The architectonic principle holds that the categories must be derived from logic, and Peirce so derived them in the "New List." But the discovery of the new logic effectively overthrew the logical basis of the "New List." Peirce had there assumed the traditional subject-predicate theory of the proposition, and his method of deriving the categories and of proving their universality rests on that assumption. The "New List" seemed to explain the relation of subject and qualitative predicate by showing that the representative relation connects them. But the logic of relations showed that there are propositions whose predicates are dyadic or triadic relations and which do not involve qualities at all. Hence the question at once arises, how are relations connected to their correlates—and specifically, how is the representative relation connected to its correlates? Nor can this question be answered by postulating another relation between the correlate and the representative relation, since the same question will recur respecting this new relation. Peirce was now faced with a complicated logical problem to which he had in 1870 no immediate answer and which threatened the categorical foundations of his system.

Although the logic of relations raised some serious problems, it also suggested to Peirce certain revisions in his theories of meaning and inquiry. These revisions were carried out in the early 1870s,[88] and were published in six articles on the philosophy of science which appeared in 1877-78 in *Popular Science Monthly*.[89] In his earlier work, Peirce had thought of the meaning of a symbol as the qualitative conception which it conveys.[90] Such a quality involves reference to a ground or abstraction— "*embodying blackness* is the equivalent of *black*"[91]—and it is not perfectly clear whether Peirce regards the quality or the abstraction as the true meaning: thus when he describes the object as "expressing" the abstraction, it is apparently the abstraction which is the meaning. In any case, however, the meaning was conceived as qualitative. But once relations are admitted as propositional constituents just as fundamental as qualities, there is no reason why the meaning may not be relational rather than qualitative. Thus the meaning of the concept of an object may just as well consist in a law relating operations performed upon the object or conditions of perceptions to perceived effects as in any purely qualitative essence. In fact, Peirce had already come very close to saying this, for the doctrine that sensation varies with our relation to the object is tantamount to asserting that all qualities of objects are disposition properties, so the meaning of the concept of an object cannot be simply a property but must be a conditional or law. And if the distinction between essential and accidental properties is given up, it will then follow that the meaning of the concept of an object consists of all the conditionals whose antecedents describe operations upon the objects or conditions of perception and whose consequents describe perceived effects.

We have noted earlier the difficulties which Peirce confronted when he tried to explain how we can know abstractions, and how these difficulties led him to the concept of an unconscious idea. This problem was one of many which were clarified by his study of the scholastics, for he learned from them the difference between an idea being in the mind *actualiter* and *habitualiter*. In the former case, the idea is directly before the mind; in the latter it is not directly before the mind but is nevertheless in the mind in the sense of being able to produce a conception.[92] The scholastic doctrine refers to qualitative concepts, but it is easily extended to relations, and this use of the term *habitualiter* at once suggests the identification of laws and rules with habits. Thus principles of inference, rules of conduct, and indeed any general lawlike connections governing behavior may be said to exist as habits in the mind. Hence if the meaning of the concept of an object is to consist in the conditionals relating operations on the object to perceived effects, these conditionals will in fact be habits. Accordingly, Peirce argues,

> To develop its meaning, we have, therefore, simply to determine what habits it produces, for what a thing means is simply what habits it involves. Now, the identity of a habit depends on how it might lead us to act, not merely under such circumstances as are likely to arise, but under such as might possibly occur, no matter how improbable they may be. What the habit is depends on *when* and *how* it causes us to act. As for the *when,* every stimulus to action is derived from perception; as for the *how,* every purpose of action is to produce some sensible result. Thus, we come down to what is tangible and practical, as the root of every real distinction of thought, no matter how subtle it may be; and there is no distinction of meaning so fine as to consist in anything but a possible difference of practice.[93]

This is the pragmatic theory of meaning. As Peirce stated it in the famous maxim of 1878, "Consider what effects, which might conceivably have practical bearings, we conceive the object of our conception to have. Then, our conception of these effects is the whole of our conception of the object."[94] Actually, this statement is a poor one, for it implies that the meaning consists in the effects or consequents only, whereas it is clear from the former statement that it is the habits or conditionals themselves which constitute the meaning. Pragmatism is thus an assertion that all concepts, qualitative or other, are definitionally equivalent to the set of all conditionals relating operations on the object of the concept, or conditions of perception, to experienced effects.

The pragmatic theory of meaning is a further step in Peirce's attempt to combine realism and idealism. For what he is asserting here is that the concept of a real object is definitionally equivalent to a set of conditionals which refer only to phenomenal experience. He had previously held that regularities in phenomenal experience are explained by postulating the reality of an object and hence that the concept of the object implies such conditionals; pragmatism involves the stronger assertion that the concept of the object means nothing more than the set of conditionals.

The pragmatic theory of meaning is but a part of a broader theory which Peirce elaborated in the early 1870s—the doubt-belief theory of inquiry. In this theory Peirce sought to bring his 1868 theory of cognition into line both with the new theory of meaning and with broader evolutionary doctrines by describing inquiry in terms of the organism-environment relation. In order to satisfy its needs, an organism must develop habits of action which are adjustive with respect to its environment, and these habits will relate its own behavior to experienced effects. Following the English psychologist, Alexander Bain,[95] Peirce notes that such habits are in fact beliefs concerning the relations existing in the world, and clearly on the pragmatic principle they are also beliefs about the objects themselves: indeed, to believe that there is a particular sort of object is precisely to believe that certain acts or stimuli are followed by certain consequences. Since from a functional standpoint, beliefs ensure the organism's survival by showing it how to satisfy its needs in the environment, the state of believing is one of security and satisfaction. But if belief is disrupted, either by the failure of the expected effects to ensue upon appropriate actions, or by the occurrence of unexpected effects, a state of uncertainty or doubt ensues, which, since it means that the organism does not know how to satisfy its needs, is one of anxiety and discomfort. The organism therefore seeks to escape doubt and to find belief, and this process of passing from doubt to belief Peirce defines as inquiry. Any process which leads to settled belief may thus be considered as a type of inquiry, and the problem is to discover those methods which lead most surely to the desired establishment of belief.[96]

In the famous paper on the "Fixation of Belief,"[97] which Peirce published in 1877, he discussed four alternative methods of fixing belief. The first is the method of tenacity, by which an arbitrarily chosen belief is dogmatically held, come what may. The second is the method of authority, by which some social institution enforces acceptance of a particular belief. The third is the a priori method, which consists in accepting any belief which is agreeable to reason. Finally, there is the scientific method.[98] Peirce quickly rejected the first three methods, on the ground that they will inevitably fail to produce the desired agreement. This leaves only the scientific method, which he claims will fix belief by leading to one true conclusion.

To satisfy our doubts, therefore, it is necessary that a method should be found by which our beliefs may be caused by nothing human, but by some external permanency—by something upon which our thinking has no effect . . . Such is the method of science. Its fundamental hypothesis, restated in more familiar language, is this: There are Real things, whose characters are entirely independent of our opinions about them; those realities affect our senses according to regular laws, and, though our sensations are as different as our relations to the objects, yet, by taking advantage of the laws of perception, we can ascertain by reasoning how things really are; and any man, if he have sufficient experience and reason enough about it, will be led to the one True conclusion.[99]

The validity of the scientific method thus rests for Peirce upon the hypothesis of real things. Peirce makes this even clearer in the fourth paper of the *Popular Science Monthly* series, when he asserts "that the rule of induction will hold good in the long run may be deduced from the principle that reality is only the object of the final opinion to which sufficient investigation would lead."[100] That is, to say that there are real things is to say that inquiry converges to a limiting proposition, for the real is defined to be the object of that limiting proposition. Thus Peirce asserts, "all that we can know or conceive of the existence of real things is involved in two premises: first that investigation will ultimately lead to a settled opinion, and, second, that that [*sic*] this opinion is entirely determined by the observations."[101]

The position which Peirce had reached by 1878 was a peculiar combination of doctrines. By his denial of intuition Peirce had adopted a position which is virtually a conceptualistic idealism, for although there are by hypothesis sensory stimuli to thought, all that is ever actually known is conceptual. Yet by defining truth as the limit to which inquiry converges, and the real object as the object asserted to exist in a true statement, Peirce believed he could make this idealism support not only the reality of objects, but the reality of universals as well. But Peirce's whole position rests upon certain assumptions respecting possibility, the consequences of which he had not yet perceived. We explain our experience, Peirce holds, by postulating real objects which cause sensations in us according to the laws of perception. Is the object then identical with its actual sensible effects? If it is, then the hypothesis of the real object adds nothing. If it is not, in what further can the reality of the object consist? Peirce says that the real object is a possibility of sensation, and he equates this with the assertion that inquiry will come to one conclusion. But how is the future convergence of inquiry related to the present reality of a possibility? Is Peirce saying that the fact that inquiry converges proves the present reality of possibilities which are themselves not now ac-tualized? This is the question of the status of disposition properties when the object is not under test. Peirce's answer is the following:

There is absolutely no difference between a hard thing and a soft thing so long as they are not brought to the test. Suppose, then, that a diamond could be crystalized in the midst of a cushion of soft cotton, and should remain there until it was finally burned up. Would it be false to say that the diamond was soft? . . . We may . . . ask what prevents us from saying that all hard bodies remain perfectly soft until they are touched, when their hardness increases with the pressure until they are scratched. Reflection will show that the reply is this: there would be no *falsity* in such modes of speech. They would involve a modification of our present usage of speech with regard to the words hard and soft, but not of their meanings. For they represent no fact to be different from what it is; only they involve arrangements of facts which would be exceedingly maladroit. This leads us to remark that the question of what would occur under circumstances which do not actually arise is not a question of fact, but only of the most perspicuous arrangement of them.[102]

The difficulty here involved is fundamental for Peirce's whole doctrine, for what he is asserting is that nothing is possible which is not actual or will not become actual. To be cognizable, therefore, implies to be cognized sometime, and since Peirce also denies that anything incognizable is real, it follows that all there is, is cognized sometime. But on this view a present unactualized possibility is impossible, even if a similar possibility is actualized later, for possibility now and possibility then are two different things.

It is the problem of the possible which underlies Peirce's commitment to the infinite future, for as we have already seen, it is the endlessness of the future which persuaded him that the possible could be transformed into the actual without compromising either. And it is just this use of the infinite future which raises so many difficulties in Peirce's system. For as Thompson has noted,[103] that inquiry will go on forever is an incognizable fact, and so on Peirce's grounds it cannot be real. Further, to argue that if inquiry were to go on forever, it would converge is to employ a subjunctive conditional, and so to fall into the problem that for Peirce the conditional cannot be true unless inquiry in fact does go on forever, which is incognizable. But even if inquiry does go on forever and does converge, does it follow that there were real possibilities of sensation at times when no one cognized those sensations? I think it is clear that Peirce would have to deny this, and so even the infinite future is not sufficient for his purpose.[104]

It seems quite clear that Peirce was not aware of these difficulties when he wrote the paper "How to Make Our Ideas Clear"[105] in 1878, from which the passage about the diamond is quoted. And this fact helps to explain why his statement of the pragmatic maxim in that same paper implies that the concept of the object is definitionally equivalent to a conjunction of phenomenal experiences. Other passages in this article show very clearly that Peirce thought the meaning was the set of habits which the object is conceived to involve. But it is nevertheless true that the maxim itself states that the concept of the effects is equivalent to the object. The point is that Peirce himself at this point did not clearly distinguish the law from the set of all actual instances of the law, and the reason he did not is that to make such a distinction would have required admitting possible instances which are never actualized. It was just because Peirce was trying to merge phenomenalism and realism that he confused the difference between the two. And this fact also helps to explain Peirce's identification of the Universal Mind with the community. For the identity of the Universal Mind, which contains the Archetypal Ideas, both qualitative and relational, with the community, which can contain at most all actual instances of these ideas, is simply another case of the same confusion.

5. The Revision of the Eighties

By 1880, then, Peirce's second system was in serious trouble. His failure to solve the problem of the status of the possible threatened to reduce his realism to Humean skepticism. Moreover, since the categorical theory of the "New List" was invalidated by the logic of relations, Peirce had the choice of either revising the categories to bring his theory into line with the new logic or abandoning the architectonic theory upon which his early philosophy was based. To solve these problems, Peirce had to make drastic changes in his system—changes which first appear in his work in 1885.

The changes which Peirce made in his system in the 1880s were based, as one might expect from a philosopher who subscribed to the architectonic theory, upon new developments in logic and mathematics. The first of these was the development of the theory of quantification which Peirce completed in 1885.[106] In the development of this theory, Peirce received substantial assistance from one of his students at Johns Hopkins, O. H. Mitchell.[107] Peirce described Mitchell's work as follows:

> But tokens alone do not state what is the subject of discourse; and this can, in fact, not be described in general terms; it can only be indicated. The actual world cannot be distinguished from a world of imagination by any description. Hence the need of pronoun and indices, and the more complicated the subject the greater the need of them. The introduction of indices into the algebra of logic is the greatest merit of Mr. Mitchell's system. He writes F_1 to mean that the proposition F is true of every object in the universe, and F_u to mean that the same is true of some object. This distinction can only be made in some such way as this.[108]

The significance of quantification for the theory of the categories is that it introduces a new type of sign which is capable of referring directly to an object without describing it, and so introduces what is essentially the distinction between membership and inclusion. In his earlier work, Peirce had held that an object can only be referred to through a descriptive property: thus even a proper name is interpreted as "concrete form"[109] and "It" as a concept. But with quantification theory, the individual variable is introduced, and with it the concept of the individual. For if an individual variable can refer directly to its object without the reference being mediated by a description, then Peirce concluded that the object must possess some nonqualitative characteristics by which it can be identified. Peirce, therefore, introduced into his own system the Scotian concept of *haecceity* or "thisness"—the nonqualitative, positive, individuating principle by virtue of which each individual is just "this" thing. To possess *haecceity* is to be just this unique, self-identical individual, irrespective of what qualitative properties the individual does or does not possess. Accordingly, such individuals are not identifiable by properties alone: they can only be indicated by a variable.[110]

Second, in 1884 Peirce first became acquainted with Cantor's set theory.[111] The revolutionary effect of Cantor's work on mathematics and logic is well known, and Peirce was no less influenced by it than were Frege and Russell. In his later years, Peirce wrote extensively upon the foundations of mathematics and developed theories of the cardinal and ordinal numbers which differ sharply from those in vogue today. While Peirce's technical work in these fields lies beyond the purview of this book,[112] there are several technical results which must be briefly treated, since Peirce based much of his later philosophy upon them.

We have seen already that Peirce made extensive use of the concept of infinity in his earlier work. Even in the 1850s, Peirce not only believed that one could reason about the infinite, but that there were orders of infinities which could be subjected to mathematical manipulations.[113] What lay behind such doctrines is Peirce's acceptance of the theory of the real infinitesimal. This doctrine was once a widely accepted basis for the calculus: it was held by Peirce's father,[114] and by Peirce himself throughout his life. The theory holds that if x is infinite, then the infinitesimal quantity i is defined by the equation $i = 1/x$. Obviously, $x = 1/i$. But i may be divided by x; hence, $i/x = (1/x)/x = 1/x^2 = i^2$. This process can clearly be continued to generate two series, one of infinities and one of infinitesimals, corresponding members of which are reciprocals of each other.[115] To Peirce, then, it was clear that the existence of real infinite numbers implied the existence of real infinitesimals, and of course in Cantor's theory of transfinite numbers he found the proof that there were real infinite numbers.[116]

But as Peirce continued to explore the domain of transfinite numbers, he came to the conclusion that there was a paradox involved in the notion of a greatest cardinal number. The paradox Peirce found was not Cantor's paradox of the same name,[117] of which he apparently never knew,[118] but is instead a spurious paradox which resulted from certain technical errors of his own in the construction of transfinite cardinals. In brief, Peirce generated his series of transfinite cardinals by the method of power classes only, and he assumed that these cardinals were the alephs. By Cantor's theorem, it is obvious that this power-class series is enumerably infinite at least. Now the sum set of an enumerably infinite series, each member of which has a yet greater successor, is itself greater than any member of the series: hence the sum set of the series of power classes must be greater than any member of that set. Since we represent the cardinals of the members of the power series by the symbols $\aleph_0, 2^{\aleph_0}, 2^{2^{\aleph_0}} \ldots$, we may represent the cardinal of the sum set as $2^{\aleph \aleph_0}$, where the first power represents the fact that the series of 2s is enumerably infinite. But then Peirce argues $2^{2^{\aleph_0}} = 2^{\aleph \aleph_0}$, for the addition of another two can make no difference. And since Peirce generates transfinite cardinals only by power classes, this equality implies that $2^{\aleph \aleph_0}$ is the greatest cardinal. But this contradicts Cantor's theorem. The paradox is spurious, for the aleph-null representing the series of 2s should be an omega and $\omega \neq \omega + 1$. But spurious or not, Peirce believed he had a true paradox, and he sought an escape from it.[119]

The paradox, as Peirce believed he had shown, was that there both is and is not a greatest cardinal, and so a greatest collection. Peirce's solution to this paradox is to show that the greatest collection is not a collection of the same sort as the lesser collections, and the argument for this rests upon Peirce's definition of a "discrete" collection. To be "discrete" means, for Peirce, to possess a unique designation.[120] It follows that *haecceities* are discrete, but so too are abstract objects which have unique designations. A collection is called a "discrete collection" only if every member of the collection is discrete. It is important to stress that the universal quantifier is taken distributively here and not collectively, for it is this fact that permits infinite collections to be regarded as discrete. Thus the collection of natural numbers is defined by an initial element, zero, and a "generating" rule which specifies that each element has a successor. We may enumerate as many elements of this collection as we like, assigning to each a unique designation, yet Peirce notes, "there must always be a latter part of the collection which is not individually designated but is only generally described,"[121]—i.e., which we have not yet actually enumerated. If a discrete collection were defined as one *all* members of which are discrete—are enumerated—then infinite collections would not be discrete; but Peirce takes the definition as meaning that any member is discrete—can be enumerated—so infinite collections can be discrete.

Peirce then shows that if any collection is discrete, its power collection is discrete:

> . . . if a collection is not too great to be discrete, that is, to have all its units individually distinct, neither is the collection of sets of units that can be generally formed from that collection too great to be discrete.
> For we may suppose the units of the smaller collection to be independent characters, and the larger collection to consist of individuals possessing the different possible combinations of those characters. Then, any two units of the larger collection will be distinguished by the different combinations of characters they possess, and being so distinguished from one another they must be distinct individuals.[122]

It follows that the power series of transfinite collections starting with $\aleph_0$. is discrete. But Peirce emphasizes that as the cardinality of the collection increases, the "proportion" of the collection which can be actually enumerated constantly decreases.[123] But the limit of this power series, Peirce holds, is not a discrete collection, for if it were, it would in turn have a discrete power collection, and that fact creates the paradox. Hence Peirce avoids the paradox by claiming that the limit of the power series is not a discrete collection: it is rather a nondiscrete "potential collection," or collection of possibilities, "greater in multitude than any possible multitude of individuals."[124] This potential collection is not strictly speaking a sum set, since it is not discrete, but it can be regarded as analogous to a sum collection in the sense that any collection of the series may be regarded as the actualization of a selection of the possibilities it affords.

Peirce identifies this potential set with the linear continuum. "Since then there is a multiplicity or multiplicities greater than any discrete multitude, we have to examine continuous multiplicities . . . . although it is true that a line is nothing but a collection of points of a particular mode of multiplicity, yet in it the individual identities of the units are completely merged, so that not a single one of them can be identified . . ."[125] This identification itself involves certain technical problems. Continuity is traditionally a characteristic of certain geometrical entities; it is also, since Descartes, alleged to be a characteristic of the real numbers; and, since Newton, it has been taken to be a characteristic of certain functions. Whether the term "continuity" is used univocally in these three cases was much less clear in Peirce's day than it has since become. It was, after all, one of Cantor's major contributions to define precisely the meaning of "continuity" as applied to the real numbers and to show that the geometrical continuum may be regarded as a set of discrete points having certain order properties and certain cardinality.[126] With these results of Cantor's, Peirce strongly disagreed. He regarded the continuum of the real numbers as what he called a "pseudo-continuum" which he claimed was not sufficient for geometry, for the calculus, or for physics. This view is not necessarily in conflict with analytic geometry—it simply requires that one interpret Cartesian coordinates as defining a lattice on the plane rather than as establishing a one-to-one correspondence between the reals and the points on the plane.

It is perhaps easiest to review first Peirce's geometrical argument against Cantor's definition of continuity, since the geometrical argument really underlies the others. It must be borne in mind that the period in which Peirce lived was one of dramatic developments in geometry: between the discovery of the non-Euclidean geometries in 1829, and Klein's Erlanger classification of geometries in 1872, the entire theory of geometry was revolutionized. The discovery that there were alternative consistent metrical geometries not only dethroned Euclidean geometry, but it also led to an intensive study of the relations among these geometries. In his great sixth memoir on quantics,[127] Arthur Cayley succeeded in showing that all metrical geometries can be derived from projective geometry by the introduction of a suitable definition of distance. The definition of distance, or choice of reference figure, is itself a postulate, so that metrical geometries are not thus reduced to projective geometry; nevertheless, projective geometry emerges as the most general geometry, presupposed by all others. But during these same years, a new and still more general geometry—topology—was undergoing rapid development. Although Euler and a few other early mathematicians had worked on topological problems, and Gauss had published papers on knots, it was not until the mid-nineteenth century that topology became recognized as a distinct geometrical field: then the work of Listing, Kirchhoff, Möbius, and particularly Riemann brought it into prominence. Klein incorporated it into the Erlanger classification as the most general of all geometries, and, therefore, as one whose axioms are presupposed by all others.[128]

Peirce was intensely interested in the theory of geometry, and he followed these developments closely. He was among the earliest nineteenth-century mathematicians to see the philosophical importance of topology, for in view of the relations between topology and the other geometries, Peirce saw that if he could prove that certain axioms were necessary in topology, he had thereby proven them true for all geometry. But the topology which existed in Peirce's day was not the set-theoretic topology of the twentieth century; rather it was an algebraic topology in which such notions as continuity and limit still lacked clear definition. Peirce was particularly taken with the work of J. B. Listing—especially with his paper, "Der Census räumlicher Complexe," which appeared in 1861.[129] In this paper, Listing attempted to generalize Euler's theorem for polyhedra into a theory which would hold for all figures in three-dimensional space. The technical details of the Census theorem need not concern us here;[130] it is sufficient to remark certain characteristics of Listing's treatment. First, Listing regards every continuum as either containing its own limit, which occurs as a singularity, or place of lower dimensionality, in the containing continuum, or else as self-returning. All infinitely extended continua are, therefore, regarded as having a common limit in the point at infinity. Second, each continuum of less than three dimensions is regarded as the limit of some continuum of higher dimensionality. The dimensional limitation is a function of the fact that Listing does not deal with hyperspaces, but the limitation is arbitrary, and the theory is easily generalized to the principle that all continua occur as singularities in continua of higher dimensionality. Third, Listing tries to prove a general theorem, called the Census theorem, respecting the possible combinations of elements in three-dimensional space. As Euler had shown that in polyhedra only certain combinations of points, lines, and surfaces are possible, so Listing sought to show that in three dimensions, only certain combinations of points, lines, surfaces, and spaces are possible.

If Listing's theorem is true, and if topology is presupposed by all geometry, it follows that no concept of continuity is acceptable in geometry which would permit a continuum to be unbounded yet not self-returning. But the Cantorian definition of a continuum permits the existence of open lines which do not contain their own limits and are not self-returning. Therefore, Peirce held that Cantor's definition could not be used in topology, and hence was not an adequate basis for a definition of the geometrical continuum. On the other hand, Peirce's own definition meets the demands of Listing's theorem, for since the continuum only contains possibilities of determination and is broken only by the occurrence of an actual singularity, Peirce can argue that on his theory, wherever the continuum ends there is a contained limit. Hence the failure of the real number system to provide a specific number corresponding to that limit merely shows that the reals are inadequate to exhaust the possibilities of the continuum.

Peirce also holds Cantor's definition of the continuum to be inadequate as a basis for the physical theory of motion. His appeal here is to the classic paradoxes of Zeno, notably the Achilles. If, in fact, the continuum consists of an infinite set of discrete points, then Peirce claims that the paradox cannot be avoided, for Achilles must, in fact, pass through an infinite series of points preceding a given point before he can reach that point. On the other hand, Peirce argues, if the continuum itself contains no points at all, the appearance of paradox is an artifact of our system of measurement. We may measure distance by discrete values, but so long as the discrete values do not constitute the continuum, nothing prevents Achilles from overtaking the tortoise.[131]

But Peirce also held that the Cantorian definition of continuity was inadequate for analysis itself. In 1890 he wrote to Newcomb,

> To my definition of the word limit, you "object totally." You "cannot comprehend what is meant by the point at which a variable upon which some function depends, passes through infinity." It would seem, then, that you are not *au fait* of what has been done of recent years concerning the foundations of the theory of functions. The fashionable definition of today, if I may use the expression, of a *limit* among the chief upholders of the doctrine of limits is the following. The limit of a variable, x, is a value, c, such that for every positive quantity, ϵ, sufficiently small, a value N can be assigned to a number n, making $\mathrm{mod}(x_n\text{-}c) < \epsilon$ for every value of n exceeding N. Here in n you have the vague (variable) to which I refer becoming infinite at the limit . . .
> My definition departs from the fashionable one in two ways. First, it removes the unnecessary restriction that n must vary by discrete steps; since I regard the conception of *limit,* when understood in the way it must be understood to make it serve its purposes, as well as in the thought of most of those who employ it, as involving or, at least, not *excluding* the idea of continuity. In the second place, in the interest of co-ordination of ideas, I regard infinity, just as in projective geometry, as a value to be "passed through."[132]

We have already noted Peirce's addiction to the theory of the real infinitesimal: as this letter makes quite clear, Peirce did not abandon infinitesimals in favor of limits, but tried to base limits on infinitesimals. And given Peirce's concept of the continuum as containing no discrete elements, it is obvious that for him the calculus must be based on the notion of infinitesimals. Moreover, Peirce is here attempting to carry into the foundations of the calculus itself the concept of projective geometry that an unbounded straight line is really an oval which "passes through" the point at infinity. That is to say, he is insisting, as Listing's argument compelled him to, that the limit must be contained in the continuum. Thus, although Peirce later admitted that Cantor's definition could be used in calculus, he was perfectly consistent in trying to base all reasoning regarding continuity on his own definition.

That fact that Peirce's theory of continuity necessarily involves a commitment to infinitesimals explains why he often gave an alternative definition of continuity in terms of what he called Kanticity: namely, something is continuous only if "every part has itself parts of the same kind."[133] This does not mean simply that the continuum is infinitely divisible, for that is also true by Cantor's definition; it rather means, what the theory of infinitesimals asserts, that the limit of such an endless process of division is an infinitesimal interval, not a point. "Kanticity" is indeed just another name for the doctrine of the real infinitesimal.

6. The Revised Categories

By 1885 Peirce had made sufficient progress in his studies of quantification, set theory, and topology, to begin exploring the implications of these new doctrines for the theory of the categories, and he had also become sufficiently aware of the weakness of his position of the 1870s to recognize the need for a sweeping revision. Accordingly, between 1885 and 1890 he reformulated his entire categorical system. Peirce here introduced for the first time a sharp division between the formal and material aspects of the categories.[134] Formally considered, Peirce says, his categories are simply a classification of irreducible relations in terms of the number of their correlates. Thus Firsts are monadic relations, Seconds are dyadic relations, and Thirds are triadic relations.[135] Peirce claims that these three types of relations are necessary and sufficient to produce all other relations. The argument rests upon the claim that combinatorial relations are inherently triadic, since they must involve a relation among two things being combined and a third thing which is the result of the combination.[136] If this be granted, then clearly monadic, dyadic, and triadic relations are irreducible. Peirce argues that all other relations are reducible to these three on the ground that once combinatorial relations exist, then n-adic relations can be generated by combinations of simpler ones. There are then only three irreducible classes of relations, and these constitute the formal aspect of the categories.[137]

The fact that relations are formally of three sorts does not of itself tell us anything about our knowledge; before it can do that, these relations must be related to experience. In view of his earlier writings, one would expect Peirce to argue, as indeed he does, that these formal relations afford the basic classification of signs, and then to argue, as he did in the "New List," that since all knowledge is in signs, it is possible to establish a priori truth concerning our objects of knowledge because they must be objects of signs. But this latter sort of argument now completely disappears from Peirce's writing. Instead, when he comes to consider the material aspect of the categories, he seeks to discover empirically in the given of experience whether or not there are elements which correspond to the formal classes of relations. In its most developed form, this endeavor is formulated as a phenomenological inquiry, the task of which is to discover the most adequate classification of the phenomenally given and to determine how this classification is related to the formal classes of relations.[138] A more striking reversal of Peirce's early procedure can hardly be imagined.

What lies behind this reversal is a fundamental change in Peirce's theory of cognition. It took Peirce a considerable period to complete this revision of his cognitive theory, so that all elements of the new formulation do not appear at once, but the basic outline of the new theory may be described as follows.

We have seen that in his early papers Peirce denied that intuitions can be known as such, and so held that we know only interpretations of the given—i.e., concepts. As a result of this position, there is in the "New List" no synthesis in intuition: the unity to which the categories of the "New List" bring the manifold is what Kant called an analytic unity—a unity of concepts. It is thus correct to describe Peirce's early position as a form of conceptualism, for all that is known is conceptual. The resulting lack of contact with an empirical·given did not concern Peirce at this point since he believed that his realism was an adequate defense against its subjectivisitic implications. But when Peirce became aware that his formulation of the realistic position was inadequate, he also saw that his earlier cognitive theory led directly to subjectivism. To escape from this situation Peirce sought to get back into contact with some phenomenal given. Yet the arguments against intuition which he had earlier endorsed remained to be dealt with, and it required considerable ingenuity to devise a theory which could justify an experiential given in the face of these early objections. Peirce found his solution in the theory of the percept and the perceptual judgment, and in the division between conscious and unconscious inference. Peirce continues to regard intuitions as instantaneous neurological stimuli which are never known as such. As experience comes before us, it appears already synthesized into percepts. There is, therefore, a synthesis in intuition, but Peirce holds that this synthesis is utterly unconscious: we are unaware of it, we cannot say by which principles it proceeds, and even if we could it would be pointless to criticize it, for the process is wholly beyond conscious control. Indeed, that there are intuitions and a synthesis in intuition are really hypotheses to explain the existence of the percept—we never know these intuitions as such. What we do know is the percept which results from this synthesis. The percept is thus an image, picture, or other synthesis of sensory elements.[139] So far as our knowledge is concerned, what is given is the percept: "The percept is the reality."[140] Yet even though the percept is presented, we cannot really be said to know the percept until we can say something about it, and what we first say about it is the perceptual judgment. The percept is a wholly nonlinguistic phenomenon; the perceptual judgment is a proposition about the percept, such as "it is blue." Such a perceptual judgment is an interpretation, a hypothesis, which tells us what we perceive. It is an automatic or unconscious inference—i.e., we are not conscious of making an inference when we say "it is blue." Since the inference is not controllable, we have no choice but to accept the perceptual judgment as indubitable. Thus the perceptual judgment is very like the constitutional nominal hypothesis of his earlier theory. It is the perceptual judgment which serves as the first premise of our knowledge.[141]

In what way does this theory of perception differ from Peirce's earlier theory? There are two critical differences. First, by introducing the percept Peirce has introduced a nonconceptual given into his theory. Strictly speaking, the theory of the "New List" contains no concept of the percept. The "It" of the "New List" stands for a confused aggregate of sensation—not for a synthesized percept. The introduction of the percept, therefore, puts Peirce in touch with something other than mere concepts. It is true that the percept itself is synthesized from nerve excitations, albeit unconsciously, and it is, therefore, true that the percept is not a copy of anything external: it is simply what we find before us. It is also true that the percept as known in the perceptual judgment is already interpreted, and that what the percept was we can only know through this interpretation. But the fact remains that the percept itself is not conceptual and is given, and that fact marks a fundamental change in Peirce's point of view. Second, cognition now has a definite starting point. Although it remains true that there is no first intuition, so that the percept may be regarded as the result of an unconscious synthesis of an endless series, it is also true that so far as conscious cognition is concerned, the perceptual judgment is the premise from which knowledge begins. The division between conscious and unconscious inference, therefore, serves to reconcile Peirce's earlier and later theories: the denial of a first impression is preserved as a truth regarding unconscious inference, while at the same time we have in the perceptual judgment a first cognition of the percept.[142]

To determine what there is, if anything, in experience which can serve as a material aspect of the categories, we must examine our perceptual experience and, therefore, our percepts. What Peirce calls phenomenology is the study of what is or can be before the mind.[143] Distinctions between inner and outer or real and illusory are not relevant here, since these are not characters given in experience but represent subsequent classifications of experience.[144] If we examine our phenomenological experience, we find that it has three characteristics. The first of these Peirce calls "quality," but the term "quality" here does not mean the same thing it meant in the "New List." What Peirce is describing is not a concept but a phenomenal suchness. The firstness of a red patch is not the concept "red" under which we classify it, but the peculiar suchness of the patch which leads us to classify it as red. A phenomenal suchness itself Peirce holds to be unanalyzable: it is as near to a wholly primitive component of experience as we can come and has no parts into which it can be analyzed. In this sense suchness has a certain analogy to the simple ideas of the British empiricist, but it must be stressed that Peirce does not conceive suchnesses as given to us separately and subsequently added together: suchnesses are given only as aspects of percepts and must be prescinded if we are to contemplate them separately. And even if the percept involves various suchnesses, not only is each of these qualia unanalyzable but the ensemble of qualia has itself a peculiar suchness which is also unanalyzable and not reducible to any combination of other suchnesses. Qualities in this sense—suchnesses—Peirce defines as the material aspect of Firstness, since they are the most primitive form of monadic predicates.[145]

The second characteristic which Peirce finds in all perceptual experience is opposition, which appears either as insistency or as resistance. What Peirce refers to as insistency is what more traditional doctrines have called the forcefulness or sense of impact by which perceptual experience is distinguished from conceptual experience. Thus, for example, Hume gives the following account of perception:

> All the perceptions of the human mind resolve themselves into two distinct kinds, which I shall call IMPRESSIONS and IDEAS. The difference betwixt these consists in the degrees of force and liveliness with which they strike upon the mind, and make their way into our thought or consciousness. Those perceptions, which enter with most force and violence, we may name *impressions* . . .[146]

What Hume describes as "force and violence" Peirce calls insistency—a sense of brute compulsion by which perceptual experience comes upon us. Such a compulsion Peirce regards as inherently dyadic, since it is a constraining of the will by something other than the will, and hence insistency may be regarded as a material aspect of secondness. Secondness has, however, another material aspect. Peirce believed that every act involves an opposing reaction or resistance which accounts for the sense of effort which distinguishes genuine action from mere wishing. This sense of effort, of being resisted by some other, is also inherently dyadic and so is also to be regarded as a material aspect of Secondness. Indeed, resistance is the felt converse of insistency: in the first case the other acts upon the will; in the second, the will acts upon the other. Both are thus fundamentally dyadic and so instance secondness.[147]

The most complex and most important of Peirce's categories is Thirdness, and to see what can serve as a material aspect of Thirdness some analysis is necessary. We have seen that Peirce regards all combinatorial relations as triadic. Now it is clearly not the case that all triadic relations are combinatorial, but it is the case, Peirce holds, that all genuine triadic relations are combinatorial. By a genuine triadic relation, Peirce means a relation such that the elimination of any correlate not only destroys the triadic relation, but also destroys the component dyadic relation between the remaining correlates. Thus the sign relation is genuine because if any correlate is removed, no semiotic relation remains between the other two, while triple brotherhood is a degenerate triadic relation since the elimination of one brother does not alter the brotherhood of the others. To be genuinely triadic and to be combinatorial are, therefore, convertible terms.[148]

In the "New List" Peirce took signhood as the fundamental synthetic relation which brought the manifold to unity, and signhood is clearly a genuine triadic relation. One might expect, therefore, that the material aspect of Thirdness must be closely related to signhood, and, in fact, Peirce wrote in 1903,

> The third element of the phenomenon is that we perceive it to be intelligible, that is, to be subject to law, or capable of being represented by a general sign

or symbol . . . The essential thing is that it is capable of being represented. Whatever is capable of being represented is itself of a representative nature. The idea of representation involves infinity, since a representation is not really such unless it be interpreted in another representation.[149]

How is being subject to law related to intelligibility and to being represented by a general sign? In the first place, Peirce regards all habits as laws, for they are universal conditionals supporting prediction. Second, all laws as known to us are beliefs concerning certain orders in phenomena and so by the definition of belief in the doubt-belief theory of inquiry they are also habits. Third, it is the point of pragmatism that meaning is a matter of habit: to be intelligible or have a meaning is, therefore, to be subject to habit or law. Peirce had earlier subscribed to the Kantian doctrine that to be intelligible means to be brought under concepts. The pragmatic principle, by translating concepts into habits, converts that doctrine into the assertion that to be intelligible is to be brought under habits. Since "what a thing means is simply what habits it involves," what involves habits has a meaning.

Whatever is subject to law is capable of representation by a sign of which that law is the meaning, and whatever is subject to law is itself a sign of the law to which it is subject. It is in this sense that Thirdness is at once the category of law and of rationality or intelligibility.[150]

We have seen above that one of the most serious problems which the logic of relations created for Peirce's early theory was the fact that the apparent synthesis effected by the sign relation turns out to involve an infinite regress. For even if the correlates are combined by the representative relation, those correlates must be joined to the representative relation and that combination can only be effected by another relation. But then the same problem recurs with respect to the new relation, etc. Although in the 1870s Peirce produced no solution to this problem, his few extant writings on the categories from that era indicate that he was seeking to develop the concept of Thirdness as continuous connection or process. Thus he remarks, "Continuity represents Thirdness almost to perfection. Every process comes under that head."[151] This line of thought he subsequently developed into the concept of continuous relations.

. . . the grammarians usually limit the term [subject] to the subject nominative, while I term anything named in the assertion a Subject, and although I do not always express myself so accurately, I regard everything to which the assertion relates and to which reference can be removed from the predicate, although what is referred to be a quality, relation, state of things, etc., as a Subject. Thus one assertion may have any number of Subjects. Thus, in the assertion "Some roses are red," i.e. possess the color redness, the color redness is one of the Subjects; but I do not make "possession" a Subject, as if the assertion were "Some roses are in the relation of possession to redness," because this would not remove relation from the predicate, since the words "are in" are here equivalent to "are subjects of," that is, are related to the relation of possession of redness. For to be in relation to X, and to be in relation to a relation to X, mean the same thing. If therefore I were to put "relation" into the subject at all, I ought in consistency to put it in infinitely many times, and indeed, this would not be sufficient. It is like a continuous line: no matter what one cuts off from it a line remains. So I do not attempt to regard "A is B" as meaning "A is identical with something that is B." I call "is in the relation to" and "is identical with" Continuous Relations, and I leave such [relations] in the Predicate.[152]

What the infinite regress in combinatorial relations really proves, Peirce holds, is that combinatorial relations are ultimately Kantistic and so continuous. And this fact is of the greatest importance, for it means that true combination involves continuous connection. Genuine triadic relations therefore are continuous connections among their correlates. Thus laws for Peirce are at bottom continuous processes whereby from antecedent states a consequent state is produced.[153] But in terms of Peirce's mathematical theory of continuity, to say that something is continuous is to say that it involves unactualized possibilities greater in multitude than any discrete collection. If, therefore, laws really are continuous connections, they are necessarily general, not only in holding for all the instances there are, but also in the sense of holding for all there can be, including those possible but never actualized instances. Thus genuine Thirdness involves continua, and so generality.

To show that phenomenal experience contains Thirdness, it is sufficient for Peirce to provide evidence that it contains either continuity or generality. That generality is given in perception Peirce asserts upon the ground that since the predicate of a proposition is always general, the predicate of a perceptual judgment must be general, and since the perceptual judgment is an indubitable description of the percept, the percept itself must be general.[154] To this argument it might be replied that the generality is not in the percept but in the perceptual judgment and is therefore not given in the percept at all. But here again Peirce falls back upon the distinction between conscious and unconscious inference. Not only is the synthesis in intuition by which the percept is generated unconscious, but the inference of the perceptual judgment is unconscious as well; it is only after the propositional formulation of knowledge has occurred that thinking becomes conscious. But Peirce holds that unconscious inference cannot be criticized, for being utterly beyond our control it makes no more sense to call such reasoning correct or incorrect than it would to criticize the growth of the hair. We cannot go behind the perceptual judgment: we must accept the description of the percept which the perceptual judgment gives as true, for we have no basis upon which to criticize it. And the perceptual judgment presents the percept to us as general.[155] But Peirce also holds that continuity is directly experienced as such. For in perception, Peirce claims, we not only perceive the object of our perception as extended in time, but we also directly perceive an interval of time as such.[156] And for Peirce time itself is a true continuum; for if it were not, memory would be impossible. Whatever else memory involves, it certainly involves a synthesis in recognition among ideas obtained at different times. If time were discontinuous—if each instant were wholly separate from every other—then, Peirce argues, there could be no relation among instants, for all relations are based upon continuous connections. Peirce then holds that the fact of memory requires us to regard time as a true continuum[157] and therefore, since we experience time intervals as such, we do directly perceive continuity. We may then regard experienced generality and continuity as constituting the material aspect of Thirdness.

The new theory of perception solves many of Peirce's earlier difficulties by bringing him back into direct contact with sense experience which can serve as a starting point for knowledge. The percept now serves as the bedrock upon which knowledge rests—"the percept is the reality"—and perceptual judgments so become the first premises of knowledge. It remains true that perceptual judgments are hypothetical inferences from percepts, and that percepts themselves are conceived as the products of unconscious syntheses of neural stimuli; it also remains true that percepts contain generality and so have some conceptual aspects. Nevertheless, the percept is not itself a concept, and that fact means that knowledge has a nonconceptual starting point. Given that starting point, Peirce can now argue that the function of knowledge is to give coherence to perceptual experience, so that our hypotheses of real objects are justified only as explaining our perceptions. It is then a legitimate way of formulating the realistic position to say that, if there are real objects which affect us according to the laws of perceptions, then, if inquiry goes on indefinitely, agreement will be reached. But the coming of final agreement is here explicitly a consequence of the reality of objects, and no claim is made that inquiry will go on indefinitely. Similarly, the case for the reality of universals can no longer rest on an a priori proof. What Peirce contends in his argument respecting the material aspect of Thirdness is that generality and continuity are given in perception. But this alone is not enough—Peirce must now go on to show that the metaphysical reality of universals provides a reasonable explanation for what we find in perception, and only on that basis can he ultimately rest his case. Thus the effect of Peirce's revisions of the 1880s is to shift his philosophy away from an a priori, subjective idealism toward a more reasonable, empirically based doctrine, albeit one which is no less idealistic.

The revision of the 1880s does much more than simply redefine the categories. The introduction of the distinction between the formal and the material aspects, and the use of phenomenal inquiry to establish the material aspect, in fact alters the whole status of the categories, and so the architectonic theory itself. What the phenomenal inquiry shows is that experience can be categorized by three classes or aspects which correspond to the three formal categories. This fact does not prove that all experience must instance these categories. We do not know, therefore, that the categories are either universal or necessary, and it is obvious that no merely inductive examination of experience can ever establish that they are. Indeed, we do not even know that they are useful. In order to show any of these things, a revision of the whole design of Peirce's philosophy was required.

To prove the utility of the categories, it will suffice to show that these ideas provide a basis for empirical science. And since this cannot now be done a priori, it must be done a posteriori by an inductive survey of the sciences. Peirce first attempted this in an unpublished paper entitled a "Guess at the Riddle,"[158] in 1890, where he sought to show that the three categories in fact serve as primitive notions in all major branches of science, and he presented essentially the same thesis a year later in published form in the first *Monist* paper on "The Architecture of Theories."[159] But this sort of proof of the significance of the categories suffers from the obvious weakness that while it may show that the categories are now basic for all science, it can prove nothing about their utility in the future. Consequently, in the later 1890s and early 1900s, Peirce made extensive studies of the classification of the sciences.[160] His model here was clearly Klein's Erlanger classification—he wanted to establish a classification by presupposition such that for any given science, the classification will show which sciences it presupposes and which sciences presuppose it. If such an ordering is once established, it then follows that the primitives of a given science are presupposed by all sciences which follow it in the classification, and so if some one science is presupposed by all others, its primitives are assumed by all others. In the classification upon which Peirce finally settled, mathematics—including the mathematics of logic and, therefore, the formal classification of relations—is the science presupposed by all others, and phenomenology—which establishes the material categories—comes next, presupposing mathematics but presupposed by all others. Next come what Peirce calls the normative sciences—aesthetics, ethics, and logic—and then metaphysics, and after these the special sciences.[161] If this classification is correct, then the special sciences presuppose the categories in both their formal and their material aspects, and also presuppose the philosophic disciplines of normative science and metaphysics. Peirce can, therefore, concentrate on the problem of proving their necessity and universality in mathematics and phenomenology or through normative science and metaphysics, with the certainty that if it can be proven there, it is proven for all science.

But the universality and necessity of the categories can only be proven in a relative sense. Peirce has shown that in fact his categories can classify present experience: to show that they will always be able to classify experience he must propound a theory about experience which will show that experience must always have these characteristics. And in view of Peirce's revised theory of perception, such a theory must define the nature of external reality, the nature of the mind, and the relations between the two. These questions are scientific, and must be answered scientifically if they are to be answered at all. Yet as Peirce sees them they are not questions of the special sciences, for they concern the general characteristics of all experience and reality, while the special sciences are concerned with particular classes of experience. Accordingly, what is here required, Peirce believes, is a scientific philosophy which will attempt to account for these general features of all experience.[162] Such a theory must obviously involve an ontology and a psychology, and, since it is to deal with the past and future as well as with the present, a cosmology. If a metaphysical theory of this sort can be created, then, relative to this theory, the categories can be shown to be necessary and universal.

7. Metaphysics and Cosmology

Peirce first presented his metaphysics in a series of articles in the *Monist* in 1891-93.[163] At the time these articles were written, he had not completely worked out his position, and so numerous revisions in the doctrine were later made. Since these revisions are refinements and clarifications of the position, rather than basic changes, it will be convenient for the most part to examine Peirce's views in their later and more developed forms.

The basic hypothesis of Peirce's ontology is the hypothesis of objective idealism—that all there is, is mind.[164] The alternatives to this hypothesis Peirce considered to be two: that all there is, is matter; or that mind and matter are equally fundamental constituents of the universe.[165] The latter hypothesis Peirce regarded as condemned by Occam's razor, at least until the other two had been tested,[166] so the issue is really between idealism and materialism. But Peirce defines the materialist position as asserting that all phenomena of the universe are ultimately explicable by Newtonian mechanics.[167] This is a very restrictive definition of materialism, although in Peirce's day it was widely held and was advanced by such writers as Spencer. If this definition is granted, it then follows that living organisms must be mechanical contrivances whose properties are derivable from mechanics. "But," Peirce argues, "what is to be said of the property of feeling? . . . the attempt to deduce it from the three laws of mechanics, applied to never so ingenious a mechanical contrivance, would obviously be futile. It can never be explained, unless we admit that physical events are but degraded or undeveloped forms of psychical events."[168] Mind, therefore, cannot be reduced to matter; but can matter be reduced to mind? To support his own hypothesis of objective idealism, Peirce must show that that hypothesis can account for all experience.

If all that is, is mind, then we must account for experience in terms of the nature and behavior of mind. But since the nature and behavior of the mind is the subject of the special science of psychology, of which the ontology is a presupposition, it would seem circular to base the ontology itself upon the results of psychology. Peirce's defense of this procedure must be that insofar as psychological principles are assumed in ontology, they cease to be merely psychological principles and become instead hypotheses of general metaphysics. As such, they must be verified, not alone by human behavior, but by all experience. The explanation of human behavior may then be regarded as a more specialized study of a particular class of phenomena, and will require, besides the general hypotheses of metaphysics, certain auxiliary hypotheses which will form the principles of the special science of psychology. An idealistic ontology is, therefore, not circular, although it does involve the classification of some principles as metaphysical which would be regarded as psychological by other philosophies.

In the third *Monist* paper, entitled "The Law of Mind,"[169] Peirce presented his theory of the nature and behavior of mind. The discussion is couched in terms of "ideas,"[170] but Peirce uses this word in a psychological—almost physiological— sense rather than in its usual epistemological meaning. It is not the "idea" as a unit of knowledge, but as a psychophysiological state, that Peirce means to describe. The first problem is to find a terminology in which to describe these states, and since the hypothesis of idealism forbids reducing mind to matter, the primitive terms must be psychological. Peirce adapts the traditional division of mind into sensation, volition, and intellect[171] to serve this purpose, although he redefines the terms as feeling, energy of action, and habit. The basic term is feeling, which Peirce takes to be the stuff of which all mental phenomena are compounded. Energy of action refers to the force with which one feeling state acts upon, or "affects," another. Habit refers to general connections among feeling states, but these connections, being themselves mental phenomena, must also be feelings, or more accurately, felt processes by which some feelings are transformed into others.[172] The relation of feeling to sensation, and of energy of action to will are fairly obvious and the translation of intellect or thought into habit is a direct consequence of the pragmatic principle.

Peirce describes feeling as being at least triply continuous. First, feelings endure and so are continuous in time.[173] Second, feelings admit of continuous variation with respect to their intensity.[174] And third, feelings are spatially continuous.[175] The latter claim Peirce supports by the example of protoplasm. When a glob of protoplasm is irritated, liquefaction ensues, and the liquefaction spreads continuously from the point of disturbance to other parts of the glob. The spreading, however, is not uniform, but tends to follow various routes or paths. There is no apparent reason why one route should be preferred to another, except that the more one route has been followed the more likely it is that it will be followed the next time. Since the belief that protoplasm feels is based upon its irritability, the evident spreading of the liquefaction means, according to Peirce, that the feeling spreads—i.e, becomes continuously extended in space.[176] But as feeling spreads, Peirce holds, it loses intensity and becomes more general—i.e., becomes continuously connected to other feelings.[177] What Peirce is trying to describe here is the process of association, although the process is described only in terms of the behavior of the ideas as mental entities, not as units of knowledge. General feelings, or feeling states connecting other feelings, Peirce regards as habits or processes by which one state is transformed into another. Such processes clearly correspond to the paths or routes by which feeling spreads in the protoplasm, and the correspondence is strengthened by the fact that those paths obey the same rules of formation and maintenance that habits follow. But the habit itself is a feeling state, just as the path followed by liquefaction is itself a continuum of feeling, and the feeling which is the habit endures through time even though it is only occasionally that the intensity of the feeling is increased sufficiently to produce noticeable effects. Like modern behaviorists, Peirce holds that the continuance of habit from actualization to actualization requires some continuously present trace in the mind, and for him this must be a continuum of feeling.

Protoplasm is mind, because it possesses feelings which act upon each other and become combined into habits. But Peirce explicitly tells us that protoplasm has no personality.[178] The three elementary components of feeling, energy, and habit define mind, but these elements admit of various combinations, and only certain types of combinations constitute personality. To be a personality, ideas must be "coordinated."

> . . . [coordination] implies a teleological harmony in ideas, and in the case of personality this teleology is more than a mere purposive pursuit of a predetermined end; it is a developmental teleology. This is personal character. A general idea, living and conscious now, it is already determinative of acts in the future to an extent to which it is not now conscious.[179]

In his 1892 paper Peirce did not fully explain what he meant by this statement. It is clear that a personality is a teleological system of ideas which possesses its own consciousness. But what is not clear is the nature of the end sought. From the above statement one might infer that the end is only generally defined as the result of certain practices or as having certain characteristics, but what these might be Peirce was not yet ready to specify.

The hypothesis of idealism asserts that all there is, is mind. If the hypothesis is true, then feeling, energy, and habit must be the elements of which the world is constructed. It follows that we are personalities, or individually conscious teleological subsystems of the Universal Mind, constructed out of these same elements. But it also follows that what we experience—the cause of our perceptions—is some portion of the Universal Mind constructed of these same elements. Accordingly, Peirce's account of perceptual experience must be framed in terms of this analysis of the nature of mind. It will be recalled that Peirce held all perceptual experience to be classifiable into suchness, insistency-resistance, and generality-continuity. To account for these characteristics of experience, Peirce argues that each of them is the subjective correspondent of an elementary component of mind. Thus the suchnesses we perceive are feelings transmitted to us from without by continuity.

> The principle with which I set out requires me to maintain that these feelings are communicated to the nerves by continuity, so that there must be something like them in the excitants themselves. If this seems extravagant, it is to

be remembered that it is the sole possible way of reaching any explanation of sensation, which otherwise must be pronounced a general fact, absolutely inexplicable and ultimate.[180]

Similarly, the insistency we experience is the impact with which external feelings act upon us, while resistance is the impact of our ideas acting upon external mind—i.e., upon mind outside our own personality system. The generality and continuity we experience are the generality and continuity of the feeling-connections or habits we meet in the World Mind. Hence Peirce seeks to account for the characteristics of our experience by the simplest hypothesis his ontology will allow—a one-to-one correspondence between the categories of experience and the categories of mind. And the process of perception itself is now converted into one of communication whereby the World Mind interacts with its subsystems through the same sort of continuous connections in feeling by which ideas within our own personality system affect each other. We are, therefore, in direct connection with the Universal Mind, whether we recognize it or not.[181]

But to account for perceptual experience Peirce must do something more than account for the elements of which that experience is composed: he must also account for the relations among those elements. It is a fact that from these elements we construct a commonsense world of objects and events, and it is also a fact that Peirce's ontology is widely at variance with our commonsense view of the world. To this objection, Peirce might easily reply that his theory is no more at variance with common sense than is Newtonian mechanics, and this is certainly true, but after all Newtonian mechanics has a rather impresssive set of verified consequences with which to support its claims. If, therefore, Peirce is to support his idealist theory, he must prove that his theory can meet several further tests. First, he must prove that Newtonian mechanics is not inconsistent with his own theory. Second, since Peirce holds that there are wide ranges of phenomena which Newtonian theory cannot explain—e.g., organic phenomena—he must show that these phenomena can also be explained in a manner which is consistent with his theory. Third, he must show that his theory can explain, or explain away, the commonsense world of objects. Fourth, he must show that his theory leads to verified consequences which are not derivable from alternative theories. And finally, Peirce must show that his theory is epistemologically adequate. For if the universe is ideal, then knowledge is a relation between one part of the Universal Mind and another. The nature of this relation, and specifically of truth, must therefore admit of ontological as well as epistemological description. If inquiry is a process by which truth is discovered, Peirce must define the ontological status of that which is discovered, and the ontological meaning of saying that an idea is true of an object.

Peirce attempted to show that Newtonian mechanics can be interpreted in such a way that it is wholly consistent with his idealism. The argument is presented in two forms—the earlier being in terms of Boscovichian atoms,[182] the later of vortex atoms[183]—but the basic nature of the argument is the same in both cases. So far as the Newtonian system is concerned, reality consists of time, space, and mass-points.[184] Time and space also occur in Peirce's ontology, so the problem lies with point-masses and the laws governing their interaction. But it is well known that mass is only implicitly defined in the Newtonian system, and that the equations by which it is defined may be interpreted as asserting that mass is the resistance to change of state of a point, and the ground of the attraction between two points. That is, the material point may be replaced by an immaterial point which is the center of inertial and attractive forces. Alternatively, as Kelvin showed, the properties of Newtonian mass-points can be reproduced by vortices in a fluid which can be reconstructed along similar idealistic lines.[185] Materiality, therefore, need not be assumed; what is required is that action be located at certain time-space points and obey certain laws of behavior. Accordingly, Peirce holds that what we usually call matter may be regarded as mind whose actions have become almost completely regulated by habit.[186] Such mind-areas will transmit feelings to those in contact with them, will act, and react when acted upon, and will do so in highly regular ways. There is then nothing which mechanics predicts which idealism cannot also predict simply by translating material entities into mental ones and laws into habits.

Since Peirce holds that Newtonian physics cannot account for organic phenomena, his idealistic reconstruction of mechanics leaves untouched the question of whether or not an idealistic reconstruction of biology is possible. And in Peirce's day, any reconstruction of biology had to begin with evolutionary theory. But since the theory of evolution presumably holds for all living phenomena, it should also hold for mind, and so, in Peirce's idealistic hypothesis, for the universe itself. Accordingly, if evolution is true, the universe must have evolved from some primordial state, and so Peirce's ontology must also be a cosmology.

The construction of a cosmology involves certain assumptions regarding what can serve as a cosmological explanation. If Peirce were asked to explain why there is anything at all rather than nothing, he would answer—as would most modern philosophers—that the question is self-contradictory. An explanation presupposes antecedent conditions and general rules or processes: to ask for an explanation of everything is, therefore, absurd. Consequently, a cosmology must assume as a starting point some initial state of a system and some processes governing its behavior. These assumptions should be as weak as possible, but some such assumptions are necessary conditions for any theory. In constructing his cosmology, then, Peirce must first choose what the initial system and processes are to be.

In making this choice, Peirce was governed by certain premises. First, in line with his general idealistic position, he holds that mind can develop from nothing but mind. The original system, therefore, must have been of a mental or ideal character. To that end, Peirce is committed to some form of the mind-stuff theory, and since on his analysis of mind the basic element of the mind is feeling, he holds that the aboriginal mind-stuff was pure feeling in some form.[187] Second, since all relations are continuous, Peirce holds that things not already in relation cannot be brought into relation, since they would have to be first brought into relation to that relation, and then into relation to that relation, and so on, and we should be involved in an infinite regress. Hence relations must always be conceived as specifications of more general relations.[188] For Peirce, then, the mind-stuff cannot be a dust of discrete particles—it must rather be some sort of very general continuum which is then differentiated in some way. And since the mind-stuff is continuous in Peirce's sense, it is, of course, also general: it must contain possibilities of actualization beyond all number. In this sense, the mind-stuff is a continuum of pure possibility, though this is true in the same way that all continua contain pure possibilities.[189] And this also means that from the mind-stuff alone, it is impossible to predict which possibilities, if any, will be actualized. In a certain sense, anything may happen.[190]

Third, the actualization of these possibilities is the result of acts of will.[191] Since will or energy of action is not identical with feeling, Peirce must be interpreted as holding that will is also an original component of the mind-stuff, for there is no other way it could enter the design. These acts of will are not regulated by habit, for habits are not postulated to exist in the original state, and so are utterly arbitrary and unpredictable. The effect of such acts of will is the actualization of possibilities inherent in the original continuum. These determinations then appear as singularities within the more general continua, but they may themselves be continua of lower dimensionality. Peirce spells this out in one of his discussions of the process of differentiation:

Let the clean blackboard be a sort of diagram of the original vague potentiality, or at any rate of some early stage of its determination. This is something more than a figure of speech; for after all continuity is generality. This blackboard is a continuum of two dimensions, while that which it stands for is a continuum of some indefinite multitude of dimensions. This blackboard is a continuum of possible points; while that is a continuum of possible dimensions of quality, or is a continuum of possible dimensions of a continuum of possible dimensions of quality, or something of that sort. There are no points on this blackboard. There are no dimensions in that continuum. I draw a chalk line on the board. This discontinuity is one of those brute acts by which alone the original vagueness could have made a step towards definiteness. There is a certain element of continuity in this line. Where did this continuity come from? It is nothing but the original continuity of the blackboard which makes everything upon it continuous.[192]

This passage involves three principles of great importance for Peirce's cosmology. First, individuality is relative. A determination may be individual with respect to one dimension but not to others. Thus Peirce defined a dimension as follows:

An element or respect of extension of a logical universe of such a nature that the same term which is individual in one such element of extension is not so in another. Thus, we may consider different persons as individual in one respect, while they may be divisible in respect to time, and in respect to different admissible hypothetical states of things, etc.[193]

Second, a continuum of n dimensions may be regarded as a law governing continua of lower dimensionality actualized within it while it is itself individual with respect to continua of higher dimensionality in which it is embedded. This follows from the fact that an n dimensional continuum embedded in an n + 1 dimensional continuum permits the determination of one variable defining the latter continuum by the n variables of the former—$x_{n+1}=f(x_1 \ldots x_n)$. Hence, for figures of less than n dimensions actualized within this n dimensional hyperspace, possibilities of variation along x_{n+1} are limited by this "law" which would otherwise have been open. So Peirce remarks, "Whatever is real is the law of something less real."[194] Consequently, a law is itself a continuum of feeling, constituting a continuous process whereby certain states of feeling are transformed into others. Third, if a series of singularities occurs within a continuum, Peirce regards it as possible that these singularities may generalize into new continua. Thus he argues,

> Once the line will stay a little after it is marked, another line may be drawn beside it. Very soon our eye persuades us there is a *new* line, the envelope of those others. This rather prettily illustrates the logical process which we may suppose takes place in things, in which the generalizing tendency builds up new habits from chance occurrences. The new curve, although it is new in its distinctive character, yet derives its continuity from the continuity of the blackboard itself.[195]

This principle does not contradict the rule that connection must be a determination of a prior connection, for the elements from which the generalization is made must lie within some higher continuum. If they did not—if they belonged to completely separate hyperspaces—there could be no possible relation among them. The rule of generalization amounts to a law of habit formation whereby a series of chance acts may become regulated under a law. It is this principle which permits the developing system to attain some degree of organization and coherence. For since the actualization of the original potentialities is random, if it were not for this rule the result of the process of differentiation would be the endless random proliferation of increasingly determinate variants with no resulting order or pattern. The rule of habit formation guarantees that these variants will themselves become organized into a coherent structure. It thus plays the part, not of a selector among variants, but of a coordinator and harmonizer of the variants.

The law of habit formation is itself a habit and so a continuum of feeling. Peirce claims that the existence of the law of habit is not a postulate of the cosmology, for the law itself can be regarded as an arbitrary determination of the original mind-stuff.[196] If this claim is granted, then the postulates of the cosmology come down to the initial state of feeling together with energy or will, and the process of determination. This is certainly, as Peirce claimed, an economical base.

Peirce regards his cosmology as a description of the evolution of the universe; does it, in fact, provide such a description? That there are marked analogies between Peirce's doctrine and Darwinian evolution is at once obvious. According to Peirce's theory, the determination of the original continuum is a purely arbitrary or chance process. This fact commits him to the position that chance is objectively real—that there is real indeterminacy or chance in the universe—and this doctrine he called the principle of tychism.[197] The claim that determination is a chance process has clear analogies to the Darwinian process of fortuitous variation: both processes lead to an unpredictable and random proliferation of variants. But Peirce differs sharply from Darwin with respect to natural selection. In the Darwinian theory, the environment imposes a set of conditions relative to which some variants provide better adaptation for survival than others and which, therefore, determine which variants will survive and which will not. But in Peirce's theory, there is no environment of the universe as a whole which can play this role. Whatever is to guide the evolutionary process in Peirce's theory cannot be something independent of the evolving organism itself, for the universe includes all there is. Accordingly, Peirce found Darwin's theory inadequate for his purposes and was forced to seek a different formulation of the evolutionary theory.[198]

The formulation which Peirce adopted he attributed to Lamarck,[199] although the connection is distant. According to Lamarck, every organism strives actively to satisfy its needs through interaction with its environment. In this process, the organism makes differential use of its abilities and members: those most extensively employed will be strengthened by constant exercise, while those little used will tend to atrophy. For any particular organism the variations produced by use or disuse will be slight, but Lamarck supposes these acquired variations to be inheritable so that over many generations the cumulative effects may be very marked. It was particularly the principle of the inheritance of acquired characteristics which commended Lamarck to Peirce, for Peirce regarded such inheritance as being "of the general nature of habit-taking."[200] This statement is not obvious until one recalls that for Peirce matter is mind, so that any enduring change in material form must be regarded as the creation of a habitual connection among acts and feeling-states at a certain point. Thus, as Peirce viewed it, the Lamarckian theory provided a formulation of evolution in which feeling and acts which first occurred as random responses to stimuli become systematized through habit:

Lamarckian evolution is thus evolution by the force of habit.—That sentence slipped off my pen . . . Of course, it is nonsense. Habit is mere inertia, a resting on one's oars, not a propulsion. Now it is energetic projaculation . . . by which in the typical instances of Lamarckian evolution the new elements of form are first created. Habit, however, forces them to take practical shapes, compatible with the structures they affect, and, in the form of heredity and otherwise, gradually replaces the spontaneous energy that sustains them. Thus, habit plays a double part: it serves to establish the new features, and also to bring them into harmony with the general morphology and function of the animals and plants to which they belong.[201]

Moreover, this theory bears a strong analogy to the doubt-belief theory of inquiry. In both, maladjustment to the environment serves as a stimulus to new behaviors through which the organism strives to attain a more satisfactory adjustment, and in both, adjustment takes the form of habits of behavior which are sufficient for need satisfaction. Furthermore, if the principle of the inheritance of acquired characteristics is read as broadly as Peirce read it, it seems clear that beliefs should be inheritable too, and Peirce adopted this idea in his theory of critical common sensism. Peirce maintains that our commonsense beliefs represent an inherited stock of ideas whose adjustive value has been established over many generations, and which have, therefore, become quasi-instinctive. These commonsense beliefs may not be true, and indeed science has shown that many of them are not true—hence our acceptance of them must be critical and they must be evaluated in the light of empirical evidence. Nevertheless, their commonsense character bears witness to the fact that they have proven adjustive in the past and this fact gives them an initial credibility as hypotheses which commands respect.[202]

But the Lamarckian doctrine does not solve Peirce's problem of what guides evolution. For Lamarck, the environment completely controls the course of evolution: the behavior of the individual organism may be purposive, but it is environmental pressure which determines the nature and direction of the adaptation.[203] Actually, the same thing is true of the doubt-belief theory of inquiry: it is doubt which compels inquiry and doubt is produced by the breakdown of the adaptation to the environment. But if there is no environment, as there obviously cannot be for the universe itself, there cannot be any maladjustment, so the Lamarckian theory is inapplicable in such a case. What Peirce's theory still lacks is some factor which can initiate and direct the striving of the organism and which is not external to the mind itself.

Such a factor must be a goal sought by the Universal Mind for reasons intrinsic to the nature of the mind itself. In the *Monist* series, Peirce tried to formulate this concept of evolution as what he called "agapasm," or evolution due to cherishing love.[204]

> The agapastic development of thought is the adoption of certain mental tendencies, not altogether heedlessly, as in tychasm [Darwinian evolution], nor quite blindly by the mere force of circumstances or of logic, as in anancasm [evolution by mechanical necessity], but by an immediate attraction for the idea itself, whose nature is divined before the mind possesses it, by the power of sympathy, that is, by virtue of the continuity of mind . . .[205]

From this description it is clear that the goal of agapasm is sought because of the inherent attractiveness of the goal itself. And recalling Peirce's discussion of

Lamarckian evolution and the role of habit, one might infer that it is the harmony of the resulting order which is the ground of that attractiveness. But in the *Monist* series Peirce did not succeed in defining the nature of his goal, or of agapastic evolution; to do that he found it necessary to introduce the theory of normative science.

Since the universe is ideal, the development of the universe is the development of thought. The cosmology is not only a theory of universal evolution, but a theory of inquiry as well. Just as the goal of evolution is the organization of feeling and will into organized systems governed by increasingly stable habits, so the goal of inquiry according to the doubt-belief theory is the explanation of experience by a stable system of beliefs. The analogy between Lamarckian evolution and the doubt-belief theory of inquiry is not accidental: insofar as the goal of the universe is the fixation of belief, the internal logic of inquiry and the objective logic of evolution are one and the same. Indeed, in an ultimate sense, the possibility of true knowledge rests for Peirce precisely upon the fact that these processes are the same—that the beliefs inquiry forms are the habits of the Universal Mind. If the process by which evolution creates these habits is identical with the process by which we discover these habits, the upshot of evolution must be a world wholly knowable and intelligible to us, for since to be intelligible or have meaning is to be governed by habit, a process of evolution which leads to the rule of habit will create a perfectly reasonable and intelligible world. Thus the same problems which affect the theory of evolution affect inquiry, for it can no more be said that the universe is trying to escape from doubt than that it is trying to adapt to its environment. If there is, then, a goal of evolution intrinsic to the nature of the mind itself, that goal must also be the goal of inquiry. One may, therefore, approach the problem of the goal of evolution by asking, what is the goal of inquiry?

Although it is implicit in the argument of the *Monist* papers that the goal of inquiry, and of evolution, is a good which we ought to seek, Peirce did not explicitly advance the normative theory of inquiry until 1902.[206] There are, Peirce says, three normative sciences—logic, ethics, and aesthetics. Logic is normative because it consists of rules of inference—deductive and synthetic—which one ought to follow if one's aim is to discover the truth. It may be a fact that if these procedures of inquiry are followed the upshot will be the truth, and that all who follow them will, in fact, finally come to agreement, but these facts provide no reason for being logical unless the attainment of truth is accepted as being desirable. Yet logic itself does not provide a reason for choosing truth as a goal—it merely tells us how to reason if truth is our goal.[207] To find a warrant for truth seeking, Peirce held we must turn to ethics. But ethics as Peirce defines it is the science of how we ought to behave to attain our ends, whatever they may be. It thus deals with goal-directed behavior in general, but it provides no warrant for the choice of the particular goals.[208] To find that warrant, Peirce holds, we must look to aesthetics, for aesthetics is the science of what is inherently desirable in and of itself.[209] Peirce's justification for this identification of the good and the beautiful is by no means clear, and is often presented in terms of a very dubious application of the categories: as logic deals with thought and ethics with action, so aesthetics must deal with feeling, for feelings are Firsts, and only Firsts are what they are independently of all else.[210] But this argument does show that for Peirce beauty is a particular kind of feeling which is ultimate and attractive in its own nature. One may be able to specify conditions upon which this feeling ensues or with which it varies, but the feeling itself is ultimately desirable and unanalyzable. Moreover, it is clear that Peirce had at least two good reasons for this position. If any idea is to exert an attraction on the mind by virtue of continuity, then since the continuity is in feeling, the attractiveness of the idea must be felt. Hence that attractiveness must be itself a communicable feeling such as Peirce holds beauty to be. Secondly, Peirce's theory of aesthetics is essentially a coherentist theory. Although beauty in itself cannot be analyzed, yet the maximum beauty is the quality of a perfectly symmetrical or harmonious aggregate.[211] And this fact enables Peirce to define the goal of evolution.

We have seen already that Lamarckian evolution as Peirce describes it should lead first to an ever-increasing proliferation of variants and second to the harmonious ordering of these variants under habits or laws of ever-increasing exactness. Indeed, the limiting state of the cosmos as Peirce describes it should be one of both infinite complexity and perfectly harmonious order under absolutely exact laws. But it is at once evident that according to Peirce's aesthetics, such a state of the cosmos will be one of perfect and infinite beauty. And since the beautiful is the good which we ought to seek, the goal of the World Mind ought to be this limiting state. Thus evolution is guided by a goal intrinsic to the mind, inherently good, yet voluntarily sought because of its attractiveness. Moreover, since inquiry and evolution are one process, this goal is also the perfect fixation of belief or ultimate agreement toward which inquiry aims. The limiting state of infinitely complex but perfect order is also a state of perfect rationality, for in it habit governs everything. Hence all there is will have a perfectly definite meaning, and all meanings will be perfectly realized. Such a state Peirce called "concrete reasonableness,"[212] and its attainment is both our objective and the universe's.

> Under this conception, the ideal of conduct will be to execute our little function in the operation of the creation by giving a hand toward rendering the world more reasonable whenever, as the slang is, it is "up to us" to do so.[213]

We ought to seek truth because by so doing we help the Universal Mind to perfection.

Peirce regarded his cosmology both as highly speculative and as scientific. If it is really scientific, it must do more than simply translate the known results of science into idealistic terms—it must also lead to verifiable consequences which are not derivable from other theories. But from the nature of Peirce's cosmology, it is clear that there are only certain types of consequences to which it can lead. The cosmology cannot, e.g., predict any particular event, nor can any particular law of science be derived from it. For according to the cosmology, the actualization of possibilities is random and unpredictable—hence, what habits will be found cannot be known in advance. Nevertheless, there are certain types of consequences to which the cosmology does lead. First, since the original continuity of the mind-stuff involves innumerable possibilities of determination but affords no basis for predicting which are specified, and since the action of will is arbitrary, determinations must occur which are not subject to law and, therefore, appear to be random or chance variations. The progressive increase in habit will decrease the chance characteristic of the world but never completely eliminate it. Hence it should be true both that there are random events, and that the laws of nature as we know them are not yet fully precise. Both consequences Peirce believed were amply supported. The first is verified by the apparent lack of perfect order in nature and by the continually increasing diversity and complexity of natural phenomena, as evidenced, e.g., in evolution.[214] The second is verified by the phenomenon of errors of observation. No matter how rigorously disturbing influences are controlled, our observations are subject to random fluctuations which can neither be eliminated nor precisely predicted. Such errors may just as well be attributed to objective indeterminacy in the phenomenon observed as to fluctuations in the conditions of observation itself.[215] Second, it is well known that the laws of mechanics are reversible: they are completely indifferent to the direction of time. And since Peirce believed that all materialistic explanations were reducible to explanations in terms of the laws of mechanics, he believed that a materialistic theory was committed to the view that all the laws of nature are reversible. Hence Peirce believed that the presence of such irreversible processes as evolution were strong arguments in favor of his view as opposed to a materialistic alternative.[216] Third, it follows from Peirce's theory that the very laws of nature are becoming ever more exact, since, as habits, the longer they continue without disruption the stronger they become. This is admittedly a difficult claim to test, since standards of observation also change over time, but in theory it is a testable consequence. Fourth, Peirce believed that the materialistic theory could not account for the existence of feeling,[217] and that the dualistic theory—the theory that mind and matter are both irreducible components of reality—could not account for the interaction of mind and matter. On the other hand, Peirce's own theory, since it treats all there is as continuously connected mind, involved no basic discontinuity between mind and matter. And using the vortex model, Peirce actually constructed some elaborate examples to show how ethers of varying degrees of consciousness could act upon each other.[218] These consequences may not be exhaustive of those which Peirce believed followed from his theory—he never enumerated them—but they perhaps suffice to show why he believed a scientific metaphysics possible, and why he thought that his own theory, however vague, still met the test.

If Peirce is right—if, indeed, the cosmology can be regarded as a reasonable hypothesis to explain experience—then his later theory succeeds in establishing most of the doctrines which his early philosophy failed to establish. First, relative to the cosmology, Peirce's categories must be true descriptions of all possible experience. For it is obvious that the elaborate theory of cosmic evolution leads at last to the conclusion that the experience of the World Mind has exactly the same basic structure as our own—a structure generated by the very composition of the World Mind itself. It follows that no future development can ever outdate this categorical scheme. Second, universals are real, not only in the sense of moderate realism, but also in the extreme sense that the objective correlate of the universal is itself a general entity. For the cosmology guarantees that the objective correlate of perceptual generality and continuity is real feeling-continua constituting habits of the World-Mind. And since these habits are real continua, they are general entities containing unactualized possibilities. This is why Peirce called his final system "synechism," or the philosophy of continuity, and claimed that it was a new form of extreme scholastic realism.[219] Third, if the cosmology is true, then in the long run evolution will create a perfectly ordered system of habits which will be at once perfectly intelligible, good, and beautiful. Such a world will be perfectly coherent, and the complete realization of rationality. Fourth, since evolution is also inquiry, the limiting state of the cosmos will also be known, for the Universal Mind is the community. Hence in the long run, the final agreement will be achieved. In the state of concrete reasonableness to which the universe tends, everything will be not only intelligible, but also understood.

This was the system which Peirce strove to build, yet when he died only the general outlines of the system had been worked out—the finer structure remained incomplete. The reason for this was, as Peirce saw it, that he had yet to solve the problem of the logic of continuity. Peirce was convinced that in the concept of continuity he had found the "master key" to philosophy, yet again and again in his late papers he posed the question "How are we to establish a method of reasoning about continuity?" Peirce never solved this question, yet one can see how he thought a solution could be found. In the 1890s Peirce began the construction of a graphic logic which he came to regard as the best of his several logical systems. In the graphs he developed the propositional calculus and the first order functional calculus with identity in essentially their modern form. But he then went on to try to develop a modal logic through which he could deal with possibility, and so with the potentiality involved in the continuum. The modal section of the graphs was never completed, and so the problem of the logic of the continuum was never solved, yet it was entirely characteristic of Peirce's architectonic method that he should have sought in logic a basis for the construction of his system.[220]

Notes—Chapter Ten

1. Paul Weiss, "Charles Sanders Peirce," *Dictionary of American Biography* (New York: Scribner's, 1934), vol. XIV; Max Fisch, "Peirce at the Johns Hopkins University," *Studies in the Philosophy of Charles Sanders Peirce,* ed. Wiener and Young (Cambridge, Mass.: Harvard University Press, 1952), pp. 277-311; Max Fisch, "Was there a Metaphysical Club in Cambridge?" *Studies in the Philosophy of Charles Sanders Peirce,* 2d ser., ed. Moore and Robin (Amherst: University of Massachusetts Press, 1964), pp. 3-32; Victor Lenzen and Robert Multhauf, "Development of Gravity Pendulums in the Nineteenth Century," *U.S. National Museum Bulletin 240: Contributions from the Museum of History and Technology* (Washington: Smithsonian Institution, 1965), pp. 301-47, Murray G. Murphey, *The Development of Peirce's Philosophy* (Cambridge, Mass.: Harvard University Press, 1961), pp. 9-19, 97-105, 291-95.

2. *Immanuel Kant's Critique of Pure Reason,* trans. Norman Kemp Smith (London: Macmillan, 1956), A832f B860f.

3. Charles S. Peirce, Untitled Manuscript, August 21, 1861, p. 42. 920. (The numbers which terminate the citations of the Peirce manuscripts refer to Richard Robin, *Annotated Catalogue of the Papers of Charles S. Peirce* (Amherst: University of Massachusetts Press, 1967).

4. Charles S. Peirce, "Analysis of Creation," p. 1. 1105.

5. *Ibid.,* pp. 1f.

6. Charles S. Peirce, "Why We Can Reason on the Infinite," October 25, 1859. 921.

7. Charles S. Peirce, "Elucidation of the Essay headed 'All Unthought is Thought-of,' " June 30, 1860. 921.

8. Peirce, Untitled Manuscript, August 21, 1861, pp. 43-44. 920.

9. *Ibid.*, pp. 15f.

10. Charles S. Peirce, "The Rules of Logic Logically Deduced," June 23, 1860, p. 6. 743.

11. *Kant's Critique*, A334 B391.

12. Charles S. Peirce, "The Synonyms of the English Language Classed according to their meaning on a definite and stated Philosophy," October 13, 1857. 1141. See also 1137.

13. Charles S. Peirce, "Analysis of Creation," p. 1. 1105.

14. *Ibid.*, pp. 2f.

15. Charles S. Peirce, "New Names and Symbols for Kant's Categories," May 21, 1859. 921.

16. *Kant's Critique*, B110f.

17. *Ibid.*, A344 B402, A415 B443, A571-83 B599-611.

18. Peirce, "New Names and Symbols for Kant's Categories." 921.

19. *Ibid.*

20. Charles S. Peirce, "On Classification," p. 1. 919.

21. Charles S. Peirce, "The Modus of the It," p. 1. 916.

22. Charles S. Peirce, *The Collected Papers of Charles Sanders Peirce*, vols. 1-6, ed. Hartshorne and Weiss (Cambridge, Mass.: Harvard University Press, 1931-35); vols. 7-8, ed. Burks (Cambridge, Mass.: Harvard University Press, 1958), 4.2. References to these volumes will be given in the form of volume number, followed by a decimal point, followed by the paragraph number.

23. Charles S. Peirce, "Logic, Chapter I," pp. 1-2. 720.

24. Murphey, *Development*, p. 56.

25. Charles S. Peirce, "A System of Logic. Chapter I. Syllogism," pp. 2f. 723.

26. Charles S. Peirce, "Distinction between *A Priori* and *A Posteriori*." 744.

27. Immanuel Kant, "Die falsche Spitzfindigkeit der vier Syllogistischen Figuren, 1762," in *Immanuel Kant Werke*, ed. Buchenau (Berlin, 1912), II: 49-65.

28. 2.792-807.

29. Murphey, *Development,* p. 60.

30. Charles S. Peirce, "Logic: 1865-1867." 339.

31. "On a New List of Categories," 1.545-59. For the others see n. 51.

32. Jean Buridan in Moody, *Truth and Consequence in Medieval Logic,* p. 21.

33. 1.547; 5.213ff; Murphey, *Development,* pp. 68ff.

34. 1.547.

35. *Ibid.*

36. Moody, *Truth and Consequence,* p. 22.

37. Murphey, *Development,* p. 90; 2.228.

38. 1.549.

39. Charles S. Peirce, "Grounds of Induction," pp. 3-4. 347.

40. 1.553.

41. Charles S. Peirce, "Logic of Science," chap. 1, p. 6. 769.

42. 1.555f.

43. Charles S. Peirce, "Appendix, No. 2," p. 3. 740.

44. *Ibid.,* p. 5.

45. *Ibid.,* p. 7.

46. 5.253; 5.284.

47. Charles S. Peirce, "Logic of Science," Lecture I, 1866, p. 9. 340.

48. *Ibid.,* p. $5^{1}/4$.

49. *Kant's Critique,* A110.

50. 1.559.

51. "Questions Concerning certain Faculties Claimed for Man," 5.213-63; "Some Consequences of Four Incapacities," 5.264-317; "Grounds of Validity of the Laws of Logic," 5.318-57.

52. 5.265.

53. 5.213.

54. 5.215ff.

55. 5.263.

56. 5.225-49.

57. 5.251.

58. 5.244-53.

59. 5.255.

60. 5.254-57.

61. 5.259ff.

62. 5.267f.

63. 5.282.

64. *Ibid.*

65. 5.299ff.

66. 5.313.

67. *Ibid.*

68. 8.13.

69. 8.15.

70. Charles S. Peirce, "Of Reality," pp. 4-6. 373.

71. Murphey, *Development,* pp. 143-44.

72. 5.312; 8.14.

73. 3.93n1.

74. 5.312.

75. Philotheus Boehner, O.F.M., "The History of the Franciscan School, Part III: Duns Scotus," mimeographed (New York, 1945); remimeographed (Detroit: Duns Scotus College, 1946), pp. 42ff.

76. 5.311.

77. Charles S. Peirce, "Lecture XI," pp. 8ff. 359.

78. *Ibid.*, pp. 22½-23½.

79. 5.313.

80. *Kant's Critique,* A104-10.

81. Charles S. Peirce, "An Unpsychological View of Logic. Chapter I. Definition of Logic," 8th page. 726.

82. 8.12.

83. Murphey, *Development,* pp. 169-70.

84. 5.345.

85. 5.349.

86. 5.353.

87. 3.45-149.

88. 7.354-61; Max Fisch, "Alexander Bain and the Genealogy of Pragmatism," *Journal of the History of Ideas* 15:413-44 (1954).

89. "The Fixation of Belief," 5.358-87; "How to Make Our Ideas Clear," 5.388-410; "The Doctrine of Chances," 2.645-68; "The Probability of Induction," 2.669-93; "The Order of Nature," 6.395-427; "Deduction, Induction, and Hypothesis," 2.619-44.

90. 5.255.

91. 1.551.

92. 8.18.

93. 5.400.

94. 5.402.

95. Fisch, "Alexander Bain," pp. 419ff.

96. 5.370-77.

97. 5.358-87.

98. 5.377-84.

99. 5.384.

100. 2.693.

101. Charles S. Peirce, "Logic. Chapter 4. Of Reality," p. 7. 372.

102. 5.403.

103. Manley Thompson, "The Parodox of Peirce's Realism," in Wiener and Young, *Studies,* p. 138.

104. Murphey, *Development,* pp. 170-71.

105. 5.388-410.

106. 3.359-403.

107. O. H. Mitchell, "On a New Algebra of Logic," *Studies in Logic by Members of the Johns Hopkins University* (Boston: Little, Brown and Co., 1883).

108. 3.363.

109. 2.415.

110. Murphey, *Development,* pp. 299ff, 309ff.

111. *Ibid.,* p. 240.

112. See *ibid.,* chap. 13.

113. Charles S. Peirce, "The Orders of Mathematical Infinite," July 13, 1860. 921.

114. Benjamin Peirce, *An Elementary Treatise of Plane and Solid Geometry* (Boston, 1841), Preface.

115. Bartholomew Price, *A Treatise on Infinitesimal Calculus* (Oxford: University Press, 1857), I: 18ff.

116. 6.113f.

117. Stephen Cole Kleene, *Introduction to Metamathematics* (New York: D. Van Nostrand, 1952), p. 36.

118. Nor did he know of Russell's paradox. Charles S. Peirce, "Mr. Bertrand Russell's Paradox." 818.

119. Murphey, *Development,* pp. 260-62.

120. 4.172; 3.568.

121. 4.198.

122. 4.180.

123. 4.211.

124. 6.185.

125. 4.219.

126. Eric T. Bell, *Men of Mathematics* (New York: Simon and Schuster, 1937), chap. 29; Bertrand Russell, *The Principles of Mathematics* (New York: W. W. Norton, 1950), chap. 42.

127. Arthur Cayley, "Sixth Memoir on Quantics," *The Collected Mathematical Papers of Arthur Cayley* (Cambridge: University Press, 1889), II: 561-92.

128. Eric T. Bell, *The Development of Mathematics* (New York: McGraw-Hill, 1945), chaps. 15, 20; Murphey, *Development,* chap. 8.

129. Johann Benedict Listing, "Der Census räumlicher Complexe," *Abhandlungen der K. Gesellschaft der Wissenschaft zu Göttingen,* 1861, vols. 9-10, pt. II, pp. 97-180.

130. See Murphey, *Development,* chap. 9.

131. 1.276.

132. Carolyn Eisele, "The Charles S. Peirce-Simon Newcomb Correspondence," *Proceedings of the American Philosophical Society* 101:419 (1957).

133. 6.168; 3.569.

134. 1.452; 1.369-78.

135. 1.293.

136. 1.515.

137. 1.363.

138. 1.294-99; 1.280.

139. 2.141; 5.115.

140. 5.568.

141. 5.115ff.

142. 5.157; 5.181; 2.141.

143. 2.197; 1.280; 1.284-88.

144. 1.287.

145. 1.357; 1.425; 1.303.

146. David Hume, *A Treatise of Human Nature* (Oxford: Clarendon Press, 1949), p. 1.

147. 7.543.

148. 1.515.

149. Ralph Barton Perry, *The Thought and Character of William James* (Boston: Little, Brown and Co., 1935), II: 429.

150. Murphey, *Development,* p. 317.

151. 1.337.

152. Charles S. Peirce, "Logic. Chapter I. Common Ground," October 28-31, 1908, pp. 13-15. 611.

153. 6.139; John Boler, *Charles Peirce and Scholastic Realism* (Seattle: University of Washington Press, 1963), pp. 76-78.

154. 5.151-58.

155. 5.115ff; 5.151-58; 5.212.

156. 6.110f; 8.123n20.

157. 6.107-11.

158. 1.354-416.

159. 6.7-34.

160. 1.417-520; 3.427f; 1.180-283.

161. 1.183-202.

162. 1.241-42.

163. "The Architecture of Theories," 6.7-34; "The Doctrine of Necessity Examined," 6.35-65; "The Law of Mind," 6.102-63; "Man's Glassey Essence," 6.238-71; "Evolutionary Love," 6.287-317. See also "Reply to the Necessitarians," 6.588-618.

164. 6.25.

165. 6.24.

166. *Ibid.*

167. 6.264; Murphey, *Development,* pp. 345-46.

168. 6.264.

169. 6.102-63.

170. 6.105ff.

171. 1.375; Jay Wharton Fay, *American Psychology Before William James* (New Brunswick, N.J.: Rutgers University Press), pp. 82, 98.

172. 6.135-42.

173. 6.109-11.

174. 6.132.

175. 6.133-34.

176. 6.246-58.

177. 6.104.

178. 6.133.

179. 6.156.

180. 6.158.

181. 6.162.

182. 6.242; 6.82.

183. Murphey, *Development,* p. 391.

184. Albert Einstein, *Essays in Science* (New York: Philosophical Library, 1934), pp. 40-41.

185. John Theodore Merz, *A History of European Thought in the Nineteenth Century* (London: William Blackwood and Sons, 1923), II: 57-66.

186. 6.264-68.

187. 6.196-98; 6.33.

188. 6.190-91; Murphey, *Development,* pp. 318-19.

189. 6.190ff.

190. 6.217ff.

191. 6.203; 6.205; 1.412f.

192. 6.203.

193. 3.624.

194. 1.487.

195. 6.206.

196. 6.262.

197. 6.47ff; 6.102.

198. 6.296-97; 6.304.

199. 6.299.

200. *Ibid.*

201. 6.300.

202. 5.173; 5.505-25; 7.220.

203. Eiseley, *Darwin's Century,* pp. 48-55.

204. 6.302.

205. 6.307.

206. 1.611f; 2.196ff; Murphey, *Development,* p. 361.

207. 1.611f; 2.198; 5.130f.

208. 1.611f; 2.198; 5.130f.

209. 1.191; 1.612f; 2.199.

210. 5.129; 5.110-14.

211. 1.615; 5.113-14.

212. 5.3.

213. 1.615.

214. 6.553; 6.58-59.

215. 6.46.

216. 6.14; 6.59.

217. 6.264.

218. 7.370-72; 8.122n19.

219. 6.163; Murphey, *Development,* p. 397.

220. J. Jay Zeman, ''Peirce's Graphs—The Continuity Interpretation,'' *Transactions of the Charles S. Peirce Society,* 4:144-154 (1968); J. Jay Zeman, ''The Graphical Logic of C.S.Peirce,''Unpublished Dissertation, University of Chicago, 1964; Don D. Roberts, *The Existential Graphs of Charles S. Peirce* (The Hague: Mouton, 1973).

Chapter Eleven

William James, the Toughminded: An Appraisal

Chapter Eleven

William James, the Toughminded: An Appraisal[1]

That James intended pragmatism as a method to mediate between the tender-minded temperament of the rationalist who goes by principles and is intellectualistic, idealistic, optimistic, free-willist, religious, and dogmatical; and the tough-minded empiricist who goes by facts and is sensationalistic, materialistic, pessimistic, fatalistic, irreligious, and skeptical, is both too explicit in James and too entrenched in tradition to be put in contest here. But the way of a mediator is hard (as James found to his sorrow), for he tends to lapse to one side or the other and his audience contributes their own bias of him (and of course their view of what the sides mean).

Our attempt to see James as a tough-minded philosopher runs into hard sledding, as we know to our sorrow; for it almost goes without saying that James's reputation largely survives as a (tender) "Boston tourist" rather than a "Rocky Mountain" tough. Virtually every Christmas sees *The Varieties of Religious Experience* in ever more deluxe editions go on sale beside Dale Carnegie and *The Prophet,* while at this writing *Some Problems of Philosophy* is unavailable. For the many to whom the name of William James triggers an association with the forced option, the cash value of an idea, the will to believe, the sentiment of rationality, and the stream of consciousness, there is scarcely one who would know the detail and the impact of his analysis of awareness, his struggle with the construction of a single space from the manifold of sensible ones, his account of the a priori, and his contributions to the issues of mind-body, idea-action, relevance, and purposive behavior. Indeed even the two-volume *Psychology* was difficult to come by until the relatively recent Dover edition, while a popular Penguin, comprehensively entitled *William James,*[2] presents a set of psychological and religious excerpts which must have had as its goal to show the archaism of James's *Psychology* and its irrelevance for philosophy. Philosophical selections are seldom more satisfactory and we know of but one which reaches back into the psychology for anything more than the inspirational passages or a few extractions from the account of consciousness and habit.[3]

There is much in James's life to suggest that he was shaping his philosophy in response to personal needs. His father had unorthodox commitments to a relatively unorthodox religion, Swedenborgianism, and as a child James was surrounded by lively discussions of religion. When he came, later on, to edit his father's works, his preface handled the mysticism with considerable sympathy. His father's writings brought him into contact with Transcendentalism, criticism, and belles lettres generally, which were also shared with the family in lively debate. James knew Emerson and his associates through his father, the current literary circles through his brother Henry, and such people as Gertrude Stein and her brother, H. G. Wells, G. K. Chesterton, as well as notables involved in psychic research, on his own. He underscored, almost on principle, the contribution that philosophy made to his rescue from a deep personal crisis: from a deep depression which he saw as despair and panic fear in the face of a deterministic and alien world, he resolved as his first act of free will to believe in free will, and never thereafter abandoned the belief.

The strong suggestion that James belongs to the tender-minded is sustained by a first view of his philosophy. Philosophy is basically a matter of temperament and James, admittedly, hoped to preserve the optimism and the religious in spite of the claims of science. He claimed that he was anti-intellectualistic, and in a dramatic moment he "renounced" logic.

He advocated the strenuous moral life and championed unpopular causes, often less because he believed in them than because he believed in their need to be heard. He strove to change the teaching profession so that education would be a delight, he sought to alert us to the novel and the new. James never ceased to be concerned with the individual's resources and capacities. In the middle of a technical psychological discussion, he discusses how to make resolves effective. He was intrigued by the unsuspected reservoirs of courage and power that transform the weak into heroes in a crisis. He constantly emphasized and warned of the intransigence of small actions in molding habit and character—and this on physiological grounds. He notes the relation between success and aspiration that leaves one man sad because he is the second-best fighter in the world and another puny fellow unperturbed because he "doesn't carry that line" and could be beaten by anyone. Above all, he was trying to make a place for decision and freedom in the making of the future.

But when one sees what uses of logic he renounced and what kind of intellectualism he opposed, the tender appraisal seems less assured. As a matter of fact the case for James as tough-minded in terms of his own dichotomy can plausibly be made in spite of his proclaimed mediational intention. After all *Pragmatism* was dedicated to John Stuart Mill "from whom I first learned the pragmatic openness of mind and whom my fancy likes to picture as our leader were he alive today." While among the last pages that James wrote, in *Some Problems of Philosophy,* he warns that "The author of this volume is weakly endowed on the rationalistic side and his book will show a strong leaning towards empiricism." And this empiricism is of the most radical kind; he is not only unwilling to accept anything save what came from experience, but he also outdid most Empiricists by insisting that the whole of knowledge, from valuation to logical implication, from objective reference to all factors of verification, should have its clear roots in the experiential. After all, the Pragmatism which he brought onto the American scene is a part of that Empirical tradition: James publicized Peirce, even if sometimes to the latter's chagrin, he sustained Dewey's early initiative, he established experimental psychology as an independent part of the curriculum as well as a part of the stock of American philosophy. Above all, he made a firm wedding between the problems of science and those of philosophy which has entered the mainstream of our philosophic tradition and is presently both commonplace and common property. In particular, the verification theory, the ultimate need to test in observation, concern about induction and its justification in the increase of knowledge, and the status of conceptual schemes and constructions, all ally him with current tough-minded discussion. He was struggling with technical problems for which we presently have more powerful resources and vocabulary. Certainly he is somewhat limited in his understanding of "is" and predication generally; he was confessedly weak in mathematics and logic (as Peirce was happy to point out). Still, this confession and Peirce's criticism jointly mask insights into the nature of analytic and formal systems and their relation to interpreted or empirical explanation. And if occasionally he got in over deep in transfinite numbers and mathematical logic, it may be remembered that in those days they were seldom even in the vocabulary of philosophers.

Moreover, we have not mentioned James's long training in the sciences and medicine, his deep involvement with the controversies of evolution, his knowledge of German physiology and physiological psychology. These studies made a claim he could not deny in any of his work, philosophy as well as psychology. And while his philosophy may not have been rooted in the work of such scientists as Poincaré, Duhem, Mach, and Ostwald, yet he was able to generalize their conventionalism, their reference to subjective criteria in the acceptance of a hypothesis, and the part that aesthetics might play in mathematics. Even the testy Peirce, of course, was not without appreciation in the very act of criticism:

> I just have one lingering wish, for your sake and that of the countless minds that, directly or indirectly, you influence. It is that you, if you are not too old, would try to learn to think with more exactitude.
>   If you had a fortnight to spare I believe I could do something for you, . . . I have often, both in my lectures and in my printed papers, pointed out how far higher is the faculty of reasoning from rather inexact ideas than of reasoning from formal definitions; and though I am so bound up in my narrow methods as often to lament that you could not furnish me with the exact forms that I am skilled in dealing with, yet I see myself, with admiration and wonder, how you, nevertheless, come to the right conclusions in most cases, and still more wonderfully how you contrive to impart to audiences as near to the exact truth as they are capable of apprehending. That faculty makes one useful, while I am like a miser who picks up things that *might be* useful to the right person at the right time, but which, in fact, are utterly useless to anybody else, and almost so to himself. What is utility, if it is confined to a single accidental person? Truth is public.[4]

James held some of the strands of empiricism in his hands and gave them a direction and an amplitude that anticipated in an interesting way many of the problems and positions which on today's spectrum are unquestionably called tough. He anticipated and helped forge not only the naturalism of Dewey and Mead, but what in general, through Dewey's influence, became known as American Naturalism. He influenced the diverse kinds of Cambridge pragmatism, especially C. I. Lewis. Wittgenstein is said to have kept as constant company only James's *Psychology* together with the *Principia Mathematica.* Husserl acknowledges his debt to James, and Whitehead regarded his functional analysis of consciousness to be a veritable Copernican revolution. And today he is critical to the growing liaison between philosophy and psychology which is to be found in cognitive studies. Furthermore, James's insights seem to open the way for a tough-minded consideration of problems which have so long been the province of the tender side—valuation and interest, problem-solving and insight, and the philosophic bases of education and action.

However, we do not wish to push James back on one or the other of the horns of *his* dichotomy. What is tough-minded is our appraisal and our category, for we want to reconstruct James in terms of a present reach of his intellectual tools. In doing this we shall accent the continuity between his psychology and his philosophy. The connection is altogether plausible, for it was most unlikely that a man who spent at least twelve years of his life preparing the larger *Principles of Psychology* (1890), then two more in reducing it into a *Briefer Course,* and was, as late as 1899, involved in the brilliant résumé to be found in the *Talks to*

Teachers, would ditch these concerns when he turned to philosophy. Furthermore, he might well assume (and did) a thorough knowledge of the *Psychology* and build on it before any audience that he was likely to confront. As a matter of fact, James's drift from medicine through physiology to psychology seems less a matter of changing than of developing interests.

A more persuasive reason, however, for taking his work to be a whole lies in the coherence of problem and outlook that is then exposed. James draws from evolution and physiology the neurological foundations necessary to account for consciousness, purpose, habit, attention, thought, and action. Radical Empiricism (section 2) extends the theory of consciousness, especially its cognitive function, as laid down in the psychology. Building on the relation that he had early established between percepts and concepts, he analyzes further the problems of selective perception and of alternate conceptual orderings, including their claims to be real. Pragmatism (section 3) continues as a theory of the meaning of "truth," concerned now with the success or warrant of one conceptualization over another, emphasizing the role of test and action (literally verification) and the increase of knowledge as an individual and social enterprise. And the whole apparatus is brought (section 4) to bear on how to face the world in the various endeavors upon which men are engaged, including philosophy.

1. Psychology

The *Principles of Psychology,* all fourteen hundred pages of it, was published in 1890. It had been twelve years in the writing, but more than two decades in the preparing. Although parts of it had earlier appeared as articles, still its impact as a book was enormous and many hold it was the most distinguished and sustained scientific effort of nineteenth-century America. While doubtless this is open to challenge, it was undeniably an important work and marked the end of provincialism in American letters; not since Jonathan Edwards had an American thinker been so widely read in Europe. Uniquely grounded in German philosophy and physiological psychology, as well as in French medicine, James wedded these to British empiricism and to the evolutionary discussions of the day in an unprecedented way. Two years later he published a reduction which "omits all the polemical and historical matter, all the metaphysical discussions, and purely speculative passages, most of the quotations, and . . . (I trust) all the impertinences . . ."[5] In short, most of the things of especial philosophic interest, and as he later wrote, "most of the sense of humor, pathos, illustration, and bibliography." But both the larger work, familiarly called the "James," and the briefer "Jimmy" (as the smaller volume was known) play a significant role in the development of psychology and of philosophy.

In the preface to "Jimmy" he responds to the reproach of his reviewers that the order of the chapters is planless, and unnatural because it was written as a collection of articles; he replies that, though some articles were indeed published in advance, he had never conceived the work as other than a whole. To the other more serious part of their reproach he answered that if they found it unshapely, it must be so; but that the arrangement of the topics was a part of the argument itself, and critical to the innovations he was attempting to provide. The traditional way of approaching psychology from Locke through James Mill and from Fechner through Wundt was to analyze experience into sensible elements first and then build experience and knowledge out of these blocks of sensation. To point is, according to James, that simple sensations are never directly experienced as such but are consequences of discrimination and analysis by philosophers and common men and are postulated in an effort to explain experience. On Locke's account, e.g., or that of the traditional associationists, the taste of lemonade would result from the combination of separate experiences of sweetness, wetness, tartness, and coldness. According to James, this is simply wrong; one has the experience of lemonade first, and only afterward—and with considerable sophistication—are we able to analyze the taste into separate qualities. And even when we fail to isolate the sensation, e.g., the dryness of wine, we can refer to it, nonetheless. If the bias of the associationists is to be avoided, then, James thought it best to begin with the concrete mental experiences with which we are best acquainted—with entire conscious states as they are concretely given to us.

Now the nature and content of consciousness or awareness is a central problem for philosophy generally, but it was particularly urgent also to rework the notion of men's distinctive faculties like reason and will, or their particular talents, like reasoning and willing, in response to the evolutionary challenge and the developing physiology. What slowly emerges from the pages of the *Psychology* (though perhaps not altogether consistently) is no narrow view of human beings and their capacities. In contrast to the passive agent of the British empiricists and the stodgy, limited creature of the German psychologists, James's notion of consciousness emerges with radical (and radiant) difference. It is akin to a romantic or almost-Hegelian view of personality, but on the most sober physiological base. Men are knowers and doers, not simply receivers of stimuli from outside; their doing is relevant to their knowing and their knowing to their doing. Experience is not just the addition of building blocks; it is a dynamic learning, cumulative and self-correcting and, above all, systematic. Human organisms are fabulously wealthy in potential responses. They are selective and adaptive; they pursue ends preferentially, and behave purposively.

Perhaps it may be said in defense of James's critics that he seldom helps the reader to grasp the architecture of this, or as a matter of fact of any other book. But the *Principles of Psychology* has a definite, in fact organic structure which is not too hard to make out. It falls into six parts. The second, pivotal, part is the analysis of stream of consciousness and self-consciousness. Earlier chapters are prefatory and preparatory to it; they clear the field and lay down the ground rules. They state the assumptions about the data of psychology and the relations between body and mind with which psychology as a science must begin. The second part gives a "rough charcoal sketch" of consciousness and mental states—of thinking and thoughts. It is this emphasis on thinking and related "meanings" which exhibits James's close connection with philosophy and which, in a way, separates him from the direction which experimental psychology was later to take. The rest of the book may be regarded as working out the implications of the stream of thought. Thus in the third part he turns to the operations of the mind: to attending and its immediate effects in conceptualizing, in discriminating and comparing, and the associating of ideas. The next three parts follow the general pattern of the reflex arc beginning with sensation and perception, which provide the materials of internal experience, e.g., time, as well as those of external constructions such as the world of objects and the various spaces and times which contain them. A fifth division examines the central part of the arc, the so-called "faculty" of reason, while the sixth part traces the consequences and the function of consciousness in activity, i.e., in impulsive and motor behavior. A final chapter on "Necessary Truths and A Priori Science" is omitted in the *Briefer Course,* doubtless because it is a "metaphysical discussion and a speculative passage": but it serves as a transition between James's psychological concerns and his philosophical ones.

Perhaps a word or two of justification is appropriate for pursuing the first or prefatory material in detail, especially as it makes all kinds of sorties (perhaps distasteful to the contemporary philosopher) into reflex arcs, the physiological base of habit, phrenology, and the behavior of brainless frogs and even guillotined criminals. But it is a mistake to think that much here is philosophically irrelevant. These chapters prepare the way for all the properties which will be predicated of consciousness in the central chapter, and to consciousness and the nature of experience as developed in Radical Empiricism. Further they lay down the commitments for any later discussion of freedom of the will or determinism, and provide simultaneously a somewhat different model for understanding the relation between behavior and feeling or thought. By raising the problem of body-mind in this context, he will at least give respectability to the question of the utility of knowledge and its relation to action which lies at the basis of his Pragmatism.

But to begin in a more orderly fashion. James starts the discussion, boldly enough for his day, with a definition of psychology which is simultaneously a manifesto and a definition of the undertaking. "Psychology is the Science of Mental Life, both of its phenomena and their conditions."[6] Each of these— science, phenomena, and conditions[7]—when amplified, carries a challenge to the reigning psychology, especially in America. It is helpful to comment on each of these at the outset.

To treat psychology as a natural science, of course, was more an innovation in his day than it is in this. His acceptance of the posture as a natural scientist gives him positive and negative benefits. Negatively it gives him leave to be partial and provisional as befitting one science among many others; it excuses him from deciding when there are no adequate grounds for deciding. This of course meant that there were many kinds of scientific problems for which he could present both sides and leave final judgment open. But it also allowed him to suspend judgment on metaphysical issues and to hold that declarations of science on these issues would exceed its evidence. Positively, the scientific attitude allowed him to make assumptions about what constitute the data of a science, which may require defending but which by the nature of the case would not require proof. It is not incumbent upon a science to prove what it accepts as its data. It also left open for him a wider view of what are interesting problems and saved him from prematurely converting generalizations about mental life into causal laws.

This forthright statement that psychology is a science announces his decision to treat of introspective phenomena—i.e., of consciousness, awareness, etc.—as natural events in a natural setting functioning in relation to an environment which they help to create. It might be thought that the appeal to introspection as a method is a first violation of the resolve to be scientific. But James is judicious and alert to the misuses of introspection and to the standard objections. He does not look for causal laws in introspective associations and in any case it must be supplemented by comparative and experimental methods. But introspection, strictly, is scarcely a method at all but rather sets the problem and yields data (*of* but not *in* consciousness) for psychology. Awareness is simply a fact; without phenomenal and introspective reports one necessary term of physiological or physical correlations would always be missing. As Dewey put it: "With William James, introspection means genuine observation of genuine events, events that most persons are too conventional or too literal to note at all, even though the facts lie close to them."[8] The data of psychology, these states of consciousness or awareness, are broadly understood to include thoughts and feelings, volitions, cognitions, desires, sensations, and decisions, or whatever the names these fleeting states of thought go by. The breadth and richness of this definition will have far-reaching consequences for James, especially the inclusion of cognitions, i.e.,knowledge of things whether they be material objects, events, or other minds. This decision, which in effect includes meanings, explains why James's *Psychology* counts also as an epistemology. What is important here is the treatment of the phenomena and their conditions as *natural.*

This commitment pursued wholeheartedly in the context of biological, or better, physiological evolution, he believed, would distinguish his *Psychology* from that of others. In the first place, his concern about functioning and adaptation will distinguish his from the structural psychologies, and his further concern about the biological conditions will mark him off from the more classic philosophic traditions, both Rationalism and Empiricism. Given the variety of conscious phenomena, the Rational Psychologists sought to explain them by appealing to an organizing agent such as the soul, ego, self, spiritual principle, etc., with its faculties of reason, will, memory, and imagination. Apart from the lack of any empirical evidence for such an ego or self, the major criticism is the theory's lack of explanatory power.

The reason we remember, say the rational psychologists, is that we have the faculty of memory. This merely names but does not explain the phenomenon; thus it does not touch the question as to why we forget proper names more quickly than common nouns, nor account for the oddities of our memory. And when rational psychology addresses the question of how conscious states are possible, it fails altogether to tie it to empirical issues.

The traditional empiricists get along well enough without the empirically dubious self or ego, and at least by the time of Hume it has been relegated to one among other impressions. But the empiricists fail too, because, for all their insights into the association of ideas, they leave so much of the phenomena untouched—the effects of drugs, old age, or of emotional context—and provide no clue to the fantastic kaleidoscope of our ideas. Indeed, repetition and reinforcement are not always needed; a single dramatic event, say witnessing an electrocution, can dominate the associations of the rest of a life. They too have ignored that consciousness operates under natural conditions, and this led to the oversight of the patent wholeness of organic behavior and the selective and adaptive responsiveness in that setting. Further, the empiricists do not get to problems of sequential acting and reasoning, nor to the problems of interest, plans, decisions, and rule-directed behavior—nor even to purposive behavior in its weakest form of attention or sense of effort.

James seeks to correct these faults by appealing to evolutionary, biological, and physiological conditions. He thereby adds a new dimension to the empiricists' view, by insisting on their relevance to an account of knowledge. But of course it brings new problems in its wake. For while James is opening up a way to introduce questions of purpose, the function of consciousness, the dynamics of activity and problem solving, he is now faced critically not only with the old problems of how we get ideas but how our motor responses are related to them, how we behave selectively and adaptively to a natural environment to which we contribute. It is a wide problem then, for what he is really asking is what is the relation between consciousness and its conditions, its internal conditions in physiology and its external conditions in evolution.

The internal conditions of mental life are clearly to be found in the body viewed as an organism responding and acting in a natural environment. More narrowly, of course, the proximate condition is the brain, but not functioning in isolation from the nervous system as a whole. An organism may be viewed as a vast system by which stimuli are processed or converted into responses. It is the marvel of this system, viewed purely as a biological entity, that James cannot forget. It is a purposive system, prepared in advance with some native reactions, directed at least toward self-maintenance. Beyond that, the nervous system must be stable enough to allow for habit, but plastic enough to permit learning. Habit, the tendency to repeat a second case with greater ease and precision, is thus advantageous to effective learning. Both habit and learning have a physiological base, and it is here that we must look for causal law. There is a neural basis for every mental phenomenon; in James's language, "there is no psychosis without neurosis." (In this pre-Freudian use, it would not be shocking to find that every neurosis points to a psychosis!) Furthermore, there is no mental modification which is not accompanied by or followed by some bodily change or action. This point will have enormous consequences for James's account of voluntary action, but the major lesson of the physiological base points to the continual change in the developing and adapting organism and the uniqueness of each moment of its life. Of course the relation of psychic states to physiological ones is opaque, but that is only one of a thousand mysteries insensitive to which we go our happy way. We may

> . . . ask ourselves whether, after all, the ascertainment of a blank un-mediated correspondence, term for term, of the succession of states of consciousness with the succession of total brain-processes, be not the simplest psycho-physic formula, and the last word of a psychology which contents itself with verifiable laws, and seeks only to be clear, and to avoid unsafe hypotheses.[9]

A greater mystery must be this fact of awareness or consciousness itself, but evolutionary biology can raise the question of its function. Now the behavior, taken in its fullest sense, of even the most primitive of organisms (and even much of human instinctive and semiautomatic behavior) may be viewed teleologically as appropriate, i.e., as having a utility for self-maintenance in an environment. The nervous system, and in higher organisms the brain, clearly has the critical role in organizing the system's adaptive responses. As we move up the evolutionary scale, i.e., as the nervous system becomes more sophisticated, what may serve as stimuli and the alternatives of response expand incalculably. With this increase reactions become less and less automatic and predictable and more "intelligent." The mark of the latter is to be sought merely in the manner in which, an end being fixed, alternative means or strategies are pressed (created) in the presence of frustrating conditions. Of course this talent is developed most highly in men, for we respond with foresight of means and consequences; future objectives appear now self-consciously to function in their selection. While consciousness may be uniquely the possession of man, still it is continuous with the developing sophistication of intelligent behavior in the animal kingdom generally.

Just where consciousness arises on the evolutionary scale does not matter, since we clearly have it on the human level, and the term may helpfully be left vague, there as well as within human behavior. But consciousness may plausibly be taken to have a function in the evolutionary sense of that term, that it may be just what it appears to be—"an organ added for the sake of steering a nervous system grown too complex to regulate itself."[10] If it is to be effective in its steering, it must be effective as a cause. This is not demonstrable, but with one fell decision James has declared his intention to talk the language of common sense and to postulate a role for decision in determining our beliefs and actions. Thus James in this prefatory material has made his working arrangements with mind-body and mind-action; his account of consciousness will make peace with mind-object.

The point then of the departure for the *Psychology* and the later philosophic theory is a discussion of consciousness (and self-consciousness). Consciousness is a large term and includes sensations, desires, cognitions, reasonings, decisions, volitions. It is just the case that mental states exist, that we think, fear, intend, feel, remember, will have pains, get angry, hold things morally right, see things as ugly, have thoughts and thoughts about thoughts, and can react to our own reactions. The existence of these mental states then is the starting point (most broadly called feelings); the problem is to describe their content and functioning.

Thinking (or thought), James holds, is *changing, continuous, cognitive, selective,* and *personal.* Now what is there about these predicates, to which most of us would now subscribe, that was so new and revolutionary that led Whitehead to consider James as revolutionary a figure as Descartes? James "clears the stage of old paraphernalia, or rather, entirely alters its lighting." Though Whitehead here refers to the discussion in "Does Consciousness Exist?" it is equally appropriate to that of the *Psychology.* Before we get lost in the intricate analysis of these five characteristics, let's briefly indicate the kind of innovation to be expected, although it has already been suggested.

James finds our experience infinitely richer in content than earlier theorists. He reinstates the vague, the peripheral, and finds there the originals of our feelings of relevance, intellectual effort, strain at doing a problem, as well as our sensations of quality and objects. Our experience is richer also in what it can do, in its patterning of perception, and in its ability to construct out of the flux of experience spatial and temporal orders, serial arrangements, and a stable and objective world. Further, these constructions are in some sense options—even his own theory doubtless represents an alternative among explanations. Moreover, our thought is systematic in character, knowledge is cumulative and verifiable, and above all it leads somewhere. There is novelty and discovery as well as corrigibility. And perhaps first among the empiricists, he establishes an intimate relation between knowledge and action. Not only is knowledge for the sake of action, but, because there is a feedback and knowledge is tested in action, the latter is epistemologically relevant.

That consciousness is *personal* means briefly that the self is felt as a peculiar kind of appropriation. "It seems to me as if the elementary psychic fact were not *thought* or *this thought* or *that thought,* but *my thought,* every thought being *owned.* "[11] The personal refers to the warm way we regard experience that we call distinctively our own. Perhaps these comments are sufficient here since the role of the self is developed later in Radical Empiricism in connection with the ways experience is organized and unified.

If we are to share with James his effort to capture the richness and fullness of experience as lived, then a patent feature of our thinking is that it is constant *change*. True to the general emphasis of the nineteenth century that no historical event ever repeats itself and no moment of an individual's history is ever repeated, James argues that no experience is ever identical with any other segment of experience. Clearly this is the case physiologically: since every sensation is related to cerebral action, it would be impossible for a sensation to reoccur identically in a brain which is being modified constantly. Thus the immediate past of a sense organ conditions successive sensation and the particular susceptibility of an organ is created by all of its past. Psychologically speaking, that is to say from the point of view of awareness and thinking, similar considerations pertain. If there is any consciousness at all, it is a sequence of different feelings—of seeing, expecting, loving, and recollecting. Such feelings cannot be explained, as was done by Classic Empiricism, as though sensations were the bricks of experience and identical sensations of redness and hardness, etc., could then be combined. Every new sensation meets an ever-changing context. The kind of sensation required by the earlier theories is never directly felt at all, but is a consequence of a higher order of analysis, and although these units may be of use in explanation, they don't describe experience as experienced.

What holds for sensation is equally true for the larger masses of our thinking, for our complex ideas, topics, and problems. Every thought is unique: we see every fact in a fresh manner and in different relations, for experience is remolding us at every moment and our reaction on every given thing is a resultant of our whole experience at that moment. The scale sung up is different from the scale sung down, thunder succeeding thunder is different from thunder succeeding silence; the presence of certain lines in a paper will change the apparent form and quality of other lines; and in music, most clearly of all, any second note is different from a first note by virtue of being second, while the sounds of chords are almost altogether contextual.

The movement and change of experience mean that it is unstable, but such instability is an advantage, for by it knowledge can increase in more than an additive way. Later, *Pragmatism* makes full use of this instability to explain the growth both of the individual's abundant experience and of science as well, for instability makes for responsiveness to the new and to the pressure of the past in remolding the present and preparing for the future. The emphasis on the change and flux of sensation has another advantage over preceding theories since it is more faithful to experience. The green of the grass in the shade is sensibly different from the green of the grass in the sun. Clearly James is storing up for himself here a serious problem since he now has to account for the claim that it is the "same" green in spite of the fact that a painter would use different colors. In a way this is Heraclitus's problem *in extremis;* but whereas Heraclitus had said, "No man steps into the same river twice," James would have had to add that it isn't the "same" man and then to explain why we generally take him to be so. Locke had had no need to face this problem because he supposed that the sensation of green was always the same and hence recognizable. But James is confronted with the problem of explaining what is stable in experience that allows us to reidentify its segments. His starting point is that we seldom do attend to our sensations as the unique and subjective facts they are; rather we use them as signs to clue us in to an objective and stable order.

Not only is our thinking in change, but the change is sensibly *continuous*. The classic image of a train of ideas is misleading when it suggests a succession of separate, boxcar, atomic mental states. There are neither lapses in time nor breaks in quality. Of course a man may sleep, faint, or be knocked insensible, but such gaps are not registered as breaks in personal identity, which has a felt continuity of its own. The metaphor for which James is famous is rather that of a river or stream of thought. To extend James's image rather considerably, the river not only flows at different rates, now quickly and now slowly, it also widens and narrows, and even under a given bridge the water flows differentially in eddies and currents.

In usual Jamesean fashion the metaphor changes abruptly, for the stream of thought has its flights and perchings. The perchings, or substantive and stable parts, correspond to sensory images—to conceptions and to other items which can be held before the mind; these are generally represented by the nouns in a language. Such labeled items loom large in experience as events and objects. But there are other experiences equally felt which often go unlabeled and overlooked. These are the flights or transitive parts—feelings of tendency, direction, and activity. They are interstitial and lead from one substantive phase to another. If we look to language to help us catch these feelings, we should have to search among the prepositions, adverbial phrases, syntactic forms, and inflections of the voice. As was just said, these feelings of tendency help movement from one substantive part of the stream to others and without them the particular meaning of a sentence would evaporate. It is a point which James never tires of making, that we ought to speak of feelings of "nextness," "andness," and "ifness" no less than feelings of coldness and redness.

There are other modifications of our feelings, also unnamed, which go unrecognized. Wait! Hark! and Look! each arouse very different expectancies and are felt in distinctive ways, yet there is no name which distinguishes between them. In like manner, we can only say that we've forgotten a name or forgotten a verse, as if all forgetting of names or of verses were the same. In the particular case often more is going on; a sign is that we can reject "Smith," or "Brown," as incorrect without knowing the right name. And even when we can't recall a forgotten verse, the rhythm sometimes virtually dances on our tongue. And then again, there is the felt difference between interrogatives and declaratives, between the different skeletons of logical relations, between the use of "man" to intend an individual or to intend humanity. Such feelings of tendency, and unnamed feelings of relation generally, are quite as genuine parts of experience as are any properly labeled substantive state. They constitute a halo or psychic fringe—omnipresent accompaniments to the grosser furniture of experience.

The examples of logical form suggest that even reasoning processes in their most antiseptic form have their fringe of feelings. In all voluntary thinking there is an accompanying feeling of focus and interest; when this interest is well developed it may be a topic or a problem. But there is always a feeling of appropriateness or of irrelevance to an argument. The sense of direction in our thought, too, is a perfectly definite feeling. Sometimes our sense of rationality is negative, and when a discourse satisfies all grammatical rules, we may be lulled into accepting nonsense as sense. For example in greeting one's hostess, the most ridiculous statement may pass as a salutation if only it is intoned properly. (James suggests that the only reason English Hegelian nonsense passes is because it satisfies these grammatical demands.) However, our sense of rationality is usually more reliable, but in any case a most important part of the fringe is the relevancy and rightness or wrongness felt in the direction of our thought.

Now the difference between James's theory and the orthodox empirical analysis of experience begins to emerge. As long as James just emphasizes the subtleties and variety of felt experience he has only enlarged the data with which empiricism had previously worked. Of course he has raised the question of the *same* or *stable* in experience in a new context; but even this does not alter his basic orientation in empiricism. However, by pointing to the constructive function of thinking, by adding the feltness of rational processes, and by intertwining the rational and cognitive with the sensibly experienced, he is starting out on a new line.

To emphasize the point further, the intention to speak or to say something before one has said it is an entirely definite and cognitive awareness; the anticipatory intention is there for a moment, initiating the sentence; but as the words succeed one another "it welcomes them successively and calls them right if they agree with it." Further, the sense of conclusion, of the termination of a sentence or an argument is itself a part of experience and is totally different from just stopping.

Indeed meaning could not lie in the substantive terms alone (the apparent consequence of earlier empiricism). We could never solve problems on Hume's psychology, nor use strategies: we could scarcely restate the sense of a novel or a paragraph without simply repeating the same words. Meaning and understanding, therefore, are not functions just of the substantive parts of experience, but of experience as a whole, which includes the transitive parts as well—the parts that carry us along or lead somewhere. Even a sentence such as "Columbus discovered America in 1492" is not about the substantive kernels "Columbus" or "America," or even the "discovery of America." They are at best the topic of thought. Its object is the entire content or deliverance.

> Nothing but this can possibly name its delicate idiosyncrasy. And if we wish to *feel* that idiosyncrasy we must reproduce the thought as it was uttered, with every word fringed and the whole sentence bathed in that original halo of obscure relations, which, like an horizon, then spread about its meaning.[12]

Again, thinking is *cognitive;* it has the function of knowing. It is always about something—a topic or an object, an event, or about one's self or other thoughts.

We believe that our thoughts refer to something, mean something: i.e., that they claim objective reference. For James, at least as a psychologist, what is at stake here is not the truth of the claim but just the fact that we make it, that we believe in an external world having an existence outside human thought. Doubtless we should never have made this claim to an independent reality did we not suppose that we meet the same object constantly and suppose that other people's objects are the same as ours. The talent for identifying the same object, of course, is fundamental to the construction of a stable world or worlds; but the point of larger importance here is that we construct this world out of alternatives. Thus, to repeat, that we believe in an external world depends on the fact that we believe we can refer to and mean the same things repeatedly. We do not passively respond to external stimuli, but are actively constructing the world out of various possibilities. This capacity to select is another of the characteristics of the stream of thought: it is pervasive and characterizes not only our thinking but our willing and our doing as well.

We do not receive all that bombards our senses; too much is potentially presented. The sensory organs are themselves *selective,* but there is even further selection from what is received by them. Clearly we can narrow our focus and attend only to some sensations, suppressing the rest. We are almost wholly unaware of blind spots or marginal changes of color, and the boxer scarcely notices the pain of his opponent's blows during the fight. Generally we attend to present sensations which are signs of things. We promote certain groups of sensations into objects, and assign a preference to some of them as true representations of these things. Thus a tabletop is square, and a penny round—despite the fact that such things are seldom experienced in just this way. Out of simultaneous possibilities, then, consciousness carves out objects of interest, selecting and rejecting all the while. This again is important to the increase of knowledge. The language that we use always reflects its remote ancestry. Perhaps it might have been different if earlier cuts of experience had been made along different lines. The language of common sense preserves the history of our successful experiences in its categories, the most fundamental of which are those of thing and object, of what is mine and what is another's, of what is subjective and what is objective. Such distinctions might well have been made otherwise; they are always open to review and recasting, though it is unlikely that we shall ever desert our commonsense terms for everyday use. But our physical science is always engaged in drastic alteration, and philosophy and psychology ought to be equally open-minded.

The selectivity of consciousness does not apply just to what is empirically sensed but also to reasoning, to the connecting of ideas. Reasoning depends on our ability to break up the totality of phenomena and to select what will meet the situation—*reasons,* if the need is theoretical, and *means,* if it is practical. Even a work of art is but an example of selective construction, not unlike our prosaic constructions of the table as square. In ethics, matters of choice and construction are even more obvious: "The problem with the man is less what act he shall now choose to do, than what being he shall now resolve to become." In summary, James writes:

> . . . the mind is at every stage a theatre of simultaneous possibilities. Consciousness consists in the comparison of these with each other, the selection of some, and the suppression of the rest by the reinforcing and inhibiting agency of attention . . . The mind, in short, works on the data it receives very much as a sculptor works on his block of stone. In a sense the statue stood there from eternity. But there were a thousand different ones beside it, and the sculptor alone is to thank for having extricated this one from the rest . . . Other sculptors, other statues from the same stone! Other minds, other worlds from the same monotonous and inexpressive chaos! My world is but one in a million alike embedded, alike real to those who may abstract them. How different must be the worlds in the consciousness of ant, cuttlefish, or crab![13]

At the risk of redundancy, the point about attention and selectivity may be made again in a slightly different way, because it explains why James rejected the traditional analysis that began with atomic sensations. Strictly speaking, there are not any raw and unstructured sensations (they are consequences of sophisticated discriminations by both common sense and philosophy). We never just see, but "see-as" in patterns and with emphases. Indeed, it is just this organizing even at the perceptual level that enables us to grasp as much detail as we do. For example, we make "tick-tocks" out of a clock's "equal" beats (and can change the tock to tick) or a rhythm out of a series of equivalent notes; by such grouping we increase the span of attention. If we did not ignore, focus, abstract, and cut into experience (in a word respond and attend selectively to some aspects rather than others of a series), we should never be able to respond at all to the overwhelming variety of sensory stimuli and to the uniqueness of each lived moment. We should never be able to respond by principles or rules or in ways learned from other experiences; we could not notice the *same* tree or the same *kinds* of trees, nor then make judgments about them. We could not begin to think about the *same* problem and attack *it* in various ways. The necessity for limiting and focusing our responses forces us to exchange the variety of the perceptual for a more restricted conceptual order of relative stability. Yet even so, we create the worlds of our experience—these conceptual orders—out of larger possibilities according to our interests. If we are hungry, the grapefruit there will generally become a sign of food; but if we are sated, it may become a lovely patch of yellow against the brown of the bowl and the turquoise of the wall. An architect and a businessman will walk down the same street and give different descriptions of it. Attention effects a dynamic construction of our theoretical as well as our practical life; it affects the way we perceive the present and thus the shape of all that we shall experience in the future.

Nowhere is our selective attention more obvious than in language. We do not hear in separate sounds, nor read in letters, but in full words and groups of words; the silences and cadences play a full role in our listening and reading. Language determines also much of further perception and of scientific knowledge generally. We have little eye for what we have not been taught to discern; the only things which we commonly see are those that we preperceive—and we preperceive only what has been labeled for us. "Without our stock of labels we should be intellectually lost . . ." Even novelty must be knitted into the things of which we have preperceptions and labels.

The features of consciousness we have been discussing are not to be thought of as independent of one another. And as is obvious, they are also dynamic and function to lead to further thought and to action. In the Lockean tradition that then prevailed, once having considered the (static) elements of experience, it next proceeded to the operations of the mind—combining, comparing, abstracting, using association as the explanatory device. But James's version of the processing of experience must be different since consciousness has activity already built in. Thus his discussion of operations is largely commentary and extension of the capacities already laid down, especially those dealing with the cognitive or referential and the selective attention.

There are three cooperating capacities which organize experience and help translate the perceptual into the conceptual. We have already noted the most obvious, the ability to conceptualize, that is to cut into sensible experience in such a way as to identify and later to recognize or to mean the *same* thing. James calls this the "principle of constancy in the mind's meaning." We further clearly discriminate (i.e., attend discriminatively) and order experiences in simple comparisons and in series. Coordinately with such analytic orderings of sensible modalities in linear series, there is association—the uniting of sensations into objects and the connecting of what has been discriminated into successions of thought.

Our sense of sameness, as mentioned above, is the very backbone of our thinking; the awareness both of personal identity and of other objects depends upon it. Conception names the way attention singles out and identifies some part of the perceptual flow and makes a subject of discourse and allows reidentification. A conception is properly "neither the mental state nor what the state signifies, but the relation between the two, namely the function of the mental state in signifying just that particular thing."[14] "A polyp would be a conceptual thinker if a feeling of 'Hollo! thingumbob again!' ever flitted through its mind."[15] Without the sense of sameness, the world could be orderly and we should not know it, and with it the world could be chaotic and we should structure it.

Now conceptions can be of virtually anything, of events, of qualities of things, even of mere *thises*. But a conception is what it is; it is unchangeable and cannot develop into something else. The white paper may turn yellow without the conception of whiteness changing at all. Even where the topic is a problem and we are aware only of some of the conditions which the answer must meet, and even when we are learning more of these conditions, we must know it to be the same problem in order to recognize any solution as correct for that problem.

But if conceptions, like definitions in a given context, cannot be altered or corrected, they can be replaced by more adequate ones. This replacement also contributes to a topic's development and the increase of knowledge. Where knowledge grows through empirical discovery, it is through the continued exposure to things with their power to impress our senses constantly with new sensations. Similarly the conceptual develops by replacement and discarding, and by insight into new connections. Though new conceptions may arise in various ways, from new sensations, comparisons, emotions, movements, and the like, still each new conception is carved by attention out of the continuum of felt experience and provisionally isolated to become a topic of discourse. These new conceptions have ways of suggesting other parts of the continuum from which they were taken. Sometimes it is a matter of mere association, but sometimes it is rather like an invitation to be inventive with the materials—to make new cleavages and new groupings. Thus higher-ordered conceptions arise, and incompatibilities and new relations between conceptions are exposed. New truth, then, affirms a relation between an original subject and a new subject conceived at a later moment. Conceptions weave essentially changeless and discontinuous systems which translate the flux of perceptual experience, the data arising from sensations, into entirely different orders, those of a conceived world or worlds.

Sameness, thus, is a characteristic of meanings and not a characteristic of the objects meant. Consistently with the analysis of the continuous change of consciousness, thought is unified though it may be of a multiplicity of objects and relations. True enough we do not get the same sensation twice; what we do get twice over is the same object. The conceptual grass *is* the same green in the sun as in the shade. Things may be discrete without the thought of them being so; conceptual time may have boundaries. We ignore the variety of phenomenal experience if it clues us in to a stable external order; it is not the sensible flux but the relations which are stable. An "identical" or "same" object always experientially is presented in new company since our reaction at any given moment is a resultant of our experience of the whole world to date.

But we not only construct our world, we "fix" it, so to speak, by our cognitive claim for its objective reference. Questions of validity apart, that we make such objective claims, believe things are really out there, believe there is an orderly world such that today's experiences may be reliably projected (reliably enough, i.e., to support successful decisions for action) is itself no less a matter of fact for James than it was for Hume. There are even real mirror-images, real neuroses, and even real hallucinations in appropriate contexts. This discussion of conception sets both the problems and the resources for James's later discussion of reality which in its turn introduces the discussion of truth. The whole account of the real, of objective reference or "pointing to," must take place in experience and between experiences; even the need and the substance of truth must also arise in experience as a matter of successful or satisfactory pointings to or leadings.

Considerations such as these rule out for James's later philosophy any straightforward or simple correspondence theory of truth. Since awareness is not limited to imaged thought, and the fringe and relations are always as relevant and as experienced as the focus, any naive realism that relates idea to object is also ruled out. More importantly the constructive, changing, and cumulative character of knowledge—its forward and anticipatory reference—rules out any realistic epistemology, at least as ordinarily taken.

The search for a stable world is only a part of the story. In the first place, we are doomed to disappointment, for despite such spectacular achievements as the public world of commonsense objects, of a single sensory space from the multiplicity of sensory spaces, etc., we never truly get all the pieces of the kaleidoscope into a single unified world—at least not for long. Indeed, we never get it permanently into a single world at all and are left with more-or-less effective worlds of common sense, of morals, of physics, law, art, play, and fiction, each subserving particular interests. Even those worlds cannot stay put for long before the bombardment of ever-new sensory experience, of the reappraisals of the logic of our experience, and of the interest and purposes which are ever arising out of our new needs and our newly understood old needs.

Such plasticity and open texture, far from being a disaster, are a boon; for in company with the ability to construct permanent features we have an almost limitless ability to make further and new discriminations. This opens the way to the possibility and the need for the expansion of experience. We work two ways, synthesizing and analyzing. Such notions as red, sweet, etc., are not given as originals in experience but are only available by analysis. The taste of lemonade is perceived as a whole out of which we learn afterward to pull the sweetness, the tartness, etc. In truth we can scarcely abstract any quality which does not elsewhere have a setting among other associates. If tartness and sweetness were always joined, we should likely not separate them, although we may isolate and arrange a comparative series and even project an idea limit for a quality like the dryness of wine which we never experience alone. Of course, discrimination may often be involuntary. If a white billiard ball is presented with an egg, the shape will likely shake out as a difference; if presented with a tennis ball, then probably the texture; and if the white billiard ball is presented with a red one, then in all probability the color. Discrimination depends on a felt difference in experience; likewise, similarity depends upon an experienced likeness. Felt likenesses and unlikenesses, then, are original relations rooted in experience and are both susceptible of degree. Even the most remote of inferred similarities and unlikenesses must have their feet ultimately in direct experience.

But the capacity to discriminate does not just stop here. We also compare and order discriminations in roughly linear series. Doubtless some series are constructed by simple addition—one object may simply have an added quality that another one lacks in comparison. But James holds that not all differences in quality, at least psychologically speaking, are differences in quantity. A merely additive theory might be adequate if all differences were felt in the same direction—if carpets always got darker as they got richer in pile, or if decreasing pitch were always associated with increasing loudness. Unfortunately for the neatness of experience, carpets may differ in pile, color, and roughness, and tones in pitch, loudness, and timbre, along divergent lines. In fact, everything could be compared with everything else since the directions of differences are indefinitely great. In short, the linear modalities intersect and crisscross in fantastic ways and we have labeled only a very few. We thus travel through the world discovering likenesses in the different and differences in the like. The discernment of these degrees is an ultimate cognitive power and the notion of identity or absolute sameness, as well as that of absolute difference, are but conceptual and ideal projections of termini of the continua or orderings.

Set down thus in the middle of the course we can move in either direction toward analysis or toward synthesis. Such options, together with choices among discriminations and their continua, and among objects, relations, external worlds, and selves, only further illustrate the selectivity and the adaptiveness for which biological and evolutionary grounds were laid earlier. Selective interest and preference appear on every level from the more-or-less involuntary notice of figures against backgrounds, patterns of rhythm, etc., to the sustained preferences found in the voluntary pursuit of interest, problem, plan, or strategy. Nowhere is selective attention more obvious than in association, especially in guided or goal-oriented sequences of reasoning. Classically the theory of the association of ideas had been largely an effort to determine the rules by which ideas succeed one another. By the time of Hume, the most commonly accepted rules were those of contiguity, similarity, and cause and effect. James clarifies an ambiguity resident in the problem. The rules sought concern not the order of our thoughts, but the order of the things thought of. The ranging and flights of our thinking and thought processes could scarcely ever be accurately described. Classic writers had often thought that they had discovered the laws of the generation of thoughts, and had supposed they were giving causal laws; but, as James says, the associative rules are but generalized descriptions about the ways in which the objects of succeeding thoughts are related. The only causal laws are those to be sought in the physiology of brain processes and neural habit.

The problem is not how to start the flow of traffic along paths established in experience, for that is already a given for James. The serious question now lies in the nature of traffic signals, especially in those reasoned sequences which involve solution seeking, or mediated inference. We share with animals that kind of behavior that joins the sign and the thing signified immediately. The sound of the bell may signal the Good Humor Man; a particular clearing of the professor's throat signal the end of the lecture; or a red moon, a warm day to follow. The successes of this sort of learning depend on the richness and rich use of past experiences, and when achieved to a high degree is *wisdom*—the mature wisdom say of a judge. On the whole, however, this kind of wisdom is conservative and reflects the widest uses of classifications that have already been established.

In the assimilation of all impressions we seek to accept the new as mere addition to the old with a minimum of jar. Thus a child may assimilate a new experience of ferns by identifying them as green feathers. Nowhere is the conservative tendency clearer than in the way we address the new with the labels which we already have; as noted above, we tend to perceive what we preperceive, and we preperceive mainly that for which we have ready-made labels. A great deal lies thus not only in the stock of names we have, but also upon the appropriate choice. "What's in a name?" Virtually everything from the legitimacy of American policy in Vietnam ("a civil war" or "an invasion from the north") to the appropriate labeling of an area as a "slum" (marked for clearance) or an "impoverished neighborhood" (marked for redevelopment). But contentment with old labels of any sort leads us often to ignore what is genuinely foreign and novel to our experience.

Beyond wisdom (in the sense specified), there is reasoning or mediated inference: some "essential" quality of an empirical concrete is seized upon to represent or to substitute for the whole. Such qualities have associates not connected with the original and carry us far beyond it. This abstracting is amenable to no rules—it involves genius of a sort and is a major source of novelty. A power and scope to knowledge are thus achieved by these reasoned thought sequences which mere association by contiguity could never give. The abstracted qualities are general, having many and familiar associates, and thus give the reach into broader experience. On the other hand, the properties of the abstracted quality, its consequences, relations, etc., are fewer and are therefore more obvious. This kind of reasoning characterizes the most trivial cases, like fixing a doorjamb, to the most sophisticated science. "The reason why physics grows more deductive the more the fundamental properties it assumes are of a mathematical sort . . . is that the immediate consequences of these notions are so few that we can survey them all at once and promptly pick out those which concern us."[16]

Perhaps an illustration would help. Consider a concrete experience of vermilion; it is a dye, a red color, a marketable item, an import from China, mercuric sulfate. It is all of these and many more. There are countless other classifications and as experience increases there will be many other appropriate labels. To know it completely would, at least theoretically, require completed knowledge. To seize on any one of these is, in a way, to mutilate the experience; but the only way we can deal with it at all is to deal with it abstractly, choosing some properties at the expense of others. But no property is essential; it becomes essential because it was chosen for some interest or purpose. If it is an appropriate way of conceiving the object at all, it is equally true with all other ways. Even the naming is but a selection of an ordinarily useful way of handling the object. Thus water is not more truly H_2O than a thirst quencher; indeed it is no more proper to say that water is nothing but H_2O than it is to say that H_2O is nothing but water. Our classifications, or names in general, reflect settled ways of looking at things—they prepare us for what to see, and largely determine what we do see. The individual's own language and his linguistic community thus cooperate to make the world in which he lives. Yet at any moment we may take hold by a less familiar handle which may open up a host of new relations. This way of discovery and insight is a distinctively human way of learning. Man alone has the deliberate intention to apply signs to everything and to generalize and systematize their use. The development of knowledge, science, society, and even ethics and aesthetics rest on this base.

Association comes to have a larger meaning for James, summarizing the consequences of our capacity to attend selectively from conception and discrimination to association in the narrow sense. This broader sense of association is the virtual equivalent of apperception or assimilation; it is the full account of the manner in which we receive a thing into our minds, a kind of fusion of the new with the old factors in which it is impossible to distinguish the share of either. Clearly the things which a given experience suggests to an individual will depend upon the nature and stock of ideas that he already had, in other words his character, habits, memory, education, previous experience, and momentary mood. It includes all recognition, classing, naming, and perceptive and apperceptive process generally. It is this sense of association that provides a bridge between James's psychology, his metaphysics, especially insofar as it has to do with the cognitive, and his theory of verification and truth.

It is clear that as the experiential base and the operations of the mind are enriched, say in contrast to Locke's account, a responsive complexity is needed in the account of how we acquire knowledge. Indeed, a new view of knowledge itself as tentative and corrigible is called for. The problem has become one of education in its broadest sense—i.e., of acquiring conceptions and perceptual sensibilities which will be adequate both to meet new situations and to assess and reassess what these new situations will be. James can no longer be content with accounting for how knowledge accumulates merely but he must also be concerned with the uses of past experience, with their adequacy before continual need of adaptation and with the mechanism of self-criticism and reappraisal. Viewing the problem thus it is clear that James has built into his account of knowledge the normative and the corrective, with emphasis now on the problem of how we acquire new ideas.

By the end of volume one James had made his point—had challenged the philosophic-psychological establishment both by substance and arrangement. From now on he seems content to handle a host of problems in the more orthodox framework of the reflex arc: the input by way of sensation and perception, the central processing and the motor output. Insofar as this is another way of organizing the material, it rather fills in and enlarges much that is already before us. Thus the functional status of consciousness, perception, and sensation is stressed as well as such constructive achievements as a single conceptual space and time from various sensorial ones, and a commonsense real world in preference to other possible worlds. However, the account of movement is fresh, and since belief leads into this by its relation to activity and motor output, we shall consider belief first.

As an empiricist James holds that all knowledge has its origin in sensible experience. What James now adds is the insistence that knowledge must be tested in a return to sensible experience as well. Psychologically, this means that he must account for behavior and activity; but philosophically, this means that there is a strong mutual relation between action and knowledge, that doing and testing have an epistemic status, which of course is a tenet of pragmatism generally.

Belief is the function of cognizing reality. It is a psychic attitude toward a proposition involving acquiescence or consent, which, as in Hume's *Treatise,* is allied with the emotional. There are degrees of belief and its opposite is not disbelief, but doubt and inquiry. The sense that anything we think is unreal can only come when that thing is contradicted by something else we believe, when something inadmissible is said about it. Then there is a choice of what to believe. We may stand by the present perception, or by the old. Propositions are believed through the very act of being conceived unless they clash with other propositions believed at the same time about the same thing. Generally we do not count as existents what we have discarded and labeled errors, fancies, or dreams, though as fancies and dreams they have their role in the world. "The complete philosopher is he who seeks not only to assign to every given object of his thought its right place in one or other of these sub-worlds, but he also seeks to determine the relation of each sub-world to the others in the total world which *is.* "17

Among these subworlds is the world of common sense, of physical objects as we actually take them, of empirical science, and the world of ideal relations (literature and mathematics). Each world is real after its own fashion while it is attended to. We do have a commitment to a basic world, that of common sense. It results from dominant habits of attention and, in effect, we elect it from among alternates. An object may appear to us, but this is not sufficient to call it real; it must additionally be interesting and important. Thus the real world, reality, means simply a relation to our own emotional and active life. In the long run, the origin of all reality is subjective. A whole system may be real if we turn to it with a will—if it hangs together with one stinging, immediate experience. Our own reality, then, the sense of our own life, which we possess at every moment, is the ultimate ground of belief. Whatever has continuous connection with it, we can't help but believe.

We believe as much as we can; when objects are presented unsystematically, they conflict but little. As objects, however, become permanent and their relations fixed, we note discrepancies and feel contradictions. We must settle among these in some stable and rulelike way. Generally, the ability of a contradicted object to maintain itself is related to its liveliness and its frequency. However, even lively and frequent objects may be discarded if they contradict other lively and frequent objects. A conceived thing, say a vision, may be deemed more real than a vivid sensible thing if it in its turn is related to more interesting or vivid sensible things. Under any circumstances, for a conception to prevail it must terminate in the world of orderly, sensible experiences. This is what scientific verification requires. Sensible objects are thus either realities or the tests of our realities when once the connecting and conflicting have begun.

A necessary condition for believing that any conceptual system is true of the world is a belief that it denotes actual objects of that world. That system will be preferred which is *richest* in sensible objects, i.e., includes most of the facts of sense; simplest, by being deducible from the smallest number of primitives; and systematic or organized. Objects of will and of belief then differ only in the manner of our attending them.

We come finally to the efferent processes, to the study of movement and activity. Activity as such scarcely needs explaining, for from the start the organism may be viewed as a mechanism for converting input into output. Every impression (sensation, perception, idea, memory, image, etc.) carries with it impulsive tendencies, and the intellectual part is knit up with the middle or central part of the process. We are richly endowed with native reactions, and all that we can ever do is rooted in these original responses. We find it natural to smile when we are pleased, to reach toward a light, to pull back when pained, to follow movement with the eye and head, to inhale when afraid, to duck when something is thrown at us. But these impulses are not blind after their first occurrence; they will always be modified each successive time by the outcomes associated with the earlier behavior. And as importantly, they never occur without the presence of other supportive and inhibitory responses also asking for expression. It is thus that our behavior becomes increasingly more complex.

James can treat emotions and instincts as variations on the single theme of impulse. Instincts and emotions both have been separated and categorized. James himself lists twenty-seven of them, but he does not take this list seriously, for it could be as broad as a full repertory of responses, including those which appear at later stages of maturity. The critical point is that we have such original responses and that they are modified in experience. Instinct and emotion—at least the coarser ones—are only arbitrarily separated. Shall we call anger or fear an instinct or an emotion? One way of classifying them is simply whether the impulse terminates in commerce with the world or inside our bodies.

With the discussion of impulsive behavior, James is getting a running start on that problem which more than any other single issue tormented him during his whole life, viz., the question of free agency. He has already ample resources to approach the problem; the ideomotor connections and the reflex arc, the wealth of native reactions which are originally spontaneous but quickly modified and educated in experience, and the selective character of all organic behavior (perception as well as response). Voluntary activity thus takes its place on a continuum of instinct and emotions; indeed in a larger sense volition is the entire capacity for active life. But in the narrow sense, voluntary behavior is limited to those actions which cannot be inattentively performed and which are generally attended by a feeling of resolve, fiat, or effort. (As we now know what was once regarded as involuntary may be pushed back in such phenomena as learned control of autonomic functions such as heartbeat and blood pressure.)

Intelligent behavior is more than merely adaptive behavior. The crux lies in the relation between knowledge and purposive or intentional action. Selectivity has already been built into attention, interest, intention, and the sequentially ordered associations involved in problem solving. Choice was already involved then in dealing with beliefs, and James is about to show that no new principle is involved in moving to directed action. The ideomotor theory can be trusted to take care of the translation into motor activity. That is, the problems associated with voluntary doing have been thrown back onto the central or ideational part of the reflex arc.

This joining of instinct and emotion as impulsive and as activity helps in understanding the unusual features of James's theory of emotions (independently developed by Lange). Grossly put, the theory reads: we do not see the bear, recognize the threat, feel afraid, and then run. It would be better to say that we see the bear, run, and then feel afraid. This is plausible enough to anyone who has just lived through a near collision at an intersection, has performed all the proper motions, and then has the visceral response in the next block. Still this radically opposed the more usual account which has the bodily responses follow on the feeling. James is really overstating to make the case. He does not really mean that there is a succession of three separate events, for there is but a single organic response. Further, he does not mean that cognitive elements are lacking. The response is different between a bear-uncaged and a bear-in-a-cage; we have to perceive the bear as a threat. Remarks have to be perceived as insulting to trigger resentment.

Deliberate doing is the capstone of human capacities; it is the mark of intelligence acting and molding the world and it is the beginning of the moral. Two strands are woven together here. The first is the continuity of voluntary behavior with impulsive behavior (including the emotions) as modified by learning. And the second—the theme that James uses throughout all his works—is the evolutionary utility of consciousness to lead to action and to further thought. As suggested, the first performance of any act is necessarily blind, but the individual quickly learns foresight by associating the consequences with the impulse. Ideas are instrumental; they are anticipatory and forward-looking and would have no utility if that foresight did not help to secure what is wanted or preferred. James turns to attention to ease the problem, since the crux of the matter lies in the possibility that sequences of thought can be guided, i.e., if plans can be made. If attention, interest, or purpose, playing an integral role between afferent and efferent processes, can steer thought sequences or even delay the march of ideas, then there is spontaneity and we could be said to be free in a limited sense. For, given the impulsive character of ideas (on a broadened ideomotor theory), action will result in either case.

Attention is the singling out in clear and vivid form of what seem to be several possible objects. Attention is often involuntary, e.g., in the noticing of a hidden noise or distinguishing foreground from background. In ambiguous figures, however, a command can lead us to see one or another picture and we can set ourselves to noticing shapes or colors in an abstract design. There are more significant situations in which self-generated interests seem to determine what we look for. This involves an anticipatory preparation within ideational centers and a resulting accommodation of the sense organs. It may not be possible to locate how much of our perception arises from expectant tension, and how much from without, but the preparation seems to consist in something like enactment of an imaginary rehearsal of the action. Perception always belongs to the project of an active agent; the gaze we send out to objects is like a shaft of purpose sent from a particular point of view. Memory, imagination, prior experience, immediate interest, and context contribute to that purpose. Thus once again, our entrenched experience and our labels are of determining importance. But the preparatory attention, interest, or purpose seems to be a joint product of both our internal conceptions, the way our world is ordered, and the stimulus from outside.

The most authentic kind of decision, according to James, is the one in which we feel that all the evidence is in, that reason by no imaginable feat can convince us that one course is better than another. We have the feeling that our decision, by a willful act of our own, inclines the beam either by adding living effort on the side of reason (which was by itself powerless to make the act discharge), or by making a creative contribution of something other than reason which in effect does reason's work. Phenomenally this is felt as effort, as a "slow dead heave of the will." The sense of strain is deeper here than in other cases where an alternative is rejected at the moment of decision, for in the case of authentic decision both alternatives are kept steadily in view and in choosing one option and relinquishing the other, the chooser is aware of how much he is making himself lose. There would nearly always be impulsive and inhibitory tendencies in a situation in which choice is looming, and the impelling idea is just that one which possesses the attention (where idea may be as complex as a comprehensive plan).

> *The essential achievement of the will, in short, when it is most 'voluntary' is to ATTEND to a difficult object and hold it fast before the mind.* The so-doing *is* the *fiat:* and it is a mere physiological incident that when the object is thus attended to, immediate motor consequences should ensue. A *resolve,* whose contemplated motor consequences are not to ensue until some possibly far distant future condition shall have been fulfilled, involves all the psychic elements of a motor fiat except the word *'now';* and it is the same with many of our purely theoretic beliefs.[18]

Clearly, James is attempting to deal with voluntary behavior without resorting to a faculty of will and certainly not to a supernatural agency. He relies on a relatively simple mechanism for associating motor response to perception; the richness lies in the phenomenal field, for here there is a whole mélange of tendencies—of checks from remembered unpleasantnesses, of incompatible and conflicting pulls, of long-range intentions or plans in the fringe. The relation between input and output is not simple. We carry around with us conceptual patterns or cognitive maps including prospective worlds and our place in them; impulses are mediated and the whole situation is like not a telephone exchange but an air traffic control tower. The world as it is jostles worlds as they might be or ought to be.

The practical and theoretic life of whole species, as well as of individual beings, results from the selection which the habitual direction of their attention involves . . . each of us literally *chooses,* by his ways of attending to things, what sort of universe he shall appear to himself to inhabit.[19]

James is not simply denying the picture of choice given in the mechanical juxtapositions of the faculty psychology, nor is he just drowning them out in phenomenal descriptions. He has a very definite and positive theory of his own to propound. The objects of will and of belief differ only in the manner of our attending them. The object whose existence depends on our thought, on movements of our own bodies and the facts which our movements can realize, are objects of will. Objects of belief are those which do not involve our interposition. Both belief and choice involve consent, though there is a difference: in the one case there is an immediate "sting" that makes us concede that there is a reality, while in the other it makes us say, "Let it be real."

Actually, James had the elements needed to go on to a fruitful analysis of intentional or purposive behavior. The purposes and interests which were central to the selectivity and organization of perception work for responses. If guided thinking does not need a directing faculty of consciousness, then directed acting also can get by without appeal to a will. James does go down the track of excising the will by locating the question of freedom in attention. Moreover, ideas are already impulsive and thus action does not need to be superadded, while complex ideas may involve incompatible strategies and alternate plans so that there may be conflicting motor tendencies needing reconciliation in problem-solving. Indeed, James's later pragmatism depends on a richer theory of action than he provided in the *Psychology.* For in good pragmatic tradition ideas are functional, leadings to, or plans of action, and depend on verification (literally, the making true) or testing. The pragmatic view of meaning thus emphasizes the importance of cognition to behavior as well as the importance of behavior or action to cognition. The *Psychology* is also a confrontation of the traditional dualisms of mind-body, perception-movement, and stimulus-response, which are central problems for his Radical Empiricism. But here it is important to notice that although James did not say the last word about purposive behavior, planning, and intentions, at least he insisted that a first word be said.

2. Radical Empiricism

We haven't wanted to interrupt James in the telling of the *Psychology* because we wanted to let it exhibit its own strategies and coherence and, more importantly, because it is a critical resource for dealing with philosophic issues. James could not lightly give up the scientific achievements won with such intensity of efforts. Not only was he involved with the popular outline of his psychological views in *Talks to Teachers* as late as 1899, but the posthumous *Some Problems of Philosophy* (1911) cites the *Principles* liberally while the instrumental view of consciousness is always in the background.

As we shall see, Radical Empiricism extends the model of the stream of consciousness to metaphysics. Furthermore, changes in his position would have needed mentioning since everyone interested in philosophy—from generations of Harvard students to colleagues, opponents, and Chatauqua audiences—might be expected to have firsthand acquaintance with it. The way James floated from physiology to psychology to philosophy seems less a measure of his exchange of interests than of the interpenetration of the fields in his day. One way of stating a difference between psychology and philosophy is that the former is concerned with learning whereas the latter examines its warrant and legitimacy. The technical problems of learning on the one hand and of knowledge and validity on the other tended to separate after James's day (although lately cognitive problems suggest rapprochement). But James's concern with knowing and meaning in the *Psychology* make it a very philosophical sort of psychology, and there is no doubt that his philosophy is a very psychological sort of philosophy.

There are two aspects of James's philosophic writings, Radical Empiricism and Pragmatism. James said that they were independent—at least one could be a pragmatist without being a radical empiricist. But these are difficult to disentangle; parts of *Pragmatism* (1907) duplicate *Essays in Radical Empiricism* (1912); and toward the latter part of his life James wanted to call the "tendency" which he represents Radical Empiricism. In any case they are both methods for breaking up philosophic logjams. Somewhat arbitrarily we shall distinguish them according to problem. The following section will discuss the pragmatic theory of meaning and warrant, leaving to this one the account of what is real and of knowing as experience especially as these bridge psychological issues to pragmatic ones.

The *Psychology,* though describing the content and function of thought, did not query the status of consciousness. Writing as a psychologist and evolutionist James had assumed a subject and an external environment in interaction and (at least for the most part) a self which knows other objects. Radical empiricism now has to raise problems about the nature of objective reference and the relation between thought and its object which have to be resolved before he can go on to a theory of truth. Such problems are likely to involve a series of dualisms—mind and body, self and other, thought and thing thought of, knower and that which is known. While such issues need not necessarily be related, James pools them all. Behind such questions as "How Can One State of Mind Know Another?", "How Can One Thing Be in Two Places?", "How Can Minds Meet in the Same Object?"—there lies an interesting idea: that thought and that which is thought of are ultimately one.

Modern discussions of "the mind-body problem" generally take off from Descartes, whose two different substances, once postulated, had somehow to be connected. Hence the series of perplexities: how could thought affect the material world, and how could a nonspatial entity even know what is gross and spatial? British Empiricists made something else of the dualism, but their attempt to distinguish between primary qualities, which are like the properties of the external world (size and shape), and secondary qualities, which are subjective (sweetness and redness), led Hume ultimately to challenge whether the objective world or the self was anything more than a set of impressions. However, if there are only ideas and impressions, there is an even greater danger of not getting to an objective world. Empirical theories, then, gave a particular cast to the dualism, but they too interposed an image or representation between what the mind knows and the perception. Nineteenth-century physiologists (replacing the previous century's physical model) began to look for distinctive physiological laws governing animal behavior; their comrades in psychology sought to use such physiological laws as models for their own laws of mental behavior. The dualism again is not overcome, but there is a program to correlate physiological with psychic (i.e., mental) events. Materialists and evolutionists tended to see the mind as a function of matter; idealists in opposition saw matter as a function of mind. James, in his *Essays in Radical Empiricism,* makes an even more drastic effort to dissolve the dualism.

In some ways James believes he is following Locke, who has used the word *idea* to stand for thought and thing indifferently, and Berkeley, who had held that what common sense means by realities is just what philosophers mean by ideas; and Hume's world was a single metaphysical stuff, namely impressions. It was not their empiricism, but their faintheartedness, which he set out to correct.

Radical empiricism consists first of a postulate, next of a statement of fact, and finally of a generalized conclusion. The postulate is that the only things that shall be debatable among philosophers shall be things definable in terms drawn from experience. . . . The statement of fact is that the relations between things . . . are just as much matters of direct particular experience, neither more so nor less so, than the things themselves. The generalized conclusion is that therefore the parts of experience hold together from next to next by relations that are themselves part of experience.[20]

The postulate establishes James as a thoroughgoing empiricist. He must, of course, then show how, out of this category *experience,* all the hoary categories can be constructed, viz., an external world, a self, a consciousness. Even the question of truth must ultimately be answered in terms of this experience. The statement of fact enriches beyond measure the Humean catalog of metaphysical building blocks; it is much easier to "construct" the cosmos and to explain knowledge if one allows that relations are directly experienced. Given James's scheme, the knowing need be neither an entity (the mind) nor a faculty; it can be accounted for in terms of the relations which are themselves part of experience.

James "plumply" denies that consciousness exists as a spiritual stuff or entity, neither is it a faculty; it is the name for the functioning of thought, i.e., knowing or thinking. Perhaps this is not the way we would put the question; few people ask today does consciousness exist? On the other hand, our problem is as genuine as James's: to explain the fact that experiences both are and somehow get known, that we are aware not only of things and ideas but also of our awareness.

As is clear in the *Psychology,* what we have to begin with is just pure experience, the *thats* of experience, whether called sensation, perception, datum, phenomenon, or content. Originally experience is given, it just comes or is. It belongs neither to an external world nor to a mental one. All the distinctions represented in the dualisms mentioned above between the thing referred to and the thought that does the referring, between subjective and objective, between what is presented and the representation—all these come by way of addition; i.e., as this purely given is further labeled, classified, and joined to other experiences in a system of relations. To repeat, the problem for James is to account for knowledge and the thing known (whether it be the self, or object, or another state of mind) and the relation of knowing which connects them.

The thrust of James's argument can be suggested by several weak analogies. The book on my table, which happens to be *Catch-22,* is a source of amusement to me, while to the cleaning lady it is just one more item to be dusted (if you are optimistic). To the druggist who sold it, it is a $2.95 item, associated with other equal-sized and equal-priced sundries gotten from a jobber; and to the governor, it is another ten cents in state tax. It, the *same* book, is somehow all these things. Or again, a sample of gold mixed with silver may equally well be gold debased by silver, or silver alloyed with gold, according to the context. The point is not the manner that interest or purpose generates alternate descriptions, that will come later, but rather that the *same* book or *same* piece of metal can figure in various contexts and with totally different (and possibly incompatible) associates.

With these examples in mind, let us look at one of the problems which James sets, how can one thing be in two places at the same time, in my mind and in the world? The problem so stated is simply a false one. There is one indivisible fact, and the object in mind and the object in the world are but different names given later to a single experience when, taken in a larger world, its connections are traced out in different directions. Thus when we see a white paper, the *paper seen* and the *seeing of it* are but different names given retrospectively to an experience as it gets associated systematically; the *paper seen* has its place in the history of the world, while the *seeing of it* has a part in a mental biography. Predicates which are applicable to the physical paper—it can be destroyed by fire, costs so much money, turns yellow with age—are not true of the mental paper which can be folded without creasing and can survive the disasters of time. The paper belongs as truly to one set of associates as to the other, just as a point may lie on each of two intersecting lines. Only the grossest prejudice would hold that the point belongs really to the vertical rather than the horizontal line; it belongs to both. Thought and thing coalesce in the perception; the only opposition between them lies in the added relation, context, and function. This applies to the relations of mind to body (for both are elements of explanation) as well as to the relation between thought and its object; the job is to find the systems which intersect. The point of intersection may thus legitimately have a place in the two great systems of the mental world and the physical order, as its associates are phenomenal or physical.

There is presently much discussion about whether observations are to be recorded in physicalistic or phenomenalistic language (as red, hard, pointer indication; or as *seen* red, *felt* hard, or as *sense* motion in the visual field). James's theory is not reductive in an ordinary sense for both languages are legitimate; the extent of their correlation is a problem to be worked out. Thus it is not strange that James makes a place for alternate but legitimate descriptions and, in developed theoretical knowledge, for alternate conceptual frameworks. Oftentimes the subjective and objective order are amenable to common operations, e.g., both the mental and the physical can be arranged in serial order.

> Descartes for the first time defined thought as the absolutely unextended, and later philosophers have accepted the description as correct. But what possible meaning has it to say that, when we think of a foot-rule or a square yard, extension is not attributable to our thought . . . The difference between objective and subjective extension is one of relation to a context solely. In the mind the various extents maintain no necessarily stubborn order relatively to each other, while in the physical world they bound each other stably. . . . The two worlds differ, not by the presence or absence of extension, but by the relations of the extensions which in both worlds exist.[21]

The history of science and philosophy supports the claim that secondary qualities are not "co-efficients with which experiences come to us as aboriginally stamped," but are rather later results of classifications made by us to answer particular needs. The notions of heat and sound worked well enough as objective predicates, as descriptions of the physical world, until Galileo and Descartes reclassified them as subjective along with pleasure and pain. Causation was originally thought to be a characterization of a natural process, and is still so regarded by many scientists, although Hume and others following him gave an adequate account of it as a psychological projection; space and time are conveniently used as subjective or objective categories according to their role in an explanation. According to James, then, there is neither spirituality nor materiality of experiences, but just translations or sortings of them with one kind of associate or another as the situation warrants.

While physical and mental orders are, for the most part, incompatible universes, still there is an interesting area of overlapping. In contexts of affectional experiences and language, the adjective "wavers" as though uncertain whether to affix itself to the mental or the physical. We speak indifferently of "wicked desires" or "desires of wicked object"; of "feelings of anger" or of "angry feelings." Experiences of painful objects are generally painful, while those of the morally lofty are usually lofty. It is unnecessary for these predicates to be located in one or the other realm. Their equivocality lends aesthetic and moral quality to our language, it gives affectional language the power to arouse feelings and emotions directly. The action is really mean, the situation is truly tragic. The man is really hateful and the road weary. We leave such terms ambiguous because although they are divorced from a large part of the physical world, they are in intimate connection with that part of nature which is our own bodies. Danger, beauty, morality, and the interesting aspects of things arouse our attention and have physical consequences in behavior. Having captured our attention, they rule our intellectual life as well.

What status pure experience enjoys may be perplexing. Later philosophers have built out from it in a variety of ways. It fits well enough a learning theory in which a child slowly discriminates himself from not-self and objects, things and the furniture of the world from pains and fantasies. It could be taken also as a methodological principle on a par with the Hegelian Spirit or with the materialist or idealist reductions; in that case it serves a mediating job by exposing superfluous presuppositions that make trouble and showing how a different hypothesis (James's own) might undercut the problems. Alternately, it can be read realistically as an ontological formulation of what there is, or as a phenomenological field where ontological interpretation is suspended. Again, it could simply be used, in a technical way, as the experience-matrix out of which objects of knowledge are constructed. It even has affinities with Dewey's "experience" and it gave James as much trouble as it afterward made for Dewey. Perhaps James himself wavered in his attitude. In any case, the point he is making is that experience is what is given before any categorization at all—before the divisions of internal-external, subjective-objective, apparent-real, and therefore certainly before phenomenal-physical and the rest.

There is a distinction, however, which James countenances after the fact between what is direct and unsharable in experience, the *thats* and *thises* of the just experienced in contrast to the *whats* of experience. This does not exactly parallel the usual distinction between sensation/perception and conception, because this is (true to his early commitments) a functional distinction. The first is knowledge by acquaintance and has the function of a direct introduction, while the other— knowledge about—traces out the relations and further connections in our experience. The difference may be suggested between what the average person grasps in listening and what a deaf person may learn about harmony but actually never experiences. Knowledge by acquaintance and knowledge about are both cognitive. They differ in their proximity to the origin in sense. The former has a tang and vividness which is generally absent in remembered and represented experience; it is continuous where conceptual or systematic thinking is discrete.

James usually uses the terms "percept" and "concept" to make the distinction, and both may be examined abstractly, that is nonfunctionally. In fact, we have already examined the case of knowledge by acquaintance in the example of the paper and the seeing of it. In this case, knower and known coalesce, and the knowing is direct. But concepts may also be treated abstractly, divorcing them from their role as signs for further experiences. Concepts may have roles in different conceptual systems. Thus we often speak of Hamlet as though his decisions were those of a genuinely tormented person and analyze his character, not Shakespeare's. At other times, we regard him as a character in a play, in which case he may be symbolic, necessary, well-conceived, etc. As a character we can debate his madness and his relation to Gertrude, while as a part in a play Hamlet may be well portrayed.

Conceptual systems taken abstractly do not provide *knowledge about;* that depends on the interplay between percept and concept. However, James was concerned with the traditional question of what the knower contributes to knowledge independently of experience, i.e., the a priori status of conceptual structuring. Even in the *Psychology* he had included a final chapter on "Necessary Truths and the Effects of Experience," although it was omitted in the *Jimmy* as too metaphysical.

His conclusions are in the mood of Kant, that there are at least some parts of the content of knowledge that enter by the back stairs, or rather, as James put it, "have not entered the mind at all, but got surreptitiously born in the house."[22] However, he differs importantly from Kant in attempting to give a natural explanation of their genesis (as we shall see), in allowing of a plurality rather than a fixed set of categories, and in the way in which he explores the relations between the conceptual and the perceptual. These relations are somewhat different in logic and mathematics, natural sciences, ethics, and metaphysics.

Conceptual relations in logic and mathematics are remote from the order in which our experience has initially come. Indeed, these say nothing about the world of experience at all and could not be falsified by observation. The relations in logic and mathematics are essentially matters of comparison, especially of resemblance and difference. The mind, of course, can make comparisons on comparisons and higher-ordered series over lower-ordered ones, moving ever away from the sensible. The most that can be claimed about existence is that if these ideal schemes have interpetations they will hold; but whether they have an interpretation is an empirical matter. "$1 + 1 = 2$" would be a probability judgment if it were dependent on experience. But so powerful are such conceptualizations as arithmetic that we make more numerical continuity than we spontaneously find. The relationships are true by virtue of the meanings of the terms and not because they account for anything in the physical world. The ideal systems which these relations form help order and stabilize the world as we know it.

Even the natural sciences are coerced by the more successful of our formal sciences. We sometimes forget how far removed is scientific thought from the order of experience.

> The conceiving or theorizing faculty works exclusively for the sake of ends that do not exist at all in the world of the impressions received by way of our senses, but are set by our emotional and practical subjectivity. It is a transformer of the world of our impressions into a totally different world, the world of our conception.[23]

Neither physics nor mechanics, nor other natural sciences can be taken as simply the given. Not only do our sciences have to be tested in experience and verified, but the test is not a cause of the production of the theory, but only of the preservation of one system over another. Even the testing itself may arise artificially from insights remote from the sensible. What is really remarkable is that we can assign our scientific theories interpretations; that the given order admits to being remodeled in theoretical terms.

Conceptual systems in ethics relate to the world in a different way, for they are patterns for refashioning life to make it more reasonable. Ethics (and aesthetics) cannot make the same kind of claim for their projection onto the physical world— they are not simply tested by prediction. All the same they are ways of organizing experience and of coercing it to our ends. Moral ideals serve regulatively to help refashion the world as we should like it to be. Metaphysical axioms are further ways of rendering the world intelligible. Although they cannot be directly verified in experience, they are not altogether sterile, for they serve as a reminder that we are constantly seeking to mold the world of sense into more and more comprehensive a system. That nature is simple and invariable, that the world can be understood and generalizations can be made about it, had better be called postulates of rationality, for nature would be more intelligible if she did obey them. Yet even here the choice of postulates may be rather a matter of temperament than of fact, like the choice of philosophical positions generally. James suggests that perhaps the most fundamental metaphysical axiom is that nature is such that sweeping generalizations can be made about her.

The psychogenetic problem is to account for the mode of birth of all these. It simply will not do to argue that the outer world inevitably builds up these results by the impact of repeated experience yielding automatic habits. Spencer tried to do this with the suggestion that individual adaptations were then passed on to the next generation and survived in the race. Even if a purely empirical account were allowed for the elements, it would not hold for the combinations. What happens inside after the mass is there carries one in new directions. This is true for all material masses—like a pudding, when its ingredients have been brought together, new internal forces are freed to exert their influences. So ideal and inward relations do not simply reproduce the outer, but involve new settings and new forces. In general, James inclines to explain by a kind of spontaneous variation, a summing of inward forces—morphological accidents—owing less to immediate derivation from sense than to previous thoughts and previously developed brain processes. Such variations survive when they are fitted to steer us in our active feelings with objects. In the end, after considering the origin of instincts as a parallel, and rejecting the inheritance of acquired characteristics as a way of explaining the survival of the new forms, he finds his position close to Darwin's conception of natural selection. While the conception of house-born forms commits him to no specific theory of the grounds of survival, his actual decision is altogether compatible with the contemporary view of chance variations that are stabilized by culture as a consequence of utility.

In terms of the traditional epistemological problems, James, as we may expect, stresses the creative throughout the whole range of human constructions. But his epistemological conclusions are never divorced from the psychological and their physiological roots.

But for all the utility of concepts, their misuse leads unnecessarily to dilemmas. Concepts are tailored to stay the perceptual flow and to gain the kind of stability that can make the world manageable. Since they are discrete, they cannot display or capture the vividness of experience as experienced, neither with respect to its qualitative fullness nor to its changing. There is a vast distance between a description of a symphony and its existentially experienced continuity. When we substitute the conceptual for the perceptual, not only the continuity and changing but the fugitive and the novel escape. Or, in another analogy, a map is selective and never portrays all the features of the territory.

A good example of the troubles that ensue, and a critical one for James to solve, is what conceptualization does to activity—for the whole of the *Psychology* with its account of consciousness depends on the active character of the functionings that constitute capacities such as attending and conceiving. James, of course, finds the original of activity in perceptual experience, in personal activity situations. Minimal, or as James puts it, ''bare,'' activity is an ultimate feature of the stream of consciousness as continuously changing. But often it comes with a sense of direction and of goal; there is a sense of striving, feelings of overcoming or succumbing to resistance. This is the original of the notion of agent and efficacy. Now different philosophies deny that the feeling of activity genuinely evidences real activity—some of the idealists because they want to move real activity out to a transcendent agent, some of the materialists because they want to locate it in the proximate neurological processes, and Hume who wants to deny that there is any such thing as agent. Hume is a clear example of the abuse of concepts, for he imposes the discontinuity of concepts upon the perceptual flux. The metaphysicians, idealist or materialist, when they deny the feeling of activity, treat it as illusory or surface and look for a deeper or closer cause, but their explanatory principle is simply a little spiritual or material copy of the original fact. For James, while the feeling of activity or efficacy does not certify some ulterior agency, in the end any explanation of it can only return us to the experience.

These considerations lead directly into James's view of the self, which bonds the *Psychology,* especially his account of the stream of consciousness as personal, with the account of activity and the functional view of consciousness. He steers his way between the associational view, especially of Hume, which more or less abandons a self for a sequence of impressions united only by the laws of association, and on the other hand a unifying knower behind all knowledge, in which case the self as experienced is abandoned. His problem is thus: can we account for the running of the stream of consciousness without a starter and a transcendent manager, and can we account for self-identity in experiential terms? His answer to both is: yes.

His view will have greater affinities, therefore, with empiricism, but with an empiricism that is enlarged far beyond the Humean so that it does not have to see any bonding as external. In the first place, experience already comes with a personal stamp. It isn't thought but *my* thought, and this is a primary psychic fact; it isn't, then, that feelings and thoughts exist, but my thoughts, or I think and I feel. Further, from the outset there is a kind of unity to our consciousness; the baby feels all that assails it from the outside as *one* great, blooming, buzzing confusion. And this unity is felt in experience with warmth and intimacy. But it is an empirical property which often is not found: in ordinary experience, when I am told a story about my childhood behavior, I believe it but do not feel the pride or the embarrassment which I should if I *felt* it as mine; and in unusual cases we find the divided self (e.g., in religious conversion), and pathological cases of split personality.

In the widest sense, a man's self is all that he can call his. This includes the material self of which the body is the core, but which also includes clothes, family, home, property with which we have mixed our labor, and all those instinctive preferences which we have that are tied up with the practical interests of life. And in a curious way, the loss of any of these is a shrinkage of ourselves. There are social selves as well, stemming from the way we are recognized by others; a man's honor and his fame are names for social selves, so that to cut into my reputation is to diminish me. Most of us live with a variety of social images, corresponding to our roles: the warden who is a loving parent at home might be embarrassed with this image of himself among the prison inmates. James points out that it is a fortunate man who can integrate most of his social selves, and he considers it a healthy society which allows the cultivation of many selves and provides the conditions for their integration. James also thinks in terms of a spiritual me, which includes my dispositions, my aspirations and feelings. Indeed, we subtly order our sensations as more external than our emotions and drives, and those as more external than the thinking me, and we reserve as the most internal our sense of activity and of willing.

All these may be thought of as constituents of the self. But there are also pattern properties, which are nonetheless empirical. There is, e.g., self-appreciation or self-esteem, a tone which most people carry about that is independent of the reasonable grounds for evaluating oneself. But such experiences of self-satisfaction and self-abasement are as primitive as pain and rage.

Selves are not passive, but issue in action. The bodily self yields those acts we call self-preservation, while our social selves are tied up with behavior that will win recognition. And the spiritual self prompts acts of self-improvement and self-criticism.

Our various selves are often in conflict. As James says in the *Psychology:*

> . . . I would. . . , if I could, be both handsome and fat and well-dressed, and a great athlete, and make a million a year, be a wit, a *bon-vivant,* and a lady-killer, as well as a philosopher. . . . But the thing is simply impossible. The millionaire's work would run counter to the saint's; the *bon-vivant* and the philanthropist would trip each other up; the philosopher and the lady-killer could not well keep house in the same tenement of clay.[24]

But once again there is patterning; for we tend on the whole to order ourselves hierarchically, with the spiritual selves taking priority in our esteem over the bodily selves. And this hierarchy is itself a unity won by selective industry; it is an accomplishment, not an endowment. Here too we carry about with our selves a sense of self which is rather like a cognitive map, or norm, against which we measure ourselves. Self-esteem is the ratio of success to pretension or aspiration, and it may be raised or lowered by changing either the numerator or the denominator. (How pleasant the day, James points out, when we quit striving to be young or slender. Everything added to the self is a burden as well as a pride.)

But the question remains: is there anything more than all these experiences? What about the ego or the "I," not the "me," the inner sanctuary of activity, the source of initiative and effort, the imputed or alleged author of our thoughts and acts and self-identity? James does not believe there is a separated I experienced in the traditional "cogito" (I think); he points out that the Latin does not separate the I from the thinking or feeling. James's solution is really quite simple. If, as we expect him to do by this time, one substitutes a continuity over time for an identity of substance, then the conditions of continuity would be satisfied if the experience of the present in some cumulative sense captured past experience. Just as the present state of a plant incorporates its past growth, so the present thought owns or represents all that has gone before. Memory, understanding with all its riches, and feeling with all its discriminations, are properties of the present conscious act. James works this out in considerable detail. Insofar as self-identity is a case of being the "same" I as yesterday, the constructional problems are not different from the judgment that this object is the same pen as yesterday. (Actually, it is more like the construction of a single time, space, or reality.) Again, the self is a complex structure or organization, a relatively fixed and stable ego, for most purposes. But this functional, rather than substantial, identity is only relative; for many purposes we are not the same as we were yesterday, or the man the same as the child. And finally, the fact that the I is identified with the present thought explains why there is always an experiencing I present, even when its object is its just passed self as experiencing. As James puts it explicitly, nascent thought has the trick of taking up an expiring thought and adopting it—and this is the foundation of the appropriation of the remoter constituents of the self. Thought is the vehicle of cognition and choice, and among the choices are the repudiations or appropriations of its "own." The thought, however, is never an object in its own hands—it never appropriates or disowns itself.

James's argument in all this is an obvious application of his Radical Empiricism—experiences of activity and efficacy are taken for what they are *known as*. But his approach does not involve an antitheoretical stand. Conceptualizations may be freely developed—the wide-visioned Idealist with his view of long-range teleologies or the Materialist with his short-range or close explanations in terms of the operations of brain cells—but the problem is which theory or what amalgam is to be chosen. Here James applies a pragmatic criterion: what differences do the conceptual substitutions make or what consequences do they have for the future course of experience? Radical Empiricism and Pragmatism thus go hand in hand; it is almost as if one were taking care of the perceptual, and the other (the latter) of the conceptual constructions. The pragmatic equivalent of these opposing theories is simply the recognition that on the one hand the identified feature of long-range purposes and goals actually operates in human experience, and on the other hand that microscopic physical events by their actual occurrence may make significant differences in the course of human life. Commitments to human ideals, no less than a thrombosis in a prime minister, affect the course of history. Philosophers ought to stop worrying about what effects effectuation or what makes actions act since both theories only help us recognize an actual cause when we meet one. The urgent problems of activity are concrete—which things are the causal agents and which are not, and what are the relations between longer-span and shorter-span activities.

In using this perspective, James was moving toward the question of the efficacy of human decision. These are the problems that have traditionally been associated with voluntary action and freedom. Insofar as the problem of free will rests on there being genuine novelty, James meets this related problem in the same way as he dealt with activity. We simply know from our experience that science develops, that new forms grow, and (most intimately) that the stream of consciousness is always presenting us with the unexpected and the novel. The larger consequences of these issues will be taken up after we have examined Pragmatism.

We noted at the outset of the discussion of Radical Empiricism that James asserted that it and Pragmatism were independent. Strictly he was right, for Pragmatism is a theory about the dependence of meaning and belief on experience, while Radical Empiricism is an account of the nature and content of experience. But given the background of the *Psychology,* with its account of experience, we are not surprised to find that in James's own case they are thoroughly interrelated. Most obviously Radical Empiricism builds out from the primacy and the autonomy of the stream of consciousness from which distinctions and constructions are generated, while Pragmatism builds on the purposive and forward reach of the stream expressing its evolutionary utility. Both of these are central features of James's view of experience.

3. Pragmatism: The Theory of Truth and Verification

James's pragmatic theory of truth is developed against the background of the ingredients of experience as offered in the *Psychology* and the relation between percept and concept considered in our account of Radical Empiricism. The reservation about the inability to distinguish these in any given segment of experience needs to be remembered as well as the cognitive character of both the perceptual and the conceptual. Clearly he must now go on to the central philosophical question of truth and the general problem of validity. Very briefly put, he starts from the undoubted fact that we do claim that some of our beliefs are true, that they refer to reality and are objectively warranted. That is to say, we start with a distinction between true beliefs and dreams or flights of fancy or fictions.

Nowhere in James's philosophy is the commitment to the human mark in knowledge more apparent nor its consequences so critical for the advances which his theory accomplishes. He has to go beyond, though clearly accepting, the classic empiricism of Locke, Berkeley, and Hume, and of the later associationists like Bain and James Mill. Yet he cannot agree that the knower is a passive witness, nor that knowledge is the mere accretion that results from endlessly comparing, abstracting, and compounding of ideas or psychic segments. As we have already seen, the base of experience has been expanded, and experience itself is cumulative as well as active. James must account for the corrigibility of knowledge, the fact that it develops both in an individual's learning and by society's increasing wisdom. That is to say, he has to account not only for the fact that knowledge claims are made, and for what it is that we take to be true; but he must proceed to the problem of the legitimacy and validity of such knowledge in experimental terms. In other words, he wants to account for both the role and the need of truth. Starting from the particular cases where we make truth claims, he seeks to formulate the criteria implicit therein, to consider the grounds for criticizing those criteria, and to examine the imperative or the duty to seek the truth and use it as a regulative ideal. This use of truth as a regulative ideal is the case, par excellence, where an unspecifiable objective cooperates in the solution of a problem. As we shall see in just a moment, the model for his discussion is the development of nineteenth-century science.

However, there is a sense in which James is a Kantian, but more Kantian than Kant. Kant raised the question whether the order we find in the universe might not well be an order we ourselves have placed there—that the order of nature is the order-making of the mind. James answers affirmatively. But it is clear that James, finding the originals of space and time in experience, holding that there are alternative categories and conceptual systems which develop in experience, will give a different and freer account than Kant of forms and categories. For James the distinction between true and false, the structuring and ordering of experience, are never final nor beyond correction. Not only are the most stable parts of experience alterable, but the world is in the making. We are taking a hand in it at every moment and creating it; our beliefs are at every moment under constant impact of the sensibly new, the reassessment of old experience and the reaccommodation of all parts of our knowledge. In other words, it is not the static Kantian structuring of knowledge, unmodifiable by humans in terms of their purposes, but a structuring which must constantly answer to its function.

Hume made us eternally cautious about our use of cause and about the problem of the validity of our knowledge in contrast to a description of how we arrive at our judgments. After Kant, it was no longer possible to discount the role of the observer in knowledge. After James, though perhaps we haven't taken the lesson to mind, we should be alerted to the subtleties and richness of experience, to the mutual relation between action and knowledge (even verification is an act), and to the purposiveness and directedness of thought. It isn't the bare fact of knowledge but its increase and correction that are significant. There is a dynamics to knowledge and reality. Here James shares the mood of nineteenth-century science.

. . . How short the career of what we know as 'science' has been. Three hundred and fifty years ago hardly anyone believed in the Copernican planetary theory. Optical combinations were not discovered. The circulation of the blood, the weight of air, the conduction of heat, the laws of motion were unknown; the common pump was inexplicable; there were no clocks; no thermometers; no general gravitation; the world was five thousand years old; spirits moved the planets; alchemy, magic, astrology, imposed on every one's belief. Modern science began only after 1600, with Kepler, Galileo, Descartes, Torricelli, Pascal, Harvey, Newton, Huygens, and Boyle. Five men telling one another in succession the discoveries which their lives had witnessed, could deliver the whole of it into our hands: Harvey might have told Newton, who might have told Voltaire; Voltaire might have told Dalton, who might have told Huxley, who might have told the readers of this book.[25]

But if the nineteenth-century science and its advances are the heroes in the case, then the villains are the Rationalists and their nineteenth-century extension into idealism especially English Neo-Hegelianism. And, it is against these, as in the *Psychology,* that *Pragmatism* and *The Meaning of Truth* direct their strongest polemics. Above all, it is against the idealists' view of absolute knowledge, their block universe, or Monism, that James was in revolt. As is evident from his own thought, the various conceptual schemes do not intermesh in a neat way. If unity of knowledge—as today the unity of science—is the desideratum, it is to be won and not just postulated. Completed knowledge may serve as an ideal, but if thought of as accomplished it is simply a distortion of the present situation. As he will point out, even mathematics and logic provide no single model, but alternate ones, and this had already put Classic Rationalism in question. James regarded the sketch of its rise and fall as the background for his epistemological innovations. The tremendous discoveries of Descartes that algebra and geometry were not separate sciences, but aspects of the more general analytic geometry, and that a single deductive method would suffice for the achieving of truth in any domain, had provided the model for Classic Rationalism that all knowledge could be derived from a few fundamental and self-evident axioms. The new physics of Kepler and Newton had given further grounds for believing that the nature of the world was orderly and that its structure could be penetrated. In some cases this structure was thought to be the actual structure of the world as God either created or thought it. True knowledge, thus, was regarded as a transcript of reality. The laws of logic and the laws of physics, and even the classifications of plants, revealed the divine order. In the nineteenth century, however, in the work of such men as Mach and Poincaré, Pearson and Duhem, these laws came to be looked upon as approximations rather than as eternal verities. Theories are the means for summarizing past observations and for leading to further discovery. They are not permanent homes but resting places in the march toward the newer truth which incorporates the novel and is in constant change. The notion of an absolute truth, at least an available absolute truth, had to fall before the constant replacements and discoveries in physical theory, physiology, biology, geology, and sociology. But even in the a priori sciences, in geometry and logic and algebra, uniqueness was no longer a ground for acceptance, since there were consistent and even useful alternatives. Consequently, some further criterion or set of criteria was necessary to determine which was to be used either universally or at particular times. And in the cases where these alternatives are equally consistent and where they satisfy the data equally, the choice depends upon one's preference—"the choice follows massive cues of preference."

Pragmatism, then, followed these cues. It needed to examine the particular cases where truth is decided, to be responsive to this newer and more adequate notion of truth derived from science and to generalize the criteria. We are no longer looking for absolute truth; we can no longer explain what it is by appealing to antecedent truth, for that is as foolish as asking why the rich have all the wealth.

Truth is but a class name for all sorts of working hypotheses that can carry us from some parts of experience to others, simplifying, economizing, and working securely. They help us to utilize past experiences, to deal with the unprecedented and to lead us retrospectively to examine and reassess the past. The distinction between truth and falsity itself grows up in experience along with other distinctions and with the full accompaniments of the stream of consciousness.

Another way of seeing James's problem is as an account of that characteristic of an idea, belief, or conception—or in his later, more precise moods, statements—which qualifies them as true. It must, of course, be related to their "workability," the most general term for various functions of consciousness like leading to, pointing to, resembling, meaning, or referring to. At the outset it appears then that truth is a dispositional property, just like workability, and depends on context and test.

James's theory might better be called a theory of the meaning of "truth." It is simply Peirce's theory of meaning applied to this troublesome epistemological term. If meaning is to be defined by reference to the practical effects we conceive the object of our conception to have, then what is required is an analysis of the practical bearings of calling a belief "true." James believed he was developing Peirce's notion of meaning in a way compatible with the latter's intention, though Peirce bitterly complained afterward at the bastardizing of his proposal. It is certainly the case that Peirce was concerned about general laws and intersubjective criteria, where James was going to run the consequences to ground in particular experiences; still and all, it is not clear that James had offended the letter of the theory.

White suggests that Peirce's translation of (e.g.) "X is heavy" into statements of the form "if operation O (in this case strikes) then experience E will result (in this case a scar)" can be transferred to James's theory if acceptance of belief of a statement is admissible as an operation, and satisfaction is admissible as an experience. White goes on to argue that by such means James is able "to invite back into respectability many speculative, metaphysical and theological statements that seem to be meaningless by Peirce's criterion of meaning."[26] Now this may be a fair way of reading James in his more tender moments, although even that is doubtful, but it certainly does not do justice to the tighter part of James's argument.

As has already been indicated, James starts from what he takes to be the indubitable fact that we assign objective reference to some of our ideas. He is satisfied to accept the dictionary definition of truth as agreement with objective reality if *agreement* and *reality* are examined in the light of the pragmatic method. As is evident from the discussion of Radical Empiricism, a first requirement is that reality, objectivity, and the relation of knowing must all lie within experience. In the present case, truth as a relation must itself be found within experience.

With such considerations in mind, we are now in the appropriate mood to examine James's theory of truth—remembering especially that he is going to keep this discussion close to concrete determinations of what is true. Indeed, it is a criticism he makes against most epistemologists that they forget two things: that when they examine knowledge and truth they are dealing in the highest abstractions, and that in any concrete case of knowing, of finding, or of making true, we are concerned with the particular experience and not with *Knowledge* and *Truth* at all. In the philosopher's situation, to forget this is to commit a version of what James called the "psychologist's fallacy."[27]

For a belief to be true it must agree with reality, i.e., it must guide us to it or put us in working touch with it. True beliefs are those we can verify, assimilate, corroborate, and validate. (As is later evident in a controversy with Russell, James is attentive to the variability in use of a term from context to context; it would appear that James intends by "definition" what might better be called an "informal explication.") A patient reading of James suggests that these predicates are not simply stylistic but mark out quite different functions and characteristics. Verification appears to refer especially to the function of an idea or a belief in leading us to other experiences; it calls to mind the verifying of a theory in terms of a predicted consequence, since on James's theory we have some criterion in mind which is to be successfully met in experience. To illustrate: that there are tigers in India, or salt in the sugar bowl, is true if it leads to some perception that successfully fulfills the anticipation or the prediction; however, the success must always be a matter of personal appreciation, dependent on an individual's feeling (in the broad sense of the *Psychology*). Validation is the related term suggesting retrospective assessment of the verification, which warrants future decision.

Corroboration and assimilation may be similarly paired, for they both stress the systematic character of knowledge. As a matter of fact, all four predicates might better have been used in their "-ability" form; for although knowledge must rest ultimately on a cash basis, much of it is operating on a credit system. Thus "corroborability" suggests the smooth working of our knowing, although we put only a small portion of it to test at a given time. If various books, including photographs, discuss tigers in India, we should generally be content to suppose that they are there. If three people reject their coffee after having used the material in the sugar bowl, and there is a mischievous child in the household, their claim that the bowl contains salt scarcely needs to be corroborated with a fresh test. Our truth and knowledge rest on no other base than the body of accumulated knowledge—we have no insight into any other grounds than our own experience, yet that knowledge is mutually supporting. Its strands, fully corroborated or corroborable, make a tapestry which still needs to be filled in and worked over but whose half-finished parts lend sense and pattern to the incomplete parts. Assimilability emphasizes the needed marriage of new opinion with funded knowledge. No sentence stands alone or leans wholly upon itself.

James expands the notion of verification and assimilation. It is especially by way of these that the theory of truth examines the cognitive relation between the conceptual and the perceptual in terms of its success and workability. A copying relation may be said to hold, if at all, in the limiting case of the resemblance between an image and its object. If, e.g., one looks at a clock or a cow path and then closes the eyes, the image may be said to resemble or copy the reality. Presumably then, on opening one's eyes again, the agreement of image and experience may be felt. Ultimately all knowledge must come to test by verification in such directly felt experience, in this knowledge by acquaintance.

However, the image of the clock or the cow path is functionally the least important part of our notions of such objects. What is important is their forward reference, their ability to lead to, point to, or conduct us from one part of experience to another, with each step felt to be harmonious and corroborative of every other step. The copy theory is inadequate to this functioning of an idea. Thus, though we may hold the image of a clock before us, we often cannot even fill out its detail without careful further examination; but in any case, from the surface view, we have but little image of its works and no image at all of its function of signifying that the class hour is over or that the train is late. For most of our experience and knowledge it is not the image of the clock that is important but this power to connect some portions of experience with others. Equally so with the cow path; in most situations, what is important is that it can indicate the direction of a walk, shelter, or food, though of course these indications must be fulfillable or predictive of other terminal experiences. Putting the point generally, we can test a theory by its anticipation of a conclusion, i.e., another experience which serves as its verification. In James's earlier work, he used the idea of a Memorial Hall at Harvard, but in his later writings (the social historian may note), it is a glass of beer which illustrates how one fulfills an idea—in the latter case by finding the bar, the beer, and slaking one's thirst. Whether the example be scientific, collegiate, or homely, ultimate verification consists in some felt satisfaction or agreement on the part of the observer.

Such primary verification of matters of fact is a prototype of all empirical verification, and other cases may be interpreted as interrupted, arrested, or incomplete, multiple or substitutional variations of the primary type. We accept half verifications (and the verifications of others) as corroborative, as trustworthy on the whole; thus our knowledge is given enormous potential reach. Fortunately, experience is organized in kinds, in "sames" and in regularities so that these indirect or partial verifications pass for completed ones so long as there is no clash. The intention of James's theory of truth is now apparent. It is bound to the notion of interest and of leading (in selective and purposive behavior) and not to static correspondence or copy. Truth is thus related to the property of an idea by which it initiates further experience and it is some manner of success in the leading. Since the truth of an idea then concerns its ability to put us in commerce with other parts of experience and thereby to alter or direct the course of ideas or action, it is quite literally motivational. It is precisely the lack of this property which makes what might be a "true" description in some contexts but irrelevant in this one, as worthless as a false one. The beauty or the color of a geometrical figure is of course no more helpful in the calculation of its area than is a false formula. The crux of effective truth is to be part of an idea seen as a plan of action.

Relations between ideas (i.e., between conceptions) may be true or false analytically. Truths of this kind begin with definitions or principles. "1 + 1 = 2," or "grey differs less from black than white does," if true, are true in advance of any particular verification, or of any verification whatsoever. Indeed the point is stronger than that: if the application to a given domain runs into difficulty, it is not because of falsehood of the principle, but simply its irrelevancy for that domain— always supposing, of course, that the principle is not self-contradictory. Thus neither the habits of rabbits nor chemical combination by volume threatens the truth of ordinary arithmetic.

Yet even here the notion of leading is still appropriate, for it is by relating one idea to another that we frame conceptual schemes, including those of mathematics and logic, as well as that of common sense. It is thus not just having conceptions or ideas which is central to their truth function, but their further organization into a system. And it is a most important part of James's theory that there are alternate conceptual schemes.

Common sense is the original frame; it reflects successful decisions made in antiquity and consolidated in language, and doubtless they might have gone in different directions. To make sensible experience meaningful at all, each aspect of the sensible manifold must find its place in some conceptual manifold. These ready-made frameworks constitute the very structure of our thinking, but the sensible also makes further claims on us. We are wedged in tightly between the demands of the sensibly presented and the conceptual systems which order what is presented.

Yet there is an element of freedom or scope within both the sensible and the intellectual order. We can read off our perceptions in one serial order or another, classify them variously. The sensibly presented, though intransigent in part, becomes peptonized for the particular needs of our consumption and our options: twenty-seven may be 3^3, but if there had been twenty-eight dollars in the drawer and one is missing, it is one less than twenty-eight; if, however, a twenty-six-foot board is needed and the one in my hand is twenty-seven feet, it is one more than twenty-six. Similarly the Star of David may be correctly seen as two intersecting triangles or six triangles hanging together by their two corners. Sensible reality suffers different readings, and if the question of which is more true arises, it has to be settled in terms of relevance to a context.

In general, we carve out our subjects and predicates, cut the heavens into various constellations according to our culture and our labels (a big dipper or a saucepan). Caesar was just as truly a menace to Rome's freedom as he was the bane of the American schoolboy in James's day. So our nouns and adjectives are humanized heirlooms by which the past equips us to deal with the present and prepare for the future. And theories no less than terms are heirlooms reflecting our interests.

It is then the scope for invention and discovery, this plasticity, that allows us to respond to the claims of a problem, to the unprecedented, to the novelty presented in sense, and to the inconsistencies within and between conceptual orders—in a word, to correct beliefs and increase knowledge. This, above all, exhibits the selective and active character of our knowing and distinguishes James's notion of the role of truth from that of most preceding philosophies. He asks, then, how we settle into new and truer opinions; that we come to see today's truths as tomorrow's falsities is as indubitable as our claim of objective reference for some of our ideas. This dynamic characteristic of all learning, whether individual or social, is what has to be accounted for in a theory of truth; and for James it is the problem of assimilation—of the relation between the funded resources of existing knowledge and claims which the future puts on it.

We start with a stock of old opinions taken to be true; these are never tested as a whole, never put on the line as a totality. A strain is put on them; they either meet a contradiction or turn out to be internally inconsistent; new facts are met which are incompatible with the old ones or desires arise for which old knowledge is inadequate. Against these strains some accommodation must be made, and it is here where the freedom in the sensible and the intellectual order allows the dynamics for the increase of knowledge. The ways of accommodating are various and often optional but they must ultimately meet some personal feeling of satisfactoriness which maximizes the whole of the satisfaction of our knowledge. Truth sometimes grows by simple addition: new facts of the same kind can be added, or new kinds of facts. In this case there is a minimum of alteration in the old. On the other hand sometimes a complete rearrangement of our old ideas and their radical readjustment is necessary. Even so, an altogether *outre* explanation, one totally out of connection with the old, is never acceptable. James gives the famous image of the grease spot, and like many of James's metaphors it is as sharp as it is mixed. Knowledge grows in spots: like a grease spot it spreads, although we let it spread as little as possible. Like the spot, novelty sinks in and stains the whole; but in turn it is also tinged by what absorbs it. Our past then apperceives and cooperates in each new equilibrium which is gained in the process of learning. Thus we patch and tinker more than we renew. Seldom is a new fact added raw, and the new truths are thus the resultants of the mutual accommodation of new experience and old truth. It is this successful marriage of the new with the old which we accept as true.

The fundamental ways of our thinking then are consolidated in common sense, in science, in philosophy, etc. Common sense is the best consolidated way; it had its innings first and got embedded in our language. If our biological organization had been different, say that of a lobster, or if perhaps we had started on a different foot, things might have developed differently. As it was, however, common sense uses such categories as thing, same or different, kinds, bodies, minds, one time and space, subject and attribute, the real and the fancied, and the caused and the accidental, to organize its manifold or domain. These are the simplest ways of straightening out the tangle which our sensible impressions present. However, once we pass beyond the immediately practical, the language of common sense breaks down: is the table really a mass of moving atoms? is the knife whose handle and blade are successively changed the same knife? Where common sense interpolates things between intermittent sensations, science extrapolates its elements, its atoms, its fields, etc. Yet the conceptual schemes of science yield practical utilities and control; philosophy, if nothing else, provides its intellectual satisfaction. Common sense, science, and philosophy cannot claim exclusively to be true; if they are alternatives at all then they are equally true. The characteristics of theories are economy and fruitfulness, while naturalness is the great advantage of common sense—it is even said that the physicists play ball with a commonsense football.

Language is not an entity which preexists and is eternally unrolling before decisions and uses; it exists in the making by right and wrong idioms, by correct and incorrect use, for use is being made by the creations found in its use. New idiom grafts itself on previous idiom—previous idiom, new slang or metaphor, and then new idiom. Similarly with the truth. There is no antecedent or independent truth which provides the standard for particular true judgments, for truth develops always in the making. We plunge into new experiences with the beliefs which we and our ancestors have forged and fashioned into language. These determine what we notice, and what we notice determines what we shall do. Thus truth and reality are matters of our own creation; they must meet simultaneously the sensible, the intellectual, the novel, and all of these in terms consistent with what we have of past experiences. We understand backward, but live forward.

Truth then helps handle and lead to other experiences, it welds theory and fact, it marries the old to the new, but it is always provisional and it is always just the starting point for the next day's operation. Truths make us act, and such action brings into sight new facts which redetermine belief accordingly. It is this connection of utility with truth that has earned James the title of epistemological utilitarian. True beliefs are valuable as instruments of action. To say the truth is useful, or that it is useful because it is true, are equivalent, for the truth of an idea is a leading which is worthwhile. Truth thus is a species of goodness. It is the name of whatever proves itself to be good in the way of belief. It is good for definite and assignable reasons, but its major enemy in any given case is its clash with the rest of our beliefs. The truth, then, is the expedient in the way of our thinking just as the right is the expedient in the way of our doing. Of course it is true in the long run, true for the intellectual as well as the practical. But the notion of completed truth is only an ideal. Today's truth is the calling of it "true" today.

But if the true is the name for concrete processes in men's living, the imperative to seek it is an imperative that is shared by other demands that rise in the course of our experience. Indeed, we do feel both the claims and the obligations, but these are just the concrete reasons for the expediency of believing the true—of accepting what "agrees" with reality.

4. Pluralistic Outlooks

There was a "tendency" as James's philosophy grew, to fuse the principles of radical empiricism used as a criterion of reality with the pragmatic rule as a criterion for concepts and theories. Both were to be somewhat relaxed and thinned out as he attempted to reinstate in philosophy the problems of outlook and of practical concern—those problems which philosophy even then tended to exorcise and which have increasingly moved beyond the pale as problems became more technical. This is the James who was not embarrassed to exhort, to console the teachers, to elicit the moral lessons from the nature of habit-forming. These concerns, of course, are not late interests. They were strains that appeared as early as his own awakening to philosophy in his youthful mental crisis which was vividly described in *Varieties of Religious Experience* (1902). But they were the themes which are most developed and explicit in his later works, *Pluralistic Universe* (1909) and *Some Problems of Philosophy* (1911). Broadly these are questions of the nature of world and man's place in it, of religion and morals, and of a peace between the demands of science and religion.

We said "relaxed" above, because there is no doubt that radical empiricism will now invoke marginal, fringe, and subliminal experiences where many who were sympathetic to his empiricism could not follow him. But the momentum which had carried him from the early article, "On Some Omissions of Introspective Psychology,"[28] to the full account of the stream of consciousness and its wide use as a model, will now carry him into those somewhat exotic experiences which are nearly always cleaned up before philosophers embark on a theory of knowledge or a metaphysics. Neurotic and psychopathological experiences of a sick soul are no less genuine than those of a normal and healthy soul; both classifications— abnormal and normal—are made after the fact and for special purposes. And the pragmatic criterion is also relaxed (at least from the more limited uses of the preceding section), broadening from verifying consequences in particular sensible experiences to consequences for the quality of human living. Obviously here the return appeal to experience required by the notion of verification involves a different reentry into the perceptual flow.

It is worth pausing to consider the kind of phenomenal field James has in mind—one stocked not only with the ordinary stable perceptions but with lurking and fugitive fears, aspirations and hopes, a sense of alienation from the world with its histories and goings-on, and even a sense of alienation from oneself. The overtones of floating euphoria, that all's right with the world, cross those of anxiety; despair and dependence may find release in the sense of open possibilities, of a *more* than the events of humdrum living. Implicit in these phenomenal attitudes is a belief that carries the self beyond them. Courage and regret are authentic only if danger and failure are real. Decision is serious only if what we think and do can make a difference, only if there are futures genuinely in the making. Unless there is a real evil to be overcome and a good to be realized, morals have no roots. Even scientists share this sense of incompleteness, of discovery and open future, and the story of science and technology illustrates history really in the making; it would be pointless if it amounted to reading off a novel already written. Scientists once went to the laboratory to interrogate nature, but often ended by limiting themselves to just those questions which the laboratory could answer. Similarly philosophy has often sterilized what is askable by its entrenched ways of asking questions. When it simply ignores the practical, emotional, and passional life, and insists that novelty, self-identity are illusions, that there is no point in striving in a block universe, then it had better return to its drawing board.

"Block universe," "novelty," "striving"—these terms occur over and over again in James's later works. The first refers to a depressing view of the kind of world we live in, the second and third to what gives authenticity to religion and integrity to morals. Let us explore these in turn.

The "one and the many" is James's way of lining up the conflict of monism and pluralism—whether the world is an absolute unity or an absolute discreteness. This was a central issue in the battle of the schools of his day. James's fire is directed primarily at monism. He distinguishes two kinds. The more familiar is the scientific reduction of everything to matter and its laws. This was the prevailing view of the scientist of James's day, especially as advocated by the physicist, W. K. Clifford. Implicit in this view is a hard determinism in which all events are simply an unraveling of material that is already preset. Roughly on the model of celestial mechanics, if the place-time position and the forces operating on every particle were known for any given moment, the slice of the universe of any other moment could in principle be derived. The world is thus one, complete, and without novelty.

A second kind of monism, popular among the philosophers of the time, was the monism of the Absolute. This view, to which the St. Louis Hegelians were sympathetic, was propounded especially by the British Neo-Hegelians, whose outlook dominated Oxford philosophy for almost a third of the twentieth century. James directed himself particularly against F. H. Bradley. The heart of this idealism was an attack upon both the rationalists with their belief in self-evident first principles and the empiricists with their belief in self-certifying sensations. Instead of these, the idealists see the world as a systematic whole and all propositions as attempts to introduce a greater coherence in our grasp of the whole. To regard particular things as having an isolated or self-sufficient identity is a mistake since it presupposes that a thing can be defined by its internal relations, while everything outside it (its external relations) can undergo change without its becoming essentially any different. On the contrary, says Bradley, all relations are internal and every statement that is offered as true claims that the whole of the real will "accept" the content of the statement; it is not that Mary is a subject who is baking pies, but that Reality accepts the predicate "Mary-baking-pies." For Bradley, all relations, including temporal ones, are appearances. If all relations are internal, then nothing could be different from what it is without everything else being different. The net effect is a block universe, in which everything is determined and novelty is as illusional as under scientific determinism. At bottom there is only a unity, a spiritual Absolute, in which Reality and Truth are identical. James somewhere tells the story of the little boy who, having been told that God created the world in six days, asked his father "What has God been doing since?" James suggests the father's answer might be that God has been sitting for His portrait by Bradley!

James's strategy is to insist that monisms such as these have become dogmas. They are but portraits of possible worlds without proof that our world is like them. At best they are hypotheses having the same status as alternatives, including his own. His world is *pluralistic,* not monistic. Temporal processes are genuine, novelty emerges as a genuine feature of the world, the future has real risks and is not just the production of a finished scenario; moral struggle is a genuine contest and success is not guaranteed. We believe in futures which we can affect and effect—not only our own biographies but those of civilizations. Does philosophy really conclude that cities do not grow by accident, that buildings are not designed and constructed, that medicine does not truly advance? Are we not every day faced with unprecedented problems?

The pluralistic hypothesis is, then, also one among alternative unprovable hypotheses. Not merely plausible, it has many working advantages. James proposes a pragmatic and moral criterion for deciding such large metaphysical questions as how to confront the world. If the world were really alien and determined, then our sense of initiative, of responsibility, and even of attempted scientific discovery, has no point. It thus behooves us to choose that posture in confronting the world which makes our living and our projects meaningful. In all probability James did not think the chances were fifty-fifty (we shall see later how he tackles that kind of situation) but that there is rational support for a view of the universe which is not totally indifferent to man's efforts.

James's pluralism is a mediating philosophy. If he does not accept monism, neither does he find absolute disparateness; if he rejects determinism, he certainly does not think the world thoroughly capricious. And if the world's processes are not purely habitual, neither are they pure novelty: for novelty grows out of present situations and is continuous with them. His view is neither optimistic on the one hand nor pessimistic on the other, but melioristic—steps can be taken which will make things better.

James carries the same attitudes into the philosophy of religion. He is not concerned about institutional religion or ritual (unlike his colleague, George Santayana, who called James's *Varieties of Religious Experience* religious slumming). James's criteria for accepting the religious hypothesis are openly pragmatic and moral: pragmatic with respect to its experiential consequences, and moral with respect to the impact on the quality of a person's life. As may be expected of a radical empiricist, the first and last appeal is to experienced feelings. He does not even worry about the reference of religious objects, say about the existence of God; whatever intellectual constructions be later involved, religious experience is stamped with its own authenticity. There are two kinds of judgments to be distinguished. We are making existential judgments when we seek facts and answers to the origin and history of anything, but spiritual judgments turn to the questions of the significance of some thing. Thus it is not the origin of the experience—even in a neurotic individual—but the immediate luminousness to which the validity of the spiritual judgment must turn.

> *Immediate luminousness,* in short, *philosophical reasonableness,* and *moral helpfulness* are the only available criteria. Saint Teresa might have had the nervous system of the placidest cow, and it would not now save her theology, if the trial of the theology by these other texts should show it to be contemptible. And conversely if her theology can stand these other tests, it will make no difference how hysterically or nervously off her balance Saint Teresa may have been when she was with us here below.[29]

James defines religion (much as the Supreme Court was later to do in qualifying the grounds for conscientious objection): ". . . the feelings, acts, and experiences of individual men in their solitude, so far as they apprehend themselves to stand in relation to whatever they may consider the divine."[30] In this sense of religion the religious is omnipresent throughout history in the lives of most men. But what we take to be the qualities of the divine is relative to personal crises and conditions; thus the divine shows a multitude of different faces. Yet common to all of these ways of regarding the divine is the sense of a deeper dimension. In distinctively religious experience many persons possess the objects of their belief, not in the form of mere conceptions, but in the form of quasi-sensible realities, directly apprehended. There is the most pervasive sense of something other than the self. The contradictions and antagonisms of institutional religions arise not at this level, but when an Over-Belief is superimposed upon primary religious experience and becomes doctrinaire in a theology or sect. On the level of the experience itself, especially in times of crisis, one feels coterminous with something beyond oneself—the *More*—which is cooperating in helping right the situation. Whatever this *More* may be on the farther side, on the nearer side it is often felt as a subliminal or marginal resource of psychic energy. It is a Surrounding which is receptive to aspirations, and supportive. We fall back upon this larger presence in communion and prayer. This presence, which may be called God, is rather the subconscious continuation of our conscious life, pointing not to something transcendent but to a wider self. Direct consequences follow in this world often enough from religious experiences; they can be as historically momentous as in the life of George Fox or Tolstoy, or they can be the regenerative experiences of common men that defy the patterns of long-established habit and turn careers in dramatically new directions.

When James moves away from the religious experience to intellectual formulations, he is not averse to offering a speculative hypothesis to compete with traditional formulations. He has little stomach for an infinite, omnipotent Being, indifferent to his creatures, tolerating the dreadful ills of poverty and war. He rather sees God as finite, facing uncertainty in the conquest of evil, with whom we can cooperate and who is a reservoir of spiritual strength upon which we can draw if we can make the proper bond.

The moral meaning of religion is to be found, for James, in the sense of significance contributed to the quality of life. "Is life worthwhile?" is a momentous question, constantly with us, but it is not a purely intellectual matter admitting of an open-and-shut proof. Religious experience may not answer the question intellectually, but it supports a heroic and strenuous mood in which struggle becomes meaningful and so the struggle itself worthwhile.

This phenomenon of the attitude creating the fact plays a large part in James's concept of the *will* to believe, or, as he was tempted to revise the term, the *right* to believe. In essence this was directed against a prevailing view of the scientists of the day, especially W. K. Clifford, who insisted that it was never justified to believe anything on insufficient evidence. Of course James agrees that where sufficient evidence is available the alternative supported by that evidence should be accepted. But there are cases where either there is no evidence or the evidence for and against is inconclusive. And among these there are cases where not to decide is in effect to choose one of the sides. James calls these "forced options." Genuine options are those which are living (of concern to the questioner), momentous (having serious consequences), and forced. In such cases it is justified to let one's passional nature guide the decision. James sees clearly that this would apply to self-fulfilling judgments and to indeterminate situations in which belief may become a factor in tipping the balance. However, a deeper pragmatism is involved. It may sound coldly calculating to say: where two alternatives are equally probable, believe in the one that would yield a richer quality of life. But if belief is regarded pragmatically as itself a choice of kind of life, and contributes to the quality, then it loses the character of an arbitrary selection or illusion, so often charged against the Jamesean view.

Although James presents this account in the context of religious belief, its applicability is clearly as wide as contemporary problems in decision theory. It is the problem of decision under risk and uncertainty. And it is particularly momentous in decisions of political and social policy, where long-range decisions with vast consequences have to be made in the absence of decisive evidence.

In general, James's discussion of religion follows in a Kantian vein. Kant had reversed the relation of religion and ethics, defining the religious ideas by the demands of ethics instead of conversely. As is evident from the above, pluralism, theism, and the right to believe depend upon moral criteria. The same is true of his treatment of freedom of the will. The choice of a world that is in process, open to different possibilities and in the making, not only legitimizes effort, but makes genuine regret possible and remorse meaningful, allowing them a role in conduct.

It also enables us to see great men as creators of their world, not simply as witnesses of inevitable historical processes.

James does not ignore the problems of traditional moral philosophy. Moral theory was pictured earlier as an a priori system of relations, after a legal model, that was open to review largely in terms of consistency. It transforms the sensible order into a thoroughly different one and exhibits one of the drives of philosophizing—to forge coherent and simple conceptual wholes. Such an ideal system serves regulatively. But James also warns against taking any system, however beautiful formally, as final. Genuine progress, for morals as well as knowledge, can only take place in the interplay between conceptual systems and the challenges of a particular case. We could not be sure in advance which principle, if any, will cover a situation. New problems are ever arising (as we well know in our own day—overpopulation, exhaustion of resources, new forms of war, fresh bioethical issues, etc.), making unprecedented demands on the system. Thus the picture of a corrigible and progressive morality fits hand in glove with the conception of the universe as melioristic. This takes for granted that the ends involved may be objectively worth aiming at.

Now what is the material that gets fed into the system? For James it consists of desires. Demand creates value. Value cannot lie outside of experience; if there were no experience and no sentient beings there would be no value. In a universe with only one being with one demand, its satisfaction would define the good. Conflict arises between demands, with their incompatibility and multiplicity either within the individual or between individuals. Demands make claims, every claim involves some obligation while every obligation expresses a claim. The validity of a claim does not lie outside it but merely in its being asserted. The ideal arrangement of course would be one in which all claims are satisfied. But since this is not possible the question of priority arises. There are different modes of assigning priority—authoritarian, anarchic, utilitarian, democratic. James thinks in terms of experimental modes of maximizing satisfactions and minimizing dissatisfactions rather than an antecedent calculation of a greatest good. In "The Moral Philosopher and the Moral Life" he moves into a historical perspective in which institutional inadequacies like slavery or polygamy give way, and the evils of current institutions are continually challenged as dissatisfactions become articulate.

The course of history is nothing but the story of men's struggles from generation to generation to find the more and more inclusive order. . . . Following this path, society has shaken itself into one sort of relative equilibrium after another by a series of social discoveries quite analogous to those of science. Polyandry and polygamy and slavery, private warfare and liberty to kill, judicial torture and arbitrary royal power have slowly succumbed to actually aroused complaints; and though some one's ideals are unquestionably the worse off for each improvement, yet a vastly greater total number of them find shelter in our civilized society than in the older savage ways. So far then, and up to date, the casuistic scale is made for the philosopher already far better than he can ever make it for himself.

. . . Pent in under every system of moral rules are innumerable persons whom it weighs upon, and goods which it represses; and these are always rumbling and grumbling in the background, and ready for any issue by which they may get free. See the abuses which the institution of private property covers, so that even to-day it is shamelessly asserted among us that one of the prime functions of the national government is to help the adroiter citizens to grow rich. See the unnamed and unnamable sorrows which the tyranny, on the whole so beneficent, of the marriage-institution brings to so many, both of the married and the unwed. See the wholesale loss of opportunity under our *régime* of so-called equality and industrialism, with the drummer and the counter-jumper in the saddle, for so many faculties and graces which could flourish in the feudal world.[31]

The highest ethical life consists in breaking rules which have grown too narrow for the actual situation. At any moment a situation is ambiguous and can lead off into many possible determinations. The conscientious objector can envisage an alternative world and pits the present situation against the world which the rigid rule supports. We are all to some degree "blind" in the inability to depart from entrenched habits and old ways of looking at things. But every moral dilemma faces a unique situation and the combination of ideals to be realized and those to be disappointed by each decision creates a new world to which the entrenched rules may well be inadequate.

James wrote in the *Psychology* that the individual's decision on a course of action is a choice of character:

When he debates, Shall I commit this crime? choose that profession? accept that office, or marry this fortune?—his choice really lies between one of the several equally possible future characters . . . The problem with the man is less what act he shall now choose to do, than what being he shall now resolve to become.[32]

But it is more than that, for the choice of a self is at the same time the choice of a world.

Notes—Chapter Eleven

1. A special debt is due to Professor Louis Schwartz, whose doctoral thesis "The Emergence of Accounts of Purposive Behavior within Empirical Philosophy," University of Pennsylvania, includes a chapter on William James; Eugene Beresin, whose masters thesis, "William James and Voluntary Action," University of Pennsylvania, emphasizes the neurophysiological underpinnings; to Professor James Parmenter, who shares a delight with us in reading William James.

The following are the major works by James used in the chapter in the order discussed. We have used the (fairly) standard abbreviations.

The Principles of Psychology (New York: Henry Holt and Co., 1890) 2 vols., 8vo., pp. xii+689, vi+704 [P.P.].

Psychology (Briefer Course) (New York: Henry Holt and Co., 1892), 12 mo., pp. xiii+478. [P.].

Talks to Teachers on Psychology, and to Students on Some of Life's Ideals (New York: Henry Holt and Co.; London: Longmans, Green and Co., 1899) [T.T.].

Essays in Radical Empiricism, ed. Ralph Barton Perry (London: Longmans, Green and Co., 1912) [E.R.E.].

Pragmatism: A New Name for Some Old Ways of Thinking (London: Longmans, Green and Co., 1907) [Pr.].

The Meaning of Truth: A Sequel to "Pragmatism" (London: Longmans, Green and Co., 1909) [M.T.].

A Pluralistic Universe (London: Longmans, Green and Co., 1909) [P.U.].

Some Problems of Philosophy: A Beginning of an Introduction to Philosophy (London: Longmans, Green and Co., 1911) [S.P.O.P.].

The Varieties of Religious Experience: A Study in Human Nature (London: Longmans, Green and Co., 1902) [V.R.E.].

The Will to Believe, and Other Essays in Popular Philosophy (London: Longmans, Green and Co., 1897) [W.B.].

2. The secondary sources that have been of great help are:
Alfred Schutz, *Collected Papers III* (The Hague: Martinus Nijhoff, 1966). Cf. "William James's Concept of the Stream of Thought Phenomenologically Interpreted."
John Wild, *The Radical Empiricism of William James* (New York: Anchor Books, 1970).
H. S. Thayer, *Meaning and Action: A Critical History of Pragmatism* (Indianapolis: Bobbs-Merrill, 1968).
Craig R. Eisendrath, *The Unifying Moment: The Philosophical Psychology of William James and Alfred North Whitehead* (Cambridge, Mass.: Harvard University Press, 1971).
The selections that are helpful are edited by Bruce Wiltshire, *William James: The Essential Writings* (New York: Harper Torchbooks, 1971).

3. James is fortunate in his biographer: Ralph Barton Perry's *The Thought and Character of William James* (Boston: Little, Brown and Co., 1935) is a rich picture, drawing on voluminous correspondence as well as the works. See also Gay Wilson Allen, *William James* (New York: Viking Press, 1967). Of course there are many unresolved questions about the relations between William, the philosopher, and his brother Henry, the novelist. Partisan sympathies in that debate tend to follow professional ties.

4. Perry, *Thought and Character*, II: 437.
A sample of the bad press that James enjoys among philosophers is the misunderstanding of Peirce's letter in Morton White's *The Age of Analysis* (New York: Mentor, 1955), in which this self-criticism on Peirce's part is reported as a criticism of James:

. . . His second premise raised the old question "Good for whom?" and James sometimes answered characteristically "For the individual!" On the other occasions he protested that he was not leaving truth to individual taste. His ambiguity reflected an ambiguity in utilitarian ethics and it was not surprising that Peirce should have concluded a letter to James by writing "What is utility, if it is confined to a single person? Truth is public."

5. P., p. iii.

6. P.P., I: 1.

7. James remarks patronizingly in T.T., p. 7, that there is no "new psychology worthy of the name, only the old psychology of Locke plus refinements in physiology in introspection and evaluation." This has much the flavor of "there is no new physics, just Newton plus a little spectroscopy and relativity." James was comforting the audience of teachers by telling them that the study of psychology was not essential to their craft. James's attitude was in sharp contrast to Dewey's; the latter talked to teachers as colleagues.

8. *Independent,* September 8, 1910.

9. P.P., I: 182.

10. *Ibid.,* I: 144.

11. *Ibid.,* I: 226.

12. *Ibid.,* I: 275-76.

13. *Ibid.,* I: 288-89.

14. *Ibid.,* I: 461.

15. *Ibid.,* I: 463.

16. *Ibid.,* II: 343.

17. *Ibid.,* II: 291.

18. *Ibid.,* II: 561.

19. *Ibid.,* I: 424.

20. M.T., p. XII.

21. E.R.E., pp. 30-31.

22. P.P., II: 627.

23. *Ibid.,* II: 634; cf. "Reflex Action and Theism."

24. *Ibid.,* I: 309-10.

25. S.P.O.P., p. 620.

26. White, *Age of Analysis,* p. 159.

27. The "psychologist's fallacy" is a name loosely used for a whole series of confusions that James thinks generate puzzles, dilemmas, and unnecessary philosophical problems. In its simplest version the psychologist attributes to the subject's experience the properties of his own description of the subject's situation. For example, a subject responding to a "stimulus" may in fact take as a stimulus more than the experimenter intended, or the experimenter may attribute to him the analytic complex of his theory, whereas the experience was itself simple and unified. James uses it in more sophisticated ways—e.g., to analyze nominalist-conceptualist disputes in his philosophic writings.

28. "On Some Omissions of Introspective Psychology", *Mind* 9: 1-26 (1884).

29. V.R.E., p. 18.

30. *Ibid.*, p. 31.

31. W.B., pp. 205-7.

32. P.P., I: 288.

Chapter Twelve

Josiah Royce

Chapter Twelve

Josiah Royce

1. Introduction

Josiah Royce was born November 20, 1855, in the mining camp of Grass Valley, California, the fourth child and only son of pioneer parents who had come west in the gold rush of 1849. Like most forty-niners, the Royces found no gold, and Josiah grew up in difficult financial circumstances—but he was blessed with an intelligent, devout, and strong-willed mother who made certain that her son's education was not neglected. When Royce was eleven his family moved to San Francisco, where he finished his schooling, and attended the University of California at Berkeley, from which he graduated in 1875. The university offered no work in philosophy at that time, so Royce studied science under Joseph LeConte and English literature under Edward Rowland Sill, but his major interest was always philosophy, and after his graduation he went to Germany to pursue advanced studies in that field. There for a year he studied German idealism and listened to the lectures of Lotze and Wundt. Then in 1876 Royce began graduate study at the Johns Hopkins University, from which he received his Ph.D. in 1878.

Positions teaching philosophy were not abounding in America at that time, particularly for men who were not clerics, and Royce began his career as an instructor in English at the University of California. But he continued to work on philosophic questions, and to correspond with William James, whom he had met during his graduate studies, and it was James who gave him his chance. When James went on leave in 1882-83, he arranged to have Royce appointed as his substitute for the year. Royce so impressed his Harvard colleagues that with James's support he was made an assistant professor in 1885 and a professor in

1892. From then until his death on September 14, 1916, Royce was one of the pillars of that great philosophy department at Harvard which included James, Santayana, Perry, and many others. As long as they lived, he and James remained the closest of friends and the staunchest of philosophic adversaries, and the running debate over the respective merits of Absolute idealism and pragmatism which they carried on for years to the delight and edification of their students has become legendary.[1]

2. Early Philosophy

Perhaps the easiest road into Royce's philosophy is through the problem which he posed to himself in 1880: what is the purpose of thought? Royce's answer is, "the attainment of mastery over our experience, so that we may predict the same, and know the ways in which its data are necessarily connected."[2] Not "the hidden secrets of being" but "the laws of phenomena"[3] constitute our goal. It is accordingly necessary to know what constitutes experience: what is given to us, and what—if anything—do we ourselves create? Yet it is impossible to find any very clear answer to this question in Royce. As Cotton has pointed out, "Royce never identified any given in experience because he did not believe that the given could be identified."[4] Instead, Royce chose to treat the content of the present experience as if it were the given, regardless of what the content might be: "the content of feeling or perception or idea in the present moment is absolutely forced upon me."[5] In this sense of the term,

> When I judge "This paper is white," "This book is mine," "Washington was the father of his country," "A triangle is a plane figure having three sides"; in every such case there is, when I judge, something given in my consciousness, something that I passively receive, and cannot at the time alter.[6]

What is given is experienced, but it is not necessarily sense data—the idea of a triangle can be given in my present experience just as truly as a red patch. The given is the content of the present experience, where experience is used in a very broad sense to include virtually everything which is before the mind.

Our analysis of knowledge must therefore begin with present experience, but what is meant by the present? Royce defines the present in terms of the span of time of which the mind can be simultaneously conscious.[7] What the span will be is a function of the psychological characteristics of the organism: for human beings it is a few seconds, but this is a characteristic of our species and need not be shared by other forms of life. It is possible that for some forms of life a century may be the "present," and presumably for God all eternity is present. "The present" is thus a relative concept—a fact of which Royce makes interesting use in describing the relations between man and God.

What is given in the present moment is an incoherent congeries of experiences. If our goal is the mastery of this experience, we must go beyond what is given to achieve our purpose. Royce's Kantian heritage is evident in his insistence that knowledge results not from the given but from the operation of the mind upon the given. The manifold of present experience is brought to unity by being interpreted as a sign of something not given—by being made to stand for something else which is not directly known. The concept of a real world of which our immediate experience is in some sense a representation is thus a construct of the mind which is added to the given. So, too, are the concepts of a past and a future time. We cannot in the present experience the future as future or the past as past—we construct these notions in order to give coherence to the experienced present. Thus we identify certain present experiences as memories of past experiences, and through the synthesis of recognition we explain these and other experiences by referring them to a single object. Insofar as our experience can be reduced to uniformities, we succeed in achieving coherence and unity, and because the achievement of such coherence is our goal we project these uniformities into the future.[8] As Royce comments,

> We want to have a world of a particular character; and so, from sense-impressions, we are constantly trying to build up such a world. We are prejudiced in favor of regularity, necessity, and simplicity in the world; and so we continually manipulate the data of sense for the sake of building up a notion of a regular, necessary, and simple universe.[9]

We make sense of the present by viewing it in terms of an ideal context of our own making. This context is an imaginative creation of the knower's mind: "in it is expressed his disposition, his power of attention, his skill in recognition, his interest in reality, his creative might."[10] Knowing is therefore acting: although in knowledge there is always something given, there is also always something created by the knower.

But if our knowledge is as purely an imaginative creation as Royce seems to suggest, in what sense can it be true? We do not experience the future as future, the past as past, or the real as real: what warrants can we have for asserting that they exist?

> Why are we so certain that there will be a future? . . . Try to assume a condition of things in which time has ceased, and you introduce a time-element into your assumed condition. Try to conceive an end of experience, and you conceive of your experience as continuing after it has ceased. Therefore, there will be a future, because at the present moment we actively form for ourselves the picture or notion of a future. The denying of the validity of this fundamental act is the assumption of its validity.[11]

For any proposition P, if the denial of P implies P then P is not only true, but absolutely true. To say "there will be no future," is, according to Royce, equivalent to saying "in the future there is no future"—i.e., the tense of the verb inplicitly asserts precisely the existence of the future which the proposition denies. Again, you cannot conceive of a nonfuture, except as something coming after the present time and, therefore, as future. Hence the denial of the existence of the future is self-contradictory, and so the assertion that there will be a future is an absolute truth. Obviously, an exactly parallel argument applies to the past. Thus by dialectical argument Royce claims to establish certain truths a priori and so to show that even portions of our knowledge which are purely ideal creations may be demonstrably true.

But the problem immediately arises as to how far such a priori proofs can be carried. If we can prove the existence of the future a priori, can we then prove the character of future experience a priori? Can we, for example, prove the uniformity of nature a priori? According to Royce, we can:

> The solution of our whole problem will then be at least indicated if we can be sure of the following proposition: *That by future as by past we mean only certain notions we have, that are now and here formed by a present thought-activity dealing with present data of feeling.* Then of course assertions as to the uniformity of nature become mere results of analysis. The course of nature is uniform because by the word nature we mean the complex of experience conceived in the present moment and viewed as uniform. . . . Do we conceive of the future as in definite connection with the past? Then the future is in definite connection with the past. For by past and future we mean what we now conceive to be past and future. And so our anticipation of experience will become a construction of experience.[12]

When we construct the future and the past, we do so for the purpose of giving coherence to present experience: hence we embed the present in an experience conceived as simply and uniformly as possible. But the past and future are as we conceive them to be. Since we conceive the relation of past, present, and future in terms of a necessary sequence, that sequence is true.

> How is it with the conception of necessary sequence of the present experience from the past experience? Evidently this conception carries its own validity with it in so far as what we at this moment think as past is related to what we this moment think as present, in precisely the way in which we now think the one related to the other. The same holds as to the relation of future to past. At this moment we project our world-picture into an ideal past and an ideal future. The present moment is the builder of both the branches of the conceived time-stream. The rest is pure analysis. Whatever necessary connection we see between the facts of this time-stream, is a necessary connection because we see it as such.[13]

Whatever may be the character of the present, we shall so construct past and future as to make the relation of all three involve uniformity.

Now it seems clear that this method can be extended to prove that whatever you please is true. Royce denies this and offers a definition of error which he claims will show that error is possible even in this world. For by error, he says, "we mean, first, that an expectation of experience, possessed by us in the past, has since been disappointed."[14] And Royce remarks that in fact errors so defined do occur. But since what we possessed in the past is what we now think we possessed in the past, all that is required to make us infallible is a certain spontaneity of memory. Indeed, Royce's definition of error is not a definition of error but of our own consciousness of error,[15] and to speak of error in any other sense is hardly possible on his terms. If the past and future are nothing but what we postulate them to be, we cannot be in error about them. Hence the major problem of Royce's early work is precisely the question, how is error possible?

When Royce published *The Religious Aspect of Philosophy*[16] in 1885, he made the question of error the central issue of that work. Having labored long over this problem, Royce made its solution the basis for his subsequent metaphysics. How can we be in error?

> Error is . . . generally defined as a judgment that does not agree with its object. In the erroneous judgment, subject and predicate are so combined as, in the object, the corresponding elements are not combined. And thus the judgment comes to be false.[17]

Now what is the object of which the proposition is false? Clearly it is not any randomly chosen object but only that object to which the judgment refers. We "intend" the judgment to refer to just *that* object, and it is agreement or disagreement with that object only which makes the judgment true or false. But in order to refer to a particular object, that object must be already known. I cannot intend or refer to an object of which I know nothing at all. Accordingly, I must know the object to which I refer and I can refer to it only insofar as I know it—i.e., my reference can only be to the object as I know it. But how, then, can I possibly be in error, if error is the failure of my judgment to agree with an object as I already know it to be?[18]

Royce has given a famous example of this problem. Let there be two men, John and Thomas, who converse. As Royce notes, there are six people involved in this conversation: John as he is, Thomas as he is, John as he conceives himself, Thomas as he conceives himself, John as Thomas conceives him, and Thomas as John conceives him. Now when John refers to Thomas, it is clearly to Thomas as John conceives him. And when Thomas refers to John, it is to his idea of John rather than the real and unknown John that he refers. But it seems impossible that John can be in error about his own idea of Thomas, or Thomas about his own idea of John. Hence neither John nor Thomas can be in error, for although their ideas of each other are not true of the real men, yet they are true to the concept each has of the other, and it is only to this concept of each other that they refer, since the real persons are unknown to each other.[19]

Shall we then conclude that there is no error? Again Royce turns to dialectical argument to prove that the existence of error is an absolute truth. For if we deny the existence of error, what shall we do with the statement, "there is error"? If we affirm it, there is error; if we deny it, we thereby declare it to be in error: hence there is error. On either choice, therefore, error exists.[20] But how? The only answer, Royce holds, is this:

> To explain how one could be in error about his neighbor's thoughts, we suggested the case where John and Thomas should be present to a third thinker whose thought should include them both. We objected to this suggestion that thus the natural presupposition that John and Thomas are separate self-existent beings would be contradicted. But on this natural presupposition neither of these two subjects could become object to the other at all, and error would here be impossible. Suppose then that we drop the natural presupposition, and say that John and Thomas are both actually present to and included in a third and higher thought. . . . And to sum up, let us overcome all our difficulties by declaring that all the many Beyonds, which single significant judgments seem vaguely and separately to postulate, are present as fully realized intended objects to the unity of an all-inclusive, absolutely clear, universal, and conscious thought, of which all judgments, true or false, are but fragments, the whole being at once Absolute Truth and Absolute Knowledge. Then all our puzzles will disappear at a stroke, and error will be possible, because any one finite thought, viewed in relation to its own intent, may or may not be seen by this higher thought as successful and adequate in this intent.[21]

Now this argument is the rock upon which Royce's early idealism is built, and it must, therefore, be analyzed with some care. John and Thomas cannot be in error so long as they refer only to their concepts of each other. How then can they be in error? In order for this to occur, there must be a third knower who knows that John really means to refer to real Thomas, and Thomas to real John. This impartial knower must then compare the assertions of John and Thomas to their real objects and judge that they do not agree. But this argument immediately raises two basic questions. First, the imparital knower can compare only his idea of John's judgment about Thomas and his idea about real Thomas. But how do we know that his ideas of John's judgment and of real Thomas are true? Are we not driven to postulate a fourth knower to make that judgment, and a fifth knower to guarantee the correctness of the fourth knower's judgment, etc.? We can escape such a regress, Royce holds, only if John's judgment and real Thomas, and Thomas's judgment and real John are all ideas in the mind of the third knower, for about his own ideas the third knower may be presumed to be infallible. Real John and real Thomas must, therefore, be ideal, and if we generalize to all things of which we can err, it is clear that all must be ideal. The world is, therefore, whatever the all-knower knows. But second, the argument seems to be self-contradictory.

Royce began by holding that John can refer to nothing but his idea of Thomas. What difference can it make to John that the all-knower thinks he intended real Thomas? In fact he referred to his idea of Thomas and to that idea his judgment is true. This objection is far more fundamental than Royce at first realized. Royce asserts that

> An error . . . is an incomplete thought, that to a higher thought, which includes it and its intended object, is known as having failed in the purpose that it more or less clearly had, and that is fully realized in this higher thought.[22]

But this whole argument turns on the words "more or less clearly." What if John should flatly deny that real Thomas was what he meant at all?

The problem is more general than the illustration of John and Thomas suggests—indeed, it is the problem of the whole theory of reference. If I can refer only to what I already know, in what sense is a question possible? How can I seek for an answer to a question unless I already know the answer? And how can I recognize the answer when I find it unless I already know it? Royce's answer to these questions is given more fully in *The Spirit of Modern Philosophy*[23] than in *The Religious Aspect of Philosophy*. "You mean an object, you assert about it, you talk about it, yes, you doubt or wonder about it, you admit your private and individual ignorance about it, only in so far as your larger self, your deeper personality, your total of normal consciousness already *has* that object."[24] You cannot, according to Royce, refer to an object unless you already know it. But "you" is used equivocally here. The you that refers is not necessarily the same as the you that already knows. Royce illustrates this by the example of a man trying to recall a name which has slipped his mind. Here the conscious mind seeks (and so refers to) an object which the unconscious mind possesses.[25] Just so, Royce asserts, is John related to the all-knower. For John and Thomas are themselves ideal: they are systems of ideas in the mind of the absolute knower. Just as the conscious seeking and the unconscious name exist in one mind, so Royce asserts John and Thomas exist in one mind, and John can refer to real Thomas just as the conscious mind refers to the unconscious name. More generally, Royce's argument requires that John and Thomas be conscious subsystems of the Absolute's ideas, that the Absolute be conscious of them and so of their true intentions, and also of the relations between them—even of relations of which they themselves are not conscious. All this, Royce claims, is necessary if there is to be error. John and the Absolute cannot disagree about John's real reference because the Absolute knows what John really did intend.[26]

Royce briefly considered an alternative to his doctrine: viz., that the Absolute knower is only a possible knower. On this interpretation, John could be said to be in error regarding Thomas just in case, if a third knower were to compare John's ideas with real Thomas, the third knower would conclude that John is in error.[27] In rejecting this alternative, Royce asserts a principle which is one of the fundamental premises of his philosophy:

> The idea of the barely possible, in which there is no actuality, is an empty idea. If anything is possible, then, when we say so, we postulate something as actually existent in order to constitute this possibility. The conditions of possible error must be actual. Bare possibility is blank nothingness.[28]

For Royce, "x is possible," means either that x is actual or else that we have actually confirmed that x will occur if certain conditions are realized. A hypothetical statement involves possibility only in the sense in which a well-grounded prediction involves possibility—if the antecedent is realized, then the consequent occurs. A possibility never actualized is nothing. Royce never devotes to this principle the critical attention which it merits, yet it is one of the most important premises of his philosophy. In this case, Royce employs it to prove that the present existence of error cannot be due to a possible knower, because actual error cannot consist in a bare possibility.[29] If there is actual error, Royce holds, the all-knower must also be actual. But there is error, as the dialectical argument shows. Therefore, the Absolute exists.

From this argument for the existence of the Absolute, Royce can now draw some important conclusions. "All reality must be present to the Unity of the Infinite Thought."[30] There can be no error unless the thought and its object are both present to the Absolute. But there can be error about anything about which there can be truth. Hence whatever a true judgment can refer to is present to the Absolute. But the real is that to which a true judgment refers. Therefore the Absolute knows all reality. But Royce goes further than that: not only is reality present to the Absolute mind—reality is the content of the Absolute mind. For if it were not—if the Absolute only knew *about* real things—we should need yet another knower to judge the truth or falsity of the Absolute's ideas, and so we should be driven back forever and there could still be no error. What is, is what the Absolute knows.

We have seen above that in his early work Royce held that we can know nothing but our experience. His later position still affirms this, but "our experience" now means the experience of the Absolute. Like Berkeley, Royce held that we can know only ideas, although his use of idea is much broader than Berkeley's. And so, also like Berkeley, he holds that *esse* is *percipi*.[31] The Absolute's knowledge is constitutive of the real world. So the problem which Royce could not solve in the early 1880s—viz., if we actively construct the world we know, how can our mental constructions have objective validity—receives here a resolution by making the real to be what the Absolute actively constructs and our own creations true or false as they agree or fail to agree with the work of the Absolute.

The existence of the Absolute provides Royce with a basis not only for his theories of truth and reality, but also for his ethics. The ethical theory which Royce develops in the first half of *The Religious Aspect of Philosophy* was later fundamentally altered, but these early views have considerable interest both intrinsically and historically. The ethical problem as Royce sees it lies in the seemingly capricious character of our choice of goods.[32] What we seek is a basis for deciding among these innumerable goods. Such a basis cannot be found, Royce holds, by appeal to matters of fact, to instinct, or to conscience.

> We insist then that one of the first questions of the moralist must be, *why conscience in any given case is right*. Or, to put the case otherwise, ethical doctrine must tell us why, if the devil's conscience approves of the devil's acts, as it well may do, the devil's conscience is nevertheless in the wrong.[33]

But where are we to find such a warrant? Royce examines a number of proposed solutions to this problem, and rejects them all. In fact, he concludes, no objective basis for moral ends can be found: we are left with a chaos of conflicting ends. So, having reviewed and rejected other views, Royce then proposes that we adopt provisionally a position of ethical skepticism.[34] Now in what does skepticism consist? Royce's answer is that "skepticism expresses an indifference that we feel when we contemplate two opposing aims in such a way as momentarily to share them both."[35] If we were drawn to one aim only, there would be no conflict and we would not be indifferent. "Hence it follows that moral skepticism is itself the result of an act, namely, of the act by which we seek to realize in ourselves opposing aims at the same time."[36] Now this interpretation of skepticism is anything but obvious. Why should skepticism involve any attempt to realize the conflicting aims? Indeed, why need it involve conflicting aims at all? Why cannot we simply deny that a given aim has any warrant? Royce's argument rests upon his view of the nature of ideas of the will.

> How can I know that there is anywhere a will, W, that chooses for itself some end, E? Really to know this implies something more than mere outer observation of the facts. One must repeat in one's own mind more or less rapidly or imperfectly this will, W, that one conceives to exist in somebody else.[37]

Thus, like Edwards,[38] Royce holds that ideas of reflection repeat the internal process of which they are the idea. To have an idea of E as an end of action is to will E. Skepticism cannot arise regarding E alone, since Royce holds that even to think of E is to make the choice of E which skepticism denies—"in so far forth as he reproduces this will alone, he cannot refrain from accepting the end."[39] Indecision is, therefore, possible only when simultaneously realized ends conflict. "Therefore our skepticism itself was a hesitation, resulting from the realization of several opposing ends, and from a simultaneous reproduction of the wills that aimed at them."[40] But if this is so, Royce argues, skepticism has itself an end—viz., "the effort to harmonize in one moment all the conflicting aims,"[41] in such a way as to permit all of them to be realized. And this end, Royce claims, is universally valid.

For consider its denial. That denial either returns us to skepticism, in which case, since what is denied is the end of skepticism, the denial of the aim implies its adoption, or else it asserts some other end as correct. But then, Royce holds, the choice of that other end rests on pure caprice, for as he has argued before, no objective basis can be found which will warrant the adoption of any other particular end. Hence we are returned to the chaos of conflicting ends which leads to skepticism. In either event we must come back to skepticism and so to its aim, and so by the logic of the dialectical argument Royce concludes that this aim is universally right.

But how is this harmony to be achieved?

> The highest good would be attainable if all the conflicting wills realized fully one another. For then, not abandoning each its own aim, each would have added thereto, through insight, the aims of the others. And all the world of individuals would act as one Being, having a single Universal Will. Harmony would in fact be attained.[42]

The reconciliation of aims means the reconciling of the separate individuals who hold those aims, and this can only be done by each individual realizing the aims of the others. So Royce defines our moral duty to our neighbor by the maxim: "Act as a being would act who included thy will and thy neighbor's will in the unity of one life, and who had therefore to suffer the consequences for the aims of both that will follow from the act of either."[43] Royce admits that human beings cannot completely realize each other's wills: such interpersonal insight is for us an ideal which is never attained in this life. But it is also quite clear that Royce believes we can and should approximate that ideal. Yet just how this sort of interpersonal knowledge is attained, Royce does not make clear. It may be that to know that someone wills an end E is to realize that will, but there remains the problem of how we know what someone else wills.

The objective of these moral imperatives is the merger of all men into one being. "The universal will of the moral insight must aim at the destruction of all which separates us into a heap of different selves, and at the attainment of some higher positive organic aim."[44] The goal to be sought therefore is such an organization of life and action as would result if all men were in fact mere component parts of a superhuman self in which all particular wills were realized and harmonized. And that such a superhuman self exists is just what Royce holds to be the case. What the existence of the Absolute guarantees for Royce is precisely that the good is attained in the world, for the all-knower in whom all is known and brought to unity does in fact exist. "The world then, as a whole, is and must be absolutely good. . . ."[45]

But what of evil? If the world is absolutely good, why is it so obviously partly bad? Royce's answer is that without evil to be overcome, there could be no good. For goodness, Royce claims, is not innocence. If a man were so innocent as to feel no temptation, no love of evil, his actions could no more possess goodness than those of a robot. Goodness consists in overcoming evil: "the connection is one of organic part with organic whole; . . . goodness has its life only in the instant of the discovery and inner overcoming of the evil will.''[46] Not innocence but triumph over temptation makes a saint. Evil exists because it is a necessary condition of the existence of good.

Since evil is a condition of good, its existence does not introduce disharmony into the world—rather the organic relation of good and evil is part of that harmony. Both good and evil are known to the Absolute, but in the Absolute all evil is overcome. Those evils which individual men overcome in their own lives are by that fact also overcome for the Absolute—hence the need of the injunction to each man to do good. But those evils which triumph in the lives of individual men must also be overcome in the life of the Absolute, although we cannot know how. The proof that the Absolute exists and is good therefore guarantees that good will triumph—indeed, is triumphant in the eternal world of the Absolute—yet it does not deny the existence of true evil in the world.[47]

3. The Self and the Categories

The Absolute idealism which Royce espoused in *The Religious Aspect of Philosophy* marked a considerable advance over his earlier views. But this formulation depends very much upon assumptions concerning the origin and nature of the self, and concerning the relations among selves, which remain to be explained. The self for Royce is not simply an empirical object, nor is it something immediately given[48]—it is a complex dynamic structure which involves a self-conscious organization of experience. It is therefore something which evolves in time. ''No infant begins by being self-conscious. One has to learn to be self-conscious.''[49] But how does one become a self? And what sort of thing is it that one becomes?

The evolution of our own self-consciousness Royce attributes chiefly to our social experience—i.e., our experiences with other people. We become conscious of ourselves by the contrast of our experience with that of others. ''I am consciously myself, in ordinary life, by virtue of the contrast between my inner life as I feel it and the inner life of somebody else, whose existence I believe in, and whose life I find set over against mine.''[50] Such contrasts make us aware of our differences and similarities to others, and so of our own characteristics. Moreover, Royce holds that it is from others' evaluations of us that we are made aware of our own desires and values and begin to evaluate ourselves with respect to them. Social experience is thus responsible for the formation of the conscience and the ego-ideal—the ideal of what one wishes to be—and it is this ideal which serves to give unity and stability to our lives. For the ego-ideal, once formed, is relatively stable and serves as a standard against which our variable experiences can be measured. And by so doing, it comes to define for us what we are.

Now indeed you know yourself as one Self, as a person. For, first, you know your empirical self as the Seeker, meaning, intending, aiming at, that life-ideal; and here you have a contrast of real and ideal self. And, secondly, since your ideal is *this* ideal, the expression of the meaning of your unique experience, you can rightly contrast yourself with all the real of the world's life.[51]

To make the attainment of this ideal the objective of life therefore serves to organize thought and action into a coherent plan, and to provide a reference point from which all experience can be assessed. In this sense, the ideal provides a dynamic structuring of our experience, and that structure is the ego.

. . . the true or metaphysically real ego of a man, as I venture now with emphasis to repeat, is simply the totality of his experience *in so far as* he consciously views this experience as, in its meaning, the struggling but never completed expression of his coherent plan in life, the changing but never completed partial embodiment of his one ideal. His empirical ego, or collection of egos, is constituted by his relatively self-conscious moments just as they chance to come. His metaphysically real Ego is constituted by his experiences in so far as they mean for him the struggle towards his one ideal. A man's ego, therefore, exists as one ego, only in so far as he has a plan in life, a coherent and conscious ideal, and in so far as his experience means for him the approach to this ideal. Whoever has not yet conceived of such an ideal is no *one* ego at all, whether you view him empirically or metaphysically, but is a series of chance empirical selves, more or less accidentally bound together by the processes of memory.[52]

The self or ego is thus a dynamic structure rather than a substantive one, and its unity is teleological. The purposive organization of behavior about an ideal is the true self.

There is nothing in Royce's definition of a self which requires that there be just one self for each human body, and as the phenomena of multiple personality have long since shown, there can well be more than one. But there is a further sort of multiple selfhood to which Royce's theory very clearly points. For since selfhood is a dynamic teleological unity, which arises whenever one consciously views one's experience as the expression of an ideal, it would seem that any group of men might constitute a single person if they had all a single ideal and common experiences expressing the search for that ideal. Indeed, Royce's argument in *The Religious Aspect of Philosophy*—that if individuals would only realize each other's wills they would become parts of one superorganic being—would appear to be a perfectly plausible development of this concept of the self. Yet as we saw above, there is a problem here: is it really possible for men so fully to know each other's minds that they become as it were one person?

In *The Spirit of Modern Philosophy,* published in 1892, Royce advanced the thesis that knowledge is of two sorts—appreciative and descriptive. As our experience comes to us, Royce remarks, it is a congeries of essentially private feelings. I may be said to appreciate such experience, because it "feels to me so or so. I like it or I hate it."[53] But this appreciation—this direct acquaintance with the peculiar quality of my experience—is a purely private matter. I may think that other people also have experiences like mine, but I cannot directly feel their experience—I cannot realize it in myself—and, therefore, I cannot appreciate it. Nevertheless, I can and do communicate with other people about objects which we regard as belonging to our common experience. Why is it that some experiences can be shared while others cannot? The answer, Royce claims, is because some experiences can be described as well as appreciated. To be describable, experience must have certain characteristics: (1) it must be reproducible at pleasure, by which Royce means that it must be capable of exact recall, and (2) it must fall under the forms and categories of experience.[54] By the forms of experience he means space and time—"by categories of experience we mean at present the characteristics which enable us to say, that what we experienced consisted of one or of many feelings, of like or of different feelings, or again, of feelings that differed from one another, or resembled one another, in quantity or in quality. There are many other such categories used in the work of physical science."[55] Whatever can be classified under these forms and categories can to that degree be made an object of public knowledge. Concerning the temporal and spatial location of an object—its length, its weight, its motion—we can communicate; concerning our peculiar sentimental attachments for it we cannot communicate.

The Kantian origin of this argument is evident, but Royce is far from Kantian in his development of it. It would seem at first that Royce is saying that we can only communicate concerning that which we can describe, and we can describe only that to which Kant's forms and categories apply. The question would then be, what warrant is there for the categories, and one would expect Royce to call upon the Kantian deduction. But such is not Royce's course. He accepts the fact that space and time are generic conditions of human experience,[56] but he explicitly disavows Kant's deduction of the categories[57] and instead of basing the possibility of description upon the universality of the categories, he seeks to derive the categories from the necessary conditions of universal description. Thus he argues:

> . . . the one postulate of physical science is that the real objects revealed to us in our experience are describable in universal terms, and are so whether these objects are "things" or "events." In order to be describable, the things and the events must appear, to us men, in space and in time, because these forms of our experience are actually the aspects of our conscious life that we have to use as the basis of every description. Furthermore, in order to make our description valid for all intelligent human beings, the fashions of our description have to be universal. We can't describe the unique. . . . Moreover, in order to describe, we have to reduce the transient to the permanent. Otherwise the description would *not* be independent of the appreciative content of the

moment. Hence we have to describe in terms of assumed changeless things (e.g., atoms, elements, media,—in a word, substances). And in so far as the world of experience endlessly changes, we have to refer (1) these changes of experience to changes of space and time relations amongst the assumed substances, and (2) the ways of changing themselves, so far as possible, to universal laws. The axiom of the "permanence of substance" has this very simple meaning, namely that in so far as I can describe my experience to other men, who stand quite outside of this moment, there must be elements in the thing that is the object of this experience which are quite independent of the particular time when I experienced the object itself. . . . The axiom of Causation is the axiom of the Describability of Events, in so far as they are real and public and are not merely events as privately appreciated. The axiom of the Uniformity of Nature is the axiom that the event once described, i.e., reduced to an universal type, is described forever.[58]

The categories, therefore, provide a set of concepts in terms of which we are able to describe experience and so to make it public. The warrant for the categories is not a Transcendental Deduction, but the fact that by using them we succeed in making experience public.

The belief that there is physical causation is then the belief that such mathematically exact descriptions of the things and events of the world are possible, whether we have found them as yet or not. And the genuine foundation of this belief is the observation that only by thus categorizing and formalizing our experience do we find ourselves able to make its content public property, for our later thought, or for our neighbors. I must *reconstruct* my experience, or it is not publicly mine, is not universal, is not impersonal. And to reconstruct it I must lay stress upon so much of it as exemplifies forms and categories.[59]

To such an argument there is, of course, an immediate reply: such categories may be useful but they are certainly not necessary. Indeed, the justification for such a categorical schema is entirely pragmatic. We seek stability and coherence in our experience, and we classify our experience in such a way as to maximize these characteristics. The principle of the uniformity of nature means simply that we will preserve our description as far as possible. Royce cites the example of Paul, who was stung by a viper. The "barbarians" expected Paul to die, but when he did not they pronounced him a god. "The reasoning," remarks Royce, ". . . was crude, but not extraordinary."[60] The barbarians, using the principle of the uniformity of nature, expected that Paul, being a man, would die as other men would upon being stung by a viper. But Paul did not die. "Well then, what followed? Not that one changed one's description of a man, but that one looked for another class with another description, wherein to place Paul."[61] Hence they declared him a god. Thus the description was preserved in accordance with the principle that an event or object once described is described forever, and the observed datum was reclassified to preserve the conceptual scheme. And we do not do this because there is anything necessary about the description of men as those beings who die when stung by vipers, but because it is convenient to do so.

The contingent character of the categories is also made evident by the fact that one can easily imagine that quite a different set of categories might do equally well.

> . . . conceive of beings who were mutually perfect mind-readers one of another. Their highest spiritual world would be for them what, in our finite bondage, our physical world of the outer order is not for us, a world of "one undivided soul of many a soul." The truth of it would be universal, without having to be first abstractly described . . . the community of truth, in the world of such spirits, would be rather of the Hegelian type of universality, than of the ordinary type of the more abstract universality. Forms and categories there would doubtless be in the experience of such beings, but the necessity for such forms would be of another kind.[62]

Such appreciative mind reading does not occur among men, but its failure to occur is for Royce a purely contingent fact. Why our intercommunication should be limited to the specific forms and categories which science actually employs may be known to God but not to us—this is simply an arbitrary fact of life.

But as Royce goes on to show, the fact that certain types of experience can be described does not suffice to account for our actual knowledge. When I talk of a friend, "I *mean* my friend's inner life,"[63] although I never directly experience that inner life and cannot describe it. "Neither my friend's inner life, nor the human lives all about me whose experience I try to re-word in abstractly universal terms in my descriptive science, are themselves describable objects. They are, nevertheless, real";[64] because I can be in error about them. We can communicate only because we can describe, "but we could not even mean to communicate with each other, did we not presuppose, as an objective fact, such organic spiritual relations as cannot possibly be expressed in any physical terms."[65] All our intercourse, Royce argues, presupposes a world of spiritual relations which result from the fact that all men share in the organic life of the Absolute.[66] Only so can I refer to another mind which I cannot directly experience or abstractly describe. The World of Appreciation, therefore, does really exist, for it is the world as the Absolute knows it, and "the communion of spirits, then, is genuine, although we have no consciousness of a spiritual mind-reading of other finite beings."[67] We cannot actually appreciate another's experience, but the fact that we do communicate shows that we participate in the World of Appreciation.

Now these arguments of Royce's bring out a number of interesting facts. In the first place, this is one of the very few early writings in which Royce deals with the problem of the categories, and the position which he took here was later very greatly modified. Royce was clearly dissatisfied with the Kantian deduction of the categories, and was seeking for an alternative formulation. The concept of the categories as conditions of description leads to an interpretation which is essentially pragmatic, and which was later to be developed by Royce's greatest student, C. I. Lewis, into the pragmatic interpretation of the a priori.[68] But Royce himself did not pursue this line of development, or rather pursued it only to a limited degree. Whatever his dissatisfaction with Kant, he was not prepared to abandon entirely the thesis that human knowledge rests upon absolute categories. Accordingly, when Royce returned to the subject of the categories in 1901 his doctrine took quite a different form.[69]

Second, Royce's argument is directly concerned with the interrelations among selves. In *The Religious Aspect of Philosophy* he had virtually asserted that appreciative knowledge of other minds was possible. In *The Spirit of Modern Philosophy* he restricts this assertion. It is indeed only through appreciative knowledge that we can know there are other minds, but actual communication is limited to the describable. It results from this claim that knowledge of other minds is not provable in any scientific sense. That there are other minds, that they have experiences like ours, even that they understand our descriptions, become for Royce presuppositions of science which science itself cannot test. But how on this theory can one know that other minds exist? One can dialectically prove the existence of the Absolute, but one cannot dialectically prove the existence of other finite minds, and on Royce's theory there seems to be no ground at all for asserting them except an intuitive certainty born of appreciation. Thus it is clear that for Royce the most critical epistemological question is the problem of the existence of other minds.

Third, in view of the limits upon interpersonal communication which the theory of description involves, it is clear that even if human individuals are components of superorganic selves they are not directly conscious of this fact.[70] The Absolute can appreciate our experience, but this relation does not commute. Therefore if there exist intermediate superhuman conscious selves, including groups of human beings which are themselves subsystems of the Absolute, their human members do not have appreciative access to these superminds, nor can they exchange descriptions with them. Whether any relations exist between the human members and these selves whereby their existence can be directly known, Royce does not here make clear.

Fourth, the echoes of Hegel in Royce's argument are clear and unmistakable. Description rests upon the use of class-universals, but the World of Appreciation involves "the Hegelian type of universality."[71] It is quite clear that the "absolutely organized experience"[72] of Royce's Absolute is at very least closely analogous to Hegel's concrete universal, and that the ultimate union of individuals into one being which Royce describes is the organic union of Hegel's theory. Royce is not correctly described as a follower of Hegel, but he was profoundly influenced by Hegel and many of his doctrines reflect this influence.

By 1892 Royce had developed a form of Absolute idealism which although indebted to Hegel was nevertheless distinctively his own. But the system required more careful elaboration than he had yet given it. The central argument upon which Royce rested his position was the dialectical proof of the existence of error and the argument that error is only possible if the Absolute exists. But the latter portion of this argument, which is for idealism the crucial one, rests in turn upon a theory of reference and meaning which Royce had yet to spell out in detail. To this epistemological task, and its metaphysical corollaries, he turned in *The World and the Individual*.[73]

4. The World and the Individual

Royce opened the argument of *The World and the Individual* with the following declaration:

> I am one of those who hold that when you ask the question: What is an Idea? and: How can Ideas stand in any true relation to Reality? you attack the world-knot in the way that promises most for the untying of its meshes.[74]

Such questions may be approached either epistemologically or psychologically; they can be viewed as involving problems of the functioning of mental processes as well as of the nature of knowledge. These two aspects have not always been adequately distinguished—indeed, a clear division between philosophy and psychology hardly existed before the mid-nineteenth century. Locke, Reid, Stewart, and other writers "on the mind" were regarded as much as psychologists as philosophers, and rebellions against a philosophical position, such as the Transcendentalist revolt against empiricism, usually involved asserting a new psychology as well as a new epistemology. But by the later nineteenth century, Fechner, Wundt, and other pioneers had established a science of experimental psychology which was not simply a projection of philosophic theses into psychological terms. As a result, a host of problems which had previously been dealt with only by philosophic debate now became susceptible of scientific study, and in view of the intertwining of epistemology and psychology, the results of these scientific studies bore directly upon some major philosophic claims. It was one of the marks of the genius of William James that he saw so quickly the critical role of the new psychology, and by devoting himself first to psychology, and then to the development of a philosophy which, as we have seen, is in large part based upon that psychology, James forced both his followers and his opponents to redraw the lines of philosophic debate upon a new ground of his choosing. That idealism and empiricism both survived the trial by psychology testifies to the fact that epistemology is not psychology, but the idealism and empiricism which survived were fundamentally altered by their ordeal. No empiricist after James could claim that the mind is a passive recorder of sense impressions, or that complex ideas are compounded of atomic simple ideas. In this respect James's

Principles of Psychology marked a true watershed in the history of philosophy in America.[75]

Royce was a close student of James's psychology as well as of his philosophy, and of the psychological literature of his time. Although he was never an experimental psychologist, Royce achieved sufficient eminence in that field to be elected president of the American Psychological Association in 1902,[76] and he wrote an elementary psychology text of his own which appeared in 1903.[77] This book is peculiarly useful in providing a systematic statement of Royce's own psychological views, and so of his concept of an idea. For Royce, and for any student of James, it is not atomic ideas but the stream of consciousness which is the central fact of psychology:

> Consciousness is not a shower of shot, but a stream with distinguishable ideas or other such clearer mental contents floating on its surface. What we find in any passing moment is a little portion of the "stream," a "pulse," or "wave" of mental change, some of whose contents may be pretty sharply distinguished, by what is called our attention, from the rest, while the body of the stream consists of contents that can no longer be sharply sundered from one another.[78]

The content of this stream includes our sensations, memories, associations, ideas—in short, the total content of the mind. What we term "states" of consciousness only are more or less clearly defined segments of the stream to which we happen to attend. Such states are not Lockean ideas, though by selective attention distinct qualities can be distinguished within them.[79]

It is a fundamental characteristic of human beings, Royce holds, that they can learn from experience—i.e., that they act not only in terms of the present situation, but also in terms of the relation between the present situation and their past experience.[80] This characteristic arises from the capacity to form habits—a capacity which Royce interprets as meaning that the probability that a given response is made to particular stimuli is a function of the frequency with which that response has been made to those stimuli in the past.[81] This "law of habit," as Royce calls it, gives rise with reference to conscious states to the various forms of association, all of which Royce regards as produced by habitual connections among portions of the conscious states or among the cerebral functions which are the conditions of the conscious states.[82] Such associations serve to guide the play of attention, so that one state being brought to attention calls into attention other states associated with it. In this sense Royce holds "our present conscious perception of any object which impresses our sense organs is a sort *of brief abstract and epitome of our previous experience in connection with such objects.*"[83] For the sensations we receive are linked by association to other experiences in the past, and it is in terms of these assocations that we interpret our present sensations. Every idea, therefore, is an epitome of our past learning with respect to its object.[84]

The fact that our ideas epitomize our past experience means that the recognition and interpretation of current experience is always a process of assimilation. Habits of association once established, Royce asserts, obey "the law of the conservatism of cerebral habits":[85] they are changed as little as new experience will allow. It follows both that *"novel objects, that are otherwise indifferent, and that are presented to the senses, tend to awaken our attention, and to become objects of definite consciousness, at the moment when we are able in some respect to recognize them,"*[86] and that *"the new in our experience, in so far as it is unassimilable, tends to escape our notice."*[87] Royce does not mean, of course, that old habits are never broken or new ones established, but rather that we endeavor to assimilate the new to the old until we find ourselves led into inconsistency and absurdity by doing so. Old beliefs can be overthrown by experience which we can neither assimilate nor ignore, but whenever possible we seek to conserve the old beliefs.

Despite the influence of habit upon attention, Royce does not regard the attention as determined in any mechanical way by habit. In fact our attention is very strongly influenced by our desires and aversions, our interests and our passions.

> *To attend to any action, or to any tendency to action, to any desire, or to any passion,* is the same thing as "to select," or "to choose," or "to prefer," or "to take serious interest in," just that tendency or deed. *And such attentive preference of one course of conduct, or of one tendency or desire, as against all others present to our minds at any time, is called a voluntary act.*[88]

Attention, therefore, is a form of willing: indeed, the will is "the attentive furthering of our interest in one act or desire as against another."[89] Again like James, Royce locates the will in the selective attention, so that the problem of the freedom of the will becomes the question of our freedom to attend selectively to one course of action as against another. For Royce, it is enough to prove the freedom of the will that attention is not rigorously constrained by mechanical habits, and that our selection reflects our purposes, intentions, and desires.[90] Whether in some sense we are free to choose our purposes and desires is a question upon which Royce does not here embark. But in view of the basic role which attention plays in all thinking as Royce conceives it, it must be clear that from this perspective all thought, all conscious activity, involves the action of the will. The distinction between thinking and willing is thus for Royce a false division: to attend selectively is to think and also to will. Without the will there is no thought.

But ideas do more than express our will and epitomize our past learning: they are also plans of action. For as self-conscious beings we are aware of the patterns of behavior which we have learned to associate with the object of our idea, and we can, therefore, project these patterns into plans as to how we will act in the future. Thus, Royce points out,

Whoever believes himself to have a correct general idea of a tiger, merely because he has an image of a tiger, has only to ask himself whether his general idea of a tiger is such as to permit him to believe that when you meet a tiger you pat him on the head and ask him to give you his paw, in order to see that his image of a tiger possesses what Professor James has so skillfully called a "fringe"—a fringe which at once excludes any such disposition to deal with a tiger as one does with a pet dog. . . . If one's confidence, that one's general idea is a good one, is well founded, and if one then allows one's general idea of the object in question to become explicit and fully developed, instead of remaining a mere fragmentary image or word-memory, then one discovers that *the whole general idea involves what one may as well call "a plan of action," that is, a way of behavior which is fitting to characterise and portray an object of the class in question.*[91]

Thus for Royce an idea is a complex mental phenomenon which epitomizes past learning, expresses our purposes and desires, and furnishes a plan of action by which those purposes can be realized. Royce's kinship with pragmatism could not be more evident.

This psychological analysis provides the basis for the distinction between the internal and the external meaning of ideas which Royce drew in *The World and the Individual.* Royce describes the internal meaning of an idea as follows:

I have just said that an idea is any state of mind, or complex of states, that, when present, is consciously viewed as the relatively completed embodi-ment, and therefore already as the partial fulfillment of a purpose. Now this purpose, just in so far as it gets a present conscious embodiment in the contents and in the form of the complex state called the idea, constitutes what I shall hereafter call the internal meaning of the Idea.[92]

It would be difficult to imagine a less clear definition of meaning than Royce has here given, and we must accordingly try to find out what he is talking about. Since the contrast is drawn between internal and external meanings, and the external meaning is in some sense the reference of the idea, one is led to suspect that the internal meaning might be the intension. And this suspicion finds considerable warrant in Royce's discussion of the relations between internal meaning and essence. "The *what*, also sometimes called the essence, refers to the ideal description of the object."[93] That is, the essence is for Royce the intension, the characters connoted by the idea. But as Royce remarks, "so long as the *what* and the *that* remain abstractly sundered in our investigation we shall call the *what* the *essence*, or again, the *idea* taken abstractly in its internal meaning."[94] Again, Royce asserts, ". . . your idea, as an internal meaning, presents to you a combination of characters such as, according to your definition, some Other, *i.e.* some object external to the idea, might embody."[95] It would appear then that the internal meaning is the intension. Yet Royce emphasizes that the internal meaning is a purpose, an intention. One might indeed say the intension "expresses" the intention, but hardly that they are identical. Something more is clearly involved here.

If an idea is a plan of action, it is a plan for acting according to multiple purposes. My idea of a tiger provides a plan for action in case I want to eat the tiger, and (hopefully) in case I do not want the tiger to eat me. In this sense, an idea can be said to serve a purpose if its object can be a means to the satisfaction of that purpose and the idea itself involves a plan of action according to which the object may be utilized for that end. Such a relation of idea and purpose may be called extrinsic, since the purpose—e.g., my hunger—is not part of the idea itself. Now when Royce speaks of ideas as fulfilling purposes, it is clear that he included such extrinsic relations of idea and purpose,[96] but it is also clear that this was not his primary meaning. Thus Royce remarks:

> . . . you sing to yourself a melody, you are then and there conscious that the melody as you hear yourself singing it, partially fulfills and embodies a purpose. Well, in this sense, your melody, at the moment when you sing it, or even when you silently listen to its imagined presence, constitutes a musical idea . . .[97]

Or again,

> . . . the state or complex of states called the idea, presents to consciousness the expressed although in general the incomplete fulfillment of a purpose. In presence of this fulfillment, one could, as it were, consciously say: "That is what I want, and just in so far I have it. The purpose of singing or of imagining the melody is what I want fulfilled; and, in this musical idea, I have it at least partially fulfilled." Well, this purpose, when viewed as fulfilled through the state called the idea, is the internal meaning of the idea.[98]

The relation between purpose and idea which Royce describes here is quite different from the extrinsic relations of the tiger to my hunger. What is involved here is the relation of artistic purpose to artistic work.[99] Now the purpose that is involved in artistic creation is obviously a purpose to create, but more exactly it is a purpose to achieve a certain integration of form and content. The resulting relation of idea and purpose cannot be exactly defined apart from the created idea, and the integration of experience which constitutes that idea would not exist apart from this purpose. In claiming therefore that all ideas have internal meanings, by which he means intrinsic purposes, Royce is reasserting in new terms his claim that ideas are constructed by the mind. Whatever extrinsic purposes may also be involved, the intrinsic purpose is an artistic synthesis of experience—a creation of coherence and order out of flux. To know is to create.

Ideas, however, are more than artistic creations—they also stand for or refer to something other than themselves. The idea of a tiger presumably represents some object of the real world—something beyond itself. This reference to something beyond the idea itself Royce calls the "external meaning."[100] Such reference also involves purpose, for as Royce points out, an idea does not refer to everything external to itself but only to certain intended others. When one thinks of a tiger, one "means" to refer to a particular type of object, and it is only to the intended object that the idea can be true or false. The idea, as Royce puts it, selects its own referent.[101]

The idea also selects the type of correspondence which it will bear to the referent. We say that an idea is "true of" its intended object if it "corresponds" to that object, but correspondence can be of many kinds. The relation which a photograph bears to its object is different from the relation that the number five bears to the fingers of my hand, yet both the photograph and the number truly correspond to their intended objects in an intended way. An idea cannot be false to its chosen referent unless it fails, not just to correspond to it, but to correspond to it in the intended way. Metaphor is always literally false.[102]

The external meaning of an idea is, therefore, an object to which the idea intends to refer and to which the idea itself corresponds in an intended way. What is the nature of this object? It is, according to Royce, an individual.[103] The significance of this claim depends entirely upon what is meant by "individual." If the idea is to select its object, and the object is individual, it seems clear that the particular individual referred to must be specifiable in terms of the intension of the idea. Yet Royce denies this, for he holds that the characters connoted by a finite idea are always general, so that our finite ideas always describe a type of object—a type which can be satisfied by innumerable individual objects.[104] Now this assertion implies that Royce denies the Identity of Indiscernibles, even with respect to spatiotemporal properties. For although Royce admits that no two objects can have identical spatiotemporal coordinates with respect to the same origin, he denies that the origin can be specified without assuming the concept of individuality. For in the absence of a measure, there is no intrinsic character of any one point of space which will distinguish it from any other. To define individuality in terms of spatiotemporal coordinates would therefore be circular.[105]

What then is to be the principle of individuation? If the points of space are not distinguished by their intrinsic characteristics, how can any one be specified? It can be distinguished, Royce asserts, only by an arbitrary choice—an act of will, a decision that this point and no other shall be taken. To be individual is to be the object of an exclusive interest—a choice which both distinguishes the object and denies the possibility of another such object. Royce uses the example of a child's affection for a toy, which is such that no other toy can be substituted.[106] To be individual is thus for Royce to be unique, and uniqueness is guaranteed by an exclusive interest which essentially refuses to admit any other object as equivalent.

. . . the Principle of Individuation, in us as in reality, is identical with the principle that has sometimes been called Will, and sometimes Love. Our human love is a good name for what first individuates for us our universe of known objects. We have good reason for saying that it is the Divine Love which individuates the real world wherein the Divine Omniscience is fulfilled.[107]

Love is an exclusive interest which denies the possibility that there can be an equivalent object, and it is, therefore, a particularly delightful example of exclusive interest. Moreover, there are excellent theological reasons for saying that the Divine Love individuates the world, when Love is construed in an active sense. But Royce's fondness for this mode of expression should not obscure the generality of the point he is making. In any given inquiry, we choose some unit as individual. That unit may be a social group, a human person, a biological cell, a chromosome, a molecule—in short, it can be anything we *choose*. What Royce insists upon is that what is regarded as individual is relative to our purpose or interest, and rests simply upon our decision so to regard it. Individuality is, therefore, for Royce a teleological category—a category of will. And to ask whether there are real individuals is to ask what the Absolute chooses as objects of its exclusive interest.[108]

If an idea is true, it is true of its external meaning. By the same token, if the idea is in error, it is in error about its external meaning. But how can an idea be in error? We have already described Royce's use of the dialectical argument to prove that we can only err about the content of the Absolute mind. It follows then that the external meaning is an idea in the mind of the Absolute: it therefore realizes an internal meaning of the Absolute's. Indeed, all external meanings, and therefore all that we can refer to, must be ideas realizing internal meanings of the Absolute. But if what Royce has asserted is true, what is thought by the Absolute must be individual. It is what Royce calls a "life."

> We have now defined what this object is. It is an individual life, present as a whole, *totum simul,* as the scholastics would have said. This life is at once a system of facts, and the fulfillment of whatever purpose any finite idea, in so far as it is true to its own meaning, already fragmentarily embodies. This life is the completed will, as well as the completed experience, corresponding to the will and experience of any one finite idea. In its wholeness the world of Being is the world of individually expressed meanings,—an individual life, consisting of the individual embodiments of the wills represented by all finite ideas. Now *to be,* in the final sense, means to be just such a life, complete, present to experience, and conclusive of the search for perfection which every finite idea in its own measure undertakes whenever it seeks for any object.[109]

The world, Royce holds, is individual in two senses. First, our external meanings are individuals, for they are ideas of the Absolute, and since the Absolute has chosen to create just these ideas and no others, they must be objects of exclusive interest for the Absolute.[110] But second, the world as a whole is individual, for it is the self-determined and self-chosen life of the Absolute. In this individual life, all our finite ideas are satisfied, all our external meanings found.[111] Accordingly, the life of the Absolute is both complete and determinate, since if it were not so some finite ideas would remain unsatisfied—i.e., some questions would be unanswered.[112] The life of the Absolute is, therefore, the complete determinate reality.

In choosing to state his thesis in terms of the concept of life, it is clear that Royce is using this word in a sense analogous to Hegel's, and so that he is identifying the "absolutely organized experience" of the Absolute with the concrete universal— an identification already evident in his discussion of the World of Appreciation. It is only on this interpretation that Royce's account of being can be made consistent. The experience of the Absolute is described as a "complete" and individual experience which fully satisfies our ideas. But so far as our ideas are class-universals, they are not satisfied by any individual object. This shows, according to Royce, the imperfection of class-universals:[113] we must attain the further concept of *"that absolute determination of your purpose, which would constitute an individual realization of the idea."*[114] Recalling what the purpose or internal meaning of the idea is, what Royce is describing is clearly a concept closely analogous to Hegel's system-universal. The true idea is, for Royce, so complete an organic union of experiential content and conceptual form that this constructed whole is, like any perfect work of art, a complete expression and satisfaction of the creative desire. By calling it a "life," Royce indicates that this synthesis is organic: the form or intrinsic end can only be realized in this particular content, and this content is what it is only by its relation to the organic system.

All being is the absolutely organized experience of the Absolute. The internal meanings of the Absolute are fully and perfectly realized in the Absolute's experience, and these individual realizations are the external meanings to which we refer. Our ideas are imperfect realizations of these internal meanings: being finite we lack the full range of experience and the power to complete the synthesis—hence, Royce speaks of our ideas as "fragments" of the Absolute's ideas.[115] But not only are our external meanings ideas of the Absolute: we ourselves are such ideas, as the dialectical argument regarding error shows. We have seen that Royce defines the self as a teleological unity whereby experience is viewed as expressing the quest to attain an ego-ideal. But what can such an ideal be? If it is in fact an ego-ideal—i.e., an ideal concept of the kind of ego I wish to be—then it is precisely a notion of an ideal dynamic structuring of my experience which would be that ideal ego. The goal sought is just such an organic synthesis of experience and intrinsic aim as constitutes a life. And as our ideas embody or express our own will, so the Absolute's ideas express the Absolute's will, and since we are among the Absolute's ideas, our will is the Absolute's will, and our purposes are his. The Ego-ideal we seek is also the goal sought by the Absolute and partially realized in us, so that, when we are viewed as ideas, our Ego-ideals are the external meanings corresponding to us and realized in the experience of the

Absolute. It is, therefore, at once clear why we are individuals, for as ideas of a self-conscious and self-loving God we must be objects of his exclusive interest.[116]

It seems clear from the arguments presented above that Royce conceived of the "absolutely organized experience" of the Absolute in a manner very similar to Hegel's concrete universal. But it is also clear that Royce was not wholly satisfied with Hegel's doctrine, and these dissatisfactions were greatly augmented by the arguments raised by Bradley against the possibility of a consistent account of the Absolute experience. Royce was, therefore, compelled to seek for a more adequate model for the Absolute experience, and he found it, partly by Peirce's help, in the theory of transfinite numbers.

In his famous book, *Appearance and Reality,*[117] Bradley contended that the problem of how the many are combined to form the one is incapable of solution by the human mind. We can know, according to Bradley, that such a unification does take place, but we cannot explain how it takes place. We find by experience that there is variety in the world—that everything is not the same; and we also find by experience that the elements of this variety are somehow related. But as soon as we try to explain the nature of this relatedness, we find ourselves involved in a process of endless fission. For if A stands in relation R to B, then A must be related to the relation R by some further relation R', and then A must be related to R' by yet another relation R'', etc. Accordingly, we cannot say A is R to B without becoming involved in an infinite regress, and since Bradley holds that the concept of infinity is contradictory, this means that our attempts to explicate the nature of relation run to absurdity.[118]

Bradley interprets this regress of relations as indicating that thought itself possesses no principles of combination. Whatever things we know always appear to us as separate objects external to each other—hence, apparent combinations endlessly divide as soon as we examine them. But Bradley suggests that if this were not the case,

> The remedy might be here. If the diversities were complementary aspects of a process of connection and distinction, the process not being external to the elements, or, again, a foreign compulsion of the intellect, but itself the intellect's own *proprius motus,* the case would be altered. Each aspect would of itself be a transition to the other aspect, a transition intrinsic and natural at once to itself, and to the intellect. And the Whole would be a self-evident analysis and synthesis of the intellect itself by itself. Synthesis has here ceased to be mere synthesis, and has become self-completion; and analysis, no longer mere analysis, is self-explication. And the question how or why the many are one and the one is many here loses its meaning. There is no why or how beside the self-evident process, and towards its own differences this whole is at once their how and their why, their being, substance, and system, their reason, ground, and principle of diversity and unity.[119]

It is precisely Royce's endeavor to provide such a process.

Suppose that we resolve to draw upon some part of England a perfect map of England. This resolve, or purpose, is apparently a single purpose. But if we attempt to carry it out, we find that when in our map we come to map the very area upon which we are drawing the map, we must there include a perfect map of our own map. Moreover, when in that map within a map we come to map that very place upon which we are drawing our map within a map, we shall require yet another map. Clearly, the series of maps within maps so begun will never terminate: our single resolve has led to an infinite series of maps within maps each of which is an image of the others.[120] This generation of many from one Royce takes as exemplifying what he calls a self-representative system. Abstractly, such a system, A, is defined by the stipulations following: (1) x is a member of A; (2) every member of A has a unique successor, called its "image" or "representation"; (3) no two members have the same "image"; and (4) x is not the image of any member of A. Such a series is simply infinite, having a first member but no last, and possesses the type of order exemplified by the natural numbers or by the map series.[121]

Serial order of the self-representative type provides, according to Royce, the relational basis for the self. Royce drew this conclusion from Dedekind's proof that the set of one's thoughts must be infinite. For, Dedekind argued, consider any thought S. Then it is easy to define an infinite series of which S is the first member and such that if S' is any member of the series its successor is the thought "S' is one of my thoughts."[122] Such a series involves, as Royce points out, complete self-consciousness respecting the thought S, or alternatively it may be taken as realizing my purpose to reflect upon S. In either case, the series is infinite; it is defined by my purpose to reflect; it is characteristic of self-consciousness; and it is constitutive of a self defined as experience fulfilling a purpose to reflect.[123] And since Royce has defined such experience as a life, we so obtain a further specification of the meaning of that term, whereby an infinite series of experience or acts fulfilling a single purpose will constitute a life. Clearly from this point of view, it is an immediate consequence that each self is infinite, and so, if one conceives these acts as requiring a finite time for their accomplishment, immortal.[124]

That serial order is involved in the very existence of the self, and is a necessary expression of the purpose to reflect, means to Royce that it is a fundamental form of thought.

The intellect has been studying itself, and, as the abstract and merely formal expression of the orderly aspect of its own ideally conceived complete Self, and of any ideal system that it is to view as its own deed, the intellect finds precisely the Number System,—not, indeed, primarily the cardinal numbers, but the ordinal numbers. Their formal order of first, second, and, in general, of *next* is an image of the life of sustained, or, in the last analysis, of complete

Reflection. Therefore, this order is the natural expression of any recurrent process of thinking, and, above all, is due to the essential nature of the Self when viewed as a totality.[125]

Here then is the answer to Bradley. The fact that Bradley found the relation of the one and the many to involve infinite series was not due to any defect of reason, but to the fact that serial order does combine many in one. Bradley had the answer in front of him but rejected it, believing that the concept of an infinite series was self-contradictory. But Royce, following Dedekind and Cantor, argues that the seeming contradictory character of the infinite is due either to mistaking special characteristics of finite sets for characteristics of all sets, or to misconceptions respecting what is meant by being actual. Hence, Royce concludes, the problem of the one and the many is solved, at least abstractly.[126]

It is obvious that on Royce's analysis the Absolute must be a self-conscious self, and therefore a self-representative system. For to be is to be presented in the Absolute experience; hence for the absolute experience to be it must be wholly present to itself, and therefore, the Absolute must be completely self-conscious. All reality, therefore, is developed out of the Absolute's purposes to reflect and know itself. But since all human selves are ideas of the Absolute, yet are themselves infinite series, it is clear that the structure of the Absolute must be exceedingly complex. Yet as Royce points out, any infinite series contains an infinite number of infinite subseries, so the complexity of structure which can be generated from a self-representative system is boundless.[127] Royce clearly need not, and does not, attempt an exact description of how human individuals are related within the Absolute; it suffices for him to show that selves conceived as infinite series can contain subselves which are also infinite series. At the same time, the concept of infinite series helps to clarify the question of how the internal meanings in our minds are related to the external meanings in the Absolute mind. For we may conceive the Absolute as developing its internal meanings through an infinitely extended creative process whereby an original purpose is realized in absolutely determinate form. The finished idea in this absolutely determinate form may accordingly be thought of as a limit of an infinite process of determination, or creation. Our ideas respecting that object are part of the Absolute's ideas respecting it, since we ourselves are only the Absolute's ideas. The purpose to know that object which is expressed through us in our internal meaning is part of the Absolute's purpose, but insofar as our internal meaning remains vague and indeterminate, it is merely one term, or a brief segment of terms, from the series leading to the limit. What we seek as our external meaning is, therefore, our own purpose or internal meaning in absolutely determinate form. Thus when we think of an object, we, as part of the Absolute thought, help to create that object, and what we seek in our desire to know it is the final form of that creation. What is real, for Royce as for Peirce, is what is thought in the final opinion—the upshot of our infinite process of investigation. For it is the infinite process of investigation which constructs the object.

Such a theory seems at first to be open to the objection that the real does not now exist so that there is no real object corresponding to present thought. But Royce easily disposes of this objection. To say that our experience is in time is to say that we experience the infinite series which constitutes ourselves only successively. But the Absolute does not experience in time: the Absolute knows the entire series at once. For when an infinite series is defined by some recursive formula it is completely defined: every term of the series is thereby determined. This means, according to Royce, that for the Absolute the entire series is given *totum simul*— all at once. To say that the limit of the series does not now exist is, therefore, to misunderstand the nature of reality. Although we live, so to speak, from term to term of the series, the Absolute knows the entire series at once, so that what is real—i.e., what the Absolute knows—is independent of time.[128]

It follows from Royce's analysis that we are part of the Absolute. When we will, our will is God's will, or equally, God wills in us. Are we then free? Royce replies that we are free in the same sense that the Absolute is free.[129] But is the Absolute free? Royce insists that it is, for the Absolute chooses to create just the determinate individual world that it does create, and therefore whatever is willed in this world is freely willed. But could the Absolute have willed otherwise?[130]

Royce saw the problem involved here quite clearly. For a choice to be genuine, it must be a choice among alternatives, and those alternatives must be really possible—i.e., it must really be possible to choose any one. But to be real is to be what the Absolute knows, or, equally, chooses. How then can there be real alternatives which the Absolute does not choose? Are we not forced to say that there are no real alternatives, and hence that the Absolute could not have chosen otherwise? Royce emphatically denies this:

> Determinate decisions of the will involve rendering invalid countless possibilities that, but for this choice, might have been entertained as valid. In such cases the nature of the rejected possibilities is sufficiently expressed, in concrete form, by the will that decides, *if only it knows itself as deciding, and is fully conscious of how and why it decides.* That Absolute insight would mean absolute decision, and so a refusal to get presented in experience endlessly numerous contents that, but for the decision, would have been possible,—this I maintain as a necessary aspect of the whole conception of individuality.[131]

That is to say, the Absolute knows the alternative possibilities, chooses against them, and so excludes them, and the alternatives are therefore known as excluded. They are therefore real, unactualized possibilities—real because known, unactualized because excluded. They are even, Royce says, presented, but only as excluded possibilities.[132] Hence Royce insists the Absolute could have chosen otherwise, and is free.

It seems very doubtful that Royce is entitled to this conclusion, for it involves playing fast and loose with the concept of possibility. We have seen that in earlier writings Royce denied that there could be possible facts which were not grounded in the actual. Similarly, Royce repeatedly attacked the theory that validity can rest upon possible experience by demanding to know just what sort of being is to be attributed to possible experience which does not occur.[133] But if the concept of actual experience is so broadened that unactualized possibilities are actually experienced, it is difficult to see what is left out. Royce attacked the idea that there could be two sorts of being "both known to us as valid, but the one individual, the other universal, the one empirical, the other merely ideal, the one present, the other barely possible, the one a concrete life, the other a pure form."[134] Yet when Royce describes unactualized possibilities as "defined by consciousness only in relatively general terms. As mere kinds of experience, the facts which attention thus excludes are themselves part of the very consciousness which forbids them to have any richer and more concrete Being than this character of remaining mere aspects of the whole. In this sense, but in this only, are they facts whose nature is experienced"[135]—he is granting for his own theory what he denies for others.

The use of self-representative systems to describe selfhood, and so to describe the absolutely organized experience of the Absolute, involves an attempt on Royce's part to reconstruct Hegel's notion of the concrete universal by substituting the concept of serial order for that of organic relation. Thus Royce remarks, "This observation [that the self is a self-representative system], in the present form, cannot be said to be due to Hegel, although both his analysis and Fichte's account of the self, imply a theory that apparently needs to be developed into this more modern form."[136] In making this attempted reconstruction, Royce was of course seeking to answer Bradley's denial of the possibility of systematic unity, and, for reasons which we have examined already, Royce was convinced that the concept of serial order was an adequate solution to these difficulties. But is a series an adequate substitute for the concrete universal? To see why Royce thought it was, one must look at Royce's interpretation of Hegel's theory of the concrete universal. Royce describes Hegel's doctrine as follows:

> The true universal, namely, or as Hegel calls it, the *Begriff,* whose highest expression is to be the absolute *Idee,* is the organic union of the universal truth and the individual facts, an union determined by the principle that every truth is a truth constructed by the thought of the world-self, and that as such it will exemplify just that multiplicity of individual facts in the all-embracing and so universal unity of self-consciousness. . . . This universal is no abstraction at all, but a perfectly *concrete* whole, since the facts are, one and all, not mere examples of it, but are embraced in it, are brought forth by it as its moments, and exist only in relation to one another and to it. It is the vine; they, the individuals, are the branches. It is in nature the self.[137]

Royce interprets Hegel as saying that universal and individual are related as system and part: the universal is "not an abstract something *exemplified* by the individuals, nor yet an essence that is to be found *in each individual,*"138 but it is the systematic unity of many parts combined in one whole. The unity is concrete, for it does not exist apart from the whole, and it determines the part which, without the whole, would have no existence. Such a systematic unity is called "organic" because it is the type of unity illustrated by an organism. Moreover, Royce explicitly identifies organic unity with selfhood: "For organism is selfhood or personality viewed in its outward manifestation."139 Accordingly, Royce also regards the universal as necessarily involving self-consciousness, so that every such universal is self-conscious, and all self-consciousness involves such an organic unity. "But the deeper insight into the world is revealed to us through a reflection upon the nature of self-consciousness, wherein the universal, or self, is the organic total of the facts of consciousness, which exist not save as related to one another, and to this universal."140 So to define the self in terms of serial order must imply for Royce that the concrete universal can be similarly defined.

Consider the concept of the series of natural numbers. If we examine this concept, we find that it involves a well-ordered infinite series. It cannot be said that the individual members of this series "instance" the concept of the series, yet it is also true that the concept of the series is fully and completely realized in this infinite array of numbers. The series forms a unity; moreover, what belongs to this unity is completely determined by the definition and admits neither of addition nor deletion, so that as a realization of the concept the infinite series is a complete, determinate, and final embodiment. Thus the series considered as a whole involves a unification of many into one such that the unity is not properly separable from the concrete embodiment: as Russell notes, "a *series* is the same thing as a serial relation."141 Royce's belief that the concept of serial order could produce a concrete realization having the properties of the concrete universal has a good deal to recommend it.142

But to this account an immediate objection must be raised, viz., the validity of this account depends completely upon how one chooses to define the natural numbers. For Royce's argument to hold, the natural numbers must be a specific set of entities, as, e.g., Russell-Whitehead numbers. If they were defined by the Peano axioms alone, then we would have a definition only of a general type of order admitting of an infinite number of realizations, so that the concept of the "series of natural numbers" would turn out to be a class-universal after all. Royce was very clearly aware of this difficulty and undertook to answer it in a way that was extremely ingenious. Before analyzing Royce's answer, however, we must turn to the discussion of certain other aspects of his philosophy.

In the second series of lectures on *The World and the Individual,*143 Royce returned to the question of the division between the World of Description and the World of Appreciation and so to the question of the categories, but he did so from the standpoint of his newly developed metaphysics. According to this new doctrine, to be is to fulfill a purpose of the Absolute. Any ultimate explanation of what there is must therefore be in terms of the purposes of the Absolute. But we are not generally conscious of such ultimate purposes even in the case of ourselves, and still less so with respect to other things, so in seeking to account for the behavior of other objects and to bring the experiences with which they present us into a coherent whole fulfilling our own purposes, we are often forced to deal with them by describing their overt behavior rather than by viewing them in relation to their ultimate ends.[144]

Such description always embodies our own purposes. It is one of the marks of our finitude that we cannot attend at once to all the content of the stream of consciousness—as James pointed out, we must select a very few elements to attend to, while the remainder are relegated to the background of consciousness. Every such selection by attention is an act of choice from among the objects of possible attention and expresses our purposes and interests. Moreover, when we attend to something, we do so first of all in terms of likeness and difference. Now for any two objects, A and B, Royce points out that to describe them as different is also to describe them as like, and conversely. For if they are said to differ in color, they are thereby affirmed to be like in possessing color; if they differ in length, yet they both have length. Indeed, likeness and difference are reciprocal, and the decision whether to regard things as like or different is determined, not by the intrinsic characters of the objects, but by our purposes. The importance of measurement in contemporary science reflects our decision to attend to minute quantitative differences in length, weight, etc., of objects which might with equal legitimacy be classed as like.[145]

The categories of likeness and difference are the basis of our classifications, and so our classifications are teleological through and through. We classify as same or distinct in terms of our interests, purposes, and desires.[146] Whether or not these classifications are objective, in the sense of revealing something about the true natures of the objects of our experience, is a question of how our classifications correspond to those of the Absolute. If we class together those things which the Absolute regards as like, our classifications are correct—if not, not. "God distinguishes what it pleases him to distinguish. The logical as well as the moral problem is, Does my will accord with God's Will?"[147]

The descriptions of the world about us which we construct are produced, Royce argues, by a process of discrimination[148] through which we distinguish one thing from another. But discrimination, Royce holds, involves a definite logical structure. If I discriminate two facts in space, by so doing I define something which lies between the facts discriminated, and I further define two parts of space between which the two facts lie.[149] Similarly, if I discriminate two facts in time—e.g., two states of a body—I thereby define a state between the two states, and preceding and following states between which the two states lie. And having discriminated two states, and so a third between them, I can then further discriminate each from this third, so producing again an intermediary state. The process of discrimination is thus a recurrent process capable of infinite repetition, and so involves at least the infinite divisibility of that which lies between the two states initially discriminated.

Thus if I discriminate state A of a body from state B, by doing so I define state C between A and B. But I may then discriminate A from C by finding D between them, etc. Thus I reach the dense series A . . . D . . . C . . . B, and the number of intermediaries discriminated is in theory enumerably infinite. Because Royce holds our discriminations are made between facts in space and time, we usually attribute the infinite divisibility to space and time themselves, but this attribution is not necessarily correct. It is the discriminating process which we apply which makes it necessary to suppose that the space and time of the world of description are infinite and infinitely divisible forms for such an activity.[150]

The fact that the process of discrimination has such a structure means that the result of discrimination is always a dense series. We may accordingly view the series of states connecting two states of a body as a process whereby the earlier state A is transformed into the later state B. Since likeness and difference are reciprocal, the differentiation of the terminal states also implies their similiarity in at least some respect, so that some characters of the body are unchanged by the transformation of A into B. These unvarying characteristics Royce observes may be called the "invariant characters of this system of transformations."[151] Royce then remarks:

> Wherever I can say that, in passing from A to B, through a series of stages which I have a right to view as real facts in the world, I observe, or validly conceive, that all the stages have certain uniform or "invariant" characters, I then have discovered a law which, in this way of interpreting the world, I conceive of expressing the nature and structure of the facts that I acknowledge as real.[152]

Although this formulation of the concept of physical law is clearly derived from a rather weak analogy with Klein's Erlanger classification of geometry,[153] the grounds for it are more than purely analogical. What Royce is seeking to emphasize is the role of conservation laws in physical science. The behavior of a system of material bodies is predictable in Newtonian physics just in case mass and energy are conserved, or invariant, under the transformations applied.[154] Royce's thesis is a generalization of this fact into a principle governing all laws of nature—a generalization which is speculative, since the existence of conservation laws is not proven in all domains of science, but which Royce regards as a necessary basis for an exact science.

The objective of description is the reduction of the changes observed in nature to law, defined as the stipulation of the dense series connecting prior and posterior states together with its invariants. "Observe facts, and then look for their linkages. That is the one maxim of my procedure,—the maxim of descriptive science stated in its most abstract form."[155] Royce holds that the categories of likeness and difference, betweenness, and dense series are fundamental for descriptive science. Nor are these the only categories.[156] Royce does not attempt to provide an exhaustive list, but the other examples he gives—e.g., continuity—are similar in nature to these. But these categories of description are markedly different from those he advanced in 1892. The earlier categories were essentially the primitives of physical science, and were viewed as justified by the fact that their use made experience independent of the content of the present moment and so describable. But the categories which Royce now advances are due to what may be called the logical structure of certain of our psychological processes, e.g., comparison and discrimination. Royce affirms "the thesis that the laws of the objective world are the expression of Categories which the nature of every subjective process, and the Unity of Apperception wherein all truth is embraced, together determine."[157] It is the fact that our psychological processes have such a structure which guarantees that our descriptions will embody these categories and insofar as these psychological processes are common to all knowers there will be intersubjective agreement. Accordingly, this concept of the categories is not pragmatically justified, but rests upon a deeper basis—the logical forms of the activity of the mind in knowing.

Despite the justification for the categories of description and the intersubjective agreement which our descriptions command, Royce regards the world of description as incomplete and inadequate. In the first place, we are not in fact able to produce descriptions of all the phenomena we seek to account for—the necessary intermediaries frequently elude us and we are not able to trace out the detailed connections between facts which our explanations require.[158] Second, the World of Description is the world of facts accredited by the experience of mankind—the intersubjectively real world. But the totality of human experience which gives accreditation to this descriptive account is a totality which is never experienced as such by any finite mind. The existence of this totality is therefore not a fact of the world of description, since no one can verify it, yet unless its existence is assumed the warrant for descriptive science fails. Hence unless we go beyond the world as described, we have no warrant for our descriptions.[159] Third, the laws of descriptive science are general and serve to define types of processes. The World of Description is therefore not truly individual, in Royce's sense of that term—it is only described for us in general terms. But according to Royce's metaphysics the world as it is must be truly individual. Hence the world of description cannot be the true world.[160] Finally descriptive science presents us with a world whose laws describe processes as dense series. What then becomes of the self in this scheme, for as Royce had argued at length in the Supplementary Essay, every self-conscious self, including the Absolute, is a self-representative system and so involves an infinite well-ordered series. But no such entity is known to the World of Description nor can such an entity be described in terms of the laws of that domain.[161] Furthermore, not only is the self not describable, but the activity of the self in making descriptions is also indescribable. For although discrimination yields a dense order, yet the process of infinite subdivision which discrimination involves requires a well-ordered series of acts of discrimination and so is itself of the self-representative variety. Hence were it not the fact that the activity of the self is characterized by a type of order unknown to the World of Description, the processes by which the World of Description is constructed would be impossible.[162] The World of Description is therefore not the real world but is in some sense an aspect of the World of Appreciation.

The World of Description is preeminently the world of what we call material nature. Our descriptive science is most adequate in dealing with the least animate of things, and our theory of nature is based on descriptive categories. Thus what we ordinarily take to be a fact of nature is something which must be public knowledge. As Royce remarks, if I were to affirm the existence of a physical object which no one else could see, touch, or any way experience, not only would everyone deny the existence of my object but I should do so myself if I were not irrational.[163] Thus when we talk of nature, we mean a realm of publicly or intersubjectively real objects. But this in turn implies the logical priority of other minds: without other minds there can be no public knowledge. Hence our first question about what there is is why do we assert the existence of other minds?

This question must be sharply distinguished from the question of the existence of the Absolute. The existence of the Absolute can be proven dialectically and so is an absolute or necessary truth. The question at stake here is the existence of finite minds other than my own. That there are such other finite minds is not provable dialectically and so must rest on other grounds. What, Royce asks, are these grounds? That we learn of the existence of others as empirical objects in the same way we learn of tables and chairs Royce admits, but this does not solve the problem of other minds, for we attribute minds to human objects and not to tables and chairs, and it is just this difference which is in question. Royce's answer is that while we experience tables and chairs as objects which resist our purposes, we experience our fellowmen as sources of ideas which supplement and complete our own.

Our fellows are known to be real, and to have their own inner life, because they are for each of us the endless treasury of *more ideas.* They answer our questions; they tell us news; they make comments; they pass judgments; they express novel combinations of feelings; they relate to us stories; they argue with us, and take counsel with us. Or, to put the matter in a form still nearer to that demanded by our Fourth Conception of Being: *Our fellows furnish us the constantly needed supplement to our own fragmentary meanings.*[164]

It is this fact of supplementarity which leads us to distinguish other minds from other objects, not any supposed analogy between their behavior and ours. Now this account clearly assumes the possibility of interpersonal communication as a ground for our discovery of the existence of other minds. But this assumption is legitimate, Royce argues, since everything we know from psychology about the development of the self indicates that social experience is prior to and formative in the development of the self. Without language and interpersonal communication, there would be no self to raise the question of the existence of other minds. Both genetically and logically the hypothesis of other minds would be untenable without the prior possibility of interpersonal communication.[165]

Once I can recognize other minds as centers of meanings, Royce holds, I can interpret the physical behavior of other bodies as expressions of those meanings. And I can also discover that I and my fellowman describe other objects which are common to us both. For not only can I observe another's behavior toward objects of my world, but with respect to two senses—sight and touch—I can actually observe others in the act of observing a third object. It is this fact, Royce argues, which accounts for the primacy which we accord to sight and touch over the other three senses when it comes to deciding what is real, for I can see that you are looking at the same object I am observing and I can feel you touch the same object I touch, while I cannot observe that you hear or smell or taste it.[166] Thus my assurance of a world of material objects is thoroughly social: that world consists of those objects which I find that I and my fellowmen describe and behave toward in similar ways.

But what is the true nature of the World of Description? Is it really a world of material nature, or have its objects some other sort of being? From the standpoint of Royce's idealism, it is obvious that even material nature must be ideal, but that fact does not tell us in any detail what sort of ideal being nature has. To answer this question, Royce remarks certain respects in which nature appears to be similar to mind. First, Royce stresses the significance of the difference between those laws of nature which define reversible processes and those which define irreversible ones. The processes which characterize mind are according to Royce irreversible—growth, learning, the flow of the stream of consciousness have a definite temporal direction. But nature also has such processes, e.g., evolution and the increase of entropy, and to the degree to which such processes are characteristic of nature, it is at least possible to hold that nature is really conscious mind. But nature also has other processes, such as those described by the laws of mechanics, which are reversible, and to maintain his thesis Royce must explain away these exceptions. He seeks to do this by arguing that while the laws of irreversible processes "are often perfectly literal statements of how the facts of Nature are known to behave,"[167] the laws of reversible processes are highly abstract mathematical laws which cannot be directly verified. Thus he remarks

Even the law of gravitation, one of the most exact of material laws, is an extremely ideal statement of a formula whose direct truth nobody precisely verifies at any time. What we observe, and what, by the aid of the formula of gravitation, we can predict and verify, are planets moving, stones falling, and the rest of gravitative phenomena. Nobody ever directly observes any force, such as the ideal force called gravitation. A very ideal statement about the conceived mutual attractions of particles of matter enables us to summarize all the observed facts of the realm of gravitation in one formula. The truth of the formula lies in its summary application to vast ranges of phenomena. Nobody can pretend that this formula is known to express directly the observed inner nature, or even the directly observed genuine behavior of anything.[168]

That the law of gravity differs in these respects from the second law of thermodynamics is a claim which Royce should never have advanced, but his purpose is obvious—Royce holds that laws of reversible processes are in fact descriptions of irreversible processes in which change is so slow that for vast periods their irreversibility is not empirically detectable.[169] Second, Royce argues that both nature and mind "are subject to processes which involve in general a tendency of one part of Nature to *communicate,* as it were, with another part, influencing what occurs at one place through what has already occurred at another place."[170] Third, both nature and mind show a tendency "to the appearance of processes resembling those which, in the life of a mind, we call Habits."[171] Such habits in material nature appear as laws, for here the habitual behavior has become perfectly uniform, but this interpretation of laws of course implies that the law was created and can be destroyed, so that so-called laws of reversible processes are really irreversible. Finally, Royce observes that all nature, material and mental, shows processes of evolution.[172] It need hardly be remarked that this entire argument of Royce's was heavily, and explicitly, indebted to Peirce's *Monist* papers on cosmology.[173]

On the basis of these alleged similarities between mind and material nature, Royce then propounded a cosmology which is fully as speculative as Peirce's from which it is partly derived. As Royce put it, "my hypothesis is that, in case of Nature in general, as in case of the particular portions of Nature known as our fellow-men, we are dealing with phenomenal signs of a vast conscious process, whose relation to Time varies vastly, but whose general characters are throughout the same."[174] All nature, Royce holds, is not only animate but conscious. We regard as other minds those portions of nature with which we are able to communicate and which we find to be sources of new ideas. Our general refusal to extend the category of mind to all nature rests upon the fact that we do not have communication with the rest of nature. But Royce argues we can easily explain how such a lack of communication can exist by noting that our communication is only with beings whose time span is the same as ours. We may easily conceive of so-called material nature as a portion of mind for which the time span is vastly broader than ours so that what is present to such minds would take a century or more for us. Alternatively, there are doubtless things whose time span is so brief that to them ours must seem an eon.[175] With minds of this order clearly no communication would be possible. On the other hand, when we deal with the animals Royce suggests that "the rational being with whom you deal when you observe an animal's dimmer hints of rationality, may be phenomenally represented rather by the race as a whole than by any one individual."[176] Since my dog's time span is obviously not very different from my own, it is here necessary to suppose that my dog is merely a fragment of mind which is the collective consciousness of dogdom—a superorganic group mind of the sort which we have seen that Royce's theory admits. Again, direct communication between us and such a superorganic mind is not to be expected. Thus Royce seeks to show that even so-called material nature may properly be regarded as conscious mind of some sort, and so that the whole world of our experiences is really not only ideal but composed of myriad conscious subsystems of the Absolute. The real world, the World of Appreciation, is thus a world of conscious selves of varying levels, all of which are of course ideas of the Absolute. We do not know these superorganic beings directly since we cannot communicate with them, and since for Royce communication is the basis for asserting the existence of other minds, it would seem that we can have no empirical proof of their existence. Royce admits this, and regards his cosmoontology as speculative and hypothetical only. Yet he also believed that the incompleteness of our descriptions, and the consistency of this superorganic view of the World of Appreciation with his metaphysical proof of the ideality of the world and his arguments concerning the structure of the self and the Absolute warrant us in entertaining such a view.

But if this be so, how is it that most men regard the World of Description as the true one? Royce's answer is that since in the history of mankind it has been necessary for men to organize their own activity in terms of the regularities of nature, those aspects of nature which are the most regular and predictable have come to be viewed as most characteristic of the physical world. That is, the satisfaction of human need and desire, not to mention the survival of the race, has required that we give particular attention to natural uniformities, since only by so doing could men form and carry out coherent and successful plans of action. And since it is the uniformities of nature which have thus received particular attention, we have come to characterize nature as a whole by the concept of uniformity.[177] But this Royce argues is an accident "of the human point of view"[178]—a pragmatic accident if you like—which must be corrected by rational investigation.

There is a curious corollary to Royce's view. In the World of Description, time and space are infinitely divisible, owing to the fact that discrimination produces a dense order. But if the real world is well-ordered, and so the acts of the Absolute are well-ordered, is time really infinitely divisible? Royce thought not.

> We have . . . seen reasons, which, applied to time, would lead us to declare that an absolute insight would view the temporal order as a discrete series of facts ordered as any succession of facts expressing one purpose would be ordered, viz. like the whole numbers.[179]

For the Absolute at least, time is a well-ordered series of events, and there exists a minimum temporal interval, although that interval lies far below our threshold of perception.

The second volume of *The World and the Individual* marks a major advance in Royce's attempts to bring the theory of the two worlds, the descriptive and the appreciative, to full development and to perfect a theory of the categories. But the work raises as many questions as it solves, for Royce now appears to be dealing with at least two different kinds of categories—those represented by the primitives of science, which are pragmatically justified, and a second set which are somehow derived from the logical structure of the knowing act and so appear to admit of a priori deduction. Royce was far from having resolved the relation between these two types, nor was he able to do so until further work in logic made it possible for him to reformulate his theory in a much more powerful form which he called Absolute pragmatism. The nature of description and appreciation, however, are considerably clearer here than in the earlier version and Royce has made notable progress on the question of the grounds of our knowledge of other minds. While his final formulation of this question does not appear until *The Problem of Christianity,* his basic thesis—that the postulation of other minds rests upon their communication of ideas to us—is already clear. Yet the nature of this postulation was not wholly satisfactory, for it leaves open the question of how we might establish communication with another mind with whom no method of communication already existed. Royce counters this argument with the genetic argument that since we know and communicate with other minds before we know ourselves, the question is a false one, and so it is with respect to most actual cases. Yet if one supposes a Martian suddenly appearing on earth and asks how we could establish that the Martian possessed a mind, it is not clear that Royce has an answer. For to interpret the Martian's behavior as signs having a meaning which we understand is already to assume the existence of other mind in the Martian. Indeed, it is not clear that for Royce the postulate of other minds can be handled in a way comparable to other existence postulates at all.

5. The Ethics of Loyalty

These problems were to occupy Royce in the future, but he turned next to questions of ethical theory. His interest in such problems had remained undiminished, as the publication of *Studies of Good and Evil*[180] in 1898 showed, but Royce did not attempt a major reformulation of his ethical position until he published *The Philosophy of Loyalty* in 1908.[181] In this work, which is his most important ethical treatise, he revised and restated his ethical position in the light of his revised epistemology and metaphysics.

Royce states the ethical problem in a paradoxical way. In the first place, he asserts,

Your duty is what you yourself will to do in so far as you clearly discover who you are, and what your place in the world is. This is, indeed, a first principle of all ethical inquiry.[182]

The autonomy of the moral will is therefore taken as axiomatic. But in the second place, Royce asserts, "that I can never find out what my own will is by merely brooding over my natural desires, or by following my momentary caprices."[183] For my natural desires have among themselves no order: some are periodic, some are utterly capricious, some contradict others, and nowhere among them can I find any principle of order which will bring them into a stable organization. Such chaotic impulses do not constitute a moral will, for a moral will in Royce's sense involves a consistent ordering of goods in terms of some standard or ideal, and "I have no inborn ideal naturally present within myself."[184] It follows then that the will is acquired.

By nature, then, apart from a specific training, I have no personal will of my own. One of the principal tasks of my life is to learn to have a will of my own. To learn your own will,—yes, to create your own will, is one of the largest of your human undertakings.[185]

How then is the moral will acquired? "We all of us first learned about what we ought to do, about what our ideal should be, and in general about the moral law, through some authority external to our own wills."[186] It is through social training, chiefly that of the parents and teachers, that moral principles are instilled in the child. One would expect then that if the training is thorough and systematic the result would be the creation of a perfectly adjusted moral individual. According to Royce, one would be wrong.

Teach men customs, and you equip them with weapons for expressing their own personalities. As you train the social being, you make use of his natural submissiveness. But as a result of your training he forms plans; he interprets these plans with reference to his own personal interests; he becomes aware who he is; and he may end by becoming, if not original, then at least obstreperous. And thus society is constantly engaged in training up children who may, and often do, rebel against their mother.[187]

The more perfect the training, the more it creates an independent, self-controlled, self-directing being, with a sense of self-identity apart from society and a will in conflict with society. For it is part of Royce's theory of self-consciousness that it is just the fact that we are trained to do as others do which leads us to compare our performance with theirs and so to become aware of ourselves as separate, distinct beings. Hence for Royce social training always leads to heightened self-consciousness and social differentiation, and so to conflict between the self and others.[188] Royce realized that this pattern of development typified Western European culture rather than all cultures, but like many men of his day he interpreted cultural differences in terms of a linear evolutionary scheme with Western culture as the most advanced form, so the failure of some cultures to realize this pattern represented for him evidence of the primitive character of those cultures rather than the failure of his theory.[189] He therefore holds that in all civilized societies such a process of developmental differentiation and opposition must occur.

As a result of this process, Royce holds, the individual who seeks to know what his duty is turns first to society, and, having discovered what society considers his duty to be, finds that he cannot accept society's answer and is so driven back upon himself.

> We . . . look within, at what we call our own conscience, to find out what our duty is. But, as we do so, we discover, too often, what wayward and blind guides our own hearts so far are. So we look without, in order to understand better the ways of the social world. We cannot see the inner light. Let us try the outer one. These ways of the world appeal to our imitativeness, and so we learn from the other people how we ourselves are in this case to live. Yet no, . . . Seeing the world's way afresh, I see that it is not my way. I revive. I assert myself. My duty, I say, is my own. And so, perhaps, I go back again to my own wayward heart.[190]

The effects of this circular process are disastrous for both the individual and the society. For as long as the individual cannot find a stable ideal, he remains under the rule of caprice and can so attain no true unity and no true selfhood. At the same time, a stable social order becomes impossible, for the society will be composed of restless individuals who can agree neither on private nor public objectives.

The solution to the ethical problem Royce finds in loyalty to a cause. As an example of such loyalty, Royce cites the case of patriotism. When one is under the influence of strong patriotism,

> . . . it seems at once to define a plan of life,—a plan which solves the conflicts of self-will and conformity. This plan has two features: (1) it is through and through a social plan, obedient to the general will of one's country, submissive; (2) it is through and through an exaltation of the self, of the inner man, who now feels glorified through his sacrifice, dignified in his self-surrender, glad to be his country's servant and martyr,—yet sure that through this very readiness for self-destruction he wins the rank of hero.[191]

Loyalty to such a cause, if it is strong enough, affords the individual a commanding ideal in terms of which his other goods can be ordered, and unites him with his fellows in the service of society. Yet it is by no means clear that patriotism is a typical example of loyalty to a cause. To see why Royce thought it was, we must look rather closely at Royce's concept of a cause.

Royce defines a cause as having two characteristics: (1) it must seem "to the loyal person to be larger than his private self,"[192] and (2) it must "unite him with other persons by some social tie."[193] The cause, therefore, cannot be only self-interest—it must embrace interests beyond his own. Nor can it be a "merely impersonal abstraction"[194]—it must be personal in the sense of concerning both the self and other people. And it must involve a social unity or bond: "you also cannot be loyal simply to a collection of various separate persons, viewed merely as a collection."[195] In short, Royce asserts, "Where there is an object of loyalty, there is, then, an union of various selves into one life. This union constitutes a cause to which one may indeed be loyal, if such is his disposition."[196]

As these statements make clear, a cause for Royce is not an abstract principle but a concrete universal. The cause itself is a union of the adherents into one life.

Loyalty has its metaphysical aspect. It is an effort to conceive human life in an essentially superhuman way, to view our social organizations as actual personal unities of consciousness, unities wherein there exists an actual experience of that good which, in our loyalty, we only partially apprehend.[197]

Every cause involves a union of individuals who thereby form a single superhuman self-conscious self. This union is itself the cause sought, yet it is also inseparable from its members, or, to put the matter in different terms, if we conceive this superhuman being as an idea in the mind of the Absolute (as it must be), then the cause is the Internal meaning of that idea.

The fact that the cause is the group life helps to resolve certain ambiguities in Royce's statement of his doctrine. Royce actually uses the term "cause" in several different senses: he usually uses it to mean the union of individuals itself, but he also employs it to mean that ideal loyalty to which creates the group, or brings members into the group. Thus Royce applauds loyalty to the state and to the family as unions of people—"my cause has always been a tie, an union of various individuals in one."[198] And he does not define the state or the family as created by the loyalty of their members to any ideal other than the group itself. Yet he also talks of truth as a cause, because seeking truth creates a social unit—the truth seekers, or the scientific community. But this latter case is deceptive, for Royce is at pains to justify the role of truth as a cause by pointing out that he who seeks truth seeks for a unity of experience which transcends his own fragmentary experience and can only be realized in a supernatural mind.[199] It is not just because seeking truth gives men something in common that truth is a cause, but because he who seeks truth seeks union in a greater life. Royce's ambiguous usage of the term "cause" is justified by the fact that for him the cause is the system-universal while the individuals composing the group are the components of the system. Since in the concrete universal these two aspects are inseparable, Royce is justified in using one term for both.

But loyalty to a cause is only the first part of Royce's ethical doctrine. There are innumerable causes, many of which conflict. Unless Royce is to endorse an anarchy of contradictory causes he must provide a rule whereby choices among causes can be made, and conflicts of causes resolved. The rule he proposes is, "In choosing and in serving the cause to which you are to be loyal, be, in any case, loyal to loyalty."[200] By this injunction Royce means that one should so act as to increase the total loyalty in the world and so to prevent the destruction of loyalty. Any cause, loyalty to which will involve the destruction of other loyalties, is therefore evil: "in so far as my cause is a predatory cause, which lives by overthrowing the loyalties of others, it is an evil cause, because it involves disloyalty to the very cause of loyalty itself."[201] Thus the principle of loyalty to loyalty amounts to saying that one's highest duty is to promote the development of such superhuman systems. It seems clear that Royce believed the result of such a principle would be the union of all men in one final "great community."

Since loyalty is a relation between an individual and a superhuman being, it is clearly a partially religious concept. Royce makes this clear when he asserts that *"Loyalty is the will to manifest, so far as is possible, the Eternal, that is, the conscious and superhuman unity of life, in the form of the acts of an individual self."*[202] As mere parts of the superhuman, we cannot have any direct intuition into that higher mind, although of course it knows our experience. Yet the experience of loyalty Royce regards as a religious experience, for it involves a felt identification of the finite self with the greater whole. Insofar as one is loyal, one renders service to one's ideal, and so labors to do one's part in the system of the whole. So one simultaneously acquires both an inner peace which comes with certain knowledge of one's duty, and harmony with one's fellowmen as joint servants of the divine.

We have noted above Royce's growing dissatisfaction with Hegel's organic universal and his attempts to reconstruct this notion in more precise terms. *The Philosophy of Loyalty* was a popular book, and Royce did not there undertake any detailed analysis of the structure of the concrete universal, but it is clear that such an analysis was due. And it is also clear that such an analysis must involve questions of logic and mathematics, of theology, and of the structure of knowledge. To these questions Royce turned in his last years.

6. Logic and Absolute Pragmatism

Although Royce was not himself a scientist, he was deeply and widely read in the scientific literature of his time, and was a close student of the philosophy of science. He was also intensely interested in logic and mathematics. Royce's first book, published in 1881, was a primer of logical analysis,[203] and he continued to follow the progress in that field as well as the closely related new developments in the foundations of mathematics. These interests were undoubtedly furthered by his contact with Peirce, of whose logical and mathematical work he had a very high opinion, but Peirce in his later years had lost touch with the new developments in Europe whereas Royce followed the work of Frege, Russell, and Whitehead very closely. Royce was not a great logician, but in the period from 1900 to 1914, he was as competent a student of logic as there was in America, and it was from Royce rather than from Peirce that C. I. Lewis derived his inspiration and early direction.[204] As Royce's views of the nature and structure of scientific knowledge were modified as he grew older, his earlier concept of science as description underwent considerable development.

It will be recalled that in 1892 Royce had advanced the thesis that the function of science is to reconstruct experience in such a way as to permit interpersonal communication. The possibility of such a reconstruction Royce based upon the alleged universality of the forms of time and space, and our ability to categorize experience under universal descriptive terms. Experience can only be public, Royce held, if it can be made independent of the unique appreciative content of the moment: hence we must postulate relatively permanent substances describable in general types, and redefine events in terms of changes in the spatiotemporal positions of such substances. Thus "the axiom of Causation is the axiom of the Describability of Events, in so far as they are real and public and are not merely events as privately appreciated. The axiom of the Uniformity of Nature is the axiom that the event once described, i.e., reduced to an universal type, is described forever."[205] In presenting this thesis in 1892, Royce described time and space as "forms of experience" and the basic descriptive predicates as "categories of experience"—a terminology which clearly recalls Kant's. But although Royce treats time and space as necessary and universal, he viewed the categories as contingent: in fact, they are simply the primitive terms of science and so are at most pragmatically justified. This view finds a very strong reaffirmation in Royce's later writings. Thus in a paper of 1902, after summarizing and endorsing the views of Mach, Pearson, and Hertz, Royce concluded that

. . . human thought, in the view of such modern writers, is not bound by any one definable collection of unquestionable axioms, nor yet limited in its operation by any mysteriously predetermined set of irreducible primal concepts. It is a variable and progressive process that is concerned with the adjustment of conduct to experience. In place of unquestionable axioms, one has therefore, in any science, only relative first principles, resolutions, so to speak, to treat some portion of the world of experience as describable in certain terms. The immediate purpose of any thinking process in a special science is the description of experience, and is not what used to be meant by the explanation of facts. To describe experience is to construct a conceptual model that corresponds, point for point, so far as desired, with the observed phenomena. In order to construct this conceptual model, one has to set about one's work with a definite plan of action, a plan large enough and coherent enough to cover the intended range. One's provisionally assumed first principles, or, as such writers often say, one's postulates, are therefore chosen simply, as expressions of this coherent plan of action. One constructs one's model according to these postulates, compares the results with the facts, and is judged accordingly.[206]

The position Royce takes here can certainly be called a type of pragmatism. The choice of primitives and axioms is arbitrary, and is determined by one's purpose to construct the simplest model which will adequately explain the phenomena. No "categories" of description are involved except the primitives, and there is obviously no deduction of primitives.

But when one turns to mathematics and logic, Royce views the nature of the primitives and axioms in quite a different light. Royce accepts completely Russell's reduction of mathematics to logic,[207] so that questions regarding the ultimate status of the axioms and primitives of mathematics are translatable into questions concerning the axioms and primitives of logic. But according to Royce the primitives and axioms of pure logic are not arbitrary, but rather express absolute truths. Royce's proof of this, as of all statements which he regards as absolutely true, is that they cannot be denied without contradiction. "One who says: 'I do not admit that for me there is any difference between saying yes and saying no,'—says 'no,' and distinguishes negation from affirmation, even in the very act of denying this distinction."[208] Similarly, Royce argues, to deny the law of excluded middle is impossible, for $\sim(p \vee \sim p) \rightarrow \sim p \& p$ which is clearly contradictory.

> The absoluteness of the truths of pure logic is shown through the fact that you can test these logical truths in this reflective way. They are truths such that to deny them is simply to reassert them under a new form.[209]

Consequently, however arbitrary the axioms and primitives of empirical science may be, there is nothing arbitrary about the axioms and primitives of pure logic. We thus find in logic a source of absolute truth, but absolute truth about what?

> I do not believe, as Russell believes, that one in such cases discovers truths which are simply and wholly independent of our constructive processes. On the contrary, what one discovers is distinctly what I must call a voluntaristic *truth,*—a truth about the creative will that thinks the truth. One discovers, namely, that our constructive processes, viewed just as activities, possess a certain absolute nature and conform to their own self-determined but, for that very reason, absolute laws. . . . In brief, all such researches illustrate the fact that while the truth which we acknowledge is indeed relative to the will which acknowledges that truth, still what one may call the pure form of willing is an absolute form, a form which sustains itself in the very effort to violate its own laws. We thus find out absolute truth, but it is absolute truth about the nature of the creative will in terms of which we conceive all truths.[210]

Since all thought expresses will, and is indeed only self-conscious action, the forms of thought are forms of will. And they are absolute. If we think at all, the thinking process must have this form, and the proof of this is that if we deny the necessity of these forms, the thought by which we make the denial involves these forms. This position Royce called Absolute pragmatism,[211] and he defined it as follows:

Whatever actions are such, whatever types of action are such, whatever
results of activity, whatever conceptual constructions are such, that the very
act of getting rid of them, or of thinking them away, logically implies their
presence, are known to us indeed both empirically and pragmatically (since
we note their presence and learn of them through action); but they are also
absolute. And any account which succeeds in telling what they are has
absolute truth. Such truth is a "construction" or "creation," for activity
determines its nature. It is "found," for we observe it when we act.[212]

Thus our knowledge consists of two radically different components: empirical
contingent truths which we establish by the usual means of empirical test, and
absolute truths which are established dialectically.

It is from this point of view that Royce returns to the question of the categories.
For what Royce seemed now to have discovered is that logic is a source of absolute
truths which are a priori, and which, since they characterize the creative will itself,
must be true of all thought. Logical truths are therefore not analytic but synthetic,
and since mathematical truths are reducible to logical truths, so are mathematical
propositions synthetic. Royce supports this claim by citing the authority of Peirce,
whose description of mathematical reasoning as iconic—i.e., as involving empirical experimentation with diagrams—convinced Royce of its nonanalytic character.[213] So Kant was right after all: it should be possible to derive from logic some
set of fundamental concepts or categories which are true of all we can ever
experience, precisely because they derive from absolute truths regarding the
nature of the thinking process itself. A deduction of the categories is possible.

What the categories are will, of course, depend upon what our logic is. It was
Royce's good fortune to live in the early phases of the greatest creative period in
the history of logic, and his views were greatly influenced by those of Peirce,
Dedekind, Cantor, Frege, Peano, and, above all, Russell. Yet Royce's view of
logic was and remained distinctively his own. Logic as Royce conceived it was the
theory of order. *"Logic is the General Science of Order,* the *Theory of the Forms
of any Orderly Realm of Objects,* real or ideal."[214] To understand what this
characterization means, it is necessary to look closely at Royce's major exposition
of logic—the system Σ .

Royce first published the system Σ in 1905 in a paper entitled "The Relation of
the Principles of Logic to the Foundations of Geometry,"[215] but the system, and
the point of view which it represents, are explicitly based on the earlier work of A.
B. Kempe.[216] In 1886 Kempe published an extended "Memoir on the Theory of
Mathematical Form,"[217] in which he developed his fundamental position respect-
ing the nature of mathematics, and he followed it in 1889-90 with a paper, "On the
Relation between the Logical Theory of Classes and the Geometrical Theory of
Points,"[218] in which he investigated the relations among logic, geometry, and
what he called "the base system"—a system which is the direct ancestor of
Royce's Σ . Kempe defined the base system simply as a set of elements satisfying

certain formal laws which are introduced as postulates. From this formally defined order system, Kempe holds, he can obtain logic and geometry.

> In the present paper . . . I first consider and fully discuss the properties of a special system of entities, here called the *base system,* the form of which is fully determined by laws which define the mode of distribution of certain like and unlike triads of its component entities—*i.e.* laws that specify which triads are like and which unlike. I then show that this system is precisely that which is under consideration by the logician, when discussing classes and their mutual relations. I further show that certain entities of the base system, selected in accordance with a simple law, compose a system which is precisely that which is under consideration by the geometrician when discussing points and their mutual relations.[219]

Kempe thus believed he could effect a very significant unification of systems which had hitherto been regarded as wholly separate by reducing them to a single, more encompassing base-system.

Royce fully accepted Kempe's general thesis, but he was critical of Kempe's technical development of it. Unfortunately, Kempe's major existence postulate involves a definition by negation ("No entity is absent from the system which can consistently be present") which, as Lewis comments, "renders [it] entirely obscure what properties the system may have, beyond those derivable from the other postulates without this."[220] Furthermore, there are difficulties in the treatment of infinite sets in Kempe's theory which Royce found inconvenient. Royce therefore set himself the task of establishing Kempe's thesis on a more solid basis. The development may be briefly outlined as follows.

The system Σ is defined as containing elements which are "simple and homogeneous," and also all collections of those elements, all collections of those collections, etc. Royce further defines a particular type of collection called an O-collection (written O(xy . . .) where x, y, etc., are the members), the members of which are said to be "mutual obverses" of each other. All collections which are not O-collections are called E-collections. Two elements, x and y, are said to be equivalent only if in any O-collection in which x occurs, y may be substituted, the collection remaining an O-collection. It follows then that equivalent elements have the same obverses, and that all obverses of a given element are equivalent. Since it is also provable from the axioms that every element has an obverse, we may select any given obverse of x as a representative of the class of obverses of x and call it $-x$. It is clear that in ordinary terms $-x$ is the negation of x. Similarly, if X is any collection and O(Xy)—i.e., if the union of X and the unit set of y is an O-collection—then y is called the "complement" of X.[221]

The axioms of Σ are as follows:

I. An *O*-collection remains an *O*-collection, whatever elements or collections may be adjoined to it.

II. If a collection β, consisting wholly of elements which are complements of a collection δ , is an O-collection, then δ itself is an O-collection.

III. The system Σ contains at least one pair of mutually non-equivalent elements.

IV. If any pair of mutually non-equivalent elements is given, a third element of Σ exists which forms an O-pair with *neither* of the elements of this pair, but which is such that the three elements in question together constitute an O-triad.

V. If there exists any complement of a given collection D, then, if *w* be such a complement, there exists a complement of D, viz. *v*, such that every element of D is a complement of the pair (v, w).[222]

The basic relation of Σ is the symmetrical O relation. To develop the algebra of logic, Royce requires the asymmetrical implication relation which he develops in terms of what he calls F-collections. An F-collection may be obtained from an O-collection, O(xyzw), by dividing the members of the O-collection into two not necessarily equal sets by a vertical slash, and replacing the elements on one side of the slash by their obverses, e.g., F(−x−y/zw) or F(xy/−z−w). Triadic F-collections are asymmetrical—thus F(xy/z) expresses a relation among three terms which, when applied to classes, is equivalent to x ∩ y. ⊂ z ⊂ .x ∪ y. The F-relation turns out to be marvelously flexible. As applied to areas, it may be described as "betweenness," since it yields a relation in which z lies between x and y. When applied to propositions, if either x or y be taken as the zero of ordinary logic, the relation becomes the same as implication—e.g., F(Oy/z) ≡ z→y and F(Ox/z)≡ z→x. Similarly, when applied to points in one dimension, the relation can be construed as "precedes," provided one element be again chosen as the origin or zero.[223] Accordingly, Royce claims that "the usual algebra of logic applies without restriction to the system Σ, which is insofar identical with a totality of logical classes, whereof an infinity are mutually nonequivalent, while all are capable of an unrestricted combination by the operations of logical addition and of logical multiplication."[224] Moreover, Royce holds that "the properties of the system Σ to which we have already called attention, make its array analogous to that of the points of space,"[225] so that Σ also turns out to afford a foundation for geometry,[226] and Royce proves that Veblen's axioms of geometry are either consequences of the axioms of Σ or results of restricting those axioms in various ways. And finally, Royce asserts,

. . . sets of the elements of Σ can be so selected that operations corresponding to the addition and multiplication of the ordinary algebra of quantity, will enable us to select elements that may be viewed (with reference to certain arbitrarily assumed constant triads of reference-elements, i.e., bases), as the sums or as the products of given pairs of elements. Hence *without introducing new elements*, the elements of Σ , if viewed in certain ways, enable us to define, not only the algebra of logic, but the algebra of quantity.[227]

The system Σ was Royce's most impressive achievement in logic, and the best example of what he called an "order system." Royce regarded Σ as a purely formal system: the "elements" of Σ are undefined, and may be regarded as uninterpreted variables. The postulates of the system define a complex but purely abstract order which may, or may not, be satisfied by some domain of existing things. Following Kempe, Royce has shown that if the element variables are given various appropriate interpretations, the algebra of logic, the algebra of quantity, and geometry result, and there are doubtless innumerable other more specialized order systems which can be developed from Σ. As Lewis remarks,

> Professor Royce used to say facetiously that the system Σ had some of the properties of a junk heap or a New England attic. Almost anything might be found in it: the question was, how to get these things out.[228]

Thus the approach to logic and mathematics which Royce took in 1905 would appear to be purely formalistic.

But by 1914 Royce had changed his mind. For by that year he had read Russell's work and had considered its significance. As we have seen above, Royce accepted both Russell's reduction of mathematics to logic, and his reformulation of logic itself, but he did not accept Russell's Platonism. Instead, Royce held that logic is a source of absolute truths about the creative activity of the will. But this interpretation of the nature of logic has important implications for Σ .

> *This system has an order which is determined entirely by the fundamental laws of logic, and by the one additional principle thus mentioned.* The new principle in question is precisely analogous to a principle which is fundamental in geometrical theory. This is the principle that, between any two points on a line, there is an intermediate point, so that the points on a line constitute, for geometrical theory, *at least a dense series.* In its application to the entities of pure logic this principle appears indeed at first sight to be extraneous and arbitrary. For the principle corresponding to the geometrical principle which defines dense series of points, does not apply at all to the logical world of propositions. And, again, it does not apply with *absolute* generality to the objects known as classes. But it *does* apply to a set of objects, to which in the foregoing repeated reference has been made. This set of objects may be defined as, "certain possible modes of action that are open to any rational being who can act at all, and who can also reflect upon his own modes of possible action."[229]

As Royce shows, every mode of action has a negation. Every pair of modes of action has a logical sum corresponding to the alternate occurrence of the members of the pair, and a logical product corresponding to their joint occurrence. Similarly, one mode of action may imply another. It is even possible to define a mode of action, "doing something," and its contradictory, "doing nothing," which may be treated as the one and zero of the algebra of logic.[230] Accordingly, Royce concludes that "the modes of action are a set of entities that in any case conform to the same logical laws to which classes and propositions conform."[231]

But does the calculus of modes of action satisfy the betweenness principle? Since axiom IV, which is the betweenness principle, taken together with the preceding axiom, generates an infinite number of elements in Σ, the application of Σ to the modes of action requires that there be an infinite set of modes of action. In order to guarantee this, Royce restricts himself to the modes of action of a perfectly self-conscious being.

> It is perfectly possible to define a certain set, or "logical universe" of modes of action such that all the members of this set are "possible modes of action," *in case* there is some rational being who is capable of performing some one single possible act, and is also capable of noting, observing, recording, in some determinate way every mode of action of which he is actually capable, and which is a mode of action whose possibility is *required* (that is, is made logically a necessary entity) by the *single* mode of action in terms of which this system of modes of action is defined.[232]

Royce does not require that the being in question be immortal: it suffices that it be self-conscious, since Royce regarded self-consciousness as defining an infinite series of ideas. But it must be observed that Royce here takes "knowing" or "choosing" to be a mode of action. To this set of the possible modes of action of a rational self-conscious being, Royce holds that the betweenness principle applies:

> This principle could be otherwise stated thus "for any rational being who is able to reflect upon and to record his own modes of action, if there be given any two modes of action such that one of them implies the other, there always exists at least one determinate mode of action which is implied by the first of these modes of action and which implies the second, and which is yet distinct from both of them." That this principle holds true of the modes of action which are open to any rational being to whom any one mode of action is open, can be shown by considerations for which there is here no space . . .[233]

It is very unfortunate that Royce does not tell us what these "considerations" are, and presents neither proof nor illustration for this thesis. Royce's claim is obviously aimed at Bradley, since it makes Bradley's principle of endless fission a defining characteristic of self-conscious thought, yet the sort of infinite divisibility of relations which Bradley discussed does not immediately yield Royce's axiom in the form stated above. A set of terms ordered with respect to implication generally does not form a dense order, and it is not obvious why Royce thought the modes of action do. One might indeed argue that if we restrict ourselves, as Royce so very carefully does, to the possible acts of a rational self-conscious being, then every action is deliberately chosen, and every act which is deliberately chosen is performed. In that case, one might hold that if there are two modes of action, x and y, such that x→y, then x implies choosing to do y and choosing to do y implies y. The problem, however, will be whether or not choosing to do y and choosing to choose to do y are properly distinct modes of action: if it be granted that they are, then Royce's argument will hold, but if this be denied it is not clear to me how to prove the applicability of the principle.

Supposing, however, that Royce can show that the modes of action satisfy the system Σ , what then? Royce argues as follows:

> The result of these considerations is *that it at present appears to be possible to define, upon the basis of purely logical relations, and upon the basis of the aforegoing principles concerning rational activity, an order-system of entities inclusive not only of objects having the relation of the number system, but also of objects illustrating the geometrical types of order, and thus apparently including all the order-systems upon which, at least at present, the theoretical natural sciences depend for the success of their deductions.*[234]

The metaphysical implications of this thesis are quite clear. According to Royce's idealism, reality must consist of the ideas, or acts, of the Absolute, conceived as a perfectly self-conscious rational being. Royce further believed that the "absolute"—i.e., dialectically provable—truths of logic were descriptive of the creative will of the Absolute. If these claims are true, then if there is an order-system which precisely characterizes the actions of such a self-conscious being, we should also find that that order-system furnishes all the concepts and orders necessary for the description of reality. And this is precisely what Royce believes he has proven here. Here was a new theory of the categories, indeed: the elements of Σ are the modes of action of the Absolute, and so also the modes of action of our own minds, since we are subsystems of the Absolute, and what we know when we know the world is simply another subsystem of the Absolute. The system Σ was not simply an abstract order-system—it was a description of the mind of God.

This interpretation of Σ also leads to a vindication of Royce's assertion that reality is a determinate individual whole, selected by the Absolute from among other possible worlds. For if the Absolute realized all possible modes of action, those modes would form the universal class, and so "would meet with all the difficulties which the Theory of Assemblages has recently met with in its efforts to define certain extremely inclusive classes"[235]—i.e., it would be subject to Russell's paradox. Hence Royce asserts, "there is in fact no such totality."[236] The Absolute must, therefore, be regarded as choosing from among these possibilities a certain ordered infinite aggregate of modes of action, and such an ordered system Royce regards as determinate and individual in the same sense in which he holds series to be determinate and individual. The problem of the status of these unactualized possibilities remains, but the consistency of the world-system requires that they exist.

Royce's analysis shows our knowledge to be composed on the one hand of contingent empirical propositions validated by experience, and on the other of absolute a priori truths descriptive of the absolute character of the creative will. But he also included another component in our knowledge which albeit a priori cannot be regarded as absolute in the same sense in which the truths of logic are absolute. It was particularly from Poincaré that Royce derived his concept of "leading ideas," but his clearest statement of it related to Virchow's definition of disease. Virchow asserted that "we have learned to recognize that diseases are not autonomous organisms, that they are no entities that have entered the body, that they are no parasites which take root in the body, but *that they merely show us the course of the vital processes under altered conditions.* "[237] Now, Royce asks, have the recent discoveries of the bacteriological origin of disease disproven Virchow's principle? Not at all, "for if diseases proved to be the consequences of the presence of parasites, the diseases themselves, so far as they belonged to the diseased organism, were still not the parasites, but were, as before, the reaction of the organism to the *veränderte Bedingungen* which the presence of the parasites entailed."[238] But if this is so, Royce points out, then "Virchow's theoretical principle in its most general form *could be neither confirmed nor refuted by experience.* "[239] For if the devil causes the disease, still the devil could at most merely determine the altered conditions which determine the behavior of the organism.

> I insist, then, that this principle of Virchow's is no trial supposition, no scientific hypothesis in the narrower sense—capable of being submitted to precise empirical tests. It is, on the contrary, a very precious *leading idea,* a theoretical interpretation of phenomena, in the light of which observations are to be made—'a regulative principle' of research. It is equivalent to a resolution to search for those detailed connections which link the processes of disease to the normal processes of the organism.[240]

Such regulative principles are essential to science, for they guide research and direct attention to particular lines of investigation. Yet they are not themselves empirical statements, and so are not verifiable or refutable in the ordinary sense. They are accordingly a priori truths, but they are not absolute truths since they cannot be dialectically established. These leading ideas are decisions to interpret experience in a given way, and the concept of the a priori which they involve is fundamentally pragmatic, for these ideas constitute "an interpretation rather than a portrayal or a prediction of the objective facts of nature, an adjustment of our conceptions of things to the internal needs of our intelligence, rather than a grasping of things as they are in themselves."[241] Here was a concept of the a priori the implications of which were to be developed by Royce's greatest student—C. I. Lewis.[242]

7. Christ and the Community

At the same time that Royce was trying to prove the nature of the Absolute mind through logic, he was also pursuing a different line of approach to it through theology. As an Absolute idealist, Royce had always been in one sense a theologian, but his writings had, previously, little explicit connection to Christian theology. But in the Boss lectures of 1912 on *The Sources of Religious Insight,*[243] and much more fully in *The Problem of Christianity*[244] in 1913, Royce undertook a critique and reformulation of Christian theology which is among his most remarkable works.

Royce's approach to Christian doctrine is in striking contrast to the prevailing views of his time. Royce was writing half a century after the publication of Darwin's *Origin of Species* and at the conclusion of a period which had witnessed the bitterest contest between science and religion in American history. From that contest, the sciences had emerged the unquestioned victors. The churches had had to abandon the Biblical creation story, and with it the doctrine of the literal truth of the Scripture. Similarly, many cherished doctrines of the natural theology had had either to be abandoned or substantially revised. As a result, the prestige of theology itself was considerably weakened, and the churches turned more and more to an emphasis on an atheological religion of sentiment, humanitarianism, and good works. This broad trend finds many expressions—in the Social Gospel and the reform activities of the churches, in the humanistic interpretation of Jesus, and in the identification of religion with sentiment and feeling rather than with adherence to explicit dogmas. If the appalling social problems spawned by industrialism required charity and good works, it is also true that by devoting themselves to reform the churches could avoid further conflict with science and at the same time validate their role as a major institution in society. And by shifting the emphasis to sentiment and Christian "feeling" they could avoid for a time the problems of the grounds of religious belief. In its most sophisticated form, as, e.g., in James's *Varieties of Religious Experience,*[245] this view comes to saying that religion is grounded upon needs and feelings of subconscious origin which are not otherwise explicable, and involves so minimal a commitment to specific doctrines that there is little left to conflict with science. Thus the warfare of science and religion ended with religion abandoning theology.[246]

For Royce such a surrender of theology was unthinkable. To found religion upon the "mysterious depths of the subconscious,"[247] as he accused James of doing, was to degrade religion to the level of the irrational and to abandon the task of a responsible religious thinker. Religion is not a sentiment but a belief, and this belief must be justified on rational grounds if it is to be held at all. Nor would Royce accept the claim that religion must rid itself of metaphysics. If one asserts that there is a God, Royce holds, then one is also committed to saying what sort of being that God is. Similarly, problems of the nature of Christ are not solved by historical studies of the man Jesus. Royce refused to become involved in the problem of the historical Jesus or to enter the controversy over the textual criticism of the Bible. Indeed, for him the historical Jesus remained a shadowy figure whose actual teachings are of much less importance than the interpretation put upon Him by His later followers—notably by Paul. The central fact of Christianity for Royce is rather the church itself—the Beloved Community, as he calls it—and the relation of Jesus to the church is interpreted in terms of Pauline Christology. But such an approach necessarily involves both metaphysical and epistemological problems. Thus in writing *The Problem of Christianity,* Royce was not only defending specific Christian doctrines—he was also defending the legitimacy of philosophical theology.

In formulating such a theology, Royce found himself confronting some major problems. First, he found it necessary to answer the claim made by James and others that religious conviction is based upon nonrational, emotional experience and that rational argument and abstract reasoning can contribute nothing to our faith.[248] This claim Royce regarded as the result of a false view that knowledge consists solely of sensation or feeling on the one hand and abstract ideas on the other.

In seeking for any sort of novel truth, have we only the choice between the experience of the data of sense or of feeling on the one hand and the analysis of abstract ideas and assertions upon the other? May there not be another source of knowledge? May not this source consist in the synthetic view of many facts in their unity—in the grasping of a complex of relations in their total significance? And may not just this be a source of insight which is employed in many of the processes ordinarily known as reasoning processes?[249]

Insight, Royce asserts, is not just an uncontrollable impulse to believe; it is rather the perception of order in what had previously seemed chaotic, and it yields a "knowledge that makes us aware of the unity of many facts in one whole, and that at the same time brings us into intimate personal contact with these facts and with the whole wherein they are united."[250] Such insight involves a rational synthesis, a theoretical interpretation of the data, yet the nature of this synthesis remained to be clarified. Second, Royce's emphasis on the church is closely connected with his doctrines of the superhuman character of social institutions, and so involves all the difficulties of that doctrine—notably, the problems of the nature of such superhuman beings, of their relations to their constituent members, and of the relations among the members. And these problems raise a third fundamental problem—the problem of our knowledge of other minds. This problem is for Royce the most difficult problem of epistemology. It is obvious that other minds cannot be directly known by sense experience, so if they are known at all it can only be as constructs whose existence is indirectly confirmed through observable consequences. But the problem of confirming the existence of other minds differs from that of confirming the existence of other entities in two ways. First, with respect to electrons and other unseen entities, confirmation consists in the occurrence of predicted experiences. But these predicted experiences are generally the experiences of others. If we are restricted to our own actual experience, as we must be in confirming the existence of other minds, we find ourselves with a very narrow experiential basis for such a proof.[251] But second, even if the sufficiency of such a basis be granted, can we in fact confirm the postulate? Royce holds that we cannot, without taking for granted what was to be proved. For to confirm that there is another mind—i.e., to show that self-consciousness exists in another—I must show that someone else has experiences similar to mine. But I cannot accept another's testimony regarding his experiences without assuming interpersonal communication, i.e., that we share common meanings for words, and so that he has a mind like mine. Nor can I accept his behavior as indicating such experience. For I have no reason to associate his overt behavior with any inner experience. If it be argued that I infer this relation from the analogy with myself, Royce answers that most of the overt behavior I observe in others is behavior which I never observe in myself, or observe only from so different a perspective that no similarity is visible.[252] Indeed, the inaccessibility of the other's experience makes it impossible for me to correlate his behavior with his experience, except on the assumption (which I cannot verify) that some other behavior of his is already correlated with such an experience.

Royce's answers to these problems were heavily indebted to two theories of Peirce's—the theory of the community and the theory of interpretation. Royce states that he derived these ideas from Peirce's 1867 paper, "On a New List of Categories,"[253] and from his papers in the *Journal of Speculative Philosophy* in 1868,[254] and he repeatedly cites Peirce as his authority for some of the statements he makes in respect to these theories. Yet Royce's use of these ideas is distinctively his own; although he follows Peirce very closely on many points, he also adapts Peirce's ideas to fit his own problems.

Peirce introduced the concept of interpretation in the "New List"[255] in order to explain how subject and predicate of a proposition are brought to unity. It will be recalled that for Peirce, this unification is effected by comparing the object denoted by the subject with other objects denoted by the predicate, by recognizing their similarity, and so by interpreting the subject as standing for an object for which the predicate stands. Royce elaborates Peirce's argument by pointing out that comparison, as here used, does not consist in mere contrast or juxtaposition, but requires the introduction of a "mediating" representation which defines the nature of the relation between relate and correlate. Suppose, e.g., that we compare the two letters, p and b. If we merely juxtapose them, we have a contrast but, for Royce, no comparison. To have a comparison, we must not only be aware of contrast, but we must also stipulate the nature of the difference—i.e., that b is an inverted p. This stipulation constitutes a third, or "mediating," idea, which explains the contrast by stipulating its character.

This new act consists in the invention or discovery of some third idea, distinct from both the ideas which are to be compared. This third idea, when once found, interprets one of the ideas which are the objects of the comparison, and interprets it to the other, or in the light of the other.[256]

The act of interpretation is thus an act of synthesis: it brings the two things compared into explicit relation with each other, and so makes them part of a larger unity.

The essential fact for our present study is that, in case of the comparisons which Peirce discusses, the problem, whether you call it a theoretical or a practical problem . . . is the problem either of arbitrating the conflicts; or of bringing to mutual understanding the estrangements; or of uniting in some community the separate lives of these two distinct ideas,—of ideas which, when left to themselves, decline to coalesce or to cooperate, or to enter into one life.[257]

This act of unification is not properly an act of perception, nor, Royce claims, is it an act of conception: it is not one of "linking percepts to their fitting concepts, nor . . . of paying the bank bills of conception in the gold of the corresponding perceptions,"[258] nor does it involve a mere explication of the meaning of concepts. It is, Royce claims, a third kind of mental function which is distinctively synthetic.

Comparison, however, is only a rudimentary form of interpretation. The paradigm case of interpretation for both Peirce and Royce is that of sign translation. Peirce defined a sign as something which stands for something to someone in some respect, and the someone who interprets the sign as standing for something is the interpretant idea. For Peirce, every sign is so only because it is so interpreted, and what the interpretant does is to translate the meaning of the sign and to recognize its reference. And since the interpretant is itself a sign, it must also be interpreted by a further interpretant, and that interpretant by yet another, and so we have an infinite series of interpretants.[259] All of this Royce fully accepted, and applied as Peirce did to explain the relations among ideas in the mind of the individual. These relations are both triadic and asymmetric: every thought is interpreted to another by an interpreting thought, and the direction in which interpretation takes place is always from past to future.[260] Reflective consciousness may, therefore, be regarded as a process by which present thought interprets past thought (or rather memories of past thought) to future thoughts.[261] Furthermore, since every idea must be interpreted by another, the "purpose to interpret" defines a self-representative system, in which each interpretant may be regarded as including the recognition that its predecessors belong to the self. Indeed, from this perspective, the series of interpretants is the self, and the unification of separate ideas and experiences is achieved through interpretation. And since, to Royce, mind always implies self-consciousness, it is evident that Royce, like Peirce, regards the mind itself as the sign-series.[262]

So long as a man interprets his own ideas only, the ideas being interpreted are directly present to him, and the truth of the interpretation is immediately evident. With respect to such interpretation, Royce believes we can have virtually complete certainty.[263] Yet one is often confronted with ideas which, "by virtue of their contrast with my ideas, and by virtue of their novelty and their unexpectedness, I know to be not any ideas of my own."[264] For these ideas an interpretation is required, yet no clear interpretation appears.

> When I possess certain ideas sufficiently to enable me to seek for their interpretation, but so that, try as I will, I can never clearly survey, as from above, the success of any of my attempted interpretations,—then these ideas remain, from my own point of view, ideas that never become wholly my own. Therefore these relatively alien ideas can be interpreted at all only by using the familiar hypothesis that they belong to the self of some one else.[265]

Thus I suddenly receive certain auditory sensations which at once suggest to my mind certain ideas. I cannot relate these sensations to any prior vocal sensations of my own, nor can I relate the ideas they suggest to my prior train of ideas. What, then, am I to make of them? Royce's answer is that I can solve my problem by interpreting those sensations as signs of ideas in my neighbor's mind. But, "of my neighbor's ideas I can never win, under human conditions, any interpretation but one which remains hypothetical, and which is never observed, under these human conditions, as face to face with its own object."[266] The hypothesis that there are other minds thus serves to bring my experience to coherence, but this hypothesis itself is based upon a more fundamental assumption—that all ideas are interpretable. It is only because I assume to begin with that the ideas suggested to me are signs capable of interpretation that they can be asserted to be indications of mind, and it is this principle which justifies my assertion that, since they are not indications of my own mind, they must be signs of another mind. The hypothesis of other minds can therefore be justified, but only on the basis of the far more sweeping hypothesis that all things that are, are signs.[267] This hypothesis will indeed bring my experience to unity, but it is not a hypothesis which can be verified in any ordinary sense: it is rather a resolution to treat experience in a particular way—a "leading idea" which directs me to seek coherence by interpreting experience in these terms.

The fact that interpersonal interpretation is possible provides Royce with a basis for explaining the origin and nature of the community. And here again, Royce drew heavily on Peirce. It will be recalled that in his early papers, Peirce defined the truth as the final opinion—i.e., the limiting opinion—to which an infinitely extended process of inquiry must converge, and defined reality as what is asserted to be in that true opinion.[268] But if inquiry is conceived as actually continuing forever, it is necessary to postulate the existence of investigators who can continue it, and so Peirce argues that the idea of reality involves that of a community of investigators. Actually, by the community, Peirce meant more than simply the collection of human minds—he also meant the universal mind in which human minds exist only as developing signs. This idealistic meaning of the term "community" is not spelled out in detail in those early papers, but it is strongly implied by the closing section of "Consequences of Four Incapacities,"[269] and in view of Royce's detailed knowledge of Peirce's work, there is little doubt that he knew what Peirce meant. Royce's own development of the concept of community is very similar to Peirce's, but more detailed and more extensive.

The simplest form of community Royce calls a community of interpretation. Such a community comes into existence whenever any group of people undertake to interpret their ideas to one another. The defining characteristic of such a community is a deliberate intercommunication—a purposeful attempt on the part of the members to interpret each other's ideas to one another. What Royce calls the "will to interpret"—the desire to create such interpersonal communication—is therefore a much revised form of the injunction in *The Religious Aspect of Philosophy* to realize each other's ideas. This purpose cannot be perfectly fulfilled in any human community, but it can be approached.[270]

All true communities involve a community of interpretation: intercommunication is a necessary condition for the existence of any genuine community. But the community can be further developed if its members share a common past and a common future. Since no two individuals can have identical memories, the past of personal experiences can be shared only to a limited degree. But insofar as people conceive themselves to be members of a group which has a distinctive history or tradition, they can all look back upon and fully identify themselves with the persons and events of that past which so becomes the common possession of all. Similarly, if the community as a whole is dedicated to achieving certain objectives, then its members share common goals and common anticipations of future experiences and events. Where such sharing of present ideas and of past and future experience exists, Royce holds that we have a true community.[271]

A community of interpretation of the sort described above begins to approach Royce's goal of the unification of the members into one life. To make the approach complete, one need only conceive the community as possessing a perfect interpreter. For such an interpreter, all the ideas of the members would be directly present in his own experience, and so would be directly compared and interpreted. Such an interpreter, if he existed, would be the Absolute, in whose mind all ideas are brought to perfect unity and order.[272] But on Royce's theory, the existence of the Absolute is dialectically provable, as we have already seen. Indeed, all that Royce has previously held respecting the Absolute can be carried over directly into this new formulation of the theory. All that we can err about, and therefore all reality, must be present to the Absolute, and the Absolute itself can be conceived as an infinite, ordered system of interpretation. Thus the hypothesis underlying the postulate of other minds—that all things that are, are signs—is true, for the ideas of the Absolute must form a series of interpretants.

But if all that the theory of interpretation does is to translate Royce's old doctrines into a new terminology, what is gained? There are, I believe, four significant gains to Royce in the new formulation. First, the theory of interpretation gives Royce an improved model of self-consciousness. Royce's previous model had been a series defined by an initial thought S_1, and the rule that for any x, if S_x is a thought of mine, then "S_x is a thought of mine" is a thought of mine.[273] While such a series does no doubt involve self-consciousness, it is a piteously stupid form of self-consciousness. The infinite series of interpretants, on the other hand, offers a vastly more flexible and reasonable model of reflective awareness in which each thought not only involves an awareness that the prior thought is mine but in interpreting that thought combines it with others and develops as well as translates its meaning. Second, the theory of interpretation gives Royce a much more reasonable account of our knowledge of other minds. Building upon the thesis which he had advanced in 1901 that the ground for postulating the existence of other minds is interpersonal communication, Royce is able to regard other minds as what they obviously are—constructs postulated for explanatory purposes. But at the same time the new formulation preserves Royce's central insight into the problem of other minds: the fact that the hypothesis of other minds is an interpretation of the data of experience, not a verifiable hypothesis. Third, the theory of interpretation gives Royce a much more satisfying way of explaining the relation between the Absolute and human individuals. So long as the iron division between description and appreciation was maintained, and interpersonal knowledge of an appreciative sort was denied, the formation of the community remained an inexplicable mystery. The concept of interpretation removes this problem, and Royce is now able to define the development of the community as a continuous process of intercommunication and organization of experience. He is, therefore, able to develop in a clearer way than formerly the thesis that the more perfect the community becomes the closer it approximates a superhuman self, and so to give an improved basis to his superorganicism. The phenomena of individual identification and loyalty to the community is similarly clarified, since interpretation makes possible more and more sharing of ideas and experience among the members. And the concept of the Absolute as the perfect community, while it does not compromise the superhuman character of the Absolute, nevertheless avoids any suggestion that the human individuals are annihilated or swallowed up in the Absolute. Fourth, the theory of interpretation and the community further carry out Royce's reconstruction of the concrete universal. When Peirce introduced the idea of interpretation in his early papers, he regarded the interpretation as translating the meaning of the interpreted sign, and that meaning was not itself an interpretant but an abstract property.[274] Subsequently, Peirce changed his theory of meaning, but it always remained true for him that the meaning was distinct from the interpretant sign.[275] But Royce makes no such distinction—interpretant and interpretation are used interchangeably. The reason is that for Royce the internal meaning of an idea is the purpose to create a perfectly coherent order out of certain experiences, and the combinatorial character of interpretation makes it possible to identify that process of synthesis with interpretation. The interpretation *is* the interpretant which brings other ideas to unity. *"The world is the interpretation of the problems which it presents,"*[276] and the world is the community.[277] For as human individuals are only ideas of the Absolute, so the Absolute is the perfectly ordered system which is the interpretation of those ideas. The concept of the community, so considered, is Royce's equivalent of the concrete universal, for like the organism, the community has no existence apart from its members, yet it is an ordered system in which those members participate, not as instances, but as contributing parts to a whole.

The three fundamental doctrines of Christianity, according to Royce, are the doctrines of the beloved community, sin, and the atonement.[278] Of these, the most difficult and most fundamental is the first. Royce does not claim that any such doctrine is directly stated in the teachings of Jesus; rather, he regards it as an interpretation of the teachings and life of Jesus which was added by Paul.[279] For it is Paul who first asserts the existence of the church as a spiritual unity.

> This new being is a corporate entity,—the body of Christ, or the body of which the now divinely exalted Christ is the head. Of this body the exalted Christ is also, for Paul, the spirit and also, in some new sense, the lover. This corporate entity is the Christian community itself.[280]

The invisible church of true believers is thus, as Royce interprets Paul, a true community. For the church possesses a historical and traditional past, centering about the life of Jesus and his followers, and a mission in time which involves specific goals and specific anticipations respecting future events.[281] Moreover, the church is preeminently a community of interpretation, for it is an explicit goal of the church to create perfect love and understanding among its members.[282] The church is, therefore, a superorganic person, and that person is Christ. Accordingly, Christ is the perfect interpreter who understands all, and by drawing the love of all men to Himself, harmonizes them with each other.

> . . . the literal and historical fact has always been this, that in some fashion and degree those who have thus believed in the being whom they called Christ, were united in a community of the faithful, were in love with that community, were hopefully and practically devoted to the cause of the still invisible, but perfectly real and divine Universal Community, and were saved by the faith and by the life which they thus expressed.[283]

Christ is thus the spirit of the church—the beloved community—and love to Christ now takes the form of loyalty to the beloved community. As Smith pointed out,

> The special transformation of Christian love made by Paul, according to Royce, is that he interprets love as *loyalty*. Salvation can now be defined in terms of the relation between the individual and the beloved community. The

goal of life can be found only through loyalty to that community which embraces all the "neighbors" and is at the same time the object of God's love and concern.[284]

The "neighbors" Christ told us to love are the members of the beloved community, and love to Christ is loyalty to that community. As loyalty is the will to manifest the eternal in our lives, so it is by loyalty that we are saved.

If virtue consists in our loyalty to the beloved community, it is not difficult to see that sin must consist in disloyalty or treason to the beloved community. Whoever, like Judas, betrays the beloved community or its members, or acts in such a way as to injure the community or inhibit its functions, is guilty of sin.[285] And Royce retains in his theology the same stark insistence on the reality of evil which characterizes his ethics. A sin once committed is for him ineradicable. "Whatever else the traitor may hereafter do,—and even if he becomes and remains, through all his future life, in this or any other world, a saint,—the fact will remain: There was a moment when he freely did whatever he could to wreck the cause that he had sworn to serve."[286] Our own self-consciousness makes sin irrevocable: once the deed is done, it can never be undone, and no repentance, no subsequent act can alter the pure evil character of that deed.

The doctrine of the beloved community and the definition of sin as treason constitute two of the three doctrines which Royce asserts to be the central doctrines of Christianity. The third is the doctrine of the atonement. Royce rejects at once all theories of atonement which involve the concept of the payment of a debt or the concept of a scapegoat as being wholly unworthy of Christianity. A sin once committed cannot be annulled by a subsequent good deed, nor by visiting punishment upon some substitute object. The sin itself remains unalterably sinful, and its character is in no way changed by such acts.[287] But there is nevertheless one sort of act which, if it does not revoke the sin, can yet reconcile us to it, in the sense that it can make us feel that on the whole the sin was better done than not done. If a virtuous act can be performed, which could not have been performed if the sinful act had not first been committed, so that the occurrence of the sin becomes a necessary condition for the occurrence of the subsequent act of virtue, then the virtuous act may be said to atone for the sin insofar as it leads us to conclude that we should rather have had the sin and its atoning act, than neither.[288]

> Christian feeling, Christian art, Christian worship, have been full of the sense that *somehow* (and *how* has remained indeed a mystery) there was something so precious about the work of Christ, something so divinely wise (so skilful and divinely beautiful?) about the plan of salvation,—that, as a result of all this, after Christ's work was done, the world as a whole was a nobler and richer and worthier creation than it would have been if Adam had not sinned.[289]

Atonement cannot revoke sin, but it can so bind the sin into the fabric of virtue that without that sin the world would be less good.

Royce's view of the atonement is one of his most striking and original ideas, and although it is of doubtful orthodoxy, this theory is admirably suited to his system. For among the major doctrines of Royce's ethical and religious writings are his unremitting insistence upon the reality of evil and sin, and his equally strong insistence that evil can be, and in the Absolute is, overcome. In *The Problem of Christianity* this faith in the ultimate triumph of virtue takes the form of the postulate, "No baseness or cruelty of treason so deep or so tragic shall enter our human world, but that loyal love shall be able in due time to oppose to just that deed of treason its fitting deed of atonement."[290] And it is the task of those who believe to atone for the sins of the world. This was Royce's call to the heroic life: as we are members of the beloved community, so if the Absolute does conquer evil it is we who conquer in His name.

Royce asserted that there were three fundamental doctrines in Christianity—the beloved community, sin, and atonement. Yet implicit in his whole discussion is another Christian doctrine which is equally important—the doctrine of grace. For Royce, "The problem of grace is the problem of the origin of loyalty."[291] We are saved by our love for the beloved community, but how do we acquire love for the beloved community? How, indeed, do we acquire loyalty to any cause?

It [loyalty] will always be to you the finding of an object that comes to you from without and above, as divine grace has always been said to come. . . . The cause is a religious object. It finds you in your need. It points out to you the way of salvation. Its presence in your world is to you a free gift from the realm of the spirit—a gift that you have not of yourself, but through the willingness of the world to manifest to you the way of salvation. This free gift first compels your love. Then you freely give yourself in return.[292]

You cannot merely choose a cause at random and then resolve to be loyal to it: the cause itself must be compelling to you, must somehow elicit your love, and *then* you can be loyal. Somehow—but how? For the man who has no cause and hence no unity to his life, that is the crucial question, and to that question Royce can only answer, it is given or it is not given. If it is given, it will come in some concrete human form, or as a person whose charisma first compels the response in you, and this is why Jesus had to come in the flesh to establish the beloved community.[293] But the power which made men leave their nets and follow Him—the power that first wakes loyalty in others—that power comes "from another level than our own."[294]

Notes—Chapter Twelve

1. Vincent Buranelli, *Josiah Royce* (New York: Twayne Publishing Co., 1964), chaps. 1, 2; "Josiah Royce," *Dictionary of American Biography,* ed. Malone (New York: Charles Scribner's Sons, 1946), XVI: 205-11.

2. Josiah Royce, *Fugitive Essays,* Introduction, Loewenberg (Cambridge, Mass.: Harvard University Press, 1925), p. 230. Hereafter FE.

3. FE 230.

4. James Harry Cotton, *Royce on the Human Self* (Cambridge, Mass.: Harvard University Press, 1954), p. 22.

5. FE 200.

6. *Ibid.,* p. 199.

7. Cotton, *Royce,* pp. 26-27.

8. FE 249ff, 360.

9. *Ibid.,* p. 361.

10. *Ibid.,* p. 362.

11. *Ibid.,* p. 250.

12. *Ibid.,* p. 254.

13. *Ibid.,* p. 255.

14. *Ibid.,* p. 256.

15. *Ibid.*

16. Josiah Royce, *The Religious Aspect of Philosophy* (Boston: Houghton Mifflin Co., 1885). Hereafter RAP.

17. RAP 396-97.

18. *Ibid.*, pp. 397ff.

19. *Ibid.*, pp. 408ff.

20. *Ibid.*, p. 421.

21. *Ibid.*, pp. 422-23.

22. *Ibid.*, p. 425.

23. Josiah Royce, *The Spirit of Modern Philosophy* (Boston: Houghton Mifflin Co., 1897). Hereafter SMP.

24. SMP 370.

25. *Ibid.*, pp. 371-72.

26. RAP 425ff.

27. *Ibid.*, p. 426.

28. *Ibid.*, pp. 429-30.

29. *Ibid.*, pp. 428ff.

30. *Ibid.*, p. 433. Original in italics.

31. Josiah Royce, Joseph Le Conte, G. H. Howison, and Sidney Edward Mezes, *The Conception of God* (New York: Macmillan Co., 1902), p. 195. Hereafter CG.

32. RAP 32, 127.

33. *Ibid.*, p. 57.

34. *Ibid.*, pp. 127ff.

35. *Ibid.*, p. 133.

36. *Ibid.*, p. 134.

37. *Ibid.*

38. See pp. 159-60.

39. RAP 137.

40. *Ibid.*, pp. 137-38.

41. *Ibid.*, p. 138.

42. *Ibid.*, p. 145.

43. *Ibid.*, p. 148. Original in italics.

44. *Ibid.*, p. 193. Original in italics.

45. *Ibid.*, p. 444.

46. *Ibid.*, p. 458.

47. *Ibid.*, pp. 449-59.

48. Cotton, *Royce,* p. 18.

49. CG 278.

50. *Ibid.*, p. 279.

51. *Ibid.*, p. 287.

52. *Ibid.*, p. 291.

53. SMP 389.

54. *Ibid.*, p. 390.

55. *Ibid.*

56. *Ibid.*, p. 411.

57. *Ibid.*, pp. 398, 404.

58. *Ibid.*, pp. 398-400.

59. *Ibid.*, p. 403.

60. *Ibid.*, p. 402.

61. *Ibid.*

62. *Ibid.*, pp. 395-96.

63. *Ibid.*, p. 407.

64. *Ibid.*, p. 408.

65. *Ibid.*

66. *Ibid.*, p. 407.

67. *Ibid.*, p. 408.

68. See pp. 912-16.

69. See p. 724 ff.

70. SMP 408.

71. *Ibid.*, p. 395.

72. CG 15.

73. Josiah Royce, *The World and the Individual* (New York: Macmillan, 1901). Hereafter WI.

74. WI 16-17.

75. See p. 639 ff.

76. Josiah Royce, *Royce's Logical Essays*, ed. D. Robinson (Dubuque, Iowa: William Brown and Co., 1951), p. 3. Hereafter L.

77. Josiah Royce, *Outline of Psychology* (New York: Macmillan Co., 1903). Hereafter OP.

78. OP 84.

79. *Ibid.*, p. 108.

80. *Ibid.*, p. 38.

81. *Ibid.*, p. 198.

82. *Ibid.*, p. 207.

83. *Ibid.*, p. 222.

84. *Ibid.*, pp. 222-23.

85. *Ibid.*, p. 235. Original in italics.

86. *Ibid.*

87. *Ibid.*

88. *Ibid.*, p. 368.

89. *Ibid.* Original in italics.

90. WI 469.

91. OP 289-90.

92. WI 24-25.

93. *Ibid.*, p. 49.

94. *Ibid.*, p. 52n.

95. *Ibid.*, p. 292.

96. *Ibid.*, p. 22.

97. *Ibid.*, p. 23.

98. *Ibid.*, p. 25.

99. *Ibid.*, p. 24.

100. *Ibid.*, p. 26.

101. *Ibid.*, pp. 317ff.

102. *Ibid.*, pp. 306-11.

103. *Ibid.*, p. 337.

104. *Ibid.*, p. 338; CG 248.

105. CG 247ff.

106. *Ibid.*, pp. 261ff.

107. *Ibid.*, p. 259.

108. *Ibid.*, pp. 268-70; L 350-51.

109. WI 341-42.

110. CG 266-68.

111. *Ibid.*, p. 266.

112. WI 367.

113. *Ibid.*, pp. 337, 387.

114. *Ibid.*, p. 338.

115. *Ibid.*, p. 387.

116. CG 267-68.

117. F. H. Bradley, *Appearance and Reality: A Metaphysical Essay* (Oxford: Clarendon Press, 1893).

118. See Royce's summary of Bradley's argument in WI 473-89.

119. WI 488-89.

120. *Ibid.*, pp. 503ff.

121. *Ibid.*, pp. 508-9.

122. *Ibid.*, p. 511.

123. *Ibid.*, pp. 513, 526ff, 542.

124. Josiah Royce, *The Conception of Immortality* (London: Archibald Constable and Co., 1904), pp. 141ff.

125. WI 538.

126. *Ibid.*, pp. 536-42, 553-54ff, 581-82.

127. *Ibid.*, pp. 517ff.

128. *Ibid.*, pp. 568-69.

129. *Ibid.*, pp. 467-68.

130. CG 202.

131. WI 573.

132. *Ibid.*, p. 453.

133. *Ibid.*, p. 260.

134. *Ibid.*, p.261.

135. *Ibid.*, p. 453.

136. *Ibid.*, p. 526.

137. SMP 224.

138. *Ibid.*

139. *Ibid.*, p. 225.

140. *Ibid.*, pp. 225-26.

141. Bertrand Russell, *Introduction to Mathematical Philosophy* (London: George Allen and Unwin, 1950), p. 34.

142. WI 581-88.

143. Josiah Royce, *The World and the Individual,* 2d ser. (New York: Dover Co., 1959). Hereafter WI II.

144. WI II p. 65.

145. *Ibid.*, pp. 46-50.

146. *Ibid.*, pp. 51-52.

147. *Ibid.*, p. 52.

148. *Ibid.*, p. 64.

149. *Ibid.*, p. 66.

150. *Ibid.*, pp. 66-68.

151. *Ibid.*, p. 93.

152. *Ibid.*, p. 94.

153. *Ibid.*, p. 95 n. 1.

154. *Ibid.*, p. 94.

155. *Ibid.*, p. 99.

156. *Ibid.*, pp. 95-96.

157. *Ibid.*, p. 71.

158. *Ibid.*, p. 97.

159. *Ibid.*, pp. 14ff.

160. *Ibid.*, p. 96.

161. *Ibid.*, pp. 102f.

162. *Ibid.*, pp. 103-4.

163. *Ibid.*, p. 167.

164. *Ibid.*, pp. 171-72.

165. *Ibid.*, pp. 171-73.

166. *Ibid.*, pp. 175-77.

167. *Ibid.*, p. 216.

168. *Ibid.*, p. 215.

169. *Ibid.*, p. 222.

170. *Ibid.*, p. 220.

171. *Ibid.*, pp. 220-21.

172. *Ibid.*, p. 223.

173. *Ibid.*, pp. 220-21.

174. *Ibid.*, p. 226.

175. *Ibid.*, pp. 227ff.

176. *Ibid.*, p. 232.

177. *Ibid.*, pp. 192-93.

178. *Ibid.*, p. 224.

179. *Ibid.*, p. 137.

180. Josiah Royce, *Studies of Good and Evil* (New York: D. Appleton and Co., 1906).

181. Josiah Royce, *The Philosophy of Loyalty* (New York: Macmillan Co., 1928). Hereafter PL.

182. PL 27.

183. *Ibid.*

184. *Ibid.*, p. 31.

185. *Ibid.*

186. *Ibid.*, p. 24.

187. *Ibid.*, pp. 34-35.

188. *Ibid.*, pp. 30-40; OP 295-98.

189. Josiah Royce, *The Problem of Christianity*, 2 vols. (New York: Macmillan Co., 1913), I: 142-48. Hereafter PC.

190. PL 36-37.

191. *Ibid.*, p. 40.

192. *Ibid.*, p. 51.

193. *Ibid.*, p. 52.

194. *Ibid.*

195. *Ibid.*

196. *Ibid.*

197. *Ibid.*, p. 310.

198. *Ibid.*, p. 227.

199. *Ibid.*, pp. 344-45.

200. *Ibid.*, p. 121. Original in italics.

201. *Ibid.*, p. 119.

202. *Ibid.*, p. 357.

203. Josiah Royce, *Primer of Logical Analysis* (San Francisco, 1881).

204. See below, p. 894.

205. SMP 400.

206. L 23.

207. *Ibid.*, p. 91.

208. *Ibid.*

209. *Ibid.*, pp. 91-92.

210. *Ibid.*, pp. 93-94.

211. *Ibid.*, p. 364.

212. *Ibid.*, p. 365. Original in italics.

213. PC II 196ff; WI 256.

214. L 312.

215. Josiah Royce, "The Relation of the Principles of Logic to the Foundations of Geometry," L 379-441. For a more detailed discussion of the system Σ, see Murray G. Murphey, "The Synechism of Charles Sanders Peirce" (Ph.D. diss., Yale University, 1954), chap. 3, sec. 1, "The Erlanger Logic."

216. L 379ff.

217. Alfred Bray Kempe, "Memoir on the Theory of Mathematical Form," *Philosophical Transactions of the Royal Society of London,* vol. 177, pt. I, pp. 1-70 (1886).

218. Alfred Bray Kempe, "On the Relation between the Logical Theory of Classes and the Geometrical Theory of Points," *Proceedings of the London Mathematical Society* XXI: 147-82 (1889-90).

219. Kempe, "On the Relation between etc.," p. 147.

220. Clarence I. Lewis, "Types of Order and the System Σ," *Papers in Honor of Josiah Royce on his Sixtieth Birthday, Philosophical Review* XXV, no. 3 (May 1916): 411.

221. L 388ff.

222. L 393. My numbering of these axioms differs from Royce's.

223. L 398ff, 427-38. For discussions of Σ, see Lewis, "Types of Order"; Clarence I. Lewis, *A Survey of Symbolic Logic* (New York: Dover, 1960), pp. 198ff.

224. L 428.

225. L 429.

226. L 436ff; O. Veblen, "System of Axioms for Geometry," *Transactions of the American Mathematical Society* 5:343-84 (1904).

227. L 438.

228. Clarence I. Lewis, *A Survey of Symbolic Logic* (Berkeley: University of California Press, 1918), p. 368n.

229. L 373-74.

230. *Ibid.*, p. 374.

231. *Ibid.*, p. 375. Original in italics.

232. *Ibid.*

233. *Ibid.*, p. 376.

234. *Ibid.*, p. 377.

235. *Ibid.*, p. 375.

236. *Ibid.*

237. *Ibid.*, pp. 280-81.

238. *Ibid.*, p. 281.

239. *Ibid.*

240. *Ibid.,* p. 282.

241. *Ibid.,* pp. 275-76.

242. See below, Ch. 15.

243. Josiah Royce, *The Source of Religious Insight* (New York: Charles Scribner's Sons, 1912). Hereafter SRI.

244. See above, n. 189.

245. William James, *The Varieties of Religious Experience* (New York: Modern Library, n.d.), pp. 72ff, 421ff.

246. See above, p. 541.

247 SRI 82.

248. James, *Varieties,* pp. 421-47.

249. SRI 90.

250. SRI 5-6.

251. L 78-86.

252. PC II 315-19.

253. 1.545-59.

254. 5.213-357.

255. 1.553.

256. PC II 183-84.

257. *Ibid.,* p. 183.

258. *Ibid.*

259. See p. 578.

260. PC II 147.

261. *Ibid.*, pp. 143-44.

262. *Ibid.*, pp. 193ff.

263. *Ibid.*, pp. 196-205.

264. *Ibid.*, p. 320.

265. *Ibid.*, p. 206.

266. *Ibid.*, p. 207.

267. *Ibid.*, pp. 322-25.

268. See p. 582ff.

269. 5.310-17.

270. PC II 211ff.

271. *Ibid.*, pp. 60-69.

272. *Ibid.*, pp. 216-21.

273. See p. 720.

274. See pp. 577, 589.

275. See p. 590.

276. PC II 323.

277. *Ibid.*, p. 269.

278. PC I 35ff.

279. *Ibid.*, pp. 25ff, 91ff.

280. *Ibid.*, p. 92.

281. PC II 69ff.

282. *Ibid.*, pp. 220-21.

283. *Ibid.*, p. 425. Original in italics.

284. John Smith, *Royce's Social Infinite* (New York: Liberal Arts Press, 1950), p. 139.

285. PC I 254ff.

286. *Ibid.*, pp. 263-64.

287. *Ibid.*, pp. 283ff.

288. *Ibid.*, pp. 307ff.

289. *Ibid.*, p. 319.

290. *Ibid.*, p. 322. Original in italics.

291. *Ibid.*, p. 191.

292. SRI 206.

293. PC I 186ff, 206-13.

294. *Ibid.*, p. 186.

Chapter Thirteen

George Santayana:
The Exile at Home

Chapter Thirteen

George Santayana: The Exile at Home

George Santayana (1863-1952) has been well called the Mona Lisa of philosophy; although he was admittedly a brilliant and gifted writer, most modern critics have found his philosophy as baffling and his ironic wit as confusing as the enigmatic half-smile of that celebrated lady. Certainly Santayana is a unique figure in the history of philosophy in America; despite his debts to James, he belongs to no American tradition, and had few American disciples. His philosophical terminology is radically different from that of any other American thinker, and his writings, despite their unquestionable literary merit, have often seemed almost unintelligible. In an age in which philosophy has been preoccupied with science, logic, and mathematics, Santayana has been concerned with humanism, morality, aesthetics, and what he called the life of the spirit. While philosophy generally has become increasingly technical, using the style and often the vocabulary and symbolism of science, Santayana has written with the grace and elegance befitting the poet that he was. Viewed in the context of American philosophy of the late nineteenth and early twentieth centuries, Santayana seems an alien figure—an outsider whose very presence is puzzling.[1]

Part of Santayana's strangeness is due to the bizarre set of circumstances which brought him to America in the first place. Santayana's parents were both Spaniards who first met in the Philippines. But they did not marry in the Philippines; rather Santayana's mother married a Boston merchant named Sturgis, by whom she had three children. When Sturgis died in 1857, she took her children to Boston, where the ample means of the Sturgis family guaranteed their upbringing. Several years later she visited Spain where she renewed her acquaintance with Santayana's father, with the result that they married in 1862. George Santayana was born in 1863 in Spain. The marriage, however, was not a success, and Santayana's mother returned to Boston, leaving Santayana with his father in Spain. Santayana's father was not a man of means, and by 1872, when Santayana was nine, he had decided that his son's future prospects would be much brighter in Boston than in Spain. Accordingly, he brought Santayana to Boston, where he was raised by his mother and her in-laws, his father having returned to Spain. One may only guess at the effects which this childhood, involving as it did desertion by both parents, must have had upon a child of such intelligence and sensitivity, but one can hardly repress the conviction that his subsequent pessimism and fatalism about life must have had roots in the tragedies of his early years.

In 1882 Santayana entered Harvard, where he studied under James, Royce, and Palmer. After graduation he went to Europe, where he studied Greek philosophy under Paulsen in Berlin. He returned to America to teach philosophy at Harvard from 1889 to 1912, and was thus a member of the most famous department of philosophy of which any American university has been able to boast. But even during these years Santayana was never wholly happy in America, or in his role as a professor. He spent much of his time in Europe, with which he felt a strong cultural identification, and despite the fact that he spent forty years in this country, he always saw himself as a sojourner here. In 1912 he left America for good, and spent the rest of his life in Europe, living chiefly in France and Italy, until his death in 1952.

Santayana's great virtue to the student of the history of philosophy in America lies in the radical contrast between his work and that of every other American thinker. A Catholic in a Protestant country, a humanist in an age of science, a pessimist in a nation in which optimism was a national religion, a fatalist in a culture which preached the ability of creative intelligence to master the world, a man who advocated resignation as a cardinal virtue in a land wedded to activism, Santayana provides a reference point by comparison with which the differences between other American thinkers dwindle into insignificance and their common orientations stand out starkly. Santayana was the spokesman for a tradition which has had few American philosophic champions, but which has, in recent years, become significant in the American arts, and it is not by accident that T. S. Eliot was his graduate assistant at Harvard. But however alien Santayana's voice may seem in comparison to the prevailing American tradition, it is a voice which must be heard, for the world view Santayana articulated is an authentic alternative to the optimistic, activistic, practicalist view which has dominated American thought, and it is an alternative which may well find a more sympathetic audience in the dying years of the twentieth century than it did when that century was young.

1. The Sense of Beauty

In 1896 Santayana published his first philosophical work—*The Sense of Beauty*.[2] The book grew out of a course in aesthetics which he had offered at Harvard since 1892, and, strictly speaking, it deals only with questions of aesthetics. Yet it is also one of Santayana's most characteristic and revealing productions, for not only does it contain in germinal form many of the doctrines he was to develop more fully in later writings, but it also reveals the basic orientation toward life and philosophy which Santayana was to espouse throughout his life. What the *Principles of Psychology* was for James, and the notes on excellency for Edwards, *The Sense of Beauty* was for Santayana, and much of the rest of his work can be seen as a development of the themes laid out in this early work.

The Sense of Beauty is an inquiry into the origin and nature of aesthetic experience. That there is aesthetic experience—that men have a sense of beauty— is for Santayana simply a psychological fact beyond question or denial. Like the earlier Scottish writers, Santayana regards the fact that men respond aesthetically to some stimuli as empirically certain, and sets out to provide a psychological analysis of how and why this response occurs. The standpoint of the book is therefore empirical and psychological—one might almost say scientific— although the objective is the analysis of a type of experience very different from that provided by science. As James, upon whose psychology Santayana everywhere relies, had sought to produce a scientific analysis of religious experience in the *Varieties,* Santayana is here seeking to do very much the same thing for aesthetic experience.

Aesthetic experience involves the perception of values, and so Santayana begins with the question of the basis of value. Santayana of course assumes the science-art distinction (which does not parallel the modern fact-value dichotomy), but recognizes the attainment of truth as a value. The basis of value is to be sought not in cognition, still less in the external world, but in the emotions. Value is created by desire; as Santayana paraphrases Spinoza, "we desire nothing because it is good, but it is good only because we desire it."[3] Without human desire, there could be no value to anything in the universe; values therefore are not in things independent of the valuer, but arise from the relation of the thing to the desires of the valuer. Into the origin of these desires, Santayana does not inquire; they are for him ultimate psychological facts whose existence is irrational, in the sense that they do not arise from reason but are simply given characteristics of human beings. Thus in Santayana's view, valuing is like breathing—a purely natural function of the inexplicable nature of the human animal.

Not all values are aesthetic values; to reach a definition of beauty it is necessary to differentiate the realm of value. The first restriction which Santayana introduces is to values which are positive and immediate—that which is perceived as good in itself and for its own sake.[4] The contrast here is of course with instrumental value—with that which is perceived as good because it is a means to something else. Like Peirce and many others, Santayana holds that the aesthetically valuable must be directly pleasurable in and of itself. But there is a second differentiating factor which Santayana stresses—aesthetic value must be objectified. We perceive beauty to be an objective property of an object. This is of course a projection of the pleasure we experience into the object; as Santayana has defined value, our pleasures arise from the satisfactions of our desires, so that value is essentially a local—in our case human—phenomenon. But in the case of aesthetic value the pleasure which we receive from the perception of the object is so constantly associated with its perception that we objectify the pleasure and treat it as a quality of the thing itself. Hence Santayana defines beauty as "value positive, intrinsic, and objectified" or in other words "beauty is pleasure regarded as the quality of a thing."[5]

(In *The Life of Reason* there is an evolutionary suggestion for this objectification—it fixes the character of what delights us upon an object and so gives us a perceptual way of recognizing and pursuing it. But for that matter this process underlies the whole fixing of objects out of the flux.)

In his treatment of beauty, Santayana uses three categories—matter, form, and expression. The choice of categories itself is significant—Santayana was the only American philosopher of his time for whom matter and form were concepts of major importance. By employing the category of matter Santayana is able to emphasize the dependence of beauty upon the peculiar sensory and emotional constitution of man. The materials of beauty are the various sense qualities which men are capable of perceiving, together with the basic emotions arising from man's nature. It is out of these materials that all human aesthetic experience is created—materials which obviously would be very different for beings differently constituted. As he remarks, "If any one were desirous to produce a being with a great susceptibility to beauty, he could not invent an instrument better designed for that object than sex."[6]

> What more could be needed to suffuse the world with the deepest meaning and beauty? The attention is fixed upon a well-defined object, and all the effects it produces in the mind are easily regarded as powers or qualities of that object. But these effects are here powerful and profound. The soul is stirred to its depths. Its hidden treasures are brought to the surface of consciousness. The imagination and heart awake for the first time. All these new values crystallize about the objects then offered to the mind. If the fancy is occupied by the image of a single person, whose qualities have had the power of precipitating this revolution, all the values gather about that one image. The object becomes perfect, and we are said to be in love.[7]

Certainly sexual attractiveness fits Santayana's definition of beauty with such exactness that it may well be considered a paradigm example of the theory.

Form is that characteristic of the beautiful which has traditionally received the greatest attention, and Santayana devotes more space to its examination than to any other property. Why certain forms should be pleasing to us—e.g., symmetrical forms—Santayana seeks to explain by physiological arguments concerning the movements and tensions of the perceiving organ. Without entering into these arguments, it may suffice to note that Santayana regards it as an empirical fact that some forms are more pleasing to the perceiver than others and that he regards this fact as due to physiological characteristics of the perceiver. This basic preference for certain forms carries important consequences for the role of form in organizing and giving coherence to experience. Our experience is brought to order by the development of concepts which Santayana calls "types"—class concepts by which we summarize our past experience with objects in a form which can be used to categorize new experiences. These types are instrumental for the organism and are designed to serve practical interests, but they may also be developed to serve aesthetic interests by so modifying them as to emphasize those features which are aesthetically pleasing. The type then becomes an ideal, which can serve not only to categorize objects of experience but to judge them according to their conformity to the standard thus provided. Thus the concept of a horse may at once serve to allow us to categorize animals of our experience into horses and nonhorses and—if it is a concept of a perfect horse—may provide the standard by comparison to which we may order the domain of horses in terms of perfection.

Santayana's theory of types provides a basis for integrating aesthetic considerations with other features of knowledge. Clearly, what types we will have depends upon what our experience is, and that in turn is a function of our environment and of the modes of adaptation to that environment which have proven useful. Different cultures, having different courses of experience, will develop different types and will idealize them in various ways. One need not therefore expect universal agreement upon the most beautiful type of building, or woman. But it follows too that whatever the course of experience, the resulting types can be idealized, and we may thus learn to see beauty in whatever culturally defined world we inhabit. Indeed, it is the function of education as Santayana sees it to teach us to see beauty in the world, though different observers with different experiences will do so in different ways.

There is, however, another sort of ideal upon which Santayana lays particular stress—what he calls "ideal characters": those creations of imagination and art, like Hamlet or Achilles, which are not types in the above sense, but which seem to be more real and living than many men of the actual world. Since character is not something known by sense, but a rational construction created to account for the acts and words of men, we can create characters by presenting in imagination such deeds and words as a character so conceived would do and say. And in these imaginative creations, unhindered by the constraints of the actual world, we may realize all those powers and capacities which we feel to be potential in ourselves, though alas never in our lives actualized. Such beings have individuality without having reality, because individuality is a thing acquired in the mind by the congeries of its impressions. They have power, also, because that depends on the appropriateness of a stimulus to touch the springs of reaction in the soul. And they of course have beauty, because in them is embodied the greatest of our imaginative delights—that of giving body to our latent capacities, and of wandering, without the strain and contradiction of actual existence, into all forms of possible being.[8]

Great artists such as Homer and Shakespeare have created characters of this sort that have profoundly affected generations of men, but the greatest of these ideal characters Santayana holds to be the product of the religious imagination, working through countless men over the centuries. In a passage which at once reveals much of his attraction toward Catholicism and his revulsion from Protestantism, Santayana describes the Virgin as such an ideal character.

The Virgin Mary, whose legend is so meagre, but whose power over the Catholic imagination is so great, is an even clearer illustration of this inward building up of an ideal form. Everything is here spontaneous sympathetic expansion of two given events: the incarnation and the crucifixion. The figure of the Virgin, found in these mighty scenes, is gradually clarified and developed, until we come to the thought on the one hand of her freedom from original sin, and on the other to that of her universal maternity. We thus attain the conception of one of the noblest of conceivable roles and of one of the most beautiful of characters. It is a pity that a foolish iconoclasm should so long have deprived the Protestant mind of the contemplation of this ideal.[9]

The Virgin, Christ, and even God Himself are for Santayana ideal characters whose hold upon the mind of man is due to their realization of the dreams and longings of humanity. Santayana was not a religious man in the sense of James or Edwards, yet he found in religion one of the supreme aesthetic achievements of human history, and he considered the Puritan's stubborn inability to appreciate the splendor of the Catholic tradition a foolish and lamentable failing.

By expression Santayana means objectified suggestiveness; the presented object suggests something not present. "In all expression we may thus distinguish two terms: the first is the object actually presented, the word, the image, the expressive thing; the second is the object suggested, the further thought, emotion, or image evoked, the thing expressed."[10] But mere suggestiveness alone is not enough to constitute an aesthetic value; that requires not only that the association suggested by the object be pleasurable, but that the values so suggested be objectified as properties of the presented object.

Expressiveness is thus the power given by experience to any image to call up others in the mind; and this expressiveness becomes an aesthetic value, that is, becomes expression, when the value involved in the associations thus awakened are incorporated in the present object.[11]

Thus any symbol involves suggestion, for the symbol presented stands for something besides itself. But for such a symbol to possess aesthetic value, not only must it have appropriate matter and form, but the suggested values must be so identified with the presented symbol that they seem to be properties of that symbol itself. A truly aesthetic symbol thus takes on the values which it connotes.

Expression poses a problem for Santayana, for his definition of aesthetic values as necessarily positive seems inconsistent with the fact that what is expressed by a beautiful work may be negative. Thus tragedy typically deals with death, terror, and failure, all of which are clearly negative goods; yet tragedies are among the greatest works of art. Santayana's answer to this problem is that the values in the expressive object need not be the same as those of the thing expressed, and indeed that they cannot be so when the values of the thing expressed are negative. The hideous presentation of the hideous is not art. The horrors of life can be dealt with aesthetically only when they are modified in the presentation by form and matter employed so as to acquire positive values. And this claim carries us close to the heart of Santayana's concern with aesthetics. Santayana was extraordinarily aware of the terror and horror of life. Behind his golden prose there lies a profound despair—a fatalistic view of the world as a place where inevitably all human dreams and hopes go down to defeat. In no other American thinker is so strong and pervasive a pessimism to be found. Art deals with the horrors of life, not because they are necessary to art, but because they are necessary to life, and what art does is to transform them in such a way that they can be borne.

> Art does not seek out the pathetic, the tragic, and the absurd; it is life that has imposed them upon our attention, and enlisted art in their service, to make the contemplation of them, since it is inevitable, at least as tolerable as possible.[12]

The function of art is to make life bearable: "there is no situation so terrible that it may not be relieved by the momentary pause of the mind to contemplate it aesthetically."[13] It is just because life is for Santayana so ghastly an affair that aesthetics is so important.

This view becomes particularly clear in the contrast between the beautiful and the sublime. "It is the essential privilege of beauty to so synthesize and bring to a focus the various impulses of the self, so to suspend them to a single image, that a great peace falls upon that perturbed kingdom."[14]

> But there are always two methods of securing harmony: one is to unify all the given elements, and another is to reject and expunge all the elements that refuse to be unified. Unity by inclusion gives us the beautiful; unity by exclusion, opposition and isolation gives us the sublime.[15]

One would expect that the greater of these would be beauty, and of course Santayana is devoted to the cultivation of the beautiful, yet it is quite clear that for him the sublime is the supreme aesthetic achievement. For in the sublime Santayana finds the true liberation of the self from the chains of fate—a freedom won by defiance of the worst that life can do.

> If we could count the stars, we should not weep before them. While we think we can change the drama of history, and of our own lives, we are not awed by our destiny. But when the evil is irreparable, when our life is lived, a strong spirit has the sublime resource of standing at bay and of surveying almost from the other world the vicissitudes of this.
>   The more intimate to himself the tragedy he is able to look back upon with calmness, the more sublime that calmness is, and the more divine the ecstasy in which he achieves it. For the more of the accidental vesture of life we are able to strip ourselves of, the more naked and simple is the surviving spirit; the more complete its superiority and unity, and, consequently, the more unqualified its joy. There remains little in us, then, but that intellectual essence, which several great philosophers have called eternal and identified with the Divinity.[16]

This was Santayana's answer to life—an answer that he refined and developed over the years but never fundamentally altered. For him, life was essentially tragic; like Hobbes, he perceived life as nasty, brutish, and short. His answer to this dismal decree of fate was at once resignation to the inevitable and a sublime defiance to be achieved through aesthetic appreciation of the awful spectacle of life. Standing amidst the ruin of all man cherishes, Santayana found victory, not in man's ability to conquer, nor even to endure, but in the sublime act of appreciation of his own catastrophic defeat.

2. The Life of Reason[17]

The ideas and modes of analysis that had been applied to a specific area came to full fruition in the five-volume work, *The Life of Reason,* published in 1905.[18] The product is a distinctive ethical naturalism, though it was not cast as an ethical treatise. Later, Santayana is said to have looked back on the work as his early novel. In the preface to the second edition, almost twenty years later, he says that the suggestion for the work had come from Hegel's *Phenomenology of Spirit;* and indeed the subtitle to *The Life of Reason* is "Phases of Human Progress." But it was no linear or dialectical progress that Santayana presented. Rather it was a picture of man's perennial condition, the nature of the processes that go on within him, the sober attempt to hold together in a coherent pattern the forces that would propel him in different and disruptive directions if pursued in isolation, all seen as they appear in human consciousness which reflects these variegated tendencies and in the form in which they were projected in the history of thought. The focus on consciousness is central: the frontispiece contains the Greek sentence from Aristotle which Santayana translates in *Reason in Common Sense*[19] as "life is reason in operation." And he adds, "The Life of Reason will then be a name for that part of experience which perceives and pursues ideals—all conduct so controlled and all sense so interpreted as to perfect natural happiness."

The fuller content of his ethics is seen in the four volumes on reason in society, religion, art, science. *Reason in Common Sense* sets the metaphysical and epistemological stage. Since we shall see what this became in his later works, no detailed account is here needed, nor shall we attempt to trace what were changes, what reversals of detail, what natural developments. In this first volume there is rather a general perspective, the contours of a consciousness that reflects the structure of its world, the categories in which it finds expression, and the progress and misadventures of philosophy in articulating them.

Human experience and human consciousness are permeated with the ideal. We do not remain immersed in sense, caught in the "unmitigated flux of sensations."[20] Man looks before and after, envisages the absent, recollects the past, and attempts to modify the future. Desire and regret grow into purpose, and bodily change is raised to "the dignity of action."[21] Reflection from the beginning thus engages in the functions of representation and evaluation, and there is continuity of its operations in common sense and the highest flights of philosophy.

Santayana's outlook on the world is basically Aristotelian, with a relativized concept of essence and a substitution of a Democritean causality for an Aristotelian teleology. Perhaps more explicitly, he is attempting a fusion of Plato and Democritus, in a background of Heraclitus! Heraclitus captures the flux of sensation and immediacy. Plato gives shape to the form that is involved in representation. Democritus attains the fundamental insight into the executive mechanism of matter on which all rests. These figures represent also, perhaps, the great temptations to which the great philosophers have too often yielded—for philosophy seems almost at times to be a saga of intellectual refinement plunged in misadventure: the reversion to immediacy in mysticism, the flight to the transcendent and the external, the reduction to bare skeletons of the rich quality of experience. Much of the first volume is given to tracing such a critique of philosophy, while at the same time eliciting the natural way in which, through the ideal, a representation is achieved of an order of natural objects. And a discovery of fellow minds arises naturally from the projection of feelings upon objects which gives them a steady and remembered focus. (In the case of fellow humans, this "pathetic fallacy" turns out not to be a fallacy for other beings of the species do in fact turn out to have the feelings!)

Several general theses emerge in Santayana's treatment of philosophy. There is the primacy of matter, the functional and practical character of mind, and the intimate relation of the ideal and the natural as the guarantee of authenticity in the ideal itself.

The role of matter is central. In "The Secret of Aristotle" (in *Dialogues in Limbo*[22]) Santayana has matter revealed as the basic source of all our potentialities even for Aristotle. And in the chapter on "Piety" in *Reason in Religion,* he suggests that this basic virtue may be extended to the material universe itself: "Great is this organism of mud and fire, terrible this vast, painful, glorious experiment. Why should we not look upon the universe with piety? Is it not our substance? Are we made of other clay? All our possibilities lie from eternity hidden in its bosom. It is the dispenser of all our joys."[23] And in spite of all his recognition of the different roles that matter as an idea plays in human thought, two fixed conceptions about it are central in the *Life of Reason.* One is that all categories have to be referred eventually to it and to constancies and stabilities found in its operations. Even categories of the spirit involve such a relation. Thus Santayana's theory of mind is epiphenomenal. As he says in the chapter on piety, "A soul is but the last bubble of a long fermentation in the world."[24] Consciousness may represent the trends that are shaping up in matter and be a response to the practical needs, and its enjoyments and sufferings are the fruits of these processes. But what it does not do is execute or operate causally; that is the work of material processes. The second fixed conception is that matter is physicochemical, or at most physiological. There is no general conception of material levels in Santayana's thought, as, e.g., in historical or Marxian materialism, such that one would speak of social or historical causation. The latter could be at most a mythical representation of underlying physical-material processes.

The functional and practical character of mind need not be inconsistent with this materialist doctrine. It can share with James the view that our ideas of objects express our needs and interests in their very formation; it will simply give a material interpretation of those needs and interests. It will differ from Dewey's instrumentalism not in denying the instrumental character of the ideational, but in stressing also its intrinsic values in consciousness. The larger differences from the pragmatic thinkers will be more in value attitude. Santayana remains the contemplator, not the actor; the greatest function of the mind is perhaps to let us dwell in the ideal as a relief from the suffering of this world. All this can be better spelled out in detail.

The most distinctive tenet of Santayana's ethics is his relation of the ideal and the natural. He is not only the sole American philosopher who does not shun the epithet of materialism, but he insists that the recognition of the primacy of matter is the very condition for the vitality and authenticity of the ideal. We might almost paraphrase Kant on concept and percept and say for Santayana that the ideal without the natural is empty and the natural without the ideal is blind.

This intriguing conception is best expounded in the opening pages of *Reason in Society.* "If man were a static or intelligible being, such as the angels are thought to be, his life would have a single guiding interest, under which all other interests would be subsumed. His acts would explain themselves without looking beyond his given essence, and his soul would be like a musical composition, which once written out cannot grow different and once rendered can ask for nothing but, at most, to be rendered over again."[25] So much for the essentialist or the rationalist;

man is not such an eternal essence. On the contrary, he is "an animal, a portion of the natural flux." From this Santayana concludes that "his nature has a moving centre, his functions an external reference," and—most significant—"his ideal a true ideality." Explicitly, then, a true ideality presupposes a natural or material base. Almost existentialist consequences are drawn: "What he strives to preserve, in preserving himself, is something which he never has been at any particular moment. He maintains his equilibrium by motion . . . The inmost texture of his being is propulsive, and there is nothing more intimately bound up with his success than mobility and devotion to transcendent aims. If there is a transitive function in knowledge and an unselfish purpose in love, that is only because, at bottom, there is a self-reproductive, flying essence in all existence."[26]

Santayana's relation of ideal and natural basis insists both that every ideal has a natural function and no natural function is incapable of evolving some ideal. Or more generally, "human reason lives by turning the friction of material forces into the light of ideal goods."[27] This constitutes a quite specific schema for analyzing ideals, which calls for seeing their function in the harmonious expression of human impulse and interests. If a natural need does not find ideal expression—Santayana cites breathing in one context—it is because it can be satisfied in relative isolation and usually raises no problems. On the other hand, nutrition and reproduction involve organization and cooperation; it is no wonder that they support ideals of social organization and ideals of love and human passion. Since man is born half-made, with instincts and impulses that admit of considerable plasticity, the historical and cultural forms that ideals take in their content is variable, and these different forms are capable of moral evaluation in the broad sense of the moral that is identical with the effort of the life of reason—to fashion social and cultural forms that yield a maximum harmony of human impulse and its expression. There is a basic liberalism in Santayana's assumption that every impulse is self-justifying in its occurrence till its impact on others arises (very like James's treatment of demands). The single cry of pain of a child, Santayana affirms, is a blot on the universe which cannot be rubbed out. But of course, the ideals of organization are themselves legion.

Again, an ideal does not have a constant character in the changing material of the individual. It may have a developing expression. Thus, in a spirit very much like Freud tracing the variety of libidinal attachments, Santayana traces the path of love from the mother as object to the comrade, the wife, and in later life, ideas and the pursuit of ideals. His chapter on love is at the same time a phenomenology of experience and a critique of ideals. In similar fashion, he proceeds in *Reason and Society* through the ideals embedded in family, industry, government, and war, political ideals such as aristocracy (which appeals to him), democracy (whose social forms in an industrial society he fears much in the same way as Aristotle would have people spending their lives in labor barred from citizenship), comradeship and friendship in "free society," patriotism (with its virtues and blindness), and finally ideal society with the dwelling of the spirit in religion, art, and science.

It would take us too far afield here to pursue these detailed aspects. On the whole, in spite of his liberal foundation, the outcome is traditionalist and fairly conservative. He deals with perennial values in their natural settings, and many of his conclusions express factual presuppositions about inevitable operations of society. He is skeptical of the ideals of progress resting on the growth of knowledge and control that Dewey held central and he fears the pursuit of means supplanting the appreciation of ends. Further he lacks the faith in the mass of mankind that has motivated the democratic tradition. These aspects, accentuated in the social conflicts of the first half of the century, became more prominent in his later *Dominations and Powers*[28] and explain his philosophical sympathy with what grew into the ideas of repressive social order in right-wing and even Fascist doctrines. Again, there is no attempt in *Reason and Society* to look for a social or historical basis for evaluating the progression of ideals. Ideals do not rise, grow, go out of date. Their evaluation has no systematic underlying social or historical theory, largely because, as we shall see, in Santayana's interpretation of science, social science and history have no legitimate scientific status.

While the volume on society achieves its greatest depth in its general perspective on the relation of the ideal and the natural, rather than in its specific evaluation of social ideals, the volumes on religion, art, and science are based on a systematic theory of the nature of symbols and their role in human life. In all three fields, the symbol that carries the ideal is a cultural development out of human experience. The differentiation of field comes not from any different nature among the symbols as such, but from the different roles and purposes given to the symbols. The affinities of religion, art, and science are therefore affirmed at the outset. There is no room in principle for the "two cultures" with science and religion or science and art at odds, giving us conflicting views of the world and of reality. Santayana sees all three fields as products of the imagination, put to different use. In poetry (or art generally) the symbol *supervenes* and is developed for its intrinsic satisfactions. In religion, the symbol *intervenes*; it is used to order life in an attempt to achieve the life of reason through the imagination. In science, the symbol is stripped to its fighting weight, and used to make *transitions in our experience.*

The powerful impact of this approach is seen most dramatically in Santayana's theory of religion. There is no religion in general, any more than there is language in general. There are particular religions. Each is a cultural product. It is a poetic rendering of the world, but directed to organizing human life. No religion is therefore true or false, it is simply better or worse to the extent that it humanizes men in their pursuits. The great mistake in the history of religion—characteristic, he says, of the Hebrews and Christians—was to maintain that their gods were the only gods and the gods of others were false. The Romans did better in coopting the deities of the peoples they conquered into their own pantheon, though the result was rather polyglot! Santayana means this with the utmost seriousness. He is in effect translating the dichotomy of supernatural and natural (or divine and natural) into that of ideal and natural. Hence if a god existed he would have to be material, and thus have no more ideal meaning than any great natural force. To be religiously meaningful, and an object of worship, a god must not exist.

The cultural character of religion pits Santayana's conception against James's in which it is a highly individual emotional experience. For Santayana ritual is primary, and the idea of a personal religion rather than a sociocultural form makes no more sense than a personal language. His favorite religion is the Homeric Greek, in which the gods represent natural forces and human needs quite overtly. His preference for Catholicism over Protestantism is justified by the greater social character of the former and its assistance to the individual in ordering his life. Catholicism is practically polytheistic because the functioning divinities in people's lives will be the saints, who can take all sorts of concrete expression. In Protestantism there is a great gulf between the individual and God, and the individual is left on his own for salvation or damnation. Again, as Santayana makes clear in his comparison of Dante and Shakespeare, the former gives us a rounded systematic philosophy for ordering the whole of life, as in Catholicism, while the latter simply explores isolated or fragmentary values. But of course in exercising his religious preference, Santayana sees no incompatibility between literal atheism and cultural religious form.

Santayana does not believe that he is offering a reinterpretation of religion but an analysis of what religion has always meant to the faithful, not to the intellectually minded theologian who made a science out of it. For example, the theologian has God omniscient, but the faithful pray to God, tell him about their plight, and are not put off by the argument that God knows it all in advance. This shows that the function of prayer is not to inform but to give expression to strong feelings and emotions usually when one is helpless and unable to solve one's problems (Santayana is not thinking of conventional prayer but spontaneous invocation to deity). He traces the moral effect of prayer in helping a person articulate his problem, in formulating a justification for his appeal, in seeing thus the wider system of his life in which the object of prayer is enmeshed and thus being fortified in case of a refusal, and so on. In *Reason in Religion* many phases of religious practice are thus examined—e.g., the role of renunciation in sacrifice, or the multiple functions of myth.

Santayana also carries his approach into the interpretation of religious dogma. An excellent example (in *Interpretations of Poetry and Religion*[29]) is his analysis of heaven and hell. He notes the belief that competed with the idea of eternal damnation in the early Christian fathers that God could not damn eternally because He is good. Santayana stoutly defends the moral truth of the idea of hell. What we do now is momentous, our decisions determine what we become, and so fashion our eternity (our threescore years and ten which is all we have). To say that all are eventually forgiven is morally equivalent to saying that it does not matter what we do now since it will all be the same a thousand years from now! But of course a literal hell, if we discovered its fires, would be religiously uninteresting—no more, we might say, than the discovery of the long-range effects of smoking in cancer! There is much in *Reason in Religion* that studies the history of Western religion in this vein. And in the latter part he focuses on an interpretation of the religious virtues of piety, spirituality, and charity. Piety is a reverence for the sources of our being, and the steadying of life by that attachment. Spirituality is living in the light of the ideal—"an inward aim and fixity in affection that knows what to take and what to leave in a world over which it diffuses something of its peace."[30] It is contrasted with its corruptions such as fanaticism and mysticism. (Fanaticism is elsewhere defined by Santayana in one of his best-known epigrams as redoubling one's effort after one has forgotten one's aim.) Charity is reinterpreted as recognizing—since all interests have a local base—that others may be different and have different interests, and so is a kind of empathy with what is other than oneself.

Immortality is, of course, ruled out in any literal sense. But the ideal provides one with another world to live in through the imagination, and so palliates somewhat the sorrow of the present world. Reason and the ideal are the best that men can hope to move toward.

To some extent in America, Santayana's conception of religion had considerable influence in the growth of a humanist movement. It gave an interpretation of the efforts that underlie religion without sacrificing the integrity of rational belief, and so palliated to some extent the harsh rejection that was growing up in a secular culture. It made transitions away from orthodoxy and traditional forms smoother. Whether it is an accurate analysis of the historical character of religion is another question—i.e., whether the belief in existence of religious forces may not be of greater importance than he estimated.

Reason in Art has a more comprehensive perspective than the earlier *Sense of Beauty*. Art here is very much like the classical *techné* in which there is no sharp line between making in general and the fine arts in particular. Santayana views any operation which humanizes and rationalizes objects as art. It is thus the phase of life which lies in self-conscious production. At the same time, he is not ready to see it as ideas governing or producing action, for that would go too far beyond the epiphenomenalism in which he is bound. He stresses the groping character of art and the emergence of the ideational in the midst of action.

Reason in Art thus naturalizes art as a human enterprise, seeing its basis in the full range of human life, and its justification in the full range of human activities and emotions. Like all other human enterprises, art has its basis in man's effort to maintain an equilibrium in the flux. Where this stability is built on changes in surroundings rather than simply accommodation in the self, we have art in its broadest sense. As its operation becomes conscious, an art may take shape. "Art is action which transcending the body makes the world a more congenial stimulus to the soul."[31] Whether it is industrial art or fine art, servile or liberal, close to earth or soaring, depends on the materials it deals with, the human ends it comes to subserve, the faculties it engages. Thus where the labor is sordid and merely instrumental, the industrial character is prominent; where the end is a human weakness and failure (as in war) the servility of the art is central; where the imagination is in the forefront—a region which has "pleasures more airy and luminous than those of sense, more massive and rapturous than those of intelligence"[32]—we are moving into the fine arts. In none of these are the broader relations absent: "The rose's grace could more easily be plucked from its petals than the beauty of art from its subject, occasion, and use."[33] The fantasy that characterizes the fine arts is not itself a flight into the empyrean: "An artist is a dreamer consenting to dream of the actual world; he is a highly suggestive mind hypnotised by reality."[34]

Three features accordingly characterize Santayana's analysis of specific arts. First, they will have a natural basis. Second, the basis will support or issue in some ideal fulfillment. Third, the connection of natural base and ideal supported will be found in the variety of interests and purposes of men, not in some essential connection, and the range of possible ideals will far outreach the particular, sometimes accidental forms that the arts have taken.

Santayana's treatment of music is a clear illustration of his method. The matrix out of which the art develops includes spontaneous sound, response in contagion, rhythmic movement. Music is used—e.g., to secure unison in work—long before it is refined in conscious artistry. In listening as well as sounding, education is required to yield musical judgment; what most people relish as music is rather "a drowsy revery relieved by nervous thrills."[35] In its functioning, music also taps the fund of objectless and suppressed emotion that humans build up in the complexities of life and the narrowing effect of selective feeling allied with specific interests. Music thus furnishes a mode of speech for undirected potentialities. But it also furnishes an appropriate expression to all sorts of human occasions. The intellectual essence of music is "an audible mathematics, adding sense to form,"[36] and music can build, as it were, possible worlds, set on any fine shade of emotion, giving a pure expression to joy, and likewise to sorrow, and so provide a catharsis of the emotions. In the end, music rationalizes sound, though not in any one way, nor with the momentous consequences that language does. Speech and signification build on the same base, or perhaps a wider one, since there is also gesture which took shape in communication. In comparing the way language uses sound with the way music uses it, Santayana turns the emphasis to the suspension of the flux and the way an ideal harness is loosely flung on things[37]—e.g., the way in which literature turns events into ideas.[38] Poetry remains closer to the feeling base than prose: "In poetry feeling is transferred by contagion; in prose it is communicated by bending the attention upon determinate objects; the one stimulates and the other informs."[39]

Similarly, in dealing with the domain of the plastic, Santayana moves by degrees from any action that changes the visible surroundings to conscious plastic construction—as in architecture—and then to the motif of representation which gives us sculpture and painting. Varieties of joys and satisfactions (as well as utilities) may attend the various forms, and there is a close relation of aesthetic and nonaesthetic satisfactions, but primacy lies with aesthetic sensibility.

Reason in Art does not aim to provide a methodology of aesthetic criticism for the particular arts. (Suggestions along these lines are to be found in other of Santayana's works, such as *Interpretations of Poetry and Religion* and essays on particular artists.) It aims rather to reinforce lessons of the relation of nature, ideal, and rationality in the evaluation of art as a human enterprise. It is not surprising, therefore, that the last part of the book reflects on questions of the justification of art, of taste, of the connection of art with human happiness. In these reflections he clearly has his eye on countering traditional arguments that have tried to put art into narrow confines and make it responsible to some narrow set of interests. On his side, Santayana brings out the rational aspect of aesthetic activity in dominating sensuous experience, in being a constant symbolic invitation to the good. He readily allows the criticism of art to be part of morals insofar as imaginative choices which art gives us do have a momentous character; yet he finds art justified by its very spontaneity and its deep root in human existence, and sees inner discipline as a requisite part of art rather than as an external imposition.

As to taste, there are no formulae for its exercise. "A criterion of taste is, therefore, nothing but taste itself in its more deliberate and circumspect form."[40] Intuitive reaction grows into preference which matures into judgment. Some constancy of taste is grounded in an invariable core in human nature. But no taste can be dogmatically imposed in a world of many undiscovered ideals.

In a truly rational life, art would not be isolated: mankind would not be divided into "mechanical blind workers and half-demented poets," useful would not be separated from fine art, and all would be merged into an art of life.[41] Without art life is slavish, and the more human happiness is made the test of institutions and activities, the greater would be their beauty. In the end, Santayana almost uses the place of art itself in society and human life as the measure of the quality of that life itself.

Reason in Science, the last volume of *The Life of Reason* has the task of naturalizing science, fitting it into the rational life without overwhelming it (as science and its philosophy were already beginning to overshadow all other fields), as well as being the coping stone to solution of all the philosophical problems that had emerged in the work. If, as one story in the oral tradition has it, Santayana wept in despair on beginning to write this volume, his tears were not shed in vain. What he accomplished was perhaps more significant than what he failed to solve, especially if we recall the philosophical and practical situation at the beginning of the twentieth century when he was writing—all the intellectual dichotomies that were to divide philosophic thought as well as all the irrationalisms that were to overwhelm practice. In the decades that followed science was to be increasingly set off from the rest of human activity, as the unswerving pursuit of truth without other human responsibilities, the method of science was to be cut off from the rest of human inquiry as the mathematical and experimental access to the reality of the quantitative. Reason was to be cut off from feeling and passion, as the sciences turned their backs on the humanities and the humanities dismissed science as merely practical. Values were to be divorced from facts, as a metaphysically separate domain. In practical life, irrationalism was to be elevated as a principle, and nationalisms and dogmas and superstitions were to occupy the arena of action, with irreconcilable conflicts giving no place to rational solution.

The central philosophic issues dealt with in the volume are therefore the naturalization of science (including mathematics) to exhibit the purposive structure within the whole enterprise, a reckoning once more of the nature and efficacy of reason, resolving the relations of physical science and the studies of human life and morality, and finally to underscore an orientational picture of the world and its processes. This is not, of course, Santayana's order. He begins with the types and aims of science, goes on to history as extended memory furnishing the raw materials for knowledge, establishes the basic character of the physical sciences in a chapter on "Mechanism," pauses to trace "Hesitations in Method" as science looks to the study of man, explores what goes on in psychology, intersperses a chapter on "The Nature of Intent" to reinforce the purposive base of knowledge and uses it to make sense (in the next chapter) of what dialectic and particularly mathematics are up to, and then passes on to morality for the last third of the book—not as a flight from science but to assess the possibilities of science in ethics. The concluding chapter stakes the validity of the whole life of reason on the validity of science, for science itself crowns the life of reason.

The naturalization of science lies in what are now familiar stresses on the continuities in method and experience with ordinary life and its aims. These constitute the natural basis of the ideal which is science. From the very beginning, human beings discern similarities and construct objects. Out of the former, concepts are born, out of the latter, a world of things and their relations. The exploration of concepts, i.e., constancies in meaning, leads to dialectic, deduction, and the mathematical sciences. The exploration of things and their relations leads to physics and the laws of science. These touch in their beginnings, for they express the purposive effort of stabilization in the world and the fixing of dependable features in the flux to guide future experience. The one, as Santayana puts it, imposes on the flux ideas or "concretions in discourse," the other, by separating the flux into things, provides "concretions in existence," i.e., complexes of qualities in space and time that have dynamic relations and a history that can be traced. But the purposive cement is not only at the beginning or in underlying objective. They touch in outcome, not only in the sense that mathematics has physical applications but throughout their operations. The heart of science lies in verification, systematically and persistently pursued, but what is being established are the intellectual constructions that furnish bridges from experience to experience. (We have already seen his treatment of science as symbolic, in the comparison with myth.) Moreover, the very goal of a science is to establish a successful conceptual system. Santayana focuses on this in his analysis of mechanism. To note a recurrence is, he says, to divine a mechanism. But a mechanism is simply a set of units (atoms) with discoverable dynamic operations. That is why he takes the Democritean atomism to be almost definitory of science—not that its atoms are not replaced by more complex units, but that the replacements have the same systematic-atomistic character. Science thus rests on the faith that there are underlying mechanisms to be reached by constructions out of the flux. But there is no antecedent warrant for this faith, other than its success. The validity of science, we shall see, lies in its achieving what we are all trying to do and so in its meeting our basic purposive activity.

A marked feature of Santayana's materialistic naturalism is his recognition of the great variety of possible constructions in conceptual arresting of the flux. This means that descriptions of the "same" can go in all sorts of different directions, guided by the multiplicity of specific purposes and intent. (Indeed, we shall have to ask soon how he avoids slipping into an utter intellectual relativism and is able to maintain the belief in a real material world with an order that is discoverable.) It is this variety that lies at the root of dialectic, in which every idea, every meaning, can be the source of an ideational elaboration and a possible system. But he does not let this go into the familiar route that positivism was soon to take, of regarding meanings as simply stipulations that are a matter of arbitrary selection. Neither in his epistemology nor in his ethics, is such "voluntarism" given free scope. The basis of the worlds of dialectic, and the variety of possible systems, remains the richness of the world itself. Existence is free to bloom untrammeled; that is why verification is required in science, and cannot be cut off as complete. In dialectic, in which we explore meanings through their implications, there is, in spite of the possible variety of alternatives, a responsibility to the stability of intent. If the meaning we are amplifying does not remain stable, the system as a whole is upset; indeed, the analogue of verification for dialectic is the comparison of the implications with our original, often vague, intent. (In contemporary informal analysis we often speak of an outcome as "counterintuitive," when it would force us to change our original meanings, and in formal analysis we pinpoint contradiction of our original assumptions.) Santayana's use of the notion of *intent* is at times obscure, but his intention is clear enough. It functions as the surrogate of purpose within the arena of consciousness; "Intent is action in the sphere of thought; it corresponds to transition and derivation in the natural world."[42] Its place as the practical direction of purpose in thought and similarly in consideration of all value fields is therefore basic.

The second broad philosophical issue—the question of the efficacy of reason— is open to some misunderstandings in Santayana's treatment. Over and over again he denies that reason is efficacious. Usually it is in the context of claims made by traditional philosophies that reason is a kind of pure energy which operates on its own and has its own perspective. This Santayana cannot assent to, indeed not even tolerate. The world is a material world, the executive powers are material forces, reason is a principle of order which forces exhibit in their outcome, not itself a force or energy. This is intensified by, indeed involved in, his epiphenomenalist view of mind, noted earlier; it is the physical arrangement underlying the spiritual pattern that is efficacious, not spirit itself. This metaphysical thesis may be readily translated into a methodological injunction which is clear enough in his discussions. Whenever a claim is made for reason, we should look to the context and underlying purposes, for there is no neutral rational perspective, it is always the expression of some purposive stance. It may of course be a more rational perspective in some evaluative sense, as what would yield the long-range satisfaction of the purposes involved, or the broader satisfaction, or the like. This does not mean that all systems of ideas are (in the terms of familiar controversies) to be seen as "ideologies." There can of course be differences in the degree of self-consciousness about the underlying purposive structure of aims; the very attempt to delineate the life of reason is to see with the fullest self-consciousness possible what aims operate unavoidably in all human life. Nor does it follow that the life of reason is only one perspective among others with nothing more to be said for it than that certain kinds of people go in for it (naturally reflective, sensitive, etc.). Santayana's thesis is that we are all pursuing the life of reason—it is in the later existentialist phrase, the human condition. If we do not pursue it through reason, we pursue it through the imagination, and that (in his analysis) is through one or another religion. It is no mere generosity, rather a basic consistency, which leads him to extend to irrationality the analysis that he gives of rationality. Every irrationality, every narrow ideal however abhorrent, has a basis in some understandable purposes, just as every superstition is regarded by him as a little science gone astray. The superiority of the self-conscious pursuit of the life of reason is therefore precisely that of the superiority of science over other ways of attempting to achieve knowledge of the world.

When this structure of Santayana's thesis is clear, it is evident that he is not denying the efficacy of rational effort on the part of human beings. He is able to say, without any sense of contradicting himself, in the last paragraph of the book, and so of the whole *Life of Reason*: "Could a better system prevail in our lives a better order would establish itself in our thinking. It has not been for want of keen senses, or personal genius, or a constant order in the outer world, that mankind have fallen back repeatedly into barbarism and superstition. It has been for want of good character, good example, and good government. There is a pathetic capacity in men to live nobly, if only they would give one another the chance." One might even argue that in some sense the efficacy of reason is basic in human life. For in his own analysis, the very ability of human beings to establish an order of ideas and of things in their barest experience is already reason at work in the organization of life.

Yet Santayana is far from an optimist on what men can accomplish. The epiphenomenalism is not simply an epistemological thesis. Most of human life and its causal forces scarcely come within our ken. "The thoughts of men are incredibly evanescent, merely the foam in their labouring natures . . ."[43] We live and are conscious only on the tip of the iceberg. The logical status of this attitude is not postulational, but clearly Santayana's summary of the lessons of the sciences. And so we look next into what the particular sciences are and what they have taught us, either by successes or their failures.

The most striking thing about Santayana's assessment in the roster of the sciences is his faith in the natural sciences and his skepticism about the human sciences in all their variety. It is of course what we might expect, having seen that his materialism is of the physical-biological type and the executive causes of nature are physical-physiological. In part this reflects the particular position of the sciences in his time. Physics is long entrenched and the impact of Darwin is recent and forceful; while the other areas of knowledge—history, psychology, the nascent social sciences—are shot through with myth and with obvious normative intent. It is clear sailing to see history, once it gets beyond the instrumental task of deciding what happened, for any who may have use of particular data (even here, "History is always written wrong, and so needs to be rewritten"[44]), as engaged in a kind of physico-ethical speculation with arbitrary selection of causes to serve moral purposes. It serves, Santayana thinks, to provide materials for politics and poetry, i.e., for normative practice and normative symbols. The hesitations that he finds in method are between the pursuit of a physics type of inquiry and the furthering of a purposive effort. The latter is often the real content of what is alleged to be the former, as political economy makes evident when it generalizes the sentiments of a group and a time into the nature of man and builds its institutions upon that. Psychology particularly, when it is not physiological psychology, which alone Santayana regards as scientific, uses scarcely more than a loose imaginative method in which the hearer is led to recast something in his own experience along a novel way suggested to him. It is in effect a kind of literary psychology—the kind we pick up in reading great novelists. Although the specific psychologies that Santayana criticizes are taken from the philosophical systems of the past—a Spinozistic dialectical psychology or a utilitarian association of ideas—the kinds of criticisms he offers might still hit many a mark in subsequent personality psychology or social psychology, and particularly in Freudian and depth psychology. In sum, Santayana is saying that beyond the study of the material bases of man in biology and physiology there is nothing possible but the attunement of selected phenomena to particular and partial interests. Not only history and psychology, but also the whole of social science are thus in effect moral or practical enterprises.

If we look to Santayana's procedure in this critique, it would seem that its basis is the review of the state of the sciences up to his time. It is the weakness of social science and psychology contrasted with the success of physics and biology. By itself this would seem to be looking only on the past and not thinking about the possibilities of the future; would not a similar verdict have been given in ancient times for the physical sciences? (Indeed, Plato gave such a verdict when he thought of the physical domain as too Heraclitean, too changing to admit of adequate fixed description, only of likely myths. His contrast of eternal mathematics and mythological physics is very much like Santayana's of objective physics and imaginative moral human science.) Clearly Santayana's verdict is given a metaphysical base in his physical materialism. But how far does that form of his materialism itself reflect the current state of the sciences? There is no doubt an intimate interaction in materialist philosophies (probably others as well) between the state of human knowledge and the wider philosophical sweeps which tell us what is possible and which way to turn our intellectual efforts. In his last chapter, "The Validity of Science," Santayana criticizes those philosophers who would supplement science with some ancient myth which was itself "once the best physics obtainable, from which they have not learned to extricate their affections."[45] The formulation that the metaphysics of today is often the hardened physics of yesterday became popular in later logical positivism. If it seems to apply to Santayana's treatment of the psychological and social sciences, it still faces us with the hesitations in method he describes. But they would become hesitations about which methods will yield results rather than premature despairing philosophical determinations of the nature of those sciences.

Once the arrow of method points to the moral sciences there is no hesitation in Santayana's interpretation of morality, nor in his treatment of the extent to which it can become rational-scientific. His distinctions are precise and detailed. The starting point is *prerational morality,* the fragmentary, often inchoate, often incompatible mass of intuitive reactions and judgments that constitute the codes of peoples. It represents actual interests and rooted habits or traditional growths. At times it is spontaneous formulation of human impulses and vital interests, sometimes it takes a particular narrowed though sometimes intense direction as in the early traditional religious moralities. It is inwardly turned in the sense that it rarely appreciates other forms. It is unreflective. It constitutes, as it were, the raw material for a reflection that moves to the life of reason.

Rational ethics is a kind of wisdom exercised on a prerational morality. There is no hope of so vast a material being scientifically systematized. Some ideal interests may supervene as the dialectical (Socratic) critique of one's beliefs and intuitions takes place. There may emerge a sensitivity to others' moral reactions and an understanding of the bases which they represent (as in the religious ideal of charity discussed earlier). The shift from describing the original mass as a "morality" to the rational leaven as an "ethics" is significant. It is reflection that makes the difference but it does not yield a rational morality. It yields at most a habit of greater breadth, greater consistency, greater operation under the ideal in the particular, highly unique situations in which different people and peoples find themselves and it keeps before one the distinction of what one wants and what one wants after reflection. Initial impulses are thus turned into the light of the life of reason. A rational ethics is a tenuous growth, under favorable conditions, but Santayana looking back upon the Greek experience has little hope that it can be widespread, except where science and commerce advance to reach peace and develop rational character. What comes on with force when it fails is *postrational morality.*

Postrational morality is founded originally, says Santayana, on despair. The movement toward the life of reason has failed and morality retreats to a narrow base. Some partial principle is made the foundation of an order in life, with a sizable component of myth and delusion. Stoicism, Epicureanism, the Western redemptive religions, are instances of this sort. But in spite of the fantastic shapes postrational morality may take, there underlies it the basic human effort to organize impulse and discipline it toward happiness.

The final chapter dealing with the validity of science makes clear Santayana's linkage of the life of reason and the growth of science. Science is not just one among alternative arbitrary ways of knowledge, in spite of all the special perspectives that enter into processes of description and selection on the way. It is not to be corrected from some outside perspective. There are postrational systems of nature as well as of morality that attempt such a correction and seek to transcend science. But they usually land in mysticism which represents a prescientific immersion in sense out of which science rises. His mode of criticism is very like that of postrational moralities. These are retreats from the building of knowledge and the correction of scientific results by further scientific activity.

In the light of such a conclusion we can reassess the broad philosophical problems raised earlier about the compatibility of a relativistic outlook to the rich variety of human perspectives with an insistence on the life of reason, about the efficacy of reason, and about the grounding of his basic materialism in a scientific process in which so much is regarded as constructed by the human inquirer. The answer in all three cases would seem to be the same. Santayana's theses, in the light of his last chapter, would have to be regarded as his answers based on the *results* of the growth of science; it would be a kind of category mistake to see them as presuppositions or metaphysically antecedent resolutions. If his answers are to be refined or rejected, it would have to be in terms of a changing character in the results of the growth of knowledge, not a changing fashion in philosophy. The central position of the life of reason in comparison to all other competitors for the dominant picture of human efforts depends on the thesis that however men may formulate their overall tasks in life they are in fact engaged on the enterprise that it delineates. The degree of efficacy of reason is identical with the degree to which human beings have managed to create a world they can capture in knowledge and order in their efforts; the limits of these powers are seen in their failures and in the sense of the vastness of the underlying forces that operate in their impulses and actions. And finally the very materialism that Santayana espouses seems to reflect the extent to which the physical sciences have achieved dependable results, pointing out to us what are the executive or operative forces in nature and human life as part of it, and the failure of any similar dependability in the sciences beyond the physical and natural. Indeed, Santayana's analysis of the concept of *matter* itself[46] points to the ordinary sense of things in space, and to the scientific notion of matter involved in the ability to correct different theories about its specific character. The very fact that all concepts of things involve construction and selection therefore does not make the distinction between basic material and basic executive forces and compounds and effects an arbitrary one. (Santayana's frequent criticisms of Berkeleyan idealism take the form of arguing that if we took subjective ideas to be the totality of what is we would then have to reintroduce distinctions of matter and form within that domain and in other language.) In general, then, the critique of Santayana's materialism in *the Life of Reason* would, on the terms he sets forth in that work, have to be a scientific critique of the results of the sciences at that given time.

It was remarked earlier that Santayana's materialism is fairly distinctive among American philosophers, very few of whom ventured out on the materialist philosophical limb. It did not carry through any major analysis of the basic notions in the refined and intricate way which technical philosophy of science has done since Einstein's work in close relation to specific physical treatment of space and time, matter, force and motion. And what he did do in a metaphysical fashion in his later work we shall see shortly. Santayana did set forth a remarkably insightful theory of the method of science in broad outlines very close to the pragmatic tradition, with its recognition of the pragmatic human basis, the close relation to purpose throughout and the recognition of selection and construction in human conceptualization, and in the insistence on verification as central and on the material connections combined with speculative independence of mathematics. In firm though sketchy form he did thus outline answers to many of the more technical later disputes about value and normative elements in science, the complex relation of analytic and synthetic, of the instrumental-constructive and the realistic, of the relative-variable and the underlying constant. He is here much closer to James and Dewey and even C. I. Lewis than the usual emphasis on his classicism may suggest.

Santayana's central contribution in *The Life of Reason* was, however, to lay down outlines for the naturalization of the human spirit and its works. This he did in detail, not in bare sketch. Whatever the status of specific interpretations of specific religions, specific arts, particular human institutions, particular sciences, he showed how one might envisage human ideals operative in the human enterprise under the human condition and not be driven under the growth of science to their reduction or derogation. On the contrary it was only the connection of ideal to nature that made it assessable and responsible. This whole phase of his work—the preponderant part—had great influence in the American naturalism of the twentieth century whose aim was no longer to fight the old battles for the central role of science but to show how the domains of the human spirit could be understood and fruitfully cultivated in that relation.

Santayana's specific set of values had less general influence but was for a time efficacious in the milieu of the Eastern seaboard. Particularly in New York his individualistic rational liberalism spread under teaching of Morris Raphael Cohen at the City College and Irwin Edman at Columbia. The audience to which it was addressed was in a process of transition and the analysis of the life of reason seemed to combine the acceptance of the primacy of science and the values of liberalism and relativism with a generous interpretation of the human efforts underlying the older forms that were being abandoned. For example, instead of a secular break with the orthodox religions, one could proceed with an assured secularism to work out new cultural forms for the human aims to which, Santayana furnished the assurance, the very orthodoxies had been addressed! And in general, his overview of the forms in which the human spirit had adventured gave a generous breadth to human understanding. However, as the tensions of the 1930s shaped up into the conflicts of World War II, it was the elitist and traditionalist strain in Santayana's work that came to the fore, and the influence of his specific values died away.

3. The Realms of Being

In 1927, Santayana published *The Realm of Essence*—the first of the four volumes on the realms of being in which he sought to achieve a systematic presentation of his philosophy. *The Realm of Matter* followed in 1930, *The Realm of Truth* in 1938, and *The Realm of Spirit* completed the series in 1940.[47] Although these volumes were intended to be technical philosophical works, they are written in the same graceful and elegant style as his other works, and they have proven just as baffling. Even the names given to the four realms of being have proven sources of obscurity, for at least with respect to "essence," "matter," and "spirit," Santayana certainly did not use these terms with anything like their customary meanings. Nevertheless, there is a coherent and quite remarkable position propounded in these works—a position which is an elaboration and refinement of the doctrines we have already found in his earlier works.

Santayana's naturalism—as we have seen it in *The Life of Reason*—has a close affinity on its metaphysical side to the nineteenth-century evolutionary naturalism. In the latter view, nature was originally inorganic—a purely material world describable in terms of physics and chemistry. Somehow, in the distant past by processes currently unknown to us, organic phenomena were synthesized and life began, but life is to be understood as a purely physiochemical phenomenon—no supernatural elements are involved. From those primordial living cells, millions of years ago, the biological world has evolved by the processes first discovered and described by Darwin. The biological forms produced in this process are very diverse, but natural selection has imposed upon them certain requirements of adaptation which must be met by those that survive. All animals must be able to obtain satisfactions for their biological needs or they will perish. In the lower forms, this adaptation to the environment is accomplished through hereditary instincts—innate dispositions to respond to certain stimuli in particular ways which happen to be functional for that organism. Such instincts have survival value in particular environments, but their rigidity makes their owners particularly vulnerable to environmental changes; a more flexible mode of adaptation would clearly have even greater survival value. Such flexibility is provided by the evolution of mind, which arises as a purely natural phenomenon in the biological world and gives its possessors a problem-solving capacity superior to that of creatures governed only by instinct. On this view, mind is a tool functioning within a purely natural economy. Through the ability to learn which mind offers, animals can develop functional patterns of behavior, or habits, and can alter these patterns when environmental changes make such alterations advantageous. This is of course a strong form of Peirce's doubt-belief theory of inquiry and of the prag-matic-instrumentalist view of mind elaborated by James and Dewey. Thought develops to solve problems arising in the organism's effort to satisfy biological wants, and all the higher intellectual creations of mind originate in the service of man's animal nature. Abstract science, theology, metaphysics—all are products of man's struggle for biological survival.

It is this general view, which underlay so much of late nineteenth-century thought, that is the basis of Santayana's materialism. Santayana's materialism does not involve any particular theory of the nature of matter. Although Santayana speaks of nature as "mechanical," he is not committed to the Newtonian model of a corpuscular physical reality, nor is he committed to any other particular theory of what matter is. Often the force of his assertion that nature is mechanical is primarily that nature is not governed by rational purpose but is fundamentally inanimate, irrational, and blind. Clearly this notion of matter requires a more detailed analysis, to which we shall turn presently, but for present purposes it may suffice to stress that fact that matter is something absurd and brute.

We find in our experience of matter that it evidences regularities—i.e., there are repeated patterns, events which occur in regular sequences, and entities which behave in regular ways. Most philosophers have referred to such regularities as laws; Santayana calls them tropes. That different material entities have different patterns of behavior means that they instance different tropes. And this is as true of biological organisms as of physical objects—indeed, the distinction between the two is simply one of the sort of tropes they instance, for biological organisms are for Santayana just as material as any physical object. What we call animation is, behavioristically considered, a certain organization of tropes characterizing the behavior of a particular thing. In this respect the higher animals capable of learning do not differ from the lower, for learned patterns of behavior are tropes too in Santayana's terminology. The organization of tropes which constitutes the dynamic structure of the organic being is what Santayana calls the psyche. This psyche is a purely dynamic construct—a structure of behaviors and dispositions— not a substantive thing. And it is this psyche which is the self—the essential animal. The animal itself is a material object, differentiated from other material objects by its particular psyche, its dynamic organization of tropes or behavior patterns.

Like all animals, men have biological needs which must be satisfied, and our behavior consists of a complex organization of responses to stimuli for the purpose of satisfying these needs. That complex organization is the psyche or self in us. Our lives therefore lie within the material economy of nature. We are governed by a complex set of tropes, partly inherited and involuntary, partly learned, which satisfy our fundamental needs. The satisfaction of the desires of our animal nature is the fundamental business for life, and the self or psyche is the organization of tropes which enables this business to be accomplished.

Somewhere in the dim prehistory of man, the psyche, in seeking to satisfy her needs, evolved consciousness. The function of consciousness is to afford psyche a wider survey of possible satisfactions and of means for their attainment than was possible for the unconscious psyche. Essentially, consciousness is the awareness of things absent as well as present, and of the relations among things, goals, and our desires. Because it provides psyche with a better overview of the world and of the possibilities of action in the world, consciousness has survival value, and has been furthered by natural selection. But it is important to stress that for Santayana consciousness is a purely natural and material product. It is not a thing but a function or act of thought which is instrumental for the psyche in its quest for material satisfactions.

Consciousness, so understood, Santayana calls spirit. The terminology could not be more confusing. For Santayana spirit is a product of matter; it results from a particular organization of matter and is essentially a by-product of the activity of the psyche. It is not a thing, but an act of mind—what Santayana calls the pure light of awareness. It is therefore not a supernatural entity in any sense; it is neither prior to nor independent of matter—indeed, it is destroyed by changes in the organization of the material being from which it arises. It is epiphenomenal rather than substantial. Clearly, spirit as Santayana defines it is radically different from spirit in the sense of orthodox theology. No other American thinker has employed the term in anything like Santayana's sense.

Furthermore, spirit as Santayana conceives it is passive. This assertion is made repeatedly; spirit is not a power—it only observes, contemplates, and describes. This claim involves a very curious distinction. As Santayana views the psyche, it is essentially active. When we act, therefore, whether consciousness is involved or not, it is psyche which acts, not spirit. What spirit contributes to psyche's action is only awareness—an overview of possibilities among which psyche can choose. That awareness is useful to psyche because it provides her with alternative patterns of action. But it is psyche which chooses and psyche which acts—the spirit yields merely the awareness of the alternatives. Thus in the late afternoon there will arise before the mind of the average middle-aged American a vision of a frosted cocktail glass filled with a clear liquid, with perhaps a yellow twist of lemon floating in it. This glorious vision will be accompanied by an image of the route which must be followed if he is to attain his heart's desire. All this is the work of the spirit; it sets before his psyche the image of a desired object and the mode of attaining it. But whether he will actually go and get the drink depends upon what psyche chooses and spirit itself is powerless to affect that choice.

Given this peculiar analysis of human nature, what sort of knowledge is it that humans can achieve? It is, in Santayana's view, animal knowledge—knowledge which arises from the peculiar condition of the animal seeking to fulfill its needs. To survive in the environment in which it finds itself, the animal must somehow learn to identify those things in the environment which will satisfy its needs. This is accomplished, in Santayana's view, by the animal receiving through sensation clues to the composition of its environment. These clues are the products of sensory stimulation, but of course what sensory stimuli the animal receives depends upon its relation to the object in the environment and its receptor apparatus. Only some animals can perceive colors at all, and the range of colors any animal can perceive depends upon the particular receptors which it has. Therefore what an animal perceives is relative to the particular nature and location of the animal. It follows at once that an animal can know an object only insofar as the animal is affected by it, and the sensory qualities so produced in the animal may have no similarity to the qualities of the object. Sensory qualities cannot therefore be said to describe the object, but they may serve as clues to it.

If we examine closely what is actually given in experience, abstracting from the external relations in which we conceive the given to stand, and attending only to the given itself, we find nothing but phenomenal qualities. This contemplation of quality, which Santayana calls intuition, is the function of spirit. Such qualities are not sensations or ideas, but what we have the sensation of—the specific blue that we see, or the tone that we hear. They are definite and precise in themselves; they are individual, static, and changeless (and therefore eternal), and repeatable (and therefore universal). These qualities, which Santayana calls essences, are very like Peirce's firsts in the later formulation of the categories. Each essence is simple, and is wholly self-contained; it is what it is, irrespective of anything else. Every congeries of things has an essence which is the sense quality of that ensemble. Even if the ensemble is composed of related parts, the resulting essence is simple and is the quality of those parts as related. Hence the relations are internal to the essence—to change the relations would amount to creating a different essence. Because essences are entirely simple, no two essences can be related in their own natures. If they are brought into relation, the result is a further essence which is the quality of those two as related, and the relation is then internal to this essence, not to the essences which form the terms of the relation.

Essences, Santayana insists, are passive, inert, infinite in number, and unordered. Since the essence is simply a quality, it is a static, changeless object. This claim carries the implication that change itself is not an essence. When change occurs, one essence is succeeded by another. That fact creates a relation of succession between the two essences. But that relation and its terms together instance an essence which is also static and inert. Hence any sequence of states is an essence which is itself a changeless, passive quality. Changes then may have essences, but change itself is not an essence. The domain of essence is not limited to those essences which are actually presented in experience; it includes any imaginable or conceivable quality, and is therefore infinite. And the fact that the realm of essence is unordered follows from the fact that the essences are simple and that the only relations they involve are internal to themselves. Hence there are no necessary relations among essences, but merely various essences some of which involve relational patterns among other essences.

Essences are used by animals as clues to the existence and behavior of objects. But how do we know that there are objects, if all that can be given to us in perception is essence? Santayana's answer is that the existence of objects rests upon an act of animal faith. If one were to demand that knowledge be limited to what is given in perception, the result would be total solipsism of the moment. Even memory requires an act of faith, for one must posit that the essence now present is the same as an essence experienced once before—there is no present intuition of the past essence. To escape from solipsism, therefore, one must make postulates which are not capable of proof, and to postulate a real world of substantial objects is simply to accept on faith what in fact animal behavior presupposes.

What is the nature of this external world? It is a world of material or substantial objects; it is matter or substance—terms which Santayana uses interchangeably—which confers thinghood. Following Spinoza, Santayana defines substance as that which exists in itself and is conceived through itself. Things are then conceived on the Aristotelian model as a union of form or essence with matter. The basis for this view lies in the phenomena of change. Objects of experience undergo change, yet through these changes they preserve some continuity in time, space, quantity, and potentiality. It is to explain this persistence through change that substance is postulated—it means specific potentialities existing at specific times and places. Change can then be conceptualized as the actualization or privation of an essence in a substance.

For Santayana it is matter or substance alone which is dynamic and can produce change. All potentiality and all power are packed into matter, while essence and spirit are defined as passive and impotent. The relation of matter and essence is therefore one in which matter as it were chooses what essence it will actualize. Since the realm of essence is infinite and unordered, there is no intrinsic reason why any given essence should be actualized at any particular time or place. Yet since material things cannot exist without embodied essence, some essences must be so actualized if anything at all is to exist. And for Santayana it is matter which is responsible both for the actualization and for which essence it is that is actualized. Again, it is Santayana's view of change which underlies this doctrine, for the cause of change cannot lie in changeless eternal states such as essences, and it must therefore lie in matter.

Santayana gives six fundamental properties of matter: (1) substance is external to the thought which posits it, (2) substance has parts and constitutes a physical space, (3) all parts of substance are external to one another, (4) substance is in flux and constitutes a physical time, (5) substance is unequally distributed, and (6) substances compose a relative cosmos—i.e., all parts of substance are on the same plane and interact dynamically. Time and space are thus derived from and characteristic of substance. The mode of being, characterizing material things, Santayana calls existence. To exist means for him to stand in external relations and this is possible only for substances. Essences exist only when they are actualized in a substance; as given—i.e., intuited—they simply are and have no external relations. Obviously, only a small fraction of the realm of essence is ever realized in existence.

There are three properties of matter which are particularly important: it is in flux, it is the seat of all power, and it is contingent. As we have seen above, change is intrinsic to matter, since matter is postulated to account for change. Were there no change, essence alone would suffice to account for all experience. But not only is matter in flux; the causes of the changes which occur in matter are to be found in matter. By change, what Santayana means is that some essences are replaced by other essences. Hence to ask for the causes of change is to ask why certain essences are actualized at certain times and places. To this question Santayana answers that no explanation can be given because matter is inherently irrational. In support of this extraordinary claim Santayana presents two arguments, one concerning existence, and one matter per se. With respect to existence, Santayana argues that an explanation of the existence of anything would consist in deriving its existence from some premises. But an existential statement, Santayana points out, can only be deduced validly from premises that contain existential statements. Hence no derivation of existence is possible which does not assume existence in the premises. Strictly speaking, of course, Santayana is right in this argument; since all universal statements are true in an empty universe and all existential statements false, no existential statement can be derived from universal premises unless the possibility of an empty universe is excluded. With respect to matter, Santayana's argument is essentially the same. From what could matter be derived? Not from spirit, for spirit is impotent, and not from essence, since essence is static and inert. Therefore the premises would have to be premises regarding matter itself, and so would afford no real explanation of matter. As Santayana has defined his terms, these arguments are doubtless true, but, as Russell has remarked, it is not obvious that either of them prove matter to be "irrational." Every theory starts with some premises which are not in that theory derivable from further premises. But it does not follow that the premises are "irrational" or that there are no grounds upon which one may rationally choose among alternative "arbitrary" axioms. Nevertheless, the conclusion Santayana drew is that existence and matter are fundamentally irrational, and therefore that no rational explanation of them is possible. Change therefore cannot be accounted for; the realization of any given essence must be regarded as a spontaneous act of matter which is utterly arbitrary. That matter is contingent follows from the fact that there are an infinite number of essences, and so there are always alternatives available to any actualized essence. Matter is therefore under no constraint in its choice of what to actualize, and since the behavior of matter is spontaneous and arbitrary, there is no necessity to its actions. It is of course a fact that there are regularities in nature which we call laws—that certain events do occur whenever certain antecedent conditions are realized. But these laws are tropes; although they describe sequences of essence, they are themselves essences. Hence the fact that matter actualizes a particular law is itself a contingent fact; tomorrow matter may well change to a completely different trope. And since matter is fundamentally inexplicable, no reasons can be given why matter should have actualized just the particular laws which it has. This is of course the reason why Santayana is not committed to any particular physical theory of matter. Any such theory is a set of tropes, and can no more capture the nature of matter than any other essence.

Thus for Santayana matter is the seat of all power and energy in the world. Only matter has potency; only matter becomes; and what it becomes by actualizing essence is actuality or existence. But that existence is always contingent and changeable and in an ultimate sense irrational. If Santayana believed in God in any literal sense, it is clear that his God would have to be matter, and surely no Calvinist ever conceived of a more mysterious and capricious God than this.

Existence consists of those combinations of essence and matter which actually occur. Any such fact, or composition of essence and matter, has a description, which is the statement of what essences were actualized at a given time and place. The sum of all such propositions constitutes what Santayana calls the truth; it is the complete comprehensive description of existence. What is true is thus also determined by matter; essence provides endless possibilities but matter determines what becomes actual and so what the truth shall be.

Can the truth be known? What is actually given to us in perception is only essence. We go beyond essence to obtain a knowledge of the world only by interpreting the essences given as signs of something not given. This "going beyond" is an act of faith; we cannot *prove* that there is a real world beyond the given—on this point Santayana regards the arguments of the skeptics as conclusive. But the act of faith is necessary, not logically, but as a matter of biological fact. The animal and what the animal knows are both material objects in nature, and the relations between them are real relations. Knowing is an event in nature, and is a necessary part of animal life without which no animal could survive. The faith by which we pass from the intuition of essence to the knowledge of the real world is thus what Santayana calls animal faith and forms the dogmatic foundation of all knowledge.

Is animal knowledge true? Santayana remarks

There is really a world, and there are real objects in each case to be described: but the images of sense used to describe those objects are not found there, but are created by the organs of sense in the observer: and the syntax of thought by which these appearances, which in themselves are pure essences, are turned into predicates of substance, is a mere expedient of human logic: so that while we gain true acquaintance with the real world, in that we distinguish its parts and their relations up to a certain point, we conceive these realities fantastically, making units of them on the human scale, and in human terms. Our ideas are accordingly only subjective signs, while we think them objective qualities; and the whole warp and woof of our knowledge is rhetorical while we think it physically existent and constitutive of the world.[48]

All existence involves the actualization of essence, and the truth is the description of that actualization. We perceive essences too, but the essences we perceive are relative to us and may not be identical with the essence actualized in the thing. Human knowledge therefore cannot be the truth, "but a view or expression of the truth; a glimpse of it secured by some animal with special organs under special circumstances."[49] Nor is error solely due to sense; men by their natures are passionate and moral beings with animal needs, and they organize and interpret experience in the interests of their desires. Our knowledge is thus a poetic imaginative construction which reflects our nature and our ideals.

But Santayana's emphasis upon the poetic element in knowledge should not be allowed to obscure the fact that he fully accepted the sciences, and that his views of the ways in which animal knowledge is established differ very little from those of James or Dewey. The test of a proposition is that an animal acting upon that proposition does experience the expected satisfactions. If the animal, having perceived certain clues, performs certain actions and thereupon has expected sensory experiences, the proposition connecting those clues and actions with the resulting effects is confirmed. Like James, Santayana understood that our scientific theories are constructed in imagination, but he was no less insistent than James upon the necessity of empirical verification. But the body of scientific knowledge so established is not identical with the truth, for it is incomplete and relative to our peculiar nature. Yet it may be partial truth; it may represent real objects and their relations to us correctly even though we can never be certain of its doing so in any particular case. Inquiry can therefore be progressive and we can come to know more of the truth, even though no human can ever know the whole truth.

The philosophic system Santayana elaborated so elegantly in his voluminous writings is certainly one of the most extraordinary ever produced in America. It is at once Platonic in its treatment of essence and materialist in its treatment of matter, but it is the role assigned to matter which is the heart of the position. By making matter the inexplicable source of all change, Santayana in effect presents the world as indeterminate, arbitrary, and irrational. Blind matter, acting spontaneously and uncontrollably, rules a world which is in fact a chaos, while essence and spirit are reduced to mere passive tools of this insane matter. And this striking contrast between the power of matter and the impotence of spirit stands out most starkly in the relation between psyche and spirit. Psyche is an organization of tropes realized in a material thing, and since she is material she is dynamic and active. Spirit on the other hand is merely the passive light of awareness, brought into existence to serve the psyche. This analysis does not make man the slave of blind matter, because man is himself material. Indeed, since the action of matter is spontaneous, man's will is always free. But man's will is psyche's will, not spirit's. Even when the animal does so act as to obtain an end conceived by spirit, it is not because of any causal efficacy in spirit, but only because psyche has chosen so to act in this case.

What then is the fate of spirit? Spirit is a product of matter, but it is an emergent one and constitutes a distinct order of being. It is the servant of psyche, yet it has a life of its own. Psyche has too many wants to be able to satisfy them all; she must therefore make compromises, harmonize her interests, and develop coherent strategies to maximize her satisfactions. Spirit helps psyche to do this by seeking universal knowledge and universal love. By her nature, therefore, spirit is devoted to the ideals of truth and justice as ultimate ends, but for psyche these ideals are merely instrumental to the satisfaction of animal desire. Hence those ideals which spirit cherishes are always prostituted to the partisan and utilitarian purposes of psyche. The fate of spirit is therefore tragic, for by her nature she seeks ideals which she can never fully achieve, and dreams of a freedom from matter which, could it be achieved, would be her own destruction. What is left to spirit therefore is resignation to the inevitable defeat of her dreams, and appreciation of the aesthetic quality of that world. As Santayana remarks:

The freedom and glory of spirit comes from its impotence; by its impotence it is guiltless, by its impotence it is universal, by its impotence it is invulnerably supreme. Its essence is to be light, not to be power; and it can never be pure light until it is satisfied with an ideal dominion, not striving to possess or change the world, but identifying itself only with the truth and beauty that rise unbidden from the world into the realm of spirit.[50]

Of all American thinkers, Santayana is the only one who has found passive resignation and aesthetic appreciation the answer to life. To use Freudian terms, Santayana views man as if the instinctive drives and the unconscious completely control behavior, while the conscious mind is utterly impotent. What is left then for the conscious mind in its helplessness is a purely spectatorial role, watching the madness proceed and seeking by irony and aesthetic appreciation to endure it. What the psychological origins of this view may be is not a question to be pursued here, but the contrast between Santayana's position and that of his American contemporaries is striking. The essential activism and optimism which have characterized American thought in general stand out in stark relief when seen against Santayana's passivism and pessimism.

Notes—Chapter Thirteen

1. Some appreciation of the kind of impact Santayana had may be gauged from the articles in *The Philosophy of George Santayana,* Library of Living Philosophers, ed. P.A. Schilpp (Evanston, Ill.: Northwestern University Press, 1940). This also contains an autobiographical essay, "Apologia pro mente sua." In many respects, a fuller view of his spiritual journey may be gained from his novel, *The Last Puritan* (New York: Charles Scribner's Sons, 1926).

2. George Santayana, *The Sense of Beauty; Being the Outline of Aesthetic Theory* (New York: Charles Scribner's Sons, 1896). *The Sense of Beauty* is conveniently available in a Dover paperback edition.

3. George Santayana, *The Sense of Beauty* (New York: Dover, Inc., 1955), p. 18.

4. *Ibid.,* p. 29.

5. *Ibid.,* p. 49.

6. *Ibid.,* p. 60.

7. *Ibid.,* pp. 60-61.

8. *Ibid.,* p. 185.

9. *Ibid.,* pp. 189-90.

10. *Ibid.,* p. 195.

11. *Ibid.,* pp. 197-98.

12. *Ibid.,* p. 221.

13. *Ibid.*, p. 220.

14. *Ibid.*, p. 235.

15. *Ibid.*

16. *Ibid.*, pp. 236-37.

17. We are particularly indebted to Abraham Edel in our interpretation of *The Life of Reason;* also to Milton Munits, *The Moral Philosophy of Santayana* (New York: Columbia University Press, 1939).

18. George Santayana, *The Life of Reason, or the Phases of Human Progress* (New York: Charles Scribner's Sons, 1905). The five volumes are entitled *Reason in Common Sense, Reason in Society, Reason in Religion, Reason in Art,* and *Reason in Science.*

19. *Reason in Common Sense,* p. 3.

20. *Ibid.*, p. 2.

21. *Ibid.*, p. 3.

22. George Santayana, *Works* (New York: Charles Scribner's Sons, 1936-48), vol. 10, *Dialogues in Limbo.*

23. *Reason in Religion,* p. 191.

24. *Ibid.*, p. 179.

25. *Reason in Society,* p. 3.

26. *Ibid.*, pp. 3-4.

27. *Ibid.*, p. 9.

28. George Santayana, *Dominations and Powers* (New York: Charles Scribner's Sons, 1951). Cf. Beth J. Singer, *The Rational Society, A Critical Study of Santayana's Social Thought* (Cleveland: Press of Case Western Reserve, 1970).

29. George Santayana, "The Poetry of Christian Dogma," in *Interpretations of Poetry and Religion* (New York: Charles Scribner's Sons, 1900).

30. *Reason in Religion,* p. 194.

31. *Reason in Art,* p. 15.

32. *Ibid.*

33. *Ibid.*, p. 16.

34. *Ibid.*, p. 39.

35. *Ibid.*, p. 51.

36. *Ibid.*, p. 52.

37. *Ibid.*, p. 72.

38. *Ibid.*, p. 82.

39. *Ibid.*, p. 98.

40. *Ibid.*, p. 192.

41. *Ibid.*, p. 215.

42. *Reason in Science,* p. 172.

43. *Ibid.*, p. 127.

44. *Ibid.*, p. 45.

45. *Ibid.*, p. 305.

46. *Ibid.*, pp. 100-101n.

47. A single volume edition of the four works with a new introduction is published as *The Realms of Being* (New York: Charles Scribner's Sons, 1942).

48. *Ibid.*, p. 458.

49. *Ibid.*, p. 469.

50. *Ibid.*, p. 643.

Dewey:
Battling Against Dualisms

Chapter Fourteen

Dewey:
Battling Against Dualisms

Dewey's philosophy resists encapsulation. Some have attempted to understand his work through a key concept: his notion of experience, his revolt against formalism, his use of evolution, etc. Yet even when this single-minded approach is most helpful, as it is in the works of Bernstein, Geiger, Hook, Randall, Schneider, and Werkmeister,[1] it confronts us finally with a variety of different and even conflicting interpretations. A historical approach, locating Dewey within orthodox tradition, also runs head on into his iconoclasm and his habit of "refracting" philosophies through his own objectives. Thus Dewey's early Hegelianism, e.g., is less a matter of detail than sympathy; his later naturalism is not marketable as empiricism nor as any other well-known brand of philosophy. Even where Dewey acknowledges debts there is little guarantee that what he acknowledges is to be found in the original; indeed it is precisely this refracting of the arguments of others that reveals a first view of Dewey himself. Thus he generalizes Peirce's account of doubt and belief into a full theory of inquiry; this he welds to a Jamesean analysis of consciousness which has been radically extended to include action; then he sets the whole in a social evolutionary context.

Dewey's use of historical materials is further confounded by his view of the dialectic of philosophic progress. He constantly attacks what he sees as outworn ways of posing problems, especially those that are framed in such custom certified dualisms as thought-action, theory-practice, interest-effort, conduct-experience, stimulus-response, mind-body, man-nature, science-value, to mention a few of an almost limitless supply. In his view problems are constantly changing and therefore require conceptual tools which must be constantly refashioned to meet the new demands. Accordingly, when Dewey tries to undercut these dualisms by revealing the underlying continuities, he has to employ expressions in which older outlooks are congealed. Thus traditional terms such as "habit," "intelligence," "logic," and "experience" depend for their meaning as much on what is going on within Dewey's work as within a more traditional context, much as the shape of a balloon depends on pressures both outside and in. There is no single meaning in these terms; they alter and shift meanings according to the job. This use of terms as context-dependent accounts in part for the alleged opacity of Dewey's writing. But it has a vital function in his philosophy: problems which may not be solved are dissolved through an understanding of the situations or contexts in which they arise. Perhaps Dewey's unwillingness to state or confront issues abstractly—i.e., outside of the particular social or historical conditions under which they arise— accounts for some of his unpopularity among professional philosophers. But even were his impact among his professional peers limited (and this is quite challenge-able), he left a strong mark on law and education, psychology, political thought and sociology. Certainly no other modern philosopher has exercised so wide an influence on the American scene. And today, when we have begun to view ourselves as part of an ecosystem altering and being altered continuously, when we struggle to capture feedback and process with a vocabulary built for a more stable view of the world, and when systems analysis and cybernetics have given us a vocabulary of their own, it is easier to sympathize with Dewey's struggles with language, even though it means a greater caution and effort in the reading.

Notwithstanding this apologia—itself a bit of ritual Deweyana—we shall offer an understanding of Dewey's philosophy and, of course, we have a key of our own. The near-century of Dewey's life witnessed radical changes in manners and morals, in political and social structures, in philosophy and science. Dewey's various and varying philosophical commitments arise in his attempt to draw lessons from the course of this experience. These lessons can be learned by philosophers—if philosophy is scientifically based. The serious question concerns the adequacy of the science and its method. When philosophy and science are properly understood, they are one: thus the distinction between fact and value is the major dualism in need of philosophical mending. Dewey's attempt to mend it charts his intellectual development, especially his search for a more adequate biosocial psychology as a grounding for philosophy. To relate value and knowl-edge is nothing new; this has been standard procedure from the time of Edwards and the Scottish-Americans to that of Dewey's fellow pragmatists. What is distinctive is the nature of his psychology and its thorough impact throughout his philosophy. It is a psychology enriched by the new biology and sophisticated enough to expose the preevolutionary dualisms within psychology. Epistemology, biologically oriented, makes knowing a part of the natural process of adjustment in a natural environment; thus knowledge and action cannot be divorced. Dewey presents a naturalistic account of purposive, valuing, planning behavior; but his naturalism is rich enough to embrace the institutional. Philosophy itself must be tested against human problems: it too is a kind of knowledge which answers human needs.

So central is the relation of psychology and philosophy that it provides a basic continuity throughout the whole of Dewey's work. It even shows the continuity in his early career underlying his shift from idealism to experimentalism as a continuing search for an adequate psychology. In line with this recognition we shall look first at that early career (sec. 1), and then explore his contribution to individual psychology in the *Syllabus* and psychological articles grouped around his revision of the concept of the reflex arc; in this section we also look at the social psychology, particularly in *Human Nature and Conduct* (sec. 2). Then we turn to Dewey's logic with its instrumental accent on discovery and consequences rather than formal relationships (sec. 3). Thereafter we track down the development of moral theory throughout his whole career, as individual decision, as institutional, and as a theory of valuation (sec. 4). Finally, and all too briefly, we look at Dewey's theory at work in the particular contexts of law, politics, and education, joining there what never should have been separated—logic from ethics, theory from practice (sec. 5). Such a picture hopefully approximates to a Deweyan interpretation of Dewey's development.

1. Absolutism and Experimentalism

Dewey's biography is peculiarly relevant to his philosophy. The development of his views is virtually a study in philosophic ecology, for successive intellectual positions are in phase with his geographic ones. Egregiously oversimplified, he may be called an intuitionist during his early academic years in Vermont, a nascent Anglo-Hegelian in Baltimore, and a fully accredited missionary for that idealism in the outer cultural regions of Michigan and Minnesota. Functionalism was baptized in Chicago and came of age there as Instrumentalism. With New York as a base his philosophy matured and was tested not only in conventional academic retreats abroad, but also in the intellectual and social ferment of China and Japan, Turkey, Russia, and Mexico.

Unfortunately for the early record, neither Dewey nor his family seems to have had that sense of destiny (or of hoarding) which marked the Jameses. The Deweys either corresponded little or did not preserve what they had written with an eye to the convenience of future biographers. Dewey's own brief recollection of his intellectual development, "From Absolutism to Experimentalism,"[2] is admittedly "fudged"; it is unreliable in details of intellectual history and vague or incorrect in chronology. For example, he appears to have misremembered H. A. P. Torrey, his teacher at the University of Vermont, as merely a Common Sense Realist even though acknowledging his influence as "decisive." Virtually everyone cites this autobiographical essay at first- or second-hand and error compounds like a game of gossip. Even in the volume of *Living Philosophers* devoted to Dewey, where a reasonable account of his life might have been expected, the materials were gathered together by Dewey's daughters who in their turn relied upon the original questionable essay.[3]

Uncontroversial at least is that Dewey was born in 1859, the same year as Bergson and Husserl, and that he began to attend the University of Vermont in his native Burlington in 1874. The courses in philosophy then were standardized and as standardly embedded in the regnant Common Sense Realism. But an educational progressiveness survived there from the reforms of James Marsh, professor of philosophy and fifth president. Marsh, it may be remembered, had given impetus to Transcendentalism by his edition of Coleridge's *Aide to Reflection*. Something of a political conservative, not to say a reactionary, Marsh's views about education were anything but conventional and he extended the boundaries of collegiate education by liberalizing the content of curriculum. Joseph Torrey, professor of philosophy, succeeded to the presidency on Marsh's death and continued the tradition which he, in turn, handed down to James N. Angell who, with others of that great generation (including Andrew White, Charles Eliot, Gilman, Coit, and McCosh) of college presidents, revolutionized American higher education. Dewey may have remembered his university training as rather "narrow and restrictive," but in 1879 when he graduated it was undoubtedly as liberal as any to be had in America and perhaps England as well.

The climax of an undergraduate career in those days was still the senior philosophy course. At Vermont it was customary to divide it into two sections: the first semester still covered many of the same topics as were outlined in S. S. Smith's *Lectures* (pp. 318-329), i.e., constitutional and international law, political economy, and the philosophy of history. The second semester included ethics, using Butler's *Analogy* and Calderwood's *Handbook of Moral Science,* psychology with Noah Porter's *Intellectual Psychology* and, probably, aesthetics using Joseph Torrey's *A Theory of Fine Art*. Dewey's particular mentor in philosophy, who taught the senior course, was H. A. P. Torrey (a nephew of Joseph's).[4] As the student body was small, contact with the professors was intimate and Dewey remained in close touch with Torrey even after leaving to teach high school in western Pennsylvania. After two years of this exile Dewey returned to Burlington to teach another high-school class. This experience was equally distressing but it was relieved by long philosophic talks with Torrey, who had spent 1877 abroad studying German philosophy. Dewey gained from Torrey a command of philosophic German. In the face of the intimacy it is difficult to understand how an older Dewey could have cast Torrey in the role of a Scottish intuitionist when the evidence makes him out to be a knowledgeable and sympathetic student of Leibniz, Schelling, "the suspiciously pantheistic" Spinoza, but above all, of Kant. Torrey in truth appears to have been an unregenerate (that is un-Hegelianized) Kantian, and to have taught the *Critique of Pure Reason* at first from his own notes, and then, as they became available, from Watson's edition of the *Critique* and Morris's critical exposition of it in the Griggs series—publishing ventures with which Dewey was later to become associated.

Dewey's years of secondary-school teaching were also philosophically productive. During them he thought out several articles which appeared later in the *Journal of Speculative Philosophy*. An older Dewey was to dismiss them as "schematic and formal," as "intellectual gymnastics" couched in the language of "intuitionalism," written when "of Hegel I was then ignorant."[5] Although there is an earnest dialectic about them that little suggests the mature Dewey, still they are not uninteresting on their own. "The Metaphysical Assumptions of Materialism"[6] makes a good case against the ordinary assumptions of materialism on the grounds that these, when extended, yield conclusions which are inconsistent with the initial premises. Using the same strategy, "Knowledge and the Relativity of Feeling"[7] attempts not a psychological account of feelings but a demonstration that this subjectivity, taken as a premise in the subjectivist's argument, will ultimately lead to conclusions that are incompatible with the initial assumptions. During this time Dewey also offered William Harris, the moving spirit behind the *Journal,* translations, apparently already completed, of German texts, in particular Rosenkranz's "Introduction to Hegel's *Encyclopedia*" (published finally as a translation by G. Stanley Hall). This of course suggests that Dewey, contrary to the implications of the autobiographical essay, was knowledgeable about Hegel as well as Kant before leaving Vermont for Johns Hopkins.

After the stint in secondary-school teaching, Dewey applied (1882) to Johns Hopkins for admission and for a scholarship to do graduate work. He won the first and was denied the second; but supported morally by Harris and Torrey, and financially by a loan from his aunt, he risked Baltimore. Now it was no inconsiderable step that Dewey took, for although in those days a philosopher might make a college presidency with ease, it was difficult to make a philosopher out of anything but a clergyman. We have already seen the difficulties that Peirce, James, and Royce had in making philosophy a career. Philosophy was just beginning to stake its claim for independence from established religion. So, with misgivings about his future, the young Dewey set off to Johns Hopkins and to study particularly with George Sylvester Morris. Morris, who spent the fall term at Hopkins and the spring term at Michigan, was learned in German philosophy, especially Hegelianism and its anglicization at Oxford and Edinburgh. Morris's "dynamic idealism," as we have already noted, was not an overseas shadow and was responsive, as British generally were not, both to the currents of biological and social science, and to an authentic Kant, that is, Kant for Kant's sake. Morris was an influential figure. He shared with the St. Louis Hegelians the messianic effort to educate Americans in the original materials of German philosophy. Royce had taken a degree under him in 1878, and Dewey, who chose to write with him on Kant's psychology, received his doctorate in 1884.

The following year, Morris left to spend full time at Michigan, and Dewey joined him as an instructor. Dewey remained there for the next decade, save for a year at the University of Minnesota. On Morris's death in 1889 he returned to head the Michigan department. Dewey's association with Morris as a student, and then as colleague, was rich and exciting. Both men shared idealistic assumptions not unlike the idealism that briefly captured Bertrand Russell. Dewey recalled, although he could not recapture, the exhilaration that the study of Hegel had given him: a sense of union, of synthesis, "of subject and object, of matter and spirit, the divine and the human." Dewey was searching for a rigor that Transcendentalism could not supply. Peirce found it in mathematics and logic, and James in psychology. In this context, Hegel's philosophy seemed worth serious investigation. Interpreters of it, especially T. H. Green, raised through it cogent criticisms of empiricism as well as grave social issues. In these early years at Michigan, Dewey and his colleagues were not seriously troubled by what they later saw as an important fault in Neo-Hegelianism, viz., its incompatibility with evolutionary biology and empirical psychology. Hegel's psychology, which preserved the Kantian notion of a self with power to synthesize, avoided the Kantian dualism between the transcendental and empirical self but in so doing appealed to a most suspiciously unempirical self. Nor were they yet disturbed by the lack of connection between Hegel's Universal Spirit and the world of science and experience and naturalistic teleology. What he and his colleagues of those early Michigan days were impressed by was the comprehensive sweep of the dialectic, which translated Manifest Destiny onto a cosmic scale implicating everything from the development of plants and animals to that of institutions. The latter embrace not only the church, state, and family, but establishments generally, including science, education, and even philosophy. Thus philosophy is not merely a matter of understanding; it has a social mission, and philosophers have a responsibility to face practical issues and to extend culture and education. This was the time of Chatauquas, labor schools, the popularization of science and the humanities in magazines, etc., and Dewey took a substantial hand. He wrote on all kinds of topics, from health, sex, and the education of women, to Browning's poetry and Renan's faith and doubt. Galton's statistical method and Austin's theory of sovereignty shared his time with American democracy and the teaching of morality in high school.

This catholicity as well as the Idealism which he shared with Morris show in the three philosophic books that were written from Michigan: *Leibniz,*[8] the *Psychology,*[9] and the *Outlines of a Critical Theory of Ethics.*[10] The *Leibniz* (1888) was written for Grigg's *Philosophical Classics,* which, as one fulsome advertisement puts it, ". . . will do much to clear the way and make the mastery of the German systems a comparatively easy task." Several are still respectable secondary sources, including Morris's *Kant's Critique of Pure Reason,* which began the series, and his *Hegel's Philosophy of the State and History.* Dewey presents Leibniz clearly and sympathetically and reserves for the final chapter the criticisms that stem from his own persuasions.

Jurist, diplomat, theologian, mathematician as well as philosopher, Leibniz used his prestige to foster political cooperation among eighteenth-century religious and national factions and community among its scholars. He envisaged academies stretching across Europe that would pool the world's total intellectual resources. Leibniz was as congenial to Dewey as later he was to Russell and C. I. Lewis; but where the latter two were more interested in the logic, Dewey finds this alien and unnecessary and turns rather to the German's emphasis on the organic— to the anticipations of biologic evolution, to the continuity of the physical and the psychical, and to his view of consciousness as dynamic. Moreover, the particular text with which Dewey was working, *New Essays on the Human Understanding,* offered a critique of Locke's sensationalism which was companionable with T. H. Green's criticism of empirical psychology and with Dewey's own objections, objections which remained permanent features of his attitude toward empiricism.

Dewey criticizes Leibniz's logic as formal; Leibniz failed "in Kantian language to criticize his categories, in Hegelian language, to develop a logic,—the results of his assuming without examination, the validity of formal logic as a method of truth."[11] Leibniz mistook the central principles of logic, such as the law of contradiction and of sufficient reason, to be laws of the universe as well. Dewey thinks that the principle of sufficient reason is used in such a way as to involve confusion. The principle of sufficient reason may indeed be used as purely formal, as equivalent to the notion that everything, no matter what, has some explanation. Thus employed, it simply declares that everything has a reason, without in the least determining the *what* of that reason—its content. This is what he meant by calling it "formal." Dewey claims that Leibniz in his better moments—when seeking an organic unity involving reference to a known world—does not use it in this way. The notion of sufficient reason cannot be formal and do the needed work; writes Dewey: "the bondage to scholastic method is so great that Leibniz can see no way but to measure intelligence by the ready made principle of identity and virtually (though not on purpose) to explain away the very principle of sufficient reason."[12]

Dewey's *Psychology,* with editions before and after the *Leibniz,* is in much the same mood. It is deeply stained with faculty psychology and reads harshly to those who know the pragmatic Dewey or are habituated to current empirical psychology. Knowledge is universal, feeling is individual, and they are mediated by the will. Thinking dissolves the particular out of the universal and ideal to discover the universal meaning of fact. The self is active but its activity is the idealistic one of agent-synthesizer, in sharpest contrast to Dewey's mature view of self as an organism that spills over into action with the natural world. Psychology in 1887 is taken (in a Hegelianized mode) to be the science of a self that has the power to recognize itself as an *I* and to know that it exists, or exists for itself. As universal, the self is not publicly observable. Through attention, the world becomes objectified self; and the self, subjectified world.

G. Stanley Hall joins Dewey's *Psychology* with the psychologies of James McCosh and Borden P. Bowne in a lethal review of them all: "Dr. Dewey's book is to Hegel as Professor Bowne's is to Lotze. In each case the spirit of the master animates the pupil, but has not gained insight or breadth of view. Dr. Dewey is a less servile disciple of a better master. . . .'' He adds: ''That the absolute idealism of Hegel could be so cleverly adapted to be 'read into' such a range of facts, new and old, is indeed a suprise as great as when geology and zoology are ingeniously subjected to the rubrics of the six days of creation.''¹³ Even the large-minded William James wrote to Croom Robertson, editor of *Mind*, ''Dewey is out with a psychology . . . I felt quite 'enthused' at the first glance, hoping for something really fresh; but am sorely disappointed when I come to read. It's no use trying to mediate between the bare miraculous self and the concrete particulars of individual mental lives; and all that Dewey effects by so doing is to take all the edge and definiteness away from the particulars when it falls to their turn to be treated.''¹⁴

The third product of Dewey's idealism, *Outlines of a Critical Theory of Ethics* (1891), was to preside over a critical moment in his thought. Written as a guide for students at Michigan, it is as cryptic as such course outlines are meant to be; even so it was widely circulated and extensively reviewed. Appreciated in it are the day's reigning conflicts between self-realization and utilitarianism, between Neo-Hegelian idealistic ethics and the evolutionary naturalism of Spencer and Leslie Stephen. Dewey proclaims allegiance to such idealists as T. H. Green, Bradley, and Caird, but, somewhat regretfully, he explains that he has ''not been able to adopt the standpoint or the method of the naturalists.'' Dewey was at work reediting the *Outlines* after the supply had been exhausted and at the same time working through James's *Psychology*. Under its impact Dewey thoroughly re-worked his ideas into a *Syllabus* (1894) which was ''in no sense a second edition of the previous work.''¹⁵ Despite its ungainly style and the residue of an idealistic vocabulary the *Syllabus* displays a shift in commitment now to empirical psychol-ogy and it is unmistakably aligned with ethical naturalism. But this was not a shift that ever led him to forgo the criticisms of atomism in psychology or in moral and social ethics; in this respect he was always to stay with Green.

The *Syllabus* appears as a somewhat reluctant pronouncement, but the conver-sion to an evolutionary naturalism is complete in *Studies in Logical Theory* (1903), a cooperative study which Dewey masterminded from the University of Chicago, where he had gone in 1894. For Dewey and the young men around him these essays served as a manifesto of functionalism, and they were to provide, together with the *Syllabus,* the psychological base for Dewey's later fully de-veloped instrumentalism. As suggested above, James had been disappointed in Dewey's *Psychology,* not even citing it in his *Principles;* yet by April 8, 1903, we find James enthusiastically hailing Chicago as a ''new school.'' James writes to F. C. S. Schiller:

It appears now that, under Dewey's inspiration, they have at Chicago a flourishing school of radical empiricism of which I for one have been entirely ignorant, having been led to neglect its utterances by their lack of ''terseness," "crispness," "raciness," and other "newspaperial" virtues, though I could discern that Dewey himself was laboring with a big freight, towards the light.[16]

Later in the same year (November 15) James again writes about the Chicago school:

> It is splendid stuff, and Dewey is a hero. A real school and real thought. At Harvard we have plenty of thought but no school. At Yale and Cornell, the other way about. . . . Dewey needs a great deal of building out and follow-ing of his principles into all sorts of questions of detail. But it is a noble work. Pity that their style should be so dry and abstract . . .[17]

In the year following the publication of the *Studies* Dewey moved from Chicago to Columbia where he "built out" his functionalism into the mature instrumental-ism which is his version of pragmatism. He went to New York as the acknowl-edged leader of a going movement whose naturalistic lines were clearly laid down.

We have followed in preparation and in his major works Dewey's long trek from Scottish orthodoxy to functionalism. On the face of it the reversal seems sharp and inexplicable, or explicable at best in terms of external influences. This is especial-ly so when we limit ourselves, as above, to the strictly philosophic books. Yet the abruptness and magnitude of the break can be overstated. When we look also to the psychological articles which interlaced the narrowly philosophic ones, the change seems not merely the "drift" he reported it to be in the autobiographical essay, but an eminently reasonable one in terms of the ever "new question" of the relation of psychological methods to philosophy. Perhaps not too much is to be served by one more account of the move; it has been traced via his view of logic by White,[18] his view of nature by Collins[19] and by others with their own insights.[20] But we want to stress the pivotal role of individual and social psychology which "mediated" between those elements that held Dewey to his idealism and the evolutionary naturalism he had been reluctant to adopt wholeheartedly. It is almost as if Dewey held off from naturalism until he should be able to integrate with it those aspects of idealism which he regarded as philosophically important: the view of knowledge as organic and relational, the social character of both self and knowledge, the unifying and purposive character of judgment. Dewey could not bring together these features with naturalism so long as the dominant model of the latter was atomistic. This atomism of classic empiricism, even John Stuart Mill's as-sociationism, had been carried over even into ethics and social philosophy and was enshrined in Spencer, for all his evolutionary underpinnings. Dewey's final position was experimental and empirical—a biologically oriented functionalism; yet the problems of the relation between body and mind, the freedom of the will, the privacy of feeling, and the relation of knowing to acting were never to be set in the orthodox empirical tradition. Our key lies in Dewey's breakthrough in psychology and how it accomplished the integration and built instrumentalism. As

Dewey claimed, it was James's *Psychology* that led the way, that gave "new direction" to his thinking; but the day was to come when Dewey was to regard even James as fainthearted in his empiricism. Dewey carries James's critique of atomism and his dynamic view of the knower far into a theory of action which, in the full social and cultural setting, gives an urban cast to pragmatism. As we shall see, the growing disenchantment with Hegel never led him to abandon the broad view of history and culture nor the critique of empiricism which he worked out partly in connection with the study of Leibniz and Green.

Armed with postgame wisdom we can find the promise of Dewey's final instrumentalism and the thoroughly naturalistic direction of his pragmatism even in the idealistic works that were sampled above. For example, Dewey's criticism of Leibniz's logic as formal has quite the same ring as the late (1937) *Logic, The Theory of Inquiry* with its concern to treat the relation between physical and psychical events organically. Again, breaking down the principle of sufficient reason into the different contexts of its use in the earlier book exhibits the situational and functional mode of analysis which was to become the hallmark of Dewey's later work. Even the *Outlines* criticizes Utilitarianism from a naturalism not unlike that of *Human Nature and Conduct* (1922). A word of explanation is in order about the *Psychology*, since it may seem to conflict with our thesis about the importance of psychology to later development. The situation is rather complicated by the fact that Dewey's *Psychology*, especially the first section on knowledge, is one of his least "psychological" works—at least in the current sense; it has its more legitimate place in rational psychology and in the philosophic tradition that begins with Edwards and worries about the existence or nonexistence of faculties of will, memory, etc., as entities of a special sort. Nonetheless, the emphasis on activity and its consequences in the world strongly hints of later instrumentalism. Furthermore, there are more charitable alternatives to Hall's lethal review even among the tough-minded. Croom Robertson sees Dewey's work as an effort to reconcile modern German Idealism, "with an adoption of the spirit and aims of the English psychological school from Locke onwards,"[21] while Brett writes, "The proclamation of a new era was definitely made by Professor John Dewey (at that time attached to Michigan University) by his *Psychology* (1886). . . ."[22] Brett notes that the soul of Porter has vanished, that the self is known only as it acts and reacts, that attention and association are taken as aspects of activity, that German experimental psychology is utilized, and that though knowledge may be universal, feelings as individual responses are stressed. He notes, too, the emphasis on biology and mental action as a function, and concludes:

> Since those days Professor Dewey has continued to make history . . . It is enough to say that he is now regarded as the leader of a definite "school," and that the so-called "functional psychology" . . . is to be considered as

the outcome of the thoughts which were partly expressed in the book here described.[23]

Retrospectively, too, it is not hard to find the roots of a tougher naturalism in the Vermont influences and in other associations at Hopkins and Michigan. Of course 1859 was not only the year Dewey and Bergson were born; it also saw the publication of Darwin's *Origin of Species.* America was already feeling the tensions of civil struggle. Thus Dewey's youth was shadowed by the social upheavals of national division and readjustment and it witnessed the scientific revolution which Darwin precipitated. Perhaps Dewey was born too late, or perhaps Burlington was too cosmopolitan a mix of "old American congregational- ists and Irish, German and French-Canadian Catholics," but in any case he was spared the anxieties of the science-religion controversy that so disturbed Boston. Indeed Dewey regarded the minister of the Congregational Church which he attended as "enlightened."

Now we have taken considerable care above (chaps. 4-6) to show the sturdiness of the Scottish Common Sense Realism, surely a substantial part of Vermont academic tradition. It made easy union with Hegel in British philosophy and uneasy connection with Darwin through McCosh; but its natural direction in America was Kantian. At least the writers revered in America—Reid, Stewart and Brown—were preoccupied with the relation of psychology to logic. The concep- tion of activity and of an individual as active and purposing is an important part of their theory. They even surpass Kant in their appreciation of the role of knower in knowledge and in their enlargement of experience to include the aesthetic and social. Brown, it may be remembered, stressed the biological basis of behavior and the organic character of human responses, while Reid was more concerned with the psychology of perception and the cognitive act of referring than with the metaphysical questions of realism. And they, with Stewart, emphasized the role of philosophy as a resource for directing human advance. Dewey's pragmatism owes a profound debt to the hardheaded American reading of Common Sense.

Dewey also did serious work at Vermont in geology, zoology, and biology and wrote his important undergraduate paper in political economy. Today's under- graduate would be hard put to match his education with Dewey's. But beyond the formal courses his education came mainly from reading. By the time he applied to Johns Hopkins he had read the prescribed books and more. The library of the University of Vermont was open but a few hours a week and the opportunity to borrow books was precious; the record of Dewey's withdrawals (there is no doubt that he read what he took) shows he was interested in Max Muller's *Lectures on the Science of Language,* Bain's *Mind and Body;* and Flint's *Physiology of the Nervous System* kept company with Herbert Spencer's *First Principles* both of psychology and philosophy. Hume, Berkeley, and most of all Mill were taken out many times. And he followed the fiery issues of the day from evolution to the legitimate limits of government in the current liberal British and American reviews.[24]

At Johns Hopkins the influences were wider than those already mentioned. Even Morris's idealism had been shaped by the Aristotelianizing and biologizing Trendelenburg. Further, Dewey's work in philosophy was supported by a minor with Herbert Baxter Adams who pioneered in the new "scientific" history, particularly in the concrete study of institutional growth. Hopkins was also the center for the new psychology. (James even visited there, on his honeymoon, it is said, with an eye toward accepting a professorial appointment.) As it was, the influential professor in these matters was G. Stanley Hall (the same who was to write the patronizing review of Dewey's *Psychology*); doubtless he served as a second-term antidote to Morris's first-term dose of idealism. (Evidence strongly points to Hall's heavy hand in the events that led to Morris's departure for Michigan in 1884.) It was in the second term of that year that Dewey read "The New Psychology" before the Metaphysical Club. Almost certainly Hall and Peirce were in the audience, for Peirce was on the faculty at that time. Scarcely a touch of idealism is to be found in the paper and only the mildest reference to religion and God, which may have been added later as a polite salute to the commitments of the *Andover Review* which published it (1884).[25] Written small, indeed very small, are important features of Dewey's later naturalism. He indicates the crucial relevance of biology and physiology for the new psychology. The characterization of sensation, experience, and environment reads like a preliminary comment for *Experience and Nature*. To an introspective account of perception, Dewey opposes a much more public account. The perception of a landscape, e.g., is not a matter of impressions falling on a passive receptor but a complex judgment involving emotional, volitional, and intellectual elements. Newer applications of physiology do not subtract but add a new dimension to perception by indicating its necessary involvement with the huge varieties of sensation, unlocalized feeling of extension, interest, attention, and interpretation. Memory no longer is a faculty nor even a storage bin but "lines of activity along which the mind habitually works"; physiologically it is based in structures which are modifiable as learning takes place. But Dewey's emphasis on the biological and physiological roots of psychology is not at the expense of the humanities and the social sciences. The life of the individual, the proper subject matter of psychology, is lived in society, is modified by education, tradition, and the multiple structures of language, myth, and culture.

Whatever influences were at work at Vermont and Hopkins, it took the progressive Midwest to give heart and shape to Dewey's philosophy. This decade (1884-94), when he hammered out his naturalistic commitments, had many dimensions. Although Dewey remained on the warmest terms with Morris and continued to write academic articles about mind-body problems, etc., still his sympathies, intellectual and political, moved off in new, independent directions. The University of Michigan, in contrast to Johns Hopkins, was a public coeducational institution and part of a full state system of education that began with primary schooling. As professor of pedagogy as well as philosophy, Dewey did not merely give education courses but was actively involved in educational planning with the high-school faculties. Perhaps it was here that Dewey first began to see epistemology in terms of learning—of learning *how* and *how to* as well as *that* and *what*. In any case he came to appreciate that education must begin with the ideas, activities, and interests of the child, and that the aim of a curriculum is not to transfer to students a static body of knowledge (what Paolo Freire calls "the banking model").

In 1887 Dewey married Alice Chipman who had already had some teaching experience but was completing her work at Michigan. Her guardian grandfather had worked among the Chippewa, and she had firsthand understanding of the social injustices which they suffered. At Michigan she belonged to the Samovar Club which was steeped in Russian literature, especially Turgenev. Thus she helped broaden his interests and supported his activist tendencies. Dewey was involved in social projects, e.g., in an effort (unsuccessful) to publish a reform newspaper which would give the news uninhibited by pressures from the Establishment. This fell well within his view of education, which he did not dissociate from the social responsibility of teachers toward the reform of institutions. Henceforth, Dewey talked in the context of public education, i.e., the education of the public.

There is no sharp line between Dewey's increasingly social concerns and his academic career. In H. Demarest Lloyd's terms, a "new conscience," a sense of responsibility for the relief of social evils, permeated the air. Colleagues outside Dewey's department shared in it, especially Henry Carter Adams, a first-rate economist with sympathy (unusual for economists of the time) for emerging trade unionism. But of greatest importance were members of Dewey's own department —Arthur H. Lloyd, James H. Tufts, and George Herbert Mead.

Dewey's writings toward the end of the Michigan period show the new Dewey firmly in the saddle. We have already mentioned the *Syllabus* (1891); here appears the critical notion of ideas as plans of action. To this period also belongs "Moral Theory and Practice" (1891)[26] in which *"oughtness"* is not defined in terms of feelings of obligation, nor is it cut off from the "is," but is itself declared to be the "is of action." In this period, too, Dewey began to work out the set of articles which were to be the turning point in his theory of psychology. These include "The Psychology of Infant Language" (1894) and two articles on the theory of emotion (1894, 1895). While these psychological articles were cast in individualistic terms, Dewey was even then working out their larger institutional aspects, what could be called social psychology. In this context, three studies are of special interest; on Lester Ward's *Psychic Factors of Civilization,* on Holmes's *The Common Law,* and on Renan's *Loss of Faith in Science.* Evidenced here are many of the concepts that were to stay at the core of his later work—intelligence, experience, logic, science as a liberating humanistic endeavor.

Dewey was much concerned with the shift in Renan's writing from the earlier faith in science of the 1850s to the later reversal and doubt of the 1890s, from the democrat influenced by the rise of science and its social mission and hopes spun out of the revolutions of '48 to the aristocrat disillusioned and reconciled to the necessity of evil and the limited access of the masses to artistic and intellectual goods. Dewey's sympathies lie clearly with the earlier Renan, and he elaborates this earlier view into a general outlook. Renan thought science, to have a social mission, must broaden its range to include the study of individual growth (not just the mature form) and social institutions. It also has to realize its potential for application in human betterment; and of course science itself is a historical product. The method of science would be the method of intelligence, and it could become the common possession of all men. Dewey here sees the goal of science to lie in "such a sense of life as will enable man to direct his conduct in relation to his fellows by intelligence and not by chance."[27] The French Revolution attempted this but construed reason too narrowly and opposed it to instinct. Renan too fell short in failing to see the reason already resident in institutions, as well as the resistance to science by entrenched interests to keep it from becoming practically effective—even where so remote a science as astronomy is concerned, as in the case of Galileo and Bruno.

Dewey's review of Ward's *Psychic Factors of Civilization*[28] picks up the same themes closer to home. Ward early challenged Social Darwinism by showing that not all the determinants of selection were to be found in the physical environment; that intelligence, operating indirectly, adds a new dimension to evolution by checking direct action. This makes intelligence into a normative tool of advantage. Dewey's criticism of Ward is that he isolates intelligence from impulse and emotion, failing to see the integral character of behavior. But truly to understand that requires reconstructing our theories of mind and of society to show the social character of mind in human development.

The dynamic social element that Dewey has been talking about stands out clearly in his brief comment on Oliver Wendell Holmes's *The Common Law*, which he titled "Anthropology and Law."[29] Dewey derives from the history of law the general lesson that all institutions undergo historical growth. Old institutions are never annihilated at one stroke, nor do they begin *de novo*. They are constantly being reinterpreted in terms of their uses and utilities, and so acquire changing functions. Lacking further utility, institutions fade away. For example, Holmes shows that what we take to be natural today—the liability of a person for the harm caused by his agents or his tools and possessions—grew out of a primitive direct action against the offending object, animal, or person. The costly procedure of destroying an offending ox, ax, or vessel gave way to a more efficient buying off or replacement. Incidentally, Dewey's often troublesome use of the terms "experience" and "logic" are illuminated in the context of Holmes's famous remark that "Experience, not logic, has been the life of the law."

There was continuity of interests and associations, between Michigan and

Chicago. Tufts left Michigan to go to Chicago via Freiburg, and Dewey and Mead came on in 1894. Dewey was to be professor of psychology, philosophy, and education. As was mentioned early in the chapter on the St. Louis Hegelians, Chicago had usurped the place of St. Louis as the gateway to the West. It was a place of great social and intellectual ferment: emerging agrindustry, a recent economic depression with riots; an influx of immigrants with different European backgrounds (many of them bringing socially advanced ideas adding to home-grown progressivism); labor conflicts and a growing political voice to labor; yet all this in a background of growing industrial power and militant laissez-faire.

Education remained at the center of Dewey's interests. It was a practical interest—quite consistent with the way he plunged into practical affairs. He was a mainstay of the Laboratory School at the University of Chicago, which was no simple adjunct of education courses but an experiment in social democracy. If the schools are indices of a nation's social maturity, then they are the necessary media for enlightened social progress. In contrast to the St. Louis Hegelians, Dewey took the responsibility of teachers to extend beyond materials and instruction; it was equally a matter of functioning in reform and refurbishing the teachers themselves.

Similarly, Dewey regarded Hull House as both a social experiment and an educational venture. There is continuity between Dewey's applied pragmatism and the objectives of Hull House as stated by Jane Addams.[30]

The University of Chicago itself was a new venture in education. Gathered on its faculty was an unusual assemblage of scholars, including Michelson, Franz Boas, and Jacques Loeb. Dewey's associations were especially close with the social scientists. He and Veblen had graduate students in common, such as Henry Waldgrave Stuart and Wesley Mitchell, the one going into philosophy, the other into economics. Dewey's "Interpretation of the Savage Mind" (1902) is a modest example of the same kind of analysis that Veblen did in his *Theory of the Leisure Class* by exploring the effects of productive processes on modes of thought. This article is congruent with the new sociology that Albion Small and W. I. Thomas were developing at Chicago.[31] Dewey's "My Pedagogic Creed" was published together with an essay by Small in *The Demands of Sociology upon Pedagogy.*[32] Dewey's association with these and other social scientists is perhaps to be regarded as an influence in distinguishing his instrumentalism from Cambridge pragmatists, whether James or C. I. Lewis, who were oriented more to the individual psychology. This is perhaps another confirmation of the point made earlier that it is not the appeal to science but the particular science appealed to which affects philosophic thought.

Of course Dewey's position was not a surrender of philosophy to science; his interests were essentially to reconstruct philosophy by bringing science into philosophy. In this he was ably abetted by Tufts and Mead and A. W. Moore, and Angell, a student of James who had joined the Chicago faculty.

The period at Chicago was immensely rich in published works. The most important of these (at least from the point of view of our hypothesis) are the psychological articles which are continuous with the psychological articles from Michigan, particularly the studies on the savage mind mentioned above and those on interest and will, effort, and above all the critique of the reflex arc. This batch of articles, together with the *Syllabus,* are the core of Functionalism. It was not intended to be a school, but was given this status by Titchener who opposed it to his Structuralism, and was baptized as the "Chicago School" by James. Dewey acknowledges the unity of these articles in an exchange with James. James, writing in March 1903 on another matter, added a postscript to Dewey: "I have just read, with almost absurd pleasure, A. W. Moore's *Existence, Meaning and Reality.* I am years behind in my reading, and don't know how close *you* may have come to anything like that since 1898. I see an entirely new 'school of thought' forming, and, as I believe, a true one."[33] Dewey, in replying to James's letter, identifies Moore as one of his group, and then adds: "As for the standpoint,—we have all been at work at it for about twelve years. Lloyd and Mead were both at it in Ann Arbor ten years ago. . . . Mead works himself (and it) out mainly in biological terms. . . . As for myself,—I don't know whether you ever read my psychological articles on 'Emotion' and the 'Reflex Arc Concept,'—the one on 'Effort' . . . doesn't appear very near, . . . but I have evolved them all from the same standpoint."[34]

In the same letter Dewey notes that he is sending the proof of *Studies in Logical Theory,* which he edited and which included an article by Moore. He asks James to glance over it, "enough to see whether you could stand for a dedication to yourself. . . . so far as I am concerned your *Psychology* is the spiritual *progenitor;* and while we won't attempt to father you with all the weak kidlets which are crying in the volume to be born, it would afford us all . . . very much satisfaction if you will permit us to dedicate the volume to you."[35] And when the volume appeared (1903) it carried the following in the preface: "For both inspiration and the forging of the tools with which the writers have worked there is a preeminent obligation on the part of all of us to William James, of Harvard University, who, we hope, will accept this acknowledgment and this book as unworthy tokens of a regard and an admiration that are coequal."

In the next section we shall explore in detail the psychological articles which may be thought of as a functional-field theory of individual psychology. Although they are deeply indebted to James, Dewey had already reached beyond James in social psychology, e.g., in the article on the savage mind. Dewey was already drawing lessons from the theory of evolution for an understanding of social development. Preview of his later study of human nature and conduct is already to be found in "Evolution and Ethics"[36] (1898), a critique of T. H. Huxley's work of the same title. Huxley faced the dilemma: how to reconcile the disparity between cosmic evolutionary processes and normative ethical ones—between the jungle governed by predatory survival laws and society governed by moral laws. The moral wars against the predatory, just as the gardener fights against an encroaching jungle. Dewey replaces this conflict model—a dualism of man and environment—

by a transactional one, placing the gardener himself within the evolutionary whole. The ethical process is itself a part of the evolutionary process once man has emerged and broadened the physical environment to include cultural products. Instinct has always been thought to be perfectly natural; intelligence is no less so. Once moral and cultural regulation have appeared, they enter in a perfectly natural way into evolutionary processes. On Dewey's view, conflicts arise when responses and habits that were adaptive to one set of conditions are taxed by novel ones. The situation is similar for the individual and the social group. Instincts and impulses are not moral nor immoral, and we are not called upon to suppress or replace them. But the struggle comes in the need for reconstituting them so that they function well with regard to the existing situations. So in the social realm, institutions adapted for one set of conditions may become hazardous under changed conditions unless they are modified and reconstructed in terms of the context of ever-changing social needs.

One year later, in 1904, Dewey went to Columbia University as the acknowledged leader of a going movement whose lines are clearly laid down, and as a distinguished naturalistic philosopher. And the rest of Dewey's life was spent in association with Columbia University where his major works were written and where his pragmatism took mature form.

2. A Naturalistic Psychology, Individual and Social

In this section we shall look at the writings which, as we said, constitute the core of Functionalism: the psychological articles[37] in which James saw "an entirely new 'school of thought,' " and the *Syllabus*.[38] These belong together because the set of articles works out the psychological base and the *Syllabus* applies it to moral judgment. These early writings blueprint strategies and arguments which, unchanged, continued to be the base of his position; often they become explicit, but almost as often they are so deeply embedded that they go unmentioned. The overall message is that the point of view of the interpreter or observer creates distinctions which,unless appropriately examined, import unrecognized biases and commitments to the setting of the problem. It is a point which Dewey makes often, e.g., when he examines the political bias in social theory, and is familiar as James's psychologist's fallacy, now cast on a grand scale. A related concern is to pull down those biases of philosophy and psychology which have created artificial problems as a result of compartmentalizing human experience, especially the divisions between acting and thinking, between sensation and reflection, and the isolating of human activity from its larger physical and social context. Dewey is attempting to capture the wholeness, integrity, and unity of human behavior.

The articles on infant language and on the savage mind are wholesale and retail illustrations respecting the point just made. Dewey in "The Psychology of Infant Language" is polemicizing against a Mr. Tracy who, while acknowledging the artificiality of grammatical categories when they are applied to a young child's speech, nonetheless went on to count the relative frequency of nouns, verbs, and interjections. The use of nouns, Tracy found, is much in excess of other categories. Dewey protests the futility of applying adult grammatical categories to a child's discourse, assuming they have the same role for the child as for the adult. Terms like "bottle" and "door" may appear. to be nouns in well-formed discourses; but when a child uses these in a context of expectation they clearly serve as requests or commands. Also, a child's broad use of, say, "ball" to refer indifferently to oranges, globes, balls, and toys may not mean either that the child has confused the orange with his ball or abstracted the property of roundness from these objects, but rather that roundness is primarily related to activity, e.g., what is throwable. Given that behavior is integrative of child and environment, one would expect a fusion of an emotional state and a tendency to react even before a clear recognition of objects and of abstract qualities. Dewey is arguing that grammatical categories may function adequately in adult speech, but that the vocabulary in a child's speech must be understood functionally. Baby talk or pidgin English are incomplete speech but an unexpectedly complete means of communication.

Dewey's "Interpretation of Savage Mind" criticizes the practice of contemporary anthropologists who, in putting together casual similarities from different cultures, tear loose the materials from their context. Such comparisons of cultural details can yield static facts only and ignore the dynamic and structured detail of a culture. Occupations integrate various elements into a functioning whole and determine the fundamental modes of activity as well as the formation of habits. Thus, they determine directly the chief modes of desire and satisfaction as well as the standards of success or failure. Indirectly, they furnish the definitions of value and the objects and relations, i.e., the materials, or emotion and attention. In effect, the patterns established by vocations are reflected in habits and customs, activities and products, particular views of marriage, religion, and war, and these in turn have a reciprocal impact on the patterns which produced them.

In a highly civilized culture, or even in an agricultural one, all kinds of intermediate terms have been inserted between need and satisfaction. In contrast, in a hunting culture there is an immediate and direct relation between need and satisfaction and a limited view of means and long-range goals. The savage life is dramatic and emotionally intense. When brought into contact with modern instruments which serve his ends the savage is not at all apathetic; it is only when confronted with tools and resources that serve alien ends that his interest wanes and his skills, workmanship and taste degenerate. Natively his art and religion, his views of death, disease, and war are woven into a coherent pattern and a functioning whole. These integrities of a culture can easily be ruptured beyond repair by today's rough and rapid modernization.

The moral that Dewey is pressing is turned not only toward the entrance of underdeveloped peoples into the twentieth century, it is also important to the understanding of ourselves. It is the job of genetic psychology to show how the immediate relation and adjustment of habit to satisfaction became separated by instrumentalities and ends until now there is a great distance between personal want and satisfaction—a distance filled with divisons of labor and all kinds of intermediate content, creating the vast social structure of modern societies. We have not simply passed through and beyond more primitive states; our past has left its indelible mark on the present. We have not effaced the hunting structure in modern society but built upon it, utilizing its factors in all kinds of objectives and idealized pursuits—in the hunt for truth, beauty, well-being, and heaven.

The remaining articles, on the reflex arc, emotion, and effort, are made of sterner stuff; they are Dewey's attack on the classic partitioning of reason, feeling, and will. The debt to James is enormous, but Dewey was working his way free of constraints that dogged James to the very end of his writing. Dewey early gave up the worries about the ego as a cause, partly because he had already come to terms with a functional view of necessity and contingency, and partly because he was persuaded by James that if the flow of consciousness requires no independent agent then neither does the flow of action or conduct. Dewey was prepared to identify the self with concrete and specific activities. Further, Dewey was not stymied by the view that intelligence is inefficacious; the most patent feature of experience is that planning and decision make a difference in the world, and if the psychologist rules out a base which will allow him to discuss the issue, so much the worse for his theory. Similarly, if a psychologist's theory makes learning inexplicable, by so much is his theory inadequate.

The reflex arc, according to Dewey, had been imported from physiology to psychology and philosophy in order to give a more unified and dynamic account of behavior than was possible under the reigning contenders of associationism and body-mind dualism. The associationists leave little room for explaining how a physical stimulus becomes translated into effective awareness and are left with a passive receiver conditioned by the order in which experience is received. For them, stimulus and response are a sequence of events. More classical philosophers entrench mind (spirit) and its ideas on one side and body and its movements on the other, with little connection between the two; sensation is a kind of *poseur* floating between them. They have no explanation as to how a spiritual or immaterial mind controls or influences a physical body. Now Dewey argues that the reflex arc, by partitioning experience into kinds—stimulus and response—preserves the same hard distinctions which it had been imported to replace, and locates them in a theoretically unassailable place. The stimulus, or receiving sensory input, is regarded as one event followed in time by the motor response, or muscular discharge, as a separate event with the registering mental idea (consciousness, will, or attention) as an intervening psychical event. This gives us no access to thought-guided action, to planning behavior, and to learning. It gives no account of how experience does more than aggregate.

Even James's *Psychology* is flawed with the same hard-and-fast distinctions that perhaps lay at the base of his anxiety about freedom and action generally. James generalized the stimulus or sensation in his treatment of constructing likeness classes or concepts—and so took a firm step in the direction of a learning theory—but he relied overmuch on the ideomotor theory to ensure the passage from idea or concept to action. A catalog of instincts provides the dynamics, but response remains a disconnected atomism of movements, even though he had successfully abolished atomism for sensation and perception.

Now Dewey is not about to patch up the picture of the elements, nor yet to provide a different causal theory. He is proposing a basic conceptual shift in our way of looking at the reflex arc. He is looking for a molar view of activity as integrated and coordinated; not only must thoughts, action, and feeling be coordinated, but they also must find a place in the context of ongoing behavior and of the particular matrix of experience.

Dewey argues stepwise, tackling first the distinction between sensation and motor activity. Take the case of a child reaching automatically for a bright object (a Christmas candy toy). The ordinary way of describing this is to say that the light serves as a stimulus at t_1, succeeded by the reaching or grasping as the response at t_2. But the stimulus is not wholly sensory, for it involves the muscular holding of the head, the convergence of the eye muscles, etc. Seeing is then ocular as well as optical. Similarly the reaching is not merely muscular, for kinesthetic and visual perception is also involved. In any case, the mere impinging of light on the retina does not constitute a stimulus, nor for that matter is any random movement a response; these are correlated and functional terms which are meaningless without reference to one another, to context, and to adaptation. It might be argued that the arc has to get started and that this is done by the light striking the eye or the sensation of light, followed temporarily by some response as a second event. This argument greatly oversimplifies what is taking place. It is the act of seeing, or looking, which begins things and that is only part of a larger act, seeing-reaching, which is simultaneous. Stimulus and response are not categories to describe the successive physical (or neural) events; they are divisions of labor in a complete act.

Let us look now at what is going on from the point of view of activity. Seeing is for the sake of reaching and the reaching is controlled throughout by the seeing. It is not a single seeing and a single reaching but involves continuous feedback. Vision throughout guides the movement of the child as he reaches toward a light; while the kinesthetic senses of the location of the arm, the sensations in the joints, etc., are in their turn a continually changing stimulus cuing further visual activity. There is, of course, a development over time which can be analyzed as $stimulus_1$-$response_1$ - $stimulus_2$ . . . These are not a series of jerks; for the second stimulus, e.g., is not just a repeat of the first, but the first reconstituted with the motor phase mediating between them in ever-enlarging experience. Only if it is understood in this way can a base be laid for learning.

But now suppose that this well-established flow of experience is interrupted—suppose that the child reaches for a bright object which in fact is a flame and the child is burned. When the burn results it is not a totally isolated experience; only because it enters into the earlier experience does he learn from the experience at all. The next time there is a bright cue it will carry pig-a-back the lessons accumulating from past experience, including the ambiguities. The situation is now indeterminate: a conflict or a block in the flow of experience, a hesitation in which the child seeks further discrimination to disambiguate the cue. There are alternative solutions which serve like very primitive working hypotheses which the future may test. A "right description" is required to restore the ongoing activity. But this can be cast either as a stimulus-description (is this a candy or a candle?), or as a response-description (is it to be reached for or shunned?). These alternate descriptions are equivalent in that context, for "stimulus" and "response," like "sensation" and "overt movement," are ways of describing aspects of a process; they are made for analysis and function only in this context. Stimulus and response are not existents or entities, not ready-made parts of the world.

When the continuity of experience is blocked, it is jointly the stimulus and response that are uncertain. If we are looking further to define or clarify the situation, if we look to the conditions which have to be met to restore or maintain activity, then we turn to the stimulus as setting the problem. But if we look rather for what will satisfy these conditions, we turn to the response. The stimulus sets the problem; it is not given but has to be made out; the response too is not given and insofar as it provides a solution, has to be constructed. Different purposes thus lead us to look now in one place and now in another, with a continual interaction and reconstruction of patterns of integrated perception and response. The indeterminateness, the problem, and the solution are always unique. A loud noise, e.g., tends to be made out as a backfire while we are in the city; in the forest it would be interpreted as a shot.

It is already apparent what translation or functional interpretation Dewey will make of the psychical part of the arc—the idea, awareness, or attention. Indeterminateness, doubt, indecision, and conflict provide the setting for reflection, as the hesitation provides the opportunity. In order for activity to resume successfully, we have to attend to what creates the indeterminateness. We have an idea or image of movements which may occur, and some idea or image of a completed possible situation. At this moment, a stimulus becomes transformed into a conscious possibility. Out of this will arise, in more mature behavior than the child's, our planning and our projected ideas. Ideas or thoughts function in a particular conflict to maintain or reestablish activity at a particular crisis. This point will be elaborated as mediation in the *Syllabus,* as intelligence in *Human Nature and Conduct,* and as the search for reasonable decision in the *Theory of Valuation.*

Another feature of Dewey's mature position is also raised here, viz., the means-end continuum. If the stimulus and the response are not existents and if they are taken functionally, the problem of teleology is raised in a double sense. Clearly, if we cut into a series of events and regard them as ordered, as, e.g., the operations of a self-binding reaper, it is the observer who imports the notion of end or objective. Similarly, instinctive behavior or well-established biological series may also raise the question of adaptation and of utility in an evolutionary sense of adjustment to the environment. Even in that case it is the observer's objectives which are imposed on the series, although this may be quite legitimate scientifically. But it is also clear that the notion of an end enters more intimately into the complex model of the reflex arc which Dewey has as a paradigm. The stimulus, insofar as it sets the condition to be met, may be regarded as an end, in this case an end which is being sought; there is an act to be carried out through an ideational process, and response is the means. But the lessons just learned about the stimulus and response as coordinate still apply; for when the focus is on determining the next moves, the stimulus in clarifying the conditions is now a means and the response an end. Yet insofar as both stimulus and response are in the service of a completed arc which restores the overall coordination, they are both means. Perhaps it would even be better not to speak of an "arc," but rather of a "circuit." But even a circuit is not isolated since it has a place in the larger development of conduct and character.

Perhaps it is not necessary to press the point now about the enormous importance of the model which Dewey used in the reflex arc for all the rest of his philosophy. Indeed, what follows can be regarded as expanding and developing the pattern laid down here. In effect he is completing the revolution which James had begun, and which Dewey may well have thought James had himself embarked on. Reflected in this model is also the Peircean view of doubt and hesitation. Lewis was later to see this article not only as furnishing the model for Dewey's functionalism but also as the root of his instrumentalism and pragmatism, his version of the classic pragmatic criterion of meaning and verification.

Even so it is worth, at the risk of repetition, to give a summary of its larger message. Most obviously, there survives in the rest of Dewey the emphasis on dynamic mode of process, of transaction, exchange and interchange, in a world of continual and continuous change. The problem is never one of how individual action (or later social action) is initiated, for we are active in one way or another all the time. It is rather one of channeling, directing, and redirecting activity. We are not merely reacting *to* a world but *in* a world in which our own actions contribute constantly toward a change in that world. Successful management of ourselves and the world depends now on knowledge of both, together with what changes and controls they will allow. Later on, Dewey will develop the social and cultural press of the environment in which the individual here operates.

The ambiguity of stimuli and the consequent hesitation are the psychological basis of the problematic situation; this is the groundwork for the theory of inquiry as well as the theory of value. Every inquiry and every appraisal is in some important way unique, being addressed to a particular context which furnishes meaning to the situation as well as criteria for successful reconstruction. We never come, however, to a new situation empty-handed or empty-minded. We are prepared in the ways of perception and in the ways of responding, but these are not simple ways: both reflect accumulating experience. The stimulus-response chain presages the later means-ends continuum, not merely in the sense that a projected end may take on a later role as means, nor even that its constantly changing relations may alter its character, but in at least two other critical senses: an end takes on the role of a stimulus and the means to it is a question of response, but that response may then be stimulus to other responses. The integrative character of stimulus and response will be carried over directly to the means-end relation. Further an end-in-view, being a response to a problem situation, may be regarded as a means to a resolution of the conflict. Insofar as there are alternatives to work out the tension or conflict, which then become working hypotheses to be tested in ensuing experience, we are introduced to Dewey's approach to the interlocking character of principles and particular situations; in both his ethics and his theory of inquiry principles are not rules to be applied but hypotheses to be tested in concrete contexts. We see also in the much extended ideomotor theory a front that sets Dewey irretrievably against all noncognitivist theories of action but which leaves him far short of being a mere cognitivist. Finally, the importance of conflict and its resolution in a way that will restore the functioning of a system and allow it to progress apply wherever Dewey talks of reconstruction in philosophy, the function of intelligence in individual and social life, or the office of liberalism in social development.

The articles on emotions and effort carry the same broad burden as the discussion of the reflex arc. Once again he is opposing the distinctions which are explanatory but which then harden and distort a problem in such a way as to miss larger integrative features of behavior. Once again he is directly attacking remnants of faculty psychology—reason, feeling, and will—which survived even in James's *attentionalism*. He is hoping to replace every suggestion of hard structure with operations, such as reasonings, feelings, willings, etc., together with a view of the self as function—as activity or disposition to act. Thus his account of emotions brings together the discrepant theories of Darwin and James, viewing them as complementary when seen as aspects of the larger activities of adjustment. Darwin, in his *Expression of the Emotions in Man and Animals* (1872), had shown that movements associated with the emotions, e.g., a dog's baring the teeth, are reductions of serviceable, or once serviceable, acts. In this example the completed expression would be the overt attack. In contrast, James had rather looked to the peripheral origin of the emotions, making the well-known claim that a man is angry because he strikes out, rather than striking out because he is angry. (Of course, this blatant refrain does not accurately capture his complex theory.) Insofar as Darwin assigns a temporal priority to emotion, and talks about the movement as an expression of *it,* i.e., of the emotion, he is simply wrong. And yet Darwin of course is clearly right in emphasizing the disposition to act as a central feature of emotion. Darwin's theory needs emending, for at stake are not so much acts useful in expressing emotion but acts having their utility in behavior directed toward the satisfying of desires or the relieving of pain, etc. Emotions are not prior to movement; the expression as expression is already a mode of adaptation, i.e., it is not a sign of anything in its first intention. Signs serve only as indications of a state to an observer; behavioral manifestations used to identify and interpret an emotion such as anger are thus possible only in a social context.

On the other hand, James's account is incomplete in another way. James emphasized the feeling side of emotion, its quality or affect, playing down the ideational part of emotion, and of course also assigned a temporal order to the disposition to act and the feeling.

According to Dewey, emotional experience, viewed as a total activity or a process of adjustment, has three dimensions: an idea, a feel or affect, and a tendency to act. Anger and fear, and the other emotions always have an intellectual object, i.e., a content or an idea, which is coordinated in habits or dispositions to act. Feeling afraid of a bear does not follow or precede the seeing of the bear as stimulus, it is simultaneous with it. Further it is not the perception of a coldly zoological specimen which arouses fear but the seeing-of-a-bear-as-threatening, a bear which is already a terrifying object in the context. The perception of a bear-in-a-cage in all probability would not be accompanied by direct fear. A full account of emotion must then take into account not merely the tendency to act and the feel or affect but also the idea. Even pathological reactions which seem objectless seldom seem so to the subject; and where there is merely free-floating anxiety, Dewey would not take this as an emotion, but merely an organic state. (He would hold the same of a tantrum.) Even in the normal person such a general state can helpfully be a call for a diagnosis of the situation. Clearly the elements of emotions may be separated as tendencies to act, as to what is intellectual and information bearing, and as to what is excitement or feeling-tone; but such partitions are analytic and made after the fact; their promotion into separable entities is unwarranted, for they are functional aspects serving purposes of explanation and understanding.

Dewey's task is to mold these diverse elements into a whole. As in the reflex arc article, discrimination or perception depends upon muscular coordination and depends on conscious awareness of our own organic responses. And as suggested there, where the stimulus and response run smoothly together, there isn't any emotion. It is only when an originally complete activity is checked that emotions arise, e.g., when we learn to stand still rather than run when facing a bear. The emotion is the report or resonance of this struggle (and mutual inhibition) between an idea or an end and an attitude or tendency to act. Anger, e.g., and its associated overt behavior, is reduced to attitudes supplying a reinforcing or checking factor in a more comprehensive activity; this provides the features of high emotional disturbance. The tendency to discharge into activity and the inhibition through some perception or idea are both present simultaneously, and the adjustment is urgent. Emotion is then the adjustment of habit and ideal, the concrete working out of adjustment. If the tension is dissolved by serial displacement in time, there is merely indifference. When there is a struggle to coordinate the various means and ends into a single activity, interest often results. Interest then is undisturbed unified action, which can be differentiated solely by reference to specific activities and objects. Scientific interest is a crucial illustration; on the one side it is the feeling of complex and relevant activity unified in a single channel of discharge. On this side it is emotion. Viewed on the other side it is the absorption of concentrated attention, the persistence and consecutiveness of activity against obstacles and through hindrances.

The discussion of effort is to be understood in connection with this analysis of interest. It is the functional counterpart of the traditional discussion of the will, and an indirect way of approaching the central part of the arc, the idea, or attention, in just the way that the work on emotion was directed toward understanding the organism's activities of adjustment. He is also avoiding James's concerns about the freedom of the will which in James's *Principles of Psychology* amounted to the ability to hold an idea in consciousness, i.e., to keep it before attention.

As with emotion, there are different theoretical positions concerning effort which make it difficult to keep the problem clean. On the one hand, effort is viewed behaviorally or biologically; this objective meaning of effort has to do with the psycho-physical energy which accompanies all conscious phenomena and is open to view by an observer. On the other hand, effort has its subjective side in the sense or awareness of effort, as, e.g., when we feel an enormous sense of strain as we try to determine the shape of a spot at the limit of vision. There seem to be certain sensory qualia which are ordinarily fused but which have fallen apart now in an alternation which is disagreeable. Motor sensations of the eye muscles which do the fixating are in rivalry with optical sensations of light and color, e.g., when we try to determine whether a line in the ceiling is a crack in the plaster or a spent spider web. As we try to discriminate, the motor sensations make their own claim on our awareness instead of being felt as fringe or as passing over into other sensations which are valued on their own, such as knowing what the line is. Where our interest lies just in resolving an ambiguity, it is disagreeable enough; but where expectations are balked even more is involved. For example, if we want to learn to ride a bicycle we have an anticipatory image of ourselves in motion and in balance, but as we start off to ride that image may be in sad variance with the motor sensations as we have them. In this case what is anticipated is the desideratum, i.e., the end, while the motor sensations are the means to the end. The sense of effort is the sense of incompatibilities between two sets of sensory images, the one representing an end to be reached and the other interfering experiences. Effort on its subjective side is the feeling of opposition between ends and means, while on its objective side it is the tension between competing habits and the movement toward their integration.

Attention falls on that phase of the activity which is least controlled by routine habit. In the effort to discriminate between a crack and a spider web, the sensory image is taken for granted and the motor activity or the fixing of the eyes is what is weak and therefore we regard it as the act. Often we take the act to be physical and the image psychical, but what we really have are just two acts to be coordinated in a third. While Dewey's analysis is restricted to these quite simple matters he intends it more generally, and as we shall see in the discussion of the *Syllabus,* it applies even to moral effort and the moral self. For we may sometimes identify ourselves with routine habits and see ourselves pulled by temptation in a "moral struggle." That is to say, we externalize the temptation when duty lies in maintaining habit. Similarly, when old habits, such as betting on horses, are regarded as weaknesses, we externalize them and identify ourselves with a new image of ourselves as thrifty citizens. But in neither case is there a spiritual self which is struggling against an external reality. All that there are are old coordinations in conflict with newer habits. Such conflict must occur if new ends are to be established. That the sensations of the bodily states of adjustment report this signifies merely that the adjustment is taking place ideally or psychically as well as practically. "The whole prejudice which supposes that the spiritual sense of effort is lost when it is given a sensational quality is simply a survival of the notion that an idea is somehow more spiritual than an act."[39]

The *Syllabus* expands the model of the reflex arc and the associated articles and applies it to ethics. It may be remembered from the above that Dewey was revising the *Outlines of Ethics* when he felt the impact of James so strongly that he abandoned it in favor of a totally revised course. The *Syllabus* brings new breath in his attitudes. Dewey uses the insights derived from James's *Psychology* to churn up the murky waters of the psychological base of moral decision, and one can see here the beginning of the radical departures of his later views of the nature of philosophy's task and of his personalized use of language. All the evidence suggests that in the *Syllabus* he was rushing to make explicit these new insights. As he says in the preface:

> The demand for the former book [the *Outlines*] seems, however, to justify the belief that, amid the prevalence of pathological and moralistic ethics, there is room for a theory which conceives of conduct as the normal and free living of life as it is. The present pages . . . undertake a thorough psychological examination of the process of active experience, and a derivation from this analysis of the chief ethical types and crises—a task, so far as I know, not previously attempted.[40]

The key words are "conduct" and "active experience." Dewey has to sharpen the reflex arc for purposes of understanding moral experience, and he upgrades it now to emphasize the reflective, the planning, and the intentional aspects of behavior. He must show how actions can be reasonable and how foresight and moral learning is possible. The domain of the moral here is comprehensive since every act done consciously is included; for any such act is done because it is thought worthwhile, which is a judgment of value. Yet such behavior is not isolated. It is but a part of a disposition to integrated action that issues from a reasonably stable disposition or pattern. But Dewey must also expand the interactive character of human action so that it embraces both the aspects of the physical environment that can accept or reject plans or be molded to them, and the social milieu of which the agent is a part. After all, the agent is modified by education and culture, by habits of thinking, by the demands and expectations made on him in the social environment. Dewey further has to expand the notion of a subject into an agent, character, or self. "Conduct" is used to include all of these aspects, for Dewey is now building through the notion of conduct a comprehensive instrument for handling the distinctive features of human behavior beyond mere movement. Conduct thus is the subject upon which moral judgment is passed; and the judgment is not only about conduct but it is itself conduct. Judgment arises in a practical situation and does not lie outside the domain of the conduct to be judged. Thus conduct itself is different after the judgment and because of it. This general point applies not only to the relatively singular efforts to decide in a particular case but also to the complex formulation of an ethical theory. To make the point more generally, even ethical theory which concerns conduct is itself, at least insofar as it systematizes and reconstructs conduct, a part of conduct. It follows then that the contemporary distinction between substantive and analytic (or metaethical) questions cannot be made under Dewey's broad understanding of conduct.

A further way of saying this is that "conduct" refers to the full situation which includes agent and environment and decision. Yet nothing static is intended by this, for the conditions modify both plan and planner throughout the execution of an action. There is a transaction between two subsystems, the agent and the environment. The agent cannot be cut from the environment, for the requirements which the environment makes are not outside the agent; and the agent's abilities and resources must count as a part of the conditions in reference to which plans are made and action emerges. The problem is one of integrating these conditions. The point is of tremendous importance for an understanding of Dewey's position. An analogy, recurrent in his later writings, between moral and physiological functions may help underscore the matter. There are occasions when we properly speak of organs, e.g., of lungs, as though they were self-contained entities. Thus we tend to identify the biological function with the point of initiation in the body, speaking e.g., of the lungs as though they operated in merely external relation to the air. Such a way of speaking is surely often sufficient for the medical illustrator, the anatomist or pathologist. Still, though perhaps of less immediate importance to those interests, the air is necessary to the function of breathing. But the point is not simple. Animals with different respiratory or nutritional systems have different organs but they have, by virtue of that, different environments. We are often made painfully aware in crisis situations of what holds generally. We know, of course, that when a miner is trapped in a cave his continued breathing modifies the environment and the environment modifies him. It is not as though there were a discrete or disjoint series of events that are occurring (although, of course, there is a constructable description of a temporal series); it is rather that mutually modifying interactions occur throughout the system. This begins to suggest what Dewey means by "situation." Writing before the day of systems analysis he was groping for a new vocabulary to express a novel idea. Language tends to bind us to the static even when we are trying to be loyal to the flow of situations; to counter this, Dewey sometimes forces recalcitrant words into unusual services. His deep commitment to process and his recognition of the limitations of language to describe it lie at the base of his hostility to dualisms of every sort.

The agent may be compared to an organ insofar as he is an instrument for exercising certain functions and, like the structure of the organ, his interests are controlled by ends or objectives to be reached which include the conditions of action as well as the instrument; for in order to be executed a plan must be responsive to the needs of the situation. On the other hand the agent, isolated, is not the final element since the environment must be modified so as to become the means for the realization of end and objectives. Clearly in the exercise of functions agent and environment are continually transformed. The fundamental lesson for moral experience, then, is that the total situation must be so reconstructed that the agent is able to express himself freely and fully.

Now the conduct or the situation may be viewed in either of two ways. Discussion can make either the agent central or the conditions of action. When the latter is the focus of attention, the topic is called "social ethics," whose special tasks are to understand the role of the physical and social environment, the historical antecedents and evolution of institutions and customs. When the discussion takes the agent as central the subject matter may be called "psychological ethics," and the *Syllabus* is occupied largely with its details. But the distinction between psychological and social ethics is not intended to enshrine a dichotomy between the individual and society; it is rather a matter of emphasis, for the agent is a social fact as well as a psychological one, while the conditions of action have psychological as well as social meaning.

All governable behavior is initially impulsive. (Dewey prefers this term to "instinct" because the latter had been tied to so many futile efforts, even on the part of James, at classification and assumes somehow that the classification is an explanation.) Although impulses appear spontaneous, they are modified in the course of experience; they cut across each other, they operate in ever-varying circumstances, they impede and reinforce one another in complex ways. All action, not just first impulses, is impulsive whenever (or insofar as) it contains something novel and is not habitual. Even this tentative description does not quite capture Dewey's view if it suggests that impulses are unitary and discrete acts with a determinate form that is then changed by interaction. On the contrary, they are energies in a functioning system and their character is always relative to the particular system and the situation.

Initially, impulsive conduct has no conscious objective or aim. As these impulses can carry us into divergent ways they need organization. Thus in animals timidity may war with hunger, although the series of acts which a given impulse triggers is relatively fixed. Humans are but half-made; growth necessitates selection. In more complex and complexly ordered ends the coordination of acts ceases to be a datum and becomes a problem.

The way in which experience is the medium in the transformation of impulsive energy is called "mediation," the rudimentary form of which has already been discussed in the reflex arc. An impulse to touch or reach a bright toy or candy may trigger a host of other impulses such as moving it to the mouth and tasting, and the resulting experience consolidates tasting with the motor impulses in such a way as to leave them integrated. Thus, in Dewey's awkward phrasing, there is a "reaction of the induced experience into the inducing impulse." Were it not that this "return factor" modifies the original impulse, no learning would take place.

However in the case of conflicting stimuli and response, as when the child is burned, hesitation arises from the ambiguity of meaning. This hesitation or doubt is the occasion and the source of reflection which attempts to resolve the conflict. It is not just that impulses have results, not just that the results modify the inducing impulse (the stimulus), but most importantly that we register and become aware that they follow. It is this awareness or consciousness of the consequences, the awareness of the manner in which consequences modify future behavior, that changes the import of the impulse. It is developing meaning and significance; it is quite literally idealized. Thus impulse, mediated by experience, is given conscious values through the reference into it of other experiences. Were it not that we become aware of consequences, learning in the distinctively human manner could not take place.

Dewey distinguishes three levels or degrees of completeness of this mediation. In the most complete, consequences cease totally to be the external results of the impulse and come to be the content of the act. For example, sounds become transformed into speech so completely that it is often difficult to attend to the sounds rather than the meaning. These, then, are completed habits, where "habit" is used in the broad sense which is characteristic of Dewey. Throughout the rest of his philosophy habit never loses the dynamic character that results from its connection with impulse. In effect, any stable pattern of tendency or action is a habit, and thus it is intelligible that Dewey should describe the self as habits and see cultural patterns in the same terms as custom or habit.

At the other extreme are the cases where there are variable acts in which the experiences which express the impulses are so numerous, complex, and conflicting that they create a real stop as we attempt to assess meanings and probabilities. In this case the consequences remain outside or external to the act.

Were all life habitual as in the first case we should go about our way routinely without ever the necessity to hesitate, doubt, or think. Habits are the tools which put accumulated experience at our immediate service. On the other hand, if all action required calculation and deliberation and could not become consolidated with our habits, we should remain in permanent hesitation and doubt and we should be totally ineffectual. Between the two extremes however lie the general plans of action, the continuous and permanent expectations that are the framework of our living. Into this we set our particular objectives and limit somewhat the caprice of circumstances. It is the tension between the relatively stable and habitual and the strongly variable which furnishes the setting for the problematic in reflection and the need for moral decision and deliberation.

Dewey puts this notion of mediation and reflection to work in an attempt to dissolve the dualisms and dilemma that have made opposing ethical positions out of contrasts of will and reason, motive and consequences, means and ends, and conduct and character. Such questions as these precede a theory of ethics and constitute its psychological base. His general strategy is to show that such distinctions are aspects or phases chosen from different points of analysis in the mediating process. As we saw above the mediating process can be viewed in terms of the inducing or stimulating impulse as a starting point. This would give an account of desire, its transformation, reinforcement, emergence as preference, and its ultimate fulfillment. On the other hand, if we take the standpoint of induced experiences, we are then led to reason and ideas; experiences reflectively brought forward as ideas determine whether and in what style an impulse is to be realized. These are the ideal or reflective goods, i.e., what is desired. The move from desire to preference and the move from a foreseeable ideal into a decision are simply descriptions of the same process viewed from opposite ends. They merge clearly in the overt acts but they are related throughout in the whole process. A plan of action, an intention or a projected end, are ideational and focus attention on the rational structure of the plan and its intellectual content. Yet all ideas are connected with impulse and action. Further, the fact that the idea or objective is entertained already suggests the worthwhileness, the interest, or the practical value, which is always an aspect of a plan. Again, when an aim is identified thoroughly with a prompting impulse, it constitutes a motive for a rational spring to action. When the whole transaction is abstracted from the intellectual content and considered in terms of the tensions arising in a coordination, we have the sense of effort as discussed earlier. Will has thus been distanced even further from the faculty psychology; it represents the whole of mediational activity.

If will is not a faculty neither is it an activity *of* a self. The self is not something separate that has impulses and habits and will. A normally honest person, if he feels he has an impulse to steal, tends to think of the impulse as coming from outside and to think of himself as tempted. In contrast, if a generous or fair-minded impulse is momentarily inhibited, say, by the threat of public disapproval, he may identify himself with the impulse (his "better self"). There are not two selves here; every impulse is a partial realization of self and the mediation of the impulse is thus a process of self-development.

The *Syllabus* provided the psychological analysis of active experience, and its implications for ethics. This, as we saw, Dewey called "psychological ethics," distinguishing it from social ethics not as two fields but as different ways of looking at experience. Three decades later, he furnished the second way in *Human Nature and Conduct,* significantly subtitled "An Introduction to Social Psychology."

> The book does not purport to be a treatment of social psychology. But it seriously sets forth a belief that an understanding of habit and of different types of habit is the key to social psychology, while the operation of impulse and intelligence gives the key to individualized mental activity. But they are secondary to habit so that mind can be understood in the concrete only as a system of beliefs, desires, and purposes which are formed in the interaction of biological aptitudes with a social environment.[41]

The social psychology is not, therefore, an addition to his previous analysis, nor even strictly an extension of it to a new field, but rather a restatement in social depth, the central concepts of which appeared in the *Syllabus.* Where the "Reflex Arc" stressed the ongoing and cumulative character of experience and the interaction of what is funded with what is novel, and where the *Syllabus* emphasized the interactive and integrative features that go into making a self, *Human Nature and Conduct* stresses the interaction of the organism with its environment and particularly the social environment. If we put aside the ethical discussions, the core of *Human Nature and Conduct* is the restatement of impulse, intelligence, and habit—and the greatest of these is habit, but in a very much broadened sense. It now has the character of a construction which extends over and enables us to understand the self, intelligence, and the shaping of impulse itself.

Of course no one in that generation could have written about habit without having James's superbly written chapter in mind. James had given a psychological base to habits and construed their formation in evolutionary terms. Accepting this orientation, Dewey departs not from the dynamic character of habit nor the opposition to atomism present in the stress on continuity and accumulation, but from the thoroughly individualistic emphasis of habits in the Jamesean account. Hume, of course, had already brought out the social aspects of habit and custom, seeking to explain the diversity in morals in terms of different physical environments and differing traditions. Hume's treatment seems to Dewey to be too one-directional, as was only to be expected from one writing before Boas almost single-handedly made a science of anthropology. Where Hume stressed the ways in which impressions and sentiments form culture, Dewey emphasized also the reciprocal force that social habits and customs exert on men's beliefs, emotions, and attitudes. Perhaps this is somewhat unfair to Hume, and would have been even more so to Adam Smith; yet Dewey's sense of the wash of the social environment and its penetration into the forming and constant support of habits belongs to the twentieth century, as well as his attempt to account for the mechanism of the reciprocal relation rather than relying as Hume does on custom as the explanatory principle. Psychological and anthropological studies since Dewey's book have more than substantiated this interactive mode of thought. For example, studies of sensory as well as social deprivation have shown how essential to self-maintenance is constant interaction with stimuli from the environment, while studies of cultural and social patterns and processes show how they provide the meaning for the slightest gesture and impulse.

Thus habits are to be understood in a biosocial setting. Whatever else they are, they are quite literally energetic—energies that constitute part of the raw material of the human makeup. Perhaps the simplest way to appreciate the distinctive use Dewey makes of the concept is by way of some of its most important properties:

Habits arise in a functional relation with the environment. Although there is a tendency to focus on the lungs in breathing, and the eye in vision, still (as discussed above) what is clearly involved is an interactive relation with an environment. The lungs clearly depend on the air and are modified by the quality of it. On the other hand, the air also is simultaneously modified by the functioning of the lungs. Thus, organically viewed, habits are dispositions to act or to maintain homeostasis, or in Dewey's language, to maintain a coordination between a changing organism and a changing environment.

Habits are dynamic. While James had endowed habits with something of this projective character, even he belongs to the long tradition which thought that activity had to be accounted for, that the analysis of behavior must start from the inert and find some motor principles to be applied to it. Dewey wryly wonders how Locke (or James) could have looked at a child without seeing the overvitality and have failed to appreciate that the problem was not to account for how activity is initiated but how to direct or control it. To depict a man's habits is to describe tendencies in action and predispositions in movement. These are multitudinous and their resources are richer than occasion allows for their full and unimpeded discharge.

Habits are also conservative. They provide the identifiable continuity in action and the funding of experience without which we would be inefficient. They make our character, as we saw in the *Syllabus,* and in this sense they transform action into conduct rather than a series of isolated events. Customs and morals in the traditional notion are such social habits. Yet Dewey objects to portraying habit merely as routinized behavior. That kind of account degenerates too quickly into a pathology of habits. While routine and even automatic responses are surely a part of habit, there are also habits of adjusting, of doubting, of experimenting, of deliberating or planning.

Habits function as the tools of purposeful activity. Where James merely urged us to make habits our allies, Dewey sees them as playing an instrumental role in the development of more mature activities. For example, once walking has become habitual, we can walk somewhere and even express anger and discontent in our mode of walking; or again the habit of reading is not an ally but an instrument in learning. Habits thus are not so much *had* as *used*.

Habits have only a relative discreteness. In addition to the underlying interactive aspect noted above, there is (as with impulses earlier) also the constant interaction of habits among themselves. Habits are never found singly. They often keep company with incompatible associates. In any case, the ongoing processes of organic adjustment to the environment are always productive of tension and instability and threats to the equilibrium. Thus it is not merely a question of controlling tendencies to act, but of selecting, choosing, and integrating multiple tendencies—not mere control but direction of control becomes the issue. Resolutions are necessary which may lead to the modification of old habits and to the constructing of new ones. Intelligence has its day both in the reconstructing of habits and refashioning of the environment.

Human Nature and Conduct had opened with the discussion of habit to drive home the importance of culture, not to deny the place of impulsive activity in conduct which the *Syllabus* had secured. Traditional philosophy and psychology had perennially sought an account of human nature that would explain behavior and social institutions from some one basic impulse, emotion, motive, or interest (or at least a limited number of basic impulses). On such a view human nature cannot change; it comes ready-made in the individual. Nor can institutions alter fundamentally since they are simply products of individual behavior. It goes without saying that Dewey disagrees, and that a part of his attack is to relate theories about human nature to the parochial institutions, science, and purposes of their time. Thus Hobbes's primary interest in peace expressed the civil instability of his time and so led him to view man as competitive, fearful, and insecure. The eighteenth-century sentiment theorists and the utilitarians emphasized altruism and benevolence, for they were writing when the barriers of the feudal past were in process of being challenged by nascent industry; the misery of the slums was open to any who would look, yet the responsibility for their welfare was not yet seen as a political responsibility. The utilitarians sought to extract a regard for general well-being from an assumption of egoism, showing in one doctrine both the needs of the time and the existent motivation of industrial development. In effect, such theories are ideologies. So also with modern theorists; William McDougall increased the number of primary instincts but even so left them totally specific and discrete. Social psychologies like his march in the wrong direction. They should not focus on the original impulses of isolated minds, but rather on how, from the overwhelmingly common capital stock of human responsiveness, the diversity of social institutions, of customs and habits, is produced and enjoyed.

Doubtless there are simple impulses, direct releases of energy. Yet unsocialized anger, e.g., is only a spasm; only the interactive context of responsive behavior of others, of language, etc., gives it significance and meaning and transforms it into sullenness, wrath, revenge, in effect makes it anger as we know it. Only in a social context can it become organized into serviceable patterns. Furthermore, even anger needs an object; consequently there are as many "angers" as there are objects and situations of response. The quality of anger differs as it is turned against others or against oneself, as it is directed toward an injustice or a slight, as there is the likelihood of remaking the situation or securing effective redress. Such terms as "anger" and "fear" more often mask than reveal the uniqueness of the situation. Doubtless a child's cry is initially a direct response to some frustration; but quickly he learns to use that sound and gesture to summon aid, while from the outset it was a sign (i.e., social) for his mother. Moreover, even sounds and gestures become standardized differently in different cultures, and the same holds even for the styles of satisfying such basic needs as hunger, thirst, and sex.

Impulses, to repeat, provide the energetic content of all habits. They have a vital role in transferring social power into personal ability. As indeterminate between old habits and new ones they are pivotal in the forming of new habits or in giving new directions and reorganizing the quality of old habits, individual and social. Sometimes this is because the impulse occurs in new conditions, and heads in new directions. Sometimes it is because a conservative and restrictive habit structure allows impulse no other release than isolated and undirected expression. Thus the release of impulse is an opportunity. Its origin may be a product of chance, but it allows us the opportunity to do old things in new ways. Nor are such opportunities rare; indeed the thoroughly routinized is the exception. Even, as in the case of language where we may intend to repeat exactly, there is always modification and novelty. We must seek the way to utilize impulse to reorganize, to liberalize, and to make habit and custom more serviceable. The job of intelligence is to find the way.

Once again the discussion in *Human Nature and Conduct* joins and advances that of the *Syllabus*. The earlier work had begun to analyze intelligence in terms of mediation or reflection, i.e., the return of experience to consolidate the lessons of experience. Intelligence is thus a process, not a separate faculty or a ghost in the machine. In *Human Nature and Conduct,* intelligence is further naturalized by exploring its role in more complex situations and problems; it is socialized by seeing its process as the social accumulation of knowledge, the social development of methods, and the return of both of these as habits of response and inquiry in individuals. It goes without saying that intelligence in this full character was central in Dewey's philosophy. Its role as scientific method is stressed in the theory of inquiry, as reflective morality in ethics, as criticism in the theory of valuation generally, as reconstructive liberalism in social philosophy.

In all of these ramifications of intelligence, Dewey never loses sight of the biosocial origins of intelligence and its necessary connection with a particular and changing environment. It is not merely that the configuration of habit-impulse offers a multitude of responses, but also there are conflicts of habits among themselves specifically as experiences are taxed by situations in which old patterns are inadequate. This gives a totally new dimension to the problematic situation in which conduct is to be determined. In the reconstruction of old habits and the institution of new ones, thinking takes its part. So long as old habits are adequate there is no occasion for thinking. Thought arises only as habit is impeded and the free flow of experience is blocked. In this sense, thought is born from impulse frustrated in impeded habit.

The pause which impeded habit provides is the occasion for deliberation, i.e., the projection of ends and alternate resolutions. Since the projection is merely imaginative, a dramatic rehearsal, we may be spared foreseeably disastrous consequences or may choose between different goods. The premium thus is placed on the auditing of the present concrete situation for its clues to future consequences. Still, the only resources in deliberation are established habits and experiences; but they are broad enough to include cumulative memory, judgment, experiences of prior goods, the sense of relevance in application, and of course the stock-in-trade of motor reaction. In short, deliberating is the use of funded experience projected toward future consequences.

The projected ends-in-view are then not preexisting objectives or fixed goals, but alternatives formed in the process of inquiry. There are winners and losers as these ends-in-view are imaginatively reviewed, but the winner in complex cases of deliberation is seldom an option which has not been shaped during the process. It may involve an integrative weaving of varieties of objectives into a long-range plan or an option not even entertained at the outset. Furthermore, the selected end-in-view, while exerting a control in the sequence of actions directed toward its attainment, is itself modified as the plan is developed. Thus an end-in-view operates like a hypothesis directed toward resolving a problem; clearly, it is not independent of the diagnosis of the problem, the conflict out of which it arose, and the possible changes and uses of the physical and social environment.

The concept of the means-end continuum has been the focus of controversy and confusion. It entails a variety of things: that what is held as an end at one time and in one context may appear as a means in another time and context; that the same things at one time may be serving both as an end and as a means to another end; that what are means for one person may be ends for another, etc., probably indefinitely. Dewey's continual insistence that there are no fixed ends certainly accepts and encourages these implications. However, they do not license a sharp distinction between means and end. In the first place, the sharpness of the distinction is usually made introspectively and may not adequately reflect the total situation; e.g., it may not help distinguish between wishes and solid planning or between fantasy and purposeful action. Then again, when ends are thought of as ends-in-view, then every end-in-view is clearly a means toward resolving the problem. Thirdly, insofar as an end-in-view is ideal its office is projective and controlling; but a realized end is existential and has actual consequences; thus, ends-in-view are also means to existential ends. Fourthly, in a continuum of events, ends and means are relative to the perspective from which a course of action is surveyed;

thus, an end is a series of acts viewed from a remote stage and a means the view of
the series from an earlier one. And finally, in the most important context of choice
and planning, ends are not separable from means at all, since choice is directed to a
total configuration of action. Practically, this last implies that in actual planning
the ends are so pervasively penetrated with means that different means in effect
make different ends while different ends make different means.

Human Nature and Conduct marks the maturing of functionalism into an
instrumentalism, but that functionalism was already many-faceted. Dewey is an
orthodox functionalist insofar as he looks at all human behavior as integrated and
adaptive. Insofar as purposive behavior and intelligent decision make a difference
in the course of events they constitute the distinctively human ways of adapting.
But Dewey's functionalism is also methodological; he examines the actual working of concepts and terms in some particular temporal sequence or inquiry. The
roots of this attitude had been well laid down in the "Reflex Arc."

3. Theory of Inquiry

A choice must now be made between two strategies. We could pursue the basic
commitments of empirical idealism that were set out in the *Syllabus* and the reflex
arc articles as they develop into moral philosophy; alternatively, we could follow
those commitments in Dewey's logic and metaphysics, his views as given in the
Studies in Logical Theory,[42] *Essays in Experimental Logic,*[43] the more popular
How We Think,[44] the comprehensive *Logic, the Theory of Inquiry,*[45] and his
central, metaphysical *Experience and Nature.*[46] The choice is largely a matter of
taste, since the domains of logic and morals, although separated as matters of
interest, are not separable in any final way for Dewey, nor, given the continuity of
experience, in any beginning way either. The evaluative and normative emerge as
we set about resolving intelligently the problems raised by interruptions in the flow
of experience. Perhaps a less formidable way of putting the point is that logic and
ethics both are rooted in a naturalistic psychology, when the psychology involves
learning, decision-making, and the correction or reconstruction of experience.

Since logic and the theory of inquiry are perhaps more difficult we shall begin
there and postpone moral philosophy to the next section. As always we need to
keep in mind the arena in which Dewey is fighting. Dewey worked out his initial
position against objective idealists such as Bradley and others whose philosophies,
once of overshadowing importance, have ceased to be household words. Some
twenty years later Dewey felt his theory viable enough to be tested against views
that grew out of formal logic and analytical philosophy. Dewey's use of "logic"
retains the flavor and the wide reference of earlier problems. If we take him to be
dealing with the crisp but narrow domain of symbolic logic we shall be disappointed, for his concern is with the philosophical presuppositions which underly
logical forms and which, on his view, are reflected in the analysis of those forms.

This usage is by no means peculiar to Dewey. After all, various kinds of inquiry legitimately fall under logic, including not only the Aristotelian tradition and mathematical logic but also Mill's inductive logic and the Marxian dialectic (logic) of history.

This tolerant view of the scope of logical problems sets the criteria for his own inquiry. His own view of logic must account for the differences in philosophical attitudes toward logic in the course of its development; it must also give an account of the origin of the discipline and its function. This commits him to a view of logic as itself developing like other sciences and in the context of increasing sophistication of content and methods. It also commits him to a naturalism which builds on continuities with biological-organic behavior in a social milieu. And finally it commits him to a radical empiricism since the subject matter of logic is itself open to observation. In somewhat more concrete terms Dewey is developing an experimental logic, a kind of twentieth-century quest for a logic of discovery, or even better, of invention—a logic that answers to the modern methods of experimental procedures. He wants to look at those cases where decision is adequate and effective and to extract from them the elements that lead to success. Logical theory must be responsive to the newer theories of knowledge that are connected to modern science with its use of designed experiment directed toward control; it must eschew its roots in the older Newtonian-based view of knowledge as passive understanding. Logic must have its role in learning, in social and cumulative experience, and in problem-solving. That is to say, logic is instrumental in the larger context of individual and cultural adjustment.

Logic then is the inquiry into inquiries. By this he means that the subject matter of logic, its forms and rules arise initially out of men's experiences of specific inquiries, stemming from situations which are doubtful and instituting the conditions in which doubt is resolved in particular cases. The relevant inquiries can be found in inquiries with symbols; but they may as well be concerned with the experiments of scientists, or the observations of an artisan who sees some methods succeeding in his craft and preserves them self-consciously as habits or rules or even rituals. The theory of inquiry is then the generalized search for the principles implicit in inquirings. It must never lose touch with this empirical subject matter. It is clear also that the methods are undergoing fantastic change as science develops, and therefore that the instances and the kinds of subject matter are changing, changes which must continually be reflected in the generalized theory. There will thus be no break between logic and scientific methodology, no break between scientific and commonsense inquiries, and as we shall see, no break between scientific and value inquiries.

As to the outcome or conclusion of inquiry, Dewey might have stayed with the terms "true belief" or "knowledge." But he rejects these in favor of "warranted assertion" in order to avoid the assumptions of theses in which the traditional terms have been involved. "Belief" conveys too much the idea of a personal mental state, and "knowledge" the idea of some fixed entity over and beyond the appropriate outcome of particular inquiry. "Warranted assertion" reinforces the relation between a conclusion or consequence and a particular inquiry, and "warranted assertibility" is the generalized term.

Dewey develops his naturalistic thesis in terms of the continuity between the biological and the cultural matrix of inquiry. Organic responses are the origin of deliberate inquiry and those activities prefigure the patterns of inquiry. In effect, one can look at this part of Dewey as a rewrite of James's *Psychology*, especially the first chapters, from the point of view of a dynamic and purposive behavior in which consciousness (not the omnipresent consciousness of James) functions as means in the securing of particular objectives.

The outlines of Dewey's version of the reflex arc are apparent, though now it is taken up in more consequential activity than to reach or not to reach. There will be the same ambiguity in the situation and the hesitation which sends back for a clarification of what the situation means; though this ambiguity will be promoted into a richer problem, and the hesitation and its related ideational aspects will be promoted into ideas as plans or purposes. This happens when experience has to be organized serially in pursuit of objectives which are spatially and temporally remote. In the case of hunger, there is an organic state of disequilibrium or tension and in seeking to overcome the disturbance human behavior does not simply react to the immediate environment. The reaction involves the pursuit of absent or distant objectives and a serial ordering of steps in the securing of the objective, in this case food. The stimulus is thus become the whole coordination of the activity of the organism over time, and the stimulus functions as a constant and a directive despite the progressive steps of the pursuit. There is a beginning, middle, and end or consummation to every search; the middle part provides the means, instrument, or method for resolving a particular problem, and its success is determined by reference to the answering of that particular need.

The sequential or ordered steps of behavior are not so many discrete items, nor do they take place in unchanging environment. The environment is changing progressively as the activity progresses. This opens the door for a most characteristic Deweyan emphasis. We use the environment as means or tools to restructure the situation that will allow the need to be satisfied. Changes in the organism are represented by the development of habits, while the changes of environment are not just any changes in the world but those which are relevant to interaction between organism and the world. The development either biologically or in the maturation of the single individual means that new functions and structural modifications expand the environment and allow thus for novelty. Habits do not cause the repetition of the action; rather the repetition occurs only after habits have been instituted. Yet no activity repeated is ever "the same activity" because the organism has changed, and because the environment has changed.

As Dewey moves from the biological to the cultural, there is no gap. For organic habits underlie cultural traits and patterns, while on the other hand the shape that organic habits take depends on the way they and the physical environment are incorporated into culture.

Naturalism thus also means that there is a continuity of the logical with the social as well as the biological. The environment about which so much was already said is in the largest way cultural. Hunger may be a need, but what will satisfy it is traditional and culturally elaborated. Even the tools of a culture do not merely have physical properties but speak to those who know their use. Dewey makes a careful distinction between sign and significance on the one hand, and symbol and meaning on the other. In the familiar example, smoke is a sign of or signifies fire, and the occurrence of smoke stands in evidential relation to the fire that is inferred. A symbol, such as a word, is arbitrary and dependent on social convention. It does not of itself make possible an inference to existence, but being inherently part of a system (as a word is in a language), it has been given a meaning. Meanings enter into relation with other meanings through implication. Even in the absence of the objects to which they refer, symbols make possible their expectation and recollection, and allow new combinations to be fashioned. Such transformations are not the equivalents of logical behavior but they are the conditions for it. When all the manifold manipulations of symbolic meanings to one another and their interrelations are made explicit and studied for their own sake, logic is born.

Although Dewey utilizes the distinction of sign-significance and symbol-meaning to get to the idea of logic, he does not neglect the continuity with animal patterns of behavior. For culture is a condition as well as a product of language, and organic modifications and habits underlie all these regularities. But the symbolic once it is developed adds a new dimension to our experience. We no longer need carry a suggestion into direct action, but can imaginatively rehearse and work out the implied consequences of alternatives. And in addition it allows us to share projected ends that are still in view in cooperative activity.

The judgment is the settled outcome of inquiry, i.e., the warranted assertion now corroborated and verified. Dewey specifically uses a legal model and compares the judgment to the verdict or the sentence. Whereas other views had taken the judgment to be a psychological act—in the dualist and idealist traditions of a mind—Dewey sees it as an event which modifies the existential situation and is itself existential. But it is not merely an item which is the final step of a linear sequence or the end of a mechanical procession. (This would be like the stimulus-response view that Dewey attacked.) A legal judgment instead takes a complex but indeterminate situation in which it is not clear what happened, what is relevant, and how it is to be described. The situation develops its clarity as partial settlements are reached along the way. It is established that A struck B, it is relevant to the verdict that it was intentional, and it becomes captured in the systematic network of the law as assault. All this is instrumental to the judge's verdict which, issuing in a sentence, has clearly reconstituted the original situation and clearly has existential consequences. Both the judgment and the intermediate instrumental appraisals and evaluations are open to future challenge and reconsideration. Furthermore, although that judgment is regarded as final for the moment, it belongs to the larger continuity of legal precedent which may itself be challenged.

Dewey examines the singular judgment and its subject-predicate structure in the light of this outline. There is no given subject or datum independent of the total situation. The subject of the judgment is extracted from a larger situation as a focus of a problem. "This is sugar" may isolate by pointing, but the pointing itself is already significant because of prior experience and the "this" is already in a measure determinate. To be a subject, it has to satisfy certain requirements; e.g., it must delimit or describe a problem so as to indicate a possible solution, and in such a way that further qualification will unite with it to form a coherent whole. But to be a substance as understood in the philosophical tradition is definitely not one of the requirements; rather, substantiality indicates nothing more than that certain qualifications hang together as dependable signs that consequences will follow. The qualifications that are so united with the subject to form the coherent whole are the predicates; thus what the predicate does is to render the situation more determinate. The joining is done by the copula, and it represents an operation, relation, or functional correspondence between subject and predicate. Indeed all the terms of a judgment are functional terms, since judging is a temporal process changing over time as experience occurs and learning takes place. No harm comes in practice from identifying functions with qualities, nor an object—e.g., a spade, or sugar—with its functions, so long as we do not reify subjects and predicates. There will then be no mystery in learning, e.g., that sugar has a dextrose and levulose form in addition to its sweetening power. Once these properties are worked into a coherent whole, we shall not have to worry as to what enters "really" into the definition.

Just as in his theory of learning, so in this whole account of judgment Dewey is clearly applying his revised concept of the reflex arc. The greater stress now falls on the ideational part which involves increasing clarification of what the situation is and the exploration of alternatives and tentative solutions that lead to the overt existential judgment that reconstitutes the situation. We shall see this pattern repeated over and over again in Dewey's ethics and social philosophy.

This is the setting for Dewey's emphasis on inquiry and judgment as practical, and for the particular treatment of judgments of practice.

Dewey's specific account of the processes of inquiry is presented by him as stages of reflective thought or patterns of inquiry. The idea of stages conveys correctly the temporal and processional character of inquiry, but is misleading in suggesting separate successive segments or discrete episodes. For there is a constant interplay, more consonant, as we shall see, with the integrated character of what goes on in the reflex arc as Dewey conceives it. In fact, his own description of the stages as functional distinctions (always relative to the current picture of the developing process) is more to the mark.

The patterns or stages of inquiry are given in different ways in different works, but the basic pattern remains the same. First there is the indeterminate or problematic situation which is nonreflective but which triggers the process of reflection. Second there is a locating and a defining or diagnosing of a difficulty. In the third step there are suggestions or ideas or alternative proposals of possible solutions. The fourth examines the consequences of alternative suggestions, and anticipates what would happen contingently on following certain lines of action. This is labeled "reasoning." The fifth step is that of corroboration and verification. The outcome is the judgment or the settlement of the inquiry in a verdict, the reconstruction of the subject matter of inquiry. It is worth examining in more detail each of these stages, since not only his more specific analysis of logical points, but also his larger philosophical position is captured in them.

The indeterminate situation of stage one is within experience and is an event in natural history. But not everything in the flow of experience is such as will give rise to inquiry. Though it is to be an impetus to cognition, it is itself not cognitive or reflective. For example, if a cloud suggests a face or an animal, and that is all there is to it, such free fancy is sufficient unto itself. But "indeterminate" does not mean that there is no identifiable qualitative character to the situation. It must at least provide a sense of the discrepant or a feeling of tension sufficient to lead to suspension of tendencies to action. It is a sense of the indeterminate, not an indeterminate sense, just as seeing a blur is not the same as blurred vision.

The category in terms of which Dewey describes this situation is that of quality, and the indeterminateness is only one feature of a qualitative whole in an experiential situation. In speaking of quality, he means to distinguish his view from the standard empiricism of sense-qualities or sense-data. For he regards qualities as neither atomic, nor as given. They are always reflective of past habits and funded experience.

The indeterminate or discrepant quality is however the most central feature, because it functions to impel inquiry. It is like the ambiguity of the stimulus in the reflex arc that leads to further clarification and to reconstitution of what the stimulus is. The indeterminate situation must be rich enough to provide materials for further discrimination and to exercise some continuing control on the direction of the thinking it inspires. This account of Dewey's is clearly developing Peirce's insight into the role of doubt and hesitation in initiating inquiry. And we shall see Peirce's influence (acknowledged) in his treatment of leading principles and rules, truth and the character of ideas.

The importance of hesitation cannot be underestimated. It occasions the stop in ongoing behavior and thereby sets the scene for the possibility of deliberation, including quite literally the time for choice, and thus in the long run for the enterprise of logic itself, to say nothing of ethics.

The first stage merges into the second and is often indistinguishable from it. It is marked by the greater definiteness of the problem, and it becomes cognitive as the indeterminate situation takes problematic shape. The recognition of a problem is the first step toward its solution. To formulate the problem is already to indicate a line of inquiry, and so to set implicit criteria for what would be a satisfactory solution. Stage two thus involves some structuring of the situation through selection and discrimination within the indeterminate situation. It parallels focusing on a subject which will receive the predicates in the process of judgment. There are alternatives even here and they must be held in abeyance, much as a doctor's tentative diagnosis often includes various possibilities. And the course of later inquiry may lead him back to these alternative diagnoses or even to look for further ones.

Stages one and two often coalesce, but even where they are separate, the intimate way in which even the first stage controls the whole process can be seen in the case where a problem is set up and, in its own terms, solved, only to find that the problem as formulated was not truly responsive to the original situation—as a successful war may be planned and fought against the wrong enemy.

By stage three then, we have already come to accept certain constituents of the problem as settled, just as asking any question presupposes some settled state of affairs at the very time it is seeking to determine others. Various suggestions now arise out of the observations, together with the background of habits and experience, for the solution of the problem. There are no rules for generating these suggestions or ideas. These are matters of art on the part of the knower. If the cry of "fire" results in panic and in immediate response on the part of the hearer, or if a situation simply leads to a debilitating belief that no effective response is possible, there is no question of inquiry and reflective thought even though there is a recognized problem of sorts; but if we take the present situation to suggest something tentatively which at the moment is not given, then we may say that we have an idea and the situation takes on a meaning. In complex cases such an idea or suggestion may be thought of as a hypothesis or a theory. We are not only awaiting more evidence, but we are led to further observations of the situation, and hopefully for richer and more suggestions. Such suggestions really operate as tools; they are ideas, i.e., plans of action.

In treating ideas as plans of action, Dewey is both following and developing the pragmatic tradition. Clearly, ideas are not just intellectual entities; they are organic in base, and insofar as an idea is part of our equipment in dealing with the world, it reflects a settled habit on our part. It has become part of the tools in our chest. To invoke an idea in facing a problem is equivalent to considering the tool in terms of the way it may fit into the development of the problem. Dewey occasionally distinguishes a suggestion from an idea; the former is the flash of a possible course of action and the latter, an appraisal of that suggestion in terms of its fitness toward solving a particular problem.

The fourth stage, reasoning, lies in the intellectual examination of consequences or implications in alternative ideas. The exploration of various hypotheses allows a kind of forevision of possible outcomes without committing us to the inexorability of overt action. Such dramatic rehearsal takes place, then, within discourse and with symbols. This is the functional context of logic and its formal rules, and logic cannot ultimately be divorced from it. A reference to the functions and objectives of logic is often overlooked by those absorbed in formal logic. Yet of course logic can be relatively separated for analysis, just as we can study separately the machines that are used in production, and the machines that may be used to make machines. Indeed Dewey often writes about logic as one would write about the history of tools in production. But he does it on principle, since he believes that the attention to particular contexts and functions is required to explain the particular shape and form that appears.

Tying the formal to the functional exhibits the normative aspect of logic. Peirce had begun in this direction by treating forms of inference as leading principles that when employed on true premises would yield true conclusions. We may compare them to recipes (or machines) that, furnished with good and appropriate materials, are completely reliable in yielding the finished product. For Dewey, the study of logic is a part of the larger inquiry into methods. It searches out of the actual inquiries that men have engaged in and the inquiry into inquiries seeks to generalize the methods of successful inquiry. Thus inquiry and logic as a part of it have a broadly empirical character, and they change as the total picture of inquiry and its resources themselves change. Twentieth-century science and its tools creates a totally different context for logic than the Greek science and the Greek view of science did for Aristotle and his logic.

This functional view does not deter Dewey from considering formal problems that belong to the Aristotelian tradition. Ideas that have been suggested for the solution of problems are not really serviceable until they are cast in symbolic form. Only in this way can the implications and commitments of the idea be extended remotely; and only in this way can the plans interlock with the rest of coherent and systematic discourse. The ultimate focus of logic for Dewey is not terms or even propositions, but full contexts of discourse. It is only through the manipulation of symbols that what is evidential for one or another solution can be determined.

The different kinds of propositions are dealt with in terms of their role in this process. All propositions are, in terms of their function, provisional, intermediate, and instrumental. Some refer to actual conditions as determined by experimental observation, and others, e.g., the universal, are conceptual and refer to interrelated meanings. Compare, e.g., what is involved in going from "I'm putting sugar in your coffee" (the particular description) to the anticipation of a sweet taste, added calories, etc. The transition is carried by the concept of sugar which moves us into systems of meanings and makes possible its relation to funded knowledge. Logic is concerned then with the rules of symbolic transformation. Thus appear the familiar logical connectives such as "if-then" and canons such as the excluded middle. These give the structure to discourse. They can be studied formally and in abstraction. But in the "if-then" there is always involved the sense of the transformations which they make possible. And the abstractness in the law of the excluded middle (either A or not-A) does not represent an abstract object but the ideal conditions to be approximated in inquiry. Thus any material disjunction which proves not to be exclusive is by so much defective—e.g., living and not-living as applied to viruses, or living and dead in contemporary medical debates.

Stage five concerns corroboration and verification. What is being corroborated and verified (or disconfirmed) is the set of hypotheses suggested in stage three and elaborated, especially through if-then statements, in stage four. We are led to particular tests and observations which, when carried out for the hypothesis and its alternatives, provide evidence for the conclusion. Thus the final step is a transformation in which a unified situation replaces the originally indeterminate situation. In being verified, what was the conclusion of a discourse becomes a warranted judgment, existential in its reference.

It has been difficult to make the distinction of stages firmly, and for good reason, since Dewey did not mean the stages to be isolated successive steps in inquiry. For one thing, inquiry proceeds to a concluding judgment only by partial judgments made along the way, so some degree of judgment is present throughout. (Just so, in the original legal comparison, the judge makes rulings throughout.) Also, the indeterminate situation is a controlling feature during the whole inquiry. Although it is of course itself being developed and changing during the very course of inquiry which it instigated, it remains a continual resource for new materials which the developing inquiry may elicit. Thus in any stage of the inquiry it is possible to have a shuttling, both backward for more and relevant data and new suggestions, and forward to further exploitation of the consequences of those ideas. And finally, the conclusion is a restructuring of the initial situation.

It is in terms of this shuttling that Dewey understands the much debated contrast of induction and deduction. Movements from observed or recollected particulars to general meaning are roughly inductive; this is a process of discovery. Yet as ideas lead to particulars, which can be tested, there is deduction. Systematic inference, then, is just this combination of induction and deduction. Induction is much less the amassing of instances than a way of controlling what is to be taken as a right instance. In this process, the identification of rightness obviously involves deduction from funded experience.

Again, although a particular inquiry is a unified and discrete process with its own markable beginning and its own markable closure, still it is not cut off at either end. It is worth exploring the continuities that Dewey emphasizes, which account for the maturing of experience.

As for beginnings, we have already seen that inquiry arises out of some indeterminate situation. But this never means that we come to that inquiry empty-handed. An indeterminate situation for an adult is made a vastly different thing than for a child because of funded experience. Such funded experience is so integral a part of the way that we take a situation that it not merely colors but constitutes the crudest perceptual experience. Thus for Dewey the problem of sense-data, the just-givens in experience, is simply not a genuine problem.

As to endings, judgment is a closing of the situation, and as such is always tied to the resolution of a particular problem. But the closing makes a difference in the situation and in the world; it is now a somewhat different world by virtue of the inquiry that has been completed. If the inquiry is now reopened, it is of course a new inquiry, directed in the light of a new problem (e.g., fresh evidence and a fresh situation). But it inherits the funded experience that emerged from the prior problem and its contexts. And precisely because that fund is always altered in the next inquiry (even with confirmation), and may come to be drastically altered, the conclusion in any one inquiry is never absolute. (Hence "warranted assertibility" rather than "truth.") A more patent appeal to the funding of experience is Dewey's emphasis on the continuum of inquiry. Just as every actor's exit from the stage is not a prelude to but an entrance into living beyond the stage, so every terminal judgment is at once means to some future inquiry.

As to maturing of experience, we want merely to underscore a feature of Dewey's discussion that might go unnoticed. Where James had introduced a new dimension into the account of accumulated experience by his emphasis on the activity of the knower, still such a learning theory is almost exclusively limited to the development of content and its classifications and reclassifications. Dewey certainly intends this much. He further sees learning not merely as an increase in subject-matter, but as the development of procedures and planning that can redesign sources of experience. Learning is not trial and error; it involves a redesigning of trials and an insight into new modes of testing. Hence his emphasis on method, the novelty and constant reconstruction, is the spine of his theory of inquiry; it is the recognition that method is not merely applied to experience, but is the very structure that arises out of the course of experience. This is evident from the continuity between his logic and his psychology. This same outlook underlies his whole treatment, as we have to some extent seen, of the relation of logic and experience. It is also basic, as we shall see, to the functional character of his metaphysics.

The relation of logic to experience can be seen more clearly if we look to various senses in which the existential enters Dewey's logical analyses. The primary one is, of course, the control which the original indeterminate situation exercises in the whole range of the inquiry. It is never left behind; the objective features which created the indeterminate situation provide obdurate criteria for the success or failure of the solution to the problem, even though they may be defined quite late in the inquiry. Similarly, resort to operations at any point throughout inquiry, to instruments, and to experiment and perception, are all existential. Again, while he distinguishes instruments such as hammers and telescopes from the instruments of symbolic discourse, still the latter are occurrences in actual behaving and discoursing. Even when we look to the internal character of discourse, Dewey is careful to distinguish the different ways of referring to existence. Within discourse, the bare "it is raining" takes on a role when cast as premise, conclusion, hypothesis, etc. And this function is an added property which it has in the natural processes of inquiry. Thus, even where a proposition is being entertained, not only where it is being asserted, there is an existential reference, for to entertain, and to draw implications, is the dramatic-rehearsal portion of inquiry, which is itself a set of natural events. That the central differences are functional ones is clearest in his attempt to distinguish generic from universal judgments. Universal propositions state possible operations and their consequences relative to solving a particular problem. Generic propositions may inhabit the same linguistic form, but they intend a reference and identity and isolate perceptual materials and in effect prepare them for empirical testing, and thus to serve as evidence or conclusions. "All philosophers are analysts" functions as a universal proposition as it is either definitive or represents the operation which would qualify John as a philosopher—even if there are no philosophers. As a generic proposition it is an empirical claim about identified philosophers, in which case it is probably false. Thus it requires that there shall exist philosophers.

The critical case comes in the question of the laws of inference and logic generally. We have already seen, in the case of the law of the excluded middle, that Dewey takes them to state the ideal conditions to be approximated in inquiry. In what sense is this reasonably to be seen as an existential reference, even though possibly a very dilute one? As we may expect, Dewey finds the tie in the fact of inquiry. Logical forms are traits which things, events, and qualities acquire as they function in inquiry and which they did not have antecedent to their appearance there. Dewey is thus threading his way between a descriptive treatment of the laws of logic and a psychological or mentalistic account of them as literally the laws of thought. As a beer can becomes a target only when it enters a behavioral context and is used in a definite functional way, so a human situation becomes clarified or a problem precised. Dewey means this literally, not figuratively. The beer can may become quite different as a result in the one case, and so may human life in the other. Dewey's theory is plausible because of the existential character of inquiry. Inquiry and its outcome, judgment, are practical in the sense that they make a difference in the world.

As was suggested at the outset, logic and scientific method generally are part of the general adjustment of humans with an environment which they are remaking in the process and at the same time as they are themselves being remade.. In this sense, logic is continuous with the biological and the cultural adaptations. Dewey attempted to capture the full and integrative character of this existential process, in the concept of *experience*. Late in his life Dewey became resigned to the fact that the term would not bear the burden of his argument, particularly because of the subjective connotations with which long tradition had clothed it. But he never abandoned the philosophical thrust against the adverse positions for which he had used the concept as weapon. These were two. On the one hand was the mind-body dualism in which inquiry became the subjective work of mind. The other was the type of materialism which treated concepts that were the outcome of inquiry (such as matter) as if they designated objects antecedent to and independent of inquiry.

In addressing this and other problems, his metaphysics imports the same functional strategy that he used with respect to logic.

In one sense, Dewey's functional treatment of metaphysics is overdetermined, for basic metaphysical categories are, after all, ideas, and thus plans for action. The metaphysical method will therefore be the contextual one of eliciting the kinds of jobs the ideas are doing and roles for which these jobs cast them. Where they pass the test of inquiry they will serve as organizing concepts, furnishing a structure for some domain of human experience. And since experience is objectively, not subjectively interpreted, the successful ideas are not bare stipulations or conventions.

Such a conception explains why in one context Dewey is ready to say he is a materialist—in recognizing the role of the evolutionary picture of man's development from the animal forms—and yet in another context will attack materialism for wanting to treat the idea of matter as an antecedent reality. It explains also why he stresses the continuity of commonsense objects and scientific objects, instead of embarking on any reductionist program. Although a table is a hard and solid object in common sense, and physics treats it as a mass of particles in motion with large spaces between them, we do not have to make a choice between incompatibles as ultimate reality. This follows from his functional view of facts and theories, from his insistence that facts are only meaningful in the context of theories or hypotheses, and conversely. Commonsense tables have their place in the context of common purposes, uses, and enjoyments. Their qualitative character is quite sufficient for guiding ordinary inquiry and practice. On the other hand, for purposes of scientific experiment and inquiry, it is generally important to leave behind the qualitative in favor of abstract relations which can be powerfully organized systematically and symbolically. In this question, Dewey can have his cake and eat it, with the assurance that the chemistry of carbohydrates does not destroy the taste of the cake. Common sense and science share common methods of inquiry; they differ in subject matter and, of course, in the degree of precision required, because the objectives of inquiry are different. If things are for certain purposes measured in money, Dewey says, it does not follow that their reality is dollars and cents.

As to body and mind, Dewey says that the dualism is so deeply embedded in ordinary language that we have no way even to refer to the integrated body-and-mind transaction, though in most contexts the latter would describe better the way we operate. Technically, he finds that the functional consequence of the duality is an unwholesome segregation of methods in studying man. On the one hand introspection limits itself to sensations and feelings and stirrings in consciousness, but will not touch behavior which it equates with physical movement. On the other hand, behaviorism studies gross motions and hopes to explain them all by their correlations; it will not touch the material that the other side has monopolized. Between the two, the important phenomena of purposive behavior, with plans and strategy and design in stretches of action, get lost; they are truncated to fit into either Procrustean bed. It is precisely his recognition of this area of purposiveness that drives Dewey to attack the dualism.

Perhaps the functional character of Dewey's metaphysical approach emerges most clearly in his account of appearance and reality. He examines a variety of quite concrete cases where "appearance" appears, dissolving the air of mystery about "appearance" by making it a contextually usable rather than an absolute term. In its simplest sense, "to appear" is simply to be found; its opposite is "not to appear," and not "to disappear." A rainbow, e.g., could appear and then disappear, without disturbing our metaphysical sense. A lawyer, says Dewey, appears for his client, in the sense of representing him; and a boy appears in school in the sense of attending. The different appearances of the moon are simply the parts that are visible under different conditions. So far the analyses are merely empirical and contextual. In the sense of appearing and disappearing, there is merely a quality or object whose existence or ceasing-to-exist, at a particular time, is noted without perplexity. In other cases there is additional reference to a relationship to the background or other elements in the context. Where that relationship is clear—as in the lawyer or the moon—there is again no perplexity. The perplexity arises when the relationship is unclear. Thus Lady Macbeth's utterance "Is this a dagger that I see before me?" does not deny the existence of the appearance, but only its relation to a source. (A Hamlet would even offer alternative hypotheses!) An appearance that constitutes a problem institutes an inquiry into the character of its relation to other parts of existence or experience. To treat the totality of the world as appearance and to demand a reality behind it, is to set a problem which precludes investigation.

The domain in which this analysis becomes most pertinent is Dewey's treatment of sense-perception. There is nothing in the nature of sense-perception that demands that it be treated as the appearance of something more real. As an event, it is a matter of physics or psychology. The question of its cognitive status is of philosophical interest, and to answer that we need to appeal once again to functional analysis. This returns us to the question of judgment, and especially the relation of the cognitive and the practical in perception and knowledge.

Empiricism has simply been wrong in supposing that the simple ideas of sensation—the Lockean reds, blues, rounds, etc.—are the psychological building blocks of knowledge, and are directly *known*. In fact, they are logical constructions (in Dewey's sense of logic), carefully refined elements (almost works of art) selected because of their utility in the process of inquiry. As we have already seen, the sensory field is much more ample than the objects of qualities discriminated. They are not knowledge, but elements in knowledge, and the question concerns their role in the process. This cannot be answered if they are regarded as completed objects of knowledge. They are incomplete without reference to the appropriate mode of response. But the response on the pragmatic view is active, whether an active attitude like belief, or overt behavior. Thus the view of ideas as plans of action is a richer analogue of stimulus-response (in Dewey's reconstruction of it). In this sense it is obvious that sense-perceptions, ideas, and judgments are practical. The example par excellence is the evaluative judgment. But in order to explore it we need first to have Dewey's moral theory before us.

4. Ethics and Valuation

We pick up the threads where we left off after the discussion of social psychology to explore the theory of inquiry. There is, of course, no answering break in Dewey's writings; for just as the whole of his work could be construed as inquiry, it could with equal ease be regarded as "moral" in the broad sense of that term found in *Human Nature and Conduct*. With almost equal plausibility it could be taken as an ethics in the narrower sense of a concern with the nature of right and wrong, good and bad, and virtue and vice. Dewey had early attended to these concepts, taking them then as relatively disparate. Yet in due course this very separateness became the setting for an emerging problem, since surely there can be no final divorce of what is good, right, and virtuous from one another or from the process of inquiry. Indeed, by the time of his last words on these matters, the *Theory of Valuation* (1939), he had worked out the connections among the ethical, the moral, and the evaluative, and between these in turn and the empirical. He sought to restore the relevance of science to ethics and to heal the breach between value and fact—divisions deeply entrenched in everyday speech and exploited in contemporary moral philosophy.

It is interesting to follow the destinies of the three concepts—good, right, and virtue—from their early appearance in connection with the psychology of the moral act to their substantial social setting in *Theory of the Moral Life*,[47] and finally as they are woven into a broad value theory.

Dewey's interest in ethics (in this narrow sense) antedated his pragmatism, but developing instrumentalism continually adds leverage to his treatment of the three central concepts. The "Reflex Arc" and companion articles distinguished their central roots. Natural good arises in spontaneous attractions and satisfactions. Right and obligation originate in the check on activity which is required for sorting out ambiguous stimuli. An oblique setting for virtue (as applied to character) is provided by the accounts of human growth as the development of an integrated and responsible personality.

The *Syllabus* extended the contexts and functions of these critical notions. Good, because of its relation to satisfaction of needs and desires, is fundamentally connected with action and learning. For example, the quenching of thirst is a natural good or satisfaction, yet only a bare preliminary, since it is only when such satisfactions and the behavior which secures them are "idealized" (when the consequences are incorporated into habit and impulse as remembered goods) that ends come to be projected and plans to be formulated. As experience enriches the diagnosis of the situation and as the consequences of particular satisfactions of the agent and others are traced out more extensively, we move into the domain of the ethical good, and "good" comes to be applied to permanent objects and objectives. Psychologially viewed, this is the movement from desire to settled preferences; but viewed ideationally, it involves the construction of moral good and value.

The precursor of moral right, as suggested above, lies in the control which anticipation forces on activity and the constraint which allows us to modify any particular expression of an impulse by the system of which it is a part. Our responsibility or duty *is* our ability (not the cause of it) to foresee consequences and to make such modifications. Many ethical theories see the ethical situation as a conflict between rational duty and emotional temptation. Dewey rejects this view unqualifiedly, especially as it assumes that what is right is antecedently known, the temptation identified, and reason pitted against emotion. Dewey rather sees this aspect of the moral situation as arising out of conflicts of loyalties and obligations so that the agent faces the constructive duty of working out what is the right decision.

The *Syllabus* (as indeed the earlier idealistic *Outlines*) refers virtue to the self—as the manifestations of an agent in his actions. It is character as a whole, the disposition to act in certain patterned ways, which is virtuous or vicious. Special virtues such as courage and benevolence are merely names for various parts of acts. In some respects, virtue seems here to be somewhat supplementary to good and duty. Viewed in connection with good or value, it generates the problem of freedom; since good concerns desires and their achievement, and some desires take shape as purposes and plans in the pursuit of objectives, men are free just to the extent that they can effectively develop such pursuits. This entails a unified self, i.e., one not distracted by incompatible, unrealizable, and incongruent ends. On the other hand, if virtue is viewed from the standpoint of duty, it creates the problem of responsibility—the responsibility for the ends which are sought and the plans made as they impinge on the developing of one's own character and in the appreciation of the claims made upon us by others. Dewey also integrates various functions of conscience with the central concepts; for insofar as an act is taken to be an expression of character, as virtuous or vicious and meriting approval or blame, conscience is affective or emotional. Insofar as the moral is cognitive, conscience involves the intellectual construction of what is good and valuable. And insofar as it has, in the more traditional sense, an aspect of authoritativeness, conscience functions as obligation or a sense of duty.

Human Nature and Conduct realigns the relations of the three notions as it develops them in a social context. Once again the good is pervasive since the objective of the book—a theory of social reform—is cast in terms of the social good. The latter is relieved of the traditional burden of reconciling egoistic interests with social wants, since the conflict between egoism and altruism is construed as different styles of institutionalizing impulse and habit. Dewey's position here comes closest to the utilitarians, expecially insofar as they all naturalize human good and ground it in economic and social positions. But he separates himself from hedonism by what was to become a hallmark of his philosophy—a thorough rejection of ultimate ends. There are no fixed ends and no fixed catalog of goods. Even pleasure as the highest individual or social good is an abstraction. Psychologically, pleasure as such is not an objective or desire; desires are always directed toward particular objects and in particular contexts. To assign pleasure the central place in moral theory is to turn deliberation into calculation of amounts of pleasure and thus to substitute accounting for the genuine process of the forming of an end responsive to the governing problem of the situation. As above with the right, the job is not to seek fixed goods but to govern action by a design or plan. Now clearly, the construction and execution of any plan depends upon the support of the environment, an important part of which is the cooperation of others. It is not merely that we need others to help us procure our objectives and that our goals are interwoven with those of others, but that both ours and theirs have their source and take their shape in a social milieu.

Dewey sees human nature and conduct as aspects of a single phenomenon, and virtue is a constant but not always explicit correlative of the good. The self is being constantly shaped in the process of selecting ends and means and by the successes and failures of experienced goods. This is the sense of his comments on egoism mentioned above. It is not selfishness as the locus of experience, but the quality of the self that is at stake; the self involves not the usual self-enclosed individual but an individuality which is a disposition to act socially, a virtue-pattern of coopera-tiveness, whose achievement is itself a social objective. As regards the nest of problems assigned to virtue in the *Syllabus,* the questions of freedom and respon-sibility are here considerably developed. At base, Dewey's view of freedom shares much with those of Spinoza, Freud, and Marx. For one thing, freedom is not opposed to determinism but is concerned with the kinds of powers that the individual develops. Dewey and Marx stress the resources of the environment in the developing of such power, but for all of them the power is not power over people but the self-understanding and control and the knowledge which make effective planning and the pursuit of the good possible. What is thoroughly distinctive is Dewey's instrumental view of the very concepts of freedom and responsibility. Since they arise in the effort at such control, they are *prospective,* and so the notion of freedom functions regulatively in the continual making of ourselves.

The notion of obligation and right is unstressed in *Human Nature and Conduct.* What ought to be done is dealt with as the question of what is the better or best thing to do and the problems of responsibility have been incorporated into virtue and the self. The distinctiveness of obligation, however, lies in the fact that we acknowl-edge demands of others as having legitimate claims on our decisions. Perhaps duty is underplayed in this book, in part as a reaction against the generally conservative character of theories of obligation and their not infrequent elevation of obligation into a transcendent or quasi-transcendent source of morality.

Theory of the Moral Life is Dewey's most mature confrontation with the traditional problems of ethics. This is the middle and theoretical part of an Ethics coauthored with Tufts. In the first part Tufts traces the historical development of Hebrew and Greek moralities through to modern forms. In the third part they test theory in the economic, political, and social issues of the day. The second part, Dewey's own, can stand independently. It had two versions (1908 and 1932). They flank Human Nature and Conduct and the later edition ("revised" in the sense of being totally rewritten) uses the sociocultural lessons learned in Human Nature and Conduct as handles to interpret patterns of good, right, and virtue. They are now seen as working in the context of customary morality and its internal conflicts. There is, however, an important difference in perspective for, as Dewey explains, in Human Nature and Conduct he saw the moral problem "above all from the psychological point of view," while in his later work he was concerned with "action proper, with the factors which intervene, laws imposed from outside, and the question of approval and of disapproval which impede the desires of the individual."[48]

Dewey seeks the roots of ethical concepts in the structure of human nature and in the social matrix; these must provide the data or raw materials from which reflective morality takes its start and on which even the most elegant construction of moral theory must rest and to which (at least to be effective) the latter must return in a responsible functional relation.

Ethical and moral reflection about the good thus does not begin in a vacuum. There is no society so primitive or so austere that it does not provide for the satisfaction of the basic needs and desires of individuals. This requirement is a corollary of any organism's need to maintain itself and grow, while making of plans and projects is merely the distinctive way which human nature has gained in the evolutionary process to secure such growth. Yet for all this beginning in individual needs, the social context into which men are born has largely socialized such needs and objectives; we find ourselves with premade patterns of ends in nearly every situation, from what qualifies as a proper noonday snack to what is of value in work and sport. Such patterns of ends and routine habits suffice for a great part of our experience; if custom were altogether consistent and adequate (and if there were no social change) there would be no need for further reflection. However the goods which custom recommends are not always congruent, especially in times of great social tension when violent challenges may appear even in the most traditional and established objectives. But apart from that, even an individual's experience in calm moments is sufficient to illustrate the incompatibility of plans of our own making—to say nothing of the patent conflicts between our own interests and those of others.

One phase of reflective morality arises in the efforts to resolve such conflicts, i.e., to determine which goods should be pursued. To ask that question is equivalent to projecting an end. Consequences among alternatives are compared as more and more inconclusive ends are framed which attempt to integrate and organize a multiplicity of desires and needs. Highly generalized ends, such as happiness, pleasure, wealth, health, and power, come to serve as rough guides to conduct. But moral theorists, in their efforts to understand what is permanently good and what ends ought to be pursued, have historically taken the next step of ordering such ends hierarchically and proposing now one and now another good as the *Summum Bonum*. Thus we have the long tradition from Epicurus to Hobbes and Bentham. Dewey was unequivocally against such hypostatized and final goods or highest ends; it is rather the job of the moral theorists to formulate a method for distinguishing truly good projected ends from transitory ones which, should we choose them, we should later repent.

The morality of obligation and law develops out of a different aspect of the social matrix than the morality of ends, viz., the mutual adaptations—rights and duties, contracts, etc.—which living in society necessitates. This dimension speaks in the language of imperatives and oughts. Bound together from the outset as conflicting and cooperating individuals, we constantly try to mold, anticipate, and stabilize the conduct of others; thus we frame expectations and make demands on their behavior. Sometimes such claims are casual or idiosyncratic, but often they are rooted deeply in the prohibitions of custom itself—its sanctions and taboos—and are woven into patterns of reciprocal expectations. Often, too, these claims are made not on individuals as such but on classes, e.g., on businessmen, welfare recipients, or human beings, and they are institutionalized as relations between parent and child, husband and wife, citizen and state. When a system of claims is sanctioned through the intellectual and emotional assent of the group, it takes on authority; it has become *jus* and appears as the reference of law and code. These claims are not merely imposed from without, for the individual, himself a part of the social fabric, internalizes and legitimizes them as a sense of duty, thereby connecting morality with legal and political justice.

What occurs in this second dimension when the inevitable conflicts arise among rules or duties? Claims meet counterclaims. No conceivable codification could determine every case unambiguously, as anyone knows who has toyed with the Ten Commandments by conjuring up situations, perhaps bizarre, where performance and nonperformance are both enjoined. When conscience begins to negotiate with such terms as "kill," "honor," "adultery," it has passed from customary to reflective morality. Or more generally, reflection is forced by conflicts among routine rules or their inadequacy to meet a concrete situation. Once again, as with the good, philosophic theories of right, law, and obligation are simply the further and critical efforts to bring coherence into the multitude of demands on action which living in society obliges us to take into account. Dewey's objection to the classical treatments of right and justice does not fall on their insistence on the enormous importance of the dimension but only on their tendency to make the foundations of authority and justice immune from criticism and to assume that acts can be judged in isolation from one another and from consequences. The task of the moral philosophers is to look at the actual functioning of the patterns of demands and claims and to create the social environment which will make intelligent reform possible.

Now this last suggests another problem. Can the function of a legalistic system be divorced from reference to the ends or goods which it serves—or more generally, granting that the domains of good and right are independent variables, how are they to be related? More often than not the good and the right are mutually supportive and ampliative; yet clearly at the level of customary and habitual morality conflicts occur not only among goods and among obligations, but also between desires and duties. Indeed this is the theater of anguish, doubt, and hesitation. The problematic situation and the need for reflection arise most urgently in such interdimensional conflicts. And it is just here that traditional theories fail most critically, either by isolating the good from the right so as to leave no room for their interplay or else by collapsing the good into the right or vice versa. Thus they miss the serious issue entirely, viz., the need to search for a resolution of the conflict that will be responsive to the complexity and richness of moral decisions which we actually have to make. There is no absolute principle which requires that the right be preferred to the good; a man has a right to ask whether the demands against him will contribute to a good in which others like him may share. He can ask fairly if it is a claim which he should identify with his own good. Thus the question of the function and the consequences of a system of laws, its relation to the context and the problems from which it arose, the character of possible reform of the system, all revert to the problem of the good. In the long run such systems of relationships and claims can only function in and be justified by some reference to good; but note that now the reference is no longer to private goods but has become what the individual will recognize as validly the common good.

The matter is further complicated (and enriched) by another aspect of morality, viz., the cultural approvals and disapprovals expressed in the virtues and vices of a society. To limit morals to the intellectual pursuit of ends and to regulative and contractual relations is to overlook the more or less spontaneous expressions of sympathy, of self- and other-regarding affections, of appropriate resentment, etc., which add up to a sense of humanity. The most unreflective of moralities has implicit standards of praise and blame and of excellence of character and act. Yet not only are the lists of virtues which embody such excellences indefinitely long and often arbitrary, but the same act may be described either as virtuously prudent or viciously stingy and another as courageous or foolhardy. Within a society the truncated morality of commerce may conflict with standards of personal integrity, while the morality of one's own group may be at variance with that of a neighboring one. The boundaries of loyalty are vague and those of charity obscure.

Reflective morality, arising from this indeterminacy and lack of definition, seeks to make explicit the standard implicit in social approbations; while moral theories such as the eighteenth-century Moral Sentiment School go even further and attempt to ensure the consistency and adequacy of the standard. Thus Hume, e.g., found the standard of approvals to be grounded in social utility although it was expressed differently according to the needs and resources of a given society. Bentham, of course, reworked this usefulness to the common good as an objective standard, seeking to quantify it and to use it as a criterion for social reform. This illustrates the close historical relation between standards of approbation or virtue and the social good; yet the distinctiveness and irreducibility of the dimension of moral excellence is preserved in a difference which exists between ends in view, goods as objectives, on the one hand, and standards on the other. Ends in view concern projective objectives—those things that would satisfy desire. Standards look instead at acts as past or, if they have not already been done, as judged retrospectively by the approval which they would gain from others or ourselves in the role of an impartial judge. Thus an element of social meaning enters into the estimation of our own ends in view and we seek to formulate them so that they will meet the test of the approvable.

   In seeking out the standard a theory of virtue must also look behind the kind of Benjamin Franklin checklist of separate virtues: courage to be cultivated on Mondays, kindness on Tuesdays, etc. Just as particular actions must be viewed in relation to the patterns of action, i.e., conduct, so virtues must not be left as discrete and isolated character traits, but as aspects of conduct or self in action. Dewey proposes that we regard virtues as qualities characteristic of interest, rather than of the objects in which interest is taken. This use of interest relates virtue to action, for interest is the identification of the self with the activity in which it is absorbed. This may seem odd, unless we keep in mind the issue: if virtue-traits as ordinarily discussed are ruled out, then what can function in the judgment of character? Virtue is thus a style of response or, if you like, a life-style. The specific properties of interest Dewey cites are that it be wholehearted or sincere, persistent, vital, and impartial. Dewey attempts to show that the traditional virtues can be understood as special cases of these; thus a man who is wholehearted in pursuit of an objective is able to postpone distracting desires and thereby exhibits temperance and self-control. In this he preserves the traditional emphasis of virtue theories on the affective and the appreciative. After all, we all live in a network of affections; the qualities of virtue are the qualities which help us feel and assign worth in such a network.

   Right and duty can also be brought into effective commerce with virtue when they are jointly related to the good. Thus the collision between justice as rendering each man his due, and beneficence as rendering each more than his due, is averted when each is taken functionally. Persons get their due when they are given a chance to become what they are capable of becoming, and happiness or the greatest good for the greatest number is interpreted as providing the social conditions for each individual on his own initiative to share generously in the good life.[49]

Now the tracing of the three fundamental moral concepts from their relative isolation in Dewey's early ethical writings to their integration in the *Theory of the Moral Life* is not only interesting in its own right, but important as it advances or foreshadows further issues. In particular the notions of self, of conflict, and above all of good reach deeply into his social philosophy. The view of the self implicated in the account of virtue is a main access to his educational concerns. The question becomes, as with James, what kinds of selves we shall become, what kinds of careers a social milieu can open up. After all, modes of education and institutional arrangements largely determine whether selves become job-oriented or self-esteem oriented, inner-directed or other-directed, outgoing or exploitative, trusting of others or suspicious, etc.; even the alleged theoretical issue of egoism versus altruism is the practical question of how social institutions can be reconstructed so as to develop responsible and cooperative character and conduct. Growth or development of selves, not attainments, is the primary educational goal, although of course education is not confined to formal schooling.

We have also witnessed the constant enrichment in the scope of conflict and the problematic situation. It had a limited role in the early psychological papers, where ambiguity of stimulus and response triggered the search for appropriate behavior that would restore the functioning of the organism. In the *Syllabus* (and in the early logic and *How We Think*) this search is amplified by the account of thinking and the use of reason and all that intervenes between input and output in the forming of ends and more general plans. The features of the problematic situation become more explicit as the pattern of conflict takes on ideational form. Both *Human Nature and Conduct* and *Logic*, though in different ways, socialize the conflict and problematic situation, because habits are seen there as cultural forms. Social habits determine both the occasions of conflict and the forms that it takes. And the *Logic* in an emphatic way even institutionalizes the social resources for the analyzing and solving of problems. By treating moralities directly as social phenomena, *Theory of the Moral Life* shows how ethical theories arise out of conflicts in custom and customary morality. In Dewey's developed social theory, conflict, the dynamics of social process, provides an opportunity for intelligent criticism and the reconstruction of social institutions—for a liberalism that mediates between violent or destructive change and conservative defenses of the status quo.

Finally, the category of good broadens into value. As already indicated, despite the authenticity assured each domain, the good holds the leading role: Conflicts among regulative rules of right must be appraised in terms of social goods. Similarly, conflicts among cherished patterns of virtue, especially as they are extended in application or compete with emerging ones, must be appraised by the contribution to a good life which the associated institutions make—chivalry, monogamy, organization into national states, etc. Still the matter can't stop with the mere priority of good, for there are all manners of possible goods and values which themselves, to complete the story, need evaluation as better or worse.

This last provides the problematic setting for the *Theory of Valuation*: Is there a better or worse among goods and objectives which hold a rational warrant for individual decision and social policy? The nonprofessional philosopher may easily miss how sharply this breaks from the traditional way of looking at things. It looks forward to a restructuring of a situation—to a solving of a many-sided problem— rather than a backward looking to established senses of "right" and "good"; it attempts to speak to an industrial society whose technology has opened wide horizons of control and planning.

But however novel his departures, Dewey has in common with other naturalists the problem of identifying the roots of value (or good in its broadest sense) in experience. Very roughly speaking the twentieth century provided three important approaches to this problem. First there are those who emphasize the intrinsic feature of value, although wide differences separate the advocates of this view. Some, like C. I. Lewis, locate the intrinsically valuable in some felt satisfaction or goodness which is unmistakable in (phenomenal) experience. Others, notably G. E. Moore, start from an appreciation of a uniquely but objective moral property. This property, good, is not further definable and although it is nonnatural it is known from experience as are red and yellow. A second option, that of the noncognitivists or emotivists, is a spin-off from Moore's nonnatural property and the uniqueness of moral experience, in conjunction with the positivists' effort to isolate meaningful from nonmeaningful assertions. On this view, moral terms are expressive of feelings, e.g., with A. J. Ayer; they evince feelings much as a cry of pain does, or more generally, moral and valuational terms are used to persuade persons and alter their behavior. Cognitive meaning is denied to sentences such as "Stealing is wrong" because they are neither true nor false. It reinforces thereby an alleged difference between valuational statements and empirical or scientific ones which are open to proof and verification. A final and prominently exploited position is that of R. B. Perry who stresses the biological and behavioral aspects of moral experience. Value or good attaches, on his theory, to any object of interest.

Dewey's objections to these views help form the specifications for the job he thinks needs doing. The first approach obscures an adequate account of conduct especially insofar as that involves a transaction in and with an environment— Lewis's, by remaining on the phenomenal level of the experienced, and Moore's, by supposing the property to be independent of human activities. The emotivists, although providing motor and affective dimensions of action, virtually leave reasonable action impossible; they entrench the difference between taste and judgment and put morals and values on the side of sentiment. Finally, Perry, while allowing for reasonable action as well as for the affective and motor, nonetheless limits the role of the ideational or reason to mere calculation and choice between isolated, atomic objects of desire. All these accounts oversimplify the complexity of behavioral responses and work in the shadow of an introspectionist or mentalist partitioning of the faculties. Indeed it must have been a matter of some discouragement that Dewey found himself facing the same kind of inadequate faculty psychology in midcentury that he had attempted to correct a full fifty years earlier in the package of articles which included the "Reflex Arc."

The emotivists, as highly visible bearers of moral anti-intellectualism and skepticism, are the particular targets of his *Theory of Valuation*. They offend their own canons in starting out with a positivistic demand that all phenomena under discussion should be observable by resorting to a thoroughly mentalistic view of affections and emotions, construing plans and purposes alike as mental even while denying their causal effectiveness. Further, by viewing moral terms as expressions *of* feelings, they make the very error Dewey had early criticized in Darwin's explanation of emotions. And finally, even were moral statements translatable into cries of anguish, when these latter are socially conditioned they become as meaning-laden as pointing. The infant cry may initially be part of an organic response, although even then it may be informative to the mother. Yet quickly the child may learn to use such cries as signs of discomfort. Once again, Dewey makes the general point of the "Infant Language": what is to count as significant in a language depends on the function and use in a social context.

The phenomena which provide the base for valuation are desirings but not those associated with merely casual likings nor even enjoyments and satisfactions which in no way are sought or won. Desirings, in Dewey's sense, are complex since they involve not only an affective motor response but an intervening (ideational) plan or intention. The latter must grow out of needs and their diagnosis and project a solution including the means of its realization. Thus all the components in this behavioral situation are public. Dewey prefers "prizings" or "placing a value on" to suggest the complexity of the conduct and the activity which is involved. As in the "Reflex Arc," prizings arise in response to particular felt dissatisfactions conjoined with foresight of a prospective object desired or prized or valued as remedying that particular discontent. And, of course, included is some notion of the conditions or means which will bridge the passage from discontent to contentment. Thus, to repeat, desirings or prizings in this restricted sense already have an ideational, motor, and affective aspect, all operating within a complex mode of behavior. The diagnosis is not cut from the planning and the purposive, while adaptive behavior is modified as the goal is pursued. The advantage of starting at this more fully developed stage, rather than, say, mere likings, is that it allows for the patent facts of development and learning. Further, it provides an interesting insight into the old dilemma of whether we prize something because it is valuable (or desirable) or it is valuable (or becomes valuable) because we prize it. The latter makes values solely subjective, introspective, and episodic. The former leaves values independent of human activity and of relations to other properties and conditions in the situation. Putting the issue in a temporal context Dewey points out that we do not come empty-handed to any valuing; we already have a store of previously experienced values, and the problem is the projection of that experience into the future. In the reflex arc, it is functionally indifferent whether we diagnose the new case as candy or candle, or as the appropriateness of reaching or pulling back. Similarly it is indifferent whether we diagnose in terms of a value property and its connections or in terms of whether to prize-and-seek or not. The pragmatic force of taking something as valuable is to provide jointly a statement of objective relations and a rule of action which lays a claim on our behavior. And both rest on the same consolidation of ongoing experience.

Thus far it is not too difficult to follow, and perhaps even assent, to the line that Dewey is taking; the anxious step is the next one, for now he must erect the normative out of such factual materials without importing a justifying principle which is discontinuous with the valuings, e.g., an egalitarian principle of how goods ought to be distributed, a principle of justice or right in ordering goods (Lewis), or some utilitarian principle as to the worth of maximizing public interest (Perry).

This old problem has many faces: can prescriptions be squeezed from descriptions, what ought to be done from that which is, the valuable from facts of valuing? Kant had made something of a virtue of the distinction between the worlds of science and morals in his contrast of nature as subject to causal laws and man as a free subject legislating for himself under the universal moral imperative. But a stumbling block for any naturalist ethics had been raised earlier by Hume. The latter's famous argument indicated that no imperative or "ought" conclusion could be validly derived from purely factual premises (and, of course, no ought premise could be established on empirical grounds). This point dovetails with Hume's view that "morals are more properly felt than judged of," and "reason is and ought to be the slave of the passions." In these matters Hume anticipated the modern positivists' underlining of logical difficulties in the derivation; to translate (it is alleged) from scientific or descriptive statements to moral or evaluative ones is illicit—in G. E. Moore's language, it is to commit the "naturalistic fallacy." It is this assumption of two worlds, two vocabularies, two realms of experience that set the emotivists off in search of special uses of moral terms, e.g., of "good" used to express or evince feelings or to channel conduct. Of course such nondescriptions are not verifiable, true or false, not even genuinely open to deliberation. Such disagreements as exist are not resolvable on rational or evidential grounds. Now for Dewey this way of putting the matter still reflects the old highest ends of philosophy. If the problem is to search for some ultimate and validating highest end or standard at the base of morality—some ground-norm, which by its very nature could not be validated—then he has not met it; but of course he does not try. His efforts, once again, are directed toward reformulating the issue so as to avoid the impasse and deflect the search. That contemporary ethical theory should have boxed itself in so that nothing in the way of scientific method or content is relevant to the solution of moral and valuational problems, that our plans and policies are to be placed beyond reasonable decision, and that human strivings are to be "meaningless," simply bespeaks its need to reexamine the setting of the issue.

Dewey's approach flows from the full resources of his work. As in *Theory of the Moral Life,* questions of right and ought become questions of long-range goods, the normative serving to secure what is good. To ask what ought to be done, then, is to ask which among available alternatives is the better; thus one can derive an answer to the ought if one can find the answer to the better. The distinctive locus of the problem lies in decision, and so the question of the *de jure* will turn out to be the question of warrant or legitimacy of the decisions which determine plans and policy. Some of the uneasiness that has met Dewey's account of valuation is occasioned by disagreement that the issue can be so reformulated, avoided, or resolved. But more often this uneasiness results from losing sight of the shift in the problem and Dewey's decisive break with tradition. Should Dewey succeed, he has gained a real advantage in making scientific advance relevant to the domain of values and opening it to "scientific method" in his sense, i.e., the intervention of intelligence, ideas, or plans in the direction of conduct.

Dewey works away with somewhat different phrasings; the *Theory of Valuation* talks rather directly to the history just sketched while "The Construction of the Good" in *Quest for Certainty*[50] is cast in terms of the relation of the desired to the desirable as formulated by John Stuart Mill. But the message is the same in both cases.

To continue first the discussion of the *Theory of Valuation.* Given that there are prizings-valuings, they are necessary but not sufficient to establish the evaluative in the distinctive sense required. Additionally it must be possible to criticize and to order valuings as warrantedly better or worse, and for such second-order evaluations or appraisals to interact with prizings in such a way as to educate further prizings (in the old terminology, thereby converting an arc into a circuit of experience).

The problem of a higher order criticism is not too serious for Dewey; it simply parallels the question of an inquiry into inquiries. Evaluations or appraisals are like predictions insofar as they reach into the future, may be based on scientific generalizations, and are warranted just to the extent to which the situation has been examined. As with predictions, we must carry some criteria in advance that show whether the prediction has been fulfilled. So, too, we must have some criteria by which we judge whether the need which triggered the valuing has been met. Yet unlike predictions such evaluations are rules or directives of what should be done—that is to say, of what needs to be brought about by means to be provided by activity. There is thus a fundamental difference between predicting that an eclipse will occur and saying that if one equips a ship, goes to a certain part of the South Atlantic, calculates correctly (and has a little luck with the weather) then observations can be made which are worth the effort to test the theory of relativity. Our experience is replete with such rules or directives which sum past experience and establish norms or standards which are regulative on the future. There are such rules, e.g., in medicine which prescribe general directives with respect to health; and in engineering there are general principles for sound construction. Indeed, all of our generalized and abstract ends-in-view, the patterns of ends which custom provides as to economic security, political power, etc., are such rules. We even carry with us a kind of schedule or priority of interest which determines our practice. In effect, Dewey has answered the question whether we can make evaluations by showing how much of our activity is rule-determined or conforms to norms and standards. Similarly, with the question of whether such evaluations modify our later behavior. Once again, the answer lies in the patent observation that they do and not only on an individual level but on a social level as well—witness the institutions which are assigned policy-making, i.e., evaluative tasks, such as the Bureau of Standards, commissions on fair employment, poverty, and pollution.

Now what is it we are about when we make appraisals—when we make prizings the objects of inquiry? As natural events they are thoroughly observable. The conditions out of which particular desires arise can be scrutinized, as well as where and how habits (joint products of past experience and the social milieu) are breaking down. We can study the adequacy of plans and projected ends in relation to the underlying problem: have they solved it, and at what cost, were the resources and obstacles properly diagnosed? What alternatives were open and how are particular desires related to the larger systems of interest? And we can compare ends-in-view, which as ideational function to direct behavior and sequential miniplans, with ends actually achieved. Involved here is not only a feedback, but also the development of the larger systematic relations of conditions and consequences. As the original prizings studied become seen in all these relations, the meaning of the experience is broadened; the very prizings and their meanings are perforce transformed and so the educative process in evaluation is unavoidable. The extent of this education is itself a matter of experience. For the envisaged consequences become, in deliberation, the grounds or reasons for action, and the lessons they embody may be tried out as hypotheses in future value experience.

The complaints which were foreshadowed tend to be filed just here. Dewey, it is said, may have successfully brought prizings and appraisals together (in contrast to the strategies of C. I. Lewis and, as we shall see momentarily, John Stuart Mill) in ways that are truer to valuing behavior. Yet, of course, so the objections proceed, ethics has seldom been stalled on the legitimacy of technical conditionals framed relative to specific ends. The problem remains, however, of the validating criteria of *better* as regards ultimate good. Dewey, it is said, has not even broached that issue, or else he has surreptitiously intruded a value appeal to growth, maturity, or problem-solving as a highest end of his own.

Dewey's rejoinder, predictably, is to bring up the full battery of his account of the means-end continuum. He simply denies the unilateral relation of means to ends. There are no antecedently valuable ends for which means are then sought; on the contrary, ends and means are instituted in the same judgment. Like stimulus and response the division is temporal and relative. On the one hand, whatever is necessary as a means functions (at least briefly) as an end to be sought. While an end-in-view functions ideationally as a guide to conduct and the resolution of conflict, still, ends achieved or actual consequences are conditions or means to further objectives and are to be evaluated as such. And the criteria used become standards rather than ends.

It is worth underlining that Dewey denies nowhere that we work with serviceable abstract standards or highly generalized ends. Of course we do; custom, prejudice, interest, and habit bathe us with patterns of ends which we may accept uncritically and which expedite and determine practice. Yet, even when generalized conceptions operate validly by consolidating past wisdom—setting criteria to be met where problems recur, and by exposing novelty—still they are far removed from the fixed ends of traditional moral theory. They serve rather as hypotheses in science, possible solutions to moral problems; they remain challengeable and tentative rules that help decision-making. They are corrigible as they serve well or badly as means to organize and express the meaning of value experience.

Is this enough to satisfy the critics? Not altogether. Perhaps an alternate setting will prove reassuring. *The Quest for Certainty* puts the problem as one of integrating the beliefs about nature which are factual or descriptive and beliefs about value which have rightful authority in the direction of conduct. Mill put it as the relation between the desired and the desirable. The former is a *de facto* statement, while the latter is *de jure* in the sense in which it makes a claim on future action. Mill had drawn a parallel between being seen and being visible on the one hand, and being desired and being desirable on the other. His adversaries were outraged by what they charged was an illicit importing of a value conclusion under "desirable." The analogy holds only if the "able-ible" ending means "capable of . . ."; Mill uses it, they claimed, to mean, "worthy of. . . ," in the case of "desirable." Perhaps, however, Mill was simply saying that just as acts of seeing are evidence for visibility, so acts of desiring are evidence for desirability, without insisting on an easy step between desiring and desirable; clearly there are things desired which are not desirable, and even things which are not desired which may come to be recognized as desirable. In short, Mill was making reference to a kind of evidence for an objective judgment of desirability; but it is only one among many conditions that has to be met. Just as Mill regarded material things as permanent possibilities of sensation, so statements of desirability are promises of future felicities.

This argument lies at the core of Dewey's treatment of the *de jure* in *The Quest for Certainty*. He stresses once again the importance of the distinction between satisfying and satisfactory, enjoyed and enjoyable, eaten and edible, valued and valuable. But he is more concerned to develop the responsibility of the second in each pair to the conditions and the consequences which knowledge brings of the context of the first. As we have seen, the learning process constantly modifies both. It is not then merely the question of enlarging experiences; it is the question of an active experimental attitude to the desirable also, since the knowledge of conditions and consequences of the desired makes possible experimenting with the production of the desirable.

Critics of Dewey's analysis have often argued that in spite of this greater refinement, his argument is open to objections somewhat like those urged against Mill. The appeal to conditions and consequences may be relevant to increasing control, but this provides no criterion for evaluating or choosing the better among different consequences: if the criterion is an appeal to the satis*factions* that ensue, then we are theoretically back to where we started; if it is an appeal to satis*factoriness*, then we are embarked on an endless progression or a begging of the question.

Is the case of desirabilities all so different? We always have a whole background of relatively stable interests, values, value generalizations, and principles in our accumulated social tradition and personal experience, which play the same role in the determination of desirabilities that a systematic network plays in the determination of truth. What is desirable in a particular case cannot be determined without an appeal to this accumulated background, including experiences of past methods of warranting. We have notions of individual freedom, cooperative action, nonrepressive social regulation, of maturity, of liberating experience and self-realization, which are surely guidelines. Even as guidelines they are constantly being refined by new experiences, and may be reformulated and even totally restructured. In effect, Dewey's position is that what can be said about the growth of scientific method and its criteria holds likewise for the field of value. This includes even the *de jure* quality or claim on future experience. If one feels tempted to oversimplify the picture in value theory, or to demand some absolute touchstone for desirability, one should try out a similar demand for truth in science.

It is easy to see how Dewey relates to the history of ethical theories we sketched above. He is perfectly agreed with Hume that morality and value judgment take their origin in a larger than cognitive situation, one having its affective, but also its ideational and its motor aspects. He would not be too unhappy either about Hume's view that reason is the slave of passion, though (if such distinctions were to be made at all) he would surely insist on reason being rather the duly constituted officer. He is even prepared, with the emotivists, to acquiesce in the persuasive role of valuative statements, though this is a rather external function than the subject matter. Indeed so far as even science is directed toward assent, all judgments have this persuasive aspect, and with Mill he insists on the intimate connection between what is desired and what is desirable. But he is unalterably opposed to the dualism between fact and value, whether it is stated in a Kantian or Moorean or positivistic form. These and other theories in the history of ethics are themselves intellectual tools arising out of particular problems. As such, they are products of a particular age and setting. There is a conservative force which often perpetuates these theories beyond the moment when they are in genuine contact with their stimulating problems. Dewey is delightfully prepared to turn his analysis onto the contemporary theories and even his own, and to examine them in terms of their instrumental relevance and effectiveness. Thus an analysis of value theories themselves is called for both as to the conditions and consequences of their use. The twentieth century cut between the *is* and the *ought* is a feature of Western culture. It reflects strands as diverse as the divorce between technology and the humanities, between the vocational and the liberal in education, between modes of production and modes of consumption or appreciation. At least one enormous and still outstanding need of the theory of evaluation is an integration which will make the methods of science relevant.

5. Social Philosophy

It is no small achievement to have come this far in discussing Dewey with so little mention of his social philosophy and those areas of practice—law, politics, art, and education—on which his nonprofessional reputation justly rests. Properly, we should go back now to pick up the strands of Dewey's career where we left off—in the move from Chicago to Columbia—for it was in New York and in active touch with social and political problems that he developed fully the institutional outlook and the connections already established with the social sciences. The detail of these decades would carry us far beyond the limits of a single chapter, but it is critical to keep in mind that Dewey's social philosophy is in contact with specific issues. These practical concerns, which often found expression in *The Nation,* the *New Republic,* the *Atlantic Monthly,* and educational journals, as well as in books, gave his pragmatism an urban cast in contrast to the rather suburban character of the Cambridge variety.

Dewey does not extend his philosophy suddenly into the social domain as an afterthought; that is clear from all the preceding. His thought had been social from the very start. Its base lay in a social as well as an individual psychology. The fundamental category, "habit," translates readily into "culture" (as Hume's "custom" translates into "tradition"). The theory of inquiry has obvious evolutionary-social roots. And his ethics moved steadily in the direction of the social formulation of issues and problems.

But now, in insisting that philosophy is social, a special and stronger sense is intended, for on his view philosophy is, even when disguised, an effort to face the clash of inherited institutions with newer social ends. On the whole, philosophies have tended to side with and justify the entrenched positions. Even so, it has been a part of a larger attempt to understand and to accommodate to the immense forces, now largely social, which seem to determine our lives and over which we seem to have but little control. If philosophy is social in this sense, then it has a social role. Negatively, and therapeutically, it must help clear away the congealed assumptions and concepts which go unchallenged in inquiry or become dogmas so cherished that they block fresh ways of perceiving new conditions and problems. By making explicit the assumptions under which we operate, the way may be opened for realistic and experimental treatment of problems. Positively, and reconstructively, we need to distinguish between those facts which we can control and those which control us, in an effort to determine the better in the light of the fullest knowledge of how institutions are actually working rather than in terms of stereotyped diagnoses.

Clearly this socializing of the task of philosophy moves in the direction of making scientific investigation relevant. But it needs a revamping of the notion of science. For as must be altogether evident, Dewey is looking at science not as content but as method. Above all, the sciences, especially those that deal with human affairs, cannot divorce themselves from normative tasks. Thus philosophy and science share reconstructive roles. They share a method, but differ in scope.

Sometimes this method is rather ponderously billed as the method of intelligence. But in straightforward language this merely means the responsibility to make social policy and decisions in an intelligent way—to determine the better on the basis of the most informed analysis of conditions and consequences, and to intervene so as to reconstruct the present and thus mold the future to realize what is judged to be good. We hope to illustrate this genetic-reconstructive method and its usefulness, by examining it at work in legal, political, and social domains.

Pragmatism had been associated with legal philosophy since the time of the Metaphysical Club, which included several lawyers, most prominently O. W. Holmes, Jr. And "the law" and its growth was a constant model for James in his exposition of knowledge as continuous and continually changing. Dewey is no exception: legal illustrations are as congenial to him as medical and engineering ones. But his use of law was more than illustrative. The early article (1893) on Holmes's *The Common Law*[51] already showed a concrete command of legal materials, and while at Columbia he gave seminars in legal philosophy, often jointly with members of the law faculty. His concern with the legal emphasis on judicial process and the growth of law helped shape his philosophical conceptions. We have already suggested that both the notion of experience and logic may well be glimpsed through Holmes's view of the life of law as experience and not (formal) logic. Whereas the early article stressed the continuity by which old forms are changed as they face new problems, a later article, "Logical Method and Law"[52] sets about describing a relevant sense of logic (viz., the logic of discovery, i.e., of consequences not antecedents). Holmes might well have changed his dictum to: the life of law is experience as well as instrumental logic.

Holmes had helped create the climate to challenge the deductive model in law. This was a fairly pervasive kind of shift in the social field—e.g., the institutional revolt against formalism in economics and against the still powerful rationalism in political theory which derived the state from contract, will, or natural right. Holmes gives an operational definition of law as probabilistic and as predictive of the remedies that are available in the courts. Holmesian themes were expanded by the legal realists with whom Dewey was in close touch; they saw law as a continuous process or experimental adaptation of decision-making to particular cases, and they sought to make the law a more effective social instrument.

For Dewey no less than Holmes, precedent is not altogether binding. Antecedent principles are neither absolute nor authoritative; at best they suggest the wisdom to be gleaned from the past. But changing conditions will always provide cases which will not fit under the older rubrics. Logically coherent systematization of law is clearly indispensable, but it is not ultimate and is in the last resort an instrumentality for reaching concrete decisions. Divorced from this, the use of precedent is simply the inertia of concepts expressing the phenomenon of habit and providing men with a specious sense of stability and assurance.

Universal legal premises or rules are not outside of or even antecedent to particular cases, nor even something abstracted from a variety of cases, but an indication of a way cases have been treated for certain purposes and consequences despite diversity. Hence legal principles and rules are always open to review. Indeed, the legal situation admirably illustrates Dewey's expanded view of the reflex arc model: we start with a confused situation and the quality of the problem takes shape as we attempt to diagnose the situation. We need to *find* the premises and the particular fact; conclusions do not follow from premises but proceed together in one operation, viz., that of problem-solving or decision-making. Legal decision is fulfillment of what precedes and liberative for what follows.

Dewey's pragmatic method with its appeal to consequences instead of antecedent properties is well illustrated in his examination of "Corporate Personality" (1926).[53] Legal concepts do not exist in isolation, law is context-bound and its meaning is heavily laden with materials referring to the larger conceptual and social background. Instead of analyzing the "essence" of corporate personality to infer what properties it has, we need only see that "corporate personality" operationally means no more than the legal consequences of assigning rights and responsibilities. The search for an essence tends to build established interest, values, and assumptions into legal ideas. A pragmatic approach, by putting the values frankly before us, allows them to be reviewed. Appeals to corporate personality have been used for diverse and even opposing purposes. At times assigning personality to the state glorifies it while at other times the assignment to churches, business corporations, etc., is used to limit political power. It is simply a social fact that people may constitute themselves a public for common purposes, altering thereby the purposes and character of individuals; appealing to "personality" does nothing more to assure its social reality.

"Nature and Reason in Law" (1914)[54] turned to the problem of liability. The appeal to "what a reasonable man would do" to determine liability is ambiguous. It may mean what is customary or habitual in the way of foresight in situations of that kind. At other times it may mean what an intelligent man could foresee and what he ought to act on, even when the customary behavior is unreasonable. The one sense refers to the existent order (which is often thought of as the natural way), and the other is clearly normative. Dewey generalizes the point to the relations of nature and reason. When nature is considered as the existing order (including the status quo with respect to the distribution of advantages) with built-in cosmic purposes which men may discover, then intelligence at best simply reports about a rationality already in nature. But when nature is thought of as what would be rational to bring into existence, then intelligence has a dynamic role in fashioning purposes and executing them.

A pervasive theme in these articles is the functional view of legal institutions. Just as legal concepts are not isolate, so neither are legal institutions to be isolated from the many other interrelated social institutions engaged in doing the heavy work for a society. What "the law" may be doing at a particular time depends both on the kinds of strains which the social situation is making and on the jobs that other institutions are successfully or haltingly carrying out. The shifting character is illustrated by the way that whole areas of sexual morality are presently being moved outside of the law while those of charity and welfare are being moved into it. This emphasis on the institutional and sociological functioning of law he shared with others on the American scene—with Brandeis and Cardozo in their appeal to broadly social empirical inquiry as essential for proper judicial decision, and above all with Roscoe Pound in the sociological dimension of jurisprudence. But Dewey, more even than Pound, stresses the total interrelatedness of institutions and assigns a more active function to law. Law has a legitimate part not only in settling conflicts between institutions, but also in refashioning prevailing patterns. Thus it may self-consciously become an instrument of social reconstruction. This contrasts with Pound's somewhat rearguard conception, at least insofar as Pound sees the law responding to recent interests that have already emerged. In short, Pound wants legal clarification and reconciliation of vested interests, where Dewey wants institutional reform and reconstruction in the face of emerging interests.

Dewey's sense of the systematic interrelations of institutions, and of the ways they change and interact, leads to a constant concern with human interests which generate these multiple institutions and associations. In this he is like A. F. Bentley (with whom Dewey was later to collaborate) whose *Process of Government* (1908) conveyed the sense of continually changing groups as they pressure for control of policies and outcomes. Dewey approaches these questions by considering how publics are formed, which he regards as the basis even of political phenomena.[55] In contrast to pressure group theory, he stresses the growth of self-consciousness and the extent to which intelligence is essential in forging a thoroughly democratic community.

Associated living is the starting point. That needs no explanation; the issue is rather what makes for such diversity in the kinds of associations. Clearly, interaction between individuals will have more or less direct consequences to the persons involved. This is a *private* matter. But such interactions may have indirect consequences upon others of an enduring and predictable sort. Perhaps the third parties at first merely suffer these consequences, but as they become aware of them, understand their sources, and see themselves as affected for good or evil, a *public* is born. (Conflicts as such remain a private matter as long as they do not have effects beyond the conflicting parties.) A public takes on genuine shape when the recognition of a common interest leads toward concerted action and demands that the consequences be made public and controlled. When these self-conscious interests become complex and control is exercised through representatives, we have political associations. Of course the representatives exert their own impact on shaping and consolidating the interests and consequently on the character of the public. All government is in some sense representative, for no one stays in a position of officialdom without representing some interests. The question is what are the specific interests, i.e., the specific public they represent and how well? "Government," in the broad sense of determining and executing policy, is found in any association in which there is perception of consequences and their importance. There are thus multiple publics; the political (the state and its public) is but one kind of public association. While often it may be the most extensive in regulating groups, at times it has a minimal role.

Even this sketch suggests how far classical political theory misses the mark when it examines the "essence" of the state to determine its legitimate functions, or when it seeks the causal origins of the state in consent, contract, coercion, fiat, divine authority, or even intention. No antecedent principle determines the scope of political institutions. That depends on conditions and customs that prevail at a particular time, including even the kinds of tools, resources, occupations, communication, schooling, and the jobs that other associations are doing.

Even democracy as a political form did not arise from intellectual forces alone; the determinants were importantly nonpolitical and nonintellectual. Transformations which touched all living were brought about by the Industrial Revolution and scientific revolutions with their great consequences in the new forms of power and communication. These combined with other forces to destroy local or face-to-face community associations. Theories of individualism, absolute natural rights, liberty, etc., were intellectual efforts to understand social phenomena; but they were also justifications used by the challenging bourgeoisie, and they entrenched the sanctity of private property and eventually the whole laissez-faire scheme. The political forms which arose then were a joint product of a limited and fairly articulate public and socioeconomic pressures. But what purported to be analytic descriptions of the working of social life (and were surely answers to social needs) entered as forces in the social process and turned into institutions establishing the norms of that life.

Laissez-faire and individualism brought real gains in increased suffrage, elected representation, majority rule, and a greater demand for participation in social decision. On the other hand, the liberating power of the newer norms diminished as the social situation was transformed by industrialization and the breakup of face-to-face community. We are left with a paradox that an individiualistic ideology was exalted precisely when the mass of men were losing their chances to be individuals and were alienated from work, from initiative, from fruitful association with others, and from themselves. Loyalty to these abstractions, unreviewed, becomes an obstacle in confronting new needs. It enshrines distinctions, such as that between the atomic and competitive and social goods.

Dewey's whole effort to see the questions in terms of public interest emerging with private ones is designed precisely to cut the cake in a new and hopefully illuminating way, and thereby to avoid the stereotyped problem of how to reconcile individual and social relations with a dynamic and ever-changing content which then becomes a matter of empirical research rather than of definition. Dewey wants, positively, to get through to the intrinsic values of shared experience and genuine community.

Dewey is not calling on us to abandon either individualism or democracy. On his view democracy as a political form is not an alternative to other political forms, but the idea of community itself. Individualism, in parallel fashion, involves responsible participation, according to capacity, in determining the activities of one's group according to its needs. On its side, the association must free the potentialities of its members in harmony with the interests and goods which are shared. But since everyone belongs to multiple associations, this last condition cannot be successfully fulfilled except when the various groups interact supportively and flexibly. It could be as mundane as not scheduling all committee meetings simultaneously or as far-reaching as stabilizing international exchange of currency or enlisting cooperative action for world peace.

Such a notion of community is an ideal and not realizable; still, it may be regulative. Fraternity, liberty, and equality, in any really rewarding sense, are fruits of community living. Equality is not mere mechanical identity; the infant is equal to the adult in a community because each has an unhampered share in the consequences of associated action. Equity is measured only by need and capacity to utilize the consequences. Liberty is not independence of social ties, but the largeness and richness of opportunity for personal realization—the power to be an individualized self making a distinctive contribution and enjoying in a unique way the fruits of association. Fraternity is another name for appreciating those goods of association which give quality to the fabric of social relations—a feature which the contractual views of political and social relations totally ignore.

The conditions for a genuinely moral association in a community go beyond the fact of association and a public aware of the consequences of that association. A community is an association in which good consequences are shared as goods. Communication is a prerequisite, generating shared meanings. The introduction of symbols and signs to memorialize consequences shared as goods adds a totally new dimension to social experience. Technology has revolutionized the media of communications but so far nothing has changed in what we communicate. Today's newspapers, or newscasts, with their stories of murder, theft, irresponsibility in high places, and war could be the events of yesterday or a decade ago with changes only in names, dates, and weaponry.

As association is a datum for Dewey, so is the interdependence that association requires. But community goes beyond interdependence, in its ideal of the sharing of good consequences as itself a good. The intrinsic value of shared goods is a distinctive mark of human existence. The child is born into a social setting, but he must learn to be human. The appreciation of this quality of social consequences fills out the new dimension. What this entails in the way of understanding, of social relations, what they are and could be, what policies would help foster community life—all this is now an intellectual matter, and the most critical responsibility of the social sciences and philosophy. We lack even a vocabulary of symbols and signs to communicate this new dimension of feeling and awareness. But sheer misery and discontent become more manageable as social problems when diagnosed as alienation or helplessness before immense social forces which the alienated cannot control nor understand. The resultant problem is both moral and intellectual.

Involved here is the question of basic attitudes toward the forces of social change. Social attitudes were divided, sometimes bitterly, on how we are to understand such change, what problems it generates, what measures are called for, and how we are to cope with them—by resignation, resistance, steering, or even initiation. Liberalism[56] is Dewey's answer to these questions under the regulative ideal of democracy. It is contrasted on the one hand with conservativism, and, especially in the latter part of his life, with Marxism and theories of class conflict on the other.

Dewey's conception of liberalism is worked out in the concrete context of the serious problems of the first half of the century. Among these were: the contest of labor, unorganized and impoverished, with growing corporate economic power; the emergence of world wars as ways of coping with international conflicts; the tardiness of law to devise new instruments for utterly changed situations; massive urbanization and the dislocation of family and community ties; religions tied to old dogmas rather than expressing a social faith; the dichotomy of work and enjoyment, engendered by a factory system that makes men cogs in a machine and their work meaningless to them; the lack of intermediate social organizations to give voice to protest and political initiative; the despair and violence of revolutionary movements and the repressive violence of reactionary forces. And with all this there was an ineffective morality that tried to cope with inherently social tasks, such as poverty, unemployment, illness, and old age, by individualistic moral tools.

Dewey's treatment of social change applies the instruments he developed in the theory of inquiry and social psychology. Conservativism, like habits that have been hardened in the mold of past solutions to past problems, persistently misunderstands the status of its own values and their institutional embodiment by making into fixed schemes what were earlier dynamic instruments for social development.

American individualism grew in response to frontier conditions, unlimited resources (there for the taking), rural ways, and it both expressed and intensified laissez-faire. It locked into a view of the individual that had grown in the English-speaking tradition. Such a view of the self as atomic, self-centered and complete, competitive, and self-sufficient is neither correct not relevant in the contemporary world. Conservativism thus infers an unchanging human nature from a type of character that was bred under the social system of the past few centuries. Conservatism acknowledges social change reluctantly and justifies only what is possible within the existing framework of law and order. In its defense of the status quo it rarely thinks of itself as violent, because the instruments of violence are themselves embedded in its social institutions.

Dewey's critique of Marxism focuses on two major points, the dynamics of change and the necessity of violence. Dewey agrees that technological change is generating the critical problems of social development, but class struggle is not the motor power of change so much as a friction which impedes progress; it could be stayed. Dewey denies, too, the inevitability of violence as a means of social change. Thus he considers adoption of a fixed means as erroneous as the conservative's fixed goals. Such inevitability is a dogma which reckons without the role which intelligent decision might play. Still, just as conservatism has a sense of continuity and of old values needing to be maintained, so Marxism has a sound sense for greater socialization especially in economic life.

The office that Dewey assigns to liberalism is to mediate social change in such a way that the full knowledge of our conditions and options is brought to bear on social problems, thus defusing violence and destructive upheaval. The liberal attitude toward change accepts it as inevitable but also as an opportunity for growth and institutional improvement. To deal with the succession of constant problems in the modern world requires the cultivation of a liberal culture—i.e., dispositions, commitments, and habits of inquiry comparable to those to be seen in a scientific community where there are established norms for resolving problems. Such a community exhibits intelligence as a social phenomenon. There is no reason why the growth of collective intelligence exhibited in the history of science and the procedures of technology should not characterize our attitudes toward social and political phenomena as well.

The cultivation of the habits of social intelligence is an educational matter. It is not surprising that Dewey's most extensive as well as intensive treatment of social philosophy is found in this area of his work. The ideal of growth, so prominent in his educational theory, is the counterpart of the liberation of energy that intelligence makes possible in experience. And the educational philosophies that he criticizes and assesses have the same shapes as the social philosophies (and psychologies) that he reckoned with.

It is striking how many of the changes that Dewey wanted for education are central to the current aspirations for the schools. There is the continuity of schooling with the community, the interaction between the needs and the opportunities and the vocations of the society. There is the continuity of the educative process in the schools with the continuing education of people for a whole lifetime. There is, above all, the demand for developing a sense of a community with shared interests and objectives between teacher and students and among students, replacing the authoritarian model of teacher-student relations and the competitive model of student-student relations. There is the confidence that such changes would have their impact when carried into the larger adult associations. There is the pluralistic approach which saves education from being enslaved to one precut pattern. And there is the general sense of the relevance of education, not only to the work opportunities of the society as it is constituted, but to adaptability for changes in vocational structures themselves, and beyond this to relevance to growing leisure—but a leisure that is integrated with work in a creative fashion. And finally, there is the role of teachers, not as an authoritative elite on the one hand, nor as the servants of society charged with perpetuating its patterns on the other hand, but as pioneers in educating the actual interests of the inexperienced, young or old, until they generate an intelligent awareness of means and ends.

The unity of Dewey's philosophy is nowhere better expressed than in his educational views, and it is not surprising that he sometimes saw philosophy, philosophy of education, and the organization of experience as one and the same. In a famous passage in *Democracy and Education* he says:

If we are willing to concede education as the process of forming fundamental dispositions, intellectual and emotional, toward nature and fellow man, philosophy may even be defined as the general theory of education . . . philosophy is [then] the theory of education as deliberately conducted practice.[57]

Notes—Chapter Fourteen

1. Richard Bernstein, ed., *John Dewey, On Experience, Nature, and Freedom* (New York: Liberal Arts Press, 1960). See especially the editor's introduction.

George Geiger, *John Dewey in Perspective* (New York: McGraw-Hill paperback, 1964).

Sidney Hook, *John Dewey, An Intellectual Portrait* (New York: John Day, 1939).

John H. Randall, Jr., "Dewey's Interpretation of the History of Philosophy," in P. A. Schilpp, ed., *The Philosophy of John Dewey,* The Library of Living Philosophers (New York: Tudor Publishing Co., 2nd edition, 1951).

Herbert W. Schneider, *A History of American Philosophy* (New York: Columbia University Press, 1946).

W. H. Werkmeister, *A History of Philosophical Ideas in America* (New York: Putnam's, 1949).

An invaluable *Guide to the Works of John Dewey* is edited by Jo Ann Boydston (Carbondale, Ill.: Southern Illinois University Press, 1970). This was issued in connection with the massive project of publishing the complete works of Dewey undertaken by the Co-operative Research on Dewey Publications Project at Southern Illinois University. It has already made available the definitive texts for the early writings which were accessible only in scattered form and sometimes obscure places. In addition to the full program of publication envisaged, the project includes collecting materials on Dewey's work and influence.

A handy and representative set of selections from Dewey's writings has been brought together by John J. McDermott in his *The Philosophy of John Dewey,* vol. I, *The Structure of Experience,* and vol. II, *The Lived Experience* (New York: Putnam's, 1973).

Milton H. Thomas and Herbert Schneider have prepared *A Bibliography of John Dewey 1882-1939* (New York: Columbia University Press, 1939).

2. "From Absolutism to Experimentalism," in *Contemporary American Philosophy,* ed. G. P. Adams and W. P. Montague (New York: Macmillan, 1930), II: 13-27.

3. "Biography of John Dewey," ed. Jane M. Dewey, in Schilpp, *Philosophy of John Dewey*, pp. 3-45.

4. For the character and progress of Dewey's learning during this period, see: Lewis S. Feuer, "John Dewey's Reading at College," *Journal of the History of Ideas*, June 1958, pp. 415-21; "H. A. P. Torrey and John Dewey: Teacher and Pupil," *American Quarterly*, 1958, pp. 34-54; George Dykhuizen, "John Dewey: The Vermont Years," *Journal of the History of Ideas*, 1959, pp. 515-44.

5. "From Absolutism to Experimentalism," p. 16. The quoted phrases in the next pages are from this article.

6. John Dewey, "The Metaphysical Assumptions of Materialism," *Journal of Speculative Philosophy* XVI: 209-13 (April 1882).

7. John Dewey, "Knowledge and the Relativity of Feeling," *Journal of Speculative Philosophy* XVII: 56-70 (January 1883); and John Dewey, "Kant and Philosophic Method," *Journal of Speculative Philosophy* XVIII: 162-74 (April 1884).

8. John Dewey, *Leibniz's New Essays Concerning the Human Understanding. A Critical Exposition* (Chicago: S. C. Griggs, 1888), p. 242. Reprinted in *John Dewey, The Early Works* (Carbondale, Ill.: Southern Illinois University Press, 1969), I.

9. John Dewey, *Psychology* (New York: Harper and Brothers, 1887 [©1886]). Also 1891, 2d ed. Reprinted in *John Dewey, The Early Works* (Carbondale, Ill.: Southern Illinois University Press, 1967), vol. 2.

10. John Dewey, *Outline of a Critical Theory of Ethics* (Ann Arbor, Register Publishing Company, 1891), viii 253 pp. Reprinted in *John Dewey, The Early Works* (Carbondale, Ill.: Southern Illinois University Press, 1969), III.

11. Dewey, *Liebniz's New Essays*, p. 242.

12. *Ibid.*, pp. 242-43.

13. G. Stanley Hall, Review of Dewey's *Psychology*, in *American Journal of Psychology*, 1887, p. 156.

14. Perry, *Thought and Character*, II: 516.

15. *Syllabus*, cf. n. 38.

16. Perry, II: 375-76.

17. *Ibid.*, II: 501.

18. Morton White, *The Origins of Dewey's Instrumentalism* (New York: Columbia University Press, 1943).

19. James Collins, "The Genesis of Dewey's Naturalism," in *John Dewey: His Thought and Influence,* ed. John Blewett (New York: Fordham University Press, 1960).

20. George Dykhuizen, *The Life and Mind of John Dewey* (Carbondale, Ill.: Southern Illinois University Press, 1973).

21. Croom Robertson, Review of Dewey's *Psychology,* in *Mind,* 1887, p. 440.

22. G. S. Brett, *History of Psychology* (London: Allen, 1912-21), III: 259.

23. *Ibid.,* p. 261.

24. Cf. n. 4. Also, Lewis S. Feuer, "John Dewey and the Back to the People Movement in American Thought," *Journal of the History of Ideas* XX, no. 4 (1959): 545-68.

25. John Dewey, "The New Psychology," *Andover Review* II: 278-89 (September 1884).

26. *International Journal of Ethics,* 1891, pp. 186-203.

27. "Renan's Loss of Faith in Science" (1893), reprinted in *John Dewey, The Early Works* (Carbondale, Ill.: Southern Illinois University Press, 1971), IV: 12.

28. *Psychological Review,* 1894, pp. 400-11.

29. 1893. Reprinted in *John Dewey, The Early Years* (Carbondale, Ill.: University of Southern Illinois Press, 1971), IV: 37-41.

30. Cf. C. Wright Mills, *Sociology and Pragmatism,* ed. Irving L. Horowitz (New York: Oxford University Press, 1966), chap. 16.

31. John Dewey, "Interpretation of Savage Mind," *Psychological Review,* May 1902, pp. 217-30. Also reprinted in *Sourcebook for Social Origins,* ed. W. I. Thomas (Chicago: University of Chicago Press, 1909), p. 909.

32. Albion W. Small, *The Demands of Sociology on Pedagogy* (New York: E. L. Kellogg and Co., 1897). Dewey's essay is reprinted in McDermott, *Philosophy of John Dewey,* vol. II.

33. Perry, *Thought and Character,* II: 519.

34. *Ibid.,* II: 520.

35. *Ibid.*, II: 520-21.

36. *Monist*, 1898, pp. 321-41.

37. "The Psychology of Infant Language," *Psychological Review*, January 1894, pp. 63-66.
"Interpretation of Savage Mind," *Psychological Review*, May 1902, pp. 217-30.
"The Reflex Arc Concept in Psychology," *Psychological Review*, July 1896, pp. 357-70. (Sometimes titled "The Unit of Behavior.")
"The Psychology of Effort," *Psychological Review*, January 1897, pp. 43-56.
"The Theory of Emotion," *Psychological Review*, November 1894, pp. 553-69, and January 1895, pp. 13-32.
All the above are conveniently reprinted in *John Dewey: Philosophy, Psychology and Social Practice,* ed. Joseph Ratner (New York: Capricorn Books, 1963).

38. John Dewey, *The Study of Ethics: A Syllabus* (Ann Arbor: Register Publishing Company, 1894). This replaced the *Outlines of a Critical Theory of Ethics.* Both are reprinted in *John Dewey, The Early Works* (Carbondale, Ill.: Southern Illinois University Press, 1971, 1969), vols. IV and III respectively.

39. "The Psychology of Effort," p. 55.

40. Preface to the *Syllabus.*

41. Introduction to *Human Nature and Conduct. An Introduction to Social Psychology* (New York: Modern Library, 1930).

42. John Dewey, *Studies in Logical Theory*, with the cooperation of others in the Department of Philosophy at the University of Chicago (Chicago: University of Chicago Press, 1903).

43. John Dewey, *Essays in Experimental Logic* (Chicago: University of Chicago Press, 1916).

44. John Dewey, *How We Think* (Boston: D. C. Heath, 1910).

45. John Dewey, *Logic, The Theory of Inquiry* (New York: Henry Holt, 1938).

46. John Dewey, *Experience and Nature* (Chicago: Open Court, 1925).

47. *Study of Ethics.*
Human Nature and Conduct.
Theory of the Moral Life is Part II of *Ethics* by John Dewey and James H. Tufts (New York: Henry Holt and Company, 1908; revised edition, Holt, 1932). Part II was written by Dewey and wholly rewritten for the revised edition. The rewritten part is published separately as a paperback, edited by Arnold Isenberg (New York: Holt, Rinehart and Winston, 1960).

"Theory of Valuation," *International Encyclopedia of Unified Science* (Chicago: University of Chicago Press, 1939), II: 4.

48. John Dewey, "Three Independent Factors in Morals," *Bulletin of the French Society of Philosophy,* November 7, 1930. Translated in *Educational Theory,* July 1966, pp. 197-209. The quotation given comes from the report of Dewey's response in the discussion on his paper, p. 208.

49. This is largely a paraphrase of *Theory of the Moral Life,* p. 109.

50. John Dewey, *The Quest for Certainty* (New York: Minton, Balch and Company, 1929, esp. chapter 10, "The Construction of the Good."

51. John Dewey, "Anthropology and Law," 1893 (see n. 29, above).

52. John Dewey, "Logical Method and Law," *Cornell Law Quarterly,* December 1924, pp. 17-27. Reprinted in *Philosophy and Civilization,* Minton, Balch and Company, 1931.

53. John Dewey, "The Historic Background of Corporate Legal Personality," *Yale Law Journal,* April 1926, pp. 655-73. Reprinted under the title "Corporate Personality," in *Philosophy and Civilization,* 1931.

54. John Dewey, "Nature and Reason in Law," *International Journal of Ethics,* 1914, pp. 25-32. Reprinted in *Philosophy and Civilization,* 1931.

55. John Dewey, *The Public and Its Problems* (New York: Henry Holt and Company, 1927).

56. John Dewey, *Liberalism and Social Action* (New York: G. P. Putnam's Sons, 1935).

57. John Dewey, *Democracy and Education* (New York: The Macmillan Company, 1915), p. 328.

C. I. Lewis:
Conceptualistic Pragmatism

Chapter Fifteen

C. I. Lewis:
Conceptualistic Pragmatism[1]

The name of C. I. Lewis (1883-1964) lacks the currency[2] of most of the American pragmatists. Much too contemporary to enjoy a revival like that of Peirce, too technical to impress the general cultured public as did James, and too wed to the academic to have Dewey's social impact, nonetheless as a philosopher's philosopher he is no marginal figure and it is largely through his work that a maturing pragmatism undeniably joined the main stream of discussion. The vaguely tragic entanglements that plagued Peirce, the spiritual crisis of James, the intellectual reversal of Dewey find no counterpart in Lewis's progress along the (relatively) smooth ruts of an academic career. He did not even have to struggle, as did Royce, for a place in the academic compound. Basically, from speech and personal deportment to political sympathies, Lewis was a conservative New England individualist. A native of the Boston area, he was associated with Harvard for most of his life, first as an undergraduate studying with James, Royce, and Santayana, and then, after a brief spate of high-school teaching and terms at the universities of Colorado and California, he returned to Cambridge in 1920. From then on Harvard was to be the base for the rest of his professional life.

Suggestions of James's style survive in such homely examples as "Mary's baking pies," "Fred's shopping," and "Oscar the happy coelanthe," but these stand side by side with the forbidding technicalities of modal logic and strict implication. In compensation, the irritation one feels with James, whose "picturesqueness will long be the despair of philosophers," is absent; in Lewis, one scarcely ever has to search for the meaning of a term. In strongest contrast to Peirce, who shuffled systems, and to Dewey, whose mature view seems to be a single sweeping thesis stated in different vocabularies, Lewis's work is architectonic. There is an orderly march of problems, a consistent development from early concerns about logic to final interests in social philosophy. A change occurs between his first book, *A Survey of Symbolic Logic,*[3] and the subsequent *Symbolic Logic* with Langford,[4] which strengthens his interest in the calculus of conceptual or intensional relations. The problems in the second book, especially those relating to choices between alternative logics, had turned Lewis in the direction of epistemology and the need to appeal to extrasystematic pragmatic criteria for such choice. Thus "The Pragmatic Element in Knowledge"[5] lays the base for his theory of the decisional and optional character of knowledge: our ways of conceptual structuring, i.e., our categorizing and classifying, are bound pragmatically to our purposes, interests, plans, and intentions. The materials of that essay became chapter eight of *Mind and the World Order,*[6] a work that spells out the manner of *construction* of reality and the objective world. Lewis insisted that our categories, once chosen, are in one sense invulnerable to correction by experience, but that this categorizing cannot prescribe or limit what experiences we shall have. The themes of *Mind and the World Order* are elaborated into a monumental analysis of empirical knowledge and its validation in *An Analysis of Knowledge and Valuation.*[7] Its first part gives a more technical account of meaning, and then applies it to what is given in experience ("the given" being thought of as the base of both knowledge and valuation). It is Lewis's thesis that evaluations are a kind of empirical judgment, justified and verified (i.e., validated) in the same ways as empirical knowledge generally. This treatment of valuation serves as prolegomena to his ethical theory, especially as it is found in *The Ground and Nature of the Right*[8] and "Rational Imperatives."[9] Valuations, although necessary for ethics, do not provide a full morality; the latter requires something in the nature of critique generating imperatives, as, e.g., justicial rules. However the pervasive need for right decision suggests that binding rules and their critique do not arise uniquely in the moral domain. Justice and the imperatively social character of knowledge and experience lead Lewis to a brief treatment of social philosophy in *Our Social Inheritance.*[10]

It was not so much that Lewis set out to make a system, but rather that his ground plan was adequate to support the subsequent developments in his thought. The fundamental consideration always falls on justification and grounds—whether of logic, of reality and the real, of empirical knowledge, of evaluations, or of prudence and justice. Facing each of these domains in turn, Lewis focuses on common features of objectivity, generality, order-making, and critique. Yet this very systematic character of Lewis's philosophy generates problems for us. No single book can be taken as canonical. Each fits into the others, showing development but little serious alteration of viewpoint. Abridgment is difficult and, worse, misleading since the precision of the argument can seldom be reproduced in less space than the original. Further, selection of some problems, say of the ethical or empirical ones, militates against the intended coherence of the whole. Thus there is no fair alternative to a detailed (and somewhat ponderous) systematic account.

Lewis well illustrates that the Cambridge Pragmatists were Kant's children. Kant provides the setting, and Lewis, no less than Kant, constantly faced the specter of skepticism.

> Kant compelled me. He had, so I felt, followed skepticism to its inevitable last stage, and laid his foundations where they could not be disturbed . . . Kant attracted me also by his intellectual integrity and by the massiveness and articulation of his structure. The evidence of Kant in my thinking ever since is unmistakable, however little I may achieve the excellences which aroused my youthful admiration.[11]

Kant, largely persuaded by Hume's analysis of causation, challenged the metaphysical claim that a reality independent of structuring by the mind can be known. However, Kant sought to avoid Hume's skepticism by reducing the claim and the limits of knowledge. Roughly speaking, this is the setting of Lewis's attack on the problem of knowledge. Nature must be orderly (for both Lewis and Kant) because we impose the order; it is then not a question of how knowledge and perception correspond to objects, but of how objects, necessarily, conform to knowledge. Yet how can we be sure that the world constructed by our knowledge is congenial with the world apparently independent of our ordering? Can we be sure that future experience will continue to fit the conceptual categories or classificatory concepts that have been serviceable in the past? With some liberty, Kant's question might be formulated: since no one particular theory necessarily follows from a finite number of observations, how, then, do we know that Euclidean geometry or Newtonian mechanics necessarily and uniquely applies to this world? These theories cannot be falsified by experience; they are constructions of the mind, i.e., they are mind-dependent, yet they are necessarily true descriptions. But such a priori knowledge is also synthetic and empirical. Thus while all knowledge about the world is doubtless based on experience, it does not all come from the content of sensible experience; the senses furnish materials but the mind organizes these in ways reflecting its own structure. Kant never doubted for a moment that such a priori synthetic judgments exist, but he was perturbed by how they are possible, and most philosophers after him felt the same, including Lewis. Lewis wants to show that this worrisome kind of knowledge is dispensable—that the interplay of a priori and the perceptually given is sufficient to account for the probable knowledge of ordinary experience and empirical science. In effect, what Lewis does is to utilize perspectives gained in the development of the formal sciences, in particular the possibilities of multiple geometries and algebras and even alternative logics. This freedom and the need for reasonable decision give a distinctive cast to his pragmatism.

Pragmatism, as ordinarily understood, seems to take things wrong end on; it is the element which mind contributes, in truth and knowledge, which may be pragmatic; the empirical brute fact of the given is absolute datum. Logic contains no material truth; it is independent of the given precisely because it dictates nothing whatever with regard to the content of experience, but determines only the mind's mode of dealing with it.[12]

Thus Lewis accepts a Kantian view of the indispensable activity of the mind in categorizing, but sees such categorizing or classifying as decisions that are optional, responsive to interests and purposes, and corrigible in the light of growing experience. "Knowledge is an interpretation, instigated by need or interest and tested by its consequences in action, which individual minds put upon something confronting them or given to them."[13]

While this way of posing the issue is Kantian (although who counts himself a Kantian is more often a matter of sympathy than theory), still empiricism, especially that of Berkeley and Hume, provides the major obstacles and resources. Thus, Lewis, like James, was attempting to mediate a Kantian rationalism with an empiricism made wiser by later psychology and biology. (And indeed his debt to Dugald Stewart is serious enough.)

Of course, Lewis's more immediate debt was to the Cambridge purveyors of pragmatism. Peirce's "pragmaticism" becomes the equally awkward "conceptualistic pragmatism" as Lewis elaborates the pragmatic criterion of meaning into a structural part of his system. Lewis appreciates with Royce and Peirce the critical importance of technical logics to epistemology. Indeed Royce put one of the first copies of the Russell-Whitehead *Principia Mathematica* into Lewis's hands when Lewis was assisting him in a logic course at Harvard. Royce's notion of an idea as a plan of action was also to find a place, although a more naturalistic and robust one, at the center of Lewis's work. Yet although Lewis could not follow Royce to his "absolute pragmatism or his metaphysical conclusion," still his social philosophy is not un-Roycean, and in the preface to *Our Social Inheritance* Lewis acknowledges "that what is here put forward represents a direction of thinking to which I was first drawn by Josiah Royce. If my thoughts have now strayed from the path to which his counsels pointed, still I hope he might not be displeased with them."

Yet for all Lewis's involvement in modal logics and the pyrotechnics of analytic tools, his mood (at least it seems to us) is closest to the James "who had a swift way of being right, but how he reached his conclusions was his own secret." The admitted debt to James is often diffuse and implicit but, as will become clear in the sequel, the rationale of many of Lewis's key views, from the functional and adaptive role of consciousness to the richness of experience, gain power when viewed from a Jamesean foundation. What is distinctively Lewis's is the analysis of cognitive frameworks, an interior view of how knowing is corrected and justified, and the pervasive role of rules and critique.

In the following we can mostly follow the order of Lewis's writings. Section 1 discusses the base of knowledge in what is sensibly presented. This is followed by a consideration of what concepts contribute in the way of structuring. Since the separation of the sensible and the conceptual is, of course, artificial, section 2 concludes with a first tentative account of their interrelation in the construction of the world of objects, properties, and events. Section 3 tackles more directly the question of empirical knowledge and the warrant of probable belief. Section 4 examines valuation as a kind of empirical knowledge, while the final section explains the connection of right decision generally to justice and community.

1. The Sensibly Presented

Lewis distinguishes polar elements in knowledge: on the one hand there is the sensibly presented or given, and on the other there is the purely conceptual activity of categorizing and classifying. In the long run, the success or failure of his reconstruction of knowledge will rest on bringing these polar elements together, for empirical knowledge arises from their interplay—in the conceptual interpretation of perceptual content. But it is quite possible and helpful to examine the conceptual independent of content (as in uninterpreted mathematical systems) and the perceptual base isolated from interpretive appraisal. Since the latter has the advantage of being simpler to state, we shall begin with it. For all its simplicity, however, it is as fundamental and distinctive (and as much criticized) as any of Lewis's more technical insights.

Now all empiricisms, insofar as they rely on sensible experience as the source of knowledge, must give some account of it. Yet such accounts vary according to what function this "base" is to serve and to what the theorist is trying to be true—psychology, evolution, physics, etc. Some have taken the base of empirical knowledge to be protocol statements, or reports in a physicalistic language (cf. Nagel's pointer-readings); again, the base can be interpreted as stimuli of some sort; or, finally, it can be stated in phenomenal terms that attempt to capture the quality of experience. James, as we have seen, took this last option, and by emphasizing the flow of experience, its overtones, flights, and perchings, drew attention to a qualitative richness which had hitherto been ignored. Lewis also appreciates this richness of the immediately sensed and our readiness to categorize it. He writes:

All of what goes on in mind, and any content of the stream of consciousness, is in some sense a datum of fact, open to our self-conscious notice. But these items are of various kinds, characterized by qualities by virtue of which they function differently and have for us modes of significance which are different. By reference to such qualities, they are classifiable as presentations of sense, as memories, as imaginings, as feelings of pleasure and pain, as emotions. . . , and in various other ways . . . Our classification of them in these different ways may sometimes be in error; for example, we may mistake imaging for memory or even for sense presentation. But at least the clues on the basis of which such classifications are to be made must be native qualities of conscious content, there to be observed.[14]

James discredited also the notion that "ideas" or "impressions" function as block units of experience; we make conceptual cuts in the stream of consciousness, and thus have a kind of freedom to find there "samenesses," since what is abstracted as a similarity shifts according to interests, purpose, and language. For James, even the originals of spatial and personal experience are rooted in the stream of awareness. Yet there is some question, in James, as to what "immediate experience" amounts to, both as to whether there is a temporally immediate sensation, and whether sensation is ever free from interpretation or inference. Sometimes he talks about the "blooming, buzzing, confusion," emphasizing the unstructured nature of a sensibly primitive; but at other times he is quite clear that "pure sensation" is nonexistent, that what is presented in sensation (in contrast to what is constructed) is merely a matter of degree. To know that one is confronted with a red fountain pen is surely to have a more structured experience than to see a red object of some sort. A red thing reflects more "constructive activity" than the mere seeing of red. James's account of sensation, even when he is being a radical empiricist, is largely determined by psychological considerations of learning, generalizing stimuli, etc.

Lewis's interests, on the other hand, are predominantly epistemological; his concern is with the reconstruction of knowledge and with questions of validity rather than psychology. Lewis holds that there is an immediately presented or given in experience (including hallucination, dream, and illusion). It is less than perception; it is what is immediately given before any question of inference, conscious or unconscious, arises. This is the "brute fact element in perception, illusion and dream." The given, the just presented, then, is much less than the lawyer's correction of a witness: "Don't say you saw him sign the will; say you saw him mark a piece of white paper." "White paper" and "mark " are, of course already classificatory notions which also carry more interpretation than Lewis wants to assign to the merely given. The given is just what "appears"—the looking-round, tasting-sweet, feeling-painful. It is what the most hardheaded astronomer and the most gullible citizen "just see" when they report UFO appearances. It is whatever there is in sensible experience that cannot be altered by our willing or displaced by our interests or thinking. It has no other certification than simply its being an indubitable character of experience, and claims no authority beyond that.

Even the attempt to describe, name, or classify in language perforce fails insofar as language imports categories and structure. The language of appearance here is expressive—i.e., presentative rather than representative. (We shall see later that this expressive sense is not the equivalent of expressing or giving vent to emotion.) It may convey a meaning, but any attempt to encapsulate such experience linguistically is distorting. Perhaps we feel this gulf between experience and its linguistic dress most strongly when our aesthetic enthusiasm or the burden of our sympathy makes words seem inadequate to convey the experience. This poignant gulf between experience as reported and simply as had can never be bridged. Lewis is more concerned than James with the giveness of the stream; yet even before experience is broken into and named as an object, property, or event, it must already contain within it such boundaries and disjunctions as attention may afterward make explicit. What Lewis is attempting to identify is just that aspect of experience that the activity of the mind cannot create. It is the seeing divested of all believing; it is the uncontrollable element which is not corrigible and for which we are not responsible.

Clearly a host of problems arise, even beyond the patent ones involved in reporting—viz., to mention, or even to notice introspectively, is already to categorize in some fashion. These problems are reflected in the many casual as well as penetrating objections that have been made: Is there really any such item as an isolatable given that is completely unstructured by knowledge or prior experience? If the experience of the given is unique, how does it come to play a role in repeatable and recognizable qualia, the generalization of stimulus and response that is essential to reliable expectations of future experience, learning, and reasonable action? Can such experience be certain and yet error be possible? Finally, if one is to distinguish between the given and the conceptual, then what is to serve as given for knowledge of the mind's operations?

Lewis addresses most of these problems. Strictly speaking, the given is the philosopher's abstraction; it is in experience and cannot literally be said to be before or antecedent to conceptual structuring. There is only a limited sense in which it can be said to precede interpretation, and that is when a new interpretation is offered, or when a correction is made. It is not a psychological state; no correlation with neural processes is intended for, among other things, finding pleasant or fearful may qualify as given along with the awareness of the sensible. Lewis grants that "givens" may be repeatable, as stimuli are generalizable in animal behavior, and further that they may include associations and passages of experience. He intends an epistemological not a psychological category, and on his own terms such immediacy is inarticulate. It is not even necessary to assume that there ever is a moment of immediate awareness without interpretation. Sometimes, most austerely, it is simply a theoretical primitive.

> This given element is never, presumably, to be discovered in isolation. If the content of perception is first given and then, in a later moment, interpreted, we have no consciousness of such a first state of intuition unqualified by thought, though we do observe alteration and extension of interpretation of given content as psychological temporal process. A state of intuition utterly unqualified by thought is a figment of the metaphysical imagination, satisfactory only to those who are willing to substitute a dubious hypothesis for the analysis of knowledge as we find it. The given is admittedly an excised

element or abstraction; all that is here claimed is that it is not an "unreal" abstraction, but an identifiable constituent in experience.[15]

Lewis restated his general position over a period of thirty years as his adversaries changed from Bergson, Holt, and Santayana to Reichenbach, Goodman, and Chisholm, but without substantial alteration. Indeed, the point is so direct there is not much that could have been changed. Many others, such as Russell, G. E. Moore, and Carnap, also debated the character and reportage of basic sensible experience, but their problems generally had a different setting and different motives. Lewis ruefully complains that the point he wants to make is so obvious that "it gives him pause that anyone should contest it." Suppose a chemist is carrying out a series of color titrations, and a single report is out of line with all the others; the experimenter will never be in a position to say that that color experience was not such as reported (although he may be justified in ignoring it). Similarly, if a piece of ice is placed on a blindfolded boy's hand in a hazing and he is told he is being branded, he may later realize that he should have felt coldness instead of a burning sensation, but nothing learned can retroactively alter the quality of experience as felt; it is incorrigible and forever beyond recall. Charges of inconsistency, which would be telling in a set of judgments or observations, are not in point. The given *as such* carries with it no objective claim, it promises nothing as to future experience, it raises no expectations and is not predictive. At best it can only be expressed (atrociously) in phenomenal terms—"looks green," "tastes sweet," "feels good." As merely experienced, these givens or takings cannot be in error, and therefore, although cognitive, strictly speaking they are not knowledge. Of course, there is all the distance in the world between such "green-patch-here-now" reports and the objective claim "This is green." Objective claims about properties or events or objects are empirical judgments, predictions which can be confirmed or infirmed, although all time cannot establish them as more than probable.

The importance of the givens, or better "takens," lies not in their presentedness, but as they are used as signs or clues of further passages of experience, as so-called terminating judgments. These take the form; if a sensory cue is given, then, under certain conditions (including conditions provided by action), other experiences are to be expected. These last experiences, upon which the success of expectations and predictions ultimately depend, also share some of the characteristic of givens. It is their recalcitrance that helps distinguish between what the mind can alter and that before which it is helpless.

The sensibly presented is private for much the same reason that one cannot adequately convey the quality of a color or taste to someone lacking the appropriate sense. The taste of apple pie is as ineffable as my enjoyment and as (strictly) unsharable. Yet what is sensibly given determines only in part and ambiguously what interpretation we shall put upon it; it sets the problem for interpretation rather than determines it uniquely; a loud noise may trigger either a belief that there is a burglar in the house or that a car has backfired. Interest, purpose, as well as habit and context always figure in what inference we make from the sensibles. Yet if there were no presented or given, thought would be contentless and arbitrary; without its intransigency, if all were of the mind's own making, there could be neither truth nor error in judgment nor could there be success in prediction or action.

The motives for this sharp distinction between what is sense-presented and what is objective knowledge belong to themes that run deeply through Lewis's philosophy; but above all the distinction helps him to respond to the skepticism that would follow the grounding of knowledge in a merely probable base. If the structure of empirical knowledge cannot build on certainty somewhere in experience, then empirical knowledge would not be probable but only probably probable. Indeed, major critics of Lewis have not so much attacked his position but argued that this kind of sensible certainty is dispensable. For example, Reichenbach makes his peace with probabilities and Goodman replaces givens that are certain and irrevocable with "initial credibilities."[16]

2. The Conceptual

General Statement

The success of Lewis's epistemology will finally rest on how well he interweaves the sensible with the conceptual, i.e., with what the mind contributes in the organization of experience. Such order-making activity can be studied in isolation, much as was done with the sensibly given. Yet the same caveat is required: the purely conceptual is also an abstraction, a product of analysis, but it is a "real" abstraction locating an identifiable ingredient in knowledge. The problem is Kantian (the categorizing of experience), the mood is open and Jamesean, but the theory is distinctively Lewis's with all the niceties that technical philosophy can provide. Perhaps Lewis was wrong in supposing that he alone among the pragmatists interprets the Kantian categories as optional orderings or conceptual devices relative to our interests and purposes, for we have already seen that James took long strides in that direction. For both Lewis and James, concepts or classifications establish likeness classes which introduce stability into what would otherwise be a chaos of sensation. Not only can we "mean the same" and "know that we mean the same" despite the uniqueness of every moment of experience, but also there are alternate ways of constructing such stabilizing "sames" or conceptions. Still Lewis differs from Kant and even from James in insisting on the pervasiveness and dynamic character of the mind's constructive capacity. He assigns the same kind of dignity and authority to reason that Kant does, but unprecedented is his view of the mind's legislative capacity, its talent for construction, critique-making, and self-correction and self-understanding. It is because we construct alternative conceptual patterns that we are able to elect the better fit to our experience and to our world. And because we construct, criticize, and choose the structures to order experience, ethics no less than logic, epistemology, metaphysics—indeed, philosophy itself—are normative critiques.

The key to this aspect of Lewis's philosophy lies in his analysis of meaning and its relation to intention. Philosophers have sweated mightily over meanings: what kind of things are they, how does something get to mean? English permits us to speak of the meaning of a symphony, of the *Guernica,* a dream, or a baby's cry. A red sunset means rain, a sallow or jaundiced complexion means illness, and a red light means stop. There seems to be no shred of univocality to these; even when we restrict ourselves to linguistic entities and discourse, which Lewis tends to do, there is no lack of bewildering complexities.

For Lewis, meanings are the fundamental cognitive phenomena; they are antecedent to language, and function as "criteria in mind" or rules, which determine, and are not determined by, syntactic relations. There would be meanings even if there were no linguistic expressions at all. Successful thinking must conform to the actual connections of meanings. Meanings are fixed, not only independent of language, but independent even of particular contexts. There are, of course, conventional elements in the choice of concepts to attend and the symbols we fix to express our meaning. Still there is as intransigent an element to meaning as was ever to be found in the given; this lies in what our meanings entail—in what the decision to use them in a certain way commits us to. Thus there is doubtless liberty to use any term to designate squareness or redness, but there is no equal freedom to relate squareness to rectangularity or redness to color.

There are many passages that suggest that meanings are entities with some special ontological status. But in his more tough-minded moments Lewis insists that, although we may inwardly observe what we mean and know meanings without reference to their application to things, still they are not to be reified as a kind of object. They are not special sorts of things, different from sensible presentations; they are rooted in a primitive kind of behavior in which some qualitative aspect of experience, generalized, is taken as a cue or sign of further experience. The aroma of the perking coffee in the morning is a sign of the taste of the coffee, and, for that matter, of the toast and butter to come. Linguistic signs are themselves surrogates for something more elementary in our experience; the meaning relation arises where anything stands as a sign for something else. Doubtless we share this kind of experience with animals generally: the dog who hears the leash's rattling takes it as a sign of a promised walk. However the peculiarly human mode of responding depends on assigning an abstract symbol to represent what is absent, thus "means," in Lewis's theory, is equivalent to the Jamesean "point to," "lead to," "represent," or "call to mind." When the thing anticipated actually comes off (later called a terminating judgment), it may be said to be verified. And, finally, when such patterns of expectation/confirmation are established, they become cognitive or belief attitudes, prepared modes of response, unreflective habit. Lewis, as a matter of fact, always adds alternatives for his ontological-sounding interpretations of meaning. The only ontological status needed for meanings is that kind of existence which still undiscovered theorems or unused numbers enjoy. Even the critical "criteria in mind" merely operationally requires that we know in advance, i.e., have some criterion or rule, for the applicability of a term or the appropriateness of a meaning. Lewis's sympathies are most certainly not behavioristic; perhaps he lived too close to Skinner in Cambridge, but he almost always provides a behavioristic alternative to the interpretation of meaning. He even offers a rather Jamesean view of the mind as constructed and inferred.

Indeed, once we become immersed in the subtleties of analysis, it is easy to overlook Lewis's deep reliance on biology, psychology, and evolution. He never appeals to these for internal questions of validity or evidence, but when it comes to external questions—the reasonableness of the search for cogency, for the role of knowledge in conduct—the pragmatic background shows. Even logic must ultimately answer to pragmatic criteria of utility.

We need to look somewhat more carefully at Lewis's claim that meanings are independent of their linguistic dress. Many hard-headed philosophers are unhappy about appealing to meaning to explain anything, since it seems to create more problems than it resolves. They would rather stay with language, indeed often with utterances that are public and observable. Lewis, of course, is not denying the importance and intimacy of the relation between language and meanings, but it is meanings that stand in initial critical need of clarification. If we sometimes feel that we don't know what we mean until we've said it, even more often we are aware that our words have failed to carry our intentions, or that others, perhaps legitimately, have interpreted our sentences contrary to our intentions. Further, changes in meaning are often out of phase with changes in vocabulary. There is even a sense in which the meaning of a term changes with each new application, e.g., when we extend "pillow" to include Oriental wooden head-rests. And of course ancient terms, such as "nation" and "right," "force" and "matter," "disease," "war," "universe," and "civilization," express radically different concepts now from those they expressed a bare hundred years ago.

Further, it is sometimes thought that words are the minimum units of meaning. But "un" and "able," "pose" as in "expose" have identifiable meanings. Grammarians and philosophers have been interested in terms that denote or name as a primary function of meaning and have supposed that other categories such as adjectives, prepositions, adverbs, etc., have no meaning except as they modify (in the sense of change) other terms in a context. But for Lewis all expressions including "if," "them," "a," have meanings in the sense of applying or naming. Traditional grammatical categories are often casual, the result of historical accident, and are ill-adapted to the analytic needs at hand. In any case, they are not the only ways of classifying; e.g., the fundamental distinction between substantives and predicates may itself be a matter of degree—after all predicables such as verbs apply to or name states of affairs. Prepositions such as "in" apply to any case of "being in" and thus signify or apply to a relational property. The important point here is that if these constituents had no firm and fixed meaning independent of a particular context, they could not contribute anything to a context. Orthodox grammar is mistaken insofar as it suggests that terms modify in the sense of change, other terms. Red does not change "rose," in "red rose" but modifies in the sense of limiting it; it would really be fairer to say that each of the constituents in a complex expression modifies the whole of it rather than one or another element. In addition to the meaning of the constituents, subtle differences of meaning depend upon the syntactic relations carried by order, etc.—e.g., the difference between red rose and rose red, halfback and back half.

Perhaps the consideration that most urgently sets Lewis to clarifying the modes of meaning is the fact that we can mean—and know that we mean—importantly different things by the same sentence or by sentences of the same form. Let us look at the following.

All police cars in Philadelphia are blue.
Countries friendly to the United States are democracies.
All slum dwellings lack hardware (euphemism for "plumbing").
Euclidean triangles have angles that sum to 180°.
Men die when bitten by vipers.
All swans are white.
All swans are birds.

On the one hand we may intend by such sentences (at least those about governments, slum dwellings, white swans, police cars) to express generalizations, that is to say, we learn by observation that the observed cases of one class belong to the other class. However, we might also intend such statements definitionally or prescriptively, registering thereby a decision not to name or classify anything that does not qualify by the criterion offered, e.g., to qualify as a swan a thing must be white. We are not here concerned with the way a particular example is identified; we are concerned with the difference between definitions (prescriptions) and generalizations (descriptions). The difference is readily seen when we ask what would be required to falsify such a statement. When the sentence is intended descriptively it is falsified or disconfirmed by a counterinstance, e.g., a slum dwelling with hardware or a green police car. When meant prescriptively, however, sentences will be held in such a way that they cannot be falsified by observation, i.e., nothing will be allowed to count as a counterinstance.

A host of interesting issues are involved. Clearly if we saw a car that was green but in every other respect like a police car, we should happily give up the color as a criterion. Perhaps it would cost us something more emotionally to admit that friendly countries are often dictatorships, but even that maneuver is possible. While the lack of plumbing has systematic connections with other inadequacies which generally are associated with slums, still, it too could be given up. (Of course when the viper's bite did not poison St. Paul, some thought he was more than human, but others would resign the generalization that the snake's venom is always lethal.) In the same line of ascending reluctance it would cause enormous difficulties in Euclidean plane geometry to regard the sentence about the sum of the angles of a triangle as anything other than a prescriptive use of words, unfalsifiable by any instance. (Of course the alternative among geometries may thereby be enlarged.) Yet the point remains that for a sufficiently .obdurate person, the decision to use any of the statements prescriptively need not be withdrawn. We shall see in the sequel that Lewis will rely heavily on analytic sentences; e.g., "all swans are birds" and "red is a color." These seem to be true by virtue of our intended meanings; indeed, a nonbird swan and a noncolor(ed) red are virtually inconceivable. Only the most bizarre alterations in our habits of thinking could allow these to be taken as generalizations. Even so Lewis seems quite clear that what is an empirical matter and intended as a generalization in one context may serve legislatively in another, and conversely. Indeed this freedom to develop in either direction is critical to learning. In the last analysis which decision we make is a pragmatic matter. Generalizations may be corrected by experience; definitions are not falsified but may be abandoned or repealed on grounds of disutility. When what is meant depends on experience, on finding actual instances to confirm or falsify, the mode of meaning is called *denotative*. Where no experience is allowed to falsify, i.e., where the decision is independent of what is actual, the mode of meaning is called *connotative*. As we shall see (at great length), Lewis insists that no inquiry at all is possible without some connotative or intensional element. This is the broadest distinction among the modes of meaning. To put the matter more formally, the denotational aspect is that "which is significant of the reality purported, to which we are able to make adjustment by our classifications." The connotative (intensional) is significant "of a classification made and of a criterion in mind which is the cue to this classification and the determinant of cognitively guided reaction."[17]

Nothing in the above suggests that we do not continually learn more about what is implicit in our meanings. Furthermore the distinctions themselves are aspects of cognitive apprehension in general separable by analysis but not independent of one another in any final sense.

This distinction between denotation and connotation and a further one (within connotation) between sense and linguistic meaning can be illustrated somewhat roughly by an example. A child can learn correctly to name as toys all such items in his playroom. He then has learned the denotative meaning of the term "toy." Of course this is a relatively unimportant achievement, except to the immediate family; the important talent is the further ability to apply the term to as yet unexamined and unobserved cases, that is to say, to all things that may be consistently and appropriately called "toys." Now of course a child, in the enthusiasm of a new word, may apply it indiscriminately to all new things, but the fact that a child uses a term incorrectly does not necessarily mean that he has no criteria in mind, no rules or generalizations from past experience. Things being what they are, he might have confused "toy" with "plastic article." What has happened in this case is merely that he has not generalized in a standard way. Great social pressures, arising from the needs of communication and a common world, lead us toward conforming our language and our criteria to those of others. Still there never is any way of being sure that the criteria we have in mind are the same as those of others. But the important talent is the rulelike ability to move from a limited number of cases to future and unobserved ones by this "criterion in mind." (As suggested above it would not matter to Lewis whether this criterion in mind is interpreted mentalistically or behavioristically as evidenced by the child's ability to extend the term to those and just those objects that are toys.) What is important is that we can do this, and presumably have some kind of meaning or rule operating in advance of possible identifications, and in terms of which we apply or refuse to apply the term. There is an old problem here as to whether the possible is as meaningful as the existent. But this is exactly the contingency for which Lewis is attempting to provide; there are always rejected plans or possible alternatives that could apply but don't. Criteria are not completely specifiable even in ideal cases. But if we did not have some criteria in advance and independent of experience, we should not recognize when a plan is fulfilled or criteria satisfied.

A child ultimately develops a third talent, viz., to give verbal criteria; here we could say that he has a criterion in mind of applicability, but in this instance it is of application of terms to other terms. Of course a child, or an adult, may be able to use criteria for new cases without being able explicitly to formulate them; and doubtless, we all know people who can give the words and the proper linguistic relations without being able to apply them. Many a beginner in chemistry can define a substance correctly without being able to identify it in the laboratory.

This example suggests a difference between denotation (i.e., the identification of the actual toys in the playroom) and two aspects of connotation. The sense meaning is the criterion of application in mind by reference to which we can apply or refuse to apply a term correctly to unobserved and unexamined objects. The linguistic meaning may also be regarded as a criterion in mind, but in this instance it is explicating one term by means of others, or explaining a statement by means of other statements. These criteria must, however, in some sense be knowable in advance and capable of being applied to unobserved or possible cases. Since neither of them is limited to actual cases, they are not denotative. These aspects of connotation may be put more accurately and elegantly: Linguistic meaning is constituted by the "pattern of definitive and analytic relationships (some might call this syntactic) of expression or word to other words." It is thus an intensional meaning in the sense that what a word means can be given in other words, and a statement in other statements. Sense meaning, on the other hand, is a criterion in mind "of sense representable characteristics by reference to which one is able to apply or refuse to apply an expression to presented things or situations (actual or imagined)."[18]

Linguistic meaning can be exhibited as a pattern of analytic relations—either in terms of the kind of systematic relations that are available in abstract deductive systems or in terms of some relation like synonymy. Its utility is clear in the powerful methods developed by logic and mathematics. Syntactic structures can be isolated from interpretation and the formal relations examined—of validity, of the relation between theorems and postulates, of transformation rules, etc. The truth that such elaborate logical patterns exhibit has a kind of certainty and finality which is generated solely through modes of distinguishing and relating. Yet not only deductive and analytic systems have such character, all concepts possess this kind of truth insofar as they are precise and their relations are worked out. Thus all concepts, even where their meaning is merely linguistic, exhibit a pattern of relations.

A further importance of linguistic meaning lies in its relation to communication and to community. We have already suggested that we can never be sure, in the example of the child's naming objects as toys, that a new case may not provide a clue to the fact that we lack common criteria. A stronger way of communicating meanings to an adult is obviously to give a definition in terms of other words, i.e., something in the order of a dictionary definition. But even then we cannot be sure that we share anything in the way of sensible experience. Indeed, the privacy of experience, and its noncommunicability, have been the grounds for doubting that common knowledge is possible. But this privacy doesn't really matter. An hour that may be long and tedious for one person and swift for another, nonetheless can serve as an appointed lapse, or for a meeting. In this sense, a mile is the same length to the weary as it is to the young. Even a color-blind man may deal effectively with color words, for what is communicable is the network or relational pattern of our concepts. What is sharable is the conceptual structure—what we indicate by red, hour, or mile is a place in the structure. My red might be your green, and, though it is unlikely, my pleasure your pain, my appreciation of a musical composition totally different from yours, but this might never be known so long as our behavior, including verbal behavior, is compatible. Community or understanding between two minds depends not on identity of sensation or imagery but on "the patterns of logical relationships set up by these inter-connected definitions of terms [which] constitute the conceptual meaning of the terms defined."[19]

The structure of our common world is not given, it is won. Of course Lewis supposes a commonality of interests by virtue of biological similarities and common social needs, but even this is unnecessary, for we can and do surmount our idiosyncrasies by concepts that are definitive for both of us. Such coincidence of patterns of meanings is a condition for cooperation and cooperatively purposeful behavior. This point about the social has a parallel for an individual's knowledge. For, as we shall see, the stable world of objects and repeatable events which an individual gains on the basis of what is presented in experience is also an intellectual construction or achievement. Even in this case knowledge is of conceptual structure alone. "One idea is 'sign of' another in the order of nature. If it be a reliable sign—i.e., if it bear constant and orderly relationships—one empirical quale is as good as another to serve this function of cognition. Knowledge of the empirical world consists of relations between one item of experience and another, not in the content of experience somehow matching the quality of an external real."[20] Nevertheless each of us must provide some sensible interpretation. It is then both our sensible interpretations and a structure which are jointly necessary to create an intelligible world.

Lewis illustrates linguistic meaning by reference to a kind of Arabic dictionary which contained no pictures (but presumably a sufficient clue to the grammar of Arabic). Then a scholar lost on a desert island with such a dictionary might pass his time by determining the relation of all elements of Arabic sufficiently to see the full and circular pattern of the definitional relations in the language yet not know in an obvious sense the meaning of any word whatsoever. The scholar would know the linguistic meaning, but without some way of connecting this language by pictures or by someone's pointing to objects, he would never be able to make the connection between language and the relevant nonlinguistic item.

It is exactly the reference to what is sense representable which linguistic meaning omits. A blind man, like the scholar, can understand the linguistic meaning of color terms, communication of a sort and exchange are therefore possible, but the sense meaning is precisely what both lack. The sense meaning provides the criterion by which we are able to apply the expression to what is presented or imagined in things or in situations.[21] Thus, sense meaning is a rule or a prescribed routine (test) together with an imagined result, which determines whether the term is applicable or not. Such criteria must be known in advance, because otherwise we should not recognize anything nor have any sense of when anticipation is satisfied. In other words, sense meaning is rather like a plan; we must know what our intention is in advance, when we are following the plan, and whether it is fulfilled. Of course miniplans may be included in more comprehensive ones. The use of such plans or rules enables us to know, e.g., what a chiliagon is; for though we cannot imagine it clearly, we can imagine the procedure of counting the sides of a polygon up to a thousand. Some imagery may generally be necessary but a clear-cut image is unnecessary. Similarly, we can look for toys, cuff links, or tigers in India lacking precise or explicit criteria, but our behavior suggests that we are operating with criteria and a rule. Indeed, we may reasonably look for cuff links and tigers, and for a solution to a problem, even though none exists. Thus sense meaning, insofar as it includes possible cases, is not denotation. Yet the ability to use language referentially clearly depends on this kind of rulelike behavior. Sense meaning is the backbone of Lewis's version of the pragmatic criterion of meaning and his account of verification. The sense-meaning of "This copper is malleable" is the total set of predictions (i.e., test operations and anticipated consequences) that would have to be true to confirm it. Thus sense meaning provides the critical connection between what is mind-legislated and what is sensibly presented. It is psychologically and cognitively derived from sensuous criteria of recognition; what is sensibly given signals other experiences and we use language to represent such order. This is no linear matter, for the analytic linguistic patterns give a dimensional structure to our knowledge. Indeed the usefulness of linguistic patterns lies "ultimately in the guidance of the sense-recognizable so as to conform to our intentions and make them consistent."[22] Either sense-meaning or linguistic meaning can serve as a starting point. Definitions must express criteria of application: "we must define our terms conformably to our applications of them; and we must apply them conformably to our definitions."[23] Definitive conventions may not be bound by antecedent fact but they are resolutions prescriptive on future observation. But which patterns and definitions are to be serviceable will depend on experience. Learning depends on the mutual adaptation and correction of sense and linguistic meaning.

Modes of Meaning

We now face a need, all too common in philosophical writings, to explore two different themes simultaneously. On the one hand, we should follow sense-meaning and its robust role in the act of interpretation through which the conceptual net *attaches* (in the sheriff's sense) the qualitatively given to yield empirical knowledge. On the other hand, we must plunge into the elaborate distinctions which fill out Lewis's analysis of meaning. This latter is important, for it clarifies the relation between meaning and what is analytic. This being the more technical, we shall (in Puritan fashion) tackle it first; but we shall also (in a manner that the Puritans might not approve) condense its import at the beginning of the next section.

Lewis is here concerned with that which the mind alone contributes to knowledge: the familiar problem of the analytic and the a priori.[24] We are going to explore the ground and nature, and validity of such truth as the mind contributes independently of experience. Classically, analytic truth has been defined alternatively as that which is true by virtue of meaning alone, or that which is true by definitions and the principles of logic. Lewis's strategy is to show that the second, properly understood, reduces to the first. Traditionally, a priori judgments are those which can be determined to be true or false without any reference being made to experience. Lewis argues that the analytic and the a priori coincide—that is to say, the truth which is mind given, which is true necessarily, which is certain, "has no reference beyond the cognitive act" itself. This leaves no place for a priori synthetic judgments.

To understand the relation of analytic truth to meaning, somewhat finer distinctions are required than were made above. The broad distinction between denotation and connotation will be preserved, but the latter needs to be analyzed further into intension, signification, and comprehension.

It is principally terms which have meaning. Terms are expressions which are capable of naming or applying to some actual or possible thing. As we have seen above, the denotation is the class of all *actual* things to which the term applies. By contrast, *comprehension* is the classification of all possible or consistently thinkable things to which the term would be correctly applicable, whether they are actual or not. (Lewis introduces the term "classification" to refer to possible classes.) Comprehension is thus the wider notion, since the actual world is obviously only one among possible worlds; but the converse is not necessarily true since there are possible worlds which are not actual. Terms like "centaur" which have obviously a comprehension (you would recognize one in a possible world if you met it) are not without denotation, but their denotation is zero.

The *signification* of a term is that property in things whose presence indicates that the term correctly applies, and in whose absence the term does not apply. Signification thus constitutes the necessary and sufficient conditions for applicability, though it does not of course guarantee that the term will actually apply to something. The *intension* of a term is the conjunction of all those terms each of which must be applicable to anything to which the given term is correctly applicable. Thus nothing would be correctly nameable by "gorgonzola" unless it were also correctly nameable by "cheese" and all the rest of the familiar gorgonzolean properties.

There is an interesting reciprocity between comprehension and intension, for the wider the intension the narrower the comprehension, and conversely. Thus the comprehension of "red-cheeked" may include both apples and children, but if we increase the intension by adding elements of meaning—e.g., "red-cheeked blond children"—we have considerably decreased the comprehension. The term "round square" has zero comprehension because nothing at all is consistently thinkable with it. But surprisingly enough it will also have universal intension; for wherever "round-square" is applicable, every other mentionable attribute will also be applicable. (The paradoxical air of this is somewhat eased if we remember that the zero or null class is included in every class.) Again, if we take a term with universal comprehension, such as "being" or "entity," which applies to all consistently thinkable things and cannot be defined by other terms since it would thus be limited and exclude some things, we may infer that such terms have zero intension, for to add them to anything else leaves it unchanged, showing that no meaning is added thereby.

Above we said that terms are the principal units of meaning. Lewis regards a proposition as a complex term. Thus the statement "Fred is buying groceries" is a propostion plus an assertion. In effect, Fred-buying-groceries is the propositional term, and it may be denied as well as asserted, or questioned, doubted, believed, prescribed, exhorted, or hoped for. The proposition is the kernel or content of meaning to which the attitudes of assertion, denial, etc., are attached. Treating the proposition as a participial phrase will later furnish Lewis with a weapon for insisting on the cognitive character of ethical judgments. It also helps him to get a purchase on the complex character of such statements as "I believe that Fred is shopping'' or ''I know that etc.'' whose truth-value is not a direct consequence of the truth or falsity of their component propositions.

A proposition signifies a state of affairs. It is critical to distinguish the denotation of a proposition which is the real world, i.e., the total state of affairs, from its signification which is only some attribute of the real world. The comprehension of a proposition is any consistently thinkable world which would incorporate the state of affairs it signifies. Of course we could never know the truth about the world, indeed we could not even know the whole truth about any object. But we might know the limited state of affairs, for it does not exhaust either reality or the infinite specificity of an object. The intension of a proposition ·is the totality of its deducible consequences which taken together exhibit its meaning discursively. Two propositions will have the same intension, then, when whatever is deducible from the one is also deducible from the other.

The same kind of reciprocity exists between intension and comprehension as existed for terms. Once again the interesting situations here are the limiting cases of null and universal, or zero and one. Since what propositions denote is the real world, 1 and 0 will represent truth and falsity taken in an extensional sense. (This is the ordinary truth-functional analysis of material implication.) But Lewis's concerns are also with intensional properties of propositions, which are different and distinct from their extensional ones. Thus he is interested in deducibility and strict implication, as we have seen, rather than derivability and material implication. As intensional properties 0 and 1 betoken logically necessary relations. On the one side will be propositions with zero comprehension and universal intension; on the other, propositions with universal comprehension and zero intension. The former are analytically false (in Lewis's terms necessarily false) propositions; the latter are analytically true (necessarily true) propositions. Lewis thus has a mode of identifying analytic statements by way of his theory of meaning. Zero intension does not mean that analytically true propositions fail to have implications, but only that they can entail only other analytic propositions which in turn apply to any consistently thinkable world. Being true of any possible world, they do not, however, distinguish the actual world, and therefore can impose no restriction or limitation upon it of a sort that could conceivably be dispensed with. Thus what is analytically true connects with the discussion above of the a priori, the purely conceptual or what the mind alone contributes—those legislations or decisions addressed to ourselves but which can determine nothing of what is actually true of the world.

Lewis here provides a tool for identifying analytic statements by intensional criteria, and of separating what is analytically true from what is analytically false, and both from synthetic propositions. For synthetic propositions in contrast to analytic ones have an intension and a comprehension which is neither zero nor universal. They entail some things and not others; their truth is compatible with some possible worlds and not others; they are deducible from some propositions but not all.

This property which distinguishes analytic statements is not, of course, sufficient to distinguish between such analytic statements as "All cats are vertebrates," "Iron is a metal," "Squares are rectangles," and "Felines have spinal
cords." For they all have that property. But obviously the statements about cats
and felines share a commonness of meaning which neither does with the rest, nor
the rest with one another. To get to a more serviceable account of meanings, one
closer to what the ordinary speaker and his own account of meaning above require,
Lewis has to take a finer look, not at the property of the expression as a whole, but
at its constituents. This latter he calls an analytic meaning of an analytic statement.
The argument is complex, but it requires in the end that the constituents and the
syntax be analytically comparable for expressions that are to be declared equivalent. This, of course, amounts to a direct appeal to intensional meanings, and to
the classic notion that the concept of vertebrates is contained in the concept of
cats.

Such analytic statements, when explicit, clearly require that all cats are necessarily animals, or by definition cats are animals. That anything is a cat strictly
implies that it is an animal or finally it requires that no nonanimal cat be possible.
In effect, whatever confirms something as a cat simultaneously confirms it as an
animal. We can see here the relation to the earlier discussion of meaning, for the
criteria or rules which establish the one carry along the other. Thus it is clear that
these explicitly analytic statements assert a relation of intensional meaning.
Explicitly analytic statements assert a necessity and deny an impossibility. And to
deny such statements must turn on the modal or necessary and possible elements.
Lewis's notion of strict implication furnishes a distinctive logic for dealing with
such problems.

There are several consequences of this discussion to be noted. In the first place,
the Kantian hybrid category of a priori synthetic judgments would seem to be
unnecessary. With their removal, the a priori and the analytic coincide because
both now are determinable by meanings alone. The a posteriori and the synthetic
also coincide because they are what is not thus knowable in effect, both are now
empirical. We are working out commitments which we ourselves have made by
our intending to mean. Once again, such meanings guarantee nothing about a
particular world, but only what is consistently entailed by our own meanings. The
grounds for the validity and certainty which explicated definitions have depend
solely on the consistency and the activity of the knower.

We need to look at a final classic alternative, that analytic truth is certified by
definitions and logical rules of derivation of what can be deduced from them. That
is correct enough, but it puts the cart before the horse for it begs the question of the
grounds by which definitions are accepted. The only test of the validity of rules is
provided by showing that they are analytic of intensional meanings. There are
certainly arbitrary and decisional elements in definition. For example, there is
freedom in what symbols we use and what we shall bother to classify or pay
attention to. There are also different ways of defining, as, e.g., a stipulative

definition. But what is involved here are explicative definitions in which it is alleged that one expression is equivalent in meaning to another. Given that meanings are independent and antecedent, then we here come up against facts, although facts of meanings, which are altogether coercive. Given the normal senses of red and square, it is no decision of ours that the meaning of red includes the meaning of colored, or that if something is a square it is necessarily a rectangle. Even in the case of stipulative definitions, though we can stipulate to our heart's content—e.g., a relation of 1/2 to 1/3 which yields 2/5—but we cannot force this into the pattern of significant arithmetic relations.

Such explicative definitions are tautologies but not of course in the sense that they are superfluous to make. The whole historical development of mathematics can attest to the difficulties of making explicit what is implicit in our meanings. This process can include genuine discovery as to what our meanings commit us to in their interrelations.

The general considerations about explicative definitions apply to logical rules as well, for logical constants have definite meanings, and it is exactly their meanings which certify some relations and operations as valid and others as not. Thus one who knows the meaning of "all" and "are" (and knows how to wield the syntax) would know the validity of the syllogistic form "All a's are b's, all c's are a's, therefore all c's are b's." Similarly the meaning of "implies" gives logical laws and rules of inference. In fact a whole logical system can be seen as explicating the meaning of "deducibility" and "derivability." It is analytic truth justifying such modes of valid inference, as illustrated in the case of the syllogism, which certifies the truth of logic. In a sense the rules of logic are heuristic—aids helping us to reason correctly—which would be unnecessary if we knew all that was implicit in the relational patterns of meaning.

Lewis believes that there is no need to appeal to a priori synthetic propositions. Once again the situation depends on the relation between criteria of applicability. We can know by a test in imagination whether one set of criteria includes or necessarily entails another. It is because our analyses may sometimes be faulty that we mistake what is analytic for a synthetic proposition; but clarifying what we intend by our meanings is sufficient to distinguish what is knowable by meanings alone, what is necessarily true, from that which depends on experience.

The Construction of the Real

We now return to the themes put aside to pursue the technical questions of intensional meaning and their connections with logic. In the previous section we discussed what was true by appeal to meanings alone; here we shall exploit the resources of sense meaning to take the first and tentative steps to an account of empirical knowledge. There are two directions. One, which the next section will fill out, works from the sensible to the conceptual. Our immediate concern here focuses on the reverse process, of how the conceptual "attaches" the sensibly given. (These are but two emphases, not two different processes, because knowledge arises in their interplay at every point; e.g., to go from sensible particulars to generalizations already requires rudimentary concepts that have attached the sensible to them.) Thus we are dealing now with the interpretive act—in Jamesean terms, how the conceptual cuts into the sensory flow to create and construct the world which we know as the real one. To put it somewhat differently, and in fact in Lewis's terms, how the conceptual net gets spread so as to capture sensible experience; how from the multitude of possible worlds the *real* one is selected.

Lewis is coming to grips here with the question Kant had raised as to how the autonomous order-making activity of the mind should find an independent world necessarily responsive to its orderings, its concepts, and classifications. To answer this Kant needed a priori synthetic judgments, and it is the legitimacy of these that Hume and his empirical successors had jeopardized. Lewis is attempting to connect the conceptual and the perceptual without resorting to this hybrid kind of judgment. Even if the argument in the previous section is persuasive—that a priori synthetic judgments arise through a confusion of analytic and synthetic judgments —this merely clears the way for a new handling of the issue. Can it be done without a metaphysical assumption of correspondence, thereby sidestepping Hume's challenge, and still stay clear of a Berkeleyan phenomenalism? It is at least worth mentioning in this connection that Lewis sometimes sees himself as extending the Common Sense Realism so long a part of American philosophy. Realists wanted to establish the relation of knowing and intention to a world whose objects are independent, yet they could see no way then to avoid the relativity of knowledge to the knower. Lewis tries to show that independence of the world is not incompatible with such relativity.

Much of what Lewis has to say about these matters has already been suggested above and the rest follows easily. Conceptualization, classification, and definition are necessary. Like rules in general these are constraints imposed by fiat or choice. Just as one cannot start a game without preliminary rules, nature could not even be interrogated without some classification as to object, properties, events, etc. Such rules, being optional, will generally have alternatives. Conceptualization is independent, not because the mind anticipates a harmony or correspondence between its ordering and the world, but because it prescribes nothing at all about it in entertaining a meaning. The conceptual represents no operation in the world of things (although, of course, inference, intentions, beliefs, as activities of subjects, are natural events).

Now the clearest cases of purely conceptual constructions are the formal structures of logic and mathematics. Logic, e.g., needs only definitions and logical rules to build the elaborate logical pattern of abstract terms; these patterns can be looked at abstractly, i.e., independently of any application and without denotation. These conceptual patterns must answer to the requirements of consistency (and presumably some sort of congruence or interconnectedness), but they are not falsifiable in or by sensible experience. Arithmetic thus is not threatened by the nonadditive ways that the volume of gases combine, nor that a male and female rabbit do not long add up to two. In making such patterns the alternatives are only limited by our ingenuity.

Thus all conceptualization—not merely mathematics and logic—including the most general categories of the real, thing, good, matter, property, as well as low-ordered concepts, like penny, red, table, share something of this model. They are embedded in patterns: they are all criteria or rules of classification and applicability in sense-representable terms. From a purely conceptual point of view these are patterns of linguistic meaning. They are legislative decisions addressed to ourselves; strictly they are not falsifiable in experience because they prescribe nothing about reality beyond the ways we shall view it. Thus we may know that if X is a dictator he must have such-and-such characteristics to satisfy the requirements. That refers to a brute element which is copresent with the conceptual and is in the long run what empirical knowledge must be true to.

A great deal of freedom of choice and alternatives is lost when we come to say what applies to the real world, when we try to cut out from the logically possible worlds which is the real one. Such efforts at application do not mean that we give up the prescriptive and legislative character of concepts, nor that they are any the less categorical decisions taken in advance. Application remains always hypothetical, tentative, and probable only. This holds not only for the reality of golden mountains or a golden nugget in an undiscovered mine (favorite philosophical examples), but also for applied mathematics. To assign an interpretation is to make the whole system synthetic and probable. I may know with certainty that *if* this is a Euclidean space, a triangle will have angles which sum to 180 degrees; but nothing can make it more than probable that this particular figure is a triangle nor that this space is Euclidean. Similarly I may know that *if* something is a peck it will fit in a bushel; but nothing I can do makes it more than probable that these apples make a peck.

Thus in addition to criteria of consistency, simplicity, etc., cogency must now be added as a criterion of empirical knowledge. In good pragmatic tradition, the utility of knowledge is in large measure determined by its serviceability as a predictive instrument.

The distinction between the real and the unreal is a most general and critical category which organizes perceptual knowledge. This is a paradigm of how the conceptual stabilizes the welter and chaos of sensible experience. We claim that this is a real penny, that the table is objectively square, that this action is truly good. On Lewis's view these already are constructions and show the imprint of the mind's activity. Thus it is not the world of objects and things, but the raw materials of such a world which we selectively order and construct into the reality as we know it. In effect, the sensibly presented, the now givens in sensation, are these raw materials. Knowledge of even the simplest of properties or objects, like the penny or roundness, embraces more than mere *qualia;* and whatever is more than that is mind-contributed. The qualia themselves are thoroughly unstructured and cannot provide their own categories of organization. The sensory locks into some conceptual pattern which connects and relates one item of experience with others in a systematic way.

It is often overlooked how much content is imported by additional premises or interest. Illusions and hallucinations, prime examples of what is unreal, are "real" in some contexts. Thus, e.g., what we see may be a mirage or an illusion, what we feel may be a psychosomatic pain, and we may be disturbed by a hallucination. Still these are, for some purposes, all real dreams, real illusions, and real pains. Further, paths of particles and theoretical entities are real in one sense, though they may not be in another. There is no danger at all that we shall find something which is inconceivable, for everything conceived is real in some context. Experience will conform because principles of interpretation state criteria of reality of a given sort. We know in advance that if what we experience does not fit, then we are free to repudiate it as unreal in that category. In any case, intelligibility is at best a matter of degree.

Now the patterns of organization are not just simultaneous, but have a temporal spread. It is this way of organizing experience which allows a presently given to become a sign or to be significant of what is not now present; in effect, to anticipate or predict further experiences. Thus to say that a table is square is an objective claim which puts a tax on the future. It summarizes a set of predictions. After all, the retinal image made by a square table is seldom square (perhaps only if one is under or over the table). The judgment shorthands a series of orderly experiences —if I walk around it to the right or approach it, it will visually alter in predictable ways. That the table is square entails a set of if-then expectations—operations and their consequences which would confirm the table being square if carried out. All naming and classification are similarly predictive; verification and interpretation are temporal processes. These expectations are parts of the meaning of the table being square, are taken in advance of an experience, and thus are in some sense true no matter what eventuates. They cannot coerce the future, they can only prescribe that if this is a square table, certain further experiences will follow. The expectations are fulfilled or not, independently of our will. Thus a meaning may not be falsifiable in experience, but it must present its credentials as useful for our anticipations and our actions. A fruitful concept proves its mettle by serving as a reliable guide.

The stable character of conceptual patterns and theories does not mean that we are committed to them eternally. Sense meanings are themselves products of experience which grow in a succession of meaning-replacements. In a way sense-meanings change by each application which extends the denotation, rather like the growth of common law. Doubtless the names of fundamental categories such as "mind," "real," "property," "thing" may remain, but their filling is clearly responsive to the growing sophistication of our knowledge and science. As with James, categories can change under the pressures of enlarging and novel experience, through the discovery of inconsistency and inadequacy and in response to the claims of economy, elegance, simplicity, and generality. Lewis faces again the problems of alterability and learning that James addressed, and he, too, is impressed with the increase in science. But Lewis deals more cautiously than James with the replacement of old truth by new truth. Of course empirical knowledge develops through the increasing scope of generalizations and the addition of new information through experiment and test, but there remains the sense in which a theory, if ever true, is eternally so. Euclidean geometries are not falsified by later geometries; the same holds for the phlogiston theory. If it were ever true, in the sense that it comprehensively organized a body of evidence and served predictably, it is always true relative to the data. (The alternative to this would require us to say that no scientific theory is now true since each day brings its further evidence, exploitable relations with other theories, and sometimes radical revision.) Lewis's concern was to show that not all of science and learning develops by the introduction of new facts. Indeed he uses to good advantage the history of the Copernican revolution and its replacement of Ptolemy. Doubtless the controversy at the time seemed to be over matters of observation, but later it became clear that matters of convenience and simplicity dictated the generalizations which state the phenomena. "Theoretically, if any system of motions is describable with respect to one set of axes, it is also describable in terms of any other set which moves with respect to the first according to any general rule."[25] Concepts may be self-consciously abandoned on pragmatic grounds but often they seem to slide into new meanings as they find places in new contexts, say the changes in "metal" which electrochemistry brought with it.

But alternate conceptual systems, large or small, and the need for choice opens the way to corrigibility. Experience, the classification of phenomena, and the discovery of law grow up together, being tested against one another. Indeed, in the very last analysis, it may be that the differences between a prescriptive or analytic statement, in contrast to descriptions or empirical generalizations, may be a matter of context.

Thus it is that we are all pragmatists, but, as Lewis says, "in the end and not in the beginning." The pragmatic element lies not in the brute fact of the given, but in the a priori and conceptual. On the whole, the application of conceptual systems is a matter of trial and error. We may try on hats in a store, and when one fits, put it on; or perhaps better, we can establish criteria for membership in a club—we can require the candidate to be a Republican truck driver with a passion for bird watching and caviar, but our initiative cannot fill the category with instances.

Not merely science in its historical development, but the conceptual systems which throughout the whole of our social history have organized the thought of successive ages, carry Lewis's point. Each age, as it were, has its own cognitive map with fundamental presuppositions, which are only infrequently explicit. Each acts, in effect, as a copartner in the theories in different fields in the given age. Thus the notion of a natural order in things in the Greek world, of a divine order in medieval thought, or of the Chain of Being in the eighteenth century underlies their theories of man, morals, and politics no less than their physics.

In the long run, truth is responsive to human need and bent; our interpretive categories are initiated by need and interest, the categories of logic as well as of justice. They are made by the mind but they are forged by and tested in experience.

3. Validation: Verification and Justification

We now have before us the ingredients which are needed to account for empirical knowledge. The preceding section, taken largely from *Mind and the World Order*, stressed perhaps unduly the way that knowledge and science grow by the abandonment of one conceptual system through its replacement by another hypothesis or theory. In any case the *Analysis of Knowledge and Valuation* tempers (although it does not fundamentally change) the account of empirical belief as knowledge by examining the roles of both the sensibly presented and the conceptual network in the corrigibility which is so critical for the enlargement and progress of knowledge.

Common and good usage makes many reasonable claims for knowing. It must be certain, true, and grounded as distinguished from what is false as well as groundless. Yet factual knowledge (or belief) is always incomplete in some sense since learning and correction take place. Finally it is assertive, i.e., it must intend or cognitively refer to something beyond what is merely mental. Because all of these requirements cannot appropriately apply to knowledge at the same time, Lewis undertakes a painstaking analysis of kinds of knowledge. As we have seen, analytic knowledge, although certain, true, and grounded, need intend no reference beyond itself. The given as such is also certain in the limited sense of promising nothing beyond itself, yet is self-certifying, requires no grounds, and cannot be in error. Lewis, in contrast to James, disqualifies it as knowledge proper although it enters as a part of cognition. Empirical knowledge will preserve groundedness as well as reference beyond the mental state, but certainty will be sacrificed, for it is always incomplete. Thus the issue becomes in what sense can uncertain or probable empirical belief be justified, i.e., be truly knowledge.

Traditionally the Rationalists have been concerned with justification and have looked for a logically secured relation—generally deductive—between grounds or evidence and conclusions. In consequence, they are reluctant to accept the merely probable as genuine knowledge. They want a warrant for a hypothesis antecedently to its trial by experience and thus find it difficult often to incorporate the lessons of trial and error. Empiricists (including some Pragmatists), on the other hand, are quite comfortable with probable knowledge, the world is hazardous. Yet, concerned with prediction, they may forget that verification follows judgment and put forward verification as though it were the whole of the story overlooking thus the grounds upon which the prediction-hypothesis was based. Frequently they ignore the difference between a well-grounded prediction that fails to be verified from a groundless one that succeeds—between, e.g., the weather bureau's forecast of a hurricane (which fortunately fails) and a child's expectation of a fair Fourth of July (which happily comes off) based merely on the fact that a picnic is scheduled. And skeptics, holding that knowledge can never be certain, suppose therefore that it can never be genuine; but there is a valid difference, which Lewis will attempt to show, between probable beliefs which are rationally credible and justified, and those irrational ones that are not.

Like James before him, Lewis regards the critique of knowledge as multidimensional, although where James had spoken loosely of verification, corroboration, assimilation, and validation, Lewis clothes these with great precision. Validation is the broadest category in the assessment of knowledge and justification and verification are its two faces. Verification is predictive and forward-looking; it formulates our expectations of the testing which will verify or falsify them. Justification looks, rather, to the warrant or rational credibility of these expectations prior to their testing. Time thus forces an absolute distinction between these two; a prediction once tested is no longer a prediction, having exchanged its credit for cash. "If I eat these peppers, I shall get indigestion" as a prediction will probably be verified. Were my interest limited to verification, I might continue testing by eating peppers and doubtless find the prediction verified again and again. Yet the success of the first prediction may hopefully leave me wiser in the ways of peppers and my digestion, thereby saving me the pain of further testing. Such utility is an important function of knowledge and learning. Knowledge is cumulative—I can and do embed the success and failure of today's predictions in the grounds for tomorrow's better predictions. This raises the question of justification for each prediction is warranted (or not) relative to a particular base; this base constantly changes, and hopefully improves, as the results of predictions accrue. Yet the ground for any possible prediction, antecedent to its test, is independent of what eventuates on that prediction. The prediction was either warranted or not; that warrant cannot be modified by the future truth or falsity of the prediction. This relation between grounds and prediction is a logical one, and as we might expect it will be a version of strict implication. Of course, a later prediction must reflect in its grounds the lessons learned by prior experience and verification.

Lewis's account of these matters suggests that he, like James and Dewey, was working with a kind of learning or feedback model. That we learn from past experience is scarcely an issue; this capacity we share with animal behavior generally. That knowing and believing are cumulative temporal processes involving action also needs no defense. What is distinctively human is how we learn from past experience; i.e., by self-conscious criticism and normative assessment. We tease out lessons implicit in our reflective judgments, those actually made, and formulate these lessons and principles as rules of critique with which to face the future. We have already seen that logic, as the critique of consistency, is normative in the sense that it is seeking in such rules the justification of commitments. What is here at stake is a critique of cogency, the search for the warrant or rational credibility of empirical beliefs as knowledge which must always remain incomplete and probable.

Verification

Prediction and verification already presuppose a conceptual system at work. Lewis, giving a general schema for them, appeals to two kinds of judgment—terminating and non-terminating. (Reference has been made to the latter in discussing sense-meaning, and to the former in discussing the given.) In terminating judgments the sensibly presented as such is not critical to knowledge, but rather its role in cuing an interpretation, i.e., its functioning as a sign of a belief—e.g., a visual appearance of white may signal that this is a piece of paper before me. Prediction is now in order, since the belief implies further expectations which must test positively if the belief is to be credited as knowledge. The tests (and their consequences) in good pragmatic tradition constitute the meaning of the belief, or equivalently, the sense meaning provides the required tests. Schematically:

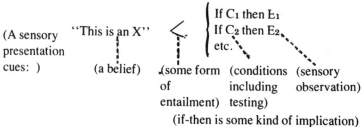

(if-then is some kind of implication)

The non-terminating judgment expresses the meaning of an objective belief as constituted by those operations and their anticipated consequences which would provide evidence for it, i.e., when tested would verify or falsify it. This is of course Peircean, but Lewis explicates in detail the relation between the belief and the relevant tests. The latter are analytic consequences of the belief and the relation between them is not empirical but the intensional relation of sense-meaning. It will be recalled that sense-meaning provides sense representable criteria or rules of applicability; we entertain such meanings without reference to particular occasions and must know in advance implicitly, if not explicitly, what tests and criteria are relevant. Otherwise we should neither recognize the evidential character of a test nor even that a prediction was verified when we made the observations. Since the actual tests which might be carried out to support a belief are inexhaustibly many and reach indefinitely into the future, objective beliefs can never be decisively verified and thus are appropriately called "non-terminating."

In contrast, terminating judgments are particular predictions or expectations which either come off or fail and thus may be verified or falsified decisively. Thus, a grainy-looking surface may suggest or signal that if certain conditions obtain a feeling of roughness will ensue. Terminating judgments are represented in the schema by: "if C, then E." Strictly speaking, terminating judgments ought to be stated entirely in expressive language, such as "rough feeling," "yellow looking," etc., since they are phenomenal and deal with passages of qualitative experience only. They make no claim about objects or events, not even that there is a piece of sandpaper.

In one sense there is the widest of gaps separating terminating judgments reporting phenomenal experience from the reality claims of non-terminating judgments which include the full range of objective beliefs from "This is a (real) piece of sandpaper" or "A penny is round" to Boyle's laws. But there is a continuity in experience too, for the ultimate ingredients' of non-terminating judgments are just those particular testings to be found in terminating judgments. These latter in Lewis's work have more or less the same role that atomic sentences, protocol sentences, or observation reports play in other philosophies. However, they differ in their dynamic character. Lewis of course is not insisting that every empirical statement must encounter sensible experience directly; there will generally be numerous intermediate statements (lower-order non-terminating judgments) which are themselves only indirectly verifiable. Nor is this distance from the sensible a defect, for on Lewis's account knowledge is not linear but systematic. Even the metaphor of cognitive map is too flat and untrue to the density and multidimensionality involved in the ramifications of a belief.

Beliefs, after the manner of James, are storage houses consolidating past experience. We share with animals the fact that a sensory stimulus may directly cue further passages of experience. But distinctively cognitive, or human, behavior depends upon the way a sensory cue locks into a conceptual system linking the consolidation of the past with what is anticipated and (with foresight) may be planned for. While Lewis has been orthodoxly pragmatic in identifying the meaning of a statement with the operations which establish it, he is here carrying the pragmatic program further by developing both the logical and the psychological account of the internal structure and processing of knowledge which James had hinted at in his talk of assimilation and corroboration. In so doing, however, Lewis is storing up problems which will force serious revisions in the neatness and simplicity of the general schema or model which we have before us. Yet such modifications will at least allow him to approach the complexity and tentativeness of knowledge as we know it. The avenue of approach to these modifications is by way of an examination of the internal economy of the terminating judgment, both the conditions (C) and the if-then relation between the conditions and experience (E). Later we shall have to look at the impact of these modifications on the analytic relation of sense meanings, i.e., at the logical relation between the objective belief and the relevant operations so critical in Lewis's account of the pragmatic criterion of significance.

The occurrence of an experience (E) depends on a fair number of conditions (C) being fulfilled. Thus a grainy appearance may not lead to a rough feeling if the sandpaper is rain-soaked. Or to speak of an objective belief, if carbon dating tests are run in the shadow of a great hospital, the anticipated readings may well be disturbed because of radiation. Properly, the conditions would include all the observable circumstances of the testing, including the state of the apparatus as well as its location, the procedures employed and even the state and competence of the observer. But a critical part of the conditions are contingent on human actions. No terminating judgment, indeed no expectation whatsoever, is entirely predictable without reference to the testings which activity may supply and alter. In the case of the sandpaper the kind of resulting feeling depends on my reaching out, touching, or pressing, i.e., If I reach, touch, or press. It is important to note that Lewis describes the activity, insofar as it enters in the terminating judgment, also in phenomenal terms; it is the *sense* of reaching, etc. which constitutes the conditions specified.

The reference to action in the terminating judgment is only one part of the active character of belief; in its case, if the analysis of a belief involves what would happen on my acting, the holding of the belief carries implicit dispositions to action under those conditions. The utility of making reliable terminating judgments derives precisely from their hypothetical form, from their contingency relative to my actions. Thus from the clouds in the sky I may anticipate that if I carry an umbrella I shall stay dry. It is even clearer in scientific inquiry: if I go to the proper location armed with the proper instruments I can (probably) observe an eclipse. In some cases, however, the point of knowing what would happen is precisely to inhibit the testing and thus to avoid the consequences. Thus the point of knowing that if I were to eat peppers I should experience pain is to protect me from the experience. In general then, the activity implicit in the judgment is set in the wider context of the funtional activity of belief itself as a guide to action. The translating of categorical prediction of objective fact into hypothetical conditionals of action makes belief useful by enabling us both to bring about what is valuable and to avoid the ills that, but for our foresight, would result. The tragedy of our situation lies not in our inability to act nor even in our inability to envisage alternative possibles, but in our ignorance—i.e., in our lack of sufficient knowledge about *if-thens*. "Both the theoretical and the moral significance of knowledge can be justly phrased by saying that what an objective fact means is certain possibilities of experience which are open to realization through our action."[26] Put with a rather different emphasis, "what is signified by the possibilities of experience which we find open to our action, is the world of objective fact" which is generally beyond our power to affect or alter. "But knowledge would not be something to be won, or valuable when obtained, if the objective fact implied categorically the experiences in which it may be verified or confirmed."[27]

The analysis of the if-then relation in the terminating judgment raises a serious problem. Is it, Lewis asks, identifiable in our logical armory? It is captured neither by logical deducibility nor strict implication since they are purely logical and make no connection with experience. Nor will material implication or formal implication do. While these make contact with experience and would allow for generalization over actual cases, still they are too weak, as is generally recognized, to support contrary-to-fact conditionals. We want to insist that not merely if I eat the peppers I shall be ill, but that if I had eaten the peppers I should have been sick. Our sense of an external world and of objective facts involves a belief in such contrary-to-fact conditionals. The nexus intends an empirical or real connection, i.e., that my action is causally related to the consequences. If logicians have not succeeded in characterizing the relation, the problem is not disposed thereby but only set. We shall return to Lewis's own contribution later in the discussion of induction.

Whatever the analysis of this real relation may eventually turn out to be, a commonsense and philosophic requirement is generality. The generalization of stimulus and response makes learning possible. It is because the sensory stimulus is repeatable, because responses are ways of acting and because anticipatable experiences are recognizable as kinds, in short because terminating judgments are generalizable for all like situations, that we can learn from the past, that whatever is sensed can become a sign, and that sense meaning and objective beliefs can be validated by sense experience.

Of course the nature of this if-then relation as representing necessary connections between matters of fact has been a perennial philosophical concern, and it has led to the challenging of the certainty of empirical knowledge. Lewis takes account of the more modest claims of common sense. Our world is not shattered nor our trust in experience completely destroyed when our expectations are not fulfilled unexceptionally. Silver may occasionally fail to adhere to glass without the need to rehaul the chemistry of mirror-making completely. A Mexican bus may occasionally be on time without altering our confidence that it will probably be late. Too often it is supposed that generalizations from past like cases must either always support beliefs about future or unobserved cases, or else that such beliefs have no validity. Lewis reduces the claim. He requires only that the connection be probable. The most that we can require is that some experiences be related to others with some reliability, i.e., that their connection be probable. This of course constitutes an emendation in the initial account of terminating judgments. A terminating judgment should now be read: if C (including the conditions of action), then *probably* E.

Introducing probable for certain as one of the qualifications forces significant emendations in the model of empirical belief. It is not merely that we do not expect the failure of a single test (or trial) to falsify a well-entrenched belief but simply to reduce confidence in it; but neither do we generally take a single successful test (trial) as verifying but only as confirming it. Even more subtle matters are raised when account is taken of various weights of the tests. The force of these matters will arise later in connection with "congruence," the mutual support that different parts of a cognitive structure lend one another. At the moment it is sufficient to note that a test has greater weight as the probability is high that the expected result will fail to occur if the belief is false. Generally a failure is less decisive a disconfirmation since it is unlikely that all tests will run in the same direction. Thus a diagnosis of malaria may be correct even when some tests are negative for some symptoms often mask, change, or exaggerate others. There are many further asymmetries between verification and falsification; a crucial experiment may weigh more heavily on one trial than a host of confirming but relatively insignificant or redundant tests. And where a belief is deeply implicated in the structure of a theory it is not easily surrendered even under the pressure of many disconfirming tests.

Of course, the pervasiveness of probability and the uncertainty of empirical belief have been implied all along. From the outset non-terminating judgments were said to include inexhaustibly many terminating judgments reaching indefinitely into the future, and thus full verification even in principle would be impossible, though the belief remains testable. To this was added the further problem that the terminating judgments were conditionals suggesting not only that there are some tests which are not carried out, but also others which could not be carried out because alternative tests are done in their place; e.g., a particular sample of butter if melted for one test could not at the same time be frozen for another, yet we have definite beliefs about what it would have done if we had frozen it instead. As noted above, the utility of knowledge (and that lurks in the background of pragmatic theory) would be lost if we did not believe in the correctness of some counterfactuals and the incorrectness of others. Not only does our sense of an objective world depend on believing that if the tests had been carried out they would have conformed to our expectations, but the value of knowledge would be considerably diminished were we not also learning when not to carry out tests—e.g., to touch a hot stove to confirm that it was hot.

Such considerations may seem to have put Lewis's model in deep water. The analytic relation of sense meaning seems suspect because it can no longer be said that the meaning of an objective belief (strictly) entails the truth of the terminating judgments. At best the objective belief is only probably related to the terminating judgments (unqualified deducibility is certainly lost). In addition, the probabilities do not attach merely to the terminating judgment but are reflected, and in no directly calculable way, in the assurance of the objective belief as well. Further, he has been relying on an inductive or causal relation whose legitimacy has long been the target of skepticism. And he has endangered his empiricism, for if knowledge is to be verified by particular sensible experiences, what has become of that solid base if the particulars themselves are only probable?

It is only fair to say that Lewis relishes such alleged infirmities as opportunities for refinement. The immediate problem for him is to reconcile the certainty of the logical and intensional character of sense meaning with the claims of probability and still keep touch with sensible experience. If this can be done, then perhaps as a bonus he would have resources to account for the cumulative and corrigible character of empirical belief. The far-reaching problem is whether a rationally credible or warranted and justified belief can qualify as knowledge.

There are important similarities between hypothetical arguments with conclusions derived from premises which are certain and those derived from premises which are probable. Lewis is concerned in both cases with the logical relation between the data or premises and the conclusion. When the premises are certain, the conclusion is certain and it follows certainly; when the premises are probable, the conclusion is probable, but it follows certainly (i.e., the conclusion is certainly probable). This amounts to looking at probability judgments as stating a relation between conclusions and the premises or data which are the evidence for them. In other words, the validity of the relation can be assessed without appealing to experience; if the belief (or judgment) is warranted or justified, relative to those data or premises, it is valid. In this sense, the validity of a probability judgment is not tested by conformity to objective facts but only to its logic. Of course, as data and premises are enlarged (as the successes and failures of predictions lead us to change the premises or grounds) then some judgments will be discarded or replaced by others.

There are important differences however between the kinds of rules of inference involved (in this case probability rules), and there must be important reservations also about the intimate relation between data and the warrant of the judgment. For example, the conjoint probability of the premises is altered as information is enlarged in the premises, and this will represent the upper limit of the probability of the conclusion. Of course, as the premises gain assurance, i.e., as the base or evidence changes, the belief itself is always changing. Even though the statement appears to be the same in linguistic form, it alters as it is relative to different premises. It is rather like James's notion that a belief is altered by each additional experience.

The situation is seriously altered when we move away from the domain of what can be established by meanings alone. Even in the case of axiomatized formal systems, once interpreted they yield only probable belief, since the interpreting premise, the rule which interprets the system, furnishes an inductive step that makes the whole empirical. It may be true necessarily that all Euclidean triangles have angles which sum to 180 degrees, and it may be equally true that *if* this plot of ground or figure before me is a Euclidean triangle, it will necessarily have angles summing to 180 degrees. Yet this does not establish that this plot or this figure has an angle sum of 180 degrees, for it does not establish with any certainty that this plot or this figure is a Euclidean triangle. A fortiori this holds for empirical generalizations such as "All Brahma bulls are ferocious" or "Manischewitz wine is sweet." Once again the now familiar problem is raised of the relation of the conceptual to experience. *Mind and the World Order*, focusing on the a priori, raised the problem largely in terms of the way the conceptual latches onto the given or sensible. *Analysis of Knowledge and Valuation* rather emphasizes the reverse direction, working from the sensibly given to belief. But the question of probability arises at the same critical point, at the interplay of the a priori or conceptual and the experiential.

So long as the relation between the data and the consequence is hypothetical it remains a logical relation; however, when the data are asserted as fact the argument is converted into an empirical one. The consequence is now asserted as a probable matter of fact. Lewis believes, however, that the categorical statement of a probability conclusion asserts something more: it asserts a probability consequence of the empirical fact of the data from which it follows, although it has a significance not merely contained in that. The probability attaches to the empirical factuality and the empirical facts or state of affairs is what we believe. The object of belief is not its probability nor just the data, but it is the fact which we find probable in some degree. (This reference is not to the real world, but to a state of affairs; see the discussion of signification above.)

In probability inferences the judgment is always relative to explicit premises. It might appear that as the premises are changed and experience accumulates we not only have different probabilities but different beliefs. And of course this is just the case, as was clear in his account of replacing beliefs and even abandoning them. Beliefs which are inferences from given data may get a better base as experiences are tested. When our felt assurance is in keeping with the degree of probability which the belief has objectively, relative to the data which are its evidence, that belief may be legitimately asserted. Thus though belief may never be certain, a rational (and cautious) man need never believe what is false if he only guides his belief to the degree warranted by the objective probability.

We have already seen that empirical knowledge must either be decisively verifiable or confirmable indefinitely; we also noted that it is claimed that knowledge must also be grounded, adding somewhat casually that knowledge was belief in what is true, objective, and certain. But does this mean that since belief is only probable, it never adds up to knowledge? Or do we sometimes know what may turn out to be false? The clue to the problem lies, for Lewis, in trying to relate psychological grounds and logical warrant. A canine example may help. Suppose a dog is lost, and its distraught owner frantically phones the police. "Have any lost dogs been found?" she begins. "Quite a few," answers the patient sergeant. "Got any identifying marks?" "Well, if it's a mongrel with a few white hairs on its left paw. . . ?" The Sergeant replies (not so patiently) that they're all more or less of that description. "Well, if its a near Alsatian, eats Gorgonzola cheeses greedily, it's probably mine . . . Oh, and if it answers to the name Netzahuacoytl, I *know* it's mine!" The conversation, so far, consists of hypothetical assertions; the relation between the antecedents and the consequents is a merely logical one. When, however, the officer goes to examine the dogs and returns to report that there is one which fits the description, and even that the tests have been made with the indicated results, then (a) the officer asserts that the conditions obtain, and then the lady (b) asserts that it *is* her dog. The data are asserted, so is the conclusion.

Justification

The issue of justification, the other face of validation, is now brought into focus, and with it problems of a new dimension—psychological and linguistic as well as logical and epistemological. If all conceptual interpretation of experience is probable only, and if beliefs always depend on premises which are fallible and incomplete and hence never more than probable, and if there is a need to maximize the reliability of our predictions before testing, then the question of warrant, ground, or evidence antecedent to the test becomes crucial. It will be remembered that justification differed absolutely from verification since prediction is future but the base upon which it is made is present and past. Predictions, since they are for Lewis contingent on possible action and testing, involve betting on one of alternate states of affairs and so choosing between possible worlds. In the testing (as James would have it) the prediction exchanges its credit for cash. Justification raises the issue of the ground or evidential base. Clearly the resources must come from past experience of like cases and whatever lessons can be elicited from them. But will the assurance thereby gleaned ever be sufficient or warrant empirical belief as *knowledge?* To put the issue more modestly, is there a difference between rationally credible beliefs and unwarranted ones? Again, if there are premises in a probability judgment that need to be made explicit, can they be made so and would we evei have them at the time of judgment? The question of the need for maximizing reliability as well as the critique of empirical knowledge is raised in connection with similar questions later, since the demand for cogency is parallel to that for consistency, prudence, and justice.

What place in all this has the concept of knowledge? If we hold to the requirement that knowledge is certain, then empirical belief cannot qualify. But if the question is whether some beliefs are better grounded than others and it is to our advantage to trust past experience and the best estimate we can make of it, then the concept of knowledge may be applied to such beliefs when the degree of assurance is warranted. Ordinary language clearly supports a use of "knowledge" for what is less than certain, and there is a kind of laxness between occasions when we say "I believe" and "I know," as is suggested by the shift from "I believe" to "I know" in the canine example.

In any case, while the philosophic construal of knowledge is sometimes antiseptic and clear, from the more modest view of human activities, knowing is a temporal process, hopefully corrigible and cumulative. In the long run knowledge is for the guidance of action (this of course is the classic pragmatic tradition) and a belief is pragmatically knowledge when we are ready to act on it. Knowing shows unmistakable evidence of its evolutionary origin, and it is continuous with animal behavior and modes of response. Even in human experience knowing is continuous with instinctive behavior and those cognitive responses that have become habitual. Such states of mind, appropriately called cognitive, are belief attitudes, which seldom contain explicitly the evidence needed to justify them. Indeed when pushed far enough it is clear that the complete grounds for our belief in anything could never be made totally explicit. For example, the hypothesis that a house is infested with termites suggests that it will soon sag; but we should need half of Mechanics to offer the necessary collateral premises. This is not fatal, for if habits of explanation and assessment of past experience have some reliability, their explicitness need not be a condition for rationality.

The account so far given of Lewis's view of knowledge may have suggested that it is linear and rather thinly and dangerously balanced on terminating judgments and the sensibly given. But a patent feature of beliefs is their systematic interconnectedness. After all we do not deal in isolated objects and properties—the tests implicit in their meanings are interrelated, making of knowledge a fabric. Even the lowly sensory cue brings into play a structure of meanings. This systematic character may contribute to the reliability of beliefs in somewhat the fashion of compounding probabilities. Corroboration may come indirectly from remote and diverse sources; items of little evidential value in themselves or highly unlikely ones may contribute in a set of tests to make the belief highly probable. What may have little initial credibility may gain assurance from its place in a pattern. For example, in the case of Netzahuacoytl, if the policeman successfully carried out the bizarre Gorgonzola test, it would have increased the credibility of the other tests and of the belief itself. Of course this does not mean that a single item could never upset a belief. Of course it could. For example, a thesis about a connection between Chinese and pre-Columbian Peruvian art is made highly probable by the parallels of form and materials, by the repetition of highly abstract design, and by the portrayal of animals that are indigenous to China and absent in Peru. However, the plausibility of this influence would have to be surrendered if there is no evidence of either a land connection or adequate means of covering the distance by water.

The idea of systematic connection is no new one to philosophy. The *deductive* model captured the imagination of the great rationalists. Royce and the British idealists emphasize *coherence* as the essence of system, often applying an organic model in which part-whole relations and purposive integration take the place of deduction. Lewis uses instead the notion of *congruence* already referred to in connection with the weight of evidence and the asymmetry of verification and falsification. It shares with the others the idea that intelligibility lies in system and interconnectedness but takes issue with specific features of their models. Against the idealist coherence model he objects to the monistic assumption, what James called the block universe, that truth is a single coherent system in which every fact implicates every other. Moreover, coherence alone could never be sufficient to distinguish this world from others equally coherent and logically possible. As against the deductive model Lewis argues that in empirical knowledge the conditions for its application seldom obtain. Deducibility would represent an ideal extension of congruent relations; but even if we had complete deducibility it would not be sufficient to distinguish the real world from alternate possible ones.

Lewis defines his distinctive notion of congruence as follows: "It is a relation such that a set of supposed facts asserted will be said to be congruent if and only if they are so related that the antecedent probability of one will be increased if the remainder of the set can be assumed as given premises."[28] Thus congruence is a stronger relation than mere consistency, but a weaker relation than deducibility, although the stronger relation may of course apply simultaneously. Thus Lewis says of a set of congruent statements that "They are not merely consistent but are such that the probability of any one of them is increased by finding the others true; hence also by any evidence increasing the probability of the remainder of the set."[29]

The appeal to congruence and incongruence is to be found at every level of experience, but it is not a sensible experience itself. It is rather a claim to the presence or absence of cognitive pattern. Thus a visual report of an unusual object becomes more assured when supported by tactile and auditory reports, whereas incongruence generally would lead to further tests and correction.

While the reliability of belief has been immeasurably increased by the supportive character of congruence, still the whole of knowledge cannot be made to stand on it alone. There must be something which is certain at the base. Lewis assigns this role to the certainties of the given and to the decisive verification of terminating judgments (coupled of course with the a priori certainties of our meanings). But the given by itself is inarticulate and establishes nothing beyond the assuredness of itself. As remarked above, even its function as a sign, as triggering an expectation of further sequences in experience, not only requires that sensory experiences be repeatable and recognizable as the *same,* but also rests on generalization from past experience. And the terminating judgments themselves, as predictions, require that such generalizations from past experience be projectible into the future, i.e., that even these primitive inductions be to some extent reliable indices of it. And of course such inductive inferences occur at every level of experience. Thus it is that Lewis faces as final problems—in the search for such warrant and justification as he can find—the validity of memory and of induction. His strategies in dealing with both of these are roughly parallel: defensively, that cogent arguments cannot be made against them without assuming them, and positively, that they are constitutive of knowledge itself.

In the case of memory, what needs to be established is that our sense of past fact is prima facie credible, i.e., that it affords some probability of remembered fact, independently of its congruence. We ordinarily assume this and would not question it if we did not also learn by experience that it is fallible. But this very experience involves memory which helps us devise rules qualifying the trustworthiness of our individual memories. Some can remember places and not dates, some faces and not names, and we all no doubt distort on pet subjects. Thus even such generalizations about the reliability of memory assume the reliability in question. To doubt the president does not mean to doubt the institution of the presidency. In short, we have no other rational alternative but to presume that anything sensed as past is more probable—to however small a degree—than that for which memory is blank and that which is incompatible with whatever else is remembered. Even the most fantastic alternative would leave us without the means to formulate or substantiate the issue.

This affords a kind of justification for seeing the present sense of pastness as constitutive of the kind of world we live in. This world, our sense of which is a memorial precipitate of past experience, is the only world with which we can be acquainted; only by reference to it could empirical judgments be meaningful or true or false. It may be phenomenal in any sense one wishes, but as Berkeley suggested there is no noticeable difference between an objectively real world and a sufficiently systematic delusion of one; we could not even discuss the difference except by assuming ourselves in and out of the phenomenal world at the same time. The problem is less to prove the objectively real and the possibility of our knowledge of it, than "to formulate correctly those criteria which delimit empirical reality and explicate our sense of it."[30] That empirical reality can be known needs neither to be postulated nor demonstrated; it is analytically the case and can only be repudiated on premises which already imply it.

If we can have the presumptive credibility of the remembered, the sensibly given and its certainty, congruence, then a case is already made for warranted empirical belief as knowledge, save the last question—that of valid generalization which does not merely summarize past experiences but provides grounds for projection into the future. This, of course, is the familiar problem of induction.

Lewis builds here on virtually all that has gone before, but especially his view of the a priori and concepts in the construction of the real, discussed in section 2, above. The connection is very tight between the problems of constructing objects, properties, and events, in terms of which we organize raw experience, and such order-making and stability as we seek in our empirical laws. It may be remembered that the problem there raised the issue of how the conceptual could "attach" the sensibly given without at the same time imposing or limiting what is real. Lewis's argument here depended not only on the ability to conceptualize, but also to make choices between alternative ways of conceptualizing. Physical objects are constructions out of actual and possible sense data ("presentations"); but from the wealth of appearances, attention selects only those qualia which have general utility: thus the real is already a selection in the direction of order. He argued there that the real world is more orderly than the flow of sensible experience, and that the search for intelligibility is directed toward making the world manageable and controllable.

The problem of induction at this point is to account for the orderliness of *experience* without assuming the uniformity of nature or without prescribing the future. Lewis needs to handle this problem not only because it is a classical issue for empiricism, but because it is vital for a pragmatism that is not to lapse into metaphysics. He has already relied on past experience as an index to expectations of the future, not only in the presumption that there are logical rules of probability inference and in the use of sensible experience to cue a belief (which requires a primitive generalization from past experience), but also inside the terminating judgment in the causal relation between an *if* of action and the anticipated consequences. And of course this characteristic in terminating judgments is carried over into non-terminating judgments and so into empirical laws. Even the analytic relation between belief and tests is itself learned from past experience.

The classic Humean formulation of the problem did not challenge that causal judgments involve a belief in necessary connections of events. It denied simply the legitimacy of the belief and hence the warrant of going from past experience to the future. Hume's argument is that when experiences of type A (events, properties, or objects) are followed with regularity by experiences of type B, the source of the necessity is psychological (custom and association), not logical. Lewis's crucial point here is that the formation of types A and B is already the construction of likeness classes out of the stream of experience which have already been selected and shaped in the interest of structure and order. In effect, the forming of such likeness classes as A and B already presumes the process of inductive inference, although on a more primitive level, in order to state the problem at all.

What minimal assumption is necessary to warrant belief in induction? No assumption of anything which could conceivably be false has to be made; anything which the wildest imagination could conjure up could fail to afford a basis for intelligibility and probable judgment. "It must be false that every identifiable entity in experience is equally associated with every other."[31] In other words, the possibilities of future experience must not be unlimited and every recognizable appearance must not be equally associated with or equally likely to be followed by every other experience. For example, it must be the case that "r" is more likely to be followed by "e" than by "q"—that "rye" is less likely to be associated with other items of discourse than with "whiskey" or "catcher."

Lewis's assumption that there is an order which is discoverable (a presumption for any inquiry) does not appeal to any specific regularity nor any particular level of specificity. Failing to find order at one level can lead the search to a more general or more specific level. Thus, if we find predictions about the weather taken from various near-lying reporting points to be unreliable, we can look toward more microcosmic phenomena in more detailed and dense reports or else (as turned out to be the case) to the macrocosmic atmospheric movements as shown by a satellite. And in the last analysis, should it turn out that nothing at all serves as a reliable base for predictions generally, at least the unreliability of experience would be reliably established.

The problem of induction opens onto a fundamental perspective in Lewis's work that has important consequences in his moral theory. He registers here his determination to let our competencies set the problem: we plan, we intend, we review past experience, and examine it seeking the wisdom which is implicit in it. No account of knowledge can but acknowledge these phenomena. We certainly make predictions and self-consciously seek to frame the wisdom that can be gleaned from their successes and failures, searching all the while for principles of criticism. Thus we forge critiques which are formulated in general principles; but such principles may be expressed as rules which are in some sense norms binding on the future. Insofar as they are thought to be valid, they carry a sense of constraint or imperative. Now this suggests, as indicated at the beginning of this section, that validation, and centrally justification, is a normative enterprise. The base of the enterprise is people actually learning; the philosopher's task is to articulate the norms of the process—the way that knowledge is corrected and the principles of such corrigibility, the way it accumulates and is systematized and the principles of such systematization. Lewis's effort itself constitutes a (normative) critique of *cogency*. This is his positive reinterpretation of the traditional epistemological question of how knowledge is possible; the job is not to justify knowledge, but to frame the most significant principles of its criticism.

The critique of cogency itself presupposes *consistency,* the rules of which are sought in logic which is the critique of consistency. This dependence of cogency on consistency also has the character of an imperative. Consistency is thus the first and cogency is the second imperative in order of priority. In similar fashion, rightness of doing is dependent on cogency or rightness in thinking. It would scarcely be possible for effective doing to ignore what is cogent and consistent.

If the question is raised why be consistent, why be cogent, why seek the most stable, reliable, and manageable world, and why direct action in the light of such knowledge, there is really no answer to the question as thus framed. In the end it is involved in what it means to be rational, to be constrained by the rules and critiques which crystallize such wisdom as we have. We shall continue the search for the rational imperatives as they apply to ethics, after an examination of value judgments.

4. Moral Theory: Values and Valuation

Lewis's moral theory readily[32] extends the views developed thus far, but it has a particular setting in the midcentury polemic against a skepticism which robustly urges that evaluations are unverifiable matters of emotion and that statements about right or obligation are not strictly true or false. Against this Lewis argues that valuations are cognitive and that ethical judgments are rational.

Skepticism and relativism about values are almost as old as philosophy itself, but the twentieth century has faced crescendoing challenges. Social scientists generally, dividing descriptive tasks sharply from evaluative ones, disclaimed professional competence for the latter while Freudians magnified the irrational and behaviorists the routinized in conduct. Everywhere science and technology were elevated over the normative. Theory echoed (or was echoed in) practice—in labor-management confrontation, in irrational wars, in cataclysmic contests of ideologies, of ethnic aspirations and countercultures; everywhere the view of value as subjective or nonobjective was reinforced. Ethical disagreements are merely matters of opposing interests and when compromise or an overriding shared interest is impossible to find, the final resource is only persuasion or coercion.

The logical positivists and their emotivist spin-offs gave substantial philosophic voice to this mood. The verifiability criterion of meaning exorcised the predicates "good," "valuable," and "right" from factual or meaningful discourse. Using scientific language as the touchstone and the necessity of observational testing as the supreme criterion of meaning, they were impressed by the contrast in which public appeal can be made to resolve scientific disagreements while moral disagreements become largely matters of personal commitment. Hence they interpreted ethical terms as emotive or persuasive, often differentiating "good" and "right" by their practical functions—"good" generally reflects a sentiment of approval, while "right" and "ought" function as commands. But in neither case are moral sentences true or false; ethical assertions are thus "noncognitive."

The conclusion about the noncognitive character of value predicates, however, was unpalatable to most contemporaries with pragmatic sympathies. Committed to the continuity of experience, pragmatists tended not to limit the scope of the Peircean view of meaning to scientific terms alone. Regardless of domain a concept has meaning when operations and observable consequences are assigned. Since values obviously have consequences in human life, the philosophic problem is to find appropriate operations and credentials for them rather than to declare the task impossible from the outset. James added another dimension by making respectable questions about the function of knowledge in purposive activity. Conceptualizing (generalizing) is part of the capacity to translate the uniqueness of the flow of sensation into a stable and manageable world. Thus inquiry itself is normative and manageability a good or utility. And yet James remained anxious to the very end about how such conceptual organizing leads to overt action in the physical world. Dewey took a next step when he transformed James's theory of concept formation into a general theory of action using an enriched view of the reflex arc in which perception and behavior are organically related. Evaluation, obligation, control, and knowledge are together tied to satisfactions and reflective goods. Thus armed Dewey confronted the challenge of noncognitivism head on. But Lewis's way is not Dewey's; he separates questions of good, needs, satisfactions, values, and purposes from those of imperatives, obligation, and rules or directives. The former, judgments of good or value are empirical; while necessary they are not sufficient to determine what is right, that is what ought to be pursued. There are thus two broad steps in Lewis's moral theory. In this section we shall consider judgments of good or value, leaving the problems of right decision, and critically social justice, until the final section.

Lewis summons the full battery of his account of knowledge to establish valuations as legitimate kinds of empirical judgments. The model which works for redness, solubility, etc., can be extended to good. But Lewis's discussion of valuation does more than merely stretch the scope of empirical belief, it also provides a critical connection between knowledge and purposive or reasonable conduct, though different from Dewey's. From the outset Lewis had argued that activity—including decisions about meaning and the design of experiments, as well as their execution—is an ingredient in learning; now the stronger point is to be urged that ultimately all knowledge is for the sake of guiding conduct.

As in the preceding, Lewis is to work with the interaction between polar elements of a given and an a priori categorizing. Value theory, like every other kind of inquiry, must start off with definitive criteria of its key notions that reflect presystematic uses. Such criteria are certainly debatable and usually there are alternatives, but in no case are they empirically true or false, for they concern what it means to say that something has value, i.e., what is the nature of value.

This decisional character of the definitions has often enough been forgotten in the heat of the disagreements which mark the history of ethical theory. We debate alternatives such as "pleasure is the good," "nothing is unqualifiedly good but a good will," "goodness is a simple unanalyzable quality," or "a thing is constituted good by being the object of interest." Inability to agree upon one among such options has long added fuel to skepticism in moral matters. But such disagreements are not themselves moral but definitional; and such debates, like those over definitions of hardness, acidity, reality, and validity, are settled in the first instance only by clarifying what meaning is intended. Of course not every analytic definition is equally serviceable, and Lewis chooses to work with a notion of value that ties it naturalistically to qualitative satisfactions disclosed in experience. Felt satisfactions, appreciations, enjoyments, and their opposites, then, have the role of the given and provide the base in experience for the long journey from phenomenal experience to objective value claims.

Found goodness in experience is reported in *expressive* terms. Particular value-apprehension, analogously with seen-red or taste-sweet, are not strictly knowledge since no error is possible except in the reporting. (And as with the sensible, there is the same difficulty in capturing the experience in words.) *Terminating judgments* are formed in expressive terms; building out from the given they predict the possible quality of an experience contingent on a particular action in such a way that the statement can be tested and decisively verified. In experimental terms a given sensory cue, say of a warm feeling or a red glow, generates a primitive expectation that, if I reach out (under certain other conditions) a feeling of pain will result. The resultant feeling would of course verify or falsify the judgment.

Non-terminating judgments are forged from sets of terminating judgments; as predictions of what is gratifying or grievous they reach far into the future for their verification. They include relatively low-ordered judgments, e.g., that a particular recording of the first Brandenburg Concerto is moving, to highest-ordered generalizations about life-styles. Such judgments are never completely verified and although they may earn "practical certainty" they remain probability assessments. Thus the broad parallel of valuations with empirical knowledge generally is complete, starting from experience reported in expressive language, cuing hypothetical predictions which are decisively established, to objective probability statements ascribing a property (value, good, etc.) to an object, situation, or state of affairs. These highest-ordered generalizations and evaluations function like scientific hypotheses; and are indefinitely testable and criticizable. As with learning generally the successes and failures of our expectations must find their way into the growing corpus of assessed experience, providing an accumulating warrant for particular value predications.

The legitimizing of valuations thus depends upon taking seriously the continuity of method in dealing with value and with empirical judgments. The whole of the previous discussion thus powers the account of valuation—from the constructive role of knowledge in converting an alien into an objective and manageable world, the problems of prediction, induction, and justification, of system and congruence. Indeed, the learning model entire, with its complexities, tentativenesses, corrigibility, and critique, is applicable. What is needed in addition are not basic changes, but refinements—further distinctions to come to grips with the subtleties of value language and experience. To rest the account of valuation on the refinements alone, as some have done, is to mistake the trimmings, tasty as they may be, for the meal; to overlook valuations is to miss a hearty part of the main course.

In simplest terms, "An object O is objectively valuable" strictly entails a set of terminating judgments of the form "Under certain conditions, including those of action, the object O with some reliability will lead to a satisfactory experience E for subject S." This formulation is admittedly relative to personal experience, but this need not disqualify it as an objective judgment, since it will be remembered that the claim of objectivity for any empirical knowledge must come ultimately to rest in the experience of someone. It may well be the case that value experiences are more variable, but the difference between felt satisfaction and looks red appears to be more a matter of degree than of kind. Admittedly too a person's judgment of satisfaction may be less stable over time than color judgments. Difficulties in interpersonal comparisons are corrigible in somewhat the manner in which color-blind and tone-deaf people also adjust. In any case these "subjective" features of the judgment are equivalent to their phenomenal status, and do not match the distinction between subjective and objective as usually applied in matters of taste. Objective value remains then the potentiality of an object, event, or state of affairs reliably to provide immediate satisfaction to someone under specifiable conditions. Only when some idiosyncrasy or some transient condition of the subject, some particular defect, is promoted into a claim about reliable prediction for others is "subjective" in a perjorative sense applicable.

The effort then is to show that value is as objective a property as, say, red, soluble, or acid. Something may well be (objectively) valuable although not valued by anyone; and clearly other things may be valued without being objectively valuable. But this situation is not unique, for looking red is not conclusive evidence that something is red (it is alleged that the walls at Smokey Joe's bar are really white although the light of day, i.e., standard conditions have never penetrated there). Similarly with "soluble": a salt may properly be said to be soluble although a sample does not dissolve when the solvent is supersaturated. And a substance, say an iron nail, might be said to "dissolve" in water, i.e., to lose an ion, even though to use the term so broadly as to make almost everything soluble is to rob it of much of its utility. The general difficulties of dispositional terms and counterfactuals are common to valuational and physical properties, and similarly for questions of utility. The identification, e.g., of a sample as an acid or not depends on which, among alternate, theory of acids is used and that choice is one of context and convenience. This dimension of choice or option relative to context or objective is found at the level of categorization in concept formation generally. But major difficulties arise in policy disputes when the commitments are not made explicit. There is no necessary contradiction between the judgment that this block of cement is a hazard and the claim that it is a lifesaver when references to the interest of motorist or pedestrian are included. Or again, an accused may be judged insane or responsible according to a psychiatrist who is protecting the defendant or a prosecutor whose concern is for the community. Of course the question of which definition, theory, or context is to be chosen is a further matter.

Now this way (the mode of simple potentiality) of expressing the meaning of the value of an object seems strong enough to make a case for the use of the empirical model for value judgments. It can handle plausibly a wide range of conditions without sacrifice of objectivity—e.g., the relativity to control or to availability (an asymmetry suggestive of the problems raised by degree of confirmation). A critically rare type of blood plasma stored in New York may be "valueless" when needed for victims in the high Andes. Current usage may label as "valueless" oil which lies inaccessibly deep (although such usage allows us not to deny its particular physical properties or market value). Generally speaking, a value is diminished as it is the less controllable while it is enhanced as it is the more controllable. Clearly we have just begun to list the conditions which help legitimize value statements and which minimize their apparent contradictoriness (when they are spelled out).

Valuations of course raise particular problems, for they occur in a multitude of other modes than that of simple potentiality. There is no neat scheme for sorting out the uses and contexts; "value," "good," etc., are systematically ambiguous in an even more complex way than "real." It is important for Lewis's general claim about the objectivity of value judgments that he consider these painstakingly if he is to make order out of the loose and elliptical ways we speak. The variety of modes requires distinctions beyond those needed for empirical knowledge generally—e.g., between instrumental and utilitarian, intrinsic and extrinsic, comparative, consummatory, social, etc. We shall illustrate only a few of the cases here. Linus's security blanket may be objectively valuable to him, but this need not contradict the claim that the security blanket is not genuinely valuable. The first is in the mode of simple potentiality, the second is in the comparative mode, i.e., comparing one security device to other possible devices, not merely one person's needs to another's. Similarly, "This concert ticket is valuable (costs sixteen dollars)" need not contradict "This concert ticket is valueless to me (because I'm tone-deaf)" or because of an uncancelable engagement (a type of situation which would be widely applicable to others in the same situation). A given ball-game ticket is not good (to anyone) if the game is called for rain.

Judgments in the mode of instrumental value are especially context-bound, yet the appearance of paradox disappears when we clarify the specification intended, e.g., "The screwdriver is no good, for it is blunted. Still save it, it will be a help (i.e., valuable) in mixing the paint" or "This coat is truly disreputable, still it will come in handy as a blanket at the shore." In many such cases there is a certain primacy to one of the uses because the function there intended has usurped the name of the instrument (screwdriver, not paint mixer). Lewis makes the point that we have the same kind of problem with the use of names in science as well as in ethics, and that disagreements in both cases can be clarified by seeing what functions are built in by the name. He also distinguishes between instrumentality and utility, the former being an efficient means for a given end, the latter assuming in addition that the end is good. Comparable problems arise in such examples as: "This is a good set of burglar tools, but the better the burglar tools the worse they are." We may compare this to nonethical judgments like "This is a slightly red dress," and "That is a very red stone," but it scarcely follows that the stone is redder than the dress. In both these cases, when the context is supplied, the paradox vanishes. Here it is not so much the functions as the conditions for the presence of a quality that need to be made explicit.

Now the problem for Lewis all along has been the question of whether assessing consequences as good or ascribing value can qualify as empirical judgments. Thus far his case has been cogently made granting that the vocabulary of values and our ways of speaking about enjoyment, grief, satisfaction, pleasure are elliptical, loose, and often confused. Still there remain two issues which are not as easily met: the first raises questions about the value base in experience and whether it can serve in the same role as the sensibly given; a second raises problems of distribution over time and over persons which has no clear analogy in the model used for empirical knowledge. Felt goodness in experience is not a simple quale (in contrast to looks red, e.g.), for there are enormous varieties of satisfactions, of prizings, distresses, anxieties, etc., and these are alike only as they are bases for preferring and choosing. Where the vocabulary of colors and pitch may be dense and precise, the vocabulary of appreciation is extraordinarily imprecise. Further the value quality of experience is scarcely a separable dimension. It has neither constant zero nor stable phenomenological threshold. Transitive ordering fails since there are complicated fusions and interactions of pains and pleasures. Indeed the quality of goodness or value is more like an atmosphere—a background euphoria or distraction or desire nearly always attaches to some other presentation such as a lovely color, acrid taste, etc. Experiences of value are seldom a function simply of the bare sensible presentation since the latter is modified by context and association and by the condition of the subject and the world at a given time. Sometimes, too, it is urged that enjoyment, etc., is affectively rather than sensibly aroused. But the potentiality of an object to arouse affective experience is as much an objective property as that which arouses the sensory. Perhaps in the end the difference between affection and perception is largely an abstraction depending upon learned physiological correlates rather than on experienced phenomenal differences. In any case affection and perception condition one another in a most intimate way and both can serve reliably as cues or signs. Actually one can follow either of two tracks in dealing with the construction of objective judgments, whether for sense or affect. In both cases objective, in the sense of veridical, non-terminating judgments could be formed. We could remain on the phenomenal level of passages of experience, directly taking the presentation as cues to further experience. At other times and for other jobs, we move indirectly from experiences to the world of objects and events. Of course the former track is of special importance in the value field. Value experiences also are more frequently sought for themselves whereas the sensible quality of the given, e.g., the redness of an apple, is primarily useful as it furnishes us with the evidence that the apple is really red or ripe. In the latter case the experience is primarily a sign of future experience, whereas the felt value is in some sense terminal. This points to the fact that as regards value the experience is the final arbiter. Thus there is a kind of reverse in value predication of the relationships between expressive and objective meanings. A thing is valuable only as it ultimately relates to some value experience—to some felt experience; objective value is derivable from and ruled by direct appreciation or felt goodness.

The fact that there can be both objective judgments of appearance (it really sounds good, looks green, excites) and of the world (the sound is good, it is green, it is exciting) reflects our casual way of talking, for a single expression may mean one or the other or both. To force clarity here a distinction is needed between intrinsic value, or a value in the quality of experience, and extrinsic value, or value ascribed to objects, situations, and events.

We have only suggested the painstaking care with which Lewis examines the variety of modes of valuations, expanding circumstances, making explicit what is unexpressed in our intentions. But even the differences in the experiential base are not infirming; if anything, learning and the generalizing of signs is quicker and more efficient as regards satisfactions and goods than in the case of other empirical knowledge.

This is not to say that valuations are not more variable and complex, and of course more exigent. Valuations are twice vulnerable to error since they are predictive both of what consequences will occur and whether such consequences will be satisfying to bring about. The judgment is thus doubly compounded by cogencies and probabilities. Which is better; a sure half-loaf, or a less probable whole one?

The most troublesome problem of valuations as empirical judgments turns on the problems of combination and collation. Pre-Jamesean psychology, following Locke, assumed that lemonade was the associated sum of discrete sensations. With the support of this model a long tradition in economics and ethics supposed that satisfactions or goods also could be added simply, whether they were goods experienced at different times or in different lives. Lewis challenges that atomism, and performs for goods something of the same operation that James did for lemonade. It was a part of James's point that no two experiences were ever exactly the same—the second sip at least different by being a second. This is essential, for James, to account for the cumulative character of experience and learning; for Lewis there may be a consummatory character as well. A good dinner with good company does not sum simply these pleasures taken separately. But even separately, their order would make a difference. Pleasures are not related as a series of juxtaposed experiences independent of collation, occurrence in time, and relation to larger passage of experience. Thus a childhood of happiness and an old age of unremitting pain is not the equivalent of a lifetime with the quality distributed in other ways, even should some kind of reckoning show the total units of pleasure-pain to be the same.

While Lewis does not desert his view that what is ultimately valuable, valuable for its own sake, is a quality of direct or immediate experience, the immediacies referred to need not be limited to those which are now present, but include those future immediacies which may be sought contingently on action and possible conditions. Thus we need to evaluate every experience beyond merely the satisfactions it affords in the present; the value of having just that experience needs to be assessed in its impact to other experiences.

Just what are to count as the relevant boundaries of a complex of experience is surely difficult to say; but undeniably we talk of a tedious journey, the value of a decade of research, the richness of a marriage (and those may overlap one another), and even the goodness of a life as a whole. We do cut into the continuum of experience to distinguish these larger unities which in turn overlap, intersect, and interplay. We assess such happenings not as mere aggregates of moments taken singly. Perhaps a wholly satisfactory passage of living could not be built of only unsatisfactory ingredients but an unsatisfactory passage sometimes follows on moments which by themselves seem satisfactory. But more importantly our experiences are self-consciously cumulative, colored by anticipations and by prior experience. Thus a small boy drudgingly carrying water for the elephants as the price of a circus ticket may find that anticipated delight lightens his work. Indeed he may even find his enjoyment of the performance enhanced by the satisfaction of having earned the ticket. Such matters are sophisticated; satisfactions of striving and succeeding are unlike those of merely striving or of securing without effort (as merely finding the ticket on the pavement). Perhaps these complex processes are understandable as a learning process, for even in a series of trials and errors that results in sudden task achievement, the learning is experienced throughout. More importantly still there are those fuller experiences (and fuller learning) in which an experience seems to reach backward and forward to contribute to the whole of which it is an ingredient. Involved here is a whole pattern or Gestalt of relations. Listening to a symphony or reading a novel is such a whole. Scarcely anything strikes one as more absurd than the favorite movements of a variety of symphonies packaged as a record, or excerpts from favorite operatic themes, twenty-four to a side. And even coming to understand a symphony may be regarded as an experience—studying its parts, repeating its themes at widely separated times, learning to subordinate parts, and grasping the structure. Putting aside for the moment questions as to what should be the ultimate boundaries for value assessment, still it is a simple fact that we do assess larger happenings and even their contribution to the quality of life as a whole.

Such assessing would require something in the way of a synthetic grasp; and now the question arises whether this need for synthetic imagination loses for Lewis his claim that these matters are open to empirical verification. If these assessments are among the most difficult, they are also the most important. We do bring together, in envisaging a path of determination, assessments that involve all modes. If such determinations cannot be quantitatively summed, still theoretically it is possible to assign them a roughly linear ordering by preference. Even the introduction of probabilities and risks can be accommodated by imagining whether we would prefer a quarter of a loaf on nine out of ten occasions, or a whole loaf three out of ten times, or similarly a whole loaf of homemade luscious bread to three loaves of the current store kind. As a matter of fact, we are called upon to make not only such homely determinations, but also choices between financing schools or hospitals with limited resources, or to vote on guns versus butter. Scientific enterprises are themselves replete with similar kinds of evaluations, e.g., in comparing large-scale theories on grounds of simplicity or congruence or predictive power. Indeed the difficulties foisted upon values may appear the more insurmountable precisely because we work with an oversimplified view of empirical knowledge. Assessments as to comprehensive plans are non-terminating judgments of the highest order, comparable to the theoretical commitments involved in a belief in the unity of science. While certainly incapable of any decisive verification, still they are capable indefinitely of correction and critique.

5. Ethics and Social Philosophy

Lewis has made a substantial case for evaluations as a kind of empirical knowledge. Whatever else their complexities they are learned, corrected, verified, and justified by methods that are open to empirical judgments generally. Objective judgments of value yielding justified expectation of good consequences in a variety of modes have a prima facie mandate to be pursued; and actions taken in the light of (or on the advice of) such predictions are reasonable. Yet, there is no direct step from these predictions of good and bad consequences to morally right decisions—i.e., to which goods ought to be pursued or to which consequences are right to bring about. Clearly, objectives which might be reasonably sought at any given time will include incompatible and competing ones, risks must be traded off against desirabilities; multiple ends must be organized and some subordinated to others in larger plans. Required then in addition to cogent predictions of valuable consequences is some principle (or principles) which legislates among the competing values and which orders goods with respect to one another. The central problem of morals beyond valuation concerns such principles or rules of right ordering and the ground of their authority, that is, of their imperativeness or obligatoriness.[33]

This ultimately critical place of right in ethical matters does not, however, displace the role of good for Lewis. Both judgments of good and decisions of right are required. Moral arguments often suppress one or the other of these considerations: a policy may be argued for because it maximizes social goods, without making explicit a rule which validates the maximization. Or again, as with the golden rule, a moral principle may be emphasized in apparent disregard of the benefits (but of course the criterion of what we would have others do to us makes implicit reference to good consequences). Indeed, long-standing antagonisms among traditional ethical theories have often resulted from exclusive allegiance to either the good or the right. The classic instance of such antagonism is the conflict between the utilitarian emphasis on good consequences and the intuitional, contractual, or Kantian emphasis on justice, obligation, and right. Lewis's account of the relation of personal and social goods as well as of distributive and contributory values is in the tradition of utilitarianism, perhaps not the rawest kind of calculating but at least in the claim that objective judgments envisaging a total personal and public good can be made. Pragmatic themes go in the same direction with their emphasis on good consequences. Both utilitarianism and pragmatism, however, have been challenged for failing to give an adequate account of obligation and justice. The challenges are twofold. One is to produce a theory of justice from within their own premises. Utilitarianism, e.g., is challenged to rule out those intuitively repugnant decisions which might maximize social welfare at an outrageous cost—the much used example of punishing an innocent man whom the judge alone knows to be innocent in order to prevent a riot which would otherwise cost many lives. A parallel objection to pragmatism is to accuse it of unavoidable opportunism in social or personal ethics. A second, but related, challenge is to provide the grounds of the authority which requires one person to consider the well-being of another as a factor in his own decision, especially when some sacrifice is involved. Once again this raises the question of the validity of a rule, e.g., of just distribution, by which some impersonal or social good has priority over (or is to be integrated with) personal ones.

Lewis's separation of the problems of right from those of good is tailored to provide a theory of obligation or justice that meets the challenges. In effect he seeks to synthesize utilitarian and Kantian ethics. But now he runs head on into further criticisms that resulted from the way ethical discussion was carried on at midcentury. It tended to force a choice between only two nonutilitarian options: emotivism and intuitionism. The intuitionist claims to grasp what is right, fair, or just, as a matter of immediate knowledge or cognition. Hard-line emotivists insist

that the distinctive meaning of right involves an imperative, directive, or persuasion which, in contrast to descriptions, can neither be true nor false and hence is
noncognitive. Lewis is too committed to naturalism to accept the first and too
committed to rationality in decision to tolerate the second. When the field is
limited to these alternatives Lewis is often classified as a noncognitivist. But
perhaps the moral is that the classification itself is too procrustean to accommodate
Lewis's theory of right (or, for that matter, Dewey's analysis of valuation). Lewis,
and perhaps pragmatism generally, can make a plausible and even convincing case
for a cognitive and naturalistic ethic which integrates the importance of consequences with a crucial place for imperatives. In what sense the theory will be
cognitive or rational will be spelled out as we go along. But since "naturalism"
has many senses let us propose one here which is compatible with Lewis's
intentions. An ethics is naturalistic when it holds that the resources and capacities
that are employed for solving problems generally are available and are sufficient to
handle moral problems. But of course this involves an ample view of human
capacities which includes learning and learning by self-conscious ways of extending knowledge to future cases (by eliciting principles of criticism of funded
experience) and the ability to foresee and to be constrained by such foresight and
such criticism of what is avoidable and achievable. Thus goal-pursuing and
rule-guided behavior and problem-solving are themselves natural capacities.
Moreover, such naturalism must embrace the presumptions and commitments
which underlie any enterprise and make it serious and significant, indeed which
make it an enterprise.

This acknowledgment of the normative in all deliberate activity provides the
clue to the strategy which Lewis will use to make the case for the cognitive
character of the morally right. He will view the morally right as a species of the
right in general, hoping thereby to relieve it of the burdens that have traditionally
beleaguered it: in particular, the prescriptive, directive, and imperative features of
the morally right, so longstandingly the stumbling block for a cognitive theory of
morals, will be installed on the generic level and so provide a wider base for
analyzing is-ought relations. As suggested earlier, though it is much more explicit
in Lewis's ethical writings, it is not only the moral—the justicial and the prudential—that will give rise to imperatives and prescriptions, but activities generally as
they are deliberate and deliberated. Philosophy itself, insofar as it seeks a critique
of cogency and consistency in determining what is valid knowledge, is a normative
enterprise. Similarly science, insofar as it makes explicit *canons* of evidence
which are constraints on its method, gives rise to imperatives.

Two kinds of considerations are interwoven here: the more or less formal
features of rightness and the more informal appeal to human nature including
rule-guided, intentional, and purposive behavior. Rightness is a property of
decision and decision-making. Wherever a choice is to be made, wherever deliberation is in point before the fact (or criticism relevant after it), a rightness is sought
that is to be complied with. Such a search is pervasive—whether giving a proof,

designing an experiment, establishing a belief, eating lobster, or baking a cake. For a decision to be right, that is, objectively right, it has to apply to all like cases; it lays out a *way* which can be formulated as a rule or directive for future cases.

What is involved here is essentially a restating of much that is already implicit in Lewis's account of knowledge. Generalizing was a critical part in the construction of a real world of objects, events, and values. (Even this involved the notion of rules and rule-guided behavior, as in the account of criterion-in-mind, intentions, and plans.) It is but a short step (at least for Lewis) from the construction of likeness classes (and the activity that moves from the sense presented to the represented) to the rules of self-governance of such activities. As learning is bound up with rule-guided generalizing, so with learning to direct and govern our ways of thinking or doing. Rules are ways of transferring the wisdom of past experience and making it available for the future. In the case of decision, for Lewis, to have made an objectively right decision is already to have laid down a rule, i.e., a constraint, that is binding until some ground is found for rejecting it. Strictly, of course, such rules or mandates are not true or false, but this is no more ground for regarding them as noncognitive in morals than it would be theoretical principles in science.

Indeed, the gap between the prescriptive and descriptive is not large; activities are directable as they answer to some mode, some generality, and are therefore amenable to some formulatable rule of procedure:

> No deliberate act can be decided otherwise than in a manner which could be formulated as a rule, and if the decision is justifiable by a rule which criticism could accept as one to be adhered to in all like cases. And no decision can be justified except by reference to some explicit rule or to some implicit rule which reflection may elicit. If critique has any criterion there is a rule.[35]

But we formulate not only low-ordered rules but go on to assess them and frame higher and more general rules which are open also to assessment and correction. And we attempt to capture in critiques even those principles of corrigibility and assessment. Thus we have the critiques of right thinking, believing and concluding, and of doing, the most developed forms of which are the ethical critiques of prudence and justice.

The most general rule or directive Lewis calls the "law of objectivity." It is an imperative to recognize that experience signifies a reality beyond what is presented and to respond to what is objective—in short, to conduct oneself with reference to those future eventualities which cognition warrantedly advises can be affected as though the effects were to be felt with the poignancy of the present. Clearly this is virtually contentless, but content is added as the domain is specified. It does, however, suggest the sanctions that past experience generates under the constraints that emerge through the recalcitrant in experience itself, constraints that are dual, stemming from the need for consistency and congruence on the one hand and the stubbornness of objective reference.

Were the question to be raised why be consistent in inferring and concluding, why be cogent in believing, whence the binding character of critique, and why the distinctions between right and wrong, valid and invalid, cogent and noncogent, fundamental to our way of learning, nothing in the way of formal proof or evidence would be available. But informal appeals may be made to the way men exercise their basic capacities—facts readily available to a descriptive psychology that admits of the ample view suggested in the definition of a naturalistic ethics. We do learn from past experience in a distinctive and self-critical way; we are required to decide and for reasons, and to find those decisions binding on the future; we are self-consciously concerned about the future and are constrained by our view of what is unavoidable and what is possible. And above all, we are responsible and feel that responsibility as a constraint to acknowledge what is more than merely presented, but what is represented and objective.

Were the question to be raised why direct our doing by what we know, once again nothing in the way of proof or evidence would be available. But the status of the practical makes no difference to the character of the imperativeness; it only adds consequences to the content of deliberation. Thus deliberation and criticism now fall on results of decision to do and what is right to bring about. Indeed there is no other way to identify an act than by reference to some aspect of the consequences—what results are hoped for, intended, interesting, accidental, etc.

Lewis's view of imperativeness can be seen by way of contrast with Kant's sharp distinction between hypothetical and categorical imperatives. According to Kant, hypothetical imperatives are contingent on their objectives being desired, while categorical imperatives are binding regardless of our desires and objectives. For Lewis hypothetical imperatives yield binding directives if, as, and when the end to which the prescribed activity is directed is either assumed or otherwise accepted. Thus for Lewis, all imperatives share the hypothetical (if-then) of technical structure, but they take on a categorical force in those cases where the if-clause is always in effect and the objective unavoidable or cannot be repudiated. If you want to drive a car, get a license; if you want to make good crêpes, let the batter rest; and although there would be some tint of irrationality in wanting an objective (all other things being equal) and not being bound by the effective rules to secure it, still such imperatives are avoidable by not engaging in the activity. But are there categories of activities, perforce general, which could not be repudiated? If so, particularly if these activities are always relevant, the imperatives would be categorical and always in force, even if sometimes justifiably overridden.

For Lewis, the imperatives involved in canons of decision in right thinking and right doing have precisely this categorical character. The most developed is that of logic, as a critique of correctness or validity of inferring and concluding. Logic is normative and if its principles generally appear as statements in the indicative, it is that the imperatives are reserved for a meta-language. The paradigms of logic are directions for valid and consistent conclusions and if they were not binding there would be no point to them. This whole critique of consistency attempts to render explicit what is implicit in our judgments, perhaps unreflective, of what is valid and invalid. Logic could not, of course, appeal to something beyond itself for validation. What criteria could determine the validity of logic when logic itself provides the criteria of validity used elsewhere, and the application of these to logic itself would beg the question. Of course nothing here commits Lewis to any particular logic; he is only pointing to a categorical distinction between valid and invalid inferring, a distinction essential to knowledge that could only be renounced at the cost of reasonableness itself.

What Lewis calls the critique of *cogent* thinking and believing is larger than the critique of consistency. Consistency alone cannot distinguish science from sophistry. The critique of cogency attempts to answer questions of objective reference, it builds out from consistent options and brings into play extralogical considerations of relevance and evidence. Cogency thus is also mandated and it is a normative industry in the sense that the canons that stand the test of time are binding. (Lewis's whole theory of epistemology could be described as a critique of cogency.)

Consistency extends beyond those intuitions and practices which logic and epistemology capture; there is a kind of consistency also between what we know and can foresee and what is right to do. Hence the imperative to conduct doing according to the advice of cognition, i.e., in the light of what is objective and has objective reference, or what is the best approximation.

The critique of doing includes but is not coextensive with prudence and justice. But these also are categorical, for in neither domain can we escape the need for right decision, and here objective reference entails the recognition that persons are not things but are capable of self-government, have needs and engage in complex interpersonal relations.

Prudence and justice will shortly be discussed in detail. But it is worth pausing to note the purchase that Lewis's emphasis on the hypothetical gives him. Just as consistency is a necessary but not sufficient condition for cogency, so cogency is a necessary but not sufficient condition for right doing. The critiques thus in some sense nest in a hierarchical order of imperativeness. Of special interest is the relation between prudence and justice. For Lewis, both are categorical, and so their claims are always relevant. Prudence is a necessary condition for justice in the sense that if prudence had no standing, justice would have none. As consistency gives alternatives for cogency to choose among, so prudence gives alternatives for justice to choose among. And even if prudence is sometimes justifiably overruled, the validity of its claims persist. And justice at least can seek creative solutions to conflicts so as to meld interests and cultivate the conditions that minimize conflicts. The critique of justice is the long-term project here, but we need to look at the critique of prudence in preparation for it.

Now prudence is the critique of our selves in our pursuit of self-determined objectives. It includes an assessment of what consequences follow on a decision, their quality as good and their larger role as contributory to a life good on the whole. Lewis takes as the *Summum Bonum,* as the reasonable objective of a life, this overall objective. Thus prudence is the critique from the point of view of one's life as a whole. There is a strong analogy between Lewis's treatment of prudence as the wise direction or ordering of values and Butler's reasonable self-love as the wise ruling of the passions. For Butler, self-love is not a passion among passions but a natural authoritative principle we find within ourselves which governs them. (Having found such a legislative principle, Butler later sees no difficulty in a parallel principle of conscience in regulating interpersonal behavior.) Lewis also finds that we do in fact order our inclinations and our values, and prudence seeks to make explicit the principles that have proved satisfactory in the implicit operation of our self-government. If one raises the question "Why be prudent?" several points have to be noted in reply. First, as a type of principle its warrant rests on no other kind of epistemological consideration than those required to warrant being cogent or being consistent—in effect, as indicated above, man is not free not to deliberate the future that he foresees. Second, we must distinguish between a particular content for prudence and the unavoidability of a prudential category. The question "Why be prudent?" with reference to the general category of prudence, thus almost answers itself—and indeed in this form has seldom been raised. It is just as if one asked a psychologist, "Why develop as a person?" rather than what kind of an ego shall we become? Third, the warrant for a particular principle of prudence, i.e., the content of the category, lies in reflection and the results of reflection.

Lewis works with a very rich notion of prudence. It is his term for the right ordering of a life, or segments and even miniplans within a life. Since a community is a community of lives, any ordering within a community or of the shared objectives of individuals will presuppose the principles of ordering an individual life, i.e., prudence. Prudence is thus not to be equated with self-love or egoism, with the self versus the other. Lewis indeed is attempting to avoid phrasing the problem of prudence in terms of selfishness versus social goods. He is not, like Hobbes, starting out with an individual's self-directed passions and bargaining with others for self-interest. Nor is he Kantian, in the sense of having the individual pure will produce a contractual effect by legislating for all pure wills (moral individuals) without inquiring into the particular interests of existent persons. Nor again is he relying, like Adam Smith, on a dependàble sentiment of sympathy of everyone for everyone else. On the other hand, he has not the resources of Dewey to challenge the dichotomy of individual/social as a basic ethical category. Lewis's own picture of a prudent life is as follows: a life in which there are mutual undertakings, common obligations, cooperative behavior in which diverse roles would be played, a reasonable competition within a cooperative institutional framework, and above all, the freedom to pursue goals which are self-determined.

Let us consider how Lewis would justify his picture of prudence. Value terms have ultimate reference to a quality of life, and all laws of learning are laws of ameliorating this quality. We share with animals generally avoidance and pursuit behavior. However, what is distinctively human in learning is the self-conscious determination of objectives which we hold to be good and the avoidance of those which we regard as bad. Men live under the tyranny of time, and their ability to foresee a future and trace out the consequences of actions in the light of past experience creates a constraint; their freedom of choice lies in the necessity of deciding. Thus for a creature who can lay out alternative futures, decision-making is unavoidable, and it would be the great betrayal if intelligence were able to foresee but impotent to modify the actions that result on such decisions. This is not to say that both the modes of value and enjoyment and the range of control and plan are limited to those which only animals enjoy. For the arts, the social values, and all that civilization contributes are products of civilization itself, and the cumulative character of our knowledge and of our institutions. Genuinely prudential judgments thus depend on cogent judgments of objective consequences, on what good consequences we can realize and are possible (thus involving consistency), and those which are avoidable. But we need not merely the intelligence of cogent thinking, but also the rational ability to be constrained by such foresight where such constraint is formulated as general principles of deliberate government.

Still, even if prudence is not selfish, how does one justify so long-range a content for the principle as a life good on the whole? Why not rather meet each situation as it comes, following the dictates of impulse? Lewis distinguishes two situations covered by such a Cyrenaic formulation. One is an unreflective merely acting on impulse. This cannot even be a candidate for a rational principle of prudence or self-government. The other could conceivably be a reflective principle, if one despairs of real foresight and real control, and is resigned to abandoning the values that can only be achieved with such foresight and control; it might conceivably be the case that planning was always abortive and the future totally unpredictable. Lewis believes such a principle to be incorrect, both as respects knowledge of the world, the possibilities of control, and scope of aspirations. In fact we shall see that he finds ample empirical grounds for meshing the content of a wise and prudent life with a just and social one. But the prudential claims will never be lost in the social, since a society is a community of lives, and so any ordering of the shared objectives of a community of individuals will presuppose the principles of wise ordering of the individual life, i.e., prudence.

If one is asked to formulate as an imperative the kind of constraint that prudence dictates, it can only derive from those distinctive features that were indicated at the outset which were involved in the fact that men must deliberate and act, with the required constraint for the future, and in ways that are derived from past experience in the light of objective knowledge. It would read: so act as to maximize the quality of individual life, a life good-on-the-whole.

In the light of the preceding what then can be said about the relation between prudence and justice; about the directives for weighing our own interests against impersonal or social ones, the rules which adjudicate conflicts between persons, and the claims of individual interests on social policy? Involved here is no single issue but a large package. Are there such rules? If so, can they be formulated in such a way as to satisfy the formal requirements of rules in general yet remain corrigible and open to advances in knowledge about ourselves and conditions? Involved here are at least two aspects of the relation of prudence to justice. One is the way in which prudential considerations are built into the system of justice itself—e.g., in what ways are individual initiatives protected in contract and the legal guarantees of ownership? The other is the way of resolving conflicts between the individual interests and the operations of the system of justice. This latter, especially, involves the question of the authority or mandate of justicial rules.

Let us examine these issues, although not altogether in the order listed. If anything, Western tradition is embarrassingly rich in directives. The most familiar is the golden rule, whether stated in its traditional form of doing or in the less familiar form of requiring respect for others. Customary morality is replete with many others, such as: love your neighbor, give each man his due, and seek peace. There are also requirements of benevolence, compassion, sympathy, and righteous resentment. Of course there have been competitors running in a different strain: private vices make public benefits, or more recently, what's good for General Motors . . . etc. Most of these explicitly concern, or could be construed as dealing with, the distribution of goods and evils, and perhaps even as extending the prudential ordering over persons and time. Of course egalitarian principles have been central in our political and moral attitudes, although this is only one method of distribution. Competing nonegalitarian principles are usually elitist, but sometimes will call for sacrifice and of giving to others more than their due. Clearly, too, there is no agreement as to what it is that is to be distributed or ordered (wealth, opportunity, liberty, etc.) and on what criteria, for example merit or need.

Materials such as these, at least on Lewis's view, are the data with which moral philosophers must begin. They do not create these commitments (any more than the logician creates the sense of consistency). Their task is to clarify, to enlarge and examine the fundamental distinctions and what is entailed by them, to tease out of judgments actually made and judgments about judgments and to forge from these the critique of what is implicit in our morally reflective judgments.

The relation of justice to prudence further illustrates the interdependence of critiques. Prudence is antecedent to justice, taken at first in the limited sense of directives governing our own actions as they affect others. If we could not represent absent and objective self-interests, we should scarcely be able to raise the question of the interests of others as comparable with our own. If we could not subordinate the immediately enticing to future goods we could not regulate our behavior toward others nor begin to weigh the claims of others on our own decisions. And finally, if we could not act in ways formulable as rules or imperatives which, if valid, are valid for all like cases, the problem of just principles could not arise.

That a category of justice is required, follows quite simply from the need for directives to govern relations to others. The rules of justice are simply the socially significant counterpart to the imperatives of prudence, given a community of human beings. Of course the necessity of the category doesn't determine the character of the rules; that will depend on other factors, including empirical ones. But the person who would ignore the question of justice would be like the unreflective Cyrenaic in the question of prudence. On the other hand, there might be limiting situations in which reflection would conclude that the only reasonable principle is for every man to follow what prudence alone dictates. In this instance prudence would be elevated to the content of justice. But Lewis, like the Utilitarians, would believe this to hold under only a very extreme and aberrant condition of turbulence.

If Western experience has not spoken in a single voice about justicial directives and their content, it has even less agreed on their justification. The major modern contenders were appeals to rationality (whether intuitive or Kantian) and utilitarianism which subordinates justicial rules to terms of good consequence and happiness. Thus far Lewis's discussion of imperatives has been designed to handle this problem, including even the preemptive (hierarchical) ordering of critiques. He has attempted all along to naturalize the problem of justification by stressing the pervasiveness of directives generally, and their continuity. For any category of objectives, rules of rightness are needed which define reasonable pursuit. Some objectives are optional, i.e., hypothetical and contingent on our interest in them. When, however, the objective is nonrepudiatable—when we have no option about whether to pursue it or not—then in Lewis's sense the imperative is categorical. Thus his problem is to demonstrate the necessity of the category of justice as nonrepudiatable. But that too is no problem for him: the category of justice is required since men are necessarily social and live in interaction with one another: and thus directives are categorical governing relations between people. The real question is what sorts of relations are there or are there to be developed—what are to be the directives of self-legislation as regards our conduct affecting others. The only kind of justification there is for such ultimate principles of justice lies in a view of the social character of human nature and an appropriate conception of person. The job then is to capture in some formula what is presystematically intended by the morally right or just. For Lewis this means the working out of the socially significant counterpart of the Law of Objectivity—the search for what constraints it lays on our actions as they affect others.

Clearly these imperatives will share the features of valid imperatives at large, with their generality and objectivity, though they will take on a special meaning in the justicial context. In this case, objectivity refers to the recognition that other persons are like ourselves in the capacity to enjoy and suffer, who makes plans, have goals, and who find it imperative to govern themselves in the light of their own knowledge and by decisions of their own making. The rule then dictates governing of one's activities toward others as one would if the effects were to be realized with the poignancy of the immediate—hence on one's own person. It is to respect others as the reality we representationally, i.e., objectively, take them to be.

The generality involved is merely the formal requirement of any valid rule, viz., that it hold under like premises of action and circumstances. As with doing generally, under the same circumstances and conditions, the right decision is right whatever the occasion and the doer. What is right for Mary would be right for Moe and Joe, all the relevant conditions being the same. In the social context then, universality has the particular connotation of impartiality or impersonality. This universality has, of course, been captured in many ways. Some of Lewis's formulations are close to the golden rule; e.g.: Take no decision of action which is a member of any class of decisions, all members of which you would call upon others to avoid. Other statements reflect more closely Kant's first familiar imperative: Act only in ways (or by rules) which you would willingly see universalized. Or again: Acknowledge as a right of freedom against others only what you would accept as a right against yourself.

Such formulations have faced traditional objections. Little guidance is given on what feature is to be universalized, but also they seem to legitimize counterintuitive judgments. For example, an employer might want to universalize the maxim of paying only minimum wages or a puritan might want to universalize an inferior status for illegitimate children even if the next depression or a correction in the birth records were to put the employer or the puritan in the weaker role! Or, and less traumatically, enthusiasts of oatmeal for breakfast or Beethoven's later quartets might be thoroughly satisfied to see these become universal fare, gastronomic or musical. Something clearly is needed to block the elevation of private preferences into moral precepts.

The way Lewis tackles the problem, though it may not altogether dispel, helps to limit the force of such "illegitimate" universalizations. In the first place, the *you* who is doing the universalizing is not intended to be personal, nor does "the moral law is no respecter of persons" intend that all that is personal in the ways of tastes, maturity, vocation, sensory defects, and special relations (familial, fiduciary) should be as irrelevant. Since for Lewis the meaning of an act cannot be specified apart from its consequences, and in this case the consequences for enjoyment and suffering are vital, then insofar as the special features modify what is experienced, the act for purposes of universalization has to be specified by this whole set of projectible consequences. Hence Lewis's argument requires that the consequences be viewed from the point of view of those who are to enjoy and suffer—i.e., as though you are to stand in their place. What is required is impersonality in the weighing, and the decision-maker is to be reckoned only as he is affected. Thus nothing should be acceptable to *you* in making a decision with consequences for Mary, Moe, and Joe, which would not be acceptable were you yourself in the place of Mary or Moe or Joe.

This necessary reference to consequences makes possible a further move on

Lewis's part, extending the formulation that we saw was close to the golden rule. There is no way of identifying or specifying an act or a way of acting except by reference to some aspect of the consequences. Thus the descriptions will be as varied and as full as the consequences which affect the enjoyment or suffering (or the quality of life) of those affected. And thus, negatively, an act is wrong insofar as it falls under a description involving harmful consequences. The maximizing of profits, e.g., is but one description of an act, while another legitimate description might be the imposing of near-starvation.

Such a rule or imperative does not provide sufficient criteria for making a particular decision. "Be just" here has the status of "Be consistent," "Be cogent," etc. At the very best, rules can do no more than to divide cases into those which are permissible and those which are not. What is spelled out here is the domain of relevant considerations as required by his pragmatic criterion of meaning when applied to "right." The exigencies of any actual situation would seldom allow the realization of all and only good consequences; but the requirement remains to examine all the consequences and all the alternate paths of action, including those which might alter the conditions so as not to necessitate harmful consequences, and to exercise ingenuity in this process and in the harmonizing of disparate interests. The right then, in the sense of one's actual duty in a concrete situation, is that decision which gives the greatest probability of contributing to a life good on the whole. It needs the support of empirical knowledge about human nature, about what is good, and the possibilities of controlling its realization. It depends too on the kind of society and practices that do or could prevail. One can well imagine austere social arrangements where independence is magnified and cooperation minimized and where the rules of prudence could be elevated into a rule of justice. One can similarly imagine an extraordinary society where everyone puts the objectives and interests of others above his own. These are limiting cases (and on Lewis's view neither would result in a very rich quality of associative living), but just what the social situation is (or could be) also depends on empirical assessment. Certain it is that the long war for civil rights seems to be moving toward human rights and that is enough to show that the content of justice may itself develop. Yet justice, at least taken narrowly, is not all of social morality and, though necessary, is not enough to guarantee any genuinely rich quality of association. This must depend surely on interpersonal relationships which go far beyond what is merely contractual.

Now Lewis is pushing a Kantian approach toward a utilitarian one, led both by his concern for universality and impersonality and by his concern that happiness be included as a genuinely moral end. It remains to be seen how far from this start, largely Kantian, he can go to resolve the stubborn problem, especially for traditional Utilitarianism, of why be just. The problem is not so urgent for Kant, since he ties morality to rationality. And Lewis has exploited the force of this part of Kant in showing the continuity of moral imperatives with right directives generally. Thus the question of imperatives as such raises no isolated problem of justification. But just where Kant runs into difficulties Lewis brings up the utilitarian reserves; he can then make an appeal to happiness or enjoyment which Kant could invoke only deviously; he can forge a criterion for choosing among alternatives that admit of universalization; and he can raise the problem (as we shall see shortly) of the ends of social institutions and criteria for their evaluation.

But Utilitarianism also has its difficulties which Lewis still has to face. At issue is not the existence but the validation of any rule requiring the overriding of prudence by social justice. Bentham seems to have thought that he had discovered in the Greatest Good for the Greatest Number a premise implicit in arguments actually advanced in moral debate, but he really offered no further proof for that principle nor for the rule that requires that each one count for one and no one for more than one. Mill, quite sensitive to the issue, seems to have thought that the principles of justice were nondemonstrable, but, like Lewis, he points out that the ultimate principles of logic are in the same condition. And yet Sidgwick, the last of the classic utilitarians, could find no justification or no rule which requires one man to take into account the interests of others so long as he requires of others no similar consideration for him.

Sidgwick has in effect painted himself into a corner from which there is no out, precisely because he has, in effect, furnished an institutional arrangement in which every man stands alone and can only have contractual relations with his fellows.

In a way the Kantians had already provided a way out, because although the categorical imperative continues to focus on the lone decision-maker, the question to be decided has shifted to what kind of practice is he ready to will universally. While this lone person still takes a contractual attitude, the situation no longer concerns a person occupied only with his own benefit. What Kant is doing is to generate a moral community of moral agents each of whom is legislating for all and thus to work out a moral order or institutional system for all. But there is still lacking a method for determining which institutions to create, and he has eliminated an evaluation of consequences to determine the value of the practice.

Lewis's effort is to bring a rapprochement between the utilitarian (especially Sidgwick's) and Kantian concerns. Sidgwick's concern reformulated by Lewis becomes: why should I refrain from doing that which I call upon others to refrain from, or better, why should I limit myself to those acts which I would willingly see as general practices? He is then in a position to ask what are the criteria for desirable practices? In contrast to Kant, Lewis looks not to the decision-maker's readiness to will but to the impact of the consequences on the quality of life of those who are to suffer or enjoy them, i.e., from the varying standpoints of the effects of the practice. Again he can ask what kind of system will contribute to enhancing the quality of life. In effect what Lewis has taken from the utilitarian is his emphasis on consequences and from Kant the maintenance of a willed or self-conscious system of institutions. But the latter is not so much contractarian in orientation but rather a way of life. The net result is a critique of practices but only indirectly related to the greatest good (and not for the greatest number, since that is indeterminate). The system of practices has become constitutive of the good life rather than merely an instrument to the summed goodnesses of individuals.

But the consequences of practices, and what would contribute to a rich life and what policies need to be implemented to achieve a genuinely desirable social order, depend on empirical considerations and much increased knowledge about ourselves and our social relations. This introduces a second prong—Lewis's account of social morality in large and of justice in particular. The first prong—just explored—faced toward epistemological concerns, to a kind of philosophic in-house effort to legitimize morally right decisions and to assure them respectable cognitive status. He tried to show that imperatives are pervasive and that they are formulatable in systems of rules which are a part of the way we utilize the past in an effort to confront the future. Thus moral imperatives are continuous with imperatives at large and are natural ingredients in human decision-making generally.

Lewis is attempting now to show not merely that we are social, but that sociability itself generates or at least modifies social imperatives. He is attempting to show not merely that groups often must act as moral agents making decisions that have assignable responsibilities, although of course they do. Again he is not primarily interested in underlining the intricate way that private goals are interwoven with social ones—the former socially modified and the latter products of individual decisions—so as to make any simple statement of the egoism-altruism problem miss the mark (although that is so too). Lewis is attempting something more intricate. He is actually insisting that the distinctive manner of intelligent and reasonable responses is itself an historical product and cannot be understood apart from the distinctively human character of social evolution and the processes of civilization.

In a way this too echoes the Kantian theme of the tensions created by man's intrinsic unsocial sociability, a theme which dialectical idealism and materialism developed. But in sharpest contrast to Kant, Lewis sees nothing in the way of social organization that is untouched by rational decision.

In this new perspective the problem is no longer concerned with the egoist reckoning a most profitable use of existent institutions for his own ends, nor even with the relation of the prudential and the social, but with the development and critique of institutions as embodying a rational human ideal. Thus in contrast to Hegelian and Kantian views of progress, which see men as witnesses of a predetermined social development, on Lewis's view they are participants. There is nothing in our knowledge, material culture, social organization, and conflicts which does not show the mark of human decision and of social memory, which self-consciously seeks out our past and constantly reassesses the lessons of our social inheritance. Success is a genuine achievement, and failure a genuine hazard. Not only is the construction of a world a cooperative matter, including what we take to be objective and what we can represent, but the projection, selection, and critique of ends for ourselves and our community is likewise a cooperative social matter. This holds also for what kinds of persons we take ourselves and others to be. All these are products of the interaction of men living in groups, and over time. This interaction has a complex producer-product character; cumulatively and progressively it modifies the material culture and the kinds of association, and vastly and exponentially alters the quality of living.

It is a basic consideration for the valid imperatives of individual human action, that the possibility of that kind of evolution which man alone exhibits, and of that progressive amelioration and enrichment of individual life found only in the species, is conditional upon the modification of individual behavior by social agencies. Indeed it requires modification of the individual mentality itself, as to its grasp and content, as an effect of social relations— relationships which themselves similarly evolve, and whose evolution is by the same instrumentalities:[36]

But for Lewis it is a datum that we are also social not because of our instincts but in spite of them. Men alone have a history and alone their history is modified by the apprehension of it. The ability to represent and accumulate the experience of the past, to start where previous generations have left off, magnifies the opportunity for gratifying experiences and complicates the modes; while knowledge, viewed as a historical and accumulative gain, extends the control and increase in the likelihood of enjoyment. Thus the sources and the certainty of goods and of knowledge are increased past anything attainable by an individual and raise for him a concern for the future that outlasts his life.

This evolution of institutions and of knowledge goes far beyond what would be required by biological evolution. There is nothing about our ways of responding that does not show the mark of social memory and our social traditions—from a common language to the construction of a common world and a shared reality. This social development is beyond any mere impact of the natural environment and evolutionary forces that make for biological adaptation and sociability.

We can look at this cultural history from the time-worn distinction between science and technology on the one hand and mores and morality (including regulatory institutions) on the other, for they highlight different features of our cultural and social inheritance. The first looks mainly toward material necessities and their distribution while the second toward the preservation and quality of group living. While this distinction is serviceable, nevertheless it points to no absolute in the culture.

The history of science illustrates, should it need illustration, the cumulative power of intelligence working through the social order. Today's school children converse about what was, in the days of a Faraday or Newton, on the frontiers of discovery. Modern science depends on the slow process by which theories are corrected and successes capitalized in pursuing a shared interest in understanding the world; clearly the achievement of any scientist today lies dramatically beyond the powers of any lone individual. The fantastic achievements of technology and economics reflect the cumulative power for reaching and sharing common interests in material things. These of course have brought about the spectacular modification in the means and materials of the quality of the life that today is open to us.

By all rights, as those most lately come and able to enjoy the consequences of this long historical process, we should be the most favored of all. No material good which is available to some should long remain unavailable to any; no life supporting resource—say of medicine—could not soon be open to each; no information which, in the marvels of communication and literacy, should not quickly become a universal resource. Education now reserved for some could be accessible to all who could use it. Clearly we are a long way from this; but even if we had thus spread the achievements in material culture, no guarantee would follow for the richness of the quality of living.

We are thus inevitably turned once again to the institutions, private and social, of control and regulation. Perhaps it is immediately in point to remark that even material culture does not rest on features which themselves are material. Should some calamity destroy the products of our culture but leave us with the know-how, with communication and cooperation it would take little more than a generation to recover; but if by some science-fiction disaster we were to lose the knowledge but be left with the artifacts merely, we should nearly have to relive the history of civilization.

And again, science itself, and the development of scientific method (publicity, intersubjective test, the importance of securing all available evidence in support of a warranted conclusion), education and communication, and even the conditions of making a social contribution—all depend on the social agencies of transmission. The norms of consistency and validity as well as particular achievement are social products—products of cultural inheritance forged over long epochs. Truth itself is a social category that depends on a common concern for objective knowledge and understanding of the natural environment. Science and technology depend on a supportive social order as the transmitting agency—not only protecting continuity, preserving the hard-won discoveries, but also institutionalizing learning and the exchange and communication of information and techniques. Indeed, insofar as freedom of inquiry and public canons of corrigibility and objectivity of method is concerned, the community of scientists comes close to being a moral association. And truth itself, as a social, cultural, and historical product adds its own imperatives and constitutive values.

Science and its values are part of a more extended pattern of mores which is itself evolving, in part at least, self-consciously and beyond the biological needs or the minimal social needs that group living requires. This evolution reflects the distinctive ways of decision-making and the self-conscious interplay of individuals and groups. These mores are marked by a heightened sense of obligation, impartial resentment, a sense of fairness, and the whole fabric of patterned expectations and expanding roles. These mores or moralities are critical not only as they provide transmitting agencies for acquired knowledge, but also as they propose common goals and long-range aspirations which include a concern for generations as yet unborn. This clearly involves a growing sense of community, of a common world (now in a moral sense), a common interest in maintaining social institutions, and a common concern for enriching the quality of associated living. Universal rights, the increasing participation in the good life (however removed from fact) are emergent directives, and as ideals they are as constitutive in the social domain as consistency and cogency are in science.

Even prudence depends on acquired modes of social response—on wisdom and experience that no man could live out for himself. It is not only that roles and opportunities are expanding enormously, but also the range and effectiveness of individual planning are increased through the accumulated products of tradition and the growing complexity of social arrangements which the division of labor, increased productivity and leisure provide. Indeed prudential ways of response as intelligent and rational depend on acquired modes which are socially modified, learned, and molded. Precious among moral achievements is also an increasing degree of liberty and autonomy, i.e., a certain independence from the community and a larger scope for individual initiative, interests, styles of living, vocations and professions. Clearly this liberty, which is not merely freedom from external restraints but freedom to participate, is implicated in the fullest sense of self-realization. Thus the discovery of ourselves, of the capacity to propose and criticize objectives and to govern ourselves in their achievement is learned in a social context and is relative to the quality of association and the social milieu. The kind of society, the quality of associations and their supportive or affiliative character, the sense of responsibility for others and for our own self-government, of loyalty, and of what is just will in large measure determine our own sense of self—of what we are or could be.

Ironically, it is just those features which could open onto so bright a future which generate in largest measure the most serious strains that tax our natural endowment. Technological and scientific progress, together with the complexities of social structure, which elicit talent and encourage independence, freedom and the sense of self, also create the need for greater restraint on the part of the individual and the need for reasonable self-government. The crisis lies in the dialectic between liberty and control, between enlarged opportunities and the erosion of privacy and liberties, between the powers of states to meliorate the human condition and to destroy civilization. Self-control is required on all sides, since there are opposing needs—for maintaining the social order and for maintaining liberties—and yet each involves human costs. Such a dialectic points to the institutionalization of criticism within the social context: the need is not merely to look for the imperatives, prescriptions that grow out of and will preserve the *status quo* and to avoid the errors of the past; it is rather, through institutionalized criticism, to invent fresh forms and articulate fresh norms that will allow the development of personality and affiliative or communal relations. Once again we are turned to the moral factors involved in self-control and self-government.

This is the setting for a final attempt to formulate the imperatives of justice. Each man in a society can recognize as right conduct toward his fellows only that which he is prepared to recognize as similarly sanctioned in their conduct toward him; in effect, no one can claim for himself a liberty or respect in his relations toward others anything which he doesn't recognize as a liberty of others against himself. Another way of putting this is that it is irrational that any given man should rightfully seek to profit from association (i.e., cooperation) with others and fail to condemn in himself modes of action which if accepted generally, i.e., generalized, would dispel the possibility that others might similarly profit from associating (cooperating) with him. This way of stating the issue suggests the importance of the quality of association for the development of personality, but it sanctions no particular social order nor determines the degree and manner by which competition and cooperation shall be regulated. For this, further appeal must be made to the empirical needs and purposes of men as regards, at any given time, the effects of initiative and its regulation. Thus an ideal or principle of social justice does not provide the decision, say, between laissez-faire and socialism (or some compromise). The choice between a greater freedom in individual enterprise and the possibly greater productivity or greater security of the individual and a possibly more equal distribution of goods according to needs is still in the balance. But even where the relation of economic competition and cooperation is determined, it is still important to remember that there are domains beyond the economic, and what might be decided there need not apply for the cooperation or competition in these other domains. Some criteria of the public good are obviously called for in such decisions. A common market, or even international commercial regulation, need not mean a discouraging of competition and initiative in science and art. Finally, no law is valid save what depends on the *consent* of the governed, since no man can rationally claim the advantages of cooperation while dissenting by his actions from those restrictions which make both cooperation possible and the common pursuit of common goals. This defines the limits of dissidence—it cannot justly be directed to the disruption or destruction of an order by those who adhere to the general framework and desire to continue sharing its benefits. Clearly this only holds insofar as the social organization reflects the willingness of those who are partners to it and so long as their constructive dissent and efforts to correct it have a fair and public hearing. But that corrigibility and that criticism also depend on the social order as a transmitting agency.

Notes—Chapter Fifteen

1. The writer's debt is large to students who shared many a seminar in which Lewis's work played a large part, but special acknowledgment is due to Robert Schwartz, Jay Hullett, Larry Foster, Foster Tait, Emily Michaels, James Gibson, and Vincent Luizzi.

2. Those who are acquainted with Nero Wolfe will, however, remember that he read through the *Symbolic Logic* while engaged in the cases recorded in *Three Men Out.*

3. C. I. Lewis, *A Survey of Symbolic Logic* (Berkeley: University of California Press, 1918).

4. C. I. Lewis and C. H. Langford, *Symbolic Logic* (New York: The Appleton Century Company, 1932).

5. C. I. Lewis, "The Pragmatic Element in Knowledge," *University of California Publications in Philosophy* VI: 205-27 (Howison Lecture, 1926).

6. C. I. Lewis, *Mind and the World Order: Outline of a Theory of Knowledge* (New York: Charles Scribner's Sons, 1929).

7. C. I. Lewis, *An Analysis of Knowledge and Valuation* (La Salle, Ill.: The Open Court Publishing Company, 1946).

8. C. I. Lewis, *The Ground and Nature of the Right* (New York: Columbia University Press, 1955).

9. C. I. Lewis, "Rational Imperatives," in *Vision and Action: Essays in Honor of Horace M. Kallen,* ed. Sidney Ratner (New Brunswick, N.J.: Rutgers University Press, 1953), pp. 148-66. Reprinted in *Clarence Irving Lewis, Values and Imperatives, Studies in Ethics,* ed. John Lange (Stanford, Cal.: Stanford University Press, 1969), pp. 156-77.

10. C. I. Lewis, *Our Social Inheritance* (Bloomington, Ind.: Indiana University Press, 1957).

11. C. I. Lewis, "Logic and Pragmatism," *Contemporary American Philosophy,* (New York: Macmillan, 1930), p. 32. Kant's impact was intensified by Lewis's influential Kant seminar, which educated Harvard philosophers for three decades.

12. *Ibid.,* p. 43.

13. Lewis, "Pragmatic Element in Knowledge," p. 206.

14. *Ground and Nature,* p. 32.

15. Lewis, *Mind and World Order,* p. 66.

16. A symposium on "The Experiential Element in Knowledge," containing "Are Phenomenal Reports Absolutely Certain?" by Hans Reichenbach, "Sense and Certainty," by Nelson Goodman, "The Given Element in Empirical Knowledge," by C. I. Lewis, *Philosophical Review,* 1952, pp. 140-64.

17. Lewis, *Knowledge and Valuation,* p. 72.

18. *Ibid.,* p. 139.

19. Lewis, "Pragmatic Element in Knowledge," p. 214.

20. Lewis, "Logic and Pragmatism," p. 49.

21. Lewis, *Knowledge and Valuation,* p. 133.

22. *Ibid.,* p. 141.

23. *Ibid.,* p. 146.

24. The problem is the focus of bk. I, *An Analysis of Knowledge and Valuation.*

25. Lewis, "Pragmatic Element in Knowledge," p. 219.

26. Lewis, *Knowledge and Valuation,* p. 208.

27. *Ibid.,* p. 208.

28. *Ibid.,* p. 338.

29. *Ibid.,* p. 345.

30. *Ibid.*, p. 361.

31. *Mind and the World Order*, p. 368.

32. The relevant materials are developed in detail in *An Analysis of Knowledge and Valuation*, Book III.

33. The relevant materials are to be found in *The Ground and Nature of the Right* and *Our Social Inheritance*. See also *Values and Imperatives* and "Subjective Right and Objective Right" in C. I. Lewis collected papers, ed. John Goheen and John Mothershead (Stanford: Stanford University Press, 1970).

34. *Ground and Nature*, p. 17.

35. "The Rational Imperatives," p. 153.

36. *Ground and Nature*, p. 90.

Epilogue

We have carried the story almost to the midpoint of the twentieth century. Although a few of the later writings of Lewis and Dewey come afterward, the period of World War II and its immediate aftermath is a great divide. The character of life undergoes vast changes, global relations reach a new level, and directions of thought in every field undergo transformations. In any case, with the growth of intercommunication and greater and more rapid mingling of thinkers, the story is now that of Western philosophy in America, rather than—if it ever was—simply of American philosophy.

Of course American philosophy all through the twentieth century responded directly to influences from revolutions in European thought. The influence of Whitehead and Russell's *Principia Mathematica* was as incalculably great here as in the rest of the Western world. Any continuation of our work would have to reckon with the tremendous influence of Whitehead's later process philosophy, which he worked out largely at Harvard and which has become essentially an American philosophic theme of growing contemporary interest. Bertrand Russell's analytic philosophy (combining a Humean sensationalism with his own logical analysis) was equally influential, though it was chiefly action at a distance. And it would have to reckon also with the formalistic approaches of Carnap at Chicago, and the informalist and more dispersed later influence of Wittgenstein's second period from abroad. Carnap was only one of the many Continental scholars driven out by Nazism who came to enrich the American scene. Many were logical positivists and their scientific and logical interests were not alien to the themes already developing in American pragmatism and naturalism. A kind of multifaceted fusion took place in the *Encyclopedia of Unified Science,* modifying both the imported philosophy and the native brand.

As for the period after World War II, perhaps we are too close to discern the major trends that are developing. But it looks as though old loyalties to philosophical -isms have given way to a regrouping around problems and fields. With the tremendous growth of philosophy accompanying the expansion of higher educa-

959

tion, and the great mobility of professors as well as students, few departments have long maintained a single stamp. Systematic textbooks from a single point of view have given way to collections presenting different approaches organized about philosophical topics or problems. Two movements are pertinent here: the inner movement among philosophical fields on the one hand, and the growth of philosophical work in relation to other domains on the other.

Logic, philosophy of science, and epistemology generally (with varyingly assigned borders among them) have had perhaps the greatest growth. In logic rapid technical progress resulted in a multiplicity of formal systems and a deepening of fundamental notions; the general dominance of systems of material implication established by *Principia Mathematica* was challenged by the rise of modal logics. Studies of axiomatization, as well as generally of the foundations of mathematics, raised problems of philosphical logic, merging with the philosophy of science and epistemology. Relations to computer developments and automation provided a fresh focus, and studies of induction, probability, decision theory—often prompted by very practical problems of the application of science—raised older issues to a new level. While the positivistic emphasis in philosophy of science had cultivated richly the logic of measurement and went on to refine operationalism and to explore the semantics of empirical theory, its own critique began to question the sharpness of the lines between theory and observation, as well as between stipulation and factual assumption. The intimate relations that grew up between logic and empirical linguistics made a rich variety of phenomena out of hitherto austere and stately concepts in strict formal relations. Oxford ordinary language analysis attacked many logical concepts in its revolt against formalism, and Harvard neo-pragmatism, which had started out with an attack on the dogmas of empiricism, has gone so far as almost to make an empirical science out of epistemology—reverting in this respect to its Jamesean progenitor. In the philosophy of science the old view of constantly cumulative growth of science has been challenged by a sociological view of theories as imaginative products replacing one another as paradigms to govern an age, to be overthrown rather than disproved. The consequence of the controversy in this field has been a growing relation between philosophy and the history of science in the attempt to ferret out the finer shades of the functioning of theory. In another wing on the epistemological stage, under phenomenological influence, attention has turned to the problem of intentionality—the question what our perceptions are ''of'' or ''about'' insofar as they are about or of things which may not exist external to thought. Many of these problems, as well as traditional problems of nominalism and realism, are discussed today in a fashion that no longer draws sharp lines even between epistemology and metaphysics.

Interest in metaphysics, for a while eclipsed by epistemological interests, revived under several stimuli, not least of which was the fact that the epistemological formulations themselves were driven increasingly—indeed, the more successful they were thought to be—to furnish accounts of what there is. Interest was also stimulated by the *Review of Metaphysics* and by the founding of the Metaphysical Society. It was accelerated at a later period by the entry of American Catholic philosophy into the mainstream of American philosophy after a long period of self-imposed isolation. To the traditional problems were added the newer problems generated by the interface of metaphysics and epistemology, such as the problems of individuals, identity, persons, mind-machine relations, etc. And the interface of metaphysics and logic has raised problems of the nature of possibility and the theory of essentialism. Whitehead's influence has grown considerably in this period, first in respect to his organic view of reality, and then in regard to his process philosophy (which has had a special influence on the philosophy of religion). With such multiplication of directions, the problem of categories has emerged and led to considerable metaphysical experimentation in an effort to determine the best concepts in terms of which to describe nature and experience as event. A further metaphysical infusion on the American scene has been the influence of phenomenology and existentialism which have come closest to the older pattern of "schools," though perhaps chiefly as a methodological emphasis.

A salutary feature of both epistemology and metaphysics has been the recognition that many of their problems are continuous with the problems long studied in the history of philosophy. But the historical works are less frequently approached these days with the assumption that the earlier formulations are only stages to our own formulations and ideas. Hence there has been a veritable renaissance in the history of philosophy in which figures and problems are studied in terms of their own context and their own problems even where the aim is to find leads for present concerns. There is increasing philosophical dialogue today with Plato and Aristotle, Descartes and Locke and Berkeley, Kant and Hegel. A great deal of this work is going on in America, if only because of the very large number of philosophers in the country who give expression to this interest. The momentum of these studies is largely a phenomenon of the last quarter of a century.

In value theory, ethics remained divided for some time between the naturalists and the ordinary language analysts. The naturalists pursued a variety of paths: bringing utilitarianism up to date both as regards the theory of measurement and investigations as to the quality of life; building an ethical theory on depth psychology or on specific psychological theories of purpose or planning behavior; showing the consequences of different scientific beliefs (particularly in psychology and the social sciences) and of different sociohistorical structures for ethical theory; exploring the value-laden character of scientific work itself. The ordinary language analysts maintained the sharp distinction between theoretical ethics or metaethics on the one hand, and normative or substantive ethics on the other, and devoted themselves almost wholly to the former, exploring particularly problems of justification and reasons for actions. Recently, interest has moved to specific moral problems—e.g., problems of bioethics or of social ethics—and concrete and serious moral issues have been the concern of moral philosophers generally.

If we turn to the second problem—the growth of philosophical work in relation to other domains—we have the paradoxical situation that some such relations, being of long standing, are thought of as parts of philosophy proper, while others quite parallel are regarded as external applications of philosophy. Among the first are aesthetics or philosophy of art, social and political philosophy, philosophy of religion, and of course philosophy of science and philosophy of mathematics. Among the latter are philosophy of literature, philosophy of physics (or of biology), philosophy of history, philosophy of economics, and philosophy of technology. Philosophy of law straddles the border; it has become so popular as to be almost "in."

Almost all these areas have experienced both growth and transformation in the past quarter of a century. Aesthetics has moved beyond traditional questions of the nature of the creative process, of the aesthetic response, and of the communication between artist and audience, to the more intensive study of particular works of art, in relation to different media and to the history of the arts, to the interpretation of art as symbolic system, and to comparative studies of the imagination in art and in science. Philosophy of religion has veered sharply away from "proofs" of the existence of God and the soul to questions of the nature of religious experience and the functions of religious systems in life processes. Finally, social and political philosophy, having emancipated themselves from the straitjacket that the stereotypes of the Cold War period had imposed on political and social thought, and recognizing the tremendous transformation in social and political problems on the global scene—the problems generated by economic development, population growth, depletion of resources, political organization, and conflict in the older colonial areas throughout the world, as well as the new social problems in the richer developed countries—have been increasingly taking the plunge into analysis close to practical issues: problems of war and peace, violence, formulae of justice and just distribution, and patterns of authority and family structure, etc. In the remainder of the philosophy-of fields it is perhaps enough to indicate general directions of change. There is a greater relation of the fields to specific bodies of knowledge based on an acquired competence in the special field—e.g., the philosophy of physics, or of biology—not merely the general features of philosophy of science, or the philosophy of literature specifically and not merely a general philosophy of art. There is a receptiveness to a variety of models rather than the imposition of one; e.g., the rise of courses in philosophy of the social sciences reflects a philosophical emancipation from a commitment to impose the model of physics on the rest of potential knowledge. And there is a greater readiness to embrace the value aspects in the philosophical consideration of fields—e.g., the current rise of studies in philosophy of technology reflects the need for evaluating the present role of technology in human life and its possibilities. In all these respects, it may be that we have a movement toward the kind of integration of knowledge and of knowledge and value that characterized the eighteenth-century philosophers whom we examined, but under the conditions of vastly great complexity.

The story of philosophy in twentieth-century America is thus a formidable one. While we have no wish to prescribe for its future historians, we would suggest at least the following:

1. It should be at least a *three-volume work!*

2. It should avoid the notion that it has to discover a distinctively American philosophy in the century, rather than explore whatever patterns of intellectual relationship are actually to be found in the Western world, and increasingly in the globe as a whole.

3. It should look for—and we may hazard the suspicion that it will find—some features of the human spirit that are distinctively emphasized on the American scene and which may still be maintaining a pattern that is consonant with the American cultural traditions.

Appendix: George Herbert Mead

George Herbert Mead was born in South Hadley, Massachusetts, in 1863, the son of a Congregational minister. In 1879 he entered Oberlin College—a school with a strong liberal tradition and a pioneer in coeducation. After graduation he spent three years surveying for the Wisconsin Central Railroad, but academic interests won out and in 1887 he went to Harvard where he studied philosophy, psychology, and classics. He was a student of Royce, Palmer, and Bowen, and a tutor for William James's children. In 1888 he went to Leipzig to study psychology, and remained in Germany for several years. In 1891 Mead made two moves which had a decisive impact upon his life: he married Helen Castle, a wealthy heiress from Hawaii, and so solved his own financial problems, and he accepted appointment as an instructor in philosophy and psychology at the University of Michigan. Here he met Dewey and Charles Cooley, the sociologist, both of whom became his intimate friends. Mead was one of the contributors to the cooperative volume, *Studies in Logical Theory*, which was edited by Dewey and dedicated to James. In 1892 the University of Chicago opened its doors and Dewey became head of its philosophy department. Dewey promptly brought Mead to Chicago, where he became associate professor in 1902, full professor in 1907, and continued his career until his death in 1931.

Dewey and Mead were certainly the leaders of the so-called Chicago School of philosophy, and although Dewey is the more famous of the two, Mead was an independent thinker of great brilliance and originality. His contributions to American pragmatism are many and varied. He outdoes James in his account of the empirical self; outdoes Dewey in his contextualism, instrumentalism, and the breadth of his use of the reflex arc model, and he developed independently the social character of Peirce's semiotic. He outdoes Lewis in making explicit the psychological presuppositions of foresight—i.e., the way the future is handled in the making of present decisions—as well as the phenomenon of the impersonal in social and moral judgment, and he was more deeply involved in questions of the evolution of mind than any of the pragmatists except Wright. Indeed, in his efforts to set British empiricism in an evolutionary social perspective, Mead's work pioneered in fields of social science as diverse as the sociology of knowledge, the process of socialization, role theory, and psychodynamics. Indeed, in some sense he was more cosmopolitan than the others, for in his effort to bring a social dimension to British empiricism and evolution, his thought makes crosscurrents with Durkheim on the sociology of knowledge, with Simmel on the processes of socialization, with Piaget on the emergence of new forms of response, and with Freud on the processes of internalization.

Why then is Mead not the subject of a chapter? The decisive factor is the state of his writings. The published articles are relatively few, and so wide-ranging that it is difficult for a reader to get a sense of systematic relatedness beyond an impression of a general way of approaching problems. His work is known chiefly through four books which were assembled and edited from various student notes, stenographic materials, and his own manuscripts which were often fragmentary. This is not as haphazard as might be thought, since he regarded the lectures as his primary mode of expression and he prepared them with the minutest care. Furthermore, the men who collated and edited the materials—such as Charles Morris, Arthur Murphy, and David Miller—are the most responsible of men. Their introductions are central to finding one's way among the texts. Still and all, they had their own interests and made original contributions, often at the tangents at which Mead had inspired them. Furthermore, there is no doubt that Mead himself was obscure. At some points reconstruction was well-nigh impossible. Again, as was the case with Dewey too, Mead was trying to respect the complexity and systematic character of transactional processes at a time when the vocabulary to do so had not yet been developed. (Indeed, we are only at the beginning of a philosophical vocabulary for this purpose even now, in spite of "feedback," "systems analysis," and the technical models for change.) The difficulties and novelty of his task thus compound the problems of the manuscripts. There is therefore a great deal of major research to be done on Mead, particularly on the Mead manuscripts, before a balanced historical interpretation of his contributions will be possible. Accordingly, we have used Mead as a resource to illuminate and at times extend or contrast problems already raised in other philosophers. This does not intend to give a full profile, but to suggest the contours of his interests, his perspective on pragmatism, and some major points at which his impact took hold. Despite all the difficulties, Mead must be reckoned among those who had a major impact upon pragmatism and upon social thought.

Evolution of Mind

We have seen above how critical the question of the evolution of mind and particularly of self-consciousness was for those involved in the evolutionary controversy. Wright's brilliant treatment of this question postulated an evolutionary process in which self-consciousness "emerged" as a result of the organism's capacity to recognize its own thoughts as representations. Thus for Wright self-awareness implied the existence of representative images, though not necessarily of a fully developed language. But Wright dealt with this developmental process from the perspective of the single organism; social interaction is not a necessary condition of the evolution of self-consciousness, though doubtless Wright assumed throughout that the animal he discussed existed within a social context.

At the same time that Wright was developing his theory, Peirce was formulating the doubt-belief theory of inquiry which was to become the starting point for all the pragmatists after him. It cannot be said that Peirce ignored the social dimensions of inquiry, for his definitions of truth and falsity as what will and what will not ever after be affirmed involve the notion of a community of investigators. Yet the social context plays no other role for Peirce in the doubt-belief theory; the process of inquiry itself is described as the effort of the individual organism to escape doubt and establish belief, and the animal's efforts to do this are not necessarily social.

For Mead on the other hand, there is neither a solitary hunter nor a solitary inquirer. Like Peirce, Mead starts from the model of the organism in an environment seeking satisfactions through action. But for Mead it is always a group of organisms who confront the environment and action is always social—hunting, playing, fighting, inquiring are social actions presupposing the presence of other animals. Accordingly, from the beginning—i.e., at the pre-self-conscious level—animals must coordinate their behavior in social action, and this obviously involves communication among animals. Such communication is not of course at a linguistic level but depends upon signal systems. Specifically, it depends upon what Mead calls the gesture. A gesture is a portion of a social act which serves as a stimulus to other organisms. Thus the cry of an animal may indicate fear on the part of the animal that makes it, but if it also arouses fear in the animal that hears it, the fear has been communicated, and one can say that the cry means fear. To the extent that a gesture arouses the same attitude in the perceiver that elicited it from the actor, meaning has been communicated and the gesture is a significant symbol. It is through such significant symbols that animal behavior is organized and coordinated.

The distinctive feature of this process is that *communication* has taken place, not just the causing of a similar state as fear. How has this happened? Mead does not limit himself to the gross phenomenon but exhibits its inner texture. While it is true that gesture is a regular part of animal behavior, and that the blocking of ongoing activity by obstacles is a feature shared by all animal behavior, what is distinctive about human response is the self-conscious intentional use of gestures in and for the process of restoring activity. Gestures are of many types: they may be facial expressions, bodily movements, sounds, etc. For the most part, the animal that makes the gesture cannot perceive it as other animals do; one cannot normally perceive one's own facial expression, and one's perception of the movements of one's body is not likely to agree with that of an onlooker. In the beginning, for children, the gesture, including vocal gestures, is part of an organic and originally meaningless response. But even in animals gestures become ritualized—Mead gives the example of dogfighting that often ends in avoiding real violence. The situation with respect to sound acquires special significance because one can hear the sound one makes just as the other animals can. We hear ourselves when we make auditory gestures while stimulating others. Thus in the end we learn to respond to our own stimulations. The meaning of our own gestures is determined in the first instance not by ourselves but it is the response of the other which gives meaning to my own action. The animal takes the role of the other animal toward his own gesture responding to his own gesture as the other does. This is the beginning of communication. A gesture then comes to be used intentionally, i.e., in terms of what we want to communicate rather than as a merely natural or organic sign. In this way a baby's cry becomes a demand for the satisfaction of a need. Quickly the situation becomes more complex. A boxer makes a feint and the anticipated response of the opponent is a stimulus for the boxer's own action. A new level of social organization and cooperation becomes possible, for gestures are not only a part of the social act, but also can be used to organize the social act, for if the first animal's gesture has reference to a subsequent phase of the act then both this animal and others can respond to that gesture in ways which will modify the subsequent course of the act. On this basis arise possibilities of purposive and planning behavior, communication and language and community, and in Mead's view self and self-consciousness.

This process of responding to one's own gestures as others do is for Mead the basis of mind—the animal responding to its own gesture by further gestures which in turn become stimuli to yet further gestures, etc. This interior dialogue, for Mead as for Peirce, is thinking. But for Mead this conversation is made possible only by the animal taking the role of the other, because each response to his gesture is the response of others. In taking the role of the other toward his own gesture, the animal treats himself as an object, just as other animals treat him, and so is able to think consciously about himself. And this self-awareness or self-consciousness makes it possible for the animal to exercise self-control, for an awareness of one's own gesture and of the response one is starting to make to it confers the power to inhibit that response from being fully actualized. Thus by taking the role of the other, the animal achieves self-consciousness and so self-control, and may then be said to possess a mind. "To the extent that the animal can take the attitude of the other and utilize that attitude for the control of his own conduct, we have what is termed mind; and that is the only apparatus involved in the appearance of mind." Thus Mead constructs a purely naturalistic evolutionary account of the origin of mind and self-consciousness—one which involves no transcendental element, but one which involves throughout a social process. The social act is there first, and mind is really the internalization of the social act in the organism.

Comparison to James and Dewey

The distinctive path that Mead was embarking on can be seen by comparing his view as so far expounded with that of James and by seeing the way in which Mead was developing the framework furnished by Dewey's analysis of the reflex arc.

Whereas most thinkers, including James, start from the notion of an individual and ask how he comes to distinguish himself from objects and how he becomes socialized, and finally even how he can have knowledge of other minds, Mead has recasted the problem from the outset. Humans are social from the beginning. Though this has no doubt become commonplace, it is usually expounded by students of culture and society in terms of the pressures that are externally applied upon the individual and they rest content with the manifest success of these pressures. Mead is broadly sympathetic to this mode of inquiry, but he has gone beyond it by looking at what goes on inside of the human being and how he comes to determine his own identity. Mead started with an appreciation of the variety of selves, such as James described. But he accounted for this in terms of role-playing which is the ability of each of us to visualize our own performances from the standpoint of others. This does not follow on an established identity, as in James, but is the beginning of becoming a self. This is the distinctive mark of Mead's views and allows him an interpretation of sympathy beyond James and Adam Smith.

The genetic account of role-playing is simply a continuation and extension of the analysis of significant gesture. In a way what is happening here is a social application of Dewey's reflex arc in all of its dimensions. There is the factor of ongoing activity, with stimulus and response as aspects of the analysis of a transaction. In role-playing, the expectations of others are internalized as rules or demands on ourselves. As anticipations of others' expectations, they are the stimulus. As following the rules of the role they are patterned responses. And such responses have associated with them not only the actions but appropriate emotions which are generated or intensified as the individual begins to accept and act in the role, e.g., of a lover or a patriot. While a social act is a temporal process, it does not follow that these aspects have causal-sequential relations. Stimulus and response are products of analysis, not a description of either learning or process. On these Mead has other ideas.

The study of specific roles—father-child, buyer-seller, promisor-promisee, etc.—is widespread by this time, both in their sociological and moral dimensions. Some philosophers have even complained that a person becomes nothing but an aggregate of roles which when peeled off, like the onion, leave nothing behind. This is certainly not Mead's view. For him, roles are not so external; they are internalized and constitutive in the growth of the self, and there is reserved for the individual a role in altering the patterns of society. Indeed there is a mutual interaction between the alterations which a self makes on society and the alterations that society makes on the individual. But it is not as if the roles were fragmented. Clearly, in highly institutionalized transactions any kind of social cooperation is facilitated by stereotyped roles, but the individual self as we shall see develops in relation to a *generalized other.*

The unit of analysis is the *act,* which is initiated by a want, directed toward a satisfaction by the use of resources to be found in a social and physical environment. An act is at once a process or a succession of adjustments, external and internal, and it is social. What he means by an act is not merely movement but a series of organized movements integrated with a purpose. His analysis parallels Dewey's account of the problematic situation in *How We Think* and *Theory of Inquiry.* One can call this behaviorism, but it is a much amplified behaviorism which legitimizes introspection and the kinds of preparations which are involved in problem diagnosis and problem-solving. The usual behaviorist account of behavior is only the final and overt phase of the act as Mead sees it. The act can be analyzed as impulse, perception, manipulation, and consummation. Like Dewey, the impulse arises in a disturbance of ongoing activities—anything from hunger pains to anxiety about next month's rent. Perception and manipulation bring the environment into relevance, for perception of an object is of something as essential to the act in a context, and which will enable the carrying out of the act and its consummation. For example, the perception of an orange as food or a brick as a doorstop is tied to a particular need and context. These are regarded by Mead as real properties, quite as real as any physical description of the things concerned. In fact on Mead's view natural objects are just as "socialized" as humans. Perception is intimately related to manipulation, for it brings the object into view as what it would be if it were manipulated in the present. Thus the anticipation, even with respect to objects, helps organize the ongoing act. Foresight of options and consequences that need not actually be enacted can be viewed as a collapsed act (i.e., Dewey's dramatic rehearsal). These collapsed acts function like hypotheses as what would happen on alternate choices. It is here of course that the full play of language is to be appreciated, for it allows the symbolic formulation of plans, the rehearsal of them, and the coordination of antagonistic objectives. The plan is confirmed in active manipulation and tested in consummation.

The Self and the Generalized Other, the I and the Me

Mead's theory of the development of mind outlined above goes without a break into his account of the self. The existence of mind implies some degree of self-consciousness, since in taking the role of others the animal makes itself an object to itself. But there are many others in the social setting, and the responses of these others to the animal's gestures may vary. Nevertheless, some responses to the animal's gestures may become "institutionalized," meaning "that the whole community acts toward the individual under certain circumstances in an identical way." Thus the whole community may condemn or approve certain gestures of the animal, so that the attitudes or response sets of all the others are the same. In this case, to take the role of any other is to take the role of the community; the others have become a generalized other. When the individual internalizes not only the role of some other but the role of *the* other—the generalized other—the self in the full sense of the term is present.

In the psychological structure of the animal, the self appears as the me. In the internal dialogue which constitutes thinking, the I is the speaker and the me is the recipient object. This me is of course a past I; the I that spoke a moment ago is the me of the next phase of discourse, but it is the past I viewed from the perspective of the generalized other, seen as the community sees it, in terms of the values, norms, and attitudes of the community. In the me there is therefore internalized the moral and ethical standards of the community, now brought within the personality as a part of the functioning psychological structure. The analogy between Mead's me and Freud's superego is striking. Because it embodies the values of the community, the me is necessarily a conventional creature. The I on the other hand is constantly reacting to the me (and through it to the community), and its responses are never wholly predictable. The I is the active, dynamic, and creative aspect of the personality, responsible for initiating action—in many ways an analogue of the Freudian ego. If there were no me, the animal would still be an I, but an I reacting directly to others, not to himself. What the addition of the me gives the animal is the capacity to act toward himself as well as others, and so to become a self-controlled and self-reflective creature. Thus from the early beginning we comprehend the nature of a cooperative venture or interpersonal transaction, and so the control of oneself with respect to an enterprise, e.g., a game. Self-control and voluntary participation develop in an internalized social context. Hence the conflicts between inclination and duty, individual and social interest, the individual and the public are cast in a new light. They are problems and conflicts in an internal forum, episodes in the development of an individual self, not the trade-offs of complete and self-centered individuals.

For Mead, as for Freud, the development of a human personality structure is thus impossible outside of a social context, for the me, like the superego, is a social product. Social life and social organization therefore precede the evolution of the mind and the self. But the social processes from which the mind and the self evolve are not the rigid, instinctively determined processes of an ant colony—they are processes involving learned cooperative behavior such as is found among the primates. Mead of course was dead long before the explosion of interest and research in comparative primatology which had led to the analysis of the social structure of primate groups and the discovery of linguistic and toolmaking capacities among the higher primates, but he would hardly have been surprised by recent findings. Indeed, Mead might justifiably have viewed these recent discoveries as confirmations of the position he developed half a century before them. And it is interesting for the distinctiveness of his approach and the depth of his insight to note that when the later psychoanalytic theorists began to question Freud's interpretation of social responses almost wholly in terms of the inner dynamics of the individual—e.g., in the work of Harry Stack Sullivan—Mead was invoked to focus on explanations in terms of patterns of interpersonal-social relations from the very early life of the child. In many respects too, on a broader sociological field, he can be seen as rescuing the category of the interpersonal from a wholly group emphasis in the category of the social.

INDEX OF NAMES

INDEX

INDEX OF SUBJECTS

Serious treatments of the American tradition in philosophy have been notable for their absence—extraordinary in the light of the impressive increase of interest in American thought. A HISTORY OF PHILOSOPHY IN AMERICA is a new and definitive work of scholarship that examines American thought from its seventeenth-century European sources to the work of C.I. Lewis in the twentieth century—a significant and unique achievement in scope and originality.

Setting out to determine the origins of American philosophy, professors Flower and Murphey have discovered debts to Europe that have not been fully considered before. They offer an original discussion of the complex relationships among philosophy, religion, and the sciences, which suggests a new genealogy for pragmatism. Their fresh approach recreates the vital exchange between academic institutions and the broader culture.

The authors initially explore the role of the Puritans in New World thinking and the impact of Newton, Locke, and other scientists on traditional Puritan beliefs. But the Puritans are not presented as a paradigm for all American thought; rather, it is the eighteenth-century Scottish philosophers, the authors believe, who introduced a fundamentally new orientation that has dominated subsequent American philosophy. The Americans naturalized this Scottish thought, retaining its sympathy to science and its realism but giving the empirical character of ethical and moral theory their own twist. The authors treat Transcendentalism, especially that of Emerson and Alcott, as a revolt against the Scottish influence—a revolt that failed.

The authors turn next to the introduction of German philosophy (in particular German idealism) into the Midwest, demonstrating how it